AFTER THE CONSTITUTION
Party Conflict in the New Republic

AFTER THE CONSTITUTION
Party Conflict in the New Republic

edited by
Lance Banning
University of Kentucky

Wadsworth Publishing Company
Belmont, California
A division of Wadsworth, Inc.

For Clinton

LIBRARY OF CONGRESS
Library of Congress Cataloging-in-Publication Data

After the Constitution : party conflict in the New Republic / edited
 by Lance Banning.
    p.   cm.
    Collection of articles previously published.
    Includes bibliographies.
    ISBN 0-534-11003-7 (pbk.)
    1. Political parties—United States—History.   2. United States-
-Politics and government—1783-1865.   I. Banning, Lance, 1942-
JK2260.A38 1989
324.273'09—dc19

88–18575
CIP

Printed in the United States of America
1 2 3 4 5 6 7 8 9 0 DO 5 4 3 2 1 0 9 8

Preface

This volume is intended for my students—or for any student who desires a richer understanding of the nation's first and most ferocious party conflict. Rising from my wishes as a teacher, it is meant to introduce a range of readers to the wealth of modern writings on the early party struggle, to provide them with a basic understanding of the way that various interpretations have developed, and thus to make it possible for them to choose among competing current views. Fifteen years ago, when I began to offer seminars and courses on the new American republic, there were several such anthologies from which to choose. All of them became outdated and eventually went out of print. Their passing left a need that this attempts to meet.

Many bitter choices were involved in editing these readings, mostly as to articles or books that had to be excluded. But the literature is so diverse (and newer contributions come in such a flow) that no anthology can offer more than a foundation. Keeping this in mind—and wanting, also, to avoid excessive editorial intrusions—I made the necessary choices in a manner that appeared consistent with my wish to lay a groundwork. If important works could not be used without extensive cutting, rearranging, and the like, I thought it better to discuss them in the introductions to the sections and selections, most of which are edited as lightly as I could. The limitations of a single volume also help explain why I could not include a wealth of brilliant writing which is less illustrative of "schools of thought" or major movements of interpretative opinion. The introductions and the numerous citations in the excerpts should provide some guidance to these works, though I apologize again to authors I could not include.

Individual selections can be read, of course, in any order that may be desired. Most were influenced in a myriad of ways by many of the others, and there are many ways in which they might have been arranged. Still, my fundamental aim was to assemble an anthology that could be used effectively by students at several different levels, interesting them all, challenging them all, and—I would hope—encouraging them all to move to further readings with a background that can deepen both their understanding and enjoyment. Thus, in choosing the selections, I have tried less hard to find the latest word than to present the articles and excerpts that may put the latest word—or even future words—in useful context. And I have sought a structure that may ease the tasks of undergraduates and graduates alike.

After a preliminary section, which is meant to place the early party battle in a broad, comparative perspective, the collection introduces topical concerns as it proceeds from the beginning of the party struggle toward its end. A framework that combines the narrative and topical approaches is often easiest and most appealing. In this case, moreover, it accords unusually well with the development of different scholarly interpretations, so that the volume also tends to move from the earliest challenges to the views that were predominant before the Second World War to the scholarship of the middle 1980s. My introductions are intended principally to make interpretative developments a little more apparent.

The University of Kentucky granted a research assistantship, which made it possible for me to enlist the aid of Melissa Baber in assembling the selections. I am grateful for that help and for the recommendations of Robert Shalhope, Drew McCoy, and the anonymous readers for the Dorsey Press. Special thanks are due to John M. Murrin, who suggested a better title, and—most of all—to Lana J. Banning, without whose help the editing might never have been finished. The work is dedicated, over his objections, to our son.

Lance Banning

Contents

PART ONE

Parties in an Anti-Party Culture

The framers of the Constitution made no plans for parties. Fearing special interests—even those of the majority in cases where majority desires seemed incompatible with private rights or long-term public needs—they framed a complex government whose multiple divisions of authority were consciously designed to defeat the workings of "faction." Dangerous majorities or interested minorities, they hoped, might both be checked or broken in the course of pushing their objectives through the several branches of a complicated, federal system.

Within three years of the adoption of the Constitution, many of its leading architects were nevertheless involved in what would soon become the most ferocious party struggle in the whole of American history. Party competition rapidly emerged as an enduring feature of their system. Many analysts, in fact, would say that parties constitute a *necessary* feature of the system. By nominating candidates for public office, parties make it possible for voters to select a winner, limiting the field sufficiently make the people's voice effective. Party loyalty and party discipline are hardly less important for the way in which they partially subvert the constitutional separation of powers, facilitating the enactment of consistent policies by linking the executive with Congress and the nation with the states. Although they thought of parties as an evil, the Founding Fathers may, withal, have framed a Constitution that does not work well without them. It is possible, in fact, that democratic government may not be feasible in any modern state without a well-developed party system.

As the first true parties of the modern sort, the Federalists and Jeffersonian Republicans have always been of interest to political scientists as well as to historians of the new American republic. This was never more the case than in the aftermath of World War II. With the United States involved in worldwide competition with a single-party state for influence in a myriad of rapidly emerging third-world nations, analysts were eager to compare developments in newly liberated African or Asian countries with the early history of the first

1

new nation. These were years, as well, when the comparative political stability of the United States, with its traditional two-party system, could scarcely fail to be contrasted with the situation in its multi-party European allies. Comparative analysis—between American experience and foreign *or* between the first American parties and later U.S. party conflicts—promised to illuminate these issues.

This section is intended to provide a broad, comparative perspective on the first party struggle. Emphasizing the concerns and contributions of political scientists (or of historians who have relied more systematically than others on the methodology and insights of political science), it offers a preliminary look at the function of parties in the American political system, but it raises questions, too, about the special features of a party conflict in a culture that was not initially receptive to such competition.

Political Parties
in a New Nation

William Nesbit Chambers

Political Parties in a New Nation: The American Experience, 1776–
1809 (New York: Oxford University Press, 1963) *was perhaps the
ablest synthesis of 1950s scholarship about the origins and course of the
first party conflict. In addition to this narrative, however, William Nesbit
Chambers, who was Edward Mallinckrodt Distinguished University Professor at Washington University in St. Louis, attempted to illuminate the
role that the development of parties may have played in the creation of an
integrated nation. Well aware that the American experience might hold
no simple lessons for societies with different problems and traditions, he
was nonetheless convinced that a comparative perspective could throw new
light on both. This excerpt, from pages 1–2, 7–15, 95–97, 103–109, and
143–147, is reprinted with the permission of Oxford University Press.*

In 1790 Alexander Hamilton, as Secretary of the Treasury in the new
government of the United States, proposed to Congress the first in a
long series of measures aimed at the economic development of the new
nation. Before he was finished he had brought into being a powerful
political engine to advance his program, to support his determined
effort to shape the destiny of the infant republic. In effect, he had
founded the Federalist party. He began this task fourteen years after
the declaration of American independence, seven years after the treaty
of peace which followed the Revolutionary War.

In 1797 Thomas Jefferson boarded a coach at Monticello, the gra-
cious home he had built on a Virginia hilltop. After three years of retirement devoted mainly to agricultural experiments and to country life, he
was on his way to the nation's capital to assume fresh duties as Vice-
President. Yet the trip of a week or so was more than just a return to
the chores of office. It was a crucial stage in a political odyssey which
was to bring him at last to full acceptance of active leadership in the
opposition Republican party, a political force which was unique for its
time.

The two events symbolize the genesis and ultimate establishment of
national political parties on the American scene. These political engines

were not only the first parties to adventure on the precarious ground of politics in an emerging nation but also the first true parties of modern times, appearing well before such formations developed in England or other European countries. They were shaped slowly and painstakingly, as part of a general progress in which the American states moved from colonial dependence and revolutionary uncertainties to become a stable, democratic, modern republic.

* * * * *

The American Revolution was a genuinely anti-colonial movement. It threw off, by violence, the ties of imperial control from London and ultimately established the thirteen colonies as legally independent entities joined in a new confederation. Many later emerging nations, however, have tended to look for inspiration more to the French Revolution of 1789 or the Russian Revolution of 1917 than to the American experience. For them, the striving for nationhood has been a long and bitter experience, a rebellion against foreign economic exploitation and foreign cultural domination as well as against foreign political control. For them, the national revolution has tended also to be a social revolution, as the French and Russian revolutions were. Like these revolutions, it has tended to bring sharp social cleavages, ideological animosities in an intense and sweeping anti-colonialism, and the hatreds toward old masters which accompany such overturns. The American rebellion was not a profound social revolution in this sense, although local "Loyalist" elites were displaced from power by American "Patriots," and the Revolution did inspire a decade of moderate reform. In this respect, the first great colonial revolt of modern times differed from many twentieth-century national movements.

Such movements have brought their own kinds of consequences. When national revolutions become also social revolutions, particularly in underdeveloped areas previously subject to substantial exploitation, the nations that emerge are likely to face difficulties in achieving a sense of national identity. Alienated from the way of life typified by their colonial "oppressors," they cannot readily build a national unity and character out of this culture, even though they aspire to the modernity the imperial power has achieved, even as they employ techniques their colonial experience has left with them. On the other hand, as leaders try to change the society "whole" into a new, advanced nation, indigenous cultural materials are likely to be still more difficult to mold into patterns of national identity and unity keyed to aspirations toward economic and social modernization. Such materials, if not primitive, are far too often pre-modern, traditionalistic, and hostile to the highly rationalized concepts of modern nationhood and an industrialized society. Also, they are often scattered by deep-reaching ethnic, regional, or tribal differences and animosities. Thus, as many national movements of the nineteenth century and later looked to the French Revolution for a model, so have many twentieth-century national movements turned to at least some aspects of the Russian experience. Often the result has been an attempt to force an idealized and still alien concept of national identity on refractory native materials. At the same time the bitterness of the colonial experience has combined with such concepts to intensify attitudes of intolerance or intransigence in politics.

In its time, the American experience and Revolution left a different kind of heritage. The English colonies in America had not in fact been subject to long or severe exploitation, despite the tightening of imperial economic policy and increasing harassments in the years from 1763 to 1775. Furthermore, even the revolutionary leaders thought of themselves as true Englishmen in America, fighting for ancient English rights, the ancient English tradition of equable law, and English liberties. The resistance to imperial power began with the argument that the colonists were being denied their English heritage by a misguided Parliament; and it was some time before Americans brought themselves to sever the ties of loyalty and obedience to the Crown and attack the King himself. Even when they did so, they did not reject their English patrimony totally, but rather built on some parts of it (such as English law and English liberal philosophy), while they sloughed off others (such as monarchy, aristocracy, and the idea of royal prerogative). Thus, they began nationhood with familiar elements that could be shaped into an indigenous and workable national outlook. They did not have to try to build national identity and unity entirely anew, out of bitter residues of conflict, chaotic or intractable native materials, or an idealism imported from a contemporaneous France or Russia, with all of its rigidities. Instead, they reshaped what they found best in their old tradition, evolved new ways as they seemed necessary, and generated ideals of their own. They were at once the heirs of a usable past, and able to be flexible as they looked to the future.

Whatever their differences, a Washington or a Jefferson, a John Adams or a Madison, or a Hamilton—with some reservations—and countless others, all worked by and large to solve the new republic's political problems in this fashion; and Washington lent his prestige to smooth the transition to new patterns of national loyalty.

The result was helpful, not only for the development of political parties as such, but ultimately also for the acceptance of opposition. In part because their Revolution was not a social revolution setting system against system, class against class, or modern against fixed and traditionalist ways on the domestic scene, Americans were able to arrive more readily than many other new nations at basic understandings on political structure, at the same time that they were arriving at a consensus on political means. Much of the emerging national outlook was summarized in the Declaration of 1776 and the Constitution of 1789, and this outlook eventually became a tradition. It countenanced substantial freedom of action in the political as well as in other realms, and over the years this basic liberal view did much to reduce the fear of parties and even of opposition parties. The first amendment to the national Constitution provided clearly for freedom of speech, assembly, publication, and petition, and the rule won ultimate acceptance. The national tradition, growing in a favorable soil in which most citizens owned at least some measure of property and in which distinctions of rich and poor were minimized, also promoted an increasing degree of social equality and political democracy, along with attitudes that kept political conflict generally within a moderate range and subject to peaceful resolution. Fear of opposition or an opposition party remained for some time, but a counter-tradition could be invoked against it. Furthermore, intolerance of opposition reinforced by an official ideology could not be invoked as a revolutionary virtue.

Still, modern parties and the party system in the United States were indeed products of a labor of Hercules, and not "natural," untended flowerings from the soil of independence and popular government. Rather, parties were ingeniously shaped "artifacts," in the sense of structures built up over years by the industrious, if often groping, activities of men. To assume that a democratic political party system in the United States in the 1790s—or in any new nation— could grow overnight from independence and a democratic constitution, or be struck off at a blow by one or two great leaders, is to underestimate the problems involved. Revolution on Monday, independence on Tuesday, a constitution on Wednesday, political parties on Thursday, orderly elections on Friday, stable democratic government by Saturday, and rest on Sunday—any such conception of political creation is the stuff of dreams. If parties and democratic party systems are the products of human ingenuity, time and energy in abundance must go into their making.

In the process of party building, American founders confronted and effectively solved a long series of political problems. Some were foreseen and some unforeseen, some were at hand from the outset and some emerged only in the course of the work. It was throughout an endeavor of pragmatic adaptation and inventiveness under necessity, guided at the beginning by immediate purposes or a general desire to prove the republican experiment, informed only later by a conception of party as a goal. The problems of establishing the republic and of establishing party overlapped, and in a sense they all involved the practical fulfillment of the national and democratic promise of the Declaration of Independence.

The first task was to fix workable patterns of legitimacy and authority in the new polity, under which the conflict of interests and opinions could go on within a larger national unity. The solution to this problem ultimately drew on elements as disparate as Washington's personal appeal and Jefferson's rationalist philosophy.

As any emerging nation must, young America faced the issue of shaping national economic development and policy, with all of its payoffs and costs for different interests. As a new national power, it also faced the trying problem of establishing national identity and effective independence in an often threatening and sometimes contemptuous world. The first great, controversial steps in economic policy were taken by Hamilton, whose party found its origins in the ties of interest and action his program brought forth. Contention over world politics and foreign policy followed, pitting Madison against Washington as well as Hamilton, and Jefferson against Adams; and full-scale party division ensued. Yet policy was evolved, and the nation survived.

To man the posts of government and the new force of party, new recruits for leadership were necessary; and the nation was fortunate in the skill and imagination of the political lieutenants, cadremen and foot soldiers who came forward to administer public affairs and develop party formations.

One task such men confronted was devising stable methods which could link a hitherto unprecedented mass public and electorate to hitherto unprecedented party structures. Another was forging sufficient unity within parties in government to enable them to govern coherently and bridge the gap between the constitutionally separated executive and legislative branches in the American system. The first great essay at governmental management was Hamilton's, and he accomplished much toward coherent policy. Within a decade, however, Jefferson and his co-workers had gone even further and achieved a near model of responsible democratic party government in office.

Given the pluralism and state-by-state fragmentation of power in the American federal system, party builders had to assemble national parties out of varied and widely scattered state and local materials. Indeed, the interplay (and often conflict) between disparate state and local elements on one hand, and national structures and concerns on the other, has been a continuing theme of American party development and action. After some years, the Republicans also developed modern organization to reinforce party strength, but the Federalists never arrived at this device.

With the establishment of parties, Americans faced the intricate problems of conducting a system of parties in competition and the delicate questions of accord in the idea of opposition and of the peaceful transfer of power from one party to another.

The eventual solution of these various problems was to become the story of America's formative political years.

American party development also touched another issue of fundamental concern. This was the question of the practical functioning of a democratic political system as a whole. Various processes have been proposed as the criteria of democracy: free entry to the political arena; widespread participation in the political system; effective representation for and balancing of varied interests in the society; open discussion and debate; free elections; government that is somehow responsive or responsible to the demands or judgments of the public or electorate; or the right to criticize government decisions. It is easy to speak broadly, as Jefferson did in the Declaration of 1776, of governments "deriving their just powers from the consent of the governed." It is more difficult in practice to realize such consent and to assure the faithfulness of governments to the governed, to meet significant criteria of democratic functioning. In practical terms, some sort of party system has proved necessary to the operation of modern democratic politics.

In the American case, the machinery of democratic functioning came to comprise three major elements. The first two developed as popular participation and the representation of varied interests. The great practical fulcrum of American democracy in a large complex society, however, became popular choice: the presentation to the public or electorate of alternatives concerning policies and leaders, and choices by the public or electorate among such alternatives, primarily in elections. It is here that parties and party competition came to play their great role, in shaping and clarifying options for popular choice or decision, and in giving such choices some effect in the conduct of government. If such choices are to be effective, they imply the operation of other crucial processes of democracy. Different patterns of democratic practice are conceivable, including the mechanisms of representative single-party systems which some later new nations have evolved. In the developing American system, however, the party Hamilton founded and the rival party Jefferson came to lead offered a remarkably useful set of political instruments.

In 1788, a Republican-to-be with a properly protesting first name, Meclancton Smith of New York, expressed his fear that the new national government would come under the control of the well-to-do and the eminent. Their "influence," he argued,

> will generally enable them to succeed in elections. [Those of] conspicuous military, popular, civil, or legal talents . . . easily form associations; the

poor and middling classes form them with difficulty. . . . A substantial yeoman, of sense and discernment, will hardly ever be chosen. From these remarks, it appears that the government will fall into the hands of the few and the great. This will be a government of oppression.

A dozen years later another Jeffersonian leader, Charles Pinckney of South Carolina, spoke of his long battle in the old-style faction politics of the state against domination by "the Weight of Talent, Wealth, and personal and family interest." From its very beginnings American democracy has been threatened by the power exerted by established wealth, status, or influence, but parties were to prove that they could do much to offset these advantages. In particular, the party of Jefferson was to emerge as a new kind of broadly-based, "popular" party which. was conspicuously effective to this end.

In the process of nation building, the American founders explored many problems generic to new nations. Their experience cannot provide literal lessons for other peoples today, who face different conditions and must devise political procedures that are appropriate to their own circumstances, as their American predecessors did. Yet there are important parallels. The American instance revealed the significance of a concern for political as well as economic development in the progress of a new nation, as it also showed that political construction is bound to be difficult and disappointing to utopian hopes, and proved the value of moderate and pragmatic approaches to political problems. It brought to light important factors which may make for national stability, underscored the role of economic development as a foundation for democracy, and underscored the crucial role of broad as well as specialized education for promoting democracy and training leaders. It also provided an early example of parties as vehicles to contain the forces of pluralism and bring coherence into public policy. It demonstrated the eventual utility of a two-party system as an instrument of democracy and a device to redress imbalances of privilege and power. Finally, the American experience set a pattern for a responsible opposition which avoided the intransigence that may disrupt a nation. In short, it uncovered viable democratic ways to conduct the conflict of politics and manage government within national unity.

Yet at the time, no one could foresee the result. Only after they had taken long steps toward the solution of the political problems they faced, only after the tasks of party development had been accomplished, could American leaders and the American public look back and see what they had achieved.

As the American founders resolved problem after problem in the shaping of the republic, they not only established the first modern political parties. They were also involved, if mostly unknowingly, in a general process of political modernization in which parties were at once an element and a catalyst in a broader change from older to newer things.

Such modernization, particularly as it showed itself first in the West, has typically revealed a variety of political developments. The tendency has been for traditionalized, highly personalized, and often parochial patterns of authority to break down, whether they have been patterns of simple custom or more complex systems of feudal hierarchy, monarchy, or social deference. Thus the sway of kings and barons, nobles and retainers, or magnates and "connexions" becomes outmoded. Authority tends to become based on rational-legal foundations in a regularized form which is expressed in constitutions or general law—although often the process may involve a transitional stage of personal foundations for authority built around an early unifying leader. The modes of conducting politics become rationalized also, in several ways. For example, the claims of political interests must be advanced more and more on allegedly rational, rather than prescriptive, grounds. The very procedures of politics and administration become more orderly, methodical, and efficient. Political formations and political action come to stand on a less personalized basis, although within the more rational politics ample opportunity may remain for new-style personal influence, as it has in much "inside" party politics. The new political culture permits innovation as against fixed, traditional ways. There is an increase in rational discussion of political values and goals, and of political methods as means to such goals. Birth and family become less important than work and achievement as keys to political success, and politics becomes more and more a matter of competition. Parties, active interest groups, press, and propaganda appear in the political arena— and often revolutionary organizations also appear. Taken over all, a new energy or *élan* comes to characterize political life.

* * * * *

American development after the Revolution of 1776 was almost a classic instance of political modernization. Thus, we find a constitution on the rationalist model, and Washington serving as a charismatic focus of acceptance and legitimacy in the transition to fully rational, legal foundations of authority; an open politics of conflicting interests; orderly administration, particularly as exhibited by Hamilton; free, formal associations of individuals on a rational basis for political action, as in the Democratic or Republican Societies, and the gradual displacement of family or fluid-faction "connexions" by the open, rationalized, stable connections of party; innovations in policy or inventions in political methods not only by Hamilton, but by men like Madison or Gallatin, and emphasis on rational discussion as typified by Jefferson and practiced by thousands; mass communication and propaganda in the two *Gazettes*, the *Aurora*, and other papers; the rise of "new men" like Beckley and Burr to labor at the "new careers" of methodical politicians as contrasted with notables in politics; and a tendency toward national outlooks and co-ordination as against parochial patterns and localism.

There were special and significant features in the American experience in modernization. As contrasted with European nations, American political shapers were not confronted with a protracted conflict to overthrow a closed, traditionalistic, or hierarchical social and political structure, for such a structure was never firmly fixed in America. Unlike most emerging nations of the twentieth century, where modernization has entailed an intense race from a slow start to bring an underdeveloped society to the level of modernity seen in alien Western societies, the new America worked from an already comparatively favorable position. It was thus able to achieve modernization as a development of existing elements and trends, rather than a forcing of alien patterns. Furthermore, in comparison with both European and latter-day underdeveloped nations, the American republic was fortunate in that it enjoyed crucial preconditions for a democratic polity. Nonetheless, the American experience followed typical paths of modernization, from the rationalization of authority to the development of political parties.

The passage from clique, faction, or junto politics to party politics has, in general, been an important aspect of political modernization. Certainly, it was so in America. As compared with faction-like formations, parties represented rationalized, comparatively ordered, and methodical ways of performing crucial political functions, even when they showed aspects of disorder on their own. Also, their public and continuing character made them less dependent than cliques or factions on particular persons, families, or "connexions," and virtually required leaders and active workers in a modern style. Yet the development of American parties also depended on national political stability and national economic development. Without these, the new America might not have continued as a democratic polity, and the first experiment in modern parties might have died with it.

An infant democracy, if it is to survive, must evolve modes of carrying on political conflict without destroying national order and unity. To Washington or to Hamilton, as to many who shared their views, such national unity was paramount, and opposition was a threat to stability. Unity and order were a delicate web which must not be strained.

To other shapers of American politics, however, democracy implied criticism, free access to politics, real options in elections. Thus, Madison, Jefferson, and the Republicans fought for the right to construct open yet peaceful competition between parties for power.

* * * * *

The party of Jefferson in the 1790s was a new political engine, the first of its kind in modern history. It exhibited little continuity with antecedent formations, and it developed political relationships which carried it well beyond the Federalists as an archetype of a modern, "popular" party. In the long process of learning and inventing in the face of need and opportunity, it had pioneered in rationalized or modernized political practices, which observers abroad later referred to as "American methods." Such practices, from the caucus to mass electoral appeals, were nonetheless frequently reproduced as democracy made its way in other nations.

Early Republicans were often stigmatized as "Anti-Federalists," a reference to the opposition to the Constitution of 1787. The idea was a plausible one, and it is true that most of those who favored the new Constitution at the convention of 1787 became Federalists in the 1790s, while those who refused to sign became Republicans. It can also be argued that many districts (and thereby presumably interests) which voted against the Constitution in the ratification controversy also stood as Republican bastions in succeeding years. Thus, for example, the argument runs that the districts which opposed the Constitution in New York in 1788 were the same as those which opposed the Federalist Jay for governor in 1792, or that the forces which had fought ratification in western Pennsylvania reappeared in the whiskey tax protests of 1793–1794 and in later Republicanism. Parallels may also be found between the elitist, "energetic" government ideas of many pro-Constitutionalists and of the Federalists, while beliefs in popular, limited government were shared by many anti-Constitutionalists and Republicans.

Nevertheless, serious difficulties attend the assumption of clear continuity from anti-Constitutionalists to Republicans. While most leaders who had opposed the Constitution became Republicans, so did many who had favored it, including Madison and Jefferson. . . . Overall, far too many pro-Constitutionalists became Republican leaders or cadre workers to sustain the notion that the "Anti-Federalists" simply metamorphosed into the Republican body of the next decade.

The point is highlighted in the Congressional divisions over Hamilton's proposals. In the House, where the strongest resistance to Hamilton's measures emerged, not more than a half-dozen members had been active against the new frame of government. Yet, in broaching federal assumption of the state debts, Hamilton touched off a stiff and continuing Congressional resistance which included friends of the Constitution.

In so far as there were lines from proponents or opponents of the Constitution to Federalists or Republicans, they were broken or badly bent in the debt assumption controversy. The party conflict Hamilton sparked was a new conflict.

Yet the crucial difficulty lies even beyond such questions as these. The argument of continuity oversimplifies the actual politics of ratification, particularly as it relates to parties. It persists in seeing the controversy as a single national battle, even a battle between "Federalist" and "Anti-Federalist" parties, each based on a broad and continuing cleavage of "business"-mercantile interests on the one side and "populist"-agrarian interests on the other. In fact, however, as we have seen, the question was not fought out on such clear, dualistic, national lines; and certainly the controversy was not fought out between national parties as we have defined parties. It is possible to trace important continuities (as well as discontinuities) between the alignments of interest groups and opinion aggregates for and against the Constitution on the one hand, and the alignments for the Federalists or the Republicans in the 1790s on the other. If parties are distinguished from other, looser political formations in terms of structure, function, and ideology, however, alignments of groups and bodies of opinion are only elements in the followings of parties, while parties as such are the durable structures of national leaders, local leaders or cadre, and actives, who perform the manifold functions of party. These functions, to be sure, include mobilizing followings as the foundations of party power, but the followings which parties mobilize are not the parties themselves. Thus, parties as structures had to be built new in the 1790s.

It is in terms of relationships between structure and following that the Republicans may be thought of as a new kind of political institution. The Federalists achieved party structure earlier and found a substantial popular power base; and yet they never quite transcended their ministerial, English-oriented, elitist origins. They represented interests, shaped opinion, and offered choices to the electorate; but they were not given to encouraging intraparty popular participation. They always depended on a comparatively close nucleus of leaders in government, and their attitude toward the public and electorate was always an uncertain mixture of condescension and fear. The Republicans on the other hand, although slower to form, finally established a close rapport between leaders and followers.

The difference is manifest in various facets of the Republican formation. Like the Federalists, the Republicans built out from a nucleus at the center of government, many of their early leaders also were notables, and Jefferson frequently showed at least a trace of condescension in his attitude toward the people, despite his republican philosophy. Yet the coruscations of republican sentiment in currents of opinion, in the

Democratic and Republican Societies, and in the furor over foreign policy, before there was a Republican party, gave the party a broad potential power base in advance. Furthermore, from the outset the Republican leaders, cadres, and actives included a large number of "politicians," of men who made their careers and achieved prominence in politics, as contrasted with notables; and the Republicans were very nearly a "party of politicians," in Max Weber's term. In this situation, the party's leaders came to look to public opinion and to the electorate as vital powers to which the party should be responsive or responsible. Thus the Republican outlook developed in terms of leaders not only acting on their following but also interacting with it. The Republican founders were the first modern party-builders to conceive of a party in a distinctively democratic role, and thus the first to create a genuinely "popular" party.

The distinction between popular and other parties raises the important question of relationships between leaders and followers which facilitate intraparty democracy. A popular party may be thought of as an open modern party which combines substantial stability in structure with responsiveness to an extended popular following and with encouragement of popular participation or initiative in party action. Not all modern or successful parties are popular parties. Thus the Federalist formation remained a semielitist party in a democratic context. It never developed strong ties of popular participation or responsiveness to popular opinion, and it continued to look upon elections as referendums or plebiscites on its established policies rather than as expressions of popular influence. In short, it operated as a plebiscitarian rather than as a democratic or popular party, as many parties in other new nations were to operate in later years. As a plebiscitarian party, the Federalists were less concerned with popular participation or initiative than with popular mobilization or manipulation, less sensitive to popular opinion than determined to mold it.

The character of the Republican formation as a popular party may be seen in its tripodal foundations. At the center of government was the party "point," exercising or seeking to exercise governmental power and providing national leadership and co-ordination. In the localities were ranged the component units of party structure proper, composed of local leaders, local cadres, and local actives, together with such local organization as they may have achieved. Also in the localities were the varied elements of the party following. Between men at the point and local leaders, and also between local party workers and their followings, there were strong lines of direct, often face-to-face, or primary interaction. Between point and following, there was a more distant, secondary relationship of action, by leaders impinging on or influencing followers. The interaction between central leaders and following, which was so important to intraparty democracy, depended heavily on indirect relationships between leaders at the "point" and the popular following by way of local party units.

* * * * *

Thus understood, Republican party structure was not only more modern and more complex than Federalist structure but also characterized by deeper and more varied foundations, which rested on broader segments of the population as a stable substructure or following. As "a body of men," in Burke's language, the Republicans were remarkably "united," determined to promote "the national interest" in terms of the principles on which they "agreed," and blessed with a degree of "popular confidence" which old-style faction politics could never have provided.

The American system was a two-party system. Many of its fundamentals, however, were representative of later multi-party patterns of politics as well as two-party patterns.

Indeed, early American experience suggests the basic outlines of plural-party systems in stable democracies generally. The defining characteristic of such systems may be taken as party interaction—a relatively durable relationship between two or more stable parties, in which they regularly compete with one another and must take one another into account in their behavior, their relationships with their followings, their bids for power, and their appeals to the uncommitted. Rivalry between parties is concerned with contesting for control or office in government, though it may involve much more than this. Thus, Federalists and Republicans in the first American party system were extraordinarily concerned also with significant issues, or with mobilizing followers behind competing programs, whereas later American parties have not always been so strongly oriented to issues. The relationship between parties may vary with the system or with historical circumstances. Yet it is possible to describe a general model of plural-party systems in terms of four basic criteria.

The first is the existence of continuing conflict between parties. This at once implies, and is in part based on, ideologies or perspectives which emerge in the parties as "we-they" perspectives. These partisan views become involved with a strong desire that the party win power for its own sake, perhaps even more than for the sake of the interests it may represent. In nominations, elections, and appointments to office, a partisan attitude tends to emphasize party loyalty, rather than eminence or ability alone. Where the political situation (and thus the parties) are significantly oriented to issues, partisanship—in the absence of strong counterpressures from local constituencies or factional forces—tends toward the adoption of general party attitudes toward issues rather than singular or "kinkish" positions. Such attitudes are likely to affect not only party leaders, cadres, and actives but also persons and even groups in the party following. When issues are drawn in this way between parties, the parties themselves tend to rally the pluralism of interests and opinions around their own standards, and thereby moderate pluralistic variety. Many crosscurrents of pluralism may remain, but generally they will not run as strongly as they would in a politics without parties or in faction politics. All of these aspects of party rivalry were observable among Federalists and Republicans in America as they joined in recurring combat with one another. The more the ties of a party become institutionalized, within its structure and with its following, and the further a party moves toward full-scale organization, the stronger the sense of partisanship is likely to become.

Despite conflict, a plural-party system need not tear a society— even a new and untried society—into fragments. Where a social system has arrived at some understandings or achieved consensus concerning political means, parties generally operate and expect to operate within such understandings or such consensus—and this marks a second direction for a plural-party system in a stable democracy. Strictly considered, this criterion implies commitment to at least two basic propositions: acceptance of the legitimacy of opposition and of opposition parties, and acceptance of freedom of access to government power for the opposition. When deep social conflict is given free play, or when the parties themselves adopt intransigent positions, consensus on these minimal propositions may be threatened and the society may thereby be seriously disturbed or even destroyed. In America many Federalists doubted the legitimacy of opposition, and the Sedition Act at least was a threat to the idea of freedom of political expression for the opposition. Yet the basic values of acceptance of opposition and its access to power triumphed. Furthermore, despite High Federalist pressures, neither party as a whole pushed matters to the extremes of intransigence.

A third criterion is the role of the parties in providing stable links between people and government as the parties contend with one another. The significance of this relationship in terms of political gratification may vary. At a maximum, it may supply effective representation in government for the interests and opinions which are joined in the party following, as both the early Federalists and Republicans in America demonstrated. It may also provide open means of participation in the political process for individuals and groups in the party following, as the Republicans in particular revealed. It may on the other hand involve little more than symbolic or emotional gratification for the sentiments or ideological perspectives which men in the party share: the rewards of victory may hinge merely on the fact that "our" symbols or rhetoric predominate, that "our" leaders hold office and set the tone. Under certain circumstances party representation may also be constricted within narrow limits of group brokerage concerning relatively insignificant issues.

The effectiveness of parties as links between public and government depends on relationships both within and between the parties. Generally, democracy within a party tends to promote effective representation of significant interests and opinions as well as substantial popular participation. On the other hand, dominance by a few leaders in a party tends to inhibit such popular representation and participation. Despite low levels of intraparty democracy, however, parties in situations where there is conflict on serious issues may, in the very competition for power and votes, differ significantly on these issues and thus offer important options to the electorate. Choice between such options is the fulcrum of interparty democracy—as it was in the interaction of elitist Federalists and popular Republicans in the American experience. Generally, however, intraparty democracy and effective representation promote interparty democracy as popular choice. Furthermore, meaningful choice for the electorate is generally encouraged when there is a significant degree of differentiation on issues between the parties and cohesion on issues within each party—once again, the American Federalists and Republicans are exhibits. Interparty democracy may be frustrated in multiparty systems where parties must make coalitions in order to govern. Similarly, in two-party systems, effective democratic choice is threatened by serious factional divisions within a party in power which may weaken the party's ability to fulfill its general commitments to the electorate. It is particularly endangered when a minority faction of a governing party, dissenting from the basic positions which that party has offered to the voters, works in alliance with a minority party and is thus able to prevent the majority party from carrying out its announced policies. Before long, intraparty factional developments on the American scene were to confuse democratic choice, and such phenomena were to recur throughout American party history. The outbreak of factionalism among Federalists in the Adams years was an omen of chronic (and more serious) difficulties to come.

Finally, if a plural-party system is to survive, each party must have a reasonable chance to win government power. If one giant party dominates the political arena persistently, even though ineffectual opposition parties are permitted to exist, a plural-party system can hardly operate in a meaningful sense as an instrument of democracy as representation and choice. Although the Federalist party was dominant at the beginning, and the Republicans finally became an overwhelmingly dominant party in turn, both parties at the peak of their rivalry enjoyed remarkably equal opportunities to exercise government authority.

The first American party system was in a sense a transitional system. It built on the experience of earlier years, with their essays in the politics of opposition in the colonies and states, and their committees and networks of correspondence in the Revolutionary endeavor. The national party system was in the process of evolution in the 1790s and did not reach its fullest development until 1800, although in the Adams years it went well beyond the personal, factional, nonparty politics of the previous decade. Even at their apogee, however, the parties of Hamilton and Jefferson were still limited in their appeal to voters and in the development of organization, and their lives were comparatively short. In the long sweep of American history, they stood as half-way houses on the road to the fully organized parties of the later Jacksonian era with their expanded mass followings. In its time, nonetheless, the first American party system revealed what parties in an emerging democracy could do.

A system in which parties interact and are balanced can provide a significant instrument for determining democratically who gets what, when, and how in government, and for shaping social and governmental policy. Yet at the same time it entails party contentions of the sort Americans were being treated to in unusually full measure during the Adams regime.

The Idea of a Party System

Richard Hofstadter

Though Chambers was aware of the peculiarities of the American experience—and of the first great party war—the very concept of a party system may exaggerate the similarities between that conflict and later party competitions. The risk of such exaggeration was a central theme of Richard Hofstadter's The Idea of a Party System: The Rise of Legitimate Opposition in the United States, 1780–1840 *(Berkeley: University of California Press, 1969). Social scientists are not insensitive to the uniqueness of the past, but they are characteristically concerned with regularities that reappear in different times and places. Historians are eager borrowers of social science methodologies and concepts, but they consider the unique and unrepeatable to be their special province. In this excerpt, drawn from pages 1–9, viii–x, 35–39, and 212, one of the most distinguished political historians of his generation argues that the absence of a concept of a party system was a distinguishing feature of the first party conflict. The selection is reprinted by permission of the University of California Press.*

When Thomas Jefferson thought of setting down the lasting achievements he wanted inscribed on his tombstone, he mentioned the writing of the Declaration of Independence and of the Virginia Statute of Religious Liberty and the founding of the University of Virginia—thus omitting almost flamboyantly all the accomplishments of his long career in national politics. Yet surely this democrat and libertarian might have taken justifiable pride in his part in creating the first truly popular party in the history of the Western world, and in his leading role in the first popular election of modern times in which the reins of government were peacefully surrendered by a governing party to an opposition. Jefferson did more than assert the claims of democracy: he was also a central figure in developing responsible constitutional opposition, an accomplishment which alone would grace any man's tombstone.

But here we are brought face to face with the primary paradox of this inquiry: Jefferson, the founder, or more accurately, co-founder, of the first modern popular party, had no use for political parties. This

SOURCE: The Idea of a Party System: The Rise of Legitimate Opposition in the United States, 1780–1840 ©Copyright 1969 (The Regents of the University of California).

seeming inconsistency is but one aspect of a larger problem: the creators of the first American party system on both sides, Federalists and Republicans, were men who looked upon parties as sores on the body politic.

Political discussion in eighteenth-century England and America was pervaded by a kind of anti-party cant. Jonathan Swift, in his *Thoughts on Various Subjects*, had said that "Party is the madness of many, for the gain of the few." This maxim, which was repeated on this side of the Atlantic by men like John Adams and William Paterson, plainly struck a deep resonance in the American mind. Madison and Hamilton, when they discussed parties or factions (for them the terms were usually interchangeable) in *The Federalist*, did so only to arraign their bad effects. In the great debate over the adoption of the Constitution both sides spoke ill of parties. The popular sage, Franklin (who was not always consistent on the subject), gave an eloquent warning against factions and "the infinite mutual abuse of parties, tearing to pieces the best of characters." George Washington devoted a large part of his political testament, the Farwell Address, to stern warnings against "the baneful effects of the Spirit of Party." His successor, John Adams, believed that "a division of the republic into two great parties . . . is to be dreaded as the greatest political evil under our Constitution."[1] Similar admonitions can be found in the writings of the arch-Federalist Fisher Ames and the "philosopher of Jeffersonian democracy," John Taylor of Caroline. If there was one point of political philosophy upon which these men, who differed on so many things, agreed quite readily, it was their common conviction about the baneful effects of the spirit of party.

That the anti-party thought and partisan action of the Founding Fathers were at odds with each other is not altogether surprising. What they were trying to resolve—and they did so, after all, with a substantial measure of success—is a fundamental problem of modern democracy. We see this problem with a new interest today when so many new

---

[1] Swift's maxim first appeared in the 1727 edition of his *Thoughts*. For Paterson on Swift, see Richard McCormick, *Experiment in Independence: New Jersey in the Critical Period, 1781–1789* (1950), 72; for Adams see *Works*, ed. by C. F. Adams (1851), VI, 508. For Hamilton and Madison on parties see especially *The Federalist* Number 9 (Hamilton) and 10 (Madison), though the subject is reverted to elsewhere throughout; see also the commentary by Benjamin F. Wright in his edition of *The Federalist* (1961), 26–41. All subsequent references to *The Federalist* are to this edition. For Franklin on parties, Max Farrand, ed., *The Records of the Federal Convention of 1787* (1911), I, 82. Elsewhere, it should be said, Franklin said of parties: "Such will exist wherever there is liberty; perhaps they help to preserve it. By the collision of different sentiments, sparks of truth are struck out, and political light is obtained." V. W. Crane, "Franklin's 'The Internal State of America, 1786,'" *William and Mary Quarterly*, 15 (1958), 226. For Adams on "the greatest political evil," see *Works*, IX, 511, and for his views on party, John R. Howe, Jr., *The Changing Political Thought of John Adams* (1966), chapter 7.

states, recently liberated from colonial status, are trying to develop viable governments and national economies. Although the political history and the particular circumstances of most of the new nations are marked less by similarities than by profound differences from, even antitheses to, the pattern of Anglo-American development, the presence in the world of so many countries undergoing rapid and formative change has awakened among scholars an interest in the general phenomena of political development almost as keen as their interest in economic development, and this has helped us to take a fresh look at our own early history. People in the new states may ask from time to time whether recognized opposition parties would be, under their circumstances, an asset to national development or, as most of their leaders appear to have concluded from the very beginning, a dangerous and inadmissible luxury. The situation of the Americans in their formative years was unusually complex, and perhaps quite unique. The Founding Fathers had inherited a political philosophy which also denied the usefulness of parties and stressed their dangers. Yet they deeply believed in the necessity of checks on power, and hence in freedom for opposition, and were rapidly driven, in spite of their theories, to develop a party system.

The problem of the Jeffersonians as our first opposition party may then be seen as a part of a larger problem: How did this nation come to develop a responsible, effective, constitutional opposition? First, perhaps, a few clarifications are in order. When we speak of an opposition as being *constitutional,* we mean that both government and opposition are bound by the rules of some kind of constitutional consensus. It is understood, on one side, that opposition is directed against a certain policy or complex of policies, not against the legitimacy of the constitutional regime itself. Opposition rises above naked contestation; it forswears sedition, treason, conspiracy, *coup d'état,* riot, and assassination, and makes an open public appeal for the support of a more or less free electorate. Government, in return, is constrained by certain limitations as to the methods it can use to counter the opposition; the free expression of oppositional views is permitted both inside and outside the halls of the parliamentary body.

When we speak of an opposition as being *responsible,* we mean that it contains within itself the potential of an actual alternative government—that is, its critique of existing policies is not simply a wild attempt to outbid the existing regime in promises, but a sober attempt to formulate alternative policies which it believes to be capable of execution within the existing historical and economic framework, and to offer as its executors a competent alternative personnel that can actually govern. Here I do not mean to prejudge the question whether a nonresponsible critique of government may not also have some value. In fact, I believe that there is a useful agitational function to be performed under certain conditions by non-responsible groups: programs and critiques that are essentially utopian in content may have practical results if they bring neglected grievances to the surface or if they open lines of thought that have not been aired by less alienated and less imaginative centers of power. But this agitational function is not the same thing as the function of a responsible opposition.

When we speak of an opposition as being *effective*, we mean not merely that its programs are expected to be capable of execution, that its alternative policy is real, but that its capability of winning office is also real, that it has the institutional structure and the public force which makes it possible for us to expect that sooner or later it will in fact take office and bring to power an alternative personnel. If opposition, no matter how constitutional its methods and realistic its programs, is too minuscule or too fragmented to offer this alternative, it hardly qualifies on the grounds of effectiveness.[2] It might then be an educational force, but it is not a political one. Now it is an essential question, to which Western theorists usually give a negative answer, whether the requirement of effectiveness can be adequately met without opposition party structures. Effectiveness and organization, they conclude, complement each other.

Free opposition, working through party organization, whether concentrated in a single party or shared by several, is regarded today in most of the Western world to be essential to a representative democracy. To the modern democratic mind, familiar as it is with the one-party states of authoritarian regimes, freedom of opposition seems almost meaningless not only in the absence of certain enforceable guarantees of political rights but also in the absence of effective oppositional *structures* in the form of one or more political parties. Such opposition as can manage to make itself felt within the framework of one-party regimes is not credited by such theorists with much effect or with a value in any way comparable to that expressed through an alternative party or parties.[3]

---

[2] It may also be argued that if the opposition program offers nothing in fact but minuscule variations of that of the government, its status as an effective opposition is doubtful. This argument is related to the modern question whether an excess of consensus does not give rise to an opposition which, however free, is excessively compliant.

[3] A new interest in the means of control over governmental decisions in one-party systems has led to a revived interest in mechanisms of control, operating both inside and outside the single party. See, for example, Jerzy J. Wjatr and Adam Przeworski, "Control without Opposition," *Government and Opposition*, I (1966), 227–239, and Ghita Ionescu, "Control and Contestation in Some One-Party States," *ibid*., 240–250.

However, for a penetrating statement on the vital differences between oppositions under one-party and multi-party conditions, see Giovanni Sartori, *Democratic Theory* (ed. 1965), especially chap. V.

"The simplest and most realistic definition of democracy," writes Maurice Duverger in his standard work on *Political Parties*, "is the following: a regime in which those who govern are chosen by those who are governed, by means of free and open elections. . . . The existence of an organized opposition is an essential feature of 'Western' democracy, its absence a feature of 'Eastern' democracy." But like most other Western democratic theorists, Duverger expresses his skepticism of the possibilities of valuable opposition without an opposition party. For example, the internal opposition, in the form of "self-criticism," as practiced in the Russian Communist party, he finds to be more like public confession than genuine opposition. "Its aim is less to give form to any resistance to the regime than to overcome such resistance. . . . In the nature of things therefore an analysis of the influence of parties upon the function of the opposition must primarily deal with systems of more than one party."[4]

Other democratic theorists concur. "Modern democracy," says Hans Kelsen, "depends directly on political parties, whose importance becomes the greater the more strongly the democratic principle is realized." "The political parties," writes E. E. Schattschneider, "created modern democracy . . . and modern democracy is unthinkable save in terms of the parties. The most important distinction in modern political philosophy, the distinction between democracy and dictatorship, can be made best in terms of party politics." "The principle of representation," says Robert MacIver, "had to be vitalized by the conflict of parties. When parties flourish we have in effect passed from a pre-democratic mode of representative government to a genuinely democratic one." "Representative government," says Herman Finer succinctly, "is party government."[5]

All of this is quite at odds with the view of party opposition that most governments have in fact adopted. The normal view of governments about organized opposition is that it is intrinsically subversive and illegitimate. Their normal procedure is to smother or suppress it, using force or more subtle techniques, depending upon what seems necessary or efficacious in the circumstances. I need hardly say that I am speaking of the present as well as the past. Robert A. Dahl has pointed out that of the 113 members of the United Nations in 1964, only 30 countries had political systems in which full legal opposition by organized political parties has existed throughout the preceding decade.[6]

---

[4] Maurice Duverger, *Political Parties* (1954), 353, 413–414.

[5] Kelsen, *Vom Wesen und Wert der Demokratie* (1929) 19; E. E. Schattschneider, *Party Government* (1942), I; Robert MacIver, *The Web of Government* (1947), 210; Herman Finer, *Theory and Practice of Modern Government* (1949), 237; Finer uses this rubric as a chapter title.

[6] Robert A. Dahl, *Political Oppositions in Western Democracies* (1966), xi, 333.

The idea of a legitimate opposition—recognized opposition, organized and free enough in its activities to be able to displace an existing government by peaceful means—is an immensely sophisticated idea, and it was not an idea that the Fathers found fully developed and ready to hand when they began their enterprise in republican constitutionalism in 1788. We will misunderstand their politics badly if we read them so anachronistically as to imagine that they had a matured conception of a legitimate organized opposition or of a party system. Such a conception would certainly have engendered different political ideas and would probably have brought about different political practices. The Federalists and Republicans did not think of each other as alternating parties in a two-party system. Each side hoped instead to eliminate party conflict by persuading and absorbing the more acceptable and "innocent" members of the other; each side hoped to attach the stigma of foreign allegiance and disloyalty to the intractable leaders of the other, and to put them out of business as a party. The high point in Federalist efforts in this direction came with the Alien and Sedition Acts of 1798. The high point in Republican efforts came after the Treaty of Ghent in 1814. Where the Federalists had failed, the Republicans succeeded: the one-party period that came with the withering away of Federalism was seen by the Republicans not as an anomalous or temporary, much less as an undesirable eventuality, but as evidence of the correctness of their views and of the success of the American system.

There are, of course, many ways of looking at what the first generation under the Constitution accomplished—setting administrative precedents, establishing the national credit, forging a federal union in the teeth of provincial loyalties, winning a national domain, resisting European attempts to force the nation back into a quasi-colonial or inferior status—but one of the most important things they did was to come to terms with the idea of opposition and to experiment, despite their theories, with its incarnation in a party system. When they began their work, they spoke a great deal—indeed they spoke almost incessantly—about freedom; and they understood that freedom requires some latitude for opposition. But they were far from clear as to *how* opposition should make itself felt, for they also valued social unity or harmony, and they had not arrived at the view that opposition, manifested in organized popular parties, could sustain freedom without fatally shattering such harmony. Their skepticism about the value of parties made it inevitable that their discovery of a party system should be the product of drift and experimentation, that the rather nice system of implicit rules under which the modern two-party duel takes place could be arrived at only after many misunderstandings and some serious missteps. All their work in party development had to be undertaken without the advantage of adequate practical precedents, either in their own pre-revolutionary provincial experience, or in the political practices of Georgian England; and it had to be undertaken without much theoretical guidance. Under such circumstances, it is entirely understandable that they should have taken a certain amount of time in developing a party democracy.

* * * * *

The Founding Fathers . . . did not believe in political parties as such, scorned those that they were conscious of as historical models, had a keen terror of party spirit and its evil consequences, and yet, almost as soon as their national government was in operation, found it necessary to establish parties. They had framed a Constitution which, among its other ends, was meant to control and counteract parties, and yet they gradually began to realize that they could not govern under it without the help of such organizations. Indeed it may appear to us, with the benefit of long historical perspective, that the new Constitution which they had so ingeniously drawn up could never have been made to work if some of its vital deficiencies, not least the link between the executive and the legislature, had not been remedied by the political party. They did not believe, as modern democrats do, that partisan competition is an asset to the political order under what they called free government; nor had they yet even conceived of a party system. Yet despite themselves they gradually gave form to the first American party system, and under it gave the world its first example of the peaceful transit of a government from the control of one popular party to another.

Of course it is important to realize that the Founding Fathers were more accurately criticizing the rudimentary parties they had seen in action or had read of in their histories than the modern parties they were themselves beginning to build for the future. They stood at a moment of fecund inconsistency, suspended between their acceptance on one side of political differences and opposition criticism, and on the other their rejection of parties as agencies to organize social conflict and political debate. They well understood that conflicts of opinion are inevitable in a state of republican freedom, but they wanted to minimize such conflicts and hoped to achieve a comprehensive unity or harmony. They did not usually see conflict as functional to society, and above all they could not see how organized and institutionalized party conflict could be made useful, or could be anything other than divisive, distracting, and dangerous.

For this reason the history of the United States during the first quarter century of government under the federal Constitution marked a focal episode in the development of the idea of legitimate opposition.

In Anglo-American experience the idea of free political criticism had made vital gains in the eighteenth century. But in England what was then called a "formed opposition"—that is, an organized and continuous opposition group, as distinct from an individual speaking his mind in or out of a parliamentary body—still fell short of respectability, and in the minds of many men was tainted with disloyalty, subversion, or treason. Even in America, where the battle with royal governors had created a strong tradition of oppositional politics, the idea of a mass party as an extension of parliamentary discussion and opposition was not widely accepted. It was held by most men to be particularly unsuited to government under a representative republic, where representative institutions themselves were believed sufficient to serve the public interest.

* * * * *

The idea that parties might perhaps be vindicated by their services to the body politic was not unknown or unthinkable here. Americans had had much experience with intense factionalism in the colonial period, and though they had not learned to like it, they had become aware that it could be endured. They were becoming conscious of the healthy plurality of interests and sects that prevailed among them, and were growing increasingly aware of the necessity for mutual tolerance that this imposed—two elements of consciousness that provided the intellectual and moral prerequisites of an understanding of the party system. To be sure, most of their discussions of parties and factions, as Bernard Bailyn has observed, dwelt at length on "their destructiveness, the history of the evils they brought upon mankind, their significance as symptoms of disease in the body politic." Yet Bailyn notices an occasional flicker of dissent, the American counterpart of that dissent Caroline Robbins has remarked on in the English scene. A writer in the *New York Gazette* in the early 1730s suggests that opposition "is not only necessary in free governments but of great service to the public," argues that parties "are a check upon one another, and by keeping the ambition of one another within bounds, serve to maintain public liberty," and postulates that "opposition is the life and soul of public zeal." Fifteen years later another argues that "parties in a free state ought rather to be considered as an advantage to the public than an evil" because they are "so many spies upon one another, ready to proclaim abroad and warn the public of any attack or encroachment upon the public liberty."[7] A full study of the development of the idea of party might show that other obscure writers were stumbling upon or toying with the idea that par-

---

[7] Bernard Bailyn, *The Origins of American Politics* (1968), 125, 126.

ties, if they could be kept in healthy competition with each other, would act as mutual checks and thus contribute to the balance of society.

Near the end of the century one finds this occurring from time to time, even among some of those whom we must on balance classify as anti-party thinkers. For example, a delegate to the Massachusetts ratifying convention of 1788, arguing for the Constitution, thought that the "competition of interest . . . between those persons who are in and those who are out of office, will ever form one important check to the abuse of power in our representatives." Arguing on the other side of the issue, a Maryland Anti-Federalist writer put it this way: "And learn this most difficult and necessary lesson: That on the preservation of parties public liberty depends. Whenever men are unanimous on great public questions, whenever there is but one party, freedom ceases and despotism commences. The object of a free and wise people should be so to balance parties, that *from the weakness of all you may be governed by the moderation of the combined judgments of the whole, not tyrannized over by the blind passions of a few individuals.*"[8] This statement of the case is so shrewd that one is disappointed to find it imbedded in a rather soggy and almost incoherent essay.

Again, Representative Robert Goodloe Harper, one of the most interesting minds among the Federalists, declared in the House in January, 1798, in the course of an argument over office-holding, that he considered parties not only inevitable but desirable. Opposition parties in government, he said, were like competitors in a public exhibition: "The public is the judge, the two parties are the combatants, and that party which possesses power must employ it properly, must conduct the Government wisely, in order to insure public approbation, and retain their power. In this contention, while the two parties draw different ways, a middle course is produced generally conformable to the public good." Party spirit, he conceded, might run to excess, as a wind gives rise to a storm or fire to a conflagration, "but its general effects, like those of the great elements of nature," he had no doubt, "were beneficial."[9] Again a highly suggestive statement; but one would be more inclined to attach profound significance to it if Harper had not been found six months later arguing zealously for the Sedition Act, which was intended to put the opposition out of business.

Even Hamilton himself, on at least one occasion, could see how partisan division within parliaments could have some merit now and

---

[8] For the Massachusetts spokesman, see Elliot's *Debates*, II, 167; for the Maryland writer, Morton Borden's collection of Anti-Federalist writings, *The Antifederalist Papers* (1965), 27.

[9] *Annals of Congress*, 5th Congress, 2d sess. , 873–874 (January 19, 1798); see below p. 116 n.

then. In *The Federalist* Number 70, at a point where he is discussing the necessity of promptitude and firmness of decision in the Executive, he pauses to concede that the same is not true to the same degree of the legislature: "In the legislature, promptitude of decision is oftener an evil than a benefit. The differences of opinion, and the jarrings of parties in that department of the government, though they may sometimes obstruct salutary plans, yet often promote deliberation and circumspection, and serve to check excesses in the majority. When a resolution too is once taken, the opposition must be at an end. That resolution is a law and resistance to it is punishable."[10] There are of course, some ambiguities in this: it is in no wise clear from this whether Hamilton saw that there might be merit in a mass party as well as a parliamentary party. Also one may ponder his assertion that opposition to a law, once passed, is "punishable." Does he mean only that the law must be obeyed, or is he trying to assert the far more objectionable proposition that criticism itself is no longer acceptable? His language indeed suggests the latter, for he speaks not of "disobedience" but of "opposition" as necessarily coming to an end. Be that as it may, we can at best make but little of this obiter dictum in behalf of opposition on the part of a man who sought to unite all parties in the general welfare.

John Adams was another anti-party theorist who had a glimmering of the possible value of an opposition. As early as 1779, speaking of the situation in Congress under the Articles, he wrote: "An opposition in parliament, in a house of assembly, in a council, in Congress, is highly useful and necessary to balance individuals, and bodies, and interests against one another, and bring the truth to light and justice to prevail." But an opposition in a foreign embassy, in the circumstances of this country and of Europe, is ruin, he went on, because it destroys the necessary secrecy and confidence. While he thus accepted the value of a parliamentary opposition, it is doubtful that he would also have accepted an opposition functioning among the people as an organized party. Certainly he did not seek such a thing for the United States. In the following year he wrote a letter in which he said: "There is nothing which I dread so much as a division of the republic into two great parties, each arranged under its leader, and concerting measures in opposition to each other. This, in my humble apprehension, is to be dreaded as the greatest political evil under our Constitution."[11]

A few observers, then, saw that parties could be good because instead of making for aggrandizement of power they offered another possible source of checks and balances in addition to those already built

---

[10] *The Federalist*, 454.
[11] *Works*, IX, 485, 511.

into the constitutional structure. A few others saw the value of opposition, short of party organization. So far as I have been able to determine, none saw that parties might perform a wide variety of positive functions necessary to representative democracy and unlikely to be performed as well by any other institutions. This seems more understandable when we consider not only the state of party in eighteenth-century thought but also the state of party development in eighteenth-century practice. The Founding Fathers did not have, in their current experience or historical knowledge, models of working parties that would have encouraged them to think in such terms. First, parties had to be created; and then at last they would begin to find a theoretical acceptance.

* * * * *

The modern idea of the political party, and with it a fully matured conception of the function of legitimate opposition, flowered first among the second generation of American political leaders—that is, among men who were in the main still children when the Federalist and Republican parties were founded. Where the Federalists and Republicans, still enchanted with eighteenth-century visions of political harmony, had schemed to devour, absorb, or annihilate each other, many Republicans raised on the one-party politics of the misnamed Era of Good Feelings, began to see clearly and consistently what such predecessors as Madison and Jefferson had seen only dimly and fitfully—the merits of the party organization as a positive principle, and of two-party competition as an asset to the public interest. The men of the second generation built firmly upon the foundations of early Jeffersonian experience with the organization of the party, but in both theory and practice they went well beyond their predecessors.

Deferential-Participant Politics:
The Early Republic's
Political Culture, 1789–1840

Ronald P. Formisano

*Ronald Formisano is especially well known for studies bridging the tran-
sition from the first party struggle to the second. His books include*
The Birth of Mass Political Parties: Michigan, 1827–1861 *(Princeton:
Princeton University Press, 1971) and* The Transformation of Political
Culture: Massachusetts Parties, 1790s–1840s *(New York: Oxford University Press, 1983). This article was an extended, systematic effort to
assess the similarities and differences between the first party conflict and
later party systems. Reprinted by permission from the* American Political
Science Review, *LXVIII (June, 1974), 473–487, it cautions us effectively
against the facile and anachronistic use of social science terms.*

Political parties in the United States took their basic form within a period
extending from the 1790s to the 1840s. Though historians perhaps have
compartmentalized this process excessively, theoretical concerns are
cutting through the time boundaries of conventional periodizations.
Amidst a still great variety of studies in this area, three general trends
may be discerned. (1) A few bold spirits venture to work with theories of modernization, national integration, and political development.
Their outlook is at least implicitly cross-national and comparative. (2)
Others, writing less ambitious histories, use the middle-range concepts of the first group, and occasionally generate their own. (3) The
great majority of historians continue to write monographs conceived
in traditional modes, tilling circumscribed plots of time, ignoring theory and comparison. Obviously, the contributions of the latter two will
attain more general interest as they lose preoccupation with the unique
and make explicit their theoretical assumptions. The theorists, in turn,
surely need continuous interaction with empirical studies at the grass-
roots. Ironically, the main point of convergence for these disparate
efforts, the concept of party, may be a source of shared illusion. In
general, catch phrases and catch-words such as "party system," "democratization" or "the decline of deference," propositions which began

as unresearched hypotheses, have almost imperceptibly become imbedded in the conventional wisdom. Generalizations about party formation, especially, seem to be outrunning their empirical bases, and "party system" may have mushroomed into an anachronism distorting the character of early national political life.

The basic idea of *party*, often loaded with cultural connotations, serves to organize political phenomena which may not fit a party mold. The era from Washington to "Tippecanoe and Tyler Too" should be thought of primarily as a transitional phase of political culture in which the passage from a traditional, notable-oriented and deferential politics on the one hand to a party electorate-oriented and egalitarian style of politics on the other, did not come about abruptly. The alleged first party system of Federalists and Republicans (1790s–1820s) reached backward into eighteenth century political culture as much as it forecast the shape of future politics. Partisan behavior was certainly present, and some men even advocated "party" as a positive good. But such precocious partisans were rare, and partisan activity is not necessarily the same as institutionalized party behavior—however haphazard that may be when fully operational in the American context. As a transition in political culture, then, the early republican era is best viewed as a deferential-participant phase somewhere between traditional forms and mass party politics, having some features of both.

This is not merely a question of timing, though even as such it has important ramifications, such as its bearing on the controversy over the causal relationship between party and democracy. Although few investigations have been designed to assess directly claims made in praise or blame of parties' role in the process of "democratization," many recent writers confidently celebrate the advent of Political Party in history. They believe that a competitive, two-party system opened up political life, brought distant governments closer to more citizens, and made power more responsive to constituent demands. In the celebratory tradition, party virtually equals democracy. Parties receive praise also as guarantors of stability. Some theorists believe that societies such as the United States, England, India, and Japan have enjoyed stable political systems because strong parties channeled newly mobilized electorates.[1] Thus, the wonders worked by parties increase, and they rise once again to almost providential proportions—even as our present parties show striking signs of decay.[2]

---

[1] J. Rogers Hollingsworth, "An Approach to the Study of Comparative Historical Politics," in *Nation and State Building in America: Comparative Historical Perspectives* ed. J. R. Hollingsworth (Boston: Little, Brown, 1971), p. 266.

[2] Walter Dean Burnham, *Critical Elections and the Mainsprings of American Politics* (New York: Norton, 1970), pp. 91–134.

Although celebrants of party have written valuable studies, even
the wisest seem mesmerized by several assumptions which rest on faith
rather than works, on values rather than data. The most sweeping
assumption is the Idea of Political Progress: that the political system
of the United States "matured" from 1789 to 1840 toward a more democratic, efficient, equitable, moral and just form, with competitive parties as the key vehicle of change. The Idea of Political Progress through
Party depends in turn on a premise which Frank Sorauf has called "the
myth of party primacy." Sorauf explained this as a tendency to consider
American parties "as independent agencies . . . —as some *élan vital*,
some autonomous, ordering force set loose in the system. It has been
customary," Sorauf added, "to speak of the parties as 'democratizing'
American politics as if they were reforming missionaries from some far-
off places."[3]

Critics of party, from Moisei Ostrogorski to Edward Pessen, have
challenged the celebrants' equations. They observe that politics remained
as much under elite control after, as before party competition in an
extended electorate. They describe "democratization" as largely a matter
of rhetoric and style. Beneath the hoopla of "The Age of the Common
Man" they discern the iron law of oligarchy at work. But the skeptics
tend to carry their critique too far, and so err in another direction.
Like the celebrants, the debunkers of party are reacting against a liberal-
conservative ideological scheme imposed earlier on parties by Progressive
historians: the result is an exaggerated view of parties as electoral
machines unrelated to conflicts over values and social belief-systems.
Thus the critics tend to empty party politics of its social, cultural and
ideological content.[4]

Critics, celebrants, and those in between often join in using a
metaphor about American parties: the party as machine: a centralized, disciplined, and rational electoral organization. Admittedly oli-
garchic, it is an institution allegedly characterized by wide participation
in internal decision making. The machine metaphor, partly as a simple
literary convenience, has exaggerated the cohesion of United States parties throughout their existence, but particularly in the early republic.
Scholars have overestimated the extent to which *institutionalized* parties
structured politics before the 1830s. To be institutionalized an organization must: (1) be well bounded or differentiated from its environ-

---

[3] Frank J. Sorauf, "Political Parties and Political Analysis," in *The American Party Systems:
Stages of Political Development*, ed. William Nisbet Chambers and Walter Dean Burnham
(New York: Oxford Univ. Press, 1967). p. 49.
[4] This point is made by: Herbert Ershkowitz and William G. Shade, "Consensus or
Conflict? Political Behavior in the State Legislatures During the Jacksonian Era," *Journal
of American History*, 58 (December, 1971), 591–621.

ment; (2) have functions that are complex and separated internally on some regular and explicit bases; and (3) use universal rather than particular criteria in conducting its internal business.[5] Above all, it has a life—and goals—of its own; its pre-eminent goal is survival. If criteria of institutionalization are applied with any rigor, then fully developed parties cannot be said to appear in the United States until the late 1830s or early 1840s, that is, parties with structures characteristic of our present relatively decentralized and undisciplined parties.[6]

Too often historians have focused on certain sectors of apparent partisan activity—Congressional debates in the 1790s, patronage under Jefferson, or cadre men organizing in the 1820s—and assumed that a party "system" existed throughout the polity. An explicit rather than a working definition of party can help avoid this simple error. Sorauf's definition of party as a "tripartite organization" can focus the historian's attention on what is "empirically observable." Sorauf thinks of party as composed of three elements: (1) the "organization proper"—party officials, activists, members, "the purposeful, organized, initiating vanguard of the party"; (2) "the party in office"—including legislative parties, caucuses, floor leaders, whips, and patronage networks; (3) "the party-in-the-electorate—the least stable, least active, least involved, and least well-organized of the three sectors," the individual voters who identify with the party and for whom it is a "symbol that provides cues and orders to the political cosmos."[7] These three elements should

---

[5] Nelson W. Polsby, "The Institutionalization of the U. S. House of Representatives," *American Political Science Review*, 62 (March, 1968), 145. Polsby's full definition of an institutionalized organization: "(1) it is relatively well-bounded, that is . . . differentiated from its environment. Its members are easily identifiable, it is relatively difficult to become a member, and its leaders are recruited principally from within the organization. (2) The organization is relatively complex, that is, its functions are internally separated on some regular and explicit basis, its parts are not wholly interchangeable, and for at least some important purposes, its parts are interdependent. There is a division of labor in which roles are specified. . . . (3) Finally, the organization tends to universalistic rather than particularistic criteria, and automatic rather than discretionary methods for conducting its internal business. Precedents and rules are followed; merit systems replace favoritism and nepotism; and impersonal codes supplant personal preferences as prescriptions for behavior.

[6] The decentralizing tendencies of American parties are discussed in Morton Grodzins, "American Political Parties and the American System," *Western Political Quarterly*, 13 (December, 1960), 974–98.

[7] Sorauf, "Political Parties and Political Analysis," pp. 37–38. Chambers recently defined party in the modern sense "as a relatively durable social formation which seeks offices or power in government, exhibits a structure of organization which links leaders at the center of government to a significant popular following in the political arena and its local enclaves, and generates in-group perspectives or at least symbols of identification or loyalty." "Party Development and the American Mainstream," in Chambers and Burnham, *American Party Systems, p. 5.*

be thought of as variables present over time in different combinations and intensity, on local, state, and national levels. Party exists when activists, officials, and voters interact and when they consciously identify with a common name and symbols. Sorauf's three analytic categories are of course transcended in reality by an entity which aspires to overarch federalism and the separation of powers. Instead, the party's inherent ambition to unify various levels of government violated the Whig heritage of the Revolution and some of the most sacred values of eighteenth-century political culture.[8]

With such a definition, party origins in the United States can be approached best in an expanded time framework. All elements of party in specific localities might be studied, or one or more elements in states or regions might be followed from the 1790s through the 1830s. Those studies carrying through the period might, as a bonus, rescue the 1820s from their relative conceptual limbo.

If guidelines such as these are pursued, the "first party system" may well become a casualty of subsequent research. As will become clear below, there is some reason to be skeptical of the concept. Although I personally do not now believe in a first party system of Federalists and Republicans as conventionally portrayed, the evidence at hand is inconclusive. When read critically, with the criteria outlined above in mind, the first system literature does not support its own conceptual burden. Nor does the residue of evidence permit us to discard the notion that some partisan activity developed in places at various times from 1800 to 1820, and that some states produced tentative party action in one or more of Sorauf's three categories of party. An institutionalized national party system, however, was most remote. I doubt there will be much justification for calling the first sporadic gropings toward national organization in 1800 and afterward the first modern parties, or for describing Federalist-Republican rivalries as a system of patterned roles, functions, and expectations. Yet this essay will achieve one of its goals if it induces even a temporary suspension of belief in the first party system. Beyond that, it might stimulate refinement of concepts describing stages of party growth.[9]

---

[8] The last sentences are paraphrases from William G. Shade, personal communication.

[9] The passages which follow will argue in effect that the first parties do not meet the criteria of party set forth by one of their leading historians, as, e.g., in William N. Chambers, *Political Parties in a New Nation: The American Experience, 1776–1809* (New York: Oxford University Press, 1963), pp. 44–48. Since then, however, Chambers has proposed a very useful taxonomy of political parties; see W. N. Chambers, review of *Political Parties Before the Constitution*, by Jackson Turner Main, *Reviews in American History*, 1 (December, 1973), 499–503.

Critique of the First Party System Literature

Although the concept of "party system" by itself reflects the impact of social science on political history (particularly Parsonian sociology),[10] the historical construct objected to here is not of recent origin. For a long time historians have believed that Hamiltonians and Jeffersonians organized parties soon after the establishment of a national arena. In older monographs, researchers seldom provided explicit definitions of party.

Absence of definitions, however, is not a fatal criticism of modern general works which support the historiographical edifice of the first party system: the well-known books of Joseph Charles, Manning Dauer, and Noble Cunningham.[11] Moreover, William Chambers's synthesis, *Political Parties in a New Nation* (1963), not only defined party politics as distinct from colonial and revolutionary political formations, but also introduced a high degree of conceptual refinement to the historical discussion.

Viewed as a group, these works display a disturbing symmetry between their methods and conclusions. In taking a nationwide perspective they quite naturally analyzed party formation *from the top down.* Party conflict originated, they found, at the center, in Washington's cabinet and the national legislature. As faction turned into party it radiated out to the states after 1794–95, with national elites stimulating local party cadres into being. It can be easily argued, as these historians know, that these activities did not constitute purposive party building.[12] Nor, in my view, did they intentionally set out to perform political functions. Policy conflicts came first, followed by attempts to reach out to state and local factions for support. Diverging elites increasingly sought electoral support to maintain, increase, or gain power, to be used to initi-

---

[10] One representative work among many is David Easton, *The Political System: An Inquiry into the State of Political Science* (New York: Knopf, 1953).

[11] Joseph Charles, *The Origins of the American Party System: Three Essays* (Williamsburg, Va.: Institute of Early American History and Culture, 1956); Manning J. Dauer, *The Adams Federalists*, 2nd ed. 1953; (Baltimore: Johns Hopkins University Press, 1968); Noble E. Cunningham, Jr., *The Jeffersonian Republicans: The Formation of Party Organization, 1789–1801* (Chapel Hill: University of North Carolina Press, 1957); Cunningham, *The Jeffersonian Republicans in Power: Party Operations, 1801–1809* (1963). A similar error is made by Lisle A. Rose, *Prologue to Democracy: The Federalists of the South, 1789–1800* (Lexington: University of Kentucky Press, 1968), which otherwise offers useful concepts.

[12] For an excellent synthesis that is not tied to the first system model and admirably eschews "party" for the period 1790s–1820s, see Roy F. Nichols, *The Invention of the American Political Parties: A Study in Political Improvisation* (New York: Macmillan, 1967), esp. pp. 158–247. On partisan consciousness in the 1790s, see Franklyn George Bonn, Jr., "The Idea of Political Party in the Thought of Thomas Jefferson and James Madison" (Doctoral dissertation, University of Minnesota, 1964).

ate, protect or change policy. This argument might be extended, but my initial objection is simply that the top down method exaggerates the extent of party penetration across the country. For example, focusing on the "apex" year of 1800, historians in search of national parties have been able to create them by piecing together a wide assortment of campaign activities up and down the Atlantic seaboard. But the fragments so assembled have not been shown to exhibit Chambers' criteria of durability over time.[13]

Moreover, recent monographs by Alfred Young, Paul Goodman, and James Banner, although written within the first system mold, contradict the thesis that party formation flowed from the center outward. All three authors emphasize internal stimuli and indigenous historic conflicts. Young concluded that "the national party appears to have been no more than a loose amalgam of state groups." Goodman spoke of Federalists and Republicans as "loose collections of provincial interests. . . . Highly local, evolving from rivalries within towns and cities, counties and states, they appealed to an electorate without firmly anchored, hereditary loyalties."[14] These studies suggest that the initial vantage point from which scholars describe party formation affects their interpretation of origins.

It would be misleading to leave the impression that only recent state monographs have questioned elements of the first system model. Take, for example, Pennsylvania, a large, heterogeneous state which is universally said to have produced sophisticated parties far in advance of other states. Given the location of the national government in Philadelphia during the 1790s, it has been taken for granted that Pennsylvanians, led by a vanguard of professional politicians, responded early to "national stimuli." Yet a close reading of the standard books covering Pennsylvania politics form 1790 to 1816, by Harry M. Tinkcom and Sanford W. Higginbotham, will not carry the burden of party institutionalization which the first system syndrome has anachronistically laid upon it.

Tinkcom made clear that party names remained uncertain throughout the 1790s. When the terms "Federalist" and "Republican" were used

---

[13] Durability and regularity are criteria suggested by Chambers, *Political Parties in a New Nation*, pp. 45–47.

[14] Alfred F. Young, *The Democratic Republicans of New York: The Origins, 1763–1797* (Chapel Hill: University of North Carolina Press, 1967), pp. 570, 578. Paul Goodman, *The Democratic Republicans of Massachusetts: Politics in a Young Republic* (Cambridge, Mass.: Harvard University Press, 1964), p. 204. James M. Banner, Jr. , *To the Hartford Convention: The Federalists and the Origins of Party Politics In Massachusetts, 1789–1815* (New York: Knopf, 1970), pp. 217, 221, 227–28. A similar point is made by Norman K. Risjord, "The Virginia Federalists," *Journal of Southern History*, 33 (November, 1967), 486–517.

before 1796, they "most accurately applied to opinion groups, to ideological 'climates,' " not to "parties which in the mass designated themselves as Federalist or Republican." Nor in 1796 did leading newspapers use consistent party labels, either in reference to their opponents or themselves.[15] County nominating meetings across the state presented "tickets" for state legislative elections, but these assemblages were not "self-avowed party groups. . . . almost invariably the candidates were sponsored by the conventional 'numerous and respectable meeting of citizens. '" Yet by 1797, Tinckom said, "general party terms were beginning to creep into editorial phraseology."[16] Tinkcom's evidence for this claim, as for many like it, came principally from Philadelphia newspapers. Indeed, it is not too unfair to say that Tinkcom's study of party emergence in Pennsylvania from 1790 to 1801 very much reflected the surfacing of partisan consciousness in the minds of two Philadelphia editors, John Fenno and Benjamin F. Bache.[17] Tinkcom did find individual instances of advanced party thinking in 1797 and 1799, but the absence of party thinking and organization impressed this reader far more. In 1799, for example, an "assembly of plain republicans" nominated ("Federalist") James Ross for governor. After the election, the victorious "Republican" candidate Thomas McKean did not call himself a Republican but favored the term "Whig" as he had throughout the decade. In that election "there was much stealing of thunder; the Republicans insisted they were the true 'Federalists,' and their opponents . . . declared with equal vigor that they were the 'real republicans.'"[18]

Higginbotham took up where Tinkcom left off. Although summaries of both books often lead one to believe otherwise, Higginbotham did not show that a party system "took off" in Pennsylvania after 1800. Rather, the Federalists "virtually disappeared" by 1802, while the Republicans, who had organized at the local level, spiralled into factionalism. By 1805 the contest for governor was between two Republican factions, with the winning coalition composed of incumbent

---

[15] Harry Martin Tinkcom, *The Republicans and Federalists in Pennsylvania, 1789–1801: A Study in National Stimulus and Local Response* (Harrisburg: Pennsylvania Historical and Museum Commission, 1950), pp. 52, 154, 161–62. Compare Charles, *Origins,* p. 42, n. 82.

[16] Tinkcom, pp. 179–80.

[17] Tinkcom, p. 191. Bache's death in 1798 interfered with Tinkcom's observation of parties because, as Tinkcom said, no other Philadelphia publisher emulated his advanced evaluation of parties.

[18] Pro-party thinking, Tinkcom, pp. 192–93, 236–37; regarding Ross, pp. 229, 309; McKean, pp. 253, 262; 1799 election, pp. 237–38. The partisan vocabulary used on a patronage list by William Duane in 1801 is quite revealing, p. 267.

Republicans and Federalist allies. Partisan conflict revived in 1808, and again in 1812, as foreign trade and war issues brought Federalism back to life. Even during the war of 1812, however, party conflict lost its edge, and an indestructible Republican factionalism persisted.

Higginbotham provided little evidence for an ongoing two-party system. For national elections the Federalists were nonexistent. Their organization was so casual "as to make it a real question whether they constituted a party or a state of mind."[19] The Republicans had local organizations, but their state party was little more than a loose collection of county groups. Higginbotham concluded that "there existed no continuing party organizations on the national level, nor even within the states. Furthermore, the course of politics in Pennsylvania was principally concerned with state and local rather than national issues."[20] Pennsylvania Republicans never developed a regular mode of nominating state candidates, and experimented with caucus, convention or mixed methods throughout the period. Does all this deserve to be called a "system"?

Doubts about the first system also arise from flaws in descriptions of party formation in Congress. One scholar discovered two self-conscious parties "crystallizing" in 1792 in the national legislature.[21] Joseph Charles put party emergence no earlier than 1794 and, on balance, favored 1795. Cunningham and Chambers located the nearly complete polarization of Congress in the Jay Treaty session of 1795–96. Dauer's evidence, as I read it, could make a case for the 1797–98, Alien-Sedition Congress.[22] Quite recently, a quantitative study of congressional roll calls from 1789 to 1796 concluded that two voting blocs "which were forged in the First Congress had reached maturity by the Third, well before the Jay Treaty controversy. By 1795 not only divisive foreign policy decisions, but also domestic matters and governmental routine, had become the objects of systematic party dispute."[23] This latter study seems to represent a severe case of the voting bloc fallacy—by which parties are equated with voting blocs—which can also be found in the general works. As James S. Young pointed out in his

---

[19] Sanford W. Higginbotham, *The Keystone in the Democratic Arch: Pennsylvania Politics, 1800–1816* (Harrisburg: Pennsylvania Historical and Museum Commission, 1952), p. 19.

[20] Higginbotham, pp. 329–30.

[21] John C. Miller, *The Federalist Era, 1789–1801* (New York: Harper and Row, 1960), p. 99.

[22] Dauer, *Adams Federalists*, pp. 132, 133, 135, 170–71.

[23] Mary P. Ryan, "Party Formation in the United States Congress, 1789 to 1796: A Quantitative Analysis," *William and Mary Quarterly*, 28 (October, 1971), 541. In a detailed critique of Ryan, Henderson accepts the first system framework, yet suggests strategies which potentially transcend it, H. James Henderson, "Quantitative Approaches to Party Formation in the United States Congress: A Comment," With a Reply by Mary P. Ryan, *William and Mary Quarterly*, 30 (April, 1973), 307–24, especially pp. 319–20.

provocative study, *The Washington Community, 1800–1828* (1966), the tendency of legislatures to form voting blocs does not automatically prove the presence of party in proportion to the cohesion of the blocs. After analyzing the early government community as a political anthropologist might, Young maintained that patterns of congressional voting correlated highly with the boarding-house residences of legislators. The members tended to live mostly with men from their own regions and, with great regularity, to vote with these same messmates. Although Young should have tested more thoroughly for partisan motivation before reading it out of the picture, his book constitutes a thrust at the very nerve center of the first system, meriting critical attention. It cannot be refuted by ignoring it. The issue is not simply one of regionalism versus party, but rather of a multiplicity of motives and influences affecting legislative behavior. A more flexible approach to party development should incorporate and transcend Young and the more conventional view.[24]

Multivariate analysis of roll calls needs to be accompanied by evidence that men ran for Congress as openly identified members of a party. To show convincingly that the core factions of Federalist and Republican interest came to think of themselves in party terms, consideration must be given to legislators' self-images, and their concepts of role, loyalty, and representation.[25]

With respect to the self-image of political leaders in the 1790s, it is generally agreed that they did not see themselves as party builders.[26] Furthermore, to the extent that Federalists or Republicans became conscious of "party," most seem to have deliberately rejected the norms of systematic party competition. Men largely remained rooted in an older politics, one that remained hostile to the idea of party as "legitimate opposition." Some states parties tried to eliminate the opposition until

---

[24] A developing rebuttal is mostly unpublished at the moment, e.g., Harry William Fritz, "The Collapse of Party: President, Congress, and the Decline of Party Action, 1807–1817." (Doctoral dissertation, Washington University, 1971); and Ronald L. Hatzenbuehler, "Foreign Policy Voting in the United States Congress, 1808–1812." (Doctoral dissertation, Kent State University, 1972). Hatzenbuehler has published an article, discussed below. Fritz showed that formal partisanship hardly existed in 1809, but from 1812 to 1815 found a high degree of voting cohesion, especially on war related issues. The return of peace, however, "demolished the party system." Fritz directly challenged Young's revisionism, but seemed to replace it at several key points only with assertions, ignoring particularly the problem of party label and self-consciousness, p. 241, n. 51, and ff.

[25] Extensive projects of congressional roll call analysis are underway, descriptions of which appear frequently in the *Historical Methods Newsletter*, e.g. 5 (June, 1972), 139.

[26] The modern party, in Paul Goodman's words, was outside the range of consciousness of that generation. Goodman, "The First American Party System," in *American Party Systems*, ed. Chambers and Burnham, p. 57.

well into the nineteenth century. Jefferson as president was not above the Sedition Law effort of trying to silence the opposition. Public officials and electorates did not believe that virtue demanded adherence to party norms.[27] Rather, many thought party at best a necessary evil and some activists did not come to revere party as a positive good until 1840 and beyond. Resistance subsided unevenly to the idea of party as an *enduring institution commanding a separate loyalty.*

Party as Organization, 1789–1840

Using Sorauf's tripartite approach to observing parties, one should be able to assess roughly the degree of institutionalization of the first parties as organizations, in office, and in electorates. This analysis can also serve to indicate some research opportunities. Federalist and Republican national organizations proper, for example, were incipient at best, and research here may have been carried as far as it's going to be.[28] Still, a long-run analysis of national organizations has not been attempted and histories of the 1824 and 1844 period are rife with conflicting claims about when national organizations took charge of campaigns. As late as 1836, however, the Whig "party" had no less than four favorite-son sectional candidates running for president. Yet historians profess to see national party organizations emerging even earlier than this national anti-Democratic coalition.[29]

Furthermore, although the study of organizations is the study of men, the organizers themselves have received little attention. We need studies of elite motivation, socialization, and recruitment. Specifically, the much heralded replacement of traditional notables by a "new class" of professional politicians should be systematically studied. Rising professionals, like declining deference, litter the entire early national period. These catch-phrases sprawl everywhere across the era

---

[27] Robert A. Dahl, ed., *Political Opposition in Western Democracies* (New Haven: Yale University Press, 1966). Richard Hofstadter, *The Idea of a Party System: The Rise of Legitimate Opposition in the United States* (Berkeley: University of California Press, 1970). Leonard W. Levy, *Jefferson and Civil Liberties: The Darker Side* (Cambridge, Mass.: Harvard University Press, 1963), pp. 46–69.

[28] James Staton Chase, "Jacksonian Democracy and the Rise of the National Nominating Convention," *Mid-America*, 45 (October, 1963), 229–49; Banner, To *the Hartford Convention*, pp. 295–312.

[29] Joel H. Silbey, "Election of 1836, in *History of American Presidential Elections, 1789–1968*, Arthur M. Schlesinger, Jr., and Fred L. Israel, eds. (New York: Mc Graw-Hill, 1971), I, 1789–1844, 577–600. Richard P. McCormick, *The Second American Party System: Party Formation in the Jacksonian Era* (Chapel Hill: University of North Carolina Press, 1966), pp. 13–15, 238–40. The essays in the Schlesinger-Israel volume testify to the absence of national organizations before 1840.

as loose, all-purpose and unexamined hypotheses. Collective biographies of local or regional elites could help resolve some of these questions empirically.[30]

Any redistribution of influence or power could be illuminated further by studies focused on public and private patronage. Carl Prince's study of New Jersey's Jeffersonian Republicans, although also conforming to first system orthodoxy, pointed to what might be done regarding state patronage.[31] Prince identified 256 Republican activists during the period 1800 to 1816, and found that nearly two-thirds held appointive office. Thus the party rewarded its activists. Or did it? The existence of an institutionalized party and unambiguous party identity is not indisputably established by Prince.[32] Appointment policy generally seems not to have become governed completely or even mostly by partisan considerations. Only slightly more than 20 percent of *all* state and federal appointees in New Jersey from 1800 to 1816 were veteran Republicans. In 1816, 22.3 percent of federal appointees were known to be active partisans.[33] On what bases were the remaining three-quarters selected? The Republicans dominated appointments during the era almost completely, and the balance could not all have been Federalist holdovers. Prince's data thus raise a question about *patronage modes* in general. The data might be taken as an index of limited penetration of party into patronage. More certainly, they suggest the need for inquiry into the universe of patronage practices from 1789 to 1840.[34]

---

[30] A provocative essay which attempts to put the professionals' rise in perspective is Lynn W. Marshall, "The Strange Stillbirth of the Whig Party," *American Historical Review*, 72 (January, 1967), 445–68; note Marshall's disagreement with Chambers, p. 462, n. 47. The approach recommended here might emulate: James Q. Wilson, *The Amateur Democrat: Club Politics in Three Cities* (Chicago: University of Chicago Press, 1962).

[31] Carl E. Prince, *New Jersey's Jeffersonian Republicans: The Genesis of an Early Political Machine, 1789–1817* (Chapel Hill: University of North Carolina Press, 1967).

[32] In an article on Jefferson's patronage policies, 1801–03, Prince showed that of 316 strategic second level offices Jefferson removed 146 (46 percent), 118 of whom Prince identified as "hardcore Federalist party cadre," "The Passing of the Aristocracy: Jefferson's Removal of the Federalists, 1801–1805," *Journal of American History*, 57 (December, 1970), 565. But activists may be dismissed or rewarded for electioneering, chairing meetings, etc., without there necessarily being a party system. Though Jefferson's removals may not have differed much from Jackson's (p. 566), one must still wonder why Jackson's patronage actions had much greater impact on what men thought about politics and spoils. That political folklore regarded Jackson's administration as a turning point was not solely a creation of Mugwump historians; see Leonard D. White, *The Jacksonians: A Study in Administrative History, 1829–1861* (New York: Macmillan, 1954), pp. 301, 308–11.

[33] Prince, *New Jersey's Jeffersonian Republicans*, pp. 223, 245.

[34] For comment on persisting "traditional local structures" within centralized, "modern" polities, see Stein Rokkan, "The Comparative Study of Political Participation: Notes Toward a Perspective on Current Research," in *Essays on the Behavioral Study of Politics*, ed. Austin Ranney (Urbana: University of Illinois Press, 1962) p. 70.

Such an approach to patronage offers a way of getting at the alleged relationship between "rising party" and "declining deference." Types of patronage probably changed from the 1780s to the 1840s. Eighteenth century patronage should have reflected a traditional social setting, characterized by a *patron-client* type of patronage. Family connections would surely be important in this milieu, and, indeed, family continued to be important in state and federal patterns of job distribution throughout the early republic.[35] With the rise of party, however, the influence of family and local notables could be expected to decline. In the context of party, expanded suffrage, and a mobilized electorate, political party patronage would increasingly mediate between citizens and government. Party elites in turn would use patronage resources to serve electoral and private ends, and these leaders would become more important relative to other elite groups.[36] The movement from a patronage centered on clients and family to one centered on interest groups and constituents might form part of the story of the decline of deference. Change from one mode to another occurred gradually: in Prince's New Jersey, for example, patron-client modes seem to have continued mixed with party directed patronage well into the nineteenth century.

Space permits only briefest mention of other possible themes of "organization proper." The role of voluntary associations and political societies has not been adequately assessed.[37] Similarly, tantalizing hints exist of the political utility of militia companies which may have contributed more than "color" to campaigns through the 1820s. In the absence of parties before the 1830s, militia outfits, political soci-

---

[35] Prince, *Jeffersonian Republicans*, pp. 240–42; Sidney H. Aronson, *Status and Kinship in the Higher Civil Service: Standards of Selection in the Administrations of John Adams, Thomas Jefferson, and Andrew Jackson* (Cambridge, Mass.: Harvard University Press, 1964).

[36] Alex Weingrod's discussion of such a change in a Sardinian village, 1870–1950, is highly suggestive. Rather than the landlord, it is "the party functionary who provides information regarding loan programs, who can contact the government's tax collector on the villager's behalf, or who can send his son on to high school. The new men of influence are thus likely to be political men, and it is their ability to deal effectively with the wider system that gives them power. Patron-client relationships may continue . . . but it is more likely that political-party directed patronage becomes increasingly significant: the party boss and his workers—the professionals—control even wider resources and they are likely better to provide for their 'constituents' than the patron can for his 'clients.'" "Patrons, Patronage and Political Parties," *Comparative Studies in Society and History*, 10 (July, 1969), 384.

[37] Eugene Perry Link, *Democratic-Republican Societies, 1790–1800* (New York: Columbia Univ. Press, 1942), made a beginning. The Society of Cincinnati was very important to the "Federalist interest" in the South in the 1790s (Rose, *Prologue to Democracy*, pp. 19–45).

eties (Cincinnati, Washington Benevolent, Democratic Republican), and secret orders such as the Freemasons may have acted as recruiting and training agents for the political establishment generally. In western New York's Genesee County, for example, militia companies and Freemasons' lodges seem to have performed just such a function in the 1820s.[38]

Some objects of inquiry obviously span two or three elements of party structure, such as the significant shift from caucuses to conventions as a means of making nominations. Solid work has been done on this process for the Federalist-Republican period and the late 1820s,[39] but not since Ostrogoski, perhaps, has anyone tried to explain the entire process. The conventions eventually assumed control of a mobilized electorate, and their rise is interwoven with the decline of deference. Whether conventions were "more democratic" or not is still a subject of debate.

The Party in Office

Historical observation of the party in office, as suggested above, is concentrating on party in legislatures. Roll-call analysis offers a direct means of measuring interparty conflict and intraparty cohesion. Yet the various quantitative techniques now being applied to early legislatures will not alone serve to dispel doubts about the presence of self-conscious parties. J. S. Young's findings for the Congress, 1800–1828, combined with other recent studies, suggest that party voting cannot be taken for granted as a fixed, all-pervasive condition. Rather, *party voting* (and bloc voting) *should be conceived of as variable within individual legislatures and across series of legislative sessions.* In Congress before the 1820s, for example, peaks of party or proto-party voting probably developed during war and foreign policy crisis of 1797–1800 and 1812–1814. Scrutiny of individual sessions in that period suggests that incipient party voting fluctuated over the course of months and weeks.[40] Roll-call analysis can be used to identify precocious partisan types, men who promoted

---

[38] Kathleen Smith Kutolowski, "The Social Composition of Political Leadership: Genesee County, New York, 1821–1860" (Doctoral dissertation. University of Rochester, 1973).

[39] George D. Luetscher, *Early Political Machinery in the United States* (Philadelphia: University of Pennsylvania Press, 1903), and David H. Fischer, *The Revolution in American Conservatism: The Federalist Party in the Era of Jefferson* (New York: Harper, 1965), are valuable on the early period. For the 1820s, Robert V. Remini, *The Election of Andrew Jackson* (Philadelphia: Lippincott, 1963).

[40] This hypothesis is based on my reading of such conflicting sources as Young, *Washington Community;* Roger H. Brown, *The Republic in Peril: 1812,* 2nd ed. (1964; New York: Norton, 1971); and particularly Ronald L. Hatzenbuehler, "Party Unity and the Decision for War in the House of Representatives, 1812," *William and Mary Quarterly,* 29 (July, 1972), 367–90. Particularly suggestive are Hatzenbuehler's charts showing Republican

norms of party regularity, and whose style looked ahead to the ethos of an institutionalized party system.

The study of legislatures in other periods offers embarrassing riches of sophistication in methods, although state legislatures before the Civil War are generally almost *terra incognita* to historians.[41] Between the 1780s and 1830s, particularly, the historical landscape with respect to state legislative behavior is a great desert, and one to be approached with caution. J. R. Pole warned that assemblies of this period in their usages and language often bore a "most deceptively modern appearance." Pole would like to know more about "what the choice between rival candidates really meant to voters in terms of interest and policy."[42] Similarly, we need to know to what extent party entered into such choices. A recent analysis of roll calls in six legislatures from 1833 to 1842 is suggestive. In it, Herbert Ershkowitz and William Shade argue that broad ideological differences separated Whig and Democratic state legislators. Indirectly, the authors indicate that party cohesion in the legislatures did not rise markedly before 1835, in some cases 1836 or 1837.[43] Such differential rates of party formation in state legislatures offer an excellent opportunity for comparative analysis.

The historical problem of applying *party labels* to political factions before 1840 must be addressed if quantitative methods are to have meaning. Too many anachronisms have been created, for example, in the name of the *Biographical Directory of Congress,* which is often not reliable for party identification. Meanwhile, the recognizable label is crucial to current definitions of party. The International Comparative Political Parties Project, now engaged in a comprehensive, comparative analysis of parties throughout the world, requires that "to qualify as a

---

and Federalist legislators' indices of cohesion values for nonunanimous Foreign Policy Roll Calls, Twelfth Congress, First Session, House, 387, 388. Congressional parties' strength in the 1840s is demonstrated in Joel H. Silbey, *The Shrine of Party* (Pittsburgh: University of Pittsburgh Press, 1967).

[41] Pertinent bibliographies appear in: Robert P. Swierenga, ed., *Quantification in American History: Theory and Research* (New York: Atheneum, 1970), pp. 127–30; and Charles M. Dollar and Richard J. Jensen, *Historian's Guide to Statistics: Quantitative Analysis and Historical Research* (New York: Holt, Rinehart, 1971), pp. 277–81.

[42] J. R. Pole, "Suffrage and Representation in Massachusetts: A Statistical Note," *William and Mary Quarterly,* 14 (October, 1957), 578.

[43] Ershkowitz and Shade, "Consensus or Conflict?" *Journal of American History,* LVIII, 597, 599, 603, 613, 594–613 *passim.* Other work is underway in this area: Peter Levine; "Party Behavior in the New Jersey Legislature: 1829–1844," and Rodney O. Davis, "The Influence of Party on Political Leadership in Illinois in the Jacksonian Era," Papers presented at the Organization of American Historians' annual meeting, Chicago, April 13, 1973.

political party, an organization must have as one of its goals that of placing its *avowed representatives* in government positions."[44] If strictly applied, this criterion of open identification would shatter confidence in the concept of the first party system. The description of party labels as "fluid" in the 1790s is an understatement, and after 1800 many Federalist and Republican candidates showed ambivalence and reluctance to run as "avowed representatives."[45] Names are hardly trivial matters, as Freud and others have taught us.

In formal terms the question of party labels amounts to whether the Federalist and Republican coalitions *as parties* constituted significant reference groups. Identification with Federalist or Republican "interests" might have been qualitatively different from later Democratic and Whig party loyalty.[46] If so, we are led again to consider a transformation of political culture.

Party and Voters, 1789–1840

Discovering the party as reference group in the electorate imposes no easy task on historical research. Interpreters of the first system readily admit the difficulty of observing electoral behavior as well as the instability of voter loyalties. To some extent the finding of instability may be related to limited visibility. The problem may be conceived of broadly as requiring the discovery of historical patterns of social cleavage which became translated into party conflicts. Considered in the mass, parties are coalitions built on hierarchies of cleavage bases, such as section, region, ethnicity, religion, economic interest group, and class, which take different ranks over time as policy and value commitments shift. Research on the early national-antebellum period can contribute much

---

[44] Kenneth Janda, *A Conceptual Framework for the Comparative Analysis of Political Parties* (Beverly Hills, Calif.: Sage Publishers, 1970) pp. 77, 83. "The project will cover some 150 political parties in 50 countries, consulting a random sample of party systems stratified equally according to 10 cultural-geographic areas of the world [for 1950–1970]," p. 77.

[45] Regarding New York in the 1790s, Young, *Democratic-Republicans;* even some ultra-Federalists after 1800, Fischer, *Revolution in Conservatism;* New York, in the 1820s, Alvin Kass, *Politics in New York State, 1800–1830* (Syracuse: Syracuse University Press, 1965). George R. Nielsen ("The Indispensable Institution: The Congressional Party During the Era of Good Feelings" (Doctoral dissertation, University of Iowa, 1968) found party labels "not available" until the late 1820s, p. 3.

[46] Michael Wallace, "Changing Concepts of Party in the United States: New York, 1815–1828," *American Historical Review,* 74 (December, 1968), 453–91; Ronald P. Formisano, "Political Character, Antipartyism, and the Second Party System," *American Quarterly,* 21 (Winter, 1970), 683–709.

to a general need for information about "the processes through which political alternatives *get set* for different local electorates."[47]

The early national electorate, at the mercy of the Law of Available Data, has tagged along as the stepchild of party history in this era. There are descriptions, old and new, of the social bases of Federalist and Republican allegiance. They tend to center on 1800, while the period of obvious party collapse after 1815 seems peculiarly invulnerable to analysis of social cleavages, except in gross sectional terms, as if only parties left behind traces of the social bases of politics.[48]

Descriptions of Federalist and Republican voters are unpersuasive, although discussions of patterns of elite division probably cannot be much improved.[49] One recent attempt to describe Federalist and Republican voters in 1800 appeared as a 26 page appendix to David H. Fischer's influential book on the Federalist party. Fischer admitted that his essay was based on impressionistic evidence and fragments of electoral returns, but managed to scan the entire nation in a suggestive analysis. His task was made easier by the vast territory which could be excluded from consideration: remote areas of low population density and poor communication, where "party consciousness was not sufficiently clear to be meaningful."[50] These included several western states and sizeable internal frontiers in older states. Fischer identified a number of variables influencing party choice, but leaving aside his findings, objection may be made to the very enterprise—common among historians of the first parties—of assuming the existence of party in the electorate, and not regarding voter loyalty *per se* as meriting its own proofs.[51]

---

[47] Seymour Martin Lipset and Stein Rokkan, "Cleavage Structures, Party Systems, and Voter Alignments: An Introduction," in *Party Systems and Voter Alignments: Cross-National Perspectives*, ed. Lipset and Rokkan (New York: Free Press, 1967), pp. 5, 6, 53; also, Stein Rokkan, *Citizens, Elections, Parties: Approaches to the Comparative Study of the Processes of Development* (New York: McKay, 1970).

[48] For detailed study of social bases of political cleavage in a pre-party situation, Van Beck Hall, *Politics Without Parties: Massachusetts, 1780–1791* (Pittsburgh: University of Pittsburgh, 1972).

[49] A recent summary of the literature on elites and voters is in Richard Buel, Jr., *Securing the Revolution: Ideology in American Politics, 1789–1815* (Ithaca: Cornell University Press, 1972), pp. 72–90, 319–24. Buel's conclusions are subject to the same criticism as Fisher's. Notable strength is indicated by Buel's comment that "during the formative stage of the first party system, the disposition of the regional leadership was often more critical than anything else in determining the political complexion of an area." p. 75.

[50] Fischer, *Revolution in Conservatism*, p. 202–03.

[51] Interyear correlations for gubernatorial elections in New York from 1792 show that stable electoral cleavage developed only from 1809 to 1816 and not again until the

Putting first things first, partisanship as such, apart from its social bases, must be shown before the group bases of party voting can be discussed sensibly. Whatever the methods, some attempt must be made to show that parties were reference groups in the electorate, that stable loyalties existed throughout the political universe. Monographs dealing with specific localities over time would be particularly welcome.

The ICPP Project considers an institutionalized party as "one that is reified in the public mind so that 'the party' exists as a social organization apart from its momentary leaders".[52] Judging by the evidence now available, this phenomenon does not seem to have emerged until the late 1830s; then followed the first classic period of party loyalty.[53]

Some historians nevertheless claim to find party loyalty of this type as early as the 1790s because they discern then the appearance of ticket voting for slates of candidates. In a preparty situation, however, ticket voting may exist without institutionalized parties. Ticket voting alone does not establish the presence of a self-conscious party in the electorate, which is a durable psychic phenomenon.[54]

Unlike party loyalty and social cleavages, one feature of voting behavior from 1789 to 1840 has been charted. J. R. Pole and others have described a gigantic leap in voter turnout in state elections after 1800. In the late 1790s turnout in some states began to rise from levels of between 15 and 40 percent. From 1804 to 1816, however, in most states "an extraordinary surge" carried participation "to unprecedented heights—68 to 98 percent of adult males." In the 1820s turnout in state elections began to decline, and presidential polls gained attention, until

---

1830s (Lee Benson, Joel Silbey, and Phyllis Field, "Toward a Theory of Stability and Change in American Voting Patterns: New York State, 1792–1972," Paper presented at the Mathematics Social Science Board Conference on Quantitative Studies in Popular Voting Behavior, Cornell University, June, 1973). A strong argument, however, for stable partisan cleavages in Maryland's electorate for two decades after 1798 has recently been made by David A. Bohmer, and John M. Rozette, "Toward the Study of Individual Level Historical Voting Data: Some Theoretical and Practical Considerations," unpublished manuscript. Bohmer and Rozette discuss a number of studies now underway using invaluable poll book data for individual voters, which should go a long way toward resolving some of the issues raised above.

[52] Janda, *Conceptual Framework*, p. 88.

[53] For general discussion of the 1830s "new politics" and of relevant literature see Edward Pessen, *Jacksonian America: Society, Personality, and Politics* (Homewood, Ill.: Dorsey, 1969), pp. 154–307, 375–83; pertinent studies include: Lee Benson, *The Concept of Jacksonian Democracy: New York as a Test Case* (Princeton: Princeton University Press, 1961), and Ronald P. Formisano, *The Birth of Mass Political Parties: Michigan, 1827–1861* (Princeton: Princeton University Press, 1971.

[54] For a case of ticket voting without party, see Tickcom, pp. 170–71, 239–40, 256.

in 1840 presidential voting equalled or surpassed earlier totals in state elections.[55]

For many writers electoral mobilization on this scale means "democratization" or "the expansion of voter participation in an increasingly open and free electoral process."[56] As noted earlier in this essay, many historians credit party competition and organization with causing boom turnouts, and thus yoke together "party" and "democracy." Others blink at the dazzling vote totals and inquire whether such electoral fireworks implied any reallocation of power. While voters responded to party "projections" of democratic procedures, according to Prince, small coteries still ran politics. McCormick wondered if high turnouts caused parties to promote and governments to enact more democratic policies, and seemed to conclude that such effects were minor.[57]

These disagreements about the democratizing role of party need more systematic study. Meanwhile, most scholars share a tendency to exaggerate the causal impact of party organization in raising turnout and creating interest in politics generally.[58] Celebrants and critics alike have neglected history and sociology in favor of too mechanistic a political science. What kinds of events and social cleavages came together to raise political consciousness in attentive publics? What historical and social conditions favor both leader activism and mass turnout? Why did some states reach high levels of turnout very quickly? Why did some counties in the same state differ substantially in turnout rates?[59] Comparative analysis here contains much potential for understanding change in political culture.

---

[55] Fischer, p. xv, summarizing works by Pole and McCormick.

[56] Fischer, p. xi.

[57] McCormick, "Political Development and the Second Party System," ed. Chambers and Burnham, p. 107. Prince, *Jeffersonian Republicans*, p. 249. Prince's discussion of these issues is excellent, and it is somewhat arbitrary to classify him in this way. Edward Pessen maintains that party's advent did not affect existing policy preferences in administration of city governments: "Who Governed the Nation's Cities in the 'Era of the Common Man'?" *Political Science Quarterly*, 87 (December, 1972), 591–614. See also, Richard B. Dawson, "Social Development, Party Competition and Policy," ed. Chambers and Burnham, pp. 203–37.

[58] Exaggerating organization: Banner, *To the Hartford Convention*, pp. 268–93; Richard P. McCormick, "New Perspectives on Jacksonian Politics," *American Historical Review*," 65 (January, 1960), 288–301. Fischer suggested that party competition, organization and turnout went together, cf. pp. xi–xx, 182–99, and especially 187–92.

[59] Compare, e.g., voting data from St. Mary's County (low) from 1790 to 1812 with those for Prince George's (and other counties with high turnouts) in Maryland; see J. R. Pole, "Constitutional Reform and Election Statistics in Maryland, 1790–1812 *Maryland Historical Magazine*, 55 (December, 1960), 285–92.

Rather than regarding organization solely as an independent variable,[60] organization and turnout should be seen also as dependent variables. Both are two forms of participation which involves several modes of action besides voting: campaigning, citizen initiated contracts with government, and cooperative activity. Studies of participation based on cross-national data conclude that voting is only weakly related to other modes and to "general political involvement."[61] This means that historians interested in shifting citizen orientations cannot be exclusively concerned with voting and need to diversify approaches to participation.

The Decline of Deference

While the rise of participation has at least a broad index for one of its modes, the long decline of deference tends to elude measurement. Any student passingly familiar with the early republic knows that deference ended sometime during these years, enjoying a decorous but rather drawn-out finale. Its definite passing away has probably been claimed for every decade from the Revolution to the Civil War. Many writers favor the 1820s, while others see declining deference permitting the growth of parties as early as the 1790s.

More than any other word, "deference" characterizes eighteenth century Whig political culture by referring directly to men's ideas and unspoken assumptions about how society actually worked.

> Fundamentally, deference meant the acceptance of the view by the whole of society that, whether by chance or simply by habit, people would naturally delegate power to a select minority. The belief that this minority would govern in the interests of the entire population was the unifying spirit that bound the society together. According to Professor Pole: "In a society whose moral cohesion was supplied by the sense of deference and dignity, it was possible for the broad mass of the people to consent to a scheme of government in which their own share would be limited.[62]

---

[60] Modern studies disagree about party organization's impact on turnout, but few political scientists claim that organization raises turnout by much more than 5 percent; see William J. Crotty, "Party Effort and Its Impact on the Vote," *American Political Science Review,* 65 (June, 1971), 439–50.

[61] Sidney Verba, Norman H. Nie, and Jae-on-Kim, *The Modes of Democratic Participation: A Cross-National Survey* (Beverly Hills, Calif.: Sage Publishers, 1971), pp. 10, 11–19, 63.

[62] John B. Kirby, "Early American Politics—The Search for Ideology: An Historiographical Critique of the Concept of 'Deference,'" *Journal of Politics,* 32 (November, 1970), 827. For a discussion of deference in relation to social science literature, Richard D. Brown, "Modernization and the Modern Personality in Early America, 1680–1865: A Sketch of a Synthesis," *Journal of Interdisciplinary History,* 2 (Winter, 1972), 214–20.

In the first-system literature, declining deference and rising parties are now virtually locked in a symbiotic embrace. In this happy union, one serves to explain the other. From 1795 to 1816, increased voting did not result simply from an enlarged franchise; rather, the inhibitions formerly imposed on the exercise of the suffrage by habits of subordination were gradually broken down by party competition. Thus, anything undermining deference prepared the way for parties, and parties hastened the departure of deference and spurred voter turnout.

Yet the matter of timing remains as a source of confusion. Apart from general disagreement, competent historians seem prone even to self-contradiction because their application of the concept is so promiscuous.[63] It is also common to associate declining deference with large, heterogeneous, differentiated states such as New York and Pennsylvania. It seems logical that states with advanced social complexity should have experienced first the decline of traditional politics and the emergence of professional politicians adept at brokerage and organization. The New York-Pennsylvania syndrome thus produces a set of nicely fitting "correlates": economic development, social complexity, heterogeneity, declining deference, rising parties: democracy. Yet we are also told, and it has long been recognized, that habits of subordination remained strong in New York for a long time. The importance of notables in Pennsylvania politics clearly manifested itself in 1799, and the tide of party there after 1800, as discovered earlier, seems to have been less than overwhelming. The assumption that "economic development leads to pluralistic, competitive political structures," by natural law as it were, has been called a "naive and culturally biased outlook [which] confuses political development with political democratization."[64]

The transition from deference to Participation, Parties, & Co., should not be seen, I believe, as absolute. New ways are hardly ever entirely devoid of the old. The content of tradition in political parties has not been sufficiently emphasized, especially during the formative period from the 1790s to the 1840s. Fascinated with parties as a sharp departure in Western political culture, historians have tended to under-

---

[63] Inconsistencies appeared in what is on the whole a stimulating essay: Paul Goodman, "The First American Party System," in Chambers and Burnham, pp. 59, 61, 69, 85, 87.

[64] Tinkcom, p. 233; Dixon Ryan Fox, *The Decline of Aristocracy in the Politics of New York, 1801–1840* (New York: Columbia University Press, 1919); Kass, *Politics in New York,* pp. 16–19; several essays by Pole stress persisting deference, including "Representation and Authority in Virginia from the Revolution to Reform," *Journal of Southern History,* 24 (February, 1958), 16–50. The quotation is from Bette A. Nesvold, "Studies in Political Development," in *Macro-Quantitative Analysis: Conflict, Development, and Democratization,* ed. John V. Gillespie and Nesvold (Beverly Hills, Calif.: Sage Publishers, 1971), pp. 283–84.

play or ignore the extent to which these organizations fused with and synthesized traditional forms.

Interest groups, for example, came to be part of a new "pluralist" order. What were the phases of transition from deference to groups? To what extent did deference to "influentials" blend with identification with groups which retained actual or symbolic leadership by notables? In nineteenth century English politics, Nossiter has observed, influence often "shades into the pressure of group membership."[65] It is a delicate historical problem, surely, to determine where group identity began and where "influence" ended. Studying leadership groups over time, with collective biography and samples of national, regional, and specific community elites, seems one obvious approach to the decline of deference.[66] (The importance of lawyers among the "new class" of politicians is often hinted at, but their role remains vague). More difficult will be the observation and measurement of "habits of subordination." Works attempting this must remember that the replacement of the traditional by the modern came in stages with mixed forms prevailing for some time.[67]

It will help, then, to see the period from 1795 to the 1830s as intermediate in the decline of deference—and political development—in which the North American states resembled the political culture characteristic of England for several decades after the Reform Bill of 1832. This halfway American phase could borrow a term from this longer English era, namely a deferential-participant political culture.[68]

---

[65] T. J. Nossiter, "Aspects of Electoral Behavior in English Constituencies, 1832–1868," in *Mass Politics: Studies in Political Sociology*, ed. Erik Allardt and Stein Rokkan (New York: The Free Press, 1970), p. 172.

[66] For a discussion of techniques: Richard Jensen "Quantitative Collective Biography: An Application to Metropolitan Elites," in *Qualification in American History*, ed. Swierenga, pp. 389–405; a bibliography is in Dollar and Jensen, *Historian's Guide to Statistics*, pp. 281–83.

[67] For an illuminating discussion of persisting traditional forms of deferential politics mixing with primitive partisan modes, Richard R. Beeman, *The Old Dominion in the New Nation, 1788–1801* (Lexington: University Press of Kentucky, 1972). Beeman's study shows the strength of deferential voting in Virginia in 1800, and maintains that Jefferson's victory ended emergent party politics and brought the return of "nonpartisan, gentlemanly style" habits (pp. 233, 234, 237–38). On the inability of the national Republicans to function as a party from 1800 to 1805, see Richard E. Ellis, *The Jeffersonian Crisis: Courts and Politics in the Young Republic* (New York: Oxford University Press), pp. 3–107.

[68] The phrase "deferential-participant" is borrowed from Gabriel Almond and Sidney Verba, who gave it a slightly different meaning: *The Civic Culture: Political Attitudes and Democracy in Five Nations*, rev. ed. (1963; Boston: Little, Brown, 1965), p. 455. On the durability of deference and influence in England, see H. J. Hanham, *Elections and Electoral Management: Politics in the Time of Disraeli and Gladstone* (London: Longmans, 1959), pp. ix, xi, xiv–xv, 200–03, and *passim;* and James Cornford, "The Adoption of Mass Organization by the British Conservative Party," in *Cleavages, Ideologies and Party Systems: Contributions to Comparative Political Sociology*, ed. Erik Allardt and Yrjö Littunen (Turku: Publs. of the Westermark Society, 1964), pp. 401–11.

Gradual mobilization and fluctuating turnouts during this phase seem related not only to certain provocative issues, elite conflict, organization, and electioneering, but also to "nonelites' maintenance of respectful and partially acquiescent attitudes toward political authority—a cultural variable."[69]

Political "Violence" and Ideological Intensity

During this transitional stage some men strained toward party norms, while many others remained powerfully attached to the codes, prerogatives, and sensitivities of men of respectability, honor, and influence. The defensiveness of a political culture in transition, in combination with other causes, helps explain the "violence" or ideological intensity of the years 1795 to 1814. ("Violence" tended to be used in the early republic to mean uncontrolled, excessive, and distorting energy of expression and emotion. The connotation of physical violence is more characteristic of our own time.)

The "violence" of ideological cleavage in the early republic is often attributed in part to the novelty of party conflict. The extremism and paranoia of some Federalists and Republicans has served to support the argument for the presence of party. Ironically, this deduction is often turned on its head by historians discussing the 1830s, some of whom claim that a hallmark of "modern" parties since Jackson has been their relatively nonideological character. The retreat from ideology resulted, it is argued, from a necessity to compromise within parties to build winning coalitions. While this line of reasoning often neglects, in my view, the generalized ideological or belief-system differences between Whigs and Democrats, the earlier Federalist-Republican conflict does seem to have been distinguished by greater ideological intensity—amounting almost to a difference in kind. Many scholars have dealt with this theme of Federalist and Republican passion recently, and most agree that it derived from a conviction that the future of the republic hung on their struggle for power. A *shared* republican mentality among Federalists and Republicans invested their rivalry with hyperbolic drama, and made them believe that the stakes were higher than they were. Roger Brown has also stressed "inexperience with political parties," and Richard Buel has noted that while moderns are not wholly nonideological, neither were early republicans innocent of electoral calculation. But

---

[69] Eric A. Nordlinger, "Political Development: Time Sequences and Rates of Change," in *Politics and Society: Studies in Comparative Political Sociology*, ed. Nordlinger (Englewood Cliffs, N.J.: Prentice-Hall, 1970) p. 346.

Buel emphasizes, correctly, that ideological tenacity went hand in hand with a rejection of party and compromise.[70] Not only were parties evil, but there was something mean and dishonorable about the behavior necessary for their operation. Therefore, "strong ideological focus"[71] before 1820 is not necessarily a clue to modern party emergence; rather, it often might have signalled the persistence of an older set of men's expectations of themselves and their enemies.

Conclusion

The analysis above of separate strands of party contains a general proposal regarding party origins. During the 1830s partisan behavior emerged in several arenas in fairly rapid sequence: in the national legislature, in state legislatures, among partisan activists, and in electoral publics for all manner of elections. The coalescence of party, a process nearly complete by 1840, can be taken as a model with which to analyze earlier, uncompleted and often unintentional anticipations of party systems. This is not to say that historians have described party institutionalization as fully as might be desired. On the contrary, a systematic, "tripartite" approach has been implicit at best in Jacksonian studies, scattered throughout monographs dealing with different elements of party. Indeed, it may be unrealistic to ask one scholar to deal comprehensively with all levels of party activity as they developed, even in a single state; but it may be expected that researchers will demarcate explicitly the arenas they intend to study, and specify the evidence needed to demonstrate party in that sector. Similarly, there are untapped possibilities for studying Jacksonian parties as organizations proper, in office, and in the electorate. To take but one example: accounts of party formation after 1828 contain perfunctory references to the importance of patronage, but hardly a glimpse of the enormous role played by cadre-men appointed to land offices, post offices, cus-

---

[70] Brown, *Republic in Peril,* pp. 182–83; John R. Howe, "Republican Thought and the Political Violence of the 1790's," *American Quarterly,* 19 (Summer, 1967), 147–65; Marshall Smelser, "The Federalist Period as an Age of Passion," *American Quarterly,* 10 (Winter, 1958), 391–419; Robert E. Shallope, "Toward a Republican Synthesis: The Emergence of an Understanding of Republicanism in American Historiography," *William and Mary Quarterly,* 29 (January, 1972), 49–80; Buel, *Securing the Revolution,* p. 91.

[71] "Strong ideological focus" prevails when political conflict concentrates "on a single, stable issue domain which presents an ordered dimension that is perceived in common terms by leaders and followers." Donald E. Stokes, "Spatial Models of Party Competition," in *Elections and the Political Order,* ed. Angus Campbell, Philip E. Converse, Warren E. Miller, and Donald E. Stokes (New York: Willey, 1966), p. 176.

toms houses and the like, in the building of organizations and possibly in forming local electoral cleavages.[72]

Subsequent studies may modify these conclusions, yet the available evidence (read with some skepticism) prompts the hypothesis that early republican politics were rooted far more deeply in preparty political culture than is conventionally allowed. Before 1834, "peaks" of elite conflict in national and state affairs generated some movement toward party action. In Congress and in many states intense policy cleavages brought forth incipient partylike behavior, especially during such war crisis years as 1797 to 1800 and 1808 to 1814. But Walter Dean Burnham correctly characterized the era as "a pre-party phase in American political development," and J. R. Pole emphasized the "incompleteness of party organization" and warned that despite high participation it would be a mistake "to see the parties of this formative period in a modern light, outlined by modern definitions." The Federalist and Republican "interests"—a very accurate contemporary word—rather remained much closer to "relatively stable coalitions" than to durable cadre parties of regular internal organization and fairly stable, self-conscious mass following.[73] The parties of the *deferential-participant* phase only approached an institutional threshold.

The partisan blocs which formed temporarily in national and state legislatures hesitated halfway between stable coalitions and party, and were ambivalently tolerated in the political culture. These temporary blocs should not be seen as exercising complete sway even over their own assembly halls. Most of the time they were smaller rings within larger circles. The universal empire of party was to come only after 1835.

Ideally, histories of party formation should recognize not only that the three elements of party eventually became related to each other, but also that they interacted with broad trends in polity and society. Some men built parties by conscious choice; others helped create them unintentionally; still others deliberately resisted the new way. None acted, however, entirely under conditions of their own choosing. Leaders of nascent parties, for example, occasionally rewrote

---

[72] Land office patronage and party in the Northwestern and Southern states are treated briefly in Malcolm J. Rohrbough, *The Land Office Business: The Settlement and Administration of American Public Lands, 1789–1861* (New York: Oxford University Press, 1968) p. 271–76.

[73] Burnham, "Party Systems and the Political Process," in Chambers and Burnham, *American Party Systems*, p. 289; Pole, "Constitutional Reform in Maryland," p. 281. "Relatively stable coalitions" as pre-party phenomena are discussed in Richard A. Pride, *Origins of Democracy: A Cross-National Study of Mobilization, Party Systems, and Democratic Stability* (Beverly Hills, Calif.: Sage Publishers, 1970), pp. 692–94.

the rules of the game (electoral, legislative, administrative) to facilitate their gaining, wielding, or maintaining power. But studies of these institutional manipulations will not be very informative if they ignore the wider social, economic, and communications changes to which elites (and electorates) responded.[74] Movements in various political theaters, split apart in researchers' division of labor, were often not only simultaneous but also intertwined responses to pervasive social change.[75]

The relationship between social change and party formation, it is assumed here, can be studied fruitfully as an aspect of political culture. So far in this essay, "political culture" has served as one of those "catchwords" described by Petter Nettl, that is, "deliberately vague conditioning concepts that follow at the end of a string of precise argument." Catchwords usually indicate the territory of another discipline, said Nettl, and permit evasion by suggesting that for the explanation to proceed further one must enter foreign territory.[76] It is time to close the escape hatch: "Political culture is, simply, the political aspect of the culture of a society . . . a historical system of widespread, fundamental, behavioral, political values . . . classified into subsystems of identity, symbol, rule and belief."[77] Most definitions stress the psychological components (especially citizen attitudes to authority). Thus Harry Eckstein defines political culture as consisting of politically relevant values (purposive desires), cognitions (conceptions of the nature of reality), and expressive symbols, from language to visual ceremony. It refers in particular to the 'internalized expectations' in terms of which the political roles of

---

[74] Burnham's discussion of realignments is relevant here (*Critical Elections*, pp. 1–10, 13, 27–28).

[75] It is easier to assert such patterns than to show them. Political scientists typically explain increased voter participation by inferences which are in effect deductive theories of mass mobilization. Thus: economic development causes changes in society, which lead to new experiences for more citizens, and hence to the growth of certain political attitudes, and thus to more participation. This hypothesis is adapted from Norman H. Nie, G. Binghem Powell, and Kenneth Prewitt, "Social Structure and Political Participation: Development Relationships, Part I," *American Political Science Review*, 63 (June, 1969), 372. Though they frequently make similar claims, historians have yet to demonstrate any of this.

[76] J. P. Nettl, *Political Mobilization: A Sociological Analysis of Methods and Concepts* (New York: Basic Books, 1967), pp. 42–43. Nettl's description of the necessary role of catchwords in social science, and of political culture as "the main catchment area of modern politics" is must reading, pp. 43–53. See also Lucian W. Pye, "Culture and Political Science: Problems in the Evaluation of the Concept of Political Culture," *Social Science Quarterly*, 53 (September, 1972), 285–96.

[77] Donald J. Devine, *The Political Culture of the United States: The Influence of Member Values on Regime Maintenance* (Boston: Little, Brown, 1972), pp. 14–18.

individuals are defined and through which political institutions (in the sense of regularized behavior patterns) come into being.[78]

Patterns of voter turnout, to illustrate, may be reflective of political culture. When from 1800 to 1840 voters shifted their attentiveness from state to national elections, turnout rates became indicators of changed cognitions and values. Aside from being attracted to vote in presidential elections, average citizens also may have found "politics in general" to be more interesting.[79] This may be one of the least studied important themes in political history. Surely citizens came to political consciousness at very different rates given the size, heterogeneity, and uneven economic development of society. In any event, voter turnouts thus reflected changes in "internalized expectations" generally entertained about political institutions. They recorded movements in men's minds as well as tidal social change. The arrival of party, whatever the final verdicts on timing, also signaled profound shifts in political culture.

---

[78] Harry Eckstein, "A Perspective on Comparative Politics, Past and Present," in *Comparative Politics: A Reader*, ed. Eckstein and David Apter (New York: Free Press, 1963) p. 26.

[79] M. Kent Jennings and Harmon Zeigler, "The Salience of American State Politics," *American Political Science Review*, 64 (June, 1970), 523–35; Moshe M. Czudowski, "A Salience Dimension for the Study of Political Culture," *American Political Science Review*, 62 (September, 1968), 878–88.

The Emergence of Political Parties in Congress, 1789–1803

John F. Hoadley

Social science methodologies, as well as social science concepts, are a well-established feature of investigations of the first party conflict. This article, which outlined central arguments of Hoadley's recent book, Origins of American Political Parties, 1789–1803 *(Lexington: University Press of Kentucky, 1986), illustrates the application of computerized techniques of quantitative roll-call analysis. Though sensitive to Formisano's cautions, Hoadley also reasserts the great cohesion of the early parties and the usefulness of the concept of a party system. The essay is reprinted by permission from the* American Political Science Review, *LXXIV (September, 1980) 757–79.*

Scholars have differed considerably in assessing the development of American political parties during the period immediately following ratification of the Constitution. The date marking the emergence of parties has been placed anywhere between the beginning of the new government and the time 50 years later when Whigs and Jacksonian Democrats were competing for power. Despite disagreements over the precise date when parties first appeared, most observers have agreed that important divisions did materialize in the first decade of the new nation. Varying explanations have been offered for these divisions, ranging across economic factors, regionalism, personalities, issues, and even the boardinghouse residences of members of Congress.[1]

---

[1] According to one traditional interpretation of American party development, political parties existed from the beginning of the national government (Beard, 1915; Ryan, 1971). Other scholars have cited the Jay Treaty as the issue which marked appearance of parties, thus placing the date at about 1795 (Bell, 1973; Chambers, 1963; Charles, 1961; Cunningham, 1957). Still others have pointed to events and issues during the Adams administration as crucial in the emergence of parties (Dauer, 1953; Libby, 1912). Finally, a group of party historians has argued that true parties did not exist in this early period and has placed the date of party emergence after 1830 (Formisano, 1974; Hofstadter, 1969; Nichols, 1967). In many cases, these different conclusions can be attributed to varying definitions of party and an assortment of methodological approaches.

This article explores the question of when and why political parties first appeared in the United States. I examine the development of parties for the period between 1789, the first year of the new government under the Constitution, and 1803, a year which directly followed the first transition of government from one party to another. This span of 14 years is of particular interest because it was dominated by individuals who themselves did not believe parties could be a positive force in a government system. It was also a critical era of national development when the United States was trying to establish itself as a newly independent nation under a democratic government, a form generally untested at that time.

To reach conclusions concerning party development which may resolve some of the confusion in the literature, I have undertaken two tasks. First, I examine carefully the concept of "party" and distinguish it from the idea of "faction." Second, I apply a new methodological approach to consider empirical evidence on the question of party development. I use spatial analysis (multidimensional scaling) of roll-call voting because it avoids some of the limitations in other methods of roll-call analysis. I then examine spatial maps of congressional voting to answer questions concerning the state of party development in the early years of the nation.

Toward a Definition of Party

As of 1789, a clear distinction between party and faction had not been established. According to eighteenth-century usage, "faction" (for which the word "party" was often substituted) usually referred to a group involved in the political arena but working toward private ends. Party, on the other hand, was "a new name for a new thing" (Sartori, 1976, p. 64). As the idea of party developed in the seventeenth and eighteenth centuries, the word gradually acquired a more distinct and positive meaning than "faction." That this distinction was not commonly recognized in 1789 is illustrated by the writings of James Madison in *The Federalist*, where he cautioned against both the "violence of faction," and the "rage of party." Although he used the terms interchangeably, he clearly had in mind the old idea of faction and not the new idea of party (Hofstadter, 1969; Sartori, 1976).[2]

Today the distinction between "party" and "faction" is much

---

[2] References are taken from *The Federalist*, No. 10 (Madison et al., 1961, p. 77) and No. 50 (p. 320). Elsewhere Madison clearly shows that he equates the two words, referring to "the most numerous party, or in other words, the most powerful faction . . ." (No. 10, p. 80).

clearer. "Faction" tends to be used in two different contexts. In one, it retains the negative connotations of the old concept, referring to a self-seeking and contentious group. In a nonpartisan setting or within a single party, it may denote a group which forms around a single issue or personality, but with limited durability and minimal organization. A political party, on the other hand, is a more permanent group which generally has a positive role in the political system. Parties "are instrumental to collective benefits. . . . [They] are functional agencies—they serve purposes and fulfill roles—while factions are not" (Sartori, 1976, p. 25). There are in fact two important and strongly related roles which can be fulfilled by parties. One is an involvement in elections. Parties may help to recruit and screen candidates, supply symbols and names to help identify candidates to voters, and provide victorious candidates a mechanism for working toward policy goals once in office. The other role is serving as what Sartori calls "channels of expression" (p. 27). The party is one institution which helps people communicate their demands to the government. Furthermore, because a party can simultaneously channel the demands of a number of people, it adds a degree of pressure which aids popular control of public policy.

While these roles are normally associated with the concept of party, the term itself is generally defined from a more structural perspective. Although numerous definitions of "party," emphasizing a variety of themes, can be found in the literature, several components are common to most of them. The following elements of the concept should be considered in any investigation of party development.[3] All parties have:

1. a common symbol or label,
2. a group of leaders in office,
3. a group of supporters in elections,
4. an organization, however minimal.

Several theories have been put forth to explain how parties come into being (Chambers, 1966; Duverger, 1959; Huntington, 1968; LaPalombara and Weiner, 1966). Integrating these considerations leads to the view that party development is a process taking place in four stages.[4] In the first stage, *factionalism*, groups form in the legislature

---

[3] This discussion on definitions of party was strongly influenced by comments of Formisano (1974, p. 475), who in turn drew heavily from Chambers (1967) and Sorauf (1967), whose ideas were also important in the present effort. An alternative definition is provided by Sartori (1976, p. 63).

[4] Huntington's terminology (1968, pp. 412–20) is used here, but the meaning of the stages has been modified to incorporate other views, particularly Duverger's (1959) idea of parliamentary origin of parties.

over a variety of issues and personalities.[5] These factions are rarely
organized and last for only a short time. In the second stage, *polarization*,
these factions are stabilized into more permanent legislative groups
which oppose each other over a broad range of issues. This coalescence
into polar groups is frequently set off by a single issue of overriding
importance or by the cumulation of several cleavages. In the third stage,
expansion, the public is drawn into the process of party development,
usually after the extension of suffrage. Electoral committees may arise at
the local level to influence decision makers or may be created by office
holders to strengthen their own positions. In either case, at this stage
party affiliations become significant factors in the electoral process. In
the fourth and final stage, *institutionalization*, a permanent linkage is
created between the parliamentary group and its electoral committees.
At this point some type of national organization should begin to direct
and coordinate the party activities.

This article examines the transition of American political parties
from factionalism to polarization and therefore focuses on parties
emerging within the Congress. The expansion of partisanship into the
electorate and the institutionalization of parties are considered only
where they amplify the party development taking place in Congress.

Methodology

The principal data for this investigation are the records of how members
of Congress voted on roll calls taken between 1789 and 1803. While there
are inherent limitations in using roll calls, the official nature of these
votes makes them a valuable source of information.[6] The chief analytic
method is multidimensional scaling of measures of agreement between
legislators. Since this method has been fully discussed elsewhere,[7] I will

---

[5] This issue of "factionalism" is not intended to carry the negative connotations often
attached to the term.

[6] Some limitations of roll-call analysis are immediately obvious. Roll-call votes may
not always be accurate records of either the scope of activity in Congress or the true
positions of members. Also, for a variety of reasons, roll calls are not taken on every issue
before the legislature. Furthermore, when votes are recorded, members may sometimes
misrepresent their positions, for reasons such as friendship or future reelection. Roll calls
nevertheless do provide an official record of positions taken on a variety of issues and
thus may be more important than a legislator's own preferences in cases where they
differ.

[7] A more detailed presentation and justification of the methodology used here is found
in Hoadley (1979). A good general discussion of multidimensional scaling is provided by
Rabinowitz (1975). The use of cluster analysis for studying legislative blocs has been
evaluated by MacRae (1970).

give only a brief summary of the approach. Multidimensional scaling employs a matrix of agreement scores, defined simply as the proportion of times two legislators agree in their votes, out of the total number of bills on which both vote. These agreement scores are transformed into distances in a geometric space of some given dimensionality. The legislators are then represented as points in this multidimensional space in such a way that those who *agree* most often in voting are *closest* to each other in the resulting configuration of points, while those who *disagree* most are *farthest* away in the space.

Interpretation of a multidimensional scaling configuration is perhaps the most important and most difficult part of the analysis. First, the quality of a solution, or the fit between the data (agreement scores) and the configuration, is indicated by a statistic called "stress," which measures the degree to which the configuration fails to reproduce accurately the relationship present in the data. Stress can range theoretically from 0.0, for a perfect fit, to 1.0, for a total lack of fit. Second, the appropriate dimensionability of a solution must be determined with respect to its stress. A solution can be derived in any number of dimensions, and the stress will always be lower when a higher dimensionality is allowed. Thus the analyst must determine the most appropriate dimensionality, according to the conflicting standards of good fit (low stress) and parsimony (a small number of dimensions). Finally, the interpretation of a configuration involves a search for meaningful dimensions, clusters, or other structural patterns. It must be emphasized that a two-dimensional solution should *not* automatically be discussed in terms of two linear dimensions, such as a factor analysis would be. The analyst must be attentive in searching for that structural interpretation which best represents the information contained in the scaling solution.

An alternative method, cluster analysis, is used to aid the interpretation and explication of the configurations derived by multidimensional scaling. In clustering, legislators are placed into blocs or clusters, based on their level of agreement with each other. Those grouped in a particular cluster are more likely to agree with others in that cluster than with those outside it. Once clusters have been obtained, it is possible to compute the average level of agreement within them. Because cluster analysis is based on the same agreement scores, the results should help to support conclusions reached from multidimensional scaling.

While cluster analysis can be used to discover blocs that exist on the basis of voting patterns, the cohesion of parties and sectional blocs, defined externally to the voting records, is of equal interest. For each group, I calculate several standard indices of partisanship, including the average level of agreement, Rice's index of cohesion, Rice's index of difference, and Lowell's party vote.[8]

Another means of studying party development is to consider the party identification of congressmen. This process is, however, far more difficult in studying the eighteenth century than the twentieth, since party labels were not commonly used in those early years of our nation. There were no formal party caucuses in Congress, nor were party labels used in most congressional elections. Nevertheless, information on the party affiliations of members of Congress has been compiled in the historical archives of the Inter-University Consortium for Political and Social Research (ICPSR), the *Biographical Directory of the American Congress, 1774–1961* (U. S. Congress, 1961), and several monographs on the early party system (Bell, 1973; Dauer, 1953). This information remains incomplete and occasionally inconsistent, particularly for the earliest years.[9] Nevertheless, party labels can aid in the assessment of partisan development. The extent to which congressional voting blocs correspond to those labels is one indication of the emergence of a party system.

Spatial Analysis of Roll-Call Voting

Once the scaling and clustering solutions are obtained, it is necessary to assess whether the resulting configurations show the existence of parties. As I have indicated, this article concentrates on the stages of factionalism and polarization. In the factional stage, congressional voting is expected to be fairly unstructured. Stress should be relatively high, as votes are cast for idiosyncratic reasons. Furthermore, the legislators should not be divided into two or three distinct blocs. Since different issues presumably produce different divisions, the individual points should be distributed fairly uniformly across the space.

---

[8] Rice's index of cohesion is the absolute difference between the percentage "yes" and percentage "no" for a particular group. His index of difference is the absolute difference between the percentage "yes" for any two groups. A party vote, according to Lowell, is one where more than 90 percent of one party opposed more than 90 percent of the other. MacRae (1970, pp. 177–84) provides a fuller discussion of these indices.

[9] It is clear, from comparisons with primary research reported in several monographs on state party development, that there are frequent errors in the ICPSR file and in the *Biographical Directory*. I have estimated an error rate of greater than 10 percent for some years and that complete and accurate information is generally available for only about 60 percent of the congressmen. A compilation of party labels from primary sources is needed, indicating the party with which a member of Congress identified at the time of each election. In the absence of such a compilation, the party codes used in this article represent the best information available in published sources.

As party development evolves from factionalism to polarization, the configurations should change correspondingly. In the second stage, groups of legislators are expected to be voting together across a set of issues, rather than shifting alignments from one issue to the next. Thus the configurations should reveal much higher clusters of legislators corresponding to these party groups. Of course, the lines of division may still shift somewhat from one issue to another, but there should be a clear consistency of groupings, which was not true in the earlier stage of development. It is impossible to denote specific thresholds of agreement or distinctive patterns which would mark the existence of a party, for many factors affect these results. But careful examination of patterns over time should allow reasonable conclusions to be drawn regarding trends in partisanship.

With the establishment of these criteria for party development, I can examine the multidimensional scaling analysis of congressional voting. Configurations have been generated in one, two, and three dimensions for both the Senate and House of Representatives of the First through the Seventh Congresses (1789–1803). In each case, all roll calls were included and weighted equally,[10] and all members were included except those who were absent on a large proportion of roll calls. The stress for each configuration, with the number of legislators and number of roll calls involved, is presented in Table 1. Configurations for the House are presented in Figures 1 through 5, and Senate configurations for illustrative years[11] are presented in Figures 6 through 9.

The two-dimensional configuration has been selected as the best representation of voting patterns in each congress, with the sole exception of the First Senate. For several congresses, three-dimensional solutions yield a distinct improvement in stress, yet in every case but one the added accuracy is counteracted by increased difficulty in visualizing the resulting configuration. In the case of the First Senate, however, a two-dimensional configuration would not accurately represent the patterns of voting agreement, and a three-dimensional configuration is presented instead. One-dimensional configurations would be adequate in

---

[10] The inclusion of all roll calls with equal weight may introduce a bias into the analysis, although its degree and nature are unknown. Because any scheme of exclusion or weighting would be difficult to justify, all votes have been included. Given the nonmetric assumptions of MDS and the strength of the results, it seems unlikely that any resulting bias has seriously affected the conclusions.

[11] Configurations for the Third, Fifth, and Sixth Senates are not included here, to conserve space. Patterns for these years differ little from those of surrounding years, and the configurations fit clearly within the overall pattern of party development.

TABLE 1.   Quality of Fit between Agreement Scores and Spatial Configurations (in 1, 2, and 3 Dimensions)

Congress	Level of Stress			Number of Members	Number of Roll Calls
	1 Dim.	2 Dim.	3 Dim.		
House of Representatives					
First (1789–1791)	.468	.337	.263	62	109
Second (1791–1793)	.438	.304	.249	65	102
Third (1793–1795)	.278	.237	.201	100	69
Fourth (1795–1797)	.282	.233	.213	100	83
Fifth (1797–1799)	.084	.070	.066	100	155
Sixth (1799–1801)	.059	.055	.053	100	96
Seventh (1801–1803)	.041	.040	.040	100	141
Senate					
First (1789–1791)	.711	.489	.275	26	100
Second (1791–1793)	.420	.275	.185	27	52
Third (1793–1795)	.278	.191	.159	29	79
Fourth (1795–1797)	.179	.161	.142	30	86
Fifth (1797–1799)	.202	.162	.150	31	202
Sixth (1799–1801)	.207	.173	.151	36	120
Seventh (1801–1803)	.107	.097	.091	33	88

SOURCE: Derived from multidimensional scaling of recorded roll-call votes in the United States Congress (collected by the Inter-University Consortium for Political and Social Research).

some cases on the basis of stress, but there is no advantage in restricting the figures to a single dimension.

It is important to reemphasize that these configurations are *not* to be interpreted in terms of two orthogonal linear dimensions. Thus I have not labeled the vertical or horizontal dimensions of the figures. Although such labeling can be appropriate in certain instances, it does not provide the best description of patterns in the period under consideration. Rather, the configurations should be seen as clusterings of legislators in a two-dimensional (or three-dimensional) space. A closely grouped cluster of congressmen indicates a cohesive voting bloc, and the relationships among voting blocs and unattached legislators are displayed in the configurations.

The series of configurations across the seven congresses, both in the House and the Senate, provides convincing evidence for the development of political parties during this period. The pattern which emerges is a clear progression from factionalism to polarization. In the following sections, the configurations are examined in greater detail.

Factionalism, 1789–1791

After the new Constitution was proposed at the Philadelphia Convention in 1787, it had to be ratified by at least nine states to become effective. The ensuing process involved considerable disagreement and very close votes in several states. This conflict between supporters and opponents of the Constitution became the major issue affecting the elections for the First Congress in 1788 and 1789. While personalities and local issues were often decisive, nearly every state experienced contests between Federalists and Antifederalists. The Federalists, who generally had more incentive to become involved in the new government, were victorious in most contests. In fact, only 10 (of 65) seats in the House and only 2 (of 26) seats in the Senate were won by Antifederalists (Paulin, 1904).

Despite the importance of divisions over the Constitution, this issue did not dominate voting in the First Congress. While Antifederalist members of the House are separated roughly at the top of the voting configuration (Figure 1), this division clearly was not the major one. This is illustrated by noting that the average agreement between Federalists and Antifederalists (49.3 percent) was not much below the average agreement within either group (Federalists, 55.1 percent; Antifederalists, 57.9 percent).

To the extent that there was any consistency in voting patterns, it was along sectional lines. In the First Senate, there is minimal evidence of consistent voting (Figure 6). Those alignments that do exist, which require three dimensions to represent spatially, are geographical and cannot be considered evidence of party voting. With certain exceptions, senators from New England, the Middle States, and the South are each isolated in a distinct region of the space. The exceptions, however, foreshadow the coming party alignment. William Maclay, from Pennsylvania's more developed party system, is aligned rather closely with Virginia's senators, an alignment consistent with the future Jeffersonian Republican party.

While it is difficult to find even factional patterns for voting in the First Senate, voting in the House of Representatives is far more structured (Figure 1). Although the stress in two dimensions is not perfect, it is far better than the stress for a two-dimensional representation of the Senate. Evident from either multidimensional scaling or cluster analysis are three principal voting blocs, which are best described as sectional groupings. One bloc includes mostly members from New England and New York. The second consists almost exclusively of southern congressmen, and the third is dominated by members from Pennsylvania and several neighboring states. The principal exceptions to this alignment come from New Jersey, Maryland, and South Carolina. The four New

FIGURE 1   Voting Patterns in the First Congress, United States House of Representatives, 1789–1791

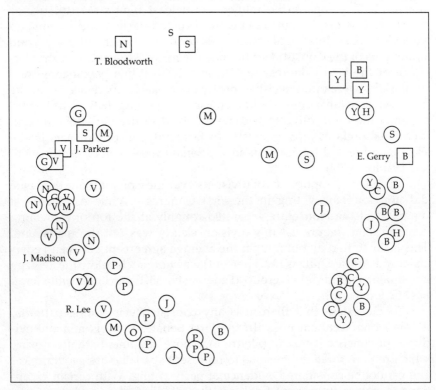

Source: Spatial configuration, derived from multidimensional scaling of recorded roll-call votes in the United States Congress (collected by the Inter-University Consortium for Political and Social Research).

Key: Each symbol indicates the state represented by a particular congressman. The circle or square drawn around the letter indicates party affiliation.

B = Massachusetts	J = New Jersey	R = Rhode Island
C = Connecticut	K = Kentucky	S = South Carolina
E = Vermont	M = Maryland	T = Tennessee
G = Georgia	N = North Carolina	V = Virgina
H = New Hampshire	P = Pennsylvania	Y = New York

Ⓧ = Federalist

☐X = Antifederalist

X = None/Unknown

Jersey congressmen are divided between the New England and Pennsylvania blocs, according to their proximity to the cities of New York and Philadelphia. Maryland congressmen are placed with or near each of the three voting blocs, perhaps in accordance with the state's location between North and South. Finally the South Carolina delegation contained two members (both representing coastal towns, Charleston and Georgetown) who voted in agreement with the New England bloc. Throughout the early years, South Carolina had the strongest Federalist party of any southern state, a fact best explained by the existence of trading interests centered in the port of Charleston.

These patterns of congressional voting in the House provide evidence that factionalism was present. At least two major sets of issues in the First Congress contributed to the appearance of this stage. One was the location of the new capital. The choice between New York, Philadelphia, the Susquehanna valley, and the Potomac valley contributed to the sectional divisions, particularly the separation of the various Middle States delegations. Another large set of votes in the First Congress concerned domestic economics, specifically relating to Hamilton's fiscal proposals. These votes have been cited as the first on which new partisan alignments arose, and they also demonstrate the lack of continuity between the old divisions over the Constitution and the newly emerging divisions. While majorities of both the North Carolina and Virginia delegations had been supporters of the Constitution, they were "federalists only in support of the Constitution and not federalists in upholding all of the centralizing measures of the new government" (Gilpatrick, 1931, p. 45).

A Period of Transition, 1791–1793

By the Second Congress, voting patterns were still best described as factional, but sectionalism was beginning to give way to partisanship. There was not yet, however, a clear movement toward polarization of legislators into two cohesive groups. Nor was there much evidence of partisanship in elections for this congress.

The circular pattern evident in the configuration for the Second Senate represents a transitional stage in the development of party voting (Figure 7). The circle actually consists of four distinct blocs of senators plus one isolated individual (Aaron Burr). These blocs are clearly dominated by senators from particular regions: a South bloc, a South-plus-Middle bloc, a Middle-plus-New England bloc, and a New England bloc. Furthermore, the third of these blocs consists exclusively of senators who were being identified as Federalists or were friendly toward Hamilton's fiscal programs. While no bloc is exclusively Republican, there is a tendency for Republicans to be at the opposite side of the figure from the Federalist core group. Clearly, voting in the Second Congress was still more determined by sectional groupings than by party, but the origins of the two parties are already evident in the configuration for this Senate.

FIGURE 2   Voting Patterns in the Second Congress, United States House of Representatives, 1791–1793

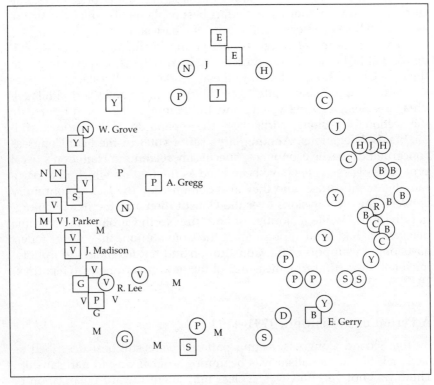

Source: Spatial configuration, derived from multidimensional scaling of recorded roll-call votes in the United States Congress (collected by the Inter-University Consortium for Political and Social Research).
Key: Each symbol indicates the state represented by a particular congressman. The circle or square drawn around the letter indicates party affiliation.

B = Massachusetts	J = New Jersey	R = Rhode Island
C = Connecticut	K = Kentucky	S = South Carolina
E = Vermont	M = Maryland	T = Tennessee
G = Georgia	N = North Carolina	V = Virgina
H = New Hampshire	P = Pennsylvania	Y = New York

Ⓧ = Federalist
X̄ = Republican
X = None/Unknown

Aaron Burr's isolated position is particularly intriguing given his special role in early American politics. His position in the spatial configuration is even more isolated than it appears in Figure 7.

FIGURE 3   Voting Patterns in the Third Congress, United States House of Representatives, 1793–1795

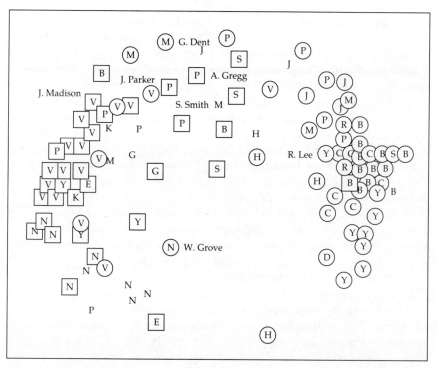

Source: Spatial configuration, derived from multidimensional scaling of recorded roll-call votes in the United States Congress (collected by the Inter-University Consortium for Political and Social Research).

Key: Each symbol indicates the state represented by a particular congressman. The circle or square drawn around the letter indicates party affiliation.

B = Massachusetts	J = New Jersey	R = Rhode Island
C = Connecticut	K = Kentucky	S = South Carolina
E = Vermont	M = Maryland	T = Tennessee
G = Georgia	N = North Carolina	V = Virginia
H = New Hampshire	P = Pennsylvania	Y = New York

Ⓧ = Federalist

☐X = Republican

X = None/Unknown

In a three-dimensional configuration, Burr alone defines the third dimension, showing his individualized voting in this congress. Chosen as a senator from New York because of a "reputation for independence which fascinated substantial men of both parties" (Young, 1967, p. 189), Burr's record in the Second Congress was truly one of independence from partisanship. Only in later years did he become a confirmed Republican, both in his congressional voting and in his political ambitions.

The configuration for the Second House (Figure 2) is not very different from that of the First House. The principal features are still the regional blocs, particularly the New England and southern blocs. Once again, the South Carolina delegation provided the main exceptions, with the continuing alliance of those from coastal districts with northern congressmen. A second notable exception was the two-member delegation from the newly admitted state of Vermont, the first state without direct access to the coast.

Delegations which changed the most from the First to the Second Congress were those from the Middle States. No longer was each state delegation a cohesive voting bloc. The New York and Pennsylvania delegations had become internally divided, with three Pennsylvanians in both the southern and northern blocs, and two others between the two blocs. In New York's delegation, two members aligned themselves with the South, and the other four voted with New England. The New Jersey delegation remained divided, but no longer along geographic lines. Finally, the Maryland delegation was still much closer to the southern bloc, but only half of it could be considered part of that bloc.

Sectionalism remained the dominant cleavage in the Second Congress. Yet geographic lines were becoming less important in certain states, especially New York and Pennsylvania. Whether this new diversity was truly a sign of partisanship, however, remains a question. In New York, most candidates could be identified as Federalists or Antifederalists, and victorious candidates later voted consistently with these affiliations. But the elections did not generally present clear partisan choices, and it would be at least two more years before the Antifederalists became known as Republicans (Young, 1967). In Pennsylvania, the 1791 elections were held on a district basis and were characterized by little political activity of any sort. Again, the candidates' political leanings were probably known to the more well-informed voters, but there was no open partisanship.

This lack of partisanship can be further illustrated by two individual cases. Elbridge Gerry, from the Middlesex district in Massachusetts, had been an Antifederalist in the Constitutional Convention, refusing even to sign the final document. He later became a leader in the Republican party, eventually serving as vice-president under James Madison. But

FIGURE 4   Voting Patterns in the Fourth Congress, United States House of Representatives, 1795–1797

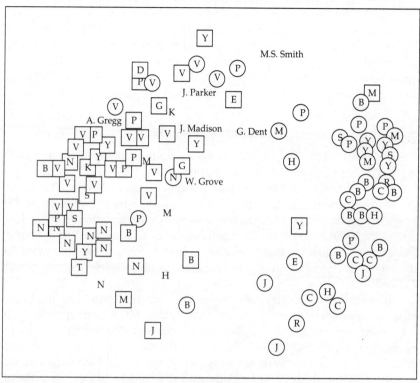

Source: Spatial configuration, derived from multidimensional scaling of recorded roll-call votes in the United States Congress (collected by the Inter-University Consortium for Political and Social Research).

Key: Each symbol indicates the state represented by a particular congressman. The circle or square drawn around the letter indicates party affiliation.

B = Massachusetts	J = New Jersey	R = Rhode Island
C = Connecticut	K = Kentucky	S = South Carolina
E = Vermont	M = Maryland	T = Tennessee
G = Georgia	N = North Carolina	V = Virgina
H = New Hampshire	P = Pennsylvania	Y = New York

Ⓧ = Federalist

☒ = Republican

X = None/Unknown

in the Second Congress, Gerry voted more often with the Federalist bloc than with his nominal Republican allies. The second case is that of William Barry Grove, who had been elected in North Carolina as a Federalist supporter of the Constitution, defeating an incumbent who was one of North Carolina's leading Antifederalists.[12] In spite of his Federalist label, his voting record placed him at the edge of the cluster of southerners, who mostly became known as Republicans. These two cases help to indicate that the patterns of voting in the Second Congress were not yet clearly determined by partisan affiliations.

Polarization and Party Politics, 1793–1797

The polarization of congressmen into two political parties occurred during Washington's second administration, from 1793 to 1797. This process is clearly indicated by the lower levels of stress for the Third and Fourth Congresses, both in the House and the Senate (Table 1). But it is even more obvious from a comparison of configurations. There is a distinctly tighter clustering in configurations of the Third and Fourth Congresses (Figures 3 and 4, House; Figure 8, Senate), as compared to the First and Second Congresses (Figures 1 and 2, House; Figures 6 and 7, Senate).

In the Fourth Congress, the Senate configuration has a clearly bipolar structure (Figure 8), with two voting blocs corresponding to the emerging Federalist and Republican parties. The parties generally retained a highly sectional character, for the Republican bloc consisted almost entirely of southern senators, while the Federalist bloc included mostly senators from New England and the Middle States. Because of this overlap of party and region, there is some difficulty in determining whether these voting blocs formed because of partisan or regional affiliation. Nevertheless, for most cases where a senator's party ties and sectional loyalties were in conflict, he voted according to his party ties.

The configurations for the House of Representatives, like that for the Senate, show a clear movement toward a pattern of polarization (Figures 3 and 4). In each congress, two distinct polar groups form the cores of the two emerging parties. In addition, there are a number of individuals who do not clearly belong to either group. While this basic

---

[12] Grove and his opponent, Bloodworth, were in sharp opposition over the wisdom of the Constitution, and the campaign was accented by a series of newspaper advertisements. In spite of an apparently heated contest where Grove won 65 percent of the 3166 votes cast, the election was very one-sided at the county level. In only two of the 12 counties in the district did the leading candidate get fewer than 90 percent of the votes, with each candidate winning those counties nearest to his home county. This "friends and neighbors" voting pattern is another clear sign of the lack of partisanship at this time (Gilpatrick, 1931; *North Carolina Chronicle*, 1791).

FIGURE 5   Voting Patterns in the United States House of Representatives, 1797–1803

A. Fifth Congress, 1797-1799

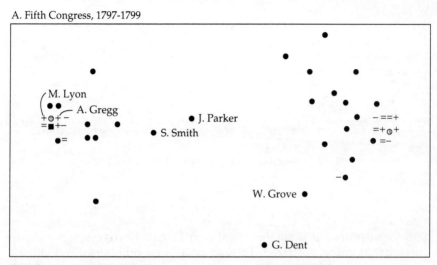

Key: Each symbol represents the number of congressmen at a particular point in space.

Symbol	Number of Members	Symbol	Number of Members
●	1	+	4
–	2	⊖	5
=	3	⊗	7
		■	9

B. Sixth Congress, 1799-1801

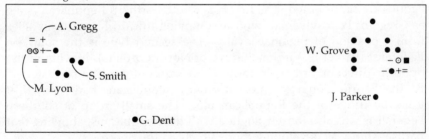

Key: Each symbol represents the number of congressmen at a particular point in space.

Symbol	Number of Members	Symbol	Number of Members
●	1	⊖	7
–	2	○	9
=	3	●	16
+	4	■	19

Source: Spatial configuration, derived from multidimensional scaling of recorded roll-call votes in the United States Congress (collected by the Inter-University Consortium for Political and Social Research).

FIGURE 5   Voting Patterns in the United States House of Representatives, 1797–1803 (continued)

C. Seventh Congress, 1801-1803

Key: Each symbol represents the number of congressmen at a particular point in space.

Symbol	Number of Members	Symbol	Number of Members
•	1	+	6
–	2	⊗	34
=	4	■	43

pattern appears for both the Third and Fourth Congresses, voting in the latter is more polarized. Instead of a large number of individuals who vote with neither cluster, nearly everyone in the Fourth Congress can be placed in one group or the other, although the groups are still not highly cohesive.

Something can be learned about the polarization process by a careful look at those congressmen who were not clustered with either polar group. In the Third Congress, over 20 of the 100 congressmen were in this intermediate position. Among these individuals, two particular categories are represented. The first type is the northern Republican (such as Gregg of Pennsylvania), who was moving toward his partisan allies from a position of regional loyalty. The second type is the southern Federalist (Parker of Virginia, Grove of North Carolina), moving in the opposite direction but again toward a position of partisan consistency. By the Fourth Congress, most northern Republicans had reached at least the fringe of the Republican bloc. The small group of southern Federalists was also loosely aligned with the Republicans, showing that partisanship was developing more slowly in the South.

Several general observations can be made about the progress of party development by the end of the Fourth Congress. First, the Federalists had developed quickly into a unified voting bloc, while cohesive voting emerged more slowly for the Republicans. This conclusion, supported by the spatial configurations, can be further confirmed by comparing the average agreement within the Federalist and Republican groups.

	Federalist	Republican
Third Congress	83.3%	73.5%
Fourth Congress	77.0%	72.7%

This difference might be partially attributed to the advantages of being in power. Because much of the agenda was set by the Federalist administration (with the active role of Hamilton), the Republicans in opposition had more difficulty reaching any kind of unity.

Second, both new parties retained a distinctive sectional character. In both the Third and Fourth Congresses, a majority of those in the Fed-

FIGURE 6   Voting Patterns in the First Congress, United States Senate, 1789–1791

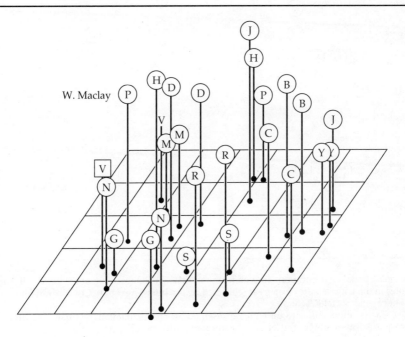

Source: Spatial configuration, derived from multidimensional scaling of recorded roll-call votes in the United States Congress (collected by the Inter-University Consortium for Political and Social Research).

Key: Each symbol indicates the state represented by a particular congressman. The circle or square drawn around the letter indicates party affiliation.

B = Massachusetts	J = New Jersey	R = Rhode Island
C = Connecticut	K = Kentucky	S = South Carolina
E = Vermont	M = Maryland	T = Tennessee
G = Georgia	N = North Carolina	V = Virgina
H = New Hampshire	P = Pennsylvania	Y = New York

Ⓧ = Federalist

☐X = Antifederalist

X = None/Unknown

FIGURE 7   Voting Patterns in the Second Congress, United States Senate, 1791–1793

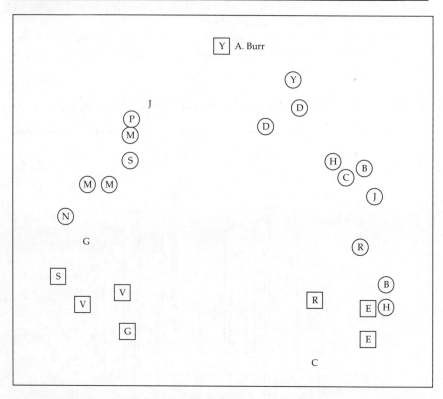

Source: Spatial configuration, derived from multidimensional scaling of recorded roll-call votes in the United States Congress (collected by the Inter-University Consortium for Political and Social Research).
Key: Each symbol indicates the state represented by a particular congressman. The circle or square drawn around the letter indicates party affiliation.

B = Massachusetts	J = New Jersey	R = Rhode Island
C = Connecticut	K = Kentucky	S = South Carolina
E = Vermont	M = Maryland	T = Tennessee
G = Georgia	N = North Carolina	V = Virgina
H = New Hampshire	P = Pennsylvania	Y = New York

Ⓧ = Federalist
☐X = Republican
X = None/Unknown

FIGURE 8   Voting Patterns in the Fourth Congress, United States Senate, 1795–1797

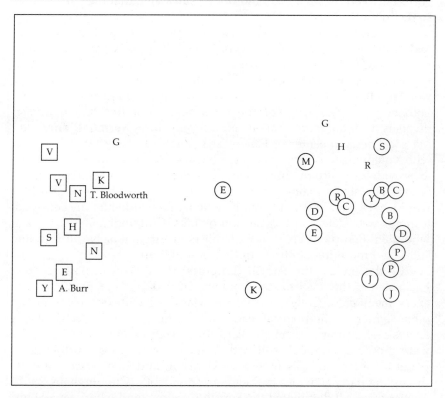

Source: Spatial configuration, derived from multidimensional scaling of recorded roll-call votes in the United States Congress (collected by the Inter-University Consortium for Political and Social Research).

Key: Each symbol indicates the state represented by a particular congressman. The circle or square drawn around the letter indicates party affiliation.

B = Massachusetts	J = New Jersey	R = Rhode Island
C = Connecticut	K = Kentucky	S = South Carolina
E = Vermont	M = Maryland	T = Tennessee
G = Georgia	N = North Carolina	V = Virgina
H = New Hampshire	P = Pennsylvania	Y = New York

Ⓧ = Federalist

☐X = Republican

X = None/Unknown

eralist bloc came from New England, and a majority of the Republican
bloc were southerners. Given the great cultural and economic differences between regions, it should not be surprising that the parties were
so distinctively regional.

Yet, in spite of the dominance of regionalism, partisan diversity
had clearly emerged within several states. This was particularly true
in the larger Middle States: New York, Pennsylvania, and Maryland.
In each, elections were revolving around partisan concerns, and they
were sending to Congress delegations which included partisans from
both emerging groups. For the other regions at this time, partisan
diversity was far more limited. New Hampshire, Vermont, and even
Massachusetts (a center of Federalist strength) had elected a few men
who voted together with the Republicans. South Carolina continued
to provide virtually the only exceptions to Republican solidarity in the
South. The sole remaining southerner to vote with the Federalist bloc
was Richard Bland Lee, of Virginia, who was rewarded for his Federalist
leanings with defeat in the election of 1795 (Cunningham, 1957). Most
who identified themselves as Federalists in Virginia or North Carolina
still voted more frequently with their Republican neighbors.

By the end of the Fourth Congress, the American party system
had reached the level of development labeled "polarization." Nearly
every member of Congress could be classified with one party or the
other, either by the political leaders of the time or on the basis of this
analysis of voting agreement. Party organization and party discipline
were growing, although still with limited effectiveness. Furthermore,
political leaders such as Jefferson, Madison, and Giles were regularly
discussing party activities in their correspondence (Cunningham, 1957).
The issue which dominated the Fourth Congress and which several historians have regarded as crucial in party development was the contest
over ratification and appropriation of funds for the Jay Treaty (Bell,
1973; Chambers, 1963; Charles, 1961). This treaty with Great Britain
marked one of the first organized attempts by the opposition to defeat
an important administration policy proposal. With Madison as party
leader, Republican strategists tried to coordinate their opposition and
defeat the treaty. In the end, they lost by a single vote, but their effort
marked a critical point in partisan development (Cunningham, 1957).

The Emergence of Parties, 1797–1803

The Jay Treaty conflict (with its final vote on April 30, 1796) had a significant impact on subsequent congressional elections. These elections,
held in late 1796 and early 1797, were dominated by the Jay Treaty
issue and were characterized by a level of partisanship not previously
seen. George Washington's retirement from politics, and the resulting

FIGURE 9   Voting Patterns in the Seventh Congress, United States Senate, 1801–1803

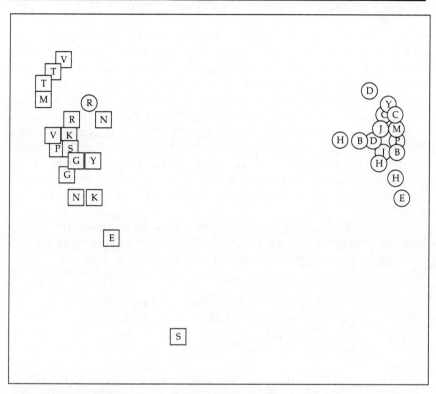

Source: Spatial configuration, derived from multidimensional scaling of recorded roll-call votes in the United States Congress (collected by the Inter-University Consortium for Political and Social Research).

Key: Each symbol indicates the state represented by a particular congressman. The circle or square drawn around the letter indicates party affiliation.

B = Massachusetts	J = New Jersey	R = Rhode Island
C = Connecticut	K = Kentucky	S = South Carolina
E = Vermont	M = Maryland	T = Tennessee
G = Georgia	N = North Carolina	V = Virgina
H = New Hampshire	P = Pennsylvania	Y = New York

Ⓧ = Federalist

☐ X ☐ = Republican

X   = None/Unknown

choice between Adams and Jefferson for president, also tended to raise the level of partisanship. Thus these elections were important for the expansion of party politics into the electoral arena.

Spatial analysis of congressional voting in the Fifth, Sixth, and Seventh Congresses reveals a set of patterns which lend support to the idea that the 1796–97 elections began a new period of partisan politics. Voting in the House had become highly polarized and extremely well defined. The stress for these three configurations is very low and supports an excellent fit even in a single dimension (Table 1). The actual configurations (Figure 5) reveal two very tight clusters with only a few individuals outside of both blocs. In fact, the clustering is so dense that individual points in these figures cannot be labeled. For this reason, the partisan and regional distributions of the major voting blocs are provided in Table 2. In the Senate (Figure 9), the voting was also polarized into two groups, although the clusters are less well defined than in the House.

Cluster analysis of House members in these three congresses helps to demonstrate further the cohesiveness of the emerging parties. Average levels of agreement within the two voting blocs are shown below.

	Federalist	Republican
Fifth Congress	82.7%	86.9%
Sixth Congress	86.4%	86.0%
Seventh Congress	89.9%	79.6%

These levels of intra-group agreement are extremely high and far above comparable levels in previous years (or, in fact, in modern times). The only real exceptions to the polarization into partisan voting blocs were in the Fifth Congress, where three individuals were noticeably unaligned: Dent (Md.), Parker (Va.), and S. Smith (Md.). All three served in Congress for several terms and had a history of inconsistent partisan ties. Yet, by the Sixth Congress, even these three men were clearly aligned with one of the party blocs.

There remains, of course, the question of whether these voting alignments can appropriately be called party blocs. This question can be examined by looking at the relationship between party labels and voting blocs, and by considering the sectional composition of these blocs. If voting blocs result from party alignments, they should be very consistent with party labels and relatively diverse in their geographical composition. The relationships in Table 2 are clearly consistent with the designation of the voting blocs as partisan.

At an individual level, this conclusion is illustrated by looking again at the voting record of Grove (N.C.). He was first elected to Congress in 1791 and was always regarded in his home state as a Federalist, the

TABLE 2.   Partisan and Regional Distributions of Members of the United States House of Representatives, by Multidimensional Scaling Blocks

Multidimensionial Scaling Bloc	Total	Party			Region			
		Feder-alist	Repub-lican	None	New England	Middle States	South	West
Fifth Congress								
Federalist	52	51	1	0	25	21	6	0
Republican	45	0	44	1	3	12	27	3
None	3	2	1	0	0	2	1	0
Sixth Congress								
Federalist	51	51	0	0	22	15	14	0
Republican	49	6	43	0	3	21	22	3
Seventh Congress								
Federalist	38	37	1	0	20	10	8	0
Republican	62	3	59	0	8	26	25	3

SOURCE: Derived for multidimensional scaling of recorded roll-call votes in the United States Congress (collected by the Inter-University Consortium for Political and Social Research).

only North Carolina Federalist chosen before 1798. Yet in the Second, Third, and Fourth Congresses, his voting record was more in line with the Republican bloc and the rest of his state delegation. By the Fifth Congress his votes placed him on the edge of the Federalist bloc; and in the Sixth and Seventh Congresses, he was clearly a partisan Federalist. Furthermore, in the latter two congresses, Grove was joined in the Federalist camp by several other North Carolina Federalists. A second southern Federalist, Parker (Va.), followed a similar path, moving from his sectional group to his party affiliation.

The issue which seems to symbolize the emergent partisanship was the passage of the Alien and Sedition Acts in 1798. These acts were at least partially an attempt by the Federalists to destroy the opposition party. Votes on these laws coincided almost perfectly with the blocs shown in the configurations, providing further evidence that these blocs were partisan groupings.

Indices of Partisanship

A more traditional type of roll-call analysis may help to amplify further the multidimensional scaling results. Three indices of party voting are employed here—Rice's index of cohesion, Rice's index of difference, and Lowell's concept of the party vote. The utility of these indices for studying partisanship across time has been demonstrated by

MacRae (1970, pp. 200–07), who showed that the degree of partisanship in Congress (as measured by party votes) rose to its highest levels immediately following party realignments. Because the emergence of new parties might be regarded as a special case of partisan realignment, a similar pattern might be expected between 1789 and 1803.

The values of the index of cohesion, the index of difference, and the percentage of party votes are presented for the House and Senate from 1789 to 1803 in Figure 10. These data readily show that cohesion in both legislative parties increased dramatically during this period, while party differences grew simultaneously. The indices of party cohesion and difference rose constantly during the first five congresses, leveling off after 1797. The timing of these changes corresponds rather closely with the polarization observed in the MDS configurations. Parties developed steadily from 1789 until 1796, the year of the Jay Treaty controversy. By the Fifth Congress, they had reached a high level of development on any measure of congressional voting, a level sustained through 1803.

For purposes of comparison, I have also calculated indices of cohesion and difference for the three regional groups: New England, Middle States, and the South. Regional cohesion remained reasonably constant across this period, although some changes did occur in the Sixth and Seventh Congresses, reflecting large partisan swings within several states in the elections of 1798 and 1800. The average regional cohesion for the entire period was 49.3, a level higher than party cohesion in the first two congresses but exceeded by party cohesion in all the remaining years. This result confirms the earlier conclusion that partisanship had become more important than sectionalism after about 1793.

In order to make a better assessment of party development in these early years, comparisons can be made between the cohesion of the early parties and twentieth-century parties. During the entire period from 1921 to 1969, the average index of cohesion of the two congressional parties was about 66, ranging from 55 to 77.[13] According to this standard of comparison, 1795 seems to mark the year when early parties reached the level of unity found in the twentieth century. Furthermore, beginning in the Fifth Congress, the level of party cohesion exceeded that in nearly any modern congress. Similarly, the average index of party difference for the twentieth-century congresses was about 41, a figure surpassed by the time of the Third Congress. The number of party votes averaged about 10 percent of all votes between 1921 and 1969; again, the early parties generally matched these levels. In fact, the proportion of party votes after 1797 had reached a level obtained at few times in American history.

---

[13] The averages for the congresses of the twentieth century were computed from tables in Cooper, Brady and Hurley (1977, pp. 138–39).

FIGURE 10   Trends in Partisanship, United States Congress, House of Representatives and Senate, 1789–1803

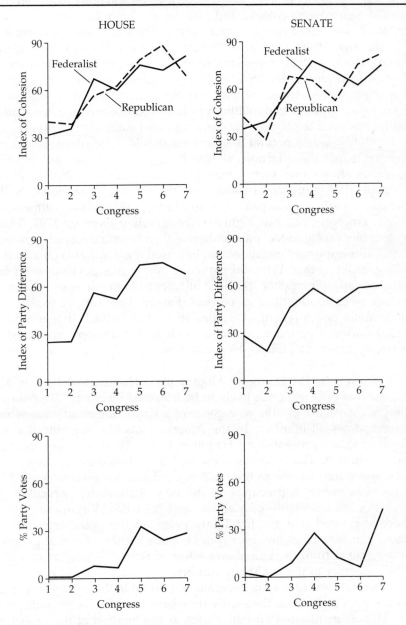

Source: Computed from recorded roll-call votes in the United States Congress (collected by the Inter-University Consortium for Political and Social Research).

Discussion and Conclusions

The loose patterns of association known as factionalism had been present in nearly every colonial and national assembly predating the Constitution, and these patterns continued in the early years of Congress. For the First House, evidence of such patterns existed in the regional voting blocs. At least minimal patterns of association characteristic of factionalism can be detected for every congress, with the exception of the unstructured voting of the First Senate. Indeed, it is difficult to imagine a legislative body without factions, particularly in a new nation with considerable geographic, economic, and cultural diversity.

While it seems natural that factions should have arisen, it was not inevitable that these factions should have polarized. Yet the empirical evidence shows that such a movement occurred. Examination of the chronological sequence of configurations, for either the House or the Senate, reveals a vivid picture of increasing polarization, culminating in the emergence of two highly cohesive voting blocs by 1797. These voting blocs were in fact more cohesive than twentieth-century parties.

Three important questions can be raised regarding this polarization of legislative voting: Why did particular alignments develop, or in fact why did any alignments appear at all? Second, should these polarized voting blocs be identified as parties? Finally, how can we explain the anomalous development of parties (if that is indeed an appropriate term) during a period when most political leaders were immersed in a strong anti-party philosophical tradition?

Reasons for the Emerging Alignments.   Huntington (1968, p. 415) argues that polarization is likely to be triggered by either "the cumulation of cleavages" or "the emergence of a single dominant issue which overshadows all others." In the American case he suggests that the fiscal program presented by Hamilton to the First Congress met this latter criterion. The evidence presented here, however, does not support this claim, for the factions did not polarize for several years. This issue was merely a precursor of the new alignments, particularly in terms of the leadership of Madison and his fellow Virginians. Others have suggested that the Jay Treaty provided the polarizing force. A more plausible case, however, can be made for the idea that polarization resulted from the cumulative effect of several issues, all of which came together in the Jay Treaty conflict.

Several cleavages were generally important in the early years of the new republic. One was the sectional division between North and South, which was manifested on issues such as the location of the capital for reasons of simple regional loyalty. A second significant conflict was that between commercial and agrarian interests (Beard, 1915), economic differences intensified by their convergence with the regional divisions.

The northern economy was built upon commercial interests (shipping, fishing, trade, banking, and manufacturing), while the southern economy (with the exception of coastal South Carolina) was more agrarian, with an abundance of plantations dependent on slavery (Dauer, 1953). A third cleavage existed between coastal and interior regions, the former naturally more concerned with trade and other commercial interests, and the latter, with agrarian economies, being concerned with internal improvements and protection of the frontier. A fourth cleavage set those wishing to maintain close relations with England against those more sympathetic to France. Against the background of the French Revolution, this division was a manifestation of a deeper philosophical disagreement over the form of democracy desired in this country, a dispute which provided the fifth major cleavage.

All five divisions were present in the political arena of 1795, and each tended to reinforce the emerging alignment of Federalists and Republicans. Federalists, coming most often from New England or the coastal regions of the Middle States and South Carolina, were generally representatives of commercial interests, sympathizers with the English, and supporters of a more aristocratic political system. Republicans, on the other hand, came generally from the interior or the South, and they were mostly allies of agrarian interests and believers in the direct democracy symbolized by the French Revolution.

At a time when these blocs of interest were coalescing, controversy arose over ratification and implementation of the Jay Treaty. The treaty itself was the outcome of negotiations with Great Britain over a number of concerns, including British activity on the western frontier, British seizure of slaves during the war, American trade debts dating to before the war, the neutrality of American shipping in the war between Britain and France, and the general status of British-American trade. As the product of the Federalist administration, the treaty was opposed by the Republicans, who were particularly concerned about the favorable trade status granted to Britain at the expense of France and the failure to provide compensation for slaves seized by Britain (Chambers, 1963; Charles, 1961; Varg, 1963). The Jay Treaty, therefore, represented in a single issue the cumulation of dominant cleavages in early American politics. The subsequent polarization of congressional voting and increased partisanship in electoral contests made this issue a crucial factor in the development of American political parties.[14]

The Existence of Party.   While there should be little question about the polarization of alignments in the early American congresses, reasonable objections can be raised to the designation of polar voting blocs

---

[14] For further discussion, see Hoadley (1979).

as parties. Formisano (1974), for example, has suggested that voting blocs may have formed not along party lines, but rather along lines related to such factors as regionalism and boardinghouse residences. Obviously, region and party were highly related during this period, a fact which itself does not run counter to the existence of parties. But the multiplicity of cleavages and the persistence of voting alliances would seem to deny a simply regional explanation. In fact, by the end of this era, the voting blocs had become less dominated by a single region (see Table 2). And, as long as the capital remained in New York or Philadelphia, boardinghouses were not a salient factor in congressional voting. Furthermore, when congress did move to Washington in 1800, there is no evidence of distinct voting blocs corresponding to boarding-house membership. Indeed, it is more likely that congressmen chose as messmates their established partisan allies.[15]

Nevertheless, there is more to the idea of party than simply the existence of congressional voting blocs. The several aspects of party identified early in this article include common symbols or labels and groups of supporters in the electorate. Formisano (1974, p. 478) has pointed out that

> multivariate analysis of roll calls needs to be accompanied by evidence that men ran for Congress as openly identified members of a party. To show convincingly that the core factions of Federalist and Republican interests came to think of themselves in party terms, consideration must be given to legislators' self-images. . . .

Although there was not a consistent use of party labels in election campaigns across the entire nation, it is clear that party labels were becoming more meaningful as legislators polarized into voting blocs. Gradually people were beginning to think about politics in explicitly partisan terms (Cunningham, 1957; Young, 1967).

The determination of whether parties existed in the 1790s has become in effect a game of definitions. Evidently, this was a decade of party development, and whether the word "party" is appropriate at any particular time is not crucial. What is important is to document the continually increasing prominence of parties in the politics of this era. In 1790, members of Congress were voting together in regional groups whose composition shifted considerably from one issue to the next. By 1792, patterns of voting were shifting from

---

[15] The boardinghouse explanation of voting cohesion was advanced by Young (1966), but his conclusions have been recently challenged (Bogue and Marlaire, 1975; Cunningham, 1978). A comparison of boardinghouse residence (found in Goldman and Young, 1973) with the location of members in the configurations for the Philadelphia and Washington years (to 1803) fails to reveal any pattern supporting Young's thesis for this period.

a regional basis to a more partisan basis built on a set of issue positions. By 1796, these voting patterns had polarized so that two blocs of congressmen opposed each other on nearly every issue. As the cohesiveness of party groups in Congress increased, party affiliation became a more significant factor in congressional elections. These trends continued until at least 1803. Only thereafter, with the decline of the Federalists, did the country experience a temporary hiatus in the process of party development.

Parties in an Anti-Party Era. When the new government was created by the Constitution, most political leaders shared a strong anti-party tradition. Parties were perceived as agencies which would hinder the progress of good government, a view expressed forcefully by Madison in *The Federalist*, No. 10 (1961, p. 77): "Among the numerous advantages promised by a well constructed Union, none deserved to be more accurately developed than its tendency to break and control the violence of faction." Yet in spite of such sentiments, parties very quickly became a prominent feature of the political system. This anti-party stigma does, however, help to account for the fact that parties had not reached the highest stages of development during this period. The reluctance of candidates to run openly for office as members of a party and the failure of leaders to develop any substantial national organization were two factors that might be explained in part by this distrust of the idea of a party system.

One explanation for the anomaly of party development within the context of an antiparty tradition lies in the lack of any positive historical precedent. Nowhere in the eighteenth-century world did parties exist by any modern definition. There was considerable factionalism, both in Great Britain and in colonial America, but no clear development of parties beyond this stage. Therefore, in their anti-party statements, American political thinkers were dealing with a concept of "party" which today would be characterized as "faction." They simply did not recognize the possibility of a more constructive political party until some time after they had actually created such parties.

A second explanation for this anomaly lies in the emerging idea of legitimate opposition. Some of the philosophical objections to the idea of party were based on the belief that parties might hinder development of the unanimity considered essential for the stability of a state. Gradually people realized that unanimity was impossible in a diverse society and that the right of opposition had to be recognized. Sartori (1976, p. 11) has suggested that "parties presuppose—for their acceptance and proper functioning—peace under a constitutional rule." The first set of elections for Congress (between 1788 and 1790) showed that the Constitution was quickly being accepted. In spite of the large numbers opposing ratification in some states, most of the new congressmen

were supporters of the Constitution. Furthermore, even an Antifederalist such as Elbridge Gerry could be found arguing in debate that, "If
this constitution, which is now ratified, be not supported, I despair of
ever having a government for these United States" (Austin, 1829, p.
103).

When it became clear that the opposition was concerned only with
specific policy alternatives within the existing constitutional system, it
was far easier for such opposition to be tolerated. Once the legitimacy
of opposition was established, the acceptance of parties followed. This
was, of course, a slow process. The Sedition Act, passed by Federalist
majorities in 1798, represented the old tradition; at least one Republican
congressman (Lyon of Vermont) won reelection after being convicted
and jailed under this act. Nevertheless, the progress of party development was not deterred seriously by this act of a declining Federalist majority. Only two years later, the Republicans were victorious in
both presidential and congressional elections. That a transfer of power
occurred peacefully in 1801 reflects growing acceptance of the legitimacy
of opposition and the idea of party.

In 1804, Thomas Jefferson wrote in a letter, "The party division in
this country is certainly not among its pleasant features. To a certain
degree it will always exist . . ." (quoted in Cunningham, 1965, p. 19). By
this time, nearly everyone in Congress was clearly associated with one
of the new parties. Acceptance of these parties, however, came reluctantly as their inevitability became more apparent. Whether recognized
by those involved or still regarded as an undesirable development, the
changing voting patterns exhibited by members of Congress between
1789 and 1803 present strong evidence that a true party system had
emerged.

References

Austin, James T. (1829). *The Life of Elbridge Gerry*, Vol. 2. Boston: Wells and
    Lilly.

Beard, Charles A. (1915). *Economic Origins of Jeffersonian Democracy*. New York:
    Macmillan.

Bell, Rudolph M. (1973). *Party and Faction in American Politics: The House of
    Representatives, 1789–1801*. Westport, Conn.: Greenwood Press.

Bogue, Allan G., and Mark Paul Marlaire (1975). "Of Mess and Men: The
    Boardinghouse and Congressional Voting, 1821–1842." *American Journal of
    Political Science* 19:207–30.

Chambers, William Nisbet (1963). *Political Parties in a New Nation: The American
    Experience, 1776–1809*. New York: Oxford University Press.

———. (1966). "Parties and Nation-Building in America." In Joseph LaPalom-
    bara and Myron Weiner (eds.), *Political Parties and Political Development*.
    Princeton, N.J.: Princeton University Press, pp. 79–106.

————. (1967). "Party Development and the American Mainstream." In William Nisbet Chambers and Walter Dean Burnham (eds.), *The American Party Systems: Stages of Political Development*. New York: Oxford University Press, pp. 3–32.

Charles, Joseph (1961). *The Origins of the American Party System: Three Essays*. New York: Harper.

Cooper, Joseph, David W. Brady, and Patricia A. Hurley (1977). "The Election Basis of Party Voting: Patterns and Trends in the U.S. House of Representatives, 1887–1969." In Louis Maisel and Joseph Cooper (eds.), *The Impact of the Electoral Process*. Beverly Hills: Sage Publications, pp. 133–65.

Cunningham, Noble E., Jr. (1957). *The Jeffersonian Republicans: the Formation of Party Organization, 1789–1801*. Chapel Hill: University of North Carolina Press.

————, ed. (1965). *The Making of the American Party System: 1789 to 1809*. Englewood Cliffs: Prentice-Hall.

————. (1978). *The Process of Government under Jefferson*. Princeton, N.J.: Princeton University Press.

Dauer, Manning J. (1953). *The Adams Federalists*. Baltimore: Johns Hopkins University Press.

Duverger, Maurice (1959). *Political Parties*, rev. ed. Translated by Barbara North and Robert North. New York: Wiley.

Formisano, Ronald P. (1974). "Deferential-Participant Politics: The Early Republic's Political Culture 1789–1840." *American Political Science Review* 68: 473–87.

Gilpatrick, Delbert H. (1931). *Jeffersonian Democracy in North Carolina*. New York: Columbia University Press.

Goldman, Perry M., and James S. Young, eds. (1973). *The United States Congressional Directories, 1789–1840*. New York: Columbia University Press.

Hoadley, John F. (1979). *The Development of American Political Parties: A Spatial Analysis of Congressional Voting, 1789–1803*. Ph. D. dissertation, University of North Carolina, Chapel Hill.

Hofstadter, Richard (1969). *The Idea of a Party System: The Rise of Legitimate Opposition in the United States, 1780–1840*. Berkeley: University of California Press.

Huntington, Samuel P. (1968). *Political Order in Changing Societies*. New Haven: Yale University Press.

LaPalombara, Joseph, and Myron Weiner (1966). "The Origin and Development of Political Parties." In Joseph LaPalombara and Myron Weiner (eds.), *Political Parties and Political Development*. Princeton, N.J.: Princeton University Press, pp. 3–42.

Libby, Orin G. (1912). "A Sketch of the Early Political Parties in the United States." *Quarterly Journal of the University of North Dakota* 2: 205–42.

McRae, Duncan, Jr. (1970). *Issues and Parties in Legislative Voting*. New York: Harper and Row.

Madison, James, Alexander Hamilton, and John Jay (1961). *The Federalist Papers*. New York: New American Library.

Nichols, Roy F. (1967). *The Invention of the American Political Parties*. New York: Macmillan.

North Carolina Chronicle or Fayetteville Gazette (1971). February 7, 1791.

Paulin, Charles O. (1904). "The First Elections Under the Constitution." *Iowa Journal of History and Politics* 2:3–33.

Rabinowitz, George B. (1975). "An Introduction to Nonmetric Multidimensional Scaling." *American Journal of Political Science* 19:343–90.

Ryan, Mary P. (1971). "Party Formation in the United States Congress, 1789 to 1796: A Quantitative Analysis." *William and Mary Quarterly*, 3rd. ser. 28: 523–42.

Sartori, Giovanni (1976). *Parties and Party Systems: A Framework for Analysis*, Vol. I. Cambridge: Cambridge University Press.

Sorauf, Frank J. (1967). "Political Parties and Political Analysis." In William Nisbet Chambers and Walter Dean Burnham (eds.), *The American Party Systems: Stages of Political Development*. New York: Oxford University Press, pp. 33–55.

United States Congress (1961). *Bibliographical Directory of the American Congress, 1774–1961*. Washington, D.C.: Government Printing Office.

Varg, Paul A. (1963). *Foreign Policies of the Founding Fathers*. Baltimore: Penguin Books.

Young, Alfred F. (1967). *The Democratic Republicans of New York: The Origins, 1763–1797*. Chapel Hill: University of North Carolina Press.

Young, James Sterling (1966). *The Washington Community, 1800–1828*. New York: Harcourt, Brace and World.

PART TWO

The Origins of Parties: The Progressives and Their Critics

Twentieth-century scholarship about the new American republic opened, as did scholarship in other fields, with Charles A. Beard. Published at the peak of the Progressive effort to control the corporations, whose resistance was entrenched behind prevailing constitutional constructions, Beard's timely masterpiece, *An Economic Interpretation of the Constitution of the United States* (New York: Macmillan, 1913), quickly proved perhaps the most important book in all of American historiography. Two years later, it was followed by his *Economic Origins of Jeffersonian Democracy.*(New York: Macmillan, 1915), which buttressed and extended the conclusions of the classic.

As the titles may suggest, Beard emphasized the economic sources of political behavior. Examining the economic interests of the members of the Constitutional Convention, the first book permanently demythologized the national charter (making it, perhaps, a less effective bulwark for contemporary special interests). The Constitution, Beard suggested, was not intended merely to provide a better national defense. Its framers also meant to further the objectives of specific economic groups that were endangered by the Articles of Confederation. Groups whose wealth was heavily invested in fluid forms of property were seriously threatened during the Confederation years by paper money and other measures that reflected the desires of debtor-oriented, agricultural majorities within the several states. Though they were a minority of voters, Beard explained, "personality" interests were united by this threat. Taking extra-legal action, they secured a document designed to end it. "Substantially all of the merchants, money lenders, security holders, manufacturers, shippers, capitalists, and financiers" were behind the Constitution, Beard insisted. Its support came mainly from the cities and from seaboard regions, where commercial, manufacturing, and speculative interests were mostly to be found. "Substantially all . . . of the opposition came from the non-slaveholding farmers and the debtors" (p. 17).

Economic Origins of Jeffersonian Democracy explained the rise and progress of the first party conflict as a continuation of this struggle between "capitalistic and agrarian interests" (p. 3). The groups that had been instrumental in securing the adoption of the Constitution, Beard maintained, continued to be dominant within the new regime. "Their material measures were all directed to the benefit of the capitalistic interests," and "the bulk of the party which supported these measures was drawn from the former advocates of the Constitution" (p. 465). Most Jeffersonians, by contrast, were former Antifederalists; but by appealing more successfully to "the mass of the people, that is, the farmers," the spokesmen for the opposition party "were able to arouse the vast mass of the hitherto indifferent voters and in the end swamp the compact minority which had dominated" the new government through its first ten years (p. 466).

For Beard, the triumph of the Jeffersonians was hardly an unmitigated victory for ordinary people. The early party battle was in many ways a clash between two segments of the early national elite, and while "the aristocracy of slave-owning planters" did repudiate the use of the federal government for the benefit of capitalistic groups, it also managed to conciliate those interests by preserving all their gains (p. 467). Still, Beard did portray the struggle partly as a clash between two "classes," one of which included the enormous bulk of ordinary people. Thus, in hands such as those of Claude G. Bowers, whose *Jefferson and Hamilton: The Struggle for Democracy in America* (Boston: Houghton Mifflin, 1925) was one of the most popular histories of the period between the two world wars, a Beardian interpretation could become the basis for a stirring narrative of popular success against the plutocratic interests. And Bowers' insistence that the early party contest pitted democrats against aristocrats in an extension of the Revolutionary struggle was immediately followed by the publication of another minor classic, Vernon Louis Parrington's *Main Currents in American Thought* (3 volumes, New York: Harcourt, Brace, 1927–1930). A leading literary critic, Parrington interpreted the whole American experience in terms of a struggle between the spirit of the Constitution and the spirit of the Declaration of Independence.

Progressive writers shaped the dominant interpretation of the first party struggle—and of American history more generally—well into the 1950s. Beard himself was active into World War II, when he and Mary R. Beard published their influential *A Basic History of the United States* (New York: New Home Library, 1944). Ten years later, in his careful study *The Adams Federalists* (Baltimore: Johns Hopkins Press, 1953), Manning J. Dauer concluded that Beard and others had been fundamentally correct in their analysis of the constituencies of the first two parties: the Federalists were dominated by commercial groups, and the Republicans by farmers. Analyzing voting records in the early congresses, together with the nature of the representatives' home districts, Dauer suggested only minor alterations of the Beardian interpretation. The Federalists, he argued, had originally received widespread support from wealthy, market-oriented farmers. But during Adams' administration, many Federalists increasingly insisted on a program whose appeal was narrowly restricted to commercial interests. By focusing on Adams and the moderates he led, Dauer was able to suggest another reason for the party's early dominance and rapid downfall. The alienation of the market farmers ended in a party split, and bitter internecine quarrels laid the groundwork for the irreversible catastrophe of 1800.

Even at this writing neither Beard nor Dauer can be easily dismissed. Their arguments continue to reward a careful study, and a larger volume of this sort would certainly include them. There can be no doubt, as many of the following selections will suggest, that themes originated by Progressive writers still inform much of the scholarship about the early national years. Several current authors are conventionally described as "NeoProgressives." Many others are responding to Progressive views.

By the middle 1950s, nonetheless, the tide of dominant opinion had begun to shift. The post-war period, for reasons mentioned briefly in the introduction to Part I, witnessed the increasing dominance of a "Consensus" school of American historiography. The new interpretive thrust was more inclined to emphasize American stability and probe the sources of a general national agreement on the fundamentals than to stress persistent conflicts. It was often hostile to interpretations stressing social class. Beard's study of the Constitution was subjected to two devastating, book-length criticisms by Forrest McDonald and Robert E. Brown. Political and intellectual developments combined to lessen the appeal of economic determinism as an explanatory theory. In these circumstances, it is not surprising that Progressive explanations of the early party conflict also faced increasing pressure.

Beard advanced at least two major themes that have been subjects for research and argument from the middle 1950s to the present: that the party conflict of the 1790s was fundamentally a clash between conflicting economic classes; and that this struggle was, in essence, a continuation of the political divisions of the previous decade. This section introduces the continuing debate about the continuity between the party struggle and the arguments of the Confederation years. It highlights both the challenge to Progressive views and their revision in the works of recent scholars.

The Development of Parties

Noble E. Cunningham, Jr.

Two important studies of the middle 1950s played a vital role in challenging Beard's argument for continuity between the first party struggle and the contest over ratification of the Constitution. Both insisted that a different set of issues came to dominate attention with the launching of the new regime and that the early years of the new government were marked by switches of position that dissolved the old alignments, most notably perhaps by James Madison (who was fully as important in the opposition to the new administration as the hero of Claude Bowers' book). Both authors argued that the new division first appeared within the infant federal government itself and only gradually reached out into the states and towns, where organizers of the nascent parties seldom simply built on pre-existing factions. Together, these two works reshaped the dominant interpretation of the early origins of parties and erected an alternative description of the character and stages of party evolution. The first was in the form of three essays by Joseph Charles, published posthumously in the William and Mary Quarterly *in 1955 and then assembled in* The Origins of the American Party System: Three Essays *(Chapel Hill: University of North Carolina Press, 1956). The second was Noble E. Cunningham's* The Jeffersonian Republicans: The Formation of Party Organization, 1789–1801 *(Chapel Hill: University of North Carolina Press, 1957), the first of many books about the new republic by this distinguished Professor of History at the University of Missouri. This selection appeared originally, under a different title, as the concluding chapter of that book, pages 249–261. ©1957 The University of North Carolina Press. Published for the Institute of Early American History and Culture, Williamsburg, Virginia. Reprinted by permission.*

When Thomas Jefferson took the oath of office as the third president of the United States on March 4, 1801, many men could remember the time twelve years before when the first president of the new nation had been inaugurated. If they paused to review in their minds the years that had passed, they must have been struck by the changes they had witnessed. They had seen a piece of paper transformed into a workable system of government and a new Union grow stronger and more respected. As they looked back over this eventful period they could well remember the excitement during the early years of the French Revolution and the controversy that was raised over Jay's Treaty. When the French Alliance was dissolved by the Convention of 1800, they must have breathed a sigh of relief as they compared the clearing diplomatic horizon with the dark days when issues of foreign policy had divided the opinions of the people so sharply. They must also have been impressed by the great changes which had taken place in the political life of the country, and although they could not have recognized the historical significance of these developments, they could see that two major parties had grown up within the American political structure and that with them far-reaching changes had been ushered into the political life of the United States.

In less than a decade, the growth of the Republican and Federalist parties significantly changed the character of American politics. At the beginning of the 1790s, elections were, for the most part, decided on a personal basis. A candidate for political office generally had to rely upon his own resources and those of his friends to promote his election. How he went about getting elected depended to a large extent on the practices and customs that prevailed in the state in which he sought election. What was considered proper in one state might lose him the election in another. In general, the solicitation of the suffrages of the voters seems to have considered improper, although the injunction against the practice was not always strictly observed, and in some states it took various subtle forms. In Virginia a candidate could scarcely expect to win the favor of the voters unless he were prepared to treat them to rum punch or other drinks on election day.[1] If he were a member of Congress and found himself unable to be in the district at the time of election, he might send letters, as Madison did in 1790, to influential citizens in each county of the district and entrust his election to their hands; or he might ask his brother or father, as Madison also did, to attend the polls and look out for his interest.[2]

New Englanders took great pride in the absence of electioneering in their choice of representatives. A Connecticut congressman boasted:

> In this state, no instance has ever been known where a person has appeared as a public candidate, and solicited the suffrages of the freemen, for a place in the legislature. Should any person have the effrontery or folly to make such an attempt, he may be assured of meeting with the

---

[1] Charles S. Sydnor, *Gentlemen Freeholders: Political Practices in Washington's Virginia* (Chapel Hill, 1952), 51–59.

[2] James Madison to A. Rose and others, August 13, 1790; Madison to James Madison, Sr., August 14, 1790, Hunt, ed., *Madison Writings*, VI, 20–21.

general contempt and indignation of the people, and of throwing an insuperable bar in the way of attaining the object of his pursuit.[3]

But in Maryland no one seemed to disapprove of a candidate's advertising his candidacy in the newspapers or otherwise seeking to forward his own election.[4]

Yet, although campaign practices were locally adapted to the prevailing public opinion concerning the proper conduct for political aspirants, there was a common condition which characterized nearly all political contests at the beginning of the 1790s. This was the fact that it was generally the personal characters of the individual candidates, their public records and private habits, their qualifications for office, and their integrity as citizens which served to commend them to the voters and furnished the issues for the electorate to decide. Men were recommended for office because of their *"diligence, consistency, integrity, and independence,"*[5] and a candidate might even by recommended for his *"facetious humor"* or *"modest aversion* to public life," or because he was *"a right up and down* honest man."[6] On election day in Philadelphia in 1791, the editor of the *General Advertiser* pointed out the qualifications required of a political candidate, declaring:

> The representative of a free people, should in the first place be a man of strict integrity, upright in his dealings as a man, and steady in his principles as a politician. Joined to a general knowledge of mankind, and of government, he should especially be well acquainted with the interests of his constituents, and with the laws of his country. Sagacity to perceive, activity and industry to pursue, eloquence to promote, and sound judgement to determine on whatever will tend to the good of his country, are among the necessary requisites.[7]

Candidates were frequently assisted in their elections by personal followings of friends and connections, and when contemporaries referred to them as "parties," they usually were thinking in terms of personal followings or political "interests." When William Smith was proposed as a representative from Maryland to the First Congress, for example, it was said that he was set up by a party in Baltimore and the voters were asked: "Does not this *party* consist chiefly of the Smiths,

---

[3] Zephaniah Swift, *A System of the Laws of the State of Connecticut* (Windham, 1795), I, 68.

[4] Annapolis, *Maryland Gazette*, September 22, October 6, 1791.

[5] Philadelphia, *General Advertiser*, October 11, 1791.

[6] Philadelphia, *National Gazette*, September 5, 1792.

[7] Philadelphia, *General Advertiser*, October 11, 1791. The Providence *United States Chronicle* reminded the citizens of Rhode Island that representatives to Congress should be men of "Liberalty, Integrity, and Information," August 2, 1792.

and their connexions and dependents? And may not this *party* with propriety be distinguished hereafter and at the next election, by the appellation of the Smithites."[8] Governor George Clinton's following, being drawn from the entire state of New York, was of considerably greater proportions than the groups which gathered around political leaders in most states and had much more the appearance of a political party, but the designation "Clintonians" which was given to Clinton's supporters suggested the basic fact that the "party" in early years was largely a personal following.

By the end of the decade of the nineties, the growth of political parties had wrought fundamental alterations in the political life of the country. The formation of parties was accompanied by a growth of compaigning; elections became more warmly contested, and even the most staid New England towns became infected with what their people had denounced as the "vile practice of electioneering."[9] Just after the election of 1800, a writer in the *Connecticut Courant* declared:

> Elections to office, in New England, have been always, till very lately, *free* beyond any example that can be found elsewhere. . . . It was not prudent for any man to express a wish for promotion. . . . Unhappily, however, our democrats have already had some influence in changing this truly republican state of things among us. The detestable practice of electioneering is, by their means, indirectly gaining ground, in these states.[10]

Another writer about the same time commented upon the growing tumult in the conduct of elections in Boston and the "confusion, wrangling and even uproar" on election day. "So loud and so indecently rude, is the noise made by the distribution of ballots for the different candidates," it was observed, "and such the illiberal reflections and uncandid remarks upon their respective characters, as cannot but excite painful sensations in every delicate mind."[11]

With the transcendency of parties over individuals, there was a decline in the feeling that is was improper to campaign for election. A candidate's efforts to win an election could now be viewed not merely as personal ambition but as a contribution to the party cause. Many candidates still did not solicit votes for themselves personally, and,

---

[8] *Queries, to the Voters of Baltimore County,* signed "Anti-smithites," January 1789, Broadside, Lib. Cong.

[9] Andrew Lee, *The Origins and Ends of Civil Government . . . A Sermon . . . May 14, 1795* (Hartford, 1795), 37. On electioneering in Massachusetts in 1800 see *The Diary of William Bentley* (Salem, Mass., 1911), II, 346–47, 354, 355.

[10] Hartford, *Connecticut Courant,* February 2, 1801.

[11] Boston, *New England Palladium,* February 10, 1801.

like Nathaniel Macon of North Carolina, they prided themselves in this conduct. After many years in public office, Macon could write: "I have never solicited any man to vote for me or hinted to him that I wished him to do so, nor did I ever solicit any person to make interest, for me to be elected to any place."[12] But such men were not prevented by their political scruples from laboring to advance the party cause and, in so doing, their own elections. Although there were still many who disapproved of campaigning for office, the development of parties was bringing respectability to electioneering.

As campaigning shifted from an individual to a party basis, a candidate's party affiliation often became of more importance than his personal qualifications for office. "It is not the personal good qualities of a candidate that are inquired for," explained one contemporary observer in 1800; "whether he is a Federalist or not, is all the question."[13] After a trip through New Jersey in 1800, a newspaper editor affirmed that "the character of the candidates is sunk in the single question—whether friendly to Adams or Jefferson."[14]

Some voters already were coming to support any candidate who carried the party standard, even when they did not approve of the candidate personally. During the election of 1796 in Maryland, one observer remarked:

> In this county, I think I never knew an election so much of *principles*. General Eccleston (the Federal candidate) is obnoxious to about one half the county and is to be opposed next year by them in a sheriff's election, yet the language is, our choice is a party question, not a personal matter—this, for a Southern election, is a pleasing feature of the People's goodness.[15]

Another Maryland voter in 1798 disapproved highly of a Federalist candidate but admitted that even his objectional conduct "will not prevent me from supporting his election, for the sake of the cause, although I wish we had an abler man."[16]

During the last decade of the eighteenth century, the voters were urged increasingly to subordinate personal considerations to the party

---

[12] Nathaniel Macon, brief autobiographical sketch in Nathaniel Macon papers, Duke University.

[13] Charles W. Harris to Robert W. Harris, May 1800, Wagstaff, ed., "The Harris Letters," *James Sprunt Historical Publications*, 14 (1916), 71.

[14] Abraham Hodge to John Steele, October 10, 1800, Wagstaff, ed., *Papers of John Steele*, I, 188.

[15] William Vans Murray to James McHenry, November 2, 1796, Steiner, *The Life and Correspondence of James McHenry*, 200–1.

[16] F. Thomas to John E. Howard, September 5, 1798, Bayard Papers, Md. Hist. Soc.

cause. "Remember that the election . . . is not a mere contest between favourite individuals," the freeholders of Virginia were told in 1799, "but a contest between principles."[17] And the voters of Massachusetts' Fourth Western District were reminded during the congressional race in 1800 that both candidates were "gentlemen of good moral characters and of respectable abilities; but of different political opinions." One candidate, it was stated, "is a friend to the administration of Washington and of Adams; the other is the advocate of Jefferson and his party. It is therefore a question of principle."[18]

With the introduction of party tickets, the voters were soon being urged to vote the straight party slate. The Newark *Centinel of Freedom* pleaded in 1799:

> Electors of New-Jersey, UNITE in support of Republican characters, be unanimous in your ticket and success will attend you. . . . Be firm, be vigilant, be enterprising and you will maintain the ground you have acquired. By your fortitude and your unanimity at this crisis, the rights and freedom of your country may be preserved and handed down to posterity; therefore remember, UNITED YOU STAND, DIVIDED YOU FALL.[19]

The Philadelphia *Aurora* exclaimed in 1800 that "every man who is not for the whole Republican Ticket, Regards the Public Good, Less than his Prejudices,"[20] and a Federalist campaign leaflet declared: *"Fellow Citizens,* let no slight dislikes or preferences induce you to relax your efforts or *break* the ticket; if you are for President Adams, be *wholly* so; by omissions of any on the *federal* nomination, or *taking up* any of the other, we shall defeat our intentions, and we may (the supposition is not too distant) ruin our Country!"[21] In recommending the ticket of Republican electors to the voters of Virginia in 1800, Republicans declared that "it must be admitted to be extremely probable that a freeholder, weak enough to be solicitous about men [rather] than principle, and who will not vote for the persons thus recommended, will throw away his suffrages. He who will not go with others must go alone."[22]

---

[17] Richmound, *Virginia Argus,* March 12, 1799.

[18] Worcester, *Masachusetts Spy,* October 15, 1800.

[19] Newark, *Centinel of Freedom,* October 6, 1799, quoted in Stewart, "Jeffersonian Journalism," 1065.

[20] Philadelphia, *Aurora,* October 11, 1800.

[21] *Address to the Federal Republicans of Burlington County,* by a Committee, appointed at the Court House, on the 30th August, 1800 (Trenton, 1800), 6. For other examples of publications encouraging straight party voting see Morristown, N. J., *Genius of Liberty,* December 18, 1800; [Circular] *In Committee,* Albany, 8th April, 1799, signed Philip S. Van Rensselaer, Chairman, Broadside, Lib. Cong.

[22] *A Vindication of the General Ticket Law,* 12.

While formerly it had been a high recommendation for a candidate to be independent of parties, by 1800 it had become a political asset to have the reputation of being a firm party man. A candidate for Congress in New York was opposed because he was

> a person of doubtful political gender—his character in public life has hitherto been fluctuating and unsettled—his conduct has been marked with extreme indecision—like a pendulum he has oscilated, now towards one party, and then to another . . . he has been in the Assembly for two or three years, during all which time he has been in a state of perpetual vibration. . . . A man, who espouses no cause, and commits himself in favor of no particular principles, is never pledged to support the true interests of his constituents, but is always understood to be open to the advances of the highest bidder.[23]

Considerable pains were taken to show that James Ross, the Federalist candidate for governor of Pennsylvania in 1799, had not been "*a firm supporter* of the administration, and a *steady* man in *federal* politics" while a member of the United States Senate. "It is deceiving their party," a campaign leaflet pointed out, "for his partizans to *pretend* that he is *firm* and *steady*."[24] By 1800 the idea that a candidate should be a consistent party man—a theory that a decade before would have been scorned as unpatriotic and incompatible with republican government—was widely accepted. In its effect, the acceptance of the virtue of party regularity together with the introduction of the party platform, which placed more of the decisions as to how the government was to be administered in the hands of the voters, tended to restrict the individual initiative and personal discretion of men elected to public office.

Under the pressure of party growth, campaign practices, the conduct of elections, the concept of what public men should be and do, and the general attitude toward the business of politics changed greatly in the brief span of three presidential terms.

Party Organization in Retrospect

Although historians have generally neglected the practical apsects of party development, the prevailing view of the emergence of the Jef-

---

[23] *To the electors of A Representative to Congress, for the First District,* signed "A Republican Elector" [1800], Broadside, N.Y. Pub. Lib. So serious was the charge that the candidate under attack wrote a lengthy refutation to the indictment. See Silas Wood, *Letters addressed to the Electors of Representatives to Congress for the First Election District in the State of New York: . . . in vindication of his public conduct* (New York, 1800), pamphlet, N.Y. Pub. Lib.

[24] *To the Citizens of Pennsylvania,* signed "An Elector" (n.p., [1799]), pamphlet, Lib. Cong., 11–15.

fersonian party pictures Jefferson personally organizing a political party to oppose Hamilton by cementing together local parties in each of the states. Claude Bowers wrote: "As Jefferson's mild eye surveyed the field, he found in almost every State local parties, some long in existence, fighting for popular rights as they understood them . . . Why not consolidate these local parties into one great national organization, and broaden the issue to include the problems of both State and Nation? . . . The philosopher-politician took up his pen. . . ."[25] More recently, Wilfred E. Binkley has repeated: "Like all our major political parties this earlier one to organize constituted a loose federation of local parties. Without precedents to guide him, Jefferson set out to negotiate the necessary connections and understanding among them."[26] Thus Jefferson is seen traveling to New York to negotiate an understanding between Virginia and New York as a first step in the organization of a party, and one is left to assume that the pattern for subsequent party development was thus established.[27]

Contemporary documents suggest the need to revise this widely accepted view. The mass of evidence points to the conclusion that the Republican party was not the outgrowth of persisting state parties. Indeed, one does not find the type of ready-made state party that needed only to affiliate with a national headquarters set up by Jefferson. In some instances (e.g., New York) the new party built upon existing state factions, and elsewhere it attracted various of the old elements of political power in the several states. But the Republican party was a new growth that sprang from the divisions in Congress and the national government; it was a product of national rather than state politics.[28] Nor did major parties appear so suddenly as the theory of the confederation of existing parties suggests; party growth rather was a process of gradual development.

---

[25] Bowers, *Jefferson and Hamilton*, 143; see also Claude G. Bowers, "Jefferson, Master Politician," *Virginia Quarterly Review*, 2 (1926), 324.

[26] Wilfred E. Binkley, *American Political Parties: Their Natural History* (New York, 2d ed., 1947), 78. Another recent work showing the acceptance of the same point of view is Herbert Agar, *The Price of Union* (New York, 1950), 88.

[27] William Goodman, *The Two-Party System in the United States* (Princeton, 1956), 165; Morison and Commager, *The Growth of the American Republic*, I, 343.

[28] Several recent studies of the development of parties on the state level have recognized the importance of national politics in the growth of state parties and have concluded that federal politics gave rise to political parties in the individual states studied. Harry M. Tinkcom, *The Republicans and Federalists in Pennsylvania, 1790–1801: A Study in National Stimulus and Local Response* (Harrisburg, 1950), 73, 153, 199, 211; Norman L. Stamps, "Political Parties in Connecticut, 1789–1819" (unpublished Ph.D. thesis, Yale University, 1950), 2; Richard P. McCormick, *The History of Voting in New Jersey: A Study of the Development of Election Machinery, 1664–1911* (New Brunswick, N. J., 1953), 87.

It was in Congress and in national politics that the early signs of party development were most noticeable. As parties developed, major party lines generally became clear in national politics and elections sooner than in state political life. As the Republican party gained strength and began presenting party tickets in the several states, it commonly started, as in Pennsylvania, by endorsing candidates for Congress and for presidential electors. Gaining popular support, the party extended its activities in state politics and initiated tickets for the legislature and other state offices. By 1800, Philadelphia Republicans added to the party ticket for the first time a candidate for the office of sheriff.[29] More and more, men came to be nominated and elected to state offices wholly on the basis of the stand which they took on national politics.

The role of members of Congress in the development of parties also should be more fully recognized. Congressmen, exposed to the growing partisan conflict in the national legislature, came to be party men before parties had reached very deeply into the political life of the country, and they played a significant role in spreading party growth. As parties developed, the members of Congress finally came to form, in essence, a national party organization and increasingly exercised a vital role in party control. Meetings of Congress, with members frequently grouped in politically oriented boarding houses, had certain aspects of party "conventions." Through the congressional caucus, the party leaders in Congress decided upon presidential nominations, and by 1800 the caucus had become strong enough to enforce its decision. As Republicans organized party machinery on a state level, as they were doing in Virginia and elsewhere in 1800, party centralization gradually lessened. But the Republican party had grown up as a national party in response to the stimulus of national politics, and this fact was still strongly reflected in the party which elected Jefferson to the presidency in 1801.

The role of Jefferson in the formation of the Republican party must be viewed in relation to the developments in Congress and to the important place of Madison's leadership in that body. Before Jefferson retired as Secretary of State at the end of 1793, he had come to be looked upon as the leader of the Republican interest. This circumstance was due both to his opposition to the Hamiltonian program and to the fact that the friends of Hamilton singled him out for their most concentrated attack. Though Jefferson's role does not correspond to

---

[29] Philadelphia, *Aurora*, October 14, 1800; a defense of the innovation appears in the *Aurora*, August 16, 1800.

the view so widely circulated in the Federalist press—that the Virginian was avidly organizing opposition to the government and constantly intriguing with members of Congress to defeat the measures of the Secretary of the Treasury—he did cooperate with Madison in bringing Freneau to Philadelphia to establish the *National Gazette* (here again the important role of Madison must be recognized), and by 1793 he was no longer maintaining that official aloofness from the proceedings of Congress to which he previously had undertaken to adhere. During 1793, the Secretary of State assisted friends in Congress in preparing resolutions designed to drive Hamilton from office, and he seemed to be thinking in terms of party when he drew up a line of policy for Republicans to follow during the controversy created by Genêt and the French issue. He appeared also to be working for party purposes when he urged Madison to prepare some replies to Hamiltonian doctrines in the press.

Although Jefferson had become something of a party leader before he retired from Washington's cabinet on the last day of December 1793, that role was abdicated when he returned to Monticello. For the next three years it was Madison who assumed the Republican leadership. By the time he left the House at the end of the Fourth Congress, the Republican party in Congress was no longer the loose and indefinite association it had been when Jefferson had retired, but a well-defined party with some measure of organization, although its members did not always display unity or follow party leadership. By 1796, party lines had tightened throughout the country, and when Jefferson returned to active political life, with his election to the vice presidency, he clearly accepted the role of party leader. His efforts in mobilizing the party for the battle with the Federalists in 1800 displayed political shrewdness and finesse.

With Vice President Jefferson its active head, the Republican party grew to maturity, and the struggle with the Federalists for political dominance was accompanied by great strides in party organization and in the introduction of party machinery. The present study has sought to display the gradual evolution of party organization and machinery and the development of the "art of electioneering." It is clear that party methods and techniques were well advanced by 1800. Although Federalists not uncommonly duplicated Republican improvements in their party organization, Republicans generally appear to have taken the initiative in introducing party machinery and new methods of winning elections. The attention which Republicans gave to these matters was in a large measure inspired by the need for an agressive campaign and superior organization to overcome the political advantage which the Federalists enjoyed as the party in power.

Effective organization and aggressive campaigning were the keys to Republican success in the election of 1800. In their attention to party organization and machinery, the Republicans remained constantly aware of the necessity of maintaining popular support. Party spokesmen therefore exploited every available agency of mass communication: official papers such as petitions against governmental measures, public circular letters from congressmen to their constituents, newspapers, pamphlets, handbills, private letters which circulated among leading figures, and personal contacts and word-of-mouth communications. The nature of democracy made it imperative that the people should play a prominent part in party activities, and political machinery was geared to win their votes.

But popular participation in politics should not be confused with popular initiative in the introduction of party machinery. In the 1790s one rarely finds effective party organization springing from the so-called "grass roots." Instead, the organization of the Republican party and the introduction of smoothly functioning party machinery were due largely to the leadership of a few dedicated and influential political leaders, such as Jefferson, Madison, members of Congress, John Beckley, and others. The newspapers report numerous popular party gatherings, but this more abundant source of information has often obscured the fact that the archives hold not a few confidential letters revealing the careful preparation that commonly preceded such meetings.

The press might announce, as the New York *Daily Advertiser* did in 1795, that "a numerous and respectable meeting of the freeholders of the town of Kingston. . . . Resolved, That in the opinion of a large majority of this meeting, Aaron Burr be nominated and recommended as a fit person for Governor at the ensuing election; and that we will support him with our votes and interest."[30] This notice might easily leave the impression that the nomination was a spontaneous expression of popular wishes, but an unpublicized letter written ten days before this meeting by the district's congressman, Peter Van Gaasbeck, to a leading political figure of his district suggests otherwise:

> I presume you will have seen the Publication of the Governor and Lieut. Governor, declining being candidates at the ensuing election—in my opinion no time ought to be lost to arrange and Publish the candidates to be supported—if we take the lead, all is secure, therefore immediately have a meeting, and announce our worthy friend Aaron Burr for Governor. . . . After this is published,—prepare your slay and Horses and meet me at Easton on Saturday the 7th February—where I have also requested some of our Kingston Friends to meet me. . . . When you go to Kingston,

---

[30] New York, *Daily Advertiser*, February 28, 1795, extra.

assure our Friends that every expense they are at will be cordially refunded from him who is not to be seen in that act; now my worthy fellow put the wheel in Motion. . . .[31]

Though it is not always possible to delve behind the newspaper reports, it seems clear that public political participation was not infrequently guided. At the same time it is important to notice that political leaders recognized the importance of public sentiment and the necessity of popular participation in politics, for, after all, the people cast the votes.

Between the inaugurations of Washington and Jefferson, the two-party system became rooted in American politics. So important had the role of parties become in the political life of the nation that the Constitution itself was soon to be amended to recognize the place of parties, whose rise had made the constitutional provisions for the election of the president and the vice president outdated and unrealistic and had led to the troublesome tie between Jefferson and Burr. In 1804, the Twelfth Amendment was added to the Constitution to provide for separate balloting for president and vice president.

With the Federalist defeat in 1800, there were many who hoped that political parties might now be set at rest. But the Federalists were not yet ready to surrender, as one New York Federalist intimated when he wrote:

It has been vainly boasted that the Sun of Federalism was about to Set and that we were about to die but Surely we are not dead yet and if it must be so let it not be without a Struggle—let us pray as Sampson did on a former Occasion that we may be avenged on our political enemies once more and that those men who are Stigmatizing us with the name of Tory and every other opprobrious Epithet might be once more Disappointed.[32]

Federalists and Republicans appeared in unaccustomed roles as the new administration began on March 4, 1801, but the party conflict had not ended.

---

[31] Peter Van Gaasbeck to Ebenezer Foote, January 26, 1795, Annie Burr Jennings Collection, Yale. See also Van Gaasbeck to Foote, February 12, 1795, *ibid*. For similar preparations for another county meeting reported in the New York *Daily Advertiser*, April 2, 1795, see Van Gaasbeck to Foote, March 17, 1795, *ibid.*, Foote to Van Gaasbeck, March 18, 1795, Katherine A. Foote, ed., *Ebenezer Foote the Founder, being an Epistolary Light on his Time as shed by Letters from his Files* (Delhi, N. Y., 1927), 54.

[32] Francis Crawford to Ebenezer Foote, March 7, 1801, Papers of Ebenezer Foote, Lib. Cong.

The Nationalists of 1781–1783 and the Economic Interpretation of the Constitution

E. James Ferguson

E. James Ferguson's The Power of the Purse: A History of American Public Finance, 1776–1790 *(Chapel Hill: University of North Carolina Press, 1961) is both a standard study of the origins and workings of Hamiltonian finance and an exciting narrative of the emergence and eventual success of a nationalist movement that attempted from the early 1780s to assert a federal responsibility for the Revolutionary debt. A student of Merrill Jensen, whose books* The Articles of Confederation *(1940) and* The New Nation *(1950) were among the great achievements of the school, Ferguson builds plainly on the old Progressive interpretation. This article, however, is at once a fine restatement of the findings of* The Power of the Purse *and a denial that the nationalists can be explained in terms of their personal interests alone. It appeared originally in* The Journal of American History, *LVI (September, 1969), 241–261, and is reprinted here by permission and without change. Copyright: Organization of American Historians, 1969.*

In spite of such leaders as George Washington, Alexander Hamilton, James Madison, Robert Morris, and others who were later enrolled among the Founding Fathers, the Nationalist movement of 1781–1783 has not made a distinct impression on historical interpretations of the early national period. Surprisingly, it is seldom brought into disputes over the economic background of the Constitution—a matter to which it is precisely relevant.[1]

---

[1] Modern studies that bring out the implications of the Nationalist movement most explicitly are Clarence L. Ver Steeg, *Robert Morris: Revolutionary Financier: With an Analysis of his Earlier Career* (Philadelphia, 1954); Merrill Jensen, *The New Nation: A History of the United States During the Confederation, 1781–1789* (New York, 1950), and E. James Ferguson, *The Power of the Purse: A History of American Public Finance, 1776–1790* (Chapel Hill, 1961). The economic phases of the movement are implicit throughout Robert A. East, *Business Enterprise in the American Revolutionary Era* (New York, 1938); and the political aspects are treated in George Bancroft, *History of the Formation of the Constitution of the United States* (2 vols., New York, 1882).

It should make a difference to historians that constitutional revision and Hamiltonian funding were first linked together not in 1787, not in 1790, but in the closing years of the Revolution. The movement to reorganize the central government was started by the Nationalists of 1781–1783. They coupled economic with political objectives, formulated a program, and lined up a body of actual and potential supporters for whom such a program had a special appeal. The merger of political and economic goals was organic, and the essential elements of Hamiltonian funding were adopted with the Constitution.

The effort to strengthen Congress began in 1780, in many ways the most discouraging year of the war, when military defeats and the depreciation of paper money seriously undermined patriot morale. Congress, convinced that any further output of Continental currency would destroy what little value it still had, ended emissions late in 1779—a courageous act, but one that left it without funds. As long as Continental currency had value, Congress enjoyed a freedom of action incommensurate with its constitutional powers under the still unratified Articles of Confederation. The stoppage of emissions disclosed its weakness.[2]

Any political change appealed to some persons more than to others and could be expected to have differential effects upon various groups of the population. In principle, central government was antithetical to liberty, which most Americans associated with local self-rule. Since the war had begun, however, there had been second thoughts on this matter. To the extent that state governments had fallen under "popular" influence, people who had opposed democratic tendencies favored a stronger central authority as the only available check upon abuses of local majorities. This sentiment was most articulated at the time by elite groups in the middle states, but it was a predisposing influence everywhere and certainly an element in the support for political reform.[3]

---

[2] Worthington C. Ford, ed., *Journals of the Continental Congress, 1774–1789* (34 vols., Washington, 1904–1937), XV, 1019–20. On the constitutional point, see James Madison to Thomas Jefferson, May 6, 1780, Edmund C. Burnett, ed., *Letters of Members of the Continental Congress* (8 vols., Washington, 1921–1936), V, 128–29.

[3] The affinity between central government and political elitism is the central theme of Merrill Jensen, *The Articles of Confederation: An Interpretation of the Social-Constitutional History of the United States* (Madison, 1940). This is made explicit in his concluding statement, pp. 239–45. The same phenomenon in late colonial times is discussed in Edmund S. and Helen M. Morgan, *The Stamp Act Crisis: Prologue to Revolution* (Chapel Hill, 1953), 11–20. With his talent for the pungent and invidious phrase, Gouverneur Morris supposed in 1774 (as paraphrased by his biographer) that an American central government would "restrain the democratic spirit, which the constitutions and local circumstances of the country had so long fostered in the minds of the people." Jared Sparks, *Life of Gouverneur Morris . . . in the Political History of the United States* (3 vols. Boston, 1832), 1, 27.

The drive for political reform was associated with changes in economic policies. By 1780, the war was supported by massive confiscations; state and federal officers seized what they needed. The people at large were surprisingly patient under these impositions, yet there was widespread resentment against arbitrary acts of government.[4] Other irritants were legal tender laws and economic controls. Such regulations were a general nuisance.[5] Merchants, especially, felt victimized by economic legislation. It could be and was argued that regulations were hopeless, that the answer to high prices and the scarcity of goods was to abolish restraints on trade, and that the solution to governmental fiscal problems was deep taxation and the abandonment of paper money. Such proposals were impractical under the circumstances, but existing policy was so clearly bankrupt that a case could be made for moving in another direction. Although merchants and other businessmen made profits amidst inflation and in the teeth of economic controls, sound money and free trade were better suited to their ethics and presumably to their interests.[6]

A different group of recruits to the cause of stronger government was the officer corps of the Continental army from Washington down. After the capture of General John Burgoyne and the formation of the French alliance, military victory seemed within sight; yet, at this very point, the American war effort faltered. In the winter of 1779–1780, the Continental army suffered as much as at Valley Forge. "We begin to hate the country for its neglect of us," warned Hamilton in 1780.[7] The officers wanted a government that could raise, pay, clothe, feed, and arm enough troops to win the war.

A more direct interest in stronger central government was that of the public creditors. As Congress fell into insolvency, it ceased paying interest on the public debt. The creditors, who emerged as a political

---

[4] On the magnitude of confiscations, see Ferguson, *Power of the Purse*, 57–64.

[5] Oscar and Mary F. Handlin, "Revolutionary Economic Policy in Massachusetts," *William and Mary Quarterly*, IV (Jan. 1947), 3–26; East, *Business Enterprise*, 195–212. See also Curtis P. Nettels, *The Emergence of a National Economy: 1775–1815* (New York, 1962), 27–29.

[6] East, *Business Enterprise*, 207, describes the repudiation of paper currency in 1781 as a victory for the "rising conservative movement" in which the viewpoint of merchants and lawyers figured prominently. Robert Morris, who frequently expressed himself on this point, looked forward in 1781 to the time when, by the removal of the "detestable tribe" of economic restrictions, people would possess "that freedom for which they are contending." Robert Morris to the Governors of North Carolina, South Carolina, and Georgia, Dec. 19, 1781, Francis Wharton, ed., *The Revolutionary Diplomatic Correspondence of the United States* (6 vols., Washington, 1889), V, 58–59.

[7] Alexander Hamilton to James Duane, Sept. 3, 1780, Harold C. Syrett, ed., Jacob E. Cooke, assoc. ed., *The Papers of Alexander Hamilton* (13 vols., New York, 1961–), II, 406.

force in 1780, had reason to urge the establishment of a government capable of paying its debts.[8]

The converging influence of these groups began to affect state and federal policy and to create a disposition toward stronger central government, more "authority," less "liberty" in the conduct of public affairs, and, in the economic sphere, sound money and the abandonment of restraints on trade.[9] The formula appealed primarily to the elite, especially in the middle states, to merchants in general, and to special interest groups such as the army officers and the public creditors. It would be a distortion, however, to attribute the Nationalist impulse wholly to the interest or influence of particular groups. The controlling factor was a national emergency which called for new measures. The degree of support, which the proposal to confer additional powers on Congress eventually received in all the states, shows that leaders at every level were alarmed by the critical state of the war and persuaded that something drastic had to be done about it.

The man who more than anyone else worked out the Nationalist program and gave the movement some degree of organization was Morris. Congress, impressed by the urgent need for reform, appointed him superintendent of finance in 1781. A wealthy Philadelphia merchant, a leader of the conservative anti-constitutionalist party in Pennsylvania, and a security holder, he combined in his own person most of the elements of the Nationalist movement. From long and ousting service in Congress he had gained an unequalled mastery of congressional administrative and business affairs. He was widely respected, also widely hated, but such duties and powers were soon conferred upon him that he became a virtual prime minister—the real director of congressional policy from the time he took office in the spring of 1781 until the close of the war. Morris proved to be a superb administrator. He was also a statesman, the first in the line of the nation's early financial ministers who tried to steer its institutional development from the treasury.[10]

Associated with Morris were some of the outstanding leaders of later movement for the Constitution. Madison, who attended Congress

---

[8] "Original Documents: A Hartford Convention in 1780," *Magazine of American History,* VIII (Oct. 1882), 688–89; Bancroft, *History of the . . . Constitution,* I, 14–16; Ferguson, *Power of the Purse,* 149–52.

[9] Jensen, *New Nation,* 45–53; East, *Business Enterprise,* 207–12; Jennings B. Sanders, *Evolution of Executive Departments of the Continental Congress, 1774–1789* (Chapel Hill, 1935), 3–5.

[10] Robert Morris is entitled to a place in the line of succession that includes Hamilton and Albert Gallatin. Although Ver Steeg in his excellent study compares Robert Morris with Hamilton, he does not give Morris enough credit. Ver Steeg, *Robert Morris,* 193–99.

from 1780 to 1783, was a strong Nationalist, and he backed Morris' program. In 1782, Hamilton served as Morris' tax receiver, a kind of personal representative, in New York before moving on to Congress to become one of the most uncompromising advocates of a national system. In the army the foremost influence for Nationalist reform was Washington. Although his military position kept him out of civil administration, he continually urged Congress and the country to give more power to the central goverment.

The Union was a league of states rather than a national system because Congress lacked the power of taxation. This was not an oversight. In drafting the Articles of Confederation, Americans registered their hatred of centralized European systems and their high regard for liberty—which they associated with the supremacy of local government—by denying Congress the power to tax. As Congress needed money to execute its functions, it was in principle dependent on the states at every turn. In practice, it had some leeway, for it could issue paper money and contract loans at home and abroad. By 1780, however, its leeway was pretty well used up. Paper money was failing fast, and neither foreign nor domestic loans were ever large enough to sustain more than a fraction of the expense of fighting the war.[11]

Early in 1781, after a last futile effort to revive Continental currency, Congress struck at the heart of its problem by requesting the states to grant a permanent 5 percent duty on imports to be collected by federal officers and placed at Congress' disposal. As an amendment to the Articles of Confederation, the impost resolution had to be ratified by every state legislature. Congress at first brought it forward as a war measure, a way of securing an income wholly under federal control and, therefore, acceptable to European nations as security for additional loans then being sought. Within a few months, however, the capture of Cornwallis and signs that Britain was ready to make peace altered its significance. The impost, and whatever federal taxes might later be added to it, were to be a fund for discharging the entire Revolutionary debt.[12]

The impost breached the primary restriction upon congressional authority and was the essential first step in building an effective central government. Of equal importance was federal control of the Revolu-

---

[11] Foreign loans became an important resource for Congrss only in 1781 as the fighting drew to a close. Ferguson, *Power of the Purse*, 125–31, 333n.

[12] *Jorunals*, XVIII, 1033–36, XIX, 110–13; Madison to Edmund Pendleton, May 29, 1781, Burnett, ed., *Letters*, VI, 103–04. The grant of the impost was to be coextensive with the existence of the Revolutionary debt.

tionary debt itself. That a federal debt existed at all was inconsistent with the structure of the Union. Congress, it is true, had authority to contract loans, but since it lacked the taxing power, it could not guarantee repayment. Under the Articles of Confederation, Congress was supposed to get money from requisitions on the states. This system never worked, not entirely because the states were negligent, but because their fiscal systems were geared to local prioritites and the use of state currency. With the best of motives, the states could often meet Continental requisitions only with great difficulty, if at all. In a country in which the operative fiscal systems were those of thirteen local and diverse entities, a federal debt was an anomaly.[13]

More compatible with the structure of the Union was the procedure outlined by the Articles of Confederation for dealing with expenses of the Revolution. Each state was to be assessed according to the value of its landed property. When requisitions proved to be ineffectual, the logical solution—one in harmony with the political system—was to give each state its share of the debt and let each state pay in its own way. In fact, something like this began to happen during the last years of the war. Various states began to settle accounts for debts owed to citizens and soldiers. They absorbed all kinds of claims—not only claims against the state goverments but also claims against Congress. There was a good chance that the entire mass of unsettled debts would slip into state possession.[14]

Loss of the debt portended disaster to the Nationalist movement. Without a debt there would be little reason to ask for a taxing power, since when the war was over, paying the debt was about the only thing Congress would need much money for. Led by Morris, the Nationalists rejected the idea that the states should take over any part of the federal debt. "There is in it," wrote Morris, "a principle of disunion implied which must be ruinous." The debt belonged wholly to Congress. "The creditors trust the Union, and there can be no right to alter the pledge which they have accepted for any other, even for a better one, without their free consent."[15] The obligation to the creditors could be honored only if Congress itself possessed the means of payment. Even if requisitions worked, which they obviously did not, they would not do. Nothing would avail but the impost and other federal taxes. In short, Morris and the Nationalists made payment of the debt contingent

---

[13] Ferguson, *Power of the Purse*, 29–31, 140–41, 221–28.

[14] *Ibid.*, 141–44, 180–83, 203–04.

[15] Robert Morris to Governors of Massachusetts, Rhode Island, New York, Delaware, Maryland, and North Carolina, July 27, 1781, Wharton, ed., *Diplomatic Correspondence*, IV, 608.

upon a revision of the Articles of Confederation to give Congress the taxing power. "The political existence of America," Morris declared, "depends on the accomplishment of this plan."[16]

Morris tried to make sure that unsettled claims against Congress would remain a federal obligation, and at his suggestion Congress resolved in 1782 to send commissioners to all parts of the country to register federal debts due to civilians.[17] The next year Congress declared the large sums owed to the Continental army to be a federal responsibility and refused to allow the states to assume payment of them.[18] Under Morris' guidance the Nationalist Congress clung to the federal debt and enlarged it. At the close of the war, the debt consisted of about $11,000,000 in loan office certificates—the government bonds of the Revolution. By 1786, when the bulk of the unsettled accounts had been examined and new securities issued in recognition of claims against Congress, the debt had risen to more than $28,000,000.[19]

A debt this large was justification enough for the impost, indeed for a whole battery of federal taxes. It was a "bond of union" in the sense of creating a need to confer additional powers upon Congress. It was a bond of union in still another way. The fact was well understood that funding the English national debt had consolidated the Revolution of 1689 by creating a vested interest in the new regime. Irrespective of historical examples, however, the primacy of economic self-interest was a maxim seldom challenged in the eighteenth century. If the federal debt could be funded—that is, the interest regularly paid by means of the impost and other federal taxes—security holders throughout the nation could be expected to give their loyalty to the central government. Economic self-interest was that "active principle of the human mind" the Nationalists sought in order to weaken the identification of Ameri-

---

[16] Robert Morris to Nathaniel Appleton, April 16, 1782, *ibid.*, V, 311. Robert Morris exempted the federal debt from the general expenses of the Revolution which were to be apportioned on the states. Robert Morris to President of Congress, Aug. 28, 1781, *ibid.*, IV, 674–75. At his insistence, Congress refused to allow the states credit for payments they had made to their own lines in the Continental army. Robert Morris to Governor of Rhode Island, June 26, 1782, *ibid.*, V, 524; Robert Morris to Daniel of St. Thomas Jenifer, March 12, 1782; Report on the New Jersey Memorial, Sept. 27, 1782; to Receivers of the several States, Oct. 5, 1782, Official Letterbook C, 97–99, Offical Letterbook D, 231–34, 277–78 Robert Morris Papers (Manuscript Division, Library of Congress); *Journals*, XXIII, 629–31. Congress backed down from this position, April 13, 1785. *ibid.*, XXVIII, 261.

[17] *Journals*, XXII, 82–86.

[18] *IBid.*, XXIV, 206–10. See Ferguson, *Power of the Purse*, 156–57.

[19] The foreign debt of about $11,000,000 was generally conceded to be a federal obligation and did not affect constitutional issues. On the foreign debt in the postwar era, see Ferguson, *Power of the Purse*, 234–38.

cans with their states and generate allegiance to the Union.[20] As Morris phrased it in a report to Congress: a peculiar advantage of domestic loans was that "they give stability to Government by combining together the interests of moneyed men for its support, and consequently in this Country a domestic debt, would greatly contribute to the Union, which seems not to have been sufficiently attended to, or provided for, in forming the national compact."[21]

Up to this point Nationalist objectives were political—to secure federal taxes and to bond the Union with the cement of self-interest. It was the economic program associated with constitutional revision, however, that gave the movement its particular character. The pursuit of political ends by economic means was certain to have economic consequences, some of them integral to and inseperable from the political changes being sought, and others not necessary, perhaps, but closely related to them.

One necessary result was an increase in business capital. That Congress, if fortified by taxation, would fund the debt was certain; otherwise, its improved status could not be actualized, and it must remain a shadow, its powers unexerted. And funding was certain to create domestic capital. After interest payments on the debt ceased in the closing years of the war, the $11,000,000 in loan office certificates, which then comprised the federal debt, had depreciated in market value. If the securities were funded, if regular taxes like the impost were devoted to paying the interest, their market value could be expected to rise, increasing the wealth of the holders.

Morris in 1782 submitted a funding program to Congress remarkably similar to Hamilton's plan in 1790. He recommended a new loan in which old securities would be received at face value in exchange for new securities. After considering a discrimination between original and present holders, he rejected it as detrimental to the public interest. In outlining his plan, he proposed that only the interest be provided for, that payment of the principal be deferred to the indefinite future, and that, in the meantime, a sinking fund be employed to purchase

---

[20] The quotation is out of context. It is taken from a comment on Hamilton's funding program by Oliver Wolcott, Jr. Hamilton to Oliver Wolcott, Sr., March 27, 1790, George Gibbs, ed., *Memoirs of the Administration of Washington and Adams From the Papers of Oliver Wolcott* (2 vol., New York, 1846), I., 43.

[21] Robert Morris to President of Congress, Aug. 5, 1782, *Journals*, XXII, 432. His report was dated July 29, 1782. Robert Morris expected the Bank of North America to create the same kind of unifying appeal. Robert Morris to John Jay, July 13, 1781, Wharton, ed., *Diplomatic Correspondence*, IV, 563, 568–69; Robert Morris to Benjamin Franklin, July 13, 1781, *ibid.*, IV, 568–69.

and retire outstanding securities. Funding on this basis, he argued, would immediately benefit the nation. Since interest on invested capital in the United States was higher than the interest payments required to support the debt, the new capital created by funding, if properly invested, would bring a net increase in national income. Moreover, since the securities were held by propertied men, the gains from an increase in security values would go to persons in a position to use them not for consumption but for investment. As Morris phrased it, funding would distribute property "into those hands which would render it most productive." He also expected that it would encourage foreign investment in federal securities. He considered the inflow of money a clear gain to the country, since Americans could employ money at rates of return higher than the interest paid to foreign investors. In short, a national debt was an economic as well as a political blessing.[22]

An increase in domestic capital implied, if it did not entail, the founding of commercial banks. Despite a growing need for banks, none had existed in colonial times, and American businessmen had been forced to rely very largely on credit extended by British merchants. But as was demonstrated by the establishment of banks in Philadelphia, New York, and Boston during and after the Revolution, American businessmen were ready to start banking enterprises with money they had made in the war. Funding the debt would provide more capital for such projects. Banking operations, in turn, would multiply the effect of the capital generated by funding, for, as was well understood, banks could expand loans to several times the reserves actually on hand.[23]

Note issues by banks were a prospective substitute for state paper money. In trying to cope with the shortage of coin and dearth of credit facilities—perennial problems of America's economy—colonial governments had employed paper currency, issuing it in public expenditures and in making loans to farmers. It was fiat money, not redeemable in gold or silver, based instead on anticipation of tax receipts and the repayment of loans. In colonial times the paper money system

---

[22] Robert Morris' report, dated July 29, 1782, is the fullest theoretical exposition of his views. *Journals*, XXII, 429–46; Wharton, ed., *Diplomatic Correspondence*, V, 619–34. He was thinking not only of the existing loan office debt but also of the enlarged federal debt that would result from the settlement of claims already under way. In his last official communication before he retired from office, he expressed his confidence that the debt would one day be funded and added that it was "a commercial problem which admits of absolute demonstration that the punctual payment of interest on our debts will produce a clear annual gain of more than such interest can possibly amount to. " Robert Morris to President of Congress, Sept. 30, 1784, *ibid.*, VI, 822.

[23] Robert Morris to Robert Smith, July 17, 1781, Wharton, ed., *Diplomatic Correspondence*, IV, 582; Alexander Hamilton to James Duane, Sept. 3, 1780, Syrett, ed., *Papers of Alexander Hamilton*, II, 415.

had worked pretty well. Businessmen in most colonies, if not always enthusiastic, were reconciled to it as the only thing possible under the circumstances. What confidence they had in it was destroyed, however, by the depreciation that occurred during the Revolution.[24] In a more democratic age, propertied men had lost faith in the integrity of legislative bodies; they were afraid that popularly controlled legislatures would deliberately undermine the currency in order to wipe out private and public debts. They wanted to end the paper money system. Because it was unlikely that the country could acquire enough coin or bullion to afford a metallic circulating medium, the only alternative was banks of issue whose notes would serve as a medium of exchange. Funding the Revolutionary debt was a way of solving this problem. The capital created by funding, placed in banks, would provide backing for bank note emissions, which, if on a sufficient scale, would afford a stable currency beyond reach of popular legislatures. The paper money era might well be brought to an end if state governments could be induced to give up paper emissions altogether and conduct their finances by borrowing from banks.[25]

During his term of office, Morris organized the nation's first bank, the Bank of North America, which began operations in 1782.[26] Its capital was only $400,000, not considered a large sum (Morris was able to

---

[24] For an appraisal of colonial experience with paper money and a bibliography of the subject up to the date of publication, see E. James Ferguson, "Currency Finance: An Interpretation of Colonial Monetary Practices," *William and Mary Quarterly*, X (April 1953), 153–80. The reorientation of scholarly opinion as to colonial monetary practices has become pretty general. It has been embraced with particular enthusiasm by the new economic historians, who are highly interested in the function of colonial currency and land banks in promoting economic development. See Ralph L. Andreano, ed., *New Views on Economic Development: A Selective Anthology of Recent Work* (Cambridge, Mass., 1965), 41–56. The current reappraisal is judiciously stated by Curtis P. Nettels, who writes that in the middle colonies land banks were prudently managed and "realized the benefits claimed for them," but that serious depreciation took place in Massachusetts, Rhode Island, and South Carolina. (He might have added that the depreciation was at an early date in South Carolina and that for forty-five years before the Revolution the colony's currency was stable.) Nettels concludes by saying that it was the depreciation that occurred during the Revolution that evoked "impassioned opposition" to paper money during the 1780s—the main reason being that creditors no longer trusted the legislatures. Nettels, *Emergence of a National Economy*, 80–81.

[25] For an expression of these ideas, see *Journals*, XVIII, 1157–64, in which a committee report of December 18, 1780, envisages a bank note currency; also, Robert Morris to Franklin, July 13, 1781; Robert Morris to Governors of the States, Sept. 4, 1781, Wharton, ed., *Diplomatic Correspondence*, IV, 562–63, 693; Madison to Pendleton, Feb. 25, 1782, Burnett, ed., *Letters*, VI, 305–06; Hamilton to Robert Morris, April 30, 1781, Syrett, ed., *Papers of Alexander Hamilton*, II, 620, 623–24, 627–30.

[26] *Journals*, XX, 545–48. Wharton, ed., *Diplomatic Correspondence*, IV, 565–68; *Journals*, XXI, 1187–90.

raise this amount only by buying $254,000 in shares for the government), and it was entirely specie. Morris was aware that he might have employed public securities as part of the bank's capital if the value of securities had been supported by regular interest payments. But, since no interest was being paid, he dared not include them in his venture.[27] In other respects, however, his plans demonstrated how well he had defined his goals and the means to reach them. He hoped to expand the bank's capital to the point where it would be "a principal pillar of American credit. " He intended, as soon as possible, to bring about a retirement of federal and state paper money and to replace it with bank notes. In fact, he made a start in this direction by floating a mercantile currency consisting of Bank of North America notes and his personal notes. In 1782 and 1783, he had about $1,000,000 of this paper outstanding. It passed at par, or nearly so, in all parts of the country. It was readily accepted by merchants and received as legal tender by most of the states.[28] Morris' larger plans for the bank were too optimistic; certainly they were unrealized. Yet they failed of at least partial accomplishment mainly because they were predicated upon political reforms which did not come to pass.

Owing in no small degree to Morris' leadership, what one might call a mercantile capitalist reorganization of the country's economic institution had become integrated with constitutional revision. Between 1781 and 1783, Morris, as virtual director of congressional policy, set forth a system that fully anticipated the later Federalist program: a government invigorated by taxation; a funded debt whose increase

---

[27] Employing federal securities as bank stock was proposed in Congress, April 12, 1781, *Journals*, XIX, 381. In the plan for a bank which he submitted to Robert Morris, Hamilton suggested that land be accepted as partial payment for shares. Robert Morris replied that he had thought of "interweaving a security" in the bank's capital, but had given up the idea as too risky. Hamilton to Robert Morris, April 30, 1781; Robert Morris to Hamilton, May 26, 1781, Syrett, ed., *Papers of Alexander Hamilton*, II, 621–22, 645–46. See also the plan of a bank Hamilton sent to Duane, Sept. 3, 1780, *ibid.*, II, 400–18. Businessmen already employed securities like money in making payments to one another. In his statement of acocunts published in 1785, Robert Morris expressed his continuing faith in the potential economic uses of the public debt, saying: "A due provision for the public debts would at once convert those debts into a real medium of commerce. The possessors of certificates, would then become the possessors of money. And of course, there would be no want of it among those who having property wish to borrow provided that the laws and administration are such, as to compel the punctual payment of debts. " Robert Morris, *A Statement of the Accounts of the United States of American During the Administration of the Superintendant of Finance* (Philadelphia, 1785), ix.

[28] On the plans, see Robert Morris to Jay, July 13, 1781; Robert Morris to Franklin, July 13, 1781, Wharton, ed., *Diplomatic Correspondence*, IV, 562–65, 568–71. Nettels is perceptive, but no more perceptive than Robert Morris himself, in seeing the implications of the flotation of currency. Nettels, *Emergence of a National Economy*, 32–33. See Robert Morris to Hamilton, Oct. 5, 1782, Syrett, ed., *Papers of Alexander Hamilton*, III, 177–79.

in market value would augment business capital; a national bank that would enhance the effect of capital accumulation, afford commercial credit, and provide a nongovernmental circulating medium beyond reach of state legislatures. Morris in 1783 even proposed the federal assumption of state debts.[29] The measures that constituted this system, and to a large extent the rationale behind them, were communicated to Congress. To what extent they were known to the country at large, or their implications grasped by persons unversed in economic reasoning, can only be conjectured; but the system and the logical relationship of its parts were plainly visible to anyone who was informed about congressional affairs.

The Nationalist movement declined rapidly at the end of the war. Although ratified by all but one state, the impost amendment of 1781 failed; hence, the debt was not funded and the economic reforms contingent upon funding did not materialize. The Bank of North America severed its connection with the government and never became a national institution. Morris lost influence over congressional policy and retired from office with his major goals unaccomplished. Yet the elements which the Nationalists had put together survived and perpetuated a need to execute their program. They had, in effect, created a national debt, vested title to it in Congress, and aroused a general expectation that the debt would be paid by means of federal taxes. In 1783, Congress submitted another request for the impost grant to the states, and for several years there was a reasonable chance of its adoption.[30]

In 1786 a new crisis reinvigorated the movement for constitutional reform. Shays' Rebellion, the paper money scandal in Rhode Island, and lesser disturbances in other parts of the country rekindled conservative fear of "unchecked democracy." Perhaps the lowest common denominator of the motives of the Founding Fathers was the desire to impose restraints upon majority rule in order to preserve a republican form of government. But sentiments like this were hardly new in 1786. What gave them peculiar urgency at this time was not entirely the disorders caused by the postwar economic depression; it was the fact that the movement to strengthen the central government had come to a dead end.

After the war, Congress and the states contested for possession of the Revolutionary debt and the consequent exercise of taxing power.[31]

---

[29] Robert Morris to President of Congress, Aug. 26, 1783, Papers of the Continental Congress, No. 137, III, 33–40 (National Archives); Ferguson, *Power of the Purse*, 209–10.

[30] Jefferson, among others, was hopeful of the impost's adoption. Jefferson to Madison, May 7, 1783, Julian P. Boyd, ed., *The Papers of Thomas Jefferson* (17 vols. Princeton, 1952–), VI, 265–67.

[31] The analysis that follows is based on Ferguson, *Power of the Purse*, 220–42.

As the all-but-unanimous agreement upon the impost amendment showed, there was a general consensus that the Union needed to be "patched together," that Congress should be allowed to fund the debt, and that, for this reason, it should be given a limited power of taxation. Yet, the impost was not unanimously ratified; and, as requisitions on the states did not raise much money, Congress lacked funds to discharge interest on the debt. Congress was in the anomalous position of asserting ownership of the debt, but not being able to pay it.

The states claimed the debt. Responding to appeals from their own citizens who were federal creditors, the states paid interest on the debt with certificates and paper money. States redeemed federal securities by accepting them for taxes and in the sale of land. Some states went further. By 1786, Maryland, Pennsylvania, and New York had carried out a transaction by which they gave their citizens state securities in exchange for federal securities. In this and other ways, various states absorbed more than $8,000,000 in securities—a sum approaching one third of the principal of the federal debt. As other states planned similar action, there was a distinct possibility that most of the debt would soon be absorbed by the states or converted into state debts.

As this unhappy prospect materialized, the impost ran into fatal difficulties. The only state that had not ratified it in one form or another by 1786 was New York. The legislature then approved it, but with stipulations that Congress would not accept. To make matters worse, Congress discovered that the earlier ratifications of Pennsylvania and Delaware were, for quite different reasons, also unacceptable. The Pennsylvania legislature refused to reconsider its position.[32]

That seemed to be just about the end of the impost amendment. In despair, Congress entertained the idea of distributing the debt among the states. The procedure proposed was simple: give each state its share of the total debt and allow it to pay its share in any way it pleased. Such a step was practical and in accord with the political realities of the Confederation.[33] It signified, however, the complete abandonment of the plan for strengthening the central government. Furthermore, a distribution of the debt was certain to promote disintegrative tendencies in the Union. When the states permanently committed their taxes to the justifiable purpose of paying Congress' creditors, it was not hard to foresee that Congress would be left with attenuated functions, little revenue, and no excuse to ask for more. Self-interest would no longer cement the Union; it would bind the creditors to their states.

---

[32] *Journals*, XXX, 439–44; James Monroe to Madison, Sept. 12, 1786, James Madison Papers (Manuscript Division, Library of Congress).

[33] Committee report of Aug. 17, 1786, *Journals*, XXXI, 521–23. See John Henry to Governor of Maryland, Aug. 30, 1786, Burnett, ed., *Letters*, VIII, 455–56.

The failure of the impost amendment in 1786 had a note of finality, for the absoprtion of the federal debt by the states destroyed any real hope of securing unanimous ratification in the future. Constitutional revision as heretofore projected had failed; some other way had to be found to achieve it. The Philadelphia Convention took place in this context. The Founders met not only to protect government from the mob but also to save the nation from disunion. It should be added that the crisis was a prospective, not an existent, one. By 1787 the country was recovering from economic depression, and it had no overwhelming problems. The real crisis involved the future of the Union.

The Philadelphia Convention of May 1787 exploited a general consensus favorable to reform and the force of economic interests in stronger central government which had arisen since the war, particularly in the matter of federal regulation of trade.[34] Throwing out the Articles of Confederation altogether, the Convention drafted a plan for a national government with powers exceeding anything the Nationalists of 1781–1783 had dared to imagine. All the delicate questions of state interest upon which the impost foundered were swept aside by the grant of unlimited power of taxation to Congress,[35] a power which George Mason observed "clearly discovers that it is a national government and no longer a Confederation. . . ."[36] Another Nationalist objective was nailed down by prohibiting the states from issuing paper money. So deep was the aversion of the Convention to fiat money that it considered denying the power to issue it even to Congress, but decided in the end to preserve this last resource for emergencies.

As the new government was being formed, the Nationalist economic program advanced in mere anticipation of its fulfillment. Federal securities sold in the market before 1787 at ten-to-fifteen cents on the dollar. But because the states paid interest on them or accepted them

---

[34] For a discussion of federal regulation of trade, see Nettels, *Emergence of a National Economy*, 66–75.

[35] Duties on exports were expected. In the struggle over ratification, the Antifederalists tried to limit congressional taxing power. Every state convention that attached amendments to its ratification requested that federal revenues be restricted to indirect taxes in the first instance, that additional sums be raised by requisitions, and that federal collection of taxes within the states be permitted only if the states themselves did not deliver the money. This proposal was considered by the first Congress, along with other amendments, but voted down thirty-nine to nine in the House of Representatives and not included among the amendments sent out to the states for ratification. Jonathan Elliot, ed., *The Debates in the Several State Conventions on the Adoption of the Federal Constitution* (2nd ed., 5 vols., Philadelphia, 1861), I, 175–77, 322–23, 325, 326, 336, II, 545; U. S. Congress, *Annals of Congress: The Debates and Proceedings in the Congress of the United States* (42 vols., Washington, 1834–1856), I, 773–77. See "Luther Martin's Letter on the Federal Convention of 1787," in Elliot, ed., *Debates*, I, 368–69.

[36] Elliot, ed., *Debates*, III, 29.

for land sales, they were a good investment at that price; and speculators bought them up. The evidence indicates that the bulk of the securities changed hands during the mid-1780s. By 1790, at least 80 percent, and almost certainly an even higher percentage, had been sold by the original holders to people of means who bought them for speculative purposes.[37] After the Constitutional Convention met, the market value of securities rose and continued to go up with every step taken in instituting the new government. At the beginning of 1787, the market value of the entire debt, principal and interest, can be estimated at $7,332,000. Three years later, in December 1789, as Hamilton was about to deliver his report on funding, the market value had shot up to about $16,628,000—a gain since the beginning of 1787 of about $9,296,000.[38]

---

[37] This is the market value of "final settlement certificates" issued in satisfaction of military and civilian claims. Loan office certificates, which represented money loaned to the government during the war, were generally higher, about twenty cents on the dollar. On speculation in the public debt, see Ferguson, *Power of the Purse*, 251–86.

[38] These estimates could be refined by exhaustive research without altering them very substantially. The principal and interest have been estimated by collating figures in the following documents: Statement of the Liquidated and Loan Office Debt to Dec. 31, 1786, Papers of the Continental Congress, No. 141, Vol. II (National Archives); Statements of the Financial Affairs of the late Confederated Government, United States, Finance (Manuscript Division, Library of Congress); *American State Papers, Finance: Documents, Legislative and Executive of the United States* (5 vols., Washington, D.C., 1832–1834), I, 12–13, 27, 239; Albert Gallatin, "A Sketch of the Finances of the United States," Henry Adams, ed., *The Writings of Albert Gallatin* (3 vols., Philadelphia, 1879), III, 124–27. Although only $27,569,000 of the debt was settled by December 31, 1786, the amount due in 1789 ($28,344,833) seems a more reliable figure because unsettled claims had value. By December 31, 1789, the principal of the debt was reduced by $960,915 received in payment for public lands; the amount was then $27,383,000. The accumulated interest due on December 31, 1789, has been computed by deducting a year's interest ($1,643,035) from the amount stated in Schedule D of Hamilton's funding report as due on December 31, 1790. *American State Papers: Finance*, I, 27–28. In the establishment of market values at the beginning of 1787, higher values of up to thirty-seven cents on the dollar in Pennsylvania and forty cents in Maryland were given to principal securities issued in these and other middle states that were funded or otherwise supported by state governments. Higher values were also assigned to loan office as opposed to final settlement certificates issued in adjustment of army and civilian claims. On the market value of securities, see Ferguson, *Power of the Purse*, 253. The market value of indents and unpaid interest has been rated at thirteen cents on the dollar. In the estimates of market values in December 1789, the principal securities have been rated at forty-seven cents on the dollar, indents and accumulated interest at thirty-three cents. These estimates are on the high side, but they reflect what New York speculators were quoting. The market fluctuated violently on the eve of Hamilton's report, prices ranging from forty cents to as high as fifty-two cents. See William Constable to Robert Morris, Dec. 17, 1789; Constable to Garret and Cottringer, Dec. 29, 1789; Constable to Thomas Fitzsimons, Jan. 1, 1790; Constable to John Inglis, Jan. 4, 1790; Constable to Robert Morris, Jan. 4, 1790; Constable to Gouverneur Morris, Jan. 7, 1790, William Constable Letterbook 1782–1790, Bayard-Campbell-Pearsall Collection (New York Public Library). Lower prices are quoted for Boston but a flurry of

In January 1790, Congress received Hamilton's report on public credit and began to draft a funding act. Many people outside Congress thought that to give one hundred cents on the dollar for securities that had for years sold at no more than one sixth or one eighth of that amount was not only unjust but unnecessary. The alternative was somehow to deal with the debt at its depreciated market value rather than its nominal value, a procedure which Congress and the states had often adopted. One way to accomplish this was to distinguish between original and secondary holders and to pay the full value of securities to original holders but only the market value to secondary purchasers. Since at least 80 percent of the debt had been transferred and the highest market value at which securities had ever sold had been about fifty cents on the dollar, this plan would have cut the federal debt nearly in half. Hamilton alluded to this idea in his report, but dismissed it as adverse to public credit.[39]

There were only a few repudiationists in Congress. Three or four members of the House of Representatives wanted to revalue the debt. Their proposition never reached the stage of definition, but it had to do with reducing securities to market value.[40] In the Senate, William Maclay pushed a scheme to accomplish the same result by other means. He proposed to fund securities at the low rate of 3 percent interest and redeem them not in cash but only by receiving them in the sale of western lands.[41] The effect would have been to keep securities nearly at current market levels and enable the government to retire them at their depreciated value as the holders offered them in bidding for western lands.

Repudiation was rejected in both houses. To advocate it was regarded as disgraceful as well as antifederal. To those concerned with implementing the political revolution that had just occurred, it was unthinkable. The proceedings of the first Federalist Congress were dominated by the logic that related sovereignty to taxation and taxation

---

speculation raised them to New York levels late in 1789, Joseph Standcliffe Davis, *Essays in the Earlier History of American Corporations* (2 vols., Cambridge, Mass., 1917), I, 339. See Andrew Craigie to Leonard Bleecker, Dec. 19, 1789; Craigie to Samuel Rogers, Jan. 11, 1790, Box 3, Andrew Craigie Papers (American Antiquarian Society); Henry Jackson to Henry Knox, Dec. 27, 1789, Henry Knox Papers (Massachusetts Historical Society).

[39] Hamilton, "Report Relative to a Provision for the support of Public Credit [Jan. 9, 1790]," Syrett, ed., *Papers of Alexander Hamilton*, VI, 73–75. Hamilton added that the idea was "sometimes" suggested of making good the difference to the original possessor, but he did not feel it necessary to discuss this. On repudiationists, see Albert Gallatin's "Sketch of the Finances," Adams, ed., *Writings of Gallatin*, III, 124, 127, 129, 148.

[40] *Annals of Congress*, I, 1148–49, 1160–62, II, 1182, 1300.

[41] William Maclay, *The Journal of William Maclay, United States Senator from Pennsylvania, 1789–1791* (New York, 1927), 195–96.

to the payment of the Revolutionary debt. Everywhere in the country congressional action on the debt was awaited as a decisive test of the difference between the new regime and the Confederation. Repudiation would have been a self-denying act, a rejection of the birthright of functions and powers conferred by the Constitution. Moreover, as Hamilton and his supporters argued, it would have undermined public credit. Any substantial scaling down of security values or discrimination between holders would have set a precedent inimical to the right of all future holders of securities to payment in full. Confidence in the government's promises, and in its securities, would have been shaken right at the beginning.[42] Finally, a repudiation would probably have ruined the valuable credit the United States possessed in Holland. Dutch bankers had invested heavily in American domestic securities at relatively high prices.

The only issue that caused any stir in the House debate over funding was Madison's motion to discriminate between original and secondary holders. His plan called for giving full value to original holders; holders of alienated securities were to get only the highest market value, presumably 50 percent. However, the remaining 50 percent was to be restored to the original holders who had sold out at a discount. Madison's proposal had a strong element of justice on its side, but it is important to note that it was not a repudiation. As a nationalist of long standing and a Virginia gentleman, Madison carefully dissociated himself from the repudiationists and refused to join them. Since his scheme called for funding the debt at its face value and paying 6 percent interest, it represented fuller payment than Hamilton's plan, which called for an immediate interest rate of about 4.5 percent. Madison's proposal neither appeased the popular desire for repudiation nor furthered the political and economic objectives of the supporters of the new regime; hence, it had few adherents in Congress.[43] It was voted down in

---

[42] Conceivably, if the debt had been funded on the basis of a repudiation or a discrimination between holders, the credit of the government might have been reestablished afterward by regular payments. But this would have been a work of time.

[43] Maclay fumed against Madison for his refusal to line up with the repudiationists. "Madison's [system] yields no relief as to the burden, but affords some alleviation as to the design the tax will be laid for; and is, perhaps on that account more dangerous, as it will be readier submitted to. . . . He will see Congress in no light than as one party. He seems to prescribe to them to follow laws already made, as if they were an executive body"; whereas, in Maclay's opinion, Congress' duty was to mediate on principles of justice between a few thousand security holders and the mass of the taxpayers. When Madison's motion was defeated, Maclay wrote: "The obstinacy of this man has ruined the opposition." But as Maclay's own remarks show, there was little opposition to Hamilton's proposal respecting the federal debt either in the House or the Senate. Maclay, *Journal*, 194–95, 197.

the House thirteen to thirty-six—nine of the minority votes being those of Virginia delegates—and it was never advocated in the Senate.[44] It seems on the whole, to have been little more than a political maneuver designed, among other things, to make a show of opposition without offering a real alternative and to court favor among Virginians who had sold out to northern speculators.[45]

Congress in the end funded at face value the Revolutionary debt, both principal and interest, in the amount of some $42,000,000. There was no promise ever to pay the principal of the debt, only the interest; however, a sinking fund was created to purchase securities in the market and retire them. This scheme was in outline what Morris had proposed in 1782, but there was one important modification of the earlier Nationalist formula. To insure that Congress would have enough revenue to pay interest on the federal debt and also on the state debts, whose assumption was contemplated, Hamilton proposed that, for a period of ten years, the interest be reduced to about 4.5 percent. So much he threw to the repudiationists on the ground of high necessity, and, not withstanding the outcries of federal creditors, Congress adopted this provision.[46] Congress saved Hamilton from further ventures into financial unorthodoxy by rejecting, as Morris had once rejected, the idea of offering payment in western lands. Congress struck out all the alternatives except specie payment or the equivalent.[47]

The assumption of state debts was in a different category from the funding of the federal debt. It was not essential to the new political establishment and was, therefore, an arguable proposition. It did, however, bear a visible relationship to national unity, and this consideration was probably foremost in Hamilton's mind. Its purpose was to sidestep divisive issues and reconcile particular states—Massachusetts and South Carolina—to the Union by equalizing the financial burdens left over from the war. For exactly the same reasons, Morris had suggested it in 1783.[48] The matter was more urgent in 1790 because Congress had taken over import duties and deprived indebted states of income. But assumption, which was contrary to the economic interest

---

[44] *Annals of Congress*, II, 1298; Irving Brant, *James Madison, Father of the Constitution*, 1787–1800 (New York, 1950), 298–99.

[45] Ferguson, *Power of the Purse*, 297–302.

[46] Robert Morris held out in the Senate for 6 percent. Maclay, *Journal*, 313–15.

[47] The final act departed from Hamilton's original proposals in other details, notably in funding accumulated interest at 3 percent rather than on equal terms with the principal, by rating old Continental currency at 100 rather than at forty-to-one of specie, and by funding state securities at a slightly lower rate of interest than federal securities. *The Public Statutes at Large* (Boston, 1848), I, 138–44.

[48] See note 29.

of several states, ran into heavy opposition, failed once in the House, and passed only as a result of the well-known trade that placed the national capital on the Potomac. Politically, its service to national unity was debatable. It appeased Massachusetts and South Carolina, and this may have been necessary at the time, but it raised lasting resentment in Virginia, North Carolina, and a few other states.[49] Economically, its contribution to Nationalist objectives was more demonstrable. It added $18,300,000 in funded securities to the federal debt, piled up another thick layer of business capital, and converted another body of creditors to national loyalty.

The next year Congress put the finishing touches on the Nationalist economic structure by incorporating the first Bank of the United States. State paper money was prohibited by the Constitution, and banks were now the only source except, possibly, for the federal government, of the paper medium that the country's economy required. The Bank of the United States was to be a truly national institution, with a capital of $10,000,000 and the authority to establish branches about the country. Federal securities, now the "real medium of commerce" that Morris had once envisaged, were directly transformed into bank capital as purchasers of shares were allowed to pay three fourths of their subscription in securities and one fourth in specie.

The demand for securities created by this transaction drove prices up to par. Early in 1792, when securities reached this level, the market value of the federal debt, including principal and accumulated interest, can be estimated at $32,378,000. The market value of federal and state debts combined, according to Hamilton, was $43,800,000.[50] Even if the rise in the value of state securities brought about by assumption is disregarded, the appreciation of the federal debt alone since the beginning of 1787 had been a little over $25,000,000. A share of the profits after 1788 went to foreign capitalists, who invested heavily in the domestic debt; and their security purchases brought a voluminous

---

49 Gallatin observed in 1796: "The additional debt laid upon the Union by the assumption, so far from strengthening government, has created more discontent and more uneasiness than any other measure." Adams, ed., *Writings of Gallatin*, III, 131.

50 *American State Papers, Finance*, I, 149–50. In the computation of the value of the debt, the ratio between the different kinds of securities that were funded was projected over the unfunded debt. The prices Hamilton gave in April, 1792 in purchasing for the sinking fund were used to compute the market value. Hamilton to William Seton, April 4, 1792, Syrett, ed., *Papers of Alexander Hamilton*, XI, 225–26. On the value of the combined debt, see Hamilton to Washington, Aug. 18, 1792, *ibid.*, XII, 232–33. At the time that Hamilton wrote, stocks had risen above par to a value of over $50,000,000.

flow of capital into the United States.[51] Within the means available, the economic revolution envisaged by the nationalists had been accomplished.

What bearing does the Nationalist movement of 1781–1783 have upon the interpretation of the Constitution? First, the economic content of the earlier movement does not necessarily imply that economic motives were primary in the actual process by which the Constitution was drafted and adopted. It does not discount the range of the Constitution's appeal to many elements of the population: to gentlemen fearful of disorder, to frontiersmen desirous of military protection, to merchants and mechanics interested in federal trade regulation, and to all kinds of people who were disgusted by the erratic government of the Confederation or alarmed by the threat of disunion. Such considerations cut across economic, class, and sectional lines; and, in 1787, they fairly well united the country's elite behind the Constitution. For this reason, it is impossible to sustain Charles A. Beard's distinction between realty and personalty interests among the gentlemen at the Convention, who, if they were so divided, were doubly united in the determination to erect barriers against popular misrule.

Second, a review of Nationalist antecedents does not tend to maximize the role of crass economic interest in the adoption of the Constitution. Certainly, there were a good many individuals who held stakes in the new government too great to be gainsaid. In 1790, the 280 largest security holders had $7,880,000, nearly two thirds of the federal securities for which ownership can be exactly established from the records. The top 100 holders had $5,000,000.[52] Beneath them was a segment of the propertied class whose holdings were large enough to

---

[51] That funding "created" new capital is of course debatable. Gallatin was perceptive enough to advance in 1796 the argument that it merely redistributed national income. Whatever the process, however, funding generated *effecitve* capital for investment—a fact which Robert Morris and Hamilton never questioned. It should also be noted that Gallatin differed with Hamilton as to the benefits from foreign investment. See Hamilton's "Report on the Subject of Manufactures," Syrett, ed., *Papers of Alexander Hamilton*, X, 278–79, 295–96, and Gallatin's "Sketch of the Finances," Adams, ed., *Writings of Gallatin*, III, 146–48.

[52] Ferguson, *Power of the Purse*, 284–85. Most of the largest holders were brokers who did not own all the securities registered in their names; hence, the figures might seem to overstate the degree of concentration. However, nearly all the records relative to $18,000,000 (out of a total of about $40,000,000) have been almost completely destroyed. These were of securities registered at the treasury, in which the really great interstate speculators, foreign as well as domestic, tended to invest. If these records were available, the degree of concentration would undoubtedly appear much higher than is suggested by the figures given here.

imply crass economic motive. Yet, if security holders were an influential group, they were only a small fraction of the population; and their motives have to be regarded as mixed. Superimposed upon what might be interpreted as a crass interest was the general allegiance of merchants and businessmen to institutional reforms long sponsored by the Nationalists, a group value system that elevated their endorsement of the Constitution and the Hamiltonian financial program to the level of moral principle.

What can be said with certainty is that the Constitution does have an economic interpretation,[53] one that does not have to be elucidated by doubtful attempts to construct the inner motives of the Founders or depend upon a Beardian or anti-Beardian assessment of the role of security holders. The relationship of economic goals to constitutional revision was neither fabricated nor foisted on the country by interested men; it was organic. If the government was to be strengthened, it had to exercise the taxing power and pay the debt. The profits of speculators were incidental—the price that had to be paid for any degree of centralized authority, even for what most of the Antifederalist leaders were ready to accept in 1787. It is hard to find a prominent man who did not admit the necessity of paying the debt and who, thereby, acquiesced in speculative gains and the advantages to be conferred on the North as opposed to the South.[54] Other Nationalist objectives, such as currency reform and the promotion of banks, were not essential to constitutional reform, yet they were inherent in the funding of the debt and made almost mandatory by the constitutional prohibition of paper money. If the nation wanted a stronger government, it had to accept part or all of the mercantile capitalist formula of economic change.

Thus, an historical necessity existed, which would continue as long as payment of the federal debt impinged upon political reform. If the establishment of a new frame of government had been delayed until circumstances changed—until the debt had disappeared and the nation faced the international crises of the French Revolution—it might well have come in a different guise. In the period immediately after the War of Independence, however, constitutional revision entailed the realization of a mercantile capitalist economic program. The nationalists

---

[53] For a powerful summary of the economic effects of the establishment of the national government, see Nettels, *Emergence of a National Economy*, 89–108.

[54] Writing in 1796, Gallatin, leading spokesman of the Republicans on financial matters, said that Republicans had never disputed the necessity of funding the debt, although he suggested mildly that they would have preferred a discrimination between creditors. He himself had no objection to the way the debt was funded. Gallatin, "Sketch of the Finances," Adams, ed., *Writings of Gallatin*, III, 128, 148.

of 1781–1783 composed the formula, kept it current after the war by preserving the federal debt, and in some measure committed the nation to an acceptance of at least their basic goals.[55] In 1787 the desire to form a more adequate government had many sources, but in certain fundamental ways the Nationalists had determined under whose auspices and to what ends the reorganization of the Union would take place.

---

[55] "The situation of our public debts and the very great embarrassments which attended all our concerns on that account, were the *principal* causes, of that revolution which has given us the Constitution." Letter on Hamilton's funding proposals dated New York, Feb. 3, 1790, *Maryland Journal and Baltimore Advertiser*, Feb. 12, 1790.

The Continental Congress and the Genesis of Parties

H. James Henderson

Party Politics in the Continental Congress (New York: McGraw-Hill, 1974) is a standard modern history of the Congress, with emphasis upon the role and evolution of its factional alignments. Drawing on computer-aided, cluster-bloc analysis, as well as on the written records, Henderson discovered voting coalitions in the Congress that seemed to him to have displayed sufficient self-identity and temporal persistence to deserve the name of parties. In his final chapter he suggested a relationship between these coalitions and the parties of the 1790s. That relationship was quite complex, but much of the complexity can be related to the stubborn force of section—an influence, to be sure, that neither the Progressives nor their critics had denied. Chapter 15 of Party Politics in the Continental Congress is reprinted by permission. The tables showing cluster blocs in the first three federal Congresses have been deleted.

Recognizing the magnitude of the problems that the Continental Congress faced, in coping with both British military might and jealousies within the states, it would be distorting the historical record not to note its accomplishments in retrospect. Within the span of a dozen years the Congress produced the Declaration of Independence, the Articles of Confederation, the alliance with France, the Treaty of Paris which ended the war, and the basis of the territorial system—probably one of the most important sets of laws ever passed by an American legislature. If the record of Congress in managing public finance was sometimes chaotic, that chaos was a logical result of the fiscal powers it was able to employ. And if its involvement in the management of military operations was sometimes meddlesome, its concern for the preservation of civic control over the military helped to sustain a principle that guided the Republic in some of its most trying moments. Despite its frailties, the Continental Congress established a record in act and principle that has rarely been equaled during a comparable time span in American legislative history. One of its achievements was laying the foundation for the first party system.

From the first Continental Congress to the time when the Articles of Confederation were replaced by the new Constitution, congressional politics was marked by partisan alignments which, if judged by behavior rather than motive or admission, took the shape of legislative parties. Considering voting patterns, contests over the control of those appointments the Congress had within its grasp, and the intensity of partisan rhetoric, party lines were as consistently drawn and battles as sharply fought in the Continental Congress as in Congress today. That these parties were concealed rather than frankly admitted and that they were restricted for the most part to the legislature rather than embracing the populace at large were natural consequences of the desire of the leaders of the Revolution to conceal conflict in a government that was on trial. The Congress was weak in its formal powers (although it displayed remarkable strength at times in the use of those powers), and sensible men committed to the cause of independence hardly wanted to compound that weakness. Perhaps more important, it was generally assumed that republics depended upon the achievement of consensus in society and in government.[1]

The existence of congressional parties was disturbing not only because it was commonly believed that stable republics depended upon consensus but also because it was assumed that consensual politics was most feasible in small geographic areas where habits and customs were similar and where the inevitable conflicts of interest that emanated from different degrees of education, attainment, and wealth could be mediated as a result of common concern for the welfare of a comprehensible community. Many believed that the states alone were sufficiently cohesive to ensure healthy republican government. In reality many of the states, particularly the larger and more populous Northern states, were becoming so economically diversified and socially pluralistic that they had lost genuine communal solidarity. But there is a frequent lag, it seems, between the fact of socioeconomic change and its translation into ideology, so if states were slow to admit the existence of conflict that somehow had to be reconciled with the ideal of a republican consensus, the existence of parties in an enlarged republic was even more troublesome to acknowledge precisely because of their predictability.

It was a stroke of genius on the part of James Madison to openly contend that many of the difficulties that had been experienced under the Confederation were due to the existence of factions (parties) within the states and that the evils of parties—particularly a majority party that tended to oppress minorities—might be checked by strengthening the national government. A national republic, according to Madison's argument in the celebrated *Federalist*, Number 10, could filter local interests and passions by channeling those interests into a centralized national legislature that would be more impartial and judicious than the separate state governments. The national legislature would naturally be composed of the "better sort," who would have a more enlightened perception of public affairs than members of the state legislatures. Whenever partial interests persisted in the national legislature, they would be canceled by opposing interests in the enlarged republic. The result of this process of refinement and cancellation would be a residuum that would constitute a filtered sense of what was acceptable to the nation, and most beneficial to its individual parts.

It was with this logic that Madison defended the Constitution, which substituted for the Confederation a massive, consolidated, democratic republic—an absurd cluster of contradictions according to the conventional political assumptions of the eighteenth century. Ironically, the Constitution sharpened rather than muted party tensions in both the states and the nation, but rather than subverting the Republic, parties helped to perpetuate it. If Madison's analysis contained errors, it also contained wisdom.

II

The first party system blossomed with extraordinary rapidity. As soon as the Federal Congress began its deliberations, voting blocs took shape.[2] By the Second Congress, firm alignments were evident to any who cared to scrutinize its proceedings. By the Third Congress, the party system was beginning to extend to the grassroots. By 1796, the year of the third presidential election, partisan politics had assumed most of the characteristics that are associated with a modern party system.

This relentless growth so contrary to the accepted precepts of stable republican government strongly suggests that the first party system was germinating during the Confederation era. Despite the fact that the House of Representatives was a popularly elected body, the initial alignments in the House showed the familiar three-way regional division that had characterized the structure of party politics in the Continental Congress.[3] New Englanders maintained a solid front; the Southerners also achieved impressive cohesion; and the Middle states divided as a section and fractured within delegations. By the Third Congress there was an increasing tendency for independent legislators to take a partisan stance and for a two-party division to take shape. The shift from three to two parties in the House produced some highly significant innovations, such as intrastate splits in delegations from the Middle states, but as the first party system crystallized, it did so basically in terms of the division between North and South that had been inherent in national politics since the beginning of the Revolution.

It was entirely natural that the first party system should have been, at least in part, an extension of the partisan politics of the Continental Congress. The major measures considered by the Federal Congresses were identical with or closely similar to the concerns that had occupied the Continental Congress. Funding the Continental debt, the location of the national capital, the development and protection of the West, and the question of diplomatic relations with England and France were the major issues during both the 1780s and 1790s. Further, the American Revolution did not "devour its own children"; almost two-thirds of the Senators and half of the members of the House during the First Congress had been delegates in the Continental Congress. Although that proportion declined by the mid-1790s to roughly 50 percent and 20 percent, respectively, the continued presence of leaders such as Elbridge Gerry, Rufus King, James Madison, and James Monroe reinforced the connection between the Continental and Federal Congresses. Indeed, John Jay, who was closely associated with important decisions during the entire era, was at the center of party conflict in 1779, in 1786 and in 1795.

The three-party formation of the First Congress was a natural consequence of the germination of the first party system in the Continental Congress. As has been previously suggested, communication between widely separated regions was a basic problem during the Confederation era in the United States, just as it has been a central difficulty in the achievement of cohesion in virtually all new nations emerging from colonial status. The major thrust toward amalgamation has usually emanated from a vital center, or core area, of the new nations. The foundation for such a coalition in the United States was established during the early eighties when the superintendency of finance under the direction of Robert Morris was sustained by the Middle states, with important support from the South and from a few New Englanders. This sort of central leadership continued when nationalist-minded Virginians who appreciated the centrality as well as the size of their state took the lead in promoting the Constitutional Convention and establishing the framework for the surprisingly centralized Constitution that was produced by the Convention. There was extremely close cooperation between Virginia and Pennsylvania at the Convention. Hamilton, Madison, and Jay combined to set forth the most persuasive arguments in support of the Constitution, and during the First Congress the Middle region agreed to establish the national capital at the northern border of Virginia—a vital issue that actually caused controversy in the Congress as prolonged as the controversy caused by Hamilton's program.

This germinal stage of the first party system reflected the fact that the American Revolution was in part—though not wholly, as will be suggested below—a colonial war for independence. The structure of the Articles of Confederation tended to reinforce traditional colonial tensions because of the one-vote rule, but even after the Constitution made it possible for the people to elect representatives to the House and to participate indirectly in the election of Senators and the President, regional loyalties and parochial distrusts continued to affect party affiliations. When the "three-party system" rapidly evolved into a two-party affair, traditional North-South divisions persisted.[4]

There were changes, of course, in the contours and accents of party politics from the 1780s to the 1790s—changes that demonstrated that the Revolution was a civil war as well as a war for independence. But these changes cannot be comprehended unless it is recognized that the Revolution was two revolutions in one. The fiscal and commercial policies of the Federalist administration converted Eastern parochialists into nationalists, and Southern nationalists into advocates of states' rights. Parochial distrusts were hard to erase, however, and New Englanders, no longer able to contend that the Southerners who were in the forefront of the emerging Republican opposition were conspiring to create a national aristocracy, now condemned the Southerners for indolent habits that had been acquired on their slave plantations—habits which prompted them to oppose orderly government and the honoring of debts. The Southern-oriented Republicans, because of Hamilton's overbearing executivism and because of the Federalist preference for trade and amity with England at a time when France was engaged in a republican revolution in the face of opposition from the monarchies of Europe, accused the Federalists of wanting to re-establish monarchy in America. This ideological inversion whereby Southern elitists became Jacobins and Eastern democrats became Anglophiles and monocrats was a good example of the gaps in communication that occur in a war for independence and its aftermath. The Easterners were not true "democrats" as the Southerners had originally supposed, and the Republicans were not the "Jacobins" that the Federalists feared.

Nonetheless, there was an element of truth in the distinctions that were drawn between Federalists and Republicans. Federalists did in fact believe in order, sometimes at the expense of liberty, and the Republicans were sometimes willing to tolerate disorder from a prior commitment to liberty. These different values permeated the party politics of the Continental Congress and the first party system; they persisted throughout the ideological inversion just referred to; and they were rooted deeply in that colonial past which so troubled the creation of national cohesion.

From the earliest settlement of the colonies there were basic differences in the way New Englanders and Southerners had occupied and used the land, New Englanders had settled in towns, had lived in close proximity, and had developed churches and schools centered about the town as a corporate unit—the basis of representation in the provincial assembly. In the South the land was more fertile, the climate less formidable, the attraction of quick wealth from rapid occupation of the land more alluring, the opportunity for economic gain through the use of slave labor seemingly irresistible, and the sense of community in the diffuse, expanding population less keenly present.[5]

While there were undeniable differences between the Yankee of the eighteenth century and the Puritan of the seventeenth century,[6] the two traditions, despite corrosion, were reinforced in the crucible of the Revolution. In New England the political organization of the Resistance centered about the town; in the South it was organized on the county level. There were comparable differences in military organization which led to relatively conventional warfare in New England and guerrilla warfare in the South. Similarly, there were regional distinctions in the accents of a broadly coherent republican ideology. The Christian Sparta of Samual Adams was markedly different from Thomas Jefferson's republic dedicated to the pursuit of happiness. Where Easterners tended to stress individual sacrifice and restraint as a necessary foundation for the welfare of the larger community, the Southerners tended to emphasize individual liberty as the ultimate rationale for the very existence of the larger political whole.[7]

These two traditions—we may call the communal and libertarian— frequently clashed. The problem of how the West should be settled and governed forced Congress to reenact the colonization of America— and thereby cast into bold relief the alternatives of town and plantation in settlement, surveillance and liberty in goverance, and restraint and exploitation in the use of the land. The Jay-Gardoqui negotiations brought to the surface many of the same tensions between liberty and restraint by pitting the interests of the settled northern seaboard against agrarian interests located mainly in the South that were attracted to the unsettled West. The problem of the West persisted for decades, and it continued to trigger disputes similar to those of the 1780s. Indeed, with the creation of a more powerful national government, the clash between the Eastern and Southern ways was intensified in this area and in many others.

As already suggested, the Eastern communal and Southern libertarian traditions were liable to startling ideological inversions. The War of Independence was a republican revolution dependent in large measure upon public support. In those terms the Eastern ideology was radically republican because it rested upon the collective will of the people to resist the enemy. But public virtue, when translated from military commitment to the honoring of public debts and the maintenance of public order as insisted upon by the preponderantly Northern (and security-rich) Federalist party, appeared coercive at the very least, and at worst, dismayingly reactionary. And when Southern Republicans encouraged public resistance to the fiscal and foreign policies of the Federalists, an aristocratic party became the party of the people.

The chance unfolding of events sometimes contributed to the alteration of party postures. The Southern party, for example, constantly tended to favor an accord with France, whether it happened to be the France of Louis XVI or the republican France of the Jacobins. Although this position was due in part to a persistent desire of Southerners who represented the most "colonial" part of the new nation to break free from British military coercion and commercial influence, the fact remains that by associating themselves with the principles of the French Revolution they were reinforcing their credibility as the party of the evolving democratic republic. Of course, the Southern Republican espousal of the French Revolution was not wholly accidental, nor was it necessarily disingenuous, but the coincidence of ideology and commercial interest that affected both North and South in connection with Hamilton's fiscal system and the furor surrounding the French Revolution conspired to cast the emerging Democratic-Republicans in the role of defenders of the liberties for which the Revolution had been fought.

The Federalists disagreed as to which party best represented the principles of the Revolution. Indeed, they claimed to be the legitimate heirs of the Revolution, just as the Eastern party had claimed to be the authentic Party of the Revolution. It was a contention that had some plausibility, particularly when connected with the charismatic leadership of Washington. But when the Federalists attempted to discredit and even to stamp out dissent—a common tendency in new nations— that contention was seriously flawed.

A major reason for the insecurities felt by the Federalists was that as the first party system matured and extended to the grassroots, the Federalists realized increasingly that they were in the minority. It was apparent that the Federalist stress upon political order and popular restraint—a derivative of the Eastern ideology—was out of tune with the ferment that accompanied the Revolution and its aftermath. The communal, corporative tradition which had sustained the Eastern party during the war was partially disfigured when it was translated into Federalism. Public virtue no longer meant sacrifices in the struggle to win the Republic but restraint in searching for opportunity now that independence had been secured. Participation in the political process had come to mean acceptance of a stratified political order rather than cooperation to regenerate a corrupt system. Consequently, Federalism was increasingly difficult to export—not simply because of its stress upon consensus, but also because of its narrowly parochial definition of the values and priorities that consensus should embody.[8] Indeed, the Federalist persuasion proved to be increasingly difficult to sustain in Massachusetts, where its most articulate exponents were located. Republican congressmen began to appear in the Massachusetts delegation by the Third Congress, and the internal tensions of Massachusetts politics filtered to the national level of politics.

III

The rejection of the Federalist argument by constantly larger segments of the whole population signified a number of important facts. Politics was becoming increasingly nationalized, for one thing, and in the process partial, parochial definitions of the political process were unacceptable to the whole of the American people. If colonial wars for independence were and are different from the classic form of internal revolution such as the French Revolution because their major problem has been the creation of a new nation rather than the destruction of a corrupt or anachronistic society, it is at least questionable whether the American Revolution fits wholly in one category or the other.[9] The American Revolution resembled a colonial revolution on the national level of politics and a series of internal revolutions within the various states. Despite the strong evidence of regional partisanship in the Continental and Federal Congresses, there were simultaneous divisions within the various states that involved sharply differing socioeconomic interests. While these interests varied somewhat from state to state, and while the conflict was serious in some areas and subdued in others, there were grave and sustained divisions between elitist and popular interests in states such as Massachusetts, Pennsylvania, and South Carolina that involved not only differing opinions about the wisdom of independence but also the implications of what the rejection of the English monarchy meant for the future of American society. Elitists wanted the perpetuation of what had been an increasingly ordered social and political system in which rank conferred esteem and position and power commanded deference. Populists challenged the revolutionary elite, and consequently they questioned assumptions that had guarded a relatively stratified society and a reasonably orderly political system. That challenge was clearly less sharp than were comparable protests in Europe. Still, America seemed to resemble Europe more and more, and the menace of changes in the relationship between men and government brought about by decisions in distant seats of power confirmed from the beginning of the Revolution that central assumption of the populists that power should be decentralized.

Indeed, the conviction that power should be rooted in local and provincial institutions rather than in any central body was so strong that there was no real controversy over the creation of a confederation that derived its energy from local rather than national sources of authority. It was this conviction that not only sustained the early war effort but also accounted for the subsequent parochialism of conservatives such as Rufus King and Theodore Sedgwick, who had strong reservations about trade conferences and a strengthened government.

But that conservatives were sometimes parochialists did not mean that there were no conflicts between interests, of course. Many good Revolutionaries believed with John Adams and Alexander Hamilton that the British constitution, purged of its monarchic elements, remained the most tested and efficacious mode of government. Others, such as the anonymous author of the essay "The People the Best Governors",[10] believed in a participatory democracy. The controversy was not simply rhetorical. The lower houses of assembly in the state legislatures were subjected to populist pressures resulting in legislation such as paper money laws that propertied interests considered inimical to their welfare and an open violation of public morality.

It was only gradually that it became apparent that there was a logical relationship between the existence of powerful central authority and the preservation of entrenched socioeconomic interests within the states. That recognition was well established by the time of the debate over the Constitution in 1787, but it was less fully comprehended during the middle years of the Revolution, when attempts were made to strengthen national finances. Indeed, it is unlikely that Robert Morris himself was primarily concerned with anything other than improving public credit and making a profit for himself and his friends in the process—a dual objective that was reprehensible only in terms of the highly charged imperatives of the early stages of the Revolution, and in terms of the extraordinarily volatile partisan politics of the state of Pennsylvania. In that state the struggle between a conservative colonial establishment which opposed independence on the one hand and an agressive radical democracy which seized power to secure independence on the other produced a genuine internal revolution.

Because the Continental Congress spent most of its time in Philadelphia, and because the parties that were involved in Pennsylvania politics were tied to the battles between parochialists and nationalists in the Continental Congress during the middle years of the Revolution, it was inevitable that the internal revolution within the states which accompanied the war of colonial liberation should have been affected by the politics of the Continental Congress. It was at that time—in late 1778 and in 1779, when so many substantive issues converged with these matters of process—that the first party system began to germinate in a clearly discernible way.

Thus the first party system arose from the different ingredients that made up the American Revolution. There were regional tensions between North and South regardless of the issues of the moment, and this was a constant of congressional partisan politics. At the same time there were internal strains common to almost all the thirteen states that commanded the attention of Congress only under special circumstances—specifically, when the alleged peculations of Deane were publicized during the Lee-Deane imbroglio; when Gérard attempted to manipulate American peace terms at the same time that he made it clear that his sympathies were with the compliant Deane rather than with the obstreperous Lee; when subsequently Robert Morris attempted to link political centralism with fiscal responsibility; when Gérard's successor Luzerne successfully maneuvered Congress to direct that American peace negotiations be directed by the French foreign office; and when menancing gestures were made by the officer corps to secure pensions at the point of the bayonet.

All these matters were highly important, and understandably controversial. But apart from their intrinsic significance in the unfolding of the Revolution, their functional importance in the development of the first party system is particularly noteworthy. Although Southerners and Easterners often shifted positions as their regional interests dictated, the radicals and conservatives of Pennsylvania were ideologically consistent during the 1780s and 1790s. The radical Pennsylvanians (the "Constitutionalists") belonged to the Eastern party during the middle years of the Revolution when that party opposed the peculations of Deane, the centralism of Robert Morris, the attempts of Gérard to dictate American peace terms, and the efforts of the army officers to secure half pay for life. In similar, that is to say, opposite, fashion, the Pennsylvanian conservatives (the "Republicans" of the 1780s) joined the Southern party—and sometimes led that party—in support of a policy that favored Morris's fiscal plans, French diplomacy, and the demands of the army. Likewise, the Pennsylvanian radicals of the 1790s joined the predominantly Southern party, which opposed Hamilton's executivism and the "monarchizing" tendencies of the Federalists. Paradoxically, the libertarian credo of the Southern party proved to be an ideology that was sufficiently spacious to absorb the social and political ferment that accompanied the Revolution in diversified societies such as Pennsylvania, and in much of the North. Consequently, the Pennsylvanian radicals shifted from the Easterners to the Democratic-Republican opposition during the Federalist decade.

IV

One of the basic problems of American politics between 1776 and 1800 was the perplexing question of whether or not it was possible to create a political structure that would at once provide cohesion in a nation of diverse parts inherited from a colonial past while at the same time absorbing the ferment associated with a civil war. Both elements of the problem seemed to invite the imposition of an authoritarian regime that could weld the nation and suppress its discontents. That the Revolutionary generation retained its republican principles by resisting the temptation to make a Caesar of its commander in chief and by establishing a stronger national authority without materially undermining the vital source of popular government in the states and at the local levels of government was a remarkable accomplishment.

That accomplishment was due in large measure, of course, to the passage of the Constitution. But it is easy to exaggerate the providential qualities of the Constitution and to underestimate the importance of the people who made it function. It is appropriate to note that Simón Bolívar warned Venezuelans not to copy the Federal Constitution of the United States because it was in his mind "a marvel" that "so weak and complicated a government" could have succeeded in the "difficult and trying circumstances of their past".[11]

The Constitution created a new national stage for the Republic, but workable government was possible only as a result of a partial transformation of the kinds of political alignments that had characterized the partisan politics of the Continental Congress and the early Federal Congresses. Regional parties had to be nationalized, and they had to be made responsive to divergent interests within as well as between states and sections. This was done, not completely—nor willingly for the most part—but sufficiently to link dissatisfied New Englanders with Virginians, and some Southerners with Northern-oriented Federalists. The most rapid and balanced nationalization of party politics occurred at the geographic center of the Union—in the Middle states, where national decisions had more immediate impact, and where parochial traditions were less distinctive and entrenched.

The provincialism that had characterized the germination of national parties in the Continental Congress was never really erased during the first system. Threats of secession punctuated the early decades of the Republic, but by 1800 it was apparent that, for the moment at least, the nation would endure. The peaceful transfer of power from the Federalists who had claimed to be the legitimate Party of the Revolution, to the Republicans, who had been chastised as being seditious, demonstrated the vitality not so much of the Constitution but of a people who had discovered the uses of party politics.

Notes

1. The assumption was almost universal, and it formed a central thread of the anti-Federalist argument against the Constitution. For an example of the argument see James Winthrop, "Agrippa, IV," in Paul Leicester Ford (ed.), *Pamphlets on the Constitution of the*

United States, Published during Its Discussion by the People, 1787–1788 (Brooklyn, N.Y., 1888), pp. 63–65.

2. Mary P. Ryan, "Party Formation in the United States Congress, 1789–1796: A Quantitative Analysis," *WMQ*, ser. 3, XXVII (1971), 523–542; H. James Henderson, "Quantitative Approaches to Party Formation in the United States Congress: A Comment," ibid., XXX (1973), 307–323.

3. Henderson, "Quantitative Approaches to Party Formation," p. 315. Party politics of the Continental Congress and the Federal Congresses has been analyzed in terms of the House rather than the Senate because the continuity (and discontinuities) between the two periods was most strikingly revealed in the House, and because the House was the more dynamic and influential of the two Federal legislative bodies.

4. For an interesting commentary on the social sources of this regional division—a commentary written over 100 years ago—see Richard Hildreth, *The History of the United States of America*, (5 vols., New York, 1851), IV, 347–348, V, 415.

5. For a recent intriguing analysis of the socioeconomic distinctions between the North and the South that complements in some ways the argument of Hildreth see David Bertleson, *The Lazy South* (New York, 1967).

6. Two excellent works which make this point are Richard L. Bushman, *From Puritan to Yankee; Character and the Social Order in Connecticut, 1690–1765* (Cambridge, Mass., 1967), and Kenneth A. Lockridge, *A New England Town; The First Hundred Years* (New York, 1970). For a different view see Michael Zuckerman, *Peaceable Kingdoms: New England Towns in the Eighteenth Century* (New York, 1970).

7. Bertleson, *The Lazy South*, passim.

8. Two valuable studies of the parochial mentality of Federalism are James Banner, *To the Hartford Convention: The Federalists and the Origins of Party Politics in Massachusetts, 1789–1815* (New York, 1970), and Linda Kerber, *Federalists in Dissent: Imagery and Ideology in Jeffersonian America* (Ithaca, N.Y., 1970). Richard Buel, *Securing the Revolution: Ideology in American Politics, 1789–1815* (Ithaca, N.Y., 1972), stresses the defensive character of the Federalist ideology.

9. Thomas Barrow has suggested that the model of the colonial war of independence is sufficient to explain the American Revolution, for while strains were present both before and after independence, they were the kinds of strains that had to do with strategies rather than values—that is, conflicts between radicals and conservatives regarding the timing of independence rather than between monarchists and republicans over the basic institutional structure of American society. While I do not agree that the American Revolution can be compartmentalized so readily, there is merit in Barrow's insightful argument and in the applicability of some sort of model of the colonial war of independence for analysis of the American Revolution. Unfortunately, no clear model exists, and if it did, the American Revolution would in all likelihood contain some major anomalies. See Thomas C. Barrow, "The American Revolution as a Colonial War for Independence," *WMQ*, ser. 3, XXV (1968), 452–464.

10. "The People the Best Governors: Or a Plan of Government Founded on the Just Principles of Natural Freedom" (Harford, 1776).

11. Simón Bolívar, address delivered at the inaguration of the Second National Congress of Venezuela in Angostura, Feb. 15, 1819, in Vincente Lecuna (comp.) and Harold A. Bierck, Jr. (ed.), *Selected Writings of Bolivar* (2 vols.; 2d ed., New York, 1951), I, 179.

PART THREE

The Social Sources
of Political Division

While Noble Cunningham and Joseph Charles were questioning the dominant interpretation of the party conflict, another challenge to Progressive views appeared amidst the flowering of state and local studies after World War II. The rapid growth of higher education in the postwar years brought an enormous increase in the number of professional historians. With more researchers working, archives everywhere were combed as they had never been before. Predictably, the virtual explosion of new knowledge was accompanied by disagreement over what the data meant.

Cunningham and Charles had both begun with close examinations of developments within the infant central government in 1789. Both suggested that the party struggle started in the cabinet and Congress over issues that did not emerge until the launching of a federal regime. Both maintained that *parties* were created as the leaders of conflicting governmental factions took their disagreement to the public, reaching out into the states and counties for popular support, but seldom simply building on existing partisan divisions. By the early 1960s, the Progressive argument for continuity between the party conflict and divisions of the 1780s had been seriously disputed. Still, many influential authors continued to insist on striking parallels between the newer quarrel and the old. State-by-state and town-by-town analyses were obviously needed if the controversy was to be resolved.

Unhappily, it proves much easier to say why scholarly researchers should have turned in this direction than it is to draw definitive conclusions from their work. Nothing like a general agreement has emerged from thirty years of careful study. Rather, different states have yielded different answers under probing from extremely able authors. In several instances, a single state has prompted a variety of different conclusions. It is tempting to suspect that the diversity of the American republic may continue to defeat a search for generalities that will apply throughout the federal union. But the fundamental task for both historians and political scientists is to discover patterns in the evidence they find.

Patterns do appear in the increasingly sophisticated studies of the last two decades. Progressive scholarship from Beard through Dauer emphasized the economic sources of the party conflict, as well as its relationship to the dispute about the Constitution. Several recent authors have continued to defend both findings, adding nuances that make for an increasingly close fit between the evidence and thesis. Meanwhile, many of the writers least impressed with continuity between the party struggle and the politics of the 1780s have also tended to reject the economic interpretation of party division, often finding that a voter's social situation was a better indicator of his likely partisan allegiance. This section offers influential writings from both points of view, asking readers to decide if they can be combined.

Patterns of Partisan Allegiance, 1800

David Hackett Fischer

Few if any essays capture the complexity of partisan division in the new republic more successfully than this selection. Few are grounded on as thorough a review of recent secondary sources, as well as on the author's own research. "Patterns of Partisan Allegiance" *appeared as Appendix I of* The Revolution of American Conservatism: The Federalist Party in the Era of Jeffersonian Democracy *(New York: Harper & Row, 1965). Copyright © 1965 by David Hackett Fischer. Reprinted by permission of Harper & Row, Publishers, Inc.*

Never was there a more singular and mysterious state of parties. The plot of an old Spanish play is not more complicated with underplot. I scarcely trust myself with the attempt to unfold it.

—Fisher Ames, 1800[1]

The difficult problem of defining Federalism in social terms was not central to this project. Nevertheless, relevant material of two kinds came to light—impressionistic opinions of Federalists and Jeffersonians, and fragmentary election returns. The evidence is grossly incomplete, and conclusions from it are necessarily tentative. But on the theory that it is better to light one candle than to curse the darkness, they are offered here, for whatever they may be worth.

I have found no single pattern of partisan allegiance in 1800, no magic monism which unlocks the inner secrets of political behavior. There was surely no simple symmetry of political conviction and economic interest, no clean-cut cleavage between wealth and poverty, between agriculture and commerce, between realty and personalty holdings, between city-dwellers and countryfolk, between northern merchants and southern planters, between subsistence and commercial farmers, between hardy frontiersmen and effete easterners, between orthodox Calvinists and other religious groups.

---

[1] Fisher Ames to Rufus King, 15 July 1800, in *King*, III, 275.

There were many patterns of political allegiance—all of them intricate in the extreme. Taken together, they present a picture of bewildering, disheartening complexity. Each serves to qualify all others; they lie superimposed one upon another, blending, shading, mixing, merging in an infinity of shapes and colors. But notwithstanding their complexity, clear patterns do appear, and some patterns are clearly more important than others. Contemporaries described them, and we can detect them in election returns. The object here is to discuss them in order of importance—to peel them back, one by one, with all due care for their fragility, caution for their intricacy and respect for many researchers who have gone before.

Before we begin, the weary reader must bear with one more qualification. Although partisan feeling was very high in 1800, higher than ever before, the two parties did not divide the nation between them. Only in the Congress, where the parties had first appeared, were men either Federalists or Jeffersonians. During the 1790s, party rivalry spread slowly outward from Philadelphia, like ripples on the surface of a pond, sweeping first through the middle states, then into New England and the southern states. The rate of diffusion seems to have been roughly proportional to the rate of travel and the density of population.[2]

The cities appear to have been well ahead of the countryside; states east of the Hudson seem to have been affected before states south of the Potomac. John Rutledge, Jr., summering in Rhode Island in 1798, noted that the "political line of distinction which separates parties here (Newport), does not extend to South Carolina." Two years later, however, the Palmetto State had caught up. "Hitherto the distinction of political parties has been marked by a very faint line," Thomas Pinckney wrote from Charleston. "This line is however becoming every day more distinct, and by the next election of President we shall probably arrive at the same acme of political rancour and malevolence which the Pennsylvanians seem to have first reached, and which has diffused itself pretty generally on all sides."[3]

In the most remote states, party distinctions appear to have had little meaning even as late as 1800. It was said of Vermont that "all goes

---

[2] Cunnigham, *Jeffersonian Republicans*, pp. 255–257; see C.O. Paullin, *Atlas of the Historical Geography of the U.S. (Washington, 1932)*, "Phyladelphia is the Heart, the Censorium, the Pineal Gland of the U. S. in Politics." John Adams to Jefferson, 3 Mar. 1814, Cappon, ed., *Adams-Jefferson Letters*, II, 426.

[3] John Rutledge, Jr., to Bishop Robert Smith, Aug. 14, 1798; Thomas Pinckney to Rutledge, 23 Sep. 1800, in Rutledge Papers, Southern Hist. Coll., Univ. of N.C. Pinckney's observations would appear to describe North Carolina as well. "Parties in this district become more and more defined. It is not the personal good qualities of a candidate that are inquired for; whether he is a Federalist or not, is all the question"; Charles W. Harris to Robert Harris, 12 May 1800, in "Harris Letters," *Sprunt Studies*, No. 14, p. 71.

there by barter and that offices are trucked off to Feds and Jacobins without much discrimination." At the opposite end of the Republic there
was scarcely any discrimination at all. A man could read the *Georgia
Gazette* in 1800 without learning that a presidential election was taking
place; in voting for Congressmen in that state in the same year there
was no visible sign of party consciousness among the electorate. Eight
years later, when party lines were clearer in most states, a Federalist
in Savannah wrote that "the ancient distinctions between federalist and
republican are almost lost in the interior of the state."[4]

Political growth in the Mississippi Valley was also retarded by distance and dispersion. A westerner declared in 1800 that the "most
numerous class" was not firmly committed to either side. Despite persistent efforts by Frederick Jackson Turner's disciples to demonstrate
that the frontier was an accelerator of political change, it would appear
that political techniques even in the most advanced western state, Kentucky, were in 1800 roughly on a par with colonial practices in coastal
settlements. Our discussion of partisan patterns might be more fruitful if we would leave by the side those distant states and territories in
which party consciousness was not sufficiently clear to be meaningful.[5]

I

The most pervasive pattern of partisan allegiance derived from
the existence of established and entrenched elites in the new republic.
Americans who analyzed the structure of their society sometimes
divided it into two groups—the better sort and the meaner sort, the
respectable and the ambitious. "Society consists of two classes," a
Friend of Order declared, "of those who have something and want to
keep it, and of the rabble who have got nothing and are ever ready to
be stirred up to get it."[6]

The distinction, of course, was not between those who had something and those who had nothing, not simply between wealth and
poverty, but between attainment and aspiration, between those who
had and those who hungered. The most hungry, the most ambitious,
the most "mean," from an elitist perspective were men who had much

---

[4] [Savannah] *Georgia Gazette*, 18 June–25 Dec. 1800; John MacPherson Berrien to John
Rutledge, Jr., 3 Oct. 1808, in Rutledge Papers, Southern Hist. Coll., Univ. of N.C.

[5] William Dunbar to Winthrop Sargent, 29 Oct. 1800, in Sargent Papers, Mass. Hist.
Soc.; see the description of electioneering practices in Kentucky in [Lexington] *Kentucky
Gazette*, 13 Mar. 1800; and an article calling for greater political sophistication on eastern
models in ibid., 27 Feb. 1800.

[6] Thomas Dwight to Hannah Dwight, 21 Jan. 1802, in Dwight-Howard Papers, Mass.
Hist. Soc.; Robinson, *Jeff. Dem. in N. Eng.*, passim.

and wanted more—men who wished to add respectability to riches, or riches to popular influence. Thus conceived, the political pattern was clear. The established elites in most states were Federalist; their challengers were Jeffersonian. Recent students of the period, even those most critical of Beard's generalizations, would appear to accept this one. "The complex array of entrenched officials, together with the older county families and their professional and mercantile allies, led the Federalist party," an anti-Beard historian of the Massachusetts Jeffersonians has recently written; the Republicans on the other hand "attracted persons either outside the elite or enjoying a recently acquired and insecure position in local society. They were often new men who came from rising families that had been excluded from the highest levels of influence and standing."[7]

It goes without saying that Federalists claimed the elites as their own. "Here as everywhere," a Connecticut gentleman wrote, "the men of talents, information and property, yea and I may add honesty and integrity are found among the Federalists." Their claims were recognized by Jeffersonians, who used different value-terms but to describe the same facts. A New England Republican labeled the Federalists of his town the "prigarchy." John Binns of Pennsylvania conceded that Federalism commanded the support of "everything that considers itself a part of the natural aristocracy." A Jeffersonian editor in Delaware wrote, "The Federalists boasted that the weight of talents is on their side; it cannot be denied that this has been the case." In South Carolina, Charles Pinckney, "Blackguard Charlie," the family Democrat, acknowledged "the weight of talent, wealth, and personal and family influence brought against us."[8]

This brute fact of early American politics explains much of the emotive power of the Jeffersonian cause. A Rhode Island Republican summarized his resentment in a stanza:

> These men I hate 'cause they despised me
>   With deep contempt—and 'cause they advis'd me,
> To hold my tongue when th'was debate
>   And not betray my want of wit.

---

[7] Goodman, *Democratic-Republicans of Mass.*, p. 75; Robinson, *Jefferson Dem. in N. Eng.*, p. 110; Purcell, *Conn. in Transition*, p. 229; Fee, *Aristocracy to Democracy* in N.J., Higginbotham, *Keystone in the Democratic Arch*, p. 382; Munroe, *Federalist Delaware*, p. 213, Ambler, *Sectionalism in Va.*, passim. Gilpatrick, *Jeff. Dem. in N.C.*, Wolfe, *Jeff. Dem. in S.C.*, pp. 6, 13, 49, 81–2.

[8] Cyrus Allen to Kilbourne Whitman, 30 Oct. 1808, in Misc. Bd. Mss., Mass. Hist. Soc.; Nathaniel Ames, "Diary," 4 Nov. 1796, *Dedham Hist. Register*, VII (1896), 116; Higginbotham, *Keystone in Demo. Arch*, p. 23; [Wilmington] *Mirror of the Times*, 16 Mar. 1804; Pinckney to Jefferson, Dec. 1800, *Amer. Hist. Rev. IV (1898)*, 122.

It also explains the immediacy of one of the most important of Jeffersonian rallying cries—"It is principles, not men, that democrats ought to support," a Marylander insisted. "It may seem like a paradox, but yet no less true, that good men may support bad political principles."[9]

The claims of Federalists and the complaints of Jeffersonians were reinforced by the observations of foreign travelers in the new republic. British or French, republican or monarchist, bourgeois or noble, nearly all agreed that in America the "gentle," the people of the "better sort" were generally Federalist; the meaner sort were Jeffersonian.[10]

Gentility in America as in England meant, most of all, old riches. By European standards, of course, personal fortunes in the new republic were neither old nor large, but they were sufficient to sustain an exclusive elitism in society and politics. There is an abundance of impressionistic testimony to a connection between established wealth and Federalist politics, but the most persuasive evidence, perhaps, appears in voting returns for the three largest American cities in 1800. New York City Federalists were strong in wards 1, 2, and 3, where assessments were high, houses were large, lots were scarce and addresses were fashionable. The Philadelphia returns reflect a traditional prejudice among the "best people" against living in the ends of the town, near the Northern Liberties and Southwark. The exclusive neighborhoods in Baltimore lay within the central and western wards; the least respectable addresses were towards Fell's Point.[11]

These patterns may have been clearer in the large cities than in rural counties, but they do not appear to have differed in kind. John Adams's observation in 1787 that three or four families comprised a little elite in almost every New England village would appear to be true in 1800; and the little elites would seem to have been generally Federalist. Similar statements appear for almost every part of the Republic—even Mississippi Territory, where Federalist Winthrop Sargent wrote of "dis-

---

[9] "To All Good People of the State of Rhode Island," n.d., in Broadsides, Amer. Antiq. Soc.; Easton *Star and Eastern Shore General Advertiser*, 5 Sep. 1809.

[10] John Howe to George Prevost, 5 May 1808, "Reports of John Howe," p. 81; Louis A.F. Beaujour, *Sketch of the United States of North America at the Commencement of the Nineteenth Century* (London, 1814), pp. 128–130; Charles William Jansen, *The Stranger in America 1739–1806*, Carl S. Driver, ed., (N.Y., 1935), p. 133; anon., *A View of the State of Parties in America* (Edinburgh, 1812), pp. 50–56.

[11] Beard, *Econ. Origins of Jeff. Dem.*, pp. 383–87; New York *Commercial Advertiser*, 5, 7 May 1800; I. N. P. Stokes, *Iconography of Manhattan Island*, 6 vols. (New York, 1895–1928), V, 502; [Philadelphia] *Aurora*, 2, 17 Oct. 1800; [Philadelphia] *Gaz. U.S.*, 16 Oct. 1800; anon., *Phila. Scrapple*, (Philadelphia, 1956), p 3; J.T. Scharf and T. Westcott, *Hist. of Philadelphia*, 3 vols. (Philadelphia, 1844), I, 511; J. T. Scharf, *Chronicles of Baltimore*, (Baltimore, 1874), p. 281; Baltimore *Telegraphe*, 11 Nov. 1800; [Baltimore] *Fed. Gazette*, 11 Nov. 1800; maps of election returns in these cities, plotted by wards, appear in my *Federalists and Democracy* on file at The Johns Hopkins University Library.

passionate men of cultivated minds" who were "firmly attached to good order by Families and Wealth."[12]

Federalists could not, of course, claim that all of the wealth of the nation was behind them. "Rich, overgrown rich men are to be found among every description of politics," a New York Federalist declared. But Friends of Order could claim most of the old wealth of the republic, and once again their claims were ratified by opponents. William Bentley, a Republican, noted that his party had "rich men not high in reputation." Many a Federal family sought to stave off the challenge of new-rich Republican rivals. The Derbys and Crowninshields of Salem are surely the most conspicuous examples. The gentry of Baltimore county, the Howards and Ridgelys and Carrolls, unwillingly surrendered their local power to parvenu Republican merchants such as the Smiths and McKims. In New Castle County, Delaware, new manufacturing families such as the Du Ponts were Republican; their influence rapidly outran that of the older Federalist gentry. The Browns of Providence faced, and outfaced, a host of rising Republican merchants and manufacturers. Jeffersonian *arrivistes* in Pittsburgh were not welcomed to the drawing rooms and dancing assemblies of the Federalist "connexion" nor into the commercial affairs of the town; and at the opposite end of Pennsylvania, Stephen Girard suffered similar snubs from Philadelphia Federalists. The same pattern appears, albeit less clearly, in Virginia and the Carolinas. Randolphs and Jeffersons notwithstanding, voting returns and impressionistic evidence suggest that the scions of splendid colonial families in the tidewater—Beverleys and Pages, Fitzhughs and Carters—either entered Federal ranks or withdrew from active politics.[13]

---

[12] Adams, *Works*, IV, 393; Winthrop Sargent in Dunbar Rowland, ed., *Mississippi Territorial Archives*, 1798–1803 (Nashville, 1905) 185; George Salmon to James McHenry, 7 Oct. 1798, McHenry Papers, Md. Hist. Soc.; Oswald Tilghman, *History of Talbot County, Md.*, I, 144; George Gibbs to Oliver Wolcott, 30 July 1812, Wolcott Papers, Library of Congress; Troup to King, 6 May 1799, *King*, III, 14; Higginbotham, *Keystone in the Democratic Arch*, 11–12, 382. "How many instances have you and I known of these monopolies of county administration! I know a county in which a particular family (a numerous one) got possession of the bench, and for a whole generation, never admitted a man on it who was not of its clan or connection. I know a country now of 1500. militia, of whom 60. are federalists. Its court is of 30. members of whom 20. are federalists." Jefferson to John Taylor, 21 July 1816, Ford, *Jefferson*, X, 53.

[13] Pickering to Hazen Kimball, 5 Jan. 1814, in Pickering Papers, Mass. Hist. Soc.; Bentley, *Diary*, III, 350; [New York] *Evening Post*, 14 Dec. 1801; Goodman, *Democratic-Republicans of Mass.*, pp. 114–115, 120–124; Munroe, *Federalist Delaware*, p. 224; Danforth, *Pictures of Providence*, R. I. *Hist.*, X (1951), 7; Tarleton Bates to Frederick Bates, 28 Jan. 1804, W. *Pa. Hist.*, XII (1930), 49; K. L. Brown, "Stephen Girard's Bank," *Pa. Mag. Hist. Biog.*, LXVI (1942), 29–55; Federalists did occasionally claim nearly all the wealth of the nation, but their claims were refuted by Jeffersonians; Ames, *Works*, II, 116; cf. [Boston] *Independent Chronicle*, 31 Dec. 1801.

A sense of elitism derived not merely from old wealth but from occupation as well. Men who held positions of power and prominence in 1800 tended toward Federalism. The same qualifications entered above also apply here, of course. Inherited power operated like ancient riches, to distinguish old families from new. Republicans, Federalists, and neutral observers agreed. John Binns of Pennsylvania, who declared that "everything that considers itself a part of the natural aristocracy" tended toward Federalism, defined aristocracy in occupational terms—"nearly all the lawyers, nearly all the merchants, most of the parsons, many of the physicians." There have been occasional efforts at quantification. Sanford Higginbotham investigated the occupations of Federalist and Republican electioneering committeemen in Philadelphia, 1811, and found that 51 percent of the Federalists were merchants and lawyers, against 17 percent of the Republicans; 27 percent of Federalists were mechanics, artisans and small shopkeepers against 37 percent of their opponents. In 1809 a Republican in Windsor, Vermont, calculated that of twenty-two lawyers in Windsor County, seventeen were Federalist; of thirty-three merchants, twenty-four were federal.[14]

Lawyers appear to have been more generally Federalist than merchants, and more active and zealous as well. Sweeping attacks upon attorneys were a common theme of Republican editors, and apparently with reason. Federal nominating meetings often coincided with court sessions and bar meetings.[15] On the other hand, a common complaint of active Federalists was the lack of enthusiasm which merchants showed for the "cause of order." Jeremiah Mason's lament in 1813 was representative. The merchants, he wrote "are of all classes of society the least apt to make a manly opposition. They have never acted with the least concert, and have always in the end quietly submitted. Gain is their great object. They will never enter into a contest with the Government in which no money can be made."[16]

"Merchant" was a term which was at once much less precise and much more inclusive than "lawyer," embracing many different kinds of entrepreneurial activity, and many different degrees of wealth and respectability. An English traveler distinguished between "principal merchants" and "small merchants," the former tending toward Federalism, the latter toward Jeffersonian principles. William Bentley noted

---

[14] Higginbotham, *Keystone in the Democratic Arch.*, pp. 326–382; Robinson, *Jeffersonian Democracy in New England*, p. 110; Fox, *Decline of Aristocracy*, ch. I; Fee, *New Jersey*, p. 269.

[15] (Portland) *Eastern Argus*, II Oct. 1804, 29 Mar. 1805; [New York] *American Citizen*, 3 May 1800; [Chillicothe]*Supporter*, II Aug. 1800; Fox, *Decline of Aristocracy*, pp. 11–17, Higginbotham, *Keystone in the Democratic Arch.*, p. 79; Benton, *Herkimer Co., N.Y.*, p. 257.

[16] Jeremiah Mason to Rev. Jesse Appleton, 21 Dec. 1813, in Hilliard, *Mason*, pp. 69–72; see above, ch. II.

that the richest and poorest citizens of Salem were generally Federalist, and the middling families Republican. In Delaware a Democrat declared that Federalists were "the wealthy and powerful," who having tasted privilege "wished to confirm themselves in it, and hand it down as a patrimony to their children by endeavoring to fix a government more energetic and more restraining to the liberties of the people." Republicans he identified as "the middling ranks" and the "industrious poor" who desired "to keep the door open, thro' which merit and industry may reach the highest summit of power, equally with the wealthiest."[17]

There were, of course, men in trade whose politics were shaped by profit-seeking in the most direct sense. Dry-goods merchants, who dealt mostly in English goods, appear to have leaned toward the "British" rather than the "French" party; merchants such as Girard who traded with France were in the other camp. But it should be noted that commercial connections with England were old and well established; merchants who operated within them were less apt to be new men than those who entered the newer sector of French trade. Similarly, contemporaries often distinguished between Federalist merchants and Democratic manufacturers. An English visitor to Philadelphia believed that "the party names they assumed were merely other terms for importers and manufacturers." The profit motive clearly operated in the case of Henry Smith, a wealthy Jeffersonian distiller in Providence, Rhode Island, who blazoned the side of his factory with the slogan "liberty, equality and no excise!" But immediate economic interest may have been less important than the transcendent fact that manufacturing money was often new money, and commercial families were more apt to be entrenched.[18]

Patterns among artisans, craftsmen, and petty shopkeepers reflect the same general theme. Occupations which appeared least "respectable," and most mobile though not necessarily the most impoverished, were markedly enthusiastic for Jefferson. The butchers of Philadelphia, often affluent but rarely respectable, were "distinguished among their fellow-citizens, for their support and attachment to Republican principles." The cartmen of New York City showed similar political attitudes. "Indigo pedlars" in Connecticut, who were regarded as a

---

[17] Lambert, *Travels*, II, 90; "To the Citizens of Newcastle County," 1804, in Broadsides, Amer. Antiq. Soc.; Bentley, *Diary*, IV, 17.

[18] [Boston] *New England Palladium*, 21 Oct. 1806; Melish, *Travels*, I, 167; see also P.A. Jay to John Jay, 7 May 1813, in Jay Papers, Columbia Univ.; Danforth "Pictures of Providence," R.I. Hist., X (1951), 7. The republicanism of manufacturers was no more than a tendency, of course. It was probably true that Federalists owned most of the manufacturing establishments of the nation, as the *Palladium* claimed. But a relative distinction between the politics of merchants and manufacturers would remain valid.

species of gypsy by the sober citizenry of that stable and conservative state, were decidedly Democratic in 1800.[19]

Two other occupational patterns of partisan allegiance, which reflected a sense of elitism and of "respectability," are sufficiently clear to be meaningful. Naval officers in the new nation appear to have been generally Federalists. Jefferson's "gunboat policy" may have been a factor, but the habit of command, as we have seen with Commodore Truxtun, provided a deeper basis for rapport with the "cause of order."[20] On the other hand, physicians more than any other profession leaned toward Jeffersonian ideas. Gideon Granger, for example, described physicians as "generally friends of equal liberty." Other observers agreed in the fact and in its explanation—no other profession was "so badly treated."[21]

Old wealth and respectable callings were but two of many distinguishing characteristics of the American elite, which tended toward Federalism in its politics in 1800. Another was education. The higher the attained level of formal schooling, the more likely was a firm Federalist commitment. Federalists often entered this claim; Jeffersonians acknowledged its validity. Gideon Granger complained to Jefferson that in Connecticut there were "at least four hundred men of public education and prospects for four or five of us to contend with." A Massachusetts Republican lamented that though his political friends were often "men of firm minds," they "were not qualified by education to plead or write."[22] A comparison of the educational level of Federalist and Jeffersonian Representatives in Congress in 1800 (see Table I) reveals a clear disparity.

The colleges of the nation were, if not Federalist, at least decidedly hostile to Jefferson. The trend was most apparent in New Eng-

---

[19] Michael Fry and Nathan Coleman to Jefferson, 17 Oct. 1801, in Jefferson Papers, Library of Congress; [New York] *Am. Citizen*, 7 May 1800; [Hartford] *Connecticut Courant*, 1 Sep. 1800; see also Timothy Dwight's strictures against boatmen in *Travels*, VII, 485.

[20] Abijah Bigelow to wife, 9 Dec. 1812, *Amer. Antiq. Soc. Procedings*, XL (1930), 345 [Exeter] *Constitutionalist*, 29 Dec. 1812; Wolfe, *Jeff. Dem. S.C.*, p. 278.

[21] Granger to Jefferson, 20 Jun. 1805, in Jefferson Papers, Library of Congress; James Wilson to Wm. Darlington, 27 Feb. 1808, in Darlington Papers, Library of Congress; [Chillicothe] *Supporter*, 4 July 1809.

[22] For Federalist claims see Warren, *Autobiography and Journals of John C. Warren*, I, 65; D.B. Ogden to Wm. Meredith, I May 1805, in Meredith Papers, Hist. Soc. Penna.; Jeremiah Smith to Wm. Plumer, 5 Jan. 1806, in Plumer Papers, Library of Congress; John Tabb to William Shaw, 25 May 1807, in Misc. Bd Mss., Mass. Hist. Soc.; Quincy, *Figures of the Past*, p. 192; for Jeffersonians, see Gideon Granger to Thomas Jefferson, 18 Oct. 1800, in Jefferson Papers, Library of Congress; Bentley, *Diary*, II, 176; Robinson, *Jeff. Dem. in New Eng.*, pp. 106, 113.

TABLE I.   Formal Education of Federalists and Republicans
           in the Sixth Congress

Attained level	Federalists Number	Percent	Republicans Number	Percent
Private tutors	5	7.5	0	0
College graduate	34	50.8	12	25.5
Attended college	6	9.0	8	17.0
Lower schools	21	31.2	22	46.9
Unknown	1	1.5	5	10.6
Total	67	100.0	47	100.0

SOURCE: Party affiliations are taken from Dauer, *Adams Federalists*; educational level, from *Biographical Directory of the American Congress* and *Dictionary of American Biography*. Efforts were also made to trace Congressmen listed here as unknown in registers, alumni catalogues and directories of American colleges founded before 1795. Those so listed in all probability did not advance beyond the lower schools.

land institutions but by no means confined to them alone. A Princeton undergraduate wrote in 1800 that "the students are in general on the federal side; this cannot, I fear, be said of the people at large." Similar evidence exists for Columbia, Brown, and even the new colleges in North Carolina, Georgia, and later in Kentucky. An exception was William and Mary, where the students refused to wear crepe for the death of Washington and received the news of Jefferson's election with "joy almost bordered on madness."[23]

The anti-Jeffersonian bias of the colleges was equally evident in the other "literary institutions" of the Republic, from the Boston Athenaeum to the Charleston Library Society. Republicans excluded from these particular associations sometimes displayed a general enmity toward literary institutions of any kind. There were of course many exceptional men in the party of Jefferson, whom New England Federalists, incidentally regarded as "a scholar among gentlemen, but not

[23] There were periodic eruptions of Republican zeal among the undergraduates, perhaps primarily because their professors were so staunchly Federalist. But for the predominantly Federal cast of trustees, teachers and students alike see Frederick Beasley to William Gaston, 3 May 1800, Gaston Papers, Univ. N.C.; Ezekiel Baer to John Bacon, 28 Dec. 1801, Gallatin Papers, N.Y. Hist. Soc.; Birdsall, *Berkshire Co.*, 137–138; Robinson, *Jeff. Dem. in New England*, 110; Fox, *Decline of Aristocracy*, 29; A.D. Murphey to John Scott, 23 Feb. 1801, Hoyt, *Murphey Papers*, I, 1–2. Gilpatrick, *Jeff. Dem. in N.C.*, 129–130; Phillips, *Sectionalism in Ga.*, 92–93; for William and Mary see J.S. Watson to David Watson, 24 Dec. 1799, 2 Mar. 1801, *William and Mary Quarterly*, 29 (1921) 152, 161–162; and [New London] *Bee*, 26 Mar. 1800. Dickinson College appears to have been divided; see James Somervell to Samuel Marsteller, I Feb. 1813, Duke Univ. Library; Dartmouth in Hilliard, *Mason*, 169; and for Transylvania, Lexington *Western Monitor*, 10 Nov. 1815.

a scholar among scholars." But there was also more than a trace of an anti-intellectual prejudice. Unlike federal fear of "visionary" philosophizing, it was directed against settled institutions of learning, against metaphysics, erudition, and formal scholarship. The most elevated expression of this prejudice is perhaps Jefferson's fulminations against "abstraction." A more crude manifestation was a New York Jeffersonian who denounced Gouverneur Morris because "he knows too much."[24]

In addition to formal education, any accomplishment, habit, custom, quality, prejudice, or predilection which tended to distinguish those who had from those who hungered, tended also to distinguish a Federalist from a Jeffersonian in a descriptive if not a causal way. Physical appearance?

> Apollo views with honest pride,
> His fav'rites all on Fed'ral side.

So at least boasted a Federalist, and he may well have been right. Modes of dress? A Democrat distinguished the parties as "ruffle-men" and "apron men." The phrase "silk-stocking district" first characterized Federalist constituencies.[25]

There were many exceptions, to be sure—exceptional men at the top and bottom of American society. Some there were who regarded themselves as full-fledged members of the elite, without any apparent reason. Some years after the fall of the Federalists, Francis Parkman came across an individual who serves as an illustration. In one of his excursions through the north woods, Parkman met a squatter who seemed at first almost a caricature of the American Democrat—and yet he was an anti-Democrat. Sitting at supper in his cabin, "squatting on his homemade chair, shirt-sleeves rolled up to the elbows, bushy hair straggling over his eyes, attacking his meal, as if his life depended on his efforts," he astonished his Brahmin guest by declaiming against "levelling democracy" and "the bed of Procrustes." This man was a Whig; thirty years earlier he would have been a Federalist.[26]

---

[24] Wolfe, *Jeff. Dem. S.C.*, p. 261; [Boston] *Independent Chronicle*, May 21, 1807; Bentley, *Diary*, II, 226; Boorstin, *Lost World of Thomas Jefferson*, pp. 128–139; Gouverneur Morris to John Parish, 9 May 1806, in Morris Papers, Library of Congress.

[25] [Boston] *New England Palladium*, 6 Nov. 1804; Cooperstown *Ostego Herald*, 3 May 1798. Charles Biddle, in his *Autobiography*, pp. 330–331n, tells an anecdote which makes clear the importance of dress as an emblem of elitism. Edward Badger, a Pennsylvania lawyer, gentleman and Federalist was riding to Lancaster, wearing a short coat which was rarely adopted by the best people. Late in the day he stopped to ask about an inn kept by a certain Mr. Slough. "Oh yes, be sure," came a stranger's reply, "Slough he keeps a good house, but that won't do for you and me, for none but gentlemen go there." Badger vowed and declared that he would never wear a short jacket again.

[26] Quoted in Howard Doughty, *Francis Parkman* (New York, 1962), p. 56.

At the upper end of American society, of course, there were others who for reasons of principle or political aggrandizement led the peaceable revolution against the entrenched elites. They qualify the general pattern but do not contradict it. "Although there are no nobles in America," a Frenchman had written in 1786, "there is a class of men denominated 'gentlemen,' and although many of these men have betrayed the interests of their order to gain popularity, there reigns among them a connection so much more intimate as they almost all of them dread the efforts of the people to despoil them of their possessions." His conclusion still held true in 1800.[27]

2

The class of men denominated "gentlemen" could not, of course account for all of the votes which Federalist candidates received in 1800. A geographical analysis of voting patterns in the elections of that year suggest that particularly heavy concentrations of Federalist voters were to be found in the following areas;[27a]

1. The North Shore of New England, including Essex County, Mass., Rockingham and Hillsborough Counties, N.H., and York and Cumberland Counties, Maine.

2. The Connecticut River Valley, including Hartford County, Conn., Worcester and Hampshire Counties in Massachusetts, Grafton and Cheshire Counties in New Hampshire and Windham, Windsor, and Caledonia Counties in Vermont.

3. The middle counties of Rhode Island—Kent and Bristol.

4. The old Dutch counties of the Hudson Valley, including Columbia, Rensselaer, and Albany Counties in New York and Bergen County in New Jersey.

5. The counties of West Jersey, and the central portions of that state—Burlington, Somerset, Middlesex, Monmouth, Hunterdon, Gloucester, Salem, Cumberland, and Cape May.

6. Philadelphia and the southeastern counties of Pennsylvania, including Adams, Chester, Delaware, and Lancaster.

7. Luzerne County in northeastern Pennsylvania.

---

[27] Otto to Vergennes, 10 Oct. 1786, in George Bancroft, *History of the Formation of the Constitution* (New York, 1882), II, 399–400.

[27a] These generalizations rest upon voting returns for the election of 1800, gathered from state archives and newspapers. Maps indicating strength in each state, plotted by town and county, appear in my "Federalists and Democracy," The Johns Hopkins University Library.

8. The "Delmarva" Peninsula, as it is now called, including Kent and Sussex Counties in Delaware; Dorchester, Worcester, and Somerset Counties in Maryland, and Virginia's Accomack and Northampton Counties.

9. Tidewater Maryland and Virginia—Charles, St. Mary's, and Prince George's Counties in the former state, Loudoun, Westmoreland, Fairfax, Stafford, James City, New Kent, Henrico, and Charles City Counties in the Old Dominion.

10. The upper Cape Fear counties of North Carolina, in Fayetteville and Salisbury Districts.

11. The southern coastal counties of North Carolina, in New Bern and Wilmington Districts.

12. The South Carolina low country, including Cheraw and Georgetown, Charleston, and Orangeburg and Beaufort Districts.

13. The Valley of Virginia, western Virginia, and western Maryland, including Alleghany County Md., and Hampshire, Hardy, Pendleton, Augusta, Rockbridge, and Greenbrier Counties in Virginia.

Manning Dauer, the only scholar since Charles Beard to publish a nationwide analysis of the socioeconomic basis of the party dispute in the 1790s, has suggested a qualified Beardian hypothesis. Extreme Federalists, he writes, were to be found in "commercial and shipping" areas of the nation. "Half-Federalists" generally in "exporting-agricultural sections," which raised cash crops and sold them abroad. The centers of Jeffersonian strength, according to Dauer, were the "more self-sufficient farming sections."[28]

Dauer's evidence does not sustain his conclusions. He suggests five specific ways of distinguishing Federalist from Republican farming areas—soil type, export statistics, ratio of slaves to whites in southern states, wealth per capita, and accessibility to markets. But voting patterns in the 1790s generally and in 1800 particularly do not correlate with any of these variables.[29]

---

[28] Dauer, *Adams Federalists*, pp. 7, 18–25, 275–287.

[29] Dauer's generalizations from soil types derive from Paullin, *Atlas of the Historical Geography of the U.S.*, Plate 2C, which does not sustain him. The brown, gravelly, and stony loams of New England and New York were farmed by Federalists and Republicans alike. In New Jersey and North Carolina, Federalists subsisted on soils which were essentially sand. The richest soil in the latter state was reputed to be in the northeastern corner—Jeffersonian country (Gilpatrick, *Jeff. Dem. in N.C.*, p. 13). By 1800, the clay loams of the Piedmont in Virginia and Baltimore, Harford, and Frederick Counties in Maryland—all Jeffersonian—were surely richer than the coastal regions where good soil had been mined nearly to exhaustion (Craven, *Soil Exhaustion*, passim) Dauer's generalizations from soil types would appear to hold for South Carolina and western Virginia, but scarcely anywhere else. Export statistics by state, from which Dauer also

There are other patterns which appear more clearly in the voting returns for 1800. Most of the Federalist regions enumerated above had one set of characteristics in common, they were mature, static, homogenous, and ingrown. Jeffersonian areas on the other hand tended to be immature, fluid, and dynamic.

---

generalizes, are not helpful. County of origin is unknown and domestic consumption is ignored; the figures are more representative of port facilities than anything else. But even assuming the relevance of state export statistics to the problem, there is certainly no "direct correlation," with Federalist voting strength, as Dauer claims. The states in which exports (excluding re-exports) were lowest—less than $5.00 per capita per year, included N.H., Vt., Conn., N.J., Del., and N.C. In all but Vt. and N.C., Federalists were strong; and in N.C., Federalism would remain stronger through the Jeffersonian era than in any other southern state. The states where exports were highest, more than $12.00 per capita, were Mass. and Md., Penna. and N.Y., R.I. and S.C., of which two were Federalist, two Republican, and two divided in 1800 and afterwards. Slave ratios are equally inconclusive. Only in S.C. do they correlate with Federalist strength. In N.C., slaves were numerous in the northeastern corner of the state, which voted Jeffersonian; they were comparatively few in the upper Cape Fear region, where Federalism was strongest. In Va., the slave ratio was high in the Federalist tidewater counties, but also in the southside counties which were Jeffersonian. The ratio was low in Federalist counties in the west. Federalist counties in Md. were in the same fastion both high (Charles) and low (Alleghany); so also, Jeffersonian counties such as Queen Anne's had a high ratio of slaves; Harford County had a very low one. Per capita wealth is generally unknown, though a conclusion could be drawn from the census of 1800 and assessments for the Federal Land Tax of 1799, a laborious task which neither Mr. Dauer nor I have undertaken to perform. Dauer does list the state land tax per capita for Massachusetts in 1796, but there is not even the "fair correspondence" which Dauer claims. Two of the three wealthiest counties, Norfolk and Middlesex, were described by a Federalist as "dens of unclean beasts" (Thomas Dwight to Theodore Sedgwick, II Apr. 1800, in Sedgwick Papers, Mass. Hist. Soc.); Hampshire County, the most Federal in the state, was less affluent according to this indicator than Worcester and Essex, which were more nearly divided, and Plymouth, which was Jeffersonian. Accessibility to markets does not correlate with party allegiance. Many Jeffersonian areas were more accessible than Federalist areas—Norfolk and Middlesex Counties in Massachusetts, Suffolk, Queens, Westchester, Rockland, Dutchess, and Orange in New York; Essex in New Jersey; Bucks, Montgomery and Berks in Pennsylvania; Harford, Anne Arundel, and Baltimore Counties in Maryland. The Jeffersonian counties of Virginia were exporting large crops as early as 1791 (Edward Carrington to Hamilton, 4 Oct. 1791, in William and Mary Quarterly, 2d series, II (1922), 139). as were the northeastern counties of North Carolina. On the other hand, the Connecticut River Valley was in Timothy Dwight's description (Dwight, Travels, III, 333) "remote from a market;" most agricultural goods appear to have been carried out by wagon across the interior of the state, rather than floated down the rock strewn river. Turnpikes and river improvements were only beginning to expand commercial opportunities.

Finally, another of Dauer's suggestions that "in general, the Half-Federalists, as those who deviated from the Hamiltonian orthodoxy are called, are to be found in farming sections," is not sustained by his evidence. Such a conclusion certainly does not appear on the face of the maps which Dauer included. As far as leading Federalists and Independents are concerned, those few who stood with Adams in 1800 (Knox, Otis, Dexter, Gerry, Reed, the Fenners, the Trumbulls, Rush, Chase, Craik, Stoddert, and

The most staunchly Federalist region in the nation was the Connecticut River Valley. Timothy Dwight wrote of it, "The inhabitants of the valley might be said in several respects to possess a common character; and, in all the different states resemble each other more than their fellow citizens, who live on the coast. This similarity is derived from their descent, their education, their local circumstances, and their mutual intercourse. In the older settlements most of the inhabitants are natives of this valley, and those who are not, yield to the influence of a character which they continually see all around them."[30]

Dwight described the "sobriety" and "good order" of the inhabitants of the Valley—and many other men of all persuasions agreed with him. "The yeomanry of the towns on and near this river in Massachusetts," another Federalist wrote, "are in their principles, habits and manners and in their police [policy] as far as a difference of government will admit, very like the stable yeomanry of Connecticut—not extremely liable to change." Still a third Federalist summarized in a sentence, "We keep more to our Old Habits, being composed chiefly of the descendants of Old Settlers."[31]

The same qualities appear among the people of the second most staunchly Federalist region, the Delmarva peninsula, including lower Delaware, Maryland's southeastern shore and the two Virginia counties. Writing of lower Delaware, John Munroe has observed, "the people were largely of English stock, inbreeding was common among them, and, with the passage of time, isolation and homogeneity bulwarked the customs and attitudes of their forbears." As Munroe succinctly states, it was a region which cherished "ancient virtues and accustomed procedures."[32]

A historian of New Jersey, Richard P. McCormick, has written of the "stability" of society in West Jersey, with its "relatively homogeneous population and its pronounced ruralness." A Pennsylvania historian has observed that the southeastern counties of that state were marked by "the habits of a mature society" early in the nineteenth century. There are similar descriptions of tidewater Maryland and Vir-

---

Marshall) were nearly all merchants or commercial lawyers. The acidulous comments of Federalists who were displeased with Adams in 1800 (nearly all the leaders in 'the first rank') suggest that commercial men were generally better pleased by Adams' temperate foreign and domestic policies than by more reckless alternatives of the "High Federalists."

[30] Dwight, *Travels*, III, 333; see also [Boston] *Repertory*, 15 May 1807, in which Federalists are described as "quiet men."

[31] Jabez Colton to Simeon Baldwin 31 Dec. 1804, Baldwin Papers, Yale University Library; Thomas Dwight to John Williams, 2 Dec. 1802, Dwight-Howard Papers, Mass. Hist. Soc.

[32] Munroe, *Federalist Delaware*, p. 239.

ginia, the Cape Fear region of North Carolina and the South Carolina low country.[33]

Jeffersonian areas, on the other hand, appear to have shown a different set of characteristics. Timothy Dwight's notorious comments upon that "Nazareth of anti-Federalism," western Vermont, as populated by "the discontented, the enterprising, the ambitious and the covetous," may perhaps be taken as something more than a measure of one Federalist's irascibility. Dynamism, expansion, and mobility appear, generally, to have distinguished Republican regions from those in which Federalism flourished.[34]

Impressionistic evidence is reinforced by demographic statistics. The single variable which correlates more closely than any other with voting behavior in 1800 is the rate of population growth as revealed in the censuses of 1790, 1800, and 1810. The most Federalist state in the nation, Connecticut, had the smallest growth rate—6 percent in the 1790s, 4 percent in the first decade of the nineteenth century. Population increase in the Connecticut Valley (except its northernmost reaches) was equally small in the period 1800–1810; 6 percent in Worcester County, Massachusetts; 5 percent in Hampshire County, Massachusetts; 2 percent in Cheshire County, New Hampshire; 4 percent in Windham County, Vermont; and 7 percent in Windsor County, Vermont.

These Valley counties were growing more slowly than the Republican counties in eastern Massachusetts, nearly all of which had growth rates of 11 percent to 25 percent in the same period. Essex County, Massachusetts, showed a low growth rate (6 percent) in the 1790s when it voted Federalist; but in the 1800s, when it drifted into the Republican camp, its rate of growth was 18 percent.[35]

In the middle states, the same generalizations can be made. The most Federal counties of New York were Albany and Columbia; the first was nearly static (2 percent population rise, 1800–1810) and in the second, population was actually declining. Rensselaer and Washington Counties, also Federalist, showed higher rates of population

[33] Richard McCormick, *Experiment in Independence; New Jersey in the Critical Period* (New Brunswick, 1950), p. 45; Philip Shriver Klein, *Pennsylvania Politics, 1817–1832* (Philadelphia, 1940), pp. 4–5; Avery O. Craven, *Soil Exhaustion as a Factor in the Agricultural History of Virginia and Maryland, 1606–1860* [Urbana, Ill.], pp. 72–121; William A. Schaper, "Sectionalism and Representation in South Carolina," *Amer. Hist. Assn. Annual Report for 1906*, I, 253–258, 433–452.

[34] Dwight, *Travels*, III, 458. See also *Providence Gazette*, 15 Nov. 1800.

[35] Growth rates of counties in eastern Massachusetts were as follows—Bristol, 11 percent; Barnstable, 15 percent; Plymouth, 17 percent; Middlesex 13 percent; Norfolk, probably more than 25 percent; Nantucket, 21 percent. Only Dukes, 5 percent, was more static than Federalist counties.

increase (20 and 23 percent respectively in 1800–1810) but were still far behind the extraordinary New York average, 78 percent. In New Jersey the three decidedly Republican counties of Morris, Essex and Sussex had growth rates of 23, 17 and 13 percent; the Federalist counties of Bergen, Burlington, and Hunterdon had rates of 10, 13 and 14 percent. Federalist counties in southeastern Pennsylvania—Adams, Delaware, Chester, and Lancaster—showed increases of 10–23 percent between 1800 and 1810, in a state which was growing at the rate of 35 percent.

States south of the Mason-Dixon line were much the same. In Delaware's one Republican county, Newcastle, growth rate during the 1790s was 30 percent; in Federalist Kent County population increase in the same period was 3 percent, and in Sussex the population was declining. Maryland's Republican counties were growing rapidly; Federalist counties in southern Maryland were losing population. Alleghany County in western Maryland, decidedly Federalist, was not a frontier area, as has sometimes been suggested, but a stagnant backwater in which population was also falling. Federalist Virginia—the Eastern shore, Potomac Valley, and the tidewater counties—was in process of depopulation. In western Virginia, the counties which showed heavy concentrations of Federalists—Berkeley, Hampshire, Hardy, Pendleton, Bath, Augusta, Rockbridge, Botetourt, and Greenbrier—were altogether losing population during the decade 1800–1810. In North Carolina, Republican Districts such as Hillsborough and Morgan were increasing during the 1790s at the rates of 34 and 47 per cent; Federalist areas—New Bern, Wilmington, and Fayetteville—were increasing at rates of 9, 15, and 21 percent.[36]

There were exceptions, of course. Grafton, Rockingham, and Hillsborough Counties in New Hampshire, Cumberland County in Maine, Caledonia and Orleans in Vermont, Oneida, Ontario, Steuben, Chenango, and Tioga Counties in New York, Luzerne County in Pennsylvania, and the Salisbury District in North Carolina were areas with high rates of population increase which voted Federalist in 1800. Nearly all of them, however would shift to the Republican side within two or three years. There were also a few Republican counties with low rates of increase—Dukes in Massachusetts, Dutchess in New York, Newport and Washington Counties in Rhode Island, Queen Anne's in Maryland; Caroline, Louisa, Isle of Wight, Surry, Nansemond, Mathews, Brunswick, Greenville, Chesterfield, Goochland, Prince Edward, Charlotte, and Montgomery Counties in Virginia, and Edenton District in

---

[36] In the absence of total population figures for Virginia and Md. counties, calculations are made from white adult males between the ages of 26 and 45. All others are taken from figures listed in the U.S. censuses of 1790, 1800, and 1810, for total county population.

North Carolina. But altogether, there are fewer exceptions to this generalization than to any other. During the period 1800–1815, the trend would become even more clear.[37]

Population increase would appear to be a more significant indicator than length of settlement or density of population. The southeastern counties of Massachusetts, for example, appear to have been surprisingly dynamic. And it might seem at first sight that the lower Hudson counties of New York, with Long Island, should have been as mature, stable, and static as the middle Hudson counties which voted Federalist. But these southern counties, particularly Suffolk, Queens, Kings, and Westchester, had been the scene of extensive confiscations of loyalist property which by the 1790s were beginning to be broken up into smaller holdings. Census returns for all these counties show growth rates of 10 to 50 percent.[38] Similarly, the most dynamic urban areas tended to be Jeffersonian—Baltimore, a rough, disorderly boom-town in the new republic, was decidedly Republican. Philadelphia, increasing more slowly, was Federalist.[39]

The descriptive pattern is clear; but causal implications are more problematical. The "meaner sort" in stable, static areas, those who voted Federalist, could be divided into two groups—those who had no objection to elitist government and those who had no opportunity or liberty to make an objection. The motivation of the first group may have been of the sort which Erich Fromm has described in *Escape from Freedom*. A stable, structured society in a world of change and conflict may have been for them a source of security, a means of identity. Economic interests may have been involved, as they surely were in the case of a Federalist barber in the District of Columbia. "What Presidents we might have, sir!" he declared. "Just look at Daggett of Connecticut and Stockton of New Jersey! (Both prominent Federalists.) What queues they have got, sir—as big as your wrist, and powdered every day, sir, like real gentlemen as they are. Such men, sir, would confer dignity upon the chief magistracy, but this little Jim Madison, with a queue no bigger than a pipe stem! Sir, it is enough to make a man

---

[37] See, e.g., on the shift of Tioga County, N.Y., populated by "a rude fierce people," and showing a high growth rate, into the Republican camp in 1802, James Kent, "Journal," in 1802, in Kent Papers, Library of Congress.

[38] Harry B. Yoshpe, *Disposition of Loyalist Estates in the Southern District of the State of New York* (New York, 1939), pp. 113–120.

[39] A related pattern which reinforces growth rates and also conforms to patterns of partisan allegiance is the fertility ratio of whites, in America. The gross reproduction rate in 1800 was generally low in Federalist areas, high in Republican ones. See A.J. Jaffe, "Differential Fertility in the White Population in Early America," *Journal of Heredity*, XXXI (1940), 407–411.

forswear his country!" A hunger for the orders and distinctions of a deferential society was not limited to the "best of people."[40]

On the other hand, there were surely other men who were so entangled in the web of social and economic connections that they were unable to escape—bound to their station not by psychic need but by fear and interest. A Pennsylvania Federalist, Charles Biddle, detailed an example:

> Enos Clark, an honest Irish tenant of mine, called upon me the morning of the election in much distress. He said just as he was putting in his ticket, one of his friends called him to come down; that he put in the ticket and came to him, when he said, "Clark, do you know what you have been doing?" "Yes, to be sure, I have been putting in the ticket that D.S.——gave me, and he, you know, is one of us." "Damn you; do you not know you have been voting against your landlord, who has been so kind, and so good to your family?" "I hope it is not so, Mr. Biddle, for I would not do that for all the world." I comforted the poor fellow, by assuring him that on this occasion I did not want his vote."[41]

Internal emigration in the new republic may have served as a social filter, to separate the "discontented, the enterprising, the ambitious and the covetous" from such men as the Washington barber, who had an economic and psychological involvement in a deferential society, and from men such as Biddle's tenant, who was perhaps in too deep to escape or even to protest. Men who remained in the most stable and slowly changing parts of the nation, whether because they were unable or willing to leave, were for the same reasons apt to be "Friends of Order" on election day.[42]

---

[40] S.G. Goodrich, *Recollections*, I, 131–32.

[41] Biddle, *Autobiography*, p. 330.

[42] To argue thus is, of course, to touch upon the wooly problem of the frontier as "safety valve" (see Murray Kane, "Some Considerations on the Safety-Valve Doctrine," *Miss. Valley Hist. Rev.*, XXIII (1936), 169–188; Carter Goodrich and Sol Davison, "The Wage Earner in the Westward Movement," *Pol. Science Quarterly*, L (1935), pp. 161–185; LI (1936), 61–116: Fred A. Shannon, "A Post Mortem on the Labor-Safety-Valve Theory," *Agricultural History*, XVII (1945), 31–37. It may be true that men who had greatest cause for discontent were least able to ameliorate their condition by emigration, either westward to the frontier or eastward to the city. But what of the men who could lead a social movement—men who had much but wanted more? From a conservative perspective, these were the "dangerous" men—and the beneficiaries of the frontier and the expanding cities. The voting patterns of Luzerne County in Penna. and western New York would suggest that many New England emigrants were Federalists. But cf. J. Cook to Jefferson, 21 Oct. 1801, Jefferson Papers, Library of Congress. "These days there is not an Emigrant from Connecticut within this country," he wrote from Marietta, "but what is really a friend to your honor and a true Republican." Boston emigrants, however, he characterized as "hauty," "overbearing," and Federalist.

3

There were, of course, many other patterns of partisan allegiance which added complexity and color to the general problem. All are important, and as many will be discussed as the limitations of time and space allow. But in the judgment of this investigator they were subordinate to major patterns described above—they were the "underplot" of this old American tragedy, the images and shadows of a larger theme.

Partisan identity in 1800 reflected, among many other things, previous and prior political loyalties. Of these, perhaps the most important allegiance was to one's state. Larger states tended toward Republicanism; smaller ones to Federalism. The three behemoths, Virginia, Pennsylvania, and New York, were the pillars of the Jeffersonian movement. Federalism flourished better in their smaller neighbors, Connecticut, New Jersey, Delaware, Maryland, and North Carolina. Clear exceptions, of course, would be Massachusetts and Rhode Island.

American statesmen demonstrated in 1800 that they were thinking of their states first when they addressed themselves to national interests. Such considerations acted upon Bayard, the young Delaware Federalist, when he shifted his vote from Burr to Jefferson. "Representing the smallest state in the Union without resources which could furnish the means of self-protection," he wrote, "I was compelled by the obligations of a sacred duty so to act as not to hazard the constitution upon which the political existence of the state depends."[43]

Ancient rivalries between state and state, often of colonial origin, also operated in 1800. Yorkers and Yankees who had traditionally viewed each other with suspicion and even with enmity, divided on the party question—New York strongly for Jefferson, Connecticut more strongly for Adams. New Jersey, the barrel bunged at both ends by its neighbors, was also affected. "Who wish to bring New-Jersey back to their *tributary* state?" a Federalist asked, "The friends of Jefferson in New York and Pennsylvania."[44]

Virginia's neighbors, Maryland and North Carolina, showed a similar jealousy of the Old Dominion. Charles Harris was one of many Federalists in his state who complained bitterly of "our republican neighbors, the Virginians." An old-school gentleman of the Old North State declared, "the real source of our divisions . . . originates in

---

[43] James A. Bayard to John Adams, 19 Feb. 1801, in Adams Papers, reel 400. Personal considerations may have been important in this case. "I fear that the Virginia pride, will never truly appreciate a Delaware character," Bayard wrote to Caesar Rodney, 10 Dec. 1803, in Bayard Papers, New York Pub. Library; see also Lewis R. Morris to Rutledge, 27 Nov. 1803, in Rutledge Papers, Univ. of N.C.

[44] "Citizens of New-Jersey," 1800, in Broadsides, N.J. Hist. Soc.

whether. Virginia shall be everything, and other states NOTHING."[45] Another state whose citizens were also jealous of Virginia was Massachusetts. Ames believed that "two causes make our affairs turbulent, the ambition of Virginia and the spirit of jacobinism." A Republican agreed. "There is much state pride in Massachusetts," he wrote, "and federalism has been kept from sinking there by raising jealousies against Virginia."[46]

In each of these state rivalries, the large state was Jeffersonian and the little one Federalist. One other rivalry operated in the opposite direction. Federalists of Massachusetts and Connecticut were neither surprised nor particularly sorry that Rhode Island should "lend the dirty mantle of its infamy to the nakedness of *Sans-culottism*." To Fisher Ames it seemed that "Rhode Island *should* be wrong."[47]

In addition to state loyalties, local attachments were reflected in voting patterns in 1800. Most apparent were rivalries between towns — Salem versus Marblehead, Providence versus Newport were two of many. Perhaps the most important conflict of this kind appeared in Maryland, between the "two great contending parties in this state, to

---

[45] Charles W. Harris to Robert Harris, 15 Sep. 1800, in Harris Papers, Univ. of N.C.; W.R. Davie to John Steele, 25 Sep. 1803, cited in Robinson, *Davie*, p. 374.

[46] Ames to Jeremiah Smith, 14 Dec. 1802, in Ames, *Works*, I, 314; Robinson, *Jeff. Dem. in N. Eng.*, p. 152; Otis to Rutledge, 18 Oct. 1801, in Rutledge Papers, Univ. of N.C.; [Boston] *Ind. Chronicle*, 15 Oct. 1801. Fear of Virginia was reinforced, of course, by the expansion of new western states which seemed her colonies to Federalists, and with reason. In 1802, four of seven U.S. Senators and Representatives from Kentucky and Tennessee were Virginia born and bred; see *Biographical Directory of the American Congress*, and compare the exaggerated fears and statistics of the [New York] *Evening Post*, 3 Mar. 1802, which reported that 57 members of Congress were natives of the Ancient Dominion. In fact only 30 were, of whom 21 represented Virginia herself. It might be noted here that although patterns of partisan allegiance did follow state boundaries they did not follow sectional lines, at least in terms of north versus south. Sectional consciousness did exist—at least one New Englander who strayed into Virginia wrote home that he felt "more secure on the other side of the Potomac." (Tristram Dalton to Gouverneur Morris, 12 Jan. 1804, in Morris Papers, Columbia University). But there were no northern and southern parties in 1800. It was the great fear of public men that such parties would soon develop. "The time is not far distant," William Plumer wrote, "when the present parties shall be no more—and parties will then derive their names from geographical lines—a southern and western party, and an eastern party will and must exist. For our separate interests will create them." (Plumer to Daniel Plumer, 7 Feb. 1804, in Plumer Papers, Library of Congress). Geographical divisions appeared in the election of the speaker of the House of Representatives in December, 1799, and cut cleanly across party lines. (John Rutledge to Bishop Smith, 3 Dec. 1799, in Rutledge Papers, Univ. of N.C)

[47] Ames to Jeremiah Smith, 14 Dec. 1802, in Ames, *Works*, I, 314; to this rivalry could be added another that was beginning to appear in 1800 between Massachusetts and the counties of Maine which sought more autonomy. It would become more important in the period 1800–1816. See Goodman, *Democratic-Republicans of Massachusetts*, pp. 118–127, 131–132, 155–162, for a discussion of the religious and economic intricacies of this rivalry.

wit: the Baltimore and Patowmack interests," of which the former was Republican, the latter Federalist.[48]

More pervasive, more generally operative, were family connections and conflicts in a society which was still strongly familial. The "Family Compact of Connecticut" is much the most famous example, which Beard enumerated in detail. The Essex clique in eastern Massachusetts was joined by marriage bonds. In Delaware the Bayards, Bassetts, and Claytons, the Dagworthys, Mitchells, and Wellses, the Johnses and Van Dykes intermarried. The Federal Party in that state was one extended cousinage, with ties to New Jersey Federalists through the Stocktons and to Maryland Federalists through the Ridgelys. In the latter state, the Harpers and the Carrolls, Taneys and Keys, Goldsboroughs, Hansons, Ridgelys, Steretts, and Platers intertwined in the same fashion.[49]

Family connections also appeared among Republicans. Gallatin married into the Nicholsons, who were connected to Randolphs, who were connected to Jeffersons and the Nicholas clan, who were tied by two marriages to the Smiths of Baltimore. The classic case is New York politics, of course. On the Republican side were two great connections— the Clinton-Osgood-Bailey clan and the Livingston-Lewis-Armstrong-Tillotson-Cutting group. On a lower level, families of Jeffersonians as well as Federalists functioned and thought as political units. In Maine, the following Republican clique, on the Federal payroll:

Joshua Wingate, esq.	Postmaster in Hallowell
Joshua Wingate, jun.	Collector at Bath
James Wingate	Postmaster at Portland
John Wingate	Commissary for troops at Hallowell
Joseph Wingate	(Indian Agent)

And another in Fredrick County, Maryland, in the same year, 1803:

David Shriver, Esq. a delegate to the General Assembly

Abraham Shriver, his son, an associate justice of Frederick County court

Andrew Shriver, ditto, a Justice of the Peace

---

[48] [Boston] *Independent Chronicle*, 9 July 1801; Robinson, *Jeff. Dem. in N. Eng.*, p. 83; [Annapolis] *Maryland Gazette*, 14 Aug. 1800; Benjamiin Stoddert to John Templeman, n.d., in Stoddert Papers, Library of Congress.

[49] Beard, *Econ. Origins of Jeff. Dem.*, p. 364; Fischer, "Myth of the Essex Junto," p. 197; J.D. Phillips in *Essex Institute Hist. Colls.*, XXXIII (1897), 299; [Boston] *New England Palladium*, 25 Mar. 1803; Munroe, *Federalist Delaware*, passim; Conrad, *Delaware*, III, 830;*Sussex Co. Records*, 295–317; G.P. Fisher, "Recollections of Dover in 1824," *Hist. Soc. Del. Papers*, LV, 24–27; Fischer, "Metamorphosis of Maryland Federalism," pp. 9–11.

Andrew Shriver, a Justice of the Levy Court

John Schley, a son-in-law of David Shriver, a Justice of the Peace

John Schley, a Justice of the Orphan's Court

Henry Leatherman, father-in-law of one of the Shrivers, a Supervisor of the Roads [and] supplier to the Jail and Courthouse, &c &c.[50]

At least one prior political conflict which had affected many parts of the new nation was reflected in the voting patterns of 1800. Men who had been Tories in the Revolution, and regions which were heavily populated with them, tended to be Federalist. Leaders of the Federal Party were, of course, more than a little uncomfortable about that fact, but in private correspondence they cheerfully acknowledged it. "Soon after we regained possession of New York," Robert Troup wrote, "we permitted the Tories to enlist under our banners; and they have since manfully fought by our side in every important battle we have had with the democracy; some of them in the character of officers, others in those of common soldiers." Areas in which Tories had been numerous and in which Federalism flourished included, in addition to New York City, downstate Delaware, Virginia's eastern shore, Norfolk, and the Cape Fear region around Fayetteville, North Carolina.[51]

Revolutionary Whigs, on the other hand, were divided; each party traced its lineage back to 1776 and cherished its own particular Revolutionary heroes. One pattern within this group appears—men who served as officers for extended periods in the Continental Army tended toward Federalism. Despite many exceptions, Monroe, Armstrong, Smith and others, Beveridge's suggestion that John Marshall's national principles, and perhaps his elitism, were strengthened if not originally implanted by his military experience.[52]

---

[50] *Letters on the Richmond Party*, #1; "To the Independent Electors of the State [of N.Y.], *N.Y. Election Broadsides*, p. 29; see John Adams in Jefferson, 15 Nov. 1813, in Cappon, ed. *Adams-Jefferson Letters*, II, 401. "In New York it is a struggle of Family Feuds"; see also Sedgwick to King, 24 Aug. 1802, in *King*, IV, 162. "The great line of division by which parties are separated in other states is more obscurely marked there [N.Y.] than anywhere else—the people are more under the dominion of personal influence." The local cliques were described by Federalists and republished in the [Boston] *N. Eng. Palladium*, 1 Mar. and 23 Sep. 1803, from local journals. Another state in which family connections were important was Rhode Island; see Hamilton to Bayard, 6 Aug. 1800, in Lodge, *Hamilton*, X, 386; the full reach of family influence in early American politics remains to be established by a careful student of genealogy and local history; this investigator can only endorse J.F. Jameson's suggestion that an important dissertation could be written upon the subject of early American mothers-in-law.

[51] Troup to King, 4 Apr. 1809, in *King* V, 148; [New York] *American Citizen*, 22 Mar. 1800; Hammond, *Pol. Parties N.Y.*, I, 223.

[52] Beveridge, *John Marshall*, I, 144–147.

Another early conflict is less easily related to the events of 1800. It is difficult to establish a clear connection between the Federalist-Republican division in 1800 and the Federalist-anti-Federalist cleavage in 1788. The cautious conclusions of Noble Cunningham are generally sustained by my research. In New York and Pennsylvania there were continuities between the parties to the argument 1787–1788, and the more structured parties of 1800. But in other states similar patterns do not appear. Of the four most prominent anti-Federalists in Maryland, three became Federalists in 1800. A Jeffersonian wrote of Delaware in 1800 that "most opponents of the Constitution in 1787 are now friends of order." In North Carolina, the Federalist regions of 1800 had been "anti-Federalist" ten years earlier. An able secondary account of Virginia politics minimizes continuities in that state as well. New England requires more thorough research—but there was surely little continuity in New Hampshire. Massachusetts and Connecticut remain doubtful.[53]

4

Ethnic voting patterns in 1800 were clear to contemporary observers of political behavior. The Irish, who were beginning to pour into the great "flour cities" of the middle states and into New England as well, were overwhelmingly Republican. Many were political refugees; all

---

[53] Cunningham, *Jeffersonian Republicans*, pp. 3, 23, 142, 218; Tinkcom, *Republicans and Federalists in Penna.*, p. 31; Young, "The Democratic-Republican Movement in New York State, 1788–97"; Harry Ammon, "The Formation of the Republican Party in Virginia," pp. 309–310; Fischer, "Metamorphosis of Maryland Federalism," p. 10; [Wilmington] *Mirror*, 5 Apr. 1800; Samuel Miller to John Jay, 17 Mar. 1800, in *Jay*, IV, 263; Goodman, *The Democratic-Republicans of Mass*, takes no clear position on this question, but stresses the "fluidity of politics" in Massachusetts during the '90s. Charles Beard's efforts to establish a relationship between the contests of 1789 and 1800 are not merely inconclusive, as Cunningham has pointed out (p. 23n) but grossly inaccurate. Forty-two members of the Convention can be clearly connected to one or the other party in 1800. Of these, seventeen (not Beard's twelve) contradict the Beardian hypothesis; twenty-five (not thirty-one) support it. Federalists of 1787 who became Jeffersonians included Baldwin, Blount, Butler, Dickinson, Few, Gilman, William Houstoun, Langdon, Madison, Alexander Martin, Charles Pinckney, Randolph, Rutledge, Spaight, and Wythe. Two anti-Federalists became Federalists in 1800, Martin and Yates. Unclassifiable are Brearly, Carroll, Franklin, Gorham, Houston, Jenifer, Livingston, McClurg, Mason, Robert Morris, Pierce, Sherman, and Williamson; cf. Beard, *Economic Origins of Jeffersonian Democracy*, pp. 34–84. There is, as Beard claims, impressionistic testimony supporting his hypothesis, but there is also much against it. In North Carolina, for example, an attempt to demonstrate in 1806 that a politician was a Federalist of the latter-day variety supplied as evidence the fact that he had opposed the Constitution in 1788! Untitled circular, July 1806, in Lenoir Papers, Southern Hist. Coll., Univ. of N.C.

felt the bite of prejudice in the Anglo-American republic. There were the inevitable exceptions—Irishmen such as Thomas FitzSimons who had emigrated before the War of Independence and became an important Federalist in Pennsylvania. But Republicans and Federalists agreed upon the rule.[54]

French immigrants appear to have been as generally Republican as the Irish, notwithstanding an occasional émigré who became a "friend of order and good government." Of 311 Frenchmen who voted in Charleston in 1812, all but seven favored the Republican ticket. The six or seven hundred Frenchmen who had settled in Philadephia by 1808 were reported to be nearly unanimous for the Democratic cause.[55]

The Germans of Pennsylvania and Maryland had generally voted for Federalist candidates in the mid 1790s, but in 1800 were generally, if not enthusiastically, Republican. Contemporaries explained the shift as a reaction to the threat of direct taxation and to the repression of Fries' Rebellion. In 1805 they would show a clear preference for moderate rather than radical Republicans. In 1814, the threat of Republican taxes would drive many of them back to the Federalists.[56]

Free Negroes, in the states which permitted them to vote, appear to have been divided; torn, perhaps, between the ideals of the Republican movement and its slave-owning leadership. Courted by both parties on election day, spurned by both parties through the rest of the year, they appear to have split their votes.[57]

Only two non-English ethnic groups leaned to Federalism in 1800 and afterwards: the old Dutch families of the Hudson valley, and Scottish merchants and factors who were sufficiently numerous to be politically significant in Richmond, Norfolk, New Bern, Wilmington, Charleston, and Savannah. Altogether, the party which in 1800 some-

---

[54] King, *Life and Corresp. of King*, II, 635–648; V, 15–20; "Federalist Persecution," 1802, in Broadsides, Library of Congress; John Adams to James Lloyd, 14 Feb. 1815, in Adams-Lloyd Letters, Harvard Univ., P.A. Jay to John Jay, 18 Feb. 1808, in Jay Papers, Columbia Univ.; Morison, *Otis*, I, 108; Howe to Prevost, c. May, 1809, *Amer. Hist. Rev.*, XVII (1913), 344; Ames to Gore, 18 Dec. 1798, in Ames, *Works*, I, 247; [Boston] *New England Palladium*, 7 Feb. 1804, 29 Aug. 1809; Robert Troup to Peter Van Schaack, 27 Oct. 1799, in Van Schaack Papers, Library of Congress.

[55] [Boston] *New England Palladium*, 21 Oct. 1808; Rutledge to Otis, to Nov. 1812, in Otis Papers, Mass. Hist. Soc.; C.J. Ingersoll to King, 11 May 1807, in *King*, V, 36; Echeverria, *Mirage in the West*, p. 187.

[56] Adams to Jefferson, 15 Nov. 1813, in Cappon, ed., *Adams-Jefferson Letters*, II 401; Adams to James Lloyd, 14 Feb. 1815, in Adams-Lloyd Letters, Harvard Univ.; C.W. Hare to Otis, 21 Oct. 1814, in Otis Papers, Mass. Hist. Soc.; Andreas Dorpalen, "The German Element in Early Penna. Politics," *Penna. Hist.*, IX (1942), 176–190.

[57] [Hartford] *Conn. Courant*, 7 Sep. 1803; Bentley, *Diary*, IV, 90; II, 366; [Boston] *Ind. Chronicle*, 3 Nov. 1800; 29 Jan. 1801; [New York] *Evening Post*, 10 Apr. 1805.

times called itself "Federal-American" or "True-American" or "American-Republican" was deeply suspicious of all men who were not old-stock Anglo-American and received their hostility in turn.[58]

5

Religious patterns were of great importance in 1800. In New England, the established Congregational churches were, despite recent attempts at reinterpretation, bastions of Federalism. But New England's establishments had acquired many enemies by 1800, both within and without their folds, and most were Jeffersonian. The ripples of revivalism which continued to overspread New England contributed to the fragmentation of the Congregational churches which had begun early in the century. And wherever a religious controversy appeared in the quiet New England countryside, it blurred into the partisan conflict. Specific alignments were difficult to predict, but from theological commitments one generalization is indisputable—a religious faction in Massachusetts, Connecticut, or New Hampshire which felt that it had more to gain than lose from a union of church and state was certain to be Federalist. Edwardsian Calvinists who suspected the establishments of a tendency toward Arminianism, Unitarianism, or worse were, in the judgment of Parson Bentley, more often Jeffersonian than not. On the other side, some Unitarians and many Universalists who found the prevailing temper of the established churches to be too orthodox, were, in John Adams's considered opinion, rarely in the Federal camp. And of course nearly all the sects and denominations which were expanding in New England were apt to be Jeffersonian—be they Irish Catholic or Anabaptist, Methodist or Episcopalian.[59]

In other parts of the Union, three religious groups were generally Jeffersonian—Baptists, Jews, and Irish Catholics. The Baptist Church

---

[58] Fox, *Decline of Aristocracy in New York*, pp. 31–34; Biddle, *Autobiography*, pp. 325–326; Baltimore *Federal Republican*, 17 July 1811; *Boston Centinel*, 22 Mar. 1800; Leonard Chester to Ephraim Kirby, 26 Sep. 1800, in Kirby Papers, Duke Univ. Library.

[59] It is very difficult to estimate the reach of Jeffersonian politics among the Congregational clergy of New England. One of them wrote from New Haven, "Being the only Democratical Preacher in the state who dares to speak I am, of course, the object of persecution." J. Gemmel to Ashbel Green, 7 Nov. 1800, in Gratz Coll. (Clergy), Hist. Soc. Penna. How many did not dare to speak out remains an open question. Bentley, *Diary*, III, 364–365; Adams to Lloyd, 14 Feb. 1815, in Adams-Lloyd Letters, Harvard Univ.; William Hart to Ephraim Kirby, 12 Apr. 1803, in Kirby Papers, Duke Univ.; Hall, *Benjamin Tallmadge*, p. 187; [Boston] *N. Eng. Palladium*, 11 June 1811; Robinson, *Jeff. Dem. N. Eng.*, p. 132; Goodman, *Democratic-Republicans of Mass.*, pp. 86–96; Sedgwick to King, 24 Aug. 1802, in *King*, IV, 161; [Warren] *Bristol Co. Register*, 1 Apr. 1809; Chase, *Johnathan Fisher*, pp. 236–237; Dwight, *Travels*, II, 65; M. Cutler to Pickering, 5 Jan. 1809, in Pickering Papers, Mass. Hist. Soc.; Mead, *Taylor*, p. 44, Joslin, *Poultney*, pp. 74–75.

in Londonderry, Vermont, which excommunicated four of its members for joining the Washington Benevolent Society, appears to have been representative in its politics if not in its zeal. Even in Virginia it was said that Baptists were "almost universally Republican."[60]

Notice was taken in chapter VIII of Jews in politics, and specifically of Benjamin Nones, who publicly declared, "I am a Jew, and if for no other reason, for that reason am I a republican." There were exceptions—Jacob Henry, the North Carolina Jew who figured in a notable test of religious liberty, had been the victim of discrimination less for his religion, perhaps, than his politics—he was a Federalist. But notwithstanding this and other exceptions, the antisemitism which appeared in Federalist tracts during the 1790s had effectively alienated another minority group.[61]

The Irish and French voters who supported Jefferson in 1800 were, of course, generally Catholic. Their religion did not cause their political commitment, but a descriptive pattern is clear. On the other hand, English Catholics in Maryland were described as Federalist "almost without exception."[62]

Two other religious groups were generally Federalist—Methodists on the Delmarva peninsula, and Scotch-Irish Presbyterians in western Virginia and the Cape Fear region of North Carolina. Jefferson himself wrote that "the string of counties at the Western foot of the Blue ridge settled originally by Irish presbyterians [composes] precisely the tory [Federalist] district of the state." Local historians have discussed the relevance of Methodism to Federalist strength in Delmarva, and of Presbyterianism in the Cape Fear region.[63]

6

Each of these patterns, as has already been noted, served to qualify all the others. Men were caught up by them in different and often conflicting and sometimes unique ways. It remains only to remind the reader that these patterns are descriptive and not necessarily causal.

---

[60] Cudworth, *Londonderry*, p. 51; [Philadelphia] *Aurora*, 2 Oct. 1800; one can wonder whether Republicans or Baptists gained more from their assocation; surely it was mutually advantageous. Bentley, *Diary*, II, 409; Dwight, *Travels*, II, 34; Jeremiah Smith to William Plumer, 11 Mar. 1804, in Plumer Papers, Library of Congress; [New London] *Bee*, 8 Oct. 1800.

[61] [Phila.] *Aurora*, 13 Aug. 1800; memo dated 8 Mar. 1801, in Jefferson Papers, Library of Congress; [Philadelphia] *Gazette of the U.S.*, 16 July 1800; Schauinger, *William Gaston*, p. 54; antisemitism was not restricted to Federalists; see Mann, *Yankee Jeffersonian*, p. 46; [Chilicothe] *Supporter*, 24 Mar. 1810.

[62] Thomas Dwight to wife, 28 Dec. 1804, in Dwight-Howard Papers, Mass. Hist. Soc.

[63] Jefferson to Horatio Gates Spofford, 10 Jan. 1816, in Ford, *Jefferson*, X, 13; Munroe, *Federalist Delaware*, pp. 239–240; Gilpatrick, *Jeffersonian Democracy in N.C.*, pp. 18 passim.

Did men take possession of the land, or did the land take possession of them? Were they masters or servants of their interests? Dilemmas such as this cannot be resolved by appeals to historical evidence. The historian must yield to the theologian.

Sectionalism

Richard Buel, Jr.

Richard Buel's Securing the Revolution: Ideology in American Politics, 1789–1815 (Ithaca, N.Y.: Cornell University Press, 1972) is a book of many facets. A history of the first party struggle from its origins to the conclusion of the War of 1812, as well as a description of the different ideologies of the warring parties, it also offers an analysis of the configuration of the partisan division. Starting with the obvious polarity between New England and the South and building on the insights of David Hackett Fischer, Paul Goodman, and others, Buel identifies the social situation of assorted regional elites as the essential key to the prevailing pattern. This selection reproduces most of Chapter 4 of Securing the Revolution, *along with a concluding word (pages 72–89 and 186). Copyright ©1972 by Cornell University. Used by permission of the publisher, Cornell University Press.*

If the first party system originated in an ideological disagreement among political leaders which afterward gradually spread to the general public, what explains the sectional character of alignments? Not that any region was ever unanimous in its political sympathies: in every state there were factional disagreements within the leadership on both local and national matters. And as might have been expected from the increasing public involvement in politics, there was no area whose political complexion was invariable. For a brief moment in 1798–1799 it seemed as if Republicanism might die in the South, and in 1803–1807 New England Federalists seemed to be threatened with extinction. Such long-term changes as did occur, though, usually confirmed the sectional character of alignments. South Carolina's shift to Republicanism after 1800 ensured homogeneity with the rest of the South. In the North, Massachusetts, Rhode Island, New Hampshire, and Vermont flirted with Republicanism in the first decade of the century but cooled toward it in the second and eventually rejoined Connecticut to confirm the Federalist character of New England during the War of 1812. The Middle Atlantic states were less decided in their allegiance, but the Republicans gradually gained ascendancy in the larger states while the smaller ones continued to show Federalist proclivities. Yet these were minor deviations from a generally sharp division in national politics which Fisher Ames of Massachusetts noticed as early as 1790, observing that in contrast to the South, "the zeal for supporting the government and the strength, too, are principally on this side of the Hudson."[1]

Because regional economic differentiation corresponded roughly to the political divisions in the first party system, some historians have offered an economic explanation for its sectionalism. Stated in its simplest form, this argument asserts that New England was Federalist because the commerce which predominated there was favored by the Federalist party, while the South was Republican because that party espoused its agrarian interests. The Middle Atlantic states shared characteristics with both regions, and consequently their loyalties were divided.[2]

Unfortunately for this explanation, many agrarians were Federalists while many merchants were Republicans. It is hard to attribute the strength of New England Federalism to commercialism once we know that the region's Republican leadership was as mercantile in orientation as its adversaries, while some of the staunchest supporters of Federalism came from isolated rural areas.[3] And it becomes less satisfactory to account for the South's Republicanism as the necessary concomitant of its agrarianism when we learn that in the 1790s the planters of the Northern Neck and eastern shore of Virginia were all Federalists, as well as inhabitants of the Shenandoah counties in the interior.[4] Southern mercantile centers were generally Federalist, and the Northern Neck and Valley counties of Virginia were the most commercial in the state, but in Maryland and Delaware this pattern was reversed. Although commercial Baltimore produced several Federalist leaders, it soon became the stronghold of the state's Republican party, obliging Federalists there to seek political allies in the rural, slaveholding counties of the south and east.[5] Similarly, in Delaware the most commercial county was Republican, while the rural southern counties were Federalist.[6]

That there were Republican merchants and Federalist farmers is not really surprising. Many of the issues which served as a focus when the first parties were being formed presented economic choices which contained elements of ambiguity, as the Jay Treaty shows. It is true that merchants who had been despoiled by the seizures in late 1793 had an economic interest in the treaty. But those who had suffered most by the Instruction of November 6, 1793, had been trading in the French empire, and may well have thought that the prospect of indemnity was not worth the risk of a war with France just when she was gaining the upper hand in Europe.[7] In raising the issue of war and peace, the treaty may have led a majority of merchants to conclude that collaboration with a power like Britain was more prudent than challenge.[8] Yet even collaboration had more than one side to it, as the controversy over the Embargo was to show some ten years later. Though the Embargo would injure commerce for a time, the long-term interests of American merchants would certainly not be served by cooperation with British efforts to control world commerce, which doomed their own to permanent, colonial subordination.[9] And if merchants came to disagree about the economic effects of certain measures, either because they had different interests or because they perceived them differently, no wonder if men of other livelihoods, with less immediate reason to look at each government measure in economic terms, were also in disagreement about them. Although the perception of economic interest did influence the politics of many individuals and some regions, it does not provide a comprehensive explanation for party alignments.

The same complexities hamper attempts to attribute sectionalism to the different military experiences of the regions during the war.[10] New England saw only sporadic action after March 1776, and that mostly favorable to the patriot cause. Even before Saratoga, British operations had been largely restricted to military objectives, and afterward it was clear that she had given up trying to conquer the North. As these hopes faded, however, she turned her attention to the South. Though she was no more successful, for the rest of the war the South suffered from the rape of the countryside by British expeditionary forces. Georgia and South Carolina were conquered for a short time, and the struggle became a vicious civil war in which no one was safe. In South Carolina it continued long after the surrender at Yorktown.[11] Though the French had failed the deep South in 1779, when the attempt to recapture Savannah aborted, southerners had to admit that the French army and navy had been essential to achieving Cornwallis's submission. It would therefore be possible to argue that the South inclined to Republicanism because she so vividly remembered the fight against Britain and the help brought by France, and because the European wars reawakened stronger feelings there than in the North.

While this was undoubtedly an ingredient in the sectionalism of foreign policy alignments from 1795 to 1815, there remain some awkward questions. Why should the leadership in that part of the South which had been most barbarously treated by Britain in the early 1780s be the most favorably inclined toward her in the 1790s? Why should the Federalist leadership of the northeastern states be pro-British? Though northerners did not hate Britain as much as southerners did, the New England coastline had suffered from British raids throughout the war, and they were far from Anglophiles. They also knew how much the French had helped in winning the war, and to judge from the observations of foreigners, not to mention the celebrations of French victories, which took place in New England ports during the early days of the European war, they had not forgotten this in the 1790s.[12] Later, when France began to disgrace herself, particularly in the XYZ affair, New

Englanders certainly did grow cool toward her. But this was also true of southerners.

Though an interpretation that emphasizes residual hatreds from the war speaks to the foreign policy orientation of the first parties, it has another serious limitation. In stressing grass-roots sentiment in the formation of the first parties, it ignores how much the national leadership took the initiative, particularly in the early phase, or how much political consciousness filtered from it down to the people, and from the metropolitan centers outward to the provinces.[13] It should not be forgotten that the character of American politics in the 1790s was still predominantly premodern; that is, many of the leadership assumed that they would be the principal force at work in shaping public opinion. Though the Revolution had proved that leaders who persistently defied the people's wishes could not hope to remain in power, and had briefly inspired a mass politics, most politicians regarded this as an anomalous interlude and looked to a gradual reversion to normality in the postwar period. The wide difference of opinion between leaders and led during 1793–1795 on the subject of accommodation with Great Britain showed that in many areas the Federalists still felt they had substantial discretion in choosing their course. It also suggests that during the formative stage of the first party system, the disposition of the regional leadership was often more critical than anything else in determining the political complexion of an area.

I

Focusing on the regional leadership seems at first to raise more problems than it solves. There was an obvious difference in their social characteristics that might explain their differing politics, but the relationship seems inverted. The aristocratic character of the southern leadership ought to have made them hostile to the French Revolution and strongly Federalist. More than any other group, southern planters had reason to fear the implications of events in France and their reflection in the rebellion on Santo Domingo. On the other hand, New Englanders, who had neither slaves nor a notably aristocratic social structure, should have been good Republicans hailing their French brothers with delight. Instead, Fisher Ames assailed southerners as "Frenchified" and "violent republicans," while the southern leadership regarded their New England counterparts as advocates of monarchy. The tension between the two parties was even increased by this incongruity, for each suspected the other of hypocrisy.[14]

Shays's Rebellion sheds some light on the anomaly. No New Englander would ever have written, as Jefferson wrote to Madison in 1787, that "a little rebellion now and then is a good thing, and as necessary in the political world as storms in the physical."[15] On the other hand, no one but a New Englander would have written, as "A Friend of Government" wrote in the *Columbian Centinel*, that "any attempt by an individual to lessen [the] respectability [of members of the government] or to alienate the affection of the publick" by insinuating "that the *General Government is pursuing measures, most destructive to the welfare and interest of the people*" threatened the country with "anarchy and confusion." In effect, this writer was asserting that any criticism of government was liable to destroy it.[16] The fear that libel would bring down government, and the accompanying desire to compensate for this by enhancing its dignity with high salaries and titles, may indeed have been produced in New England's Federalists by Shays's Rebellion. And the comparative freedom from such pressures that was enjoyed by southern leaders may have been the happy result of avoiding such disturbing upheavals.[17] Patrick Henry boasted in his state's ratifying convention that no country had been "so long without a rebellion" as Virginia, despite the burdens that the war had imposed upon her.[18]

Though differences in rhetorical and ceremonial emphasis may be attributed to Shays's Rebellion, it cannot be invoked as the sole cause of sectional alignment. As the first widespread insurrection in New England's history, it was certainly one reason why the northern leadership longed for a strong central government with power to repress such outbreaks. Yet this need was felt in the South too. The Revolution had proved that the presence of slaves was a handicap to southerners when they were obliged to defend themselves against foreign invasion, a factor which helped Federalists in South Carolina plead for ratification of the Constitution.[19] Even in peacetime there was always a danger of slave rebellion. It is possible to argue that the South had grown accustomed to the danger, and that having survived a revolution in which an invader tried to incite such rebellion, they knew now that the danger was not as great as they had formerly feared. But the experience of Santo Domingo could not have reassured them. Indeed the leading student of Negro slave revolts has found that "the dozen years following 1790 formed a period of more intense and widespread slave discontent than any that had preceded."[20] And if the fear of insurrection was the cause of New England's Federalism, Pennsylvania should have made the same response to the Whiskey and Fries's rebellions, and Virginia to her narrow escape from the aborted Gabriel's rebellion. But on the contrary, Virginia remained unshakably Republican, while in Pennsylvania the Republican party continued to gain strength.[21]

This is not to say that Shays's Rebellion had no effect upon political arguments in the 1790s, but that it was more symptomatic than causative. William L. Smith struck the proper balance when he observed to Edward Rutledge that "the influence the great body of the people in

Massachusetts have in the state government & the insurrection of Shays co-operate to make these gentlemen great favorers of monarchy."[22] Smith's comment is one of the few contemporary efforts to account precisely for the anomalous distribution of ideologies that characterized the beginning of the first party system. By and large the problem was ignored while the leadership of each section trotted out pat explanations for the acts of the other. Southerners attributed the "monarchical" inclination of New England leaders partly to the influence of commercial interests dependent on British capital, partly to the inevitable lust for power of depraved men.[23] New Englanders in turn attributed the South's Republicanism to her people's reluctance to pay their heavy debts to British creditors.[24] Both theories were attractive because they tended to enhance the stereotypes that each region already attached to the other. I know of only one studied attempt to transcend this narrow view and relate the ideological predisposition of regional leaders to their social characteristics, and that was made by Fisher Ames. He tried to analyze sectional antagonism in a letter written to George Richards Minot in 1791. This letter, together with some comments in an earlier one, provides a complex discussion of why the southern leadership was so fervently Republican. It also inadvertently sheds light on the Federalism of New England's leaders and confirms the insight of William Smith.

As early as July 1789, Ames had denounced the southern nabobs as "new lights in politics; who would not make the law, but the people, king; who would have a government all checks; who are more solicitous to establish, or rather to expatiate upon, some high-sounding principle of republicanism, than to protect property, cement the union, and perpetuate liberty."[25] In 1791 he tendered this more analytic explanation:

> To the northward, we see how necessary it is to defend property by steady laws. Shays confirmed our habits and opinions. The men of sense and property, even a little above the multitude, wish to keep the government in force enough to govern. We have trade, money, credit and industry, which is at once cause and effect of the others.
>
> At the southward, a few gentlemen govern; the law is their coat of mail; it keeps off the weapons of the foreigners, their creditors, and at the same time it governs the multitude, secures negroes, etc., which is of double use to them. It is both government and anarchy, and in each case is better than any possible change, especially in favor of an exterior (or federal) government of any strength; for that would be losing the property, the usufruct of a government, by the States, which is light to bear and convenient to manage. Therefore, and for other causes, the men of weight in the four southern states (Charleston city excepted) were more generally *antis*, and are now far more turbullent than they are with us. Many were federal among them at first, because they needed

some remedy to evils which they saw and felt, but mistook, in their view of it, the remedy. A debt-compelling government is no remedy to men who have lands and negroes, and debts and luxury, but neither trade nor credit, nor cash, nor habits of industry, or of submission to a rigid execution of law.[26]

Ames was still not free of the notion that southern leaders based their politics on the desire to dodge debts, but he went considerably beyond this in contrasting the disciplined lives of New Englanders to the "turbullent" southern aristocracy, which had no "habits of industry, or of submission to a rigid execution of the law." Here he was drawing an analogy between the political styles of Shays's rebels and the southern leadership.[27] More than this, he was suggesting that southern leaders would carry their opposition to effective government further than northern antifederalists, whom he believed "would not be the least zealous to support the Union" if the crisis that he foresaw were reached. Ames attributed southern extremism to southern strength: "Virginia, North Carolina and Georgia are large territories. Being strong, and expecting by increase to be stronger, the government of Congress over them seems mortifying to their State pride. The pride of the strong is not soothed by yielding to a stronger."[28] The statement betrayed a fear, shared by northern Federalists in general, that the political future belonged to the South. But to New Englanders there was another way in which the South appeared enviably strong. More important in shaping the ideologies of the respective leaderships was the ability of the "few gentlemen" who governed in the South to take their dominance for granted, or, in Ames's term, to regard the government as their "property." This contrasted dramatically with Smith's observation that the New England leadership felt insecure and threatened by the "influence of the great body of the people."

Federalist leaders were understandably shy of drawing this difference to public attention, yet they bore indirect witness to it by their loud and frequent criticisms of the southern leadership as lazy, undisciplined, and in Ames's words riddled with "debts and luxury." Ames's caricature became a northern stereotype of southern leaders as corrupt, debt-evading, irresponsible gentry who could be conveniently summed up in the invidious word "Jacobin."[29] Though there is some evidence that less prominent southern whites could and did indulge in a barnyard style of life, this was a grossly distorted picture of the aristocracy.[30] Virginian leaders like Jefferson and Madison had attained standing by strenuously cultivating their talents, and the economic adjustments that had to be made in the thirty years after the Revolution required that even the wealthiest plantation owner show entrepreneurial talent if he was to survive. But it did reveal what northern Federalists thought made their southern counterparts different from themselves. They believed that land-owning, slaveholding southern aristocrats could afford lax behavior because their social position was established by their property, whereas in New England there were few visible distinctions of wealth and family. Therefore, the leadership's position depended more on the less tangible claim of superior virtue and ability, which in turn rested upon ascetic discipline and the dedicated cultivation of talents.

The differences Ames hinted at were not just the product of over fertile northern imaginations. Their real existence was reflected in the contrast between the southern aristocracy's genial tolerance of different life styles and the antagonism with which northern Federalists greeted any behavior that implied a disregard for the attributes distinguishing them from the rest of the population.[31] Another striking illustration is the difference in sectional attitudes toward the code duello. In one, it was accepted as the distinguishing mark of a gentleman; in the other, it was utterly condemned. A leadership dependent on talent alone cannot tolerate a code of "honor" that might jeopardize its very existence. Honor of this kind is not a puritan virtue. It can be gained without rigorous discipline and prolonged application, demanding no more than the willingness to risk one's neck. It is the creature of impulse and chance, as open to the vulgar as to the wise and good, and the New England leadership despised it. When Thomas Blount challenged George Thacher, a representative from Massachusetts, Thacher had no hesitation in refusing. In the South, this might have cost him his reputation; in New England, it was matter for congratulation. New Englanders were not impervious to questions of honor, but believed they must be decided by public opinion rather than a bullet. Though on a few occasions New England congressmen did fight duels, this was never an accepted way of solving differences. In the North, Burr lost his reputation forever after he killed the most talented leader the Federalists possessed. But in the South right up until the Civil War the duel was a permissible indiscretion, if not a necessary part of a gentleman's background, even though society paid a price for tolerating killers among the elite.[32]

These facts could also be interpreted as showing that the southern leadership was not more but less secure in its identity, and that dueling became fashionable partly because social instability in the period between the Revolution and the Civil War created the need for a means of distinguishing the gentry. Certainly the duel performed this function, but it may well be that what was in question in the South was not so much elite rule as who was to exercise it. No elite not completely secure in its institutional foundations could tolerate such a mode of designation. Some more prominent southern leaders who were themselves distinguished for their talents did try to outlaw the custom, but the majority refused to see such statutes enforced because they would not part with so convenient a way of asserting superiority over the common man. It was different in New England. There the problem was less who belonged to the elite than whether those whose claim to membership rested upon talent would continue to wield the authority they believed themselves entitled to. Because New England Federalists thought dueling incompatible with preserving a social order dependent on their form of leadership, they condemned it unanimously and remained determined in their efforts to suppress it.[33]

II

If it is correct to say that the northern and southern elites were so differently situated in their respective societies, then their apparently anomalous ideological preferences begin to make sense. For if party affiliation depended on a judgment about the viability of republican government, it is not hard to see how this would be affected by a man's local situation. A sense of security in a leadership role would encourage faith in the republic, while the reverse would lead to doubt. It is beyond the scope of this study to discuss why the southern elite should have felt more secure than the northern elite. That is a complex subject worth a book in itself. But in retrospect, the different experiences of the elite in both regions as they tried to preserve and perpetuate themselves during the early nineteenth century show that there was reason for southern confidence and northern doubt.

In the North, Federalists experienced great difficulty in keeping the older settlements deferential to their pretensions. And for the most part, they failed to extend either their authority or their kind of leadership to the new western settlements where dissident New Englanders went in ever increasing numbers after 1780. The southern leadership could do both with apparent ease, and had a capacity for lateral extension which gave powerful testimony to its stability. The apex of Virginia's leadership continued to broaden throughout the eighteenth century. In spite of soil exhaustion, or often because of it, members of established families were willing to take up lands in the west, providing a natural leadership for the newer settlements. In the same way prominent Virginia families, like the Nicholases, the Bullitts, the Taylors, and the Breckenridges, were extended into Kentucky, while the Claibornes spread into Tennessee along with the Bentons and Blounts of North Carolina. This does not mean that the movement west did not make for greater social mobility in the Old South. Everyone knows the story of how Andrew Jackson began humble and became eminent. Such mobility as there was, however, tended to confirm the character of southern society by preserving the hegemony of the great plantation owners. Anyone on the rise usually copied their example and diverted profits into slaves. The possession of slaves then raised them above their poorer neighbors and gave them the advantage in competing for public honors, at the same time as it imposed solidarity upon all whites to gather for protection behind the plantation leadership.[34]

New England leaders had no such aids to self-preservation. Most of them were so dependent upon commerce that they could not migrate without forfeiting economic power. At the same time, diversified economic expansion was not congenial to the preservation of elite rule, because new areas of production had new and different interests and were determined to make their presence felt in politics. Sometimes expansion did strengthen the Federalist leadership because potential challengers were migrating to other states. This happened in Connecticut and Massachusetts, where already a large population was taxing limited resources. But more often, and particularly in states like New York and Pennsylvania, which still contained large unsettled areas, the long-term effect was to endanger the political hegemony of a restricted elite. Some commercial centers met the challenge well, but mostly because of their economic power. The South, on the other hand, had a simpler social structure that gave the region more flexibility. Economic uniformity produced few problems that could not be easily solved by the planters. Though the new cotton lands were often more prosperous than older areas, they posed no threat to the foundations of southern society because the old families and institutions had been extended into them. And the dependence of the elite upon slavery encouraged mutual forbearance and cooperation among themselves, as well as deference on the part of poorer whites.[35]

There were exceptions. In some parts of the South, the traditional elite was threatened by anomalous circumstances. In South Carolina there was a rift between the slaveholding planters of the eastern tidewater and the small, upcountry farmers who owned few slaves. The small farmers had gone to the uplands because they lacked the capital to turn seacoast swamps into rice-producing plantations. The large plantation owners had not followed because the region's principal cash crop could be grown only in the low-country tidal areas. Tension between the two sections was inevitable given their contrasting social systems. But it was heightened by differences in origin. The tidewater inhabitants had come from the cosmopolitan centers of the North Atlantic and retained close contact with them. The backcountry folk hailed largely from the interior of North Carolina, Virginia, and Pennsylvania. The cultural chasm between the two, described in Charles Woodmason's journal of his travels in the backcountry just before the Revolution, was made still wider by the colony's political institutions. The backcountry was virtually excluded from direct representation in the Commons House of Assembly and until the late colonial period was dependent on the tidewater even for the administration of justice.[36]

The immediate effect of the Revolution was to remove some of the grosser inequities by extending representation to the backcountry in the constitutions of 1776 and 1778. But the concessions made by no means altered tidewater planter hegemony,[37] which was not effectively challenged until the British invasion of the South in 1779. The prerevolutionary concentration of leadership along the coast and particularly around Charleston, made it vulnerable to British military operations in 1779–1780. The British occupation had disastrous results for most of the aristocracy, forcing them either to accept British protection in order to save their property, or to endure forcible removal to St. Augustine after the surrender of Charleston and the defeat at Camden. Those who escaped both fates, like Governor John Rutledge, were nevertheless obliged to rely on the backcountry for most of their political and military support. After the British had established their supremacy in conventional warfare, the patriot remnant turned to guerilla tactics which, though brilliantly effective, were also more socially disruptive than the traditional way of fighting. For two years after the fall of Charleston, American military operations in South Carolina were often conducted by partisan bands under the leadership of Frances Marion, Andrew Pickens, Thomas Sumter, and Henry Lee. Attempts to raise larger, regular forces created financial problems and ultimately forced Rutledge to call an assembly in Jacksonborough, which confiscated the estates of collaborators. When three years of vicious civil war ended, South Carolina society was a shambles and the traditional structure of authority seemed broken beyond repair by the forced exodus of most prominent loyalists.[38]

Georgia, which suffered a similar fate at the hands of the British during the war, fared differently once it was over because the displaced were less able to resist the power of challengers. This was partly because they were less solidly established in the first place, and partly because the constitutional changes that accompanied the Revolution wholly altered the centralized character of the colonial government.[39] But when the South Carolina gentlemen who had preferred imprisonment and exile to collaboration returned home in 1782–1783, they made vigorous attempts to reassert their authority. They were not deterred by a grave economic crisis that led in 1786 to a court closing at Camden or by formidable political opposition, which drew its strength from two quarters: first, from the backcountry leaders whom the war had brought to the fore and who played on local resentment of aristocrats who had failed the state in 1780; second, from the radical group in Charleston that resented repatriate attempts to restore damaged fortunes by alliance with Tory merchants. In the end, because the state constitution gave disproportionate power to the tidewater, the aristocrats succeeded in regaining much of their prewar hegemony, but their authority was not secure. Nor was it likely to become so as long as they were powerless to free the state from the burden imposed by the war debt. Any leadership that could not solve this, the principal postwar problem of its state, had reason to feel insecure.[40]

The South Carolina Federalists were an extreme example of a beleaguered aristocracy. But others in the South shared their plight, such as the slave-owning gentry of the southern and eastern counties of Maryland. They espoused Federalism because of the political challenge posed by the fast-growing commercial areas around Baltimore. Though their control of an undue number of counties, the unit of representation in the legislature, enabled them to resist this pressure, the threat to their power was unmistakable. The same was true in Delaware, where the rapid development and ethnic diversity of Newcastle County propelled the leadership of the two southern counties toward Federalism, though the construction of the state constitution confined the threat to elections for governor and congressional representative. Hamilton's fiscal policy was not an issue in either state, and party alignments did not emerge until mid-decade when the foreign policy dispute came to the fore.[41] It was very much the same in New Jersey. Hamilton's program was indeed controversial, but only because its first congressional delegation was composed of men personally interested in the fiscal policy. The state as a whole was not, and political divisions did not harden until after the neutrality controversy.[42]

By 1796 the Jay Treaty had arraigned Maryland backcountry and slave-owning Federalists against Republican commercial interests in Baltimore. Rural Federalists of the southern Delaware counties were similarly pitted against the commercial and industrial towns of Wilmington and Newcastle, and the static Federalist counties in southwest New Jersey were ranged against faster growing, more populous rivals around New York. What the Federalist leadership of these rural areas had in common with their commercial counterparts in New England, New York, and Pennsylvania, was that they all feared for their traditional status.

III

The theory that Federalism was the choice of those who felt insecure as leaders because of changes wrought by the Revolution sheds light also on the gradual transfer of power from Federalists to Republicans in the lifetime of the first party system. Neither party had ever appealed only to the elite. For instance, all who were alarmed by the speed of change, particularly in northern society, and many who were disturbed by the decline of the older religious sects, joined those whose interests were hurt by Republican policies like the Embargo in supporting the Federalists.[43] And some men, particularly in the Republican South, became Federalists primarily because their enemies were Republicans, that is, not so much for ideological reasons as for those of political identity and strategy. For one reason or another, they were alienated from the Republican coalition dominant in their state and sought to strengthen themselves in the only way they could: by alliance with external forces that had enemies in common with them. This was particularly true of the Cape Fear Federalists in North Carolina and the Federalists of the Valley in Virginia. To a lesser extent it was also true of those in the Northern Neck. Though they continued to supply more than their share of national leaders, their distinctive economy and the peculiar development of the region under the proprietorship of the Fairfax family made them a minority in their own state.[44]

In the same way wherever Federalism was the ideology of the established elite, the challengers became Republicans, and on occasion they were undoubtedly prompted by political calculation as much as by ideological conviction. When dissenting religious groups confronted a state-supported church, they aligned with its political enemies. Consequently, in an area like New England, which was the refuge of the remaining established churches, the Republicans could count on the support of many non-Congregationalists.[45] It would seem reasonable to have expected, then, that ethnic minorities would be predominantly Republican, particularly after the Federalist attempt to restrict immigration at the end of the 1790s. But the behavior of such groups was complicated by other factors. For instance, those who were more eager to preserve their distinctiveness than to assimilate often found themselves strongly in sympathy with the defensiveness of the Federalists. And though the Republicans were the principal beneficiaries of the immigration that followed the French Revolution, their identification with France at a time when all Europe was falling under her despotic sway was no help in winning over certain minorities already established, such as the Dutch in New York. In the long run, most national minorities did find it expedient to adopt Republicanism, particularly after Federalism became associated with disloyalty, but their presence did not decisively help either party in the period when these national coalitions were forming.[46]

Nevertheless, it was soon clear that Republicanism was infinitely more dynamic than Federalism, and that the espousal of one or the other in the 1790s was a good sign of who would or would not fare well with time. The unusual course pursued by the one Federalist leadership whose position improved as the first party system took shape, that of tidewater South Carolina, confirms this general interpretation. Conversion to or even acquiescence in Republicanism was rare because identification with Federalism as the ideology of the insecure tended to grow stronger with pressure. In the nation as a whole, the antagonism between Federalists and Republicans intensified throughout the 1790s, subsided briefly after the election of Jefferson in 1800, and re-emerged at the time of the Embargo. But in South Carolina, alignments began to soften with the Jay Treaty, grew confused in the election of 1800, and ended in 1808 with the state's Federalists being absorbed into a pervasive Republican establishment.

This was the more surprising since the early 1790s had seen a bitter struggle between the tidewater and the backcountry over representation. The census of 1790 had clearly shown that even though the capitol had been transferred to Columbia in the interior, the backcountry was still miserably under represented. With four times as many free citizens as the low country, it had less than a majority in both Houses. Charleston, with one-ninth of the state's free inhabitants, could elect one-third of the legislature. The tidewater argument was that the legislature should represent property as well as people. Backcountry spokesmen retorted that wealth had sufficient influence by itself, needing no special protection, and that even if wealth were to be made the basis of representation, they would still be entitled to constitutional reform. But while they lacked a staple economy dependent on slavery, the tidewater could not be persuaded. Planters feared that if farmers were given a majority in the legislature, they might seek to solve the state's fiscal problems by a discriminatory tax on two essentials of the tidewater aristocracy: commerce and slaves. And a requirement that any constitutional amendment must be approved by two-thirds of the legislature protected them even against the possibility of disagreement among themselves.[47]

The furor over the Jay Treaty, coming directly after the reapportionment controversy of 1794, should have been especially disruptive in South Carolina. In other states it certainly served to aggravate existing tensions. Here, however, it seemed to mute sectional controversy by distracting attention from it. One obvious explanation is that Article 12 of the treaty, which prohibited the export of cotton from the United States, was a threat to the economic interests of the entire state. Another was the intensity of anti-British sentiment surviving from the war. But equally significant was the radical improvement in the fortunes of the tidewater elite after 1794, brought about by the introduction of the cotton gin. By making possible the creation of a plantation aristocracy in the interior, this invention both promised to revive the state's economy and gave the tidewater elite the same potential for lateral mobility as the rest of the southern leadership had always enjoyed. In this way it ensured that with time the principal sources of antagonism between the two sections would be eliminated.

This did not take long, thanks to the reopening of the slave trade between 1803 and 1807, and the importation of almost forty thousand Africans during that time to meet the demands of the expanding upcountry economy. When formal reconciliation through revised representation was achieved in 1808, some parts of the state were still relatively free. But equitable apportionment was no longer a threat to the seacoast, for as South Carolina grew steadily more homogeneous, the planters were ever less liable to challenge. Because the implications of these developments had been clear from the start, the appeal of Federalist ideology had been muted and factional politics for personal advantage re-emerged here as it was disappearing elsewhere.[48] So the genesis and decline of Federalism in South Carolina both show that it was the ideology of those who felt their positions as leaders shaken by changes accompanying the Revolution.

Though in South Carolina the Federalists displayed less zeal than the Republicans in supporting their cause, this was not the usual pattern. Federalism may have been a symptom of elite insecurity, but the more typical response to this condition was heroic exertion. The superior dynamism of Republicanism was not the result of greater activity but of greater effectiveness in commanding mass loyalty. The Federalists labored under several disadvantages in this respect. The ideology of a threatened elite was not much of an asset either to challengers, on whom party growth should to some extent have depended, or to recognized leaders trying to recruit public support. It was not just that Federalists were anti-populist in outlook, for they proved to be remarkably successful in making isolated appeals to the people. More damaging because more visible were the public postures Federalism forced its adherents to adopt, especially the apparent liking for Britain and hostility to France. Most damning of all was Federalism's sceptical view of republics, which brought the value of revolutionary achievements into question. Republicanism, on the contrary, was admirably suited to the needs of challengers. They found its anti-elitism congenial; revolutionary loyalties were stirred by its anti-British, pro-French implications, and best of all it affirmed and exalted revolutionary achievements instead of impugning them.

The capacity of Republicanism to assimilate both revolutionary ideology and popular preferences goes a long way toward explaining why both Federalists and Republicans assumed the nation was spontaneously Republican in sympathy and why, short of national disaster, the Federalists were doomed to be the minority party after 1800 . . . When it came to competing for public opinion in 1800, the Federalists were at a decided disadvantage. Divisions in their ranks had rendered useless their greatest asset, control of the federal government, and their war measures were unpopular. These could have been passing disadvantages, but their lack of a popular ideology was a more serious and lasting one. Their efforts to compensate by harnessing Protestant piety to serve their ends were unsuccessful, and though they had two other recourses against hostile public opinion, these too disappointed them. The first was to control it punitively through the Sedition Law, which proved self-defeating. The second was to circumvent it through intrigue in the electoral college, which failed and left them in their last moment of power reduced to choosing between Jefferson and Burr in the House of Representatives.

Notes

1. Fisher Ames to Thomas Dwight, October 20, 1789, in Seth Ames, ed., *The Works of Fisher Ames* (Boston, 1854), I, 74.

2. Charles A. Beard, *Economic Origins of Jeffersonian Democracy* (New York, 1952); Charles A. and Mary R. Beard, *The Rise of American Civilization*, new ed. (New York, 1939), 336–436; Manning J. Dauer, *The Adams Federalists* (Baltimore, 1953).

3. Paul Goodman, *The Democratic-Republicans of Massachusetts: Politics in a Young Republic* (Cambridge, 1964), 70 ff; Mark D. Kaplanoff, *From Colony to State: New Hampshire 1800–1815* (unpublished Scholar of the House Dissertation, Yale University, 1970), passim.

4. Norman K. Risjord, "The Virginia Federalists," *Journal of Southern History*, XXXIII (1967), 496 ff; Lisle A. Rose, *Prologue to Democracy: The Federalists in the South, 1789–1800* (Lexington, Ky., 1968), 122.

5. Paul Goodman, "The First American Party System," in William N. Chambers and Walter Dean Burnham, eds., *The American Party Systems . . .* (New York, 1967), 68.

6. John A. Munroe, *Federalist Delaware, 1775–1815* (New Brunswick, 1954), 206–7.

7. *Annals*, 4th Cong., 996–1003.

8. Cabot to King, Aug. 4, 1795, in Henry Cabot Lodge, *Life and Letters of George Cabot* (Boston, 1877), 83–4.

9. See ch. 12.

10. Gilbert L. Lycan, *Alexander Hamilton & American Foreign Policy: A Design for Greatness* (Norman, Okla., 1970), 187.

11. David Ramsey, *The History of the Revolution of South Carolina* (Trenton, 1785), II, 372–3.

12. Francois Alexandre Frederic, duc de la Rouchefoucault Liancourt, *Travels through the United States of North America*, 2nd ed. (London, 1800), II; also Charles Downer Hazen, *Contemporary American Opinion of the French Revolution* (Gloucester, Mass., 1964), 165 ff; Benjamin W. Labaree, *Patriots and Partisans: the Merchants of Newburyport* (Cambridge, Mass., 1962), 107 ff.

13. David Hackett Fischer, *The Revolution of American Conservatism* (New York, 1965), 201–2; also William N. Chambers, *Political Parties in a New Nation* (New York, 1963); Noble T. Cunningham, Jr., *The Jeffersonian Republicans* (Chapel Hill, 1957).

14. Ames to George Richard Minot, May 3 and July 9, 1789, in Ames. I, 35, 62; unsigned, in *NG*, January 9, 1793; in *CC*, excerpt from a Connecticut paper, March 9, 1793, "New England," Oct. 3, 1792, and "A Democrat," July 23, 1793, "The Times," in *GUS*, April 30, 1794; *Annals*, 3d Cong., 628; 5th Cong., 961.

15. Jefferson to Madison, Jan. 30, 1787, in Julian P. Boyd, ed., *The Papers of Thomas Jefferson* (Princeton, 1950–), XI, 93.

16. *CC*, June 16, 1790.

17. Madison to Monroe, Dec. 4, 1794, in *WJM*, VI, 220–1. For the contrasting sentiments of Massachusetts Federalists and Virginia Republicans on the question of titles and salaries, see "Consistency," "A Spectator," "Cambridge," Massachusetts House Debates, "J," "An American," "A Federalist of 1787," in *Massachusetts Centinel*, Aug. 20, Dec. 31, 1788, Jan. 7 & 21, April 1, July 8, and Aug. 15, 1789; Jefferson to Henry Tazewell, Jan. 16 and to Madison, Jan. 30, 1797, in *WTJ*, VII, 106–7, 116. Richard H. Lee and Ralph Izard, both from the South, were exceptions to the rule.

18. Jonathan Elliot, ed., *The Debates in the several state conventions, on the adoption of the Federal Constitution* (Philadelphia, 1861), III, 397.

19. Max Farrand, ed., *The Records of the Federal Convention of 1787* (New Haven, 1911), II, 222; Elliot, III, 76–7, 192; IV, 283–4; David Ramsey, "An Address to the Freemen of South Carolina, on the subject of the Federal Constitution," in Paul Leicester Ford, ed., *Pamphlets on the Constitution of the United States* (Brooklyn, 1888), 379; Herbert Aptheker, *American Negro Slave Revolts*, new ed. (New York, 1967), 21 ff; *Marcellus; Published in the Virginia Gazette* (Richmond, 1794), 19–20.

20. Aptheker, 209 ff; Winthrop D. Jordan, *White over Black: American Attitudes towards the Negro 1580–1812*, Pelican ed. (Baltimore, 1969), 393 ff.

21. For Gabriel's plot see Aptheker, 219 ff. Pennsylvania's reaction to the Whiskey and Fries's rebellions is best traced in Harry Marlin Tinkcom, *The Republicans and Federalists in Pennsylvania, 1790–1801* (Harrisburg, 1950).

22. William L. Smith to Edward Rutledge, Aug. 9, 1789, in George C. Rogers, Jr. ed., "The Letters of William Laughton Smith to Edward Rutledge, June 6, 1788 to April 28, 1794," *South Carolina Historical Magazine*, LXIX (1968), 15; see also *Annals*, 1st Cong., 1930.

23. Jefferson to LaFayette, June 16, 1792, in *WTJ*, VI, 78.

24. Oliver Wolcott, Jr., to his father, Jan. 27, 1792 and February 8, 1793, in *MAWA*, I, 85, 86.

25. Ames to G.R. Minot, July 9, 1789, in Ames, I, 62.

26. Enclosure in Ames to Minot, Nov. 30, 1791, in *ibid.*, 103–4.

27. Ames to Minot, July 9, 1789, in *ibid.*, 62.

28. Enclosure in Ames to Minot, November 30, 1791, in *ibid.*, 105.

29. The stereotype did not come into public currency until after 1800. See Labaree, 126–7; *Connecticut Courant*, particularly Feb. 8, 1802 ff; June 1 and July 6, 1803; Feb. 6, 1805 ff.

30. Rochefoucault Liancourt, II, 76–8, 183, 231, 232; Albert Matthews ed., "Journal of William Laughton Smith, 1790–1791," *Massachusetts Historical Society Proceedings*, LI (1918), 69; also Francois Jean, Marquis de Chastellux, *Travels in North America in the Years 1780–81–82* (New York, 1827), 286.

31. Timothy Dwight, *Travels in New England and New York* (New Haven, 1821), II, 458–9.

32. "Milk" in *CC*, June 21, 1797; "Apology of Mr. Thatcher for not accepting General Blount's challenge," reprinted in the *Middlesex Gazette*, June 30, 1797; John Gardiner to H.G. Otis, March 24, 1798, in Samuel Eliot Morison, *The Life and Letters of Harrison Gray Otis, Federalist, 1765–1848* (New York, 1913), I, 91; Dwight, IV, 334–5; Jack Kenny Williams, "The Code of Honor in Antebellum South Carolina," *South Carolina Historical Magazine*, LIV (1953), 114, 117; Charles S. Sydnor, "The Southerner and the Laws" *Journal of Southern History*, VI (1940), 11–8.

33. Williams, 121 ff; Timothy Dwight, *A Sermon on duelling, preached in the chapel of Yale College* (New York, 1805); Robert Baldick, *The Duel: A History of Duelling* (New York, 1965), 121–2; Lorenzo Sabine, *Notices on Duels and Duelling* (Boston, 1859), 341–6.

34. J.D. Barnhart, *Valley of Democracy: the Frontier versus the Plantation in the Ohio Valley, 1775–1818* (Bloomington, Ind., 1953); L.H. Harrison, "A Virginian Moves to Kentucky, 1793," *WMQ*, XV (1958), 203–13; Thomas P. Abernathy, *Three Virginian Frontiers* (Baton Rouge, 1940), and *From Frontier to Plantation in Tennessee: A Study of Frontier Democracy* (University, Ala., 1967); Robert R. Russell, "The Effects of Slavery upon Non-slaveholders in the Antebellum South," *Agricultural History*, XV (1941), 112–4, 118–21; see also Robert M. Weir, "The Harmony we were Famous For: An Interpretation of Pre-Revolutionary South Carolina Politics," *WMQ*, XXVI (1969), 482–3.

35. For this interpretation I rely heavily upon Stanley Elkins and Eric McKitrick, "A Meaning for Turner's Frontier," *Political Science Quarterly*, LXIX (1954), 321–53, 565–602; Harry Ammon, "The Jeffersonian Republicans in Virginia: An Interpretation," *Virginia Magazine of History and Biography*, LXXI (1963), 153–4; Dwight, II, 461–2; Albert Laverne Olson, "Agricultural Economy and the Population in Eighteenth Century Connecticut," in *Tercentenary Commission of the State of Connecticut: Committee on Historical Publications*, XL (1935); Lois Kimball Matthews Rosenberry, "Migrations from Connecticut Prior to 1800" and "Migrations from Connecticut after 1800," in *ibid.*, XXVIII (1934), LIV (1936); James M. Banner, Jr., *To the Hartford Convention: the Federalists and the Origins of Party Politics in Massachusetts 1789–1815* (New York, 1970), 169–71; Percy W. Bidwell, "Rural Economy in New England at the Beginning of the Nineteenth Century," *Transactions of the Connecticut Academy of Arts and Sciences*, XX (1916), 241–399.

36. William A. Schaper, "Sectionalism and Representation in South Carolina," *Annual Report of the American Historical Association for the Year 1900* (Washington, 1901), I, passim; William W. Freehling, *Prelude to Civil War: The Nullification Controversy in South Carolina, 1816–1836* (New York, 1965), 7–11; Charles Woodmason, *The Carolina Backcountry on the Eve of the Revolution*, Richard J. Hooker, ed. (Chapel Hill, 1953), passim; Richard Maxwell Brown, *The South Carolina Regulators (Cambridge, 1963)*, 13 ff.

37. Schaper, 367–8, 379; *An Address to the people of South Carolina, by the General Committee of the representative reform association of Columbia* (Charleston, 1794), 27–8.

38. By far the best account of South Carolina in the revolution is David Ramsay's, *The History of the Revolution of South Carolina*, 2 vols.; I have also relied upon Edward McCrady, *The History of South Carolina in the Revolution 1775–1780* (New York, 1901), and *The History of South Carolina in the Revolution, 1780–1783* (New York, 1902). See also Richard Barry, *Mr. Rutledge of South Carolina* (New York, 1942), particularly 269–302. Some impression of the impact the British invasion had on Carolina society can be gained from Ramsay to Benjamin Rush, June 3, and to Jonathan Elmer, July 15, 1779, in Robert L. Brunhouse, ed., "David Ramsay, 1749–1815: Selections from His Writings," *Transactions of the American Philosophical Society*, new series, LV

(Part 4, 1965), 60, 62; also Aedanus Burke to Arthur Middleton, January 25, 1782, in J.L. Barnwell, annotator, "Correspondence of Hon. Arthur Middleton, Signer of the Declaration of Independence," *South Carolina Historical and Genealogical Magazine*, XXVI (1925), 192.

39. Kenneth Coleman, *The American Revolution in Georgia, 1763–1789* (Athens, Ga., 1958), especially 4–5, 15, 81–3, 179–88, 278–9.

40. Robert W. Barnwell, Jr., "Rutledge the Dictator," *Journal of Southern History*, VII (1941), 244; Edward Rutledge to Jay, November 12, 1786 and May 21, 1789 in Henry P. Johnston, ed., *The Correspondence and Public Papers of John Jay* (New York, 1890–93), III, 217, 368; see also Richard Walsh, ed., *The Writings of Christopher Gadsden, 1746–1805* (Columbia, 1966), 170 ff; Gordon S. Wood, *The Creation of the American Republic* (Chapel Hill, 1969), 367, 482–3; Rogers, 105n.

41. Malcolm C. Clark, "Federalism at High Tide: The Election of 1796 in Maryland," *Maryland Historical Magazine*, LXI (1966), 229; Dorothy M. Brown, "Maryland and the Federalist: Search for Unity," *ibid.*, LXIII (1968), 5–6, 9–10, 21; Fischer, 216; Munroe, 147, 199–200, 208, 213, 238–240, 251–4, 261.

42. Walter R. Fee, *The Transition from Aristocracy to Democracy in New Jersey, 1789–1829* (Somerville, N.J., 1933), 19 ff.

43. Kaplanoff, 79–87, 112, 256–7. Connecticut Federalists were quite explicit in appealing to the traditions of the region: see for example, Theodore Dwight, *An Oration delivered at New Haven on the 7th July, 1801, before the Society of the Cincinnati* (New Haven, 1801), and [David Daggett], *Steady habits vindicated: or a Serious Remonstrance to the People of Connecticut, against changing their government* (Hartford, 1805).

44. Risjord, 498, 505–6, 517; Jackson T. Main, "Sections and Politics in Virginia, 1781–1787," *WMQ*, XII (1955), 96–112, and "The One Hundred," *ibid.*, XI (1954), 354–84, and "The Distribution of Property in Post-Revolutionary Virginia," *Mississippi Valley Historical Quarterly*, XLI (1954–5), 241–58; Leonard L. Richards, "John Adams and the Moderate Federalists: The Cape Fear Valley as a Test Case," *North Carolina Historical Review*, XLIV (1967), 14–30.

45. Goodman, *Democratic-Republicans*, 86–96; Richard J. Purcell, *Connecticut in Transition: 1775–1818* (Middletown, Conn., 1963), 64; William A. Robinson, *Jeffersonian Democracy in New England* (New York, 1916), 141 ff; L.W. Butterfield, "Elder John Leland, Jeffersonian Itinerant," *Proceedings of the American Antiquarian Society*, N.S., LXII (1952), 207 ff.

46. Goodman, "The First American Party System," 66–7; Fischer, 223–6.

47. *An Address to the People of South Carolina*, ii, 19–21. For the opposing point of view see Henry William DeSaussere, *Letters on the questions of the justice and expediency of going into alterations of the representation of South Carolina, as fixed by the constitution* (Charleston, 1795), 10, 14–5; [Timothy Ford], *The Constitutionalist: or, an Inquiry* (Charleston, 1794), 20–2, 37–9, 41–3, 51. Schaper, 408–19 summarizes the controversy.

48. I rely for this interpretation heavily upon John Harold Wolfe, "Jeffersonian Democracy in South Carolina," *James Sprunt Studies in History and Political Science*, XXIV (1940).

The Evolution of Political
Parties in Virginia, 1782–1800

Norman K. Risjord

Gordon DenBoer

*As Fischer's excellent review of recent literature suggests, many of the state
and local studies of the 1950s and 1960s argued that the evidence would not
sustain a Beardian insistence on the economic character of partisan division or
on the continuity of the division of the 1790s with that of the Confederation
years. But other local studies argued that it did—at least if some allowance
were made for the revisions of the old Progressive thesis pioneered by Manning
Dauer, Jackson Turner Main, and others. Any number of examples might be
offered. This article, however, seems of special interest, not only as a clear
and self-contained assertion of a neo-Progressive stance, but because it focuses
on the heartland of the opposition party. It is reprinted without change from*
The Journal of American History, LX *(March, 1974), 961–984. Copyright:
Organization of American Historians, 1974.*

How and when did the first American party system develop? One way
to answer this question is by a roll call analysis of legislative behavior.
That, of course, will not tell the whole story, but it will provide an index
of party loyalty and organization, at least among the leadership élite.
Although scholars have subjected Congress to numerous quantitative
analyses, comparatively little work has been done on state legislatures.[1]
This is unfortunate, not only because American politics in the post-
Revolutionary era was state oriented but also because the state assemblies involved a sort of second-echelon élite. Thus a careful study of
assemblies would enable historians to move closer to an understanding
of the political attitudes of the "common man."

---

[1] Noble E. Cunningham, Jr., *The Jeffersonian Republicans: Formation of Party Organization,
1789–1801* (Chapel Hill, 1957): Manning J. Dauer, *The Adams Federalists* (Baltimore, 1953):
Kenneth R. Bowling, "Politics in the First Congress, 1789–1791" (doctoral dissertation,
University of Wisconsin, 1968). Richard R. Beeman analyzes the Virginia assembly in
the 1790s but includes in the program only those legislators who served three

Another difficulty with many recent analyses of early national politics is that they either begin or end with the Constitution. Historians have made the Constitution appear as an epochal break in history, but to contemporaries it was part of a chain of important political events. Those who built the first political parties in the 1790s recalled and were influenced by personal and regional rivalries that had emerged in the previous decade. A roll call analysis of the Virginia House of Delegates from 1782 to 1800 was undertaken to determine just how and when voting behavior fell into patterns of agreement that might be called parties.[2] This essay also traces contemporary observers' perceptions of this process.

The task of roll call analysis was complicated by the size of the House of Delegates and by the turnover resulting in part from annual elections (see Table I).[3] Until the Adams administration when the Quasi War caused unusual turnover in house membership, there was a decline in "new" members, from about three fifths of the house at the end of the Revolution to about two fifths by the mid-1790s. In all, 1,287 individuals served in either the legislature or the ratifying convention or both between 1782 and 1800. There was, however, a group of men, perhaps as many as twenty in any given session, whose service spanned a number of years and who provided continuity, experience, and often leadership for the legislative system.

This analysis was also complicated by the paucity of roll call votes, seldom more than ten or fifteen per session. In order to obtain enough roll calls for statistical comparisons, the sessions were grouped 1782–1784, 1785–1787, 1788–1792, 1793–1796, and 1797–1799. Delegates who did not register at least three votes on party issues, or six votes overall (about one third of the members in most sessions) were excluded from the analysis. The voting records of the remaining two thirds were

---

consecutive terms. Richard R. Beeman, *The Old Dominion and the New Nation: 1788–1801* (Lexington, Ky., 1972). Mary P. Ryan confirms at the congressional level many of the conclusions reached concerning Virginia politics in the 1790s. Her thesis, that significant blocs of partisan voting can be found as early as 1789, is a graphic demonstration of the need for a closer look at the state and congressional politics of the previous decade. Mary P. Ryan, "Party Formation in the United States Congress, 1789 to 1796: A Quantitative Analysis," *William and Mary Quarterly*, XXVIII (Oct. 1971), 523–42.

[2] The analysis was confined to the lower house because the senate was elected on a district system; analysis of the senate suffers from some of the same disadvantages as an analysis of congressional voting. Furthermore, the senate recorded few roll call votes.

[3] Each county elected two delegates, and the boroughs of Richmond, Williamsburg, and Norfolk sent one each. The increase in the number of delegates resulted from the creation of new counties; the decrease in 1792 marks the statehood of Kentucky. "New" members are those who did not serve in the previous session, even though they might have served some years before.

TABLE I.

Session	Number of Delegates	"New" Members	Percent "New"
1782	150	95	63
1783	152	83	55
1784	152	80	53
1785	156	78	50
1786	160	79	49
1787	168	80	48
1788	170	82	48
1789	173	80	46
1790	179	74	41
1791	183	86	47
1792	171	73	43
1793	171	62	36
1794	177	76	43
1795	177	71	40
1796	177	68	38
1797	177	91	51
1798	179	83	46
1799	179	82	46
1800	183	73	40

compared with those of a dozen or more "leaders," who were selected either on the basis of number of votes cast or attributed prominence in the assembly. To compare each delegate's voting record with that of every other would involve an unmanageable amount of data. In selecting "leaders" care was taken to insure that each region was represented, in order to determine whether personal and regional subgroups existed.[4]

During the years 1782–1784 the assembly was relatively disorganized. A few prominent men, such as Patrick Henry and Richard

[4] The number of individuals involved and the high rate of absenteeism precluded the use of such methods as Guttman scaling. Some scaling was attempted where the number of roll calls on related issues seemed to justify it. Though scaling failed to reveal any persistent subgroups or personal alliances, it did reveal some regional blocs within the parties—for example, a bloc of western debtor-oriented Federalists in the 1790s. Susan Lee Foard attempted to determine the degree of prominence among legislators through service on key committees. Susan Lee Foard, "Virginia Enters the Union, 1789–1792" (master's thesis, College of William and Mary, 1966). For an alternative method, see Norman K. Risjord, "The Virginia Federalists," *Journal of Southern History*, XXXIII (Nov. 1967), 486–517.

Henry Lee, commanded personal followings, but it is unlikely that these factional groups included more than half of the house membership. Contemporaries used vague terms in assessing the relative size of each faction, and the large number of new men who won seats in the annual spring elections increased the problem of identification. In each of the three year periods for which statistics were compared more than half of the delegates had not served in the previous assembly. Governor Benjamin Harrison saw in this rapid turnover a general "opposition to the old members," and others noted the appearance of an unusual number of younger men and former army officers.[5]

Most of the problems facing the assembly in these years stemmed from the Revolutionary War and the postwar depression. Of primary importance were economic issues involving debtor relief and taxation: postponement of tax collections, payment of taxes in kind, relief of sheriffs delinquent in tax collections, and regulation of relationships between private debtors and creditors. Henry was the acknowledged leader of a debtor-oriented faction in the assembly, although his absenteeism and the extensive turnover of delegates make it difficult to determine the precise size of his following. There were nine roll calls involving economic issues. Henry voted only four times. Twenty-eight delegates, most from the West and the region south of the James River, agreed with Henry on at least three of the four votes.[6] On the six roll calls that involved only domestic debts and taxation a substantial group of debtor-oriented delegates is apparent, but there is no regional pattern among them. The lack of such a pattern and the absence of a creditor-oriented group indicates the broad support for debtor-relief measures in these years. One explanation for Henry's apparent influence was that he articulated popular measures and reflected the views of a large

---

[5] Benjamin Harrison to Thomas Jefferson, April 16, 1784, Edmund Randolph to Jefferson, April 24, 1784, William Short to Jefferson, May 14, 1784, Julian P. Boyd, ed., *The Papers of Thomas Jefferson* (18 vols., Princeton, 1951–), VII, 102–03, 116–17, 257; Beverly Randolph to James Monroe, May 14, 1784, James Monroe Papers (Manuscript Division, Library of Congress). Analyzing the 1783 session, for example, Edmund Randolph identified three "corps" in the assembly; Patrick Henry, Richard Henry Lee, and Speaker John Tyler each led a faction. Henry's was the most numerous, Randolph thought, while Tyler's was "but a temporary bubble." Edmund Randolph to Jefferson, May 15, 1784, Boyd, ed., *Papers of Thomas Jefferson*, VII, 257.

[6] The Southside includes all the counties south of the James River, from the seacoast to the Blue Ridge. The Piedmont is here defined as the counties west of the fall line, from Spotsylvania to Henrico, and between the Rappahannock and the James. The Middle Tidewater includes the counties along the bay between those two rivers, as well as the Eastern Shore. The Northern Neck includes the area north of the Rappahannock and east of the Blue Ridge. The West embraces the area beyond the Blue Ridge.

majority of the assembly.[7] Even his erstwhile rival Richard Henry Lee generally voted for debtor-relief measures until 1784. Not until James Madison entered the assembly in that year did the opponents of debtor relief have a leader to rival Henry.[8]

The sharpest divisions in the 1782–1784 sessions involved the pre-war debts owed to British merchants.[9] Virginia courts were closed to British creditors during the war, but the peace settlement required the removal of impediments to debt collection. The issue involved not only the sanctity of private contracts but also national treaty obligations.[10] John Marshall objected to the law impeding British debt collection "because it affords a pretext to the British to retain possession of the forts on the lakes but much more because I ever considered it a measure tending to weaken the federal bonds which in my conception are too weak already."[11] Others recognized that it would be difficult to attract European investment capital in the future if past debts were not paid.[12] Thus, while a pro-creditor attitude on the payment of debts owed to the British went hand in hand with nationalism, there is almost no correlation between voting behavior on the debts issue and domestic debts and taxes.

The issue involved three roll call votes, one in 1783 and two in 1784, and efforts to remove the impediments to British suits were rejected

---

[7] Observers agreed that Henry was still "all powerful." George Mason to Henry, May 6, 1783, Robert A. Rutland, ed., The Papers of George Mason, 1725–1792 (3 vols., Chapel Hlll, 1970), II, 769–73; Edmund Pendleton to James Madison, May 17, 1783, David John Mays, ed., The Letters and Papers of Edmund Pendleton: 1734–1803 (2 vols., Charlottesville, 1967), II, 446.

[8] Edmund Randolph to Jefferson, May 15, 1784, Short to Jefferson, May 14, 1784, Boyd, ed., Papers of Thomas Jefferson, VII, 257, 259–61.

[9] For state and congressional action on the debts, see Benjamin R. Baldwin, "The Debts Owed by Americans to British Creditors, 1763–1802" (doctoral dissertation, Indiana University, 1932).

[10] Richard Henry Lee thought the "impeding laws" ought to be repealed "for the honour of our country." Richard Henry Lee to Madison, Nov. 26, 1784, James Madison Papers (Manuscript Division, Library of Congress). Edmund Randolph rejoiced for the national honor when Congress asked the states to comply with the debt provisions of the treaty. Edmund Randolph to Madison, April 4, 1787, ibid. See also George Washington to George William Fairfax, June 30, 1786, George Washington Papers (Manuscript Division, Library of Congress); Beverly Randolph to St. George Tucker, Nov. 29, 1784, Tucker-Coleman Papers (College of William and Mary); William Grayson to Madison, May 28, 1786, Madison Papers.

[11] John Marshall to Monroe, Dec. 2, 1784, Monroe Papers. For a similar concern see Washington to Richard Henry Lee, Dec. 14, 1784, Washington Papers; Richard Henry Lee to Madison, Nov. 20, 1784, Madison to Monroe, Dec. 24, 30, 1784, Madison Papers; Richmond Virginia Gazette, or the American Advertiser, July 12, 1786.

[12] William Lee to Thomas Lee, March 26, 1786, Lee-Ludwell Papers (Virginia Historical Society); George Mason to Arthur Lee, March 25, 1783, Rutland, ed., Papers of George Mason, II, 765–67.

by large majorities. Support for compliance with the debt repayment provisions of the peace treaty came principally from the Northern Neck and lower James River counties. Of the eighteen delegates in this group, thirteen subsequently voted for the Constitution (ten remained Federalist, three later became Republicans), one became an Antifederalist/ Republican, and the other four cannot be subsequently identified. Thirty-four delegates voted with Henry against compliance (on three of three or two of two roll calls). Of the twelve whose subsequent affiliation is known, two voted for the Constitution and later became Republicans; ten were Antifederalists in 1788.

Congress' request for authority to place an impost on imported goods for twenty-five years created a furor in 1783, but it was approved without a roll call vote. The political leadership divided along essentially the same lines as on the British debts issue, with the exception of Richard Henry Lee. Lee opposed the amendment because he was suspicious of congressional power and feared that Virginians would pay a disproportionate share of the tax.[13] Lee and his following also associated the impost with their old enemy Robert Morris. They had led an unsuccesful fight against the amendment when Morris first proposed it in 1781 and persuaded the assembly to withdraw its approval in 1782.

On other roll calls in the 1782–1784 sessions alignments varied with the issue, and there is no correlation among them. Religious issues, such as the move to incorporate the Episcopal church and the effort to assess taxpayers for religious purposes, produced divisions that followed regional lines. Anti-establishment feeling was strongest among delegates from the transmontane West and the northern Piedmont, where religious dissenters were particularly strong. A series of four votes defining citizenship—aimed at preventing certain Loyalists from returning to the state—revealed a rather lenient attitude toward the returnees. Tolerance for Loyalists was greatest in the counties near urban centers such as Alexandria, Richmond, Williamsburg, and Norfolk. Although the issue revealed some lingering bitterness, the voting alignments have no particular relationship to those on other issues.

Henry's move from the assembly to the governorship in November 1784 and Madison's rapid ascendancy in the assembly encouraged fiscal conservatives and nationalists. In autumn 1785 George Washing-

---

[13] Richard Henry Lee to Landon Carter, June 3, 1783, Lee-Ludwell Papers. For an analysis of political attitudes on the issue, see Edmund Randolph to Madison, May 9, June 28, 1783, Joseph Jones to Madison, May 25, June 8, 1783, Madison Papers; Thomson Mason to John F. Mercer, June 27, 1783, John F. Mercer Papers (Virginia Historical Society); Jefferson to Madison, May 7, June 17, 1783, Madison to Jefferson, Dec. 10, 1783, Boyd, ed., *Papers of Thomas Jefferson,* VI, 266, 277, 377.

ton outlined a program in a letter to David Stuart: an additional grant of power to Congress to regulate commerce, legislation that would encourage the development of Virginia seaports, improvement in the court system to accelerate civil suits, continuation of current taxation policies with no further delays in collection, and state support for projects to improve inland navigation.[14] The appearance of such a comprehensive, issue-oriented program marked a significant change from the piecemeal approach to issues and the emphasis on personalities that had characterized the 1782–1784 sessions. At the opening of the 1785 session Madison watched with bemused indifference while the partisans of John Tyler and Harrison engaged in complicated "intrigues" for the speaker's chair. By 1786 Madison's following was clearly in control. Joseph Prentis of Williamsburg, who subsequently became a Federalist, won the speakership over Theodorick Bland, an ally of Henry and an Antifederalist, by a vote of 49 to 37. Edmund Randolph was chosen governor by a "considerable majority" over Bland and Richard Henry Lee.[15] Furthermore, the congressional delegation was solidly pro-Madison.[16]

Clearly, an issue-oriented coalition was beginning to form. Madison welcomed the election of George Mason in 1786 as "an inestimable acquisition on most of the great points," but concluded that when the interests of Mason's locality were involved "he is to be equally dreaded." Madison also suspected that Mason was not "fully cured of his antifederal prejudices."[17] Henry was still to be feared, especially if he should endorse some popular measure such as paper money, but by 1787 Madison was able to count votes shortly after the spring elections and determine that Henry would be "powerfullly opposed" on such issues in the House of Delegates.[18]

The development of Madison's coalition between 1785 and 1787 can be seen by comparing votes on two key issues—the commerce amendment and British debts. In 1785 a proposal to grant Congress authority to regulate commerce for thirteen years was rejected in two successive votes.[19] Tactical maneuvers caused some realignment, but if

---

[14] George Washington to David Stuart, Nov. 30, 1785, John C. Fitzpatrick, ed., *The Writings of George Washington* (39 vols., Washington, 1931–1944). XXVIII, 328–29. Archibald Stuart thought Madison's power in the assembly was "almost absolute." Archibald Stuart to Jefferson, Oct. 17, 1785, Boyd, ed., *Papers of Thomas Jefferson*, VIII, 645–46.

[15] Madison to Jefferson, April 27, 1785, Boyd, ed., *Papers of Thomas Jefferson*, VIII, 110–16; Jan. 22, 1786, *ibid.*, IX, 194–95; Dec. 4, 1786, *ibid.*, X, 577; Oct. 23, 1786, *Journal of the House of Delegates of Virginia, 1776–1790* (Richmond, 1827–1828).

[16] The delegates were William Grayson, Edward Carrington, Henry Lee, Joseph Jones, and Madison.

[17] Madison to Monroe, May 13, 1786, Monroe Papers. Ill health prevented Mason from serving. Note the early use of them term "antifederal."

[18] Madison to Jefferson, April 24, 1787, Boyd, ed., *Papers of Thomas Jefferson*, XI, 310.

[19] Nov. 30, Dec. 1, 1785, *Journal of . . . Delegates . . . 1785–1786*, pp. 65–67.

those who participated in both roll calls are regarded as either "pro" or "anti" Congress, the geographical distribution was clear (see Table II). As in earlier sessions, personalities were still important: the votes of delegates from the Northern Neck reflect the continuing influence of the Lees on this particular issue; the West was voting with Patrick Henry.

By 1787 both regions were solidly aligned with the nationalists. This can be seen in the controversy over British debts, which was revived in that year by a congressional resolution calling on the states to repeal all laws in conflict with the peace treaty. The request seemed like congressional dictation to some Virginians, and the issue was discussed in the assembly when measures dealing with the proposed Constitution—calls for a state ratifying convention and a second federal convention—were generating heated feelings. The close correlation between voting behavior on the British debts issue and later stands on the Constitution suggests that the issue was, as it had been in 1783–1784, as much a federal-state question as an economic one.[20]

The repeal measure requested by Congress finally passed, but only after strenuous efforts by opponents to weaken it. The bill, in its final form, suspended repeal until Britain evacuated the Northwest posts and compensated Virginians for slaves carried off during the war. The four roll calls on the issue (counting only those delegates who voted consistently on four of four or three of three) disclose three distinct groups.

TABLE II.

Region	Pro-nationalist	Anti-nationalist
Northern Neck	3	10
Middle Tidewater	9	11
Piedmont	4	4
Southside	2	22
West	4	16

---

[20] For a discussion of this relationship, see Emory G. Evans, "Private Indebtedness and the Revolution in Virginia, 1776 to 1796," William and Mary Quarterly, XXVIII (July 1971), 349–74. It could be argued, of course, that American debts owed to British creditors were still fundamentally an economic matter and that one's subsequent stand on the Constitution was determined by indebtedness or lack of it. This may have influenced some delegates, but the Constitution posed so many issues—political as well as economic—that it seems unlikely that stands for or against ratification were dictated by the single issue of indebtedness to the British.

The creditor nationalist element favored repeal of all state laws inter-
fering with payment of the debts and opposed all efforts to dilute the
resolution of compliance. Westerners unanimously favored this stand,
evidently in the belief that strict adherence to the peace treaty would
induce the British to evacuate the Northwest posts and thus reduce
the Indian menace on the frontier.[21] A group of twenty-eight delegates wanted to suspend the repeal measure or attach conditions that
would impede payment. They were willing, however, to pay the debts
in installments (conceivably recognizing that ultimate payment was
inevitable and this was one means to delay it). The third group, led by
Henry, opposed all measures to repay the debts, even by installments.
There was also a regional and political distribution (see Tables III and
IV).

Issues involving domestic debts—primarily efforts to delay payment of taxes—show less clear divisions. Five roll calls were spread over
the three sessions, 1785–1787, and because of high turnover relatively
few delegates registered the four or five votes necessary to establish a
pattern. Eleven men favored strict tax collections on at least four of the
five votes: five from the West, six from the Tidewater. Seven became
Federalists; two became Antifederalists; and the affiliations of two are
unknown. Although this is a very small sample, it indicates that some
westerners were creditor-minded on domestic taxation as well as on
foreign debts.

Conversely, of the fourteen who voted against strict tax collections,
five were from the Southside, four from the Piedmont, three from the
Tidewater, and two from the West. Eight became Antifederalists; two

TABLE III.

Region	Creditor/ nationalists	Moderate debtor/ anti-nationalists	Henryite debtor/ anti-nationalists
West	21	0	0
Northern Neck	9	1	0
Middle Tidewater	5	6	0
Piedmont	1	6	1
Southside	6	15	8
Total	42	28	9

[21] Jackson Turner Main, *The Antifederalists: Critics of the Constitution 1781–1788* (Chapel
Hill, 1961), 229.

TABLE IV.

Subsequent Party Affiliation

Federalists	20	4	0
Antifederalists	1 (Mason)	17	7
Middle-of-road	2	0	0
Unknown	19	7	2
	—	—	—
Total	42	28	9

became Federalists; and the affiliations of four are unknown. Again the sample is very small, but the regional division complements the votes on the British debts issue. The spectrum of economic issues—involving both domestic and foreign debts—presents a vaguely defined dichotomy between debtor-oriented anti-nationalism, concentrated in the Southside and Piedmont, and a creditor-oriented nationalism, concentrated in the Tidewater—or more specifically the Northern Neck—and the West.

Closely related to these economic issues were four roll calls dealing with judical reform. In general, they involved efforts led by Madison to establish additional courts and to speed up the judicial process. Again, only a few delegates registered a significant pattern because the votes occurred in all three sessions, but there are some interesting correlations, even if the analysis is limited by counting only those who voted consistently on four of four or three of three roll calls (see Table V). The similarity of this breakdown to that involving debt issues is apparent—only one of the delegates opposed to judicial reform was creditor-oriented on debt and taxation issues, while all those who favored judicial reform also favored paying debts and taxes. Both sides clearly felt that the establishment of additional courts would facilitate the collection of debts.

Thus by the time the Constitutional Convention assembled in Philadelphia to draft a blueprint for a stronger central government, two coalitions based on regional interests could be clearly discerned in the Virginia assembly. The conflict involved mostly economic issues[22]—domestic and foreign debts, taxation, and the judiciary—and the Constitution affected every one of these in one way or another. Therefore,

---

[22] Roll calls on social issues such as religion and slavery (private manumission bills) followed regional patterns that bore little relation to votes on other issues; apparently they had no effect on party development.

TABLE V.

Region	Favored Judicial Reform	Opposed Judicial Reform
West	4	2
Northern Neck	4	0
Middle Tidewater	3	2
Piedmont	0	4
Southside	3	7
Lower James River	4	0
	—	—
Total	18	15
Subsequent Party Affiliation		
Federalists	12	3
Antifederalists	1	7
Unknown	5	5
	—	—
Total	18	15

it was assumed that popular reaction to the Constitution would follow the regional and partisan lines evident in the assembly. One of Madison's Federalist friends thought it certain "that the honest part of the community whether merchants or planters are for it. People in debt, and of dishonesty and cunning in their transactions are against it. This will apply universally to those of this class who have been members of the legislature."[23] By December 1787—three months before the election of delegates and six months before the ratifying convention met— Madison was able to predict the regional distribution of the vote on the Constitution with considerable accuracy.[24]

At that point Madison could distinguish three basic "parties" (the term was beginning to lose its pejorative connotation, for Madison applied it to his friends as well as his opponents). One party favored ratification of the Constitution as it stood. A second party, led by Mason and Randolph, approved the substance of the Constitution but desired "a few additional guards in favor of the Rights of the States and of the People." Then there was a "third Class, at the head of which is Mr. Henry. This class concurs at present with the patrons of amendments, but will probably contend for such as strike at the essence of the System. . . ."[25]

---

[23] Washington to Henry Knox, Oct. 15, 1787, Washington Papers; Benjamin Hawkins to Madison, Feb. 14, 1788, Madison Papers.
[24] Madison to Jefferson, Dec. 9, 1787, Boyd, ed., *Papers of Thomas Jefferson*, XII, 408–12.
[25] *Ibid.*

The middle group embraced a wide assortment of attitudes, ranging from those who desired some minor additions delineating the rights of citizens to those who would delete some of the substantive powers of Congress. But this middle group had to sort itself out before long because only two responses were ultimately possible—yea or nay.[26]

James Monroe subsequently claimed that he was elected to the ratifying convention without formally committing himself on the Constitution. If this is true, he was almost the only one who was.[27] Washington, noting that delegates were chosen on the basis of their stand, anticipated that the fate of the Constitution would be known as soon as the election results were tallied.[28] Indeed, even before the March elections were completed "an accurate list" of delegates, together with the stand of each on the Constitution, was circulating in Richmond.[29] When the balloting ended, the Winchester *Virginia Centinel* listed thirty-eight counties for the Constitution, twenty-five against, three divided, and seventeen (including six of the seven Kentucky counties) as doubtful. With somewhat more precision Charles Lee estimated that the Federalists had a majority of ten or twelve.[30]

The debate over ratification focused attention on issues—rather than personalities—polarized opinion, and enhanced the importance of the electorate. Both sides carefully tested the political temper, and the voters, in turn, were unusually quick to express their views. Shortly after the Constitution was published, Madison was informed that "The freeholders of Fairfax have, in the most pointed terms directed Col. Mason to vote for a convention [in the assembly], and have as pointedly assured him he shall not be in it."[31] Mason wisely moved over to neighboring Stafford County, where he possessed additional property, to run for a seat in the ratifying convention. But George Nicholas of Albemarle County, who had been one of Henry's chief lieutenants in

[26] For examples of this sorting process, see Jefferson to Edward Carrington, Dec. 21, 1787, Jefferson to Alexander Donald, Feb. 7, 1788, Boyd, ed., *Papers of Thomas Jefferson*, XII, 445–47, 570–72; John Page to Jefferson, March 7, 1788, *ibid.*, XII, 650–54; Joseph Jones to Madison, Oct. 29, 1787, Monroe to Madison, Oct. 13, 1787, Feb. 7, 1788, Madison Papers.

[27] Monroe to Jefferson, July 12, 1788, Boyd, ed., *Papers of Thomas Jefferson*, XIII, 351–53. Carrington complained that some of the Southside candidates were evasive on the question. Edward Carrington to Madison, Feb. 10, April 8, 1788, Madison Papers.

[28] Washington to John Jay, March 3, 1788, Washington to Benjamin Lincoln, March 10, 1788, Washington Papers.

[29] Winchester *Virginia Centinel, or the Winchester Mercury*, April 2, 1788.

[30] *Ibid.*, April 9, 1788; Charles Lee to Richard Henry Lee, April 6, 1788, Washington Papers.

[31] John Dawson to Madison, Oct. 19, 1787, Madison Papers. See also Instructions from a Committee of Voters in Fairfax County [Oct. 2, 1787], Rutland, ed., *Papers of George Mason*, III, 1000–01.

the early 1780s, evidently sampled local opinion and decided to support the Constitution "however contrary it may be to his own opinions."[32] Political rivalry was clearly expanding beyond the narrow confines of the assembly chamber.

The controversy over ratification also revealed a growing sophistication in political techniques—the ability to identify interests, predict votes, and secure commitments on voting behavior. Yet the "parties"—to use Madison's term—that divided over the Constitution were political coalitions, not parties in any modern sense. The requirement that the delegates vote "on the single question of Union or No Union," as Governor Randolph put it, concealed a wide variety of opinions. On June 25 the convention ratified by a vote of 89 to 79, after the Federalists agreed to attach amendments to the act of ratification. Some were concerned only with guarding the procedural rights of citizens and some were substantive alterations in the powers of the new government, but all obtained considerable support. Approving an amendment that would curtail the federal power to tax, for instance, were sixteen delegates who had voted for the Constitution, including Randolph himself and such erstwhile Madison allies as Edmund Pendleton, William Fleming, and Paul Carrington.[33] Madison pushed the Bill of Rights through Congress in the summer of 1789 in the hope of undercutting the Antifederalists' demand for amendments, but his limited procedural safeguards did not satisfy their desire for changes in the structure and powers of the government. As a result, the twin demands for a second federal convention and substantive amendments to the Constitution agitated the Virginia assembly for the next five years.

The debate on the Constitution also provided a national forum for political divisions. Federalists developed an interstate network for exchanging views and information during the ratification process, and the Antifederalists belatedly imitated their methods. In this respect the first federal election was a continuation of the contest, as both sides recognized the importance of controlling the new government. "To be shipwrecked in sight of the port," warned Washington, "would be the severest of all possible aggravations to our Misery. . . . "[34] Thus began the transformation from Federalists-as-framers to Federalists-as-party controlling the executive and legislature of the new government.

"The parties feds and anti have in most transactions been pretty distinguishable," reported Joseph Jones when the Virginia assembly

---

[32] James McClurg to Madison, Sept. 10, 1787, Madison Papers.

[33] David Robertson, *Debates and Other Proceedings of the Convention of Virginia . . . June 1788 . . .* (Richmond, 1805), 470–75.

[34] Washington to Madison, Sept. 23, 1788, Washington Papers.

met in the fall of 1788.[35] But Henry and his allies were in solid control of the house, and this presented two problems for the Federalists. The assembly was certain to elect two Antifederalists to the United States Senate, and it might design the congressional districts to the advantage of the Antifederalists. Since two senators were to be chosen, each legislator would cast two ballots; and Federalists hoped Madison would get enough second votes to slip in. Antifederalist ranks held firm, however, and the result was ninety-eight for Richard Henry Lee, eighty-six for William Grayson, seventy-seven for Madison, twenty-six for Henry (who was not a candidate), and the rest scattered. Edward Carrington concluded that "two thirds of the assembly are anti's who meditate mischief against the Govt."[36]

Madison accordingly ran for a seat in the House of Representatives, and the assembly, as expected, manipulated his northern Piedmont district to include as many Antifederalist counties as possible. "The party" even persuaded Madison's old friend Monroe to run against him.[37] By an ingenious combination of new and old tactics, Madison's friends kept him informed of the sentiment in each county of the district, identified the wavering regions, and enlisted prominent members of the gentry to endorse him at strategic moments. Such "electioneering"—distasteful as it was—succeeded, and Madison won by a substantial majority.[38] He even managed to remain on good terms with Monroe.[39]

It was anticipated that the congressional contest would be close everywhere, except in the Southside where no Federalist was even willing to step forward.[40] As a result, both sides developed some rudimentary nominating procedures in order to avoid internal divisions. In the northern congressional districts, Henry Lee reported, "It is probable that each party will fix on one man, & that the election will decide the will of the people, provided the districts have not been artfully

---

[35] Jones to Madison, Nov. 21, 1788, Madison Papers.

[36] Theodorick Bland to Richard Henry Lee, Nov. 9, 1788, Richard Henry Lee Papers (University of Virginia); Edward Carrington to Madison, Nov. 9, 1788, Madison Papers.

[37] Madison to Jefferson, Dec. 8, 1788, Boyd, ed., *Papers of Thomas Jefferson*, XIV, 340; Edward Carrington to Madison, Nov. 15, 1788, Joseph Jones to Madison, April 5, 1789, Madison Papers; Bland to Richard Henry Lee, Nov. 9, 1788, Richard Henry Lee Papers; James Duncanson to James Maury, Feb. 17, 1789, James Maury Papers (University of Virginia).

[38] Edward Carrington to Madison, Dec. 30, 1788, Henry Lee to Madison, Jan. 14, 1789, Edward Stevens to Madison, Jan. 31, 1789, Madison Papers. The vote was 1308 to 972. Fredericksburg *Virginia Herald*, Feb. 12, 1789.

[39] Monroe to Jefferson, Feb. 15, 1789, Boyd, ed., *Papers of Thomas Jefferson*, XIV, 557–59; Monroe to Madison, April [26], 1789, Madison Papers.

[40] Edward Carrington to Madison, Dec. 19, 30, 1789, Madison papers; Bland to St. George Tucker, Feb. 8, 1789, Tucker-Coleman Papers.

designated."[41] The Antifederalists in the assembly even drew up a slate of ten candidates for Congress and twelve presidential electors, which they then circulated around the state.[42] In the end, eight Federalists and two Antifederalists were sent to Congress. The balloting clearly reflected a feeling that the new government ought to be given a chance, sentiment that also marked the transition from Antifederalist-critic-of-the-Constitution to Republican-critic-of-the-administration.

The political issues presented by the Constitution—a possible second convention, amendments, arrangement of congressional districts, and an act disqualifying federal officials from serving the state—agitated the assembly for the next two years. For a time Henry ruled, and the assembly passed resolutions endorsing a second convention and substantive amendments. But the smooth establishment of the federal government and congressional passage of the Bill of Rights undermined his support. In 1789 an effort to add to the Bill of Rights the substantive amendments suggested by the Virginia ratifying convention was defeated on three successive votes. Henry went home in the middle of the session—disappointed at his lack of support, so Federalists said.[43]

Alexander Hamilton's fiscal system, especially the proposal that the federal government assume the war debts of the states, created new controversies in 1790. Virginians disliked Hamilton's proposals because it seemed to them that speculators in the public debt, most of them northern merchants, would get an undeserved windfall at the expense of taxpayers. The proposal was particularly obnoxious because Virginia had paid off much of its war debt; it now appeared that the state would be taxed again to pay the debts of others. Even so staunch a Federalist as Henry Lee, who was not above speculating in lands at the falls of the Potomac in the hope that the President would locate the nation's capital there, denounced the funding system for perverting the Constitution and placing the country in the hands of merchants.[44] Henry was considered a prophet for having predicted that northern mercantile interests would dominate the new government, and even the "strongest antifederalists" praised

[41] Henry Lee to Madison, Dec. 8, 1788, Madison Papers. For examples of conscious efforts to settle on candidates, see Henry Lee to Madison, Dec. 8, 1788, Jan. 14, 1789, Madison Papers; Washington to David Stuart, Dec. 2, 1788, Washington to Henry Knox, Jan. 1, 1789, Washington to Henry Lee, Dec. 12, 1788, Washington Papers; Isaac Avery to John Cropper, Dec. 29, 1788, Jan. 30, 1789, John Cropper Papers (Virginia Historical Society).

[42] Duncanson to Maury, Feb. 17, 1789, James Maury Papers.

[43] Edward Carrington to Madison, Dec. 20, 1789, Madison Papers; David Stuart to Washington, Dec. 3, 1789, Washington Papers.

[44] Henry Lee to Madison, March 4, 1790, Madison Papers; Henry Lee to [a member of Congress], Jan. 8, 1792, Charles Carter Lee Papers (Virginia State Library, Richmond).

Madison for his opposition to Hamilton's proposals.[45] In the assembly, Henry's resolution denouncing assumption of state debts as "repugnant to the Constitution" passed by a vote of 75 to 52.[46]

Madison's creation of an anti-administration following in Congress and Henry's transformation from critic to interpreter of the Constitution laid the foundation for a new political alignment. Toward the end of 1791 Madison's brother William transmitted the news that Henry desired to open a correspondence. Madison replied cautiously that he was gratified by any "friendly sentiments" Henry might have, but since he had never written to Henry in his life he feared that the "abrupt commencement" of a correspondence might seem odd.[47] Henry, in short, would have to write the first letter, and he never did. Madison had no reason to regret it. Henry was an unpredictable ally and a potential rival for leadership. Madison had won Henry's following—where else could they go? What the new Republican party needed was more disaffected Federalists.

How many did they get? To what extent was there continuity from the factional contest of the late 1780s to the parties that divided over national issues in the 1790s? Treating the 1788–1792 assembly sessions as a unit, there were eight roll calls during these years on issues that determined party. These ranged from Federalist/Antifederalist splits over amendments and a second convention to Federalist/Republican divisions over assumption of state debts and the establishment of new congressional districts after the census of 1790.[48] A total of 426 men served in the House of Delegates during these five sessions. Of these, 150 cast enough votes to be identified: Federalist, 41; leaning Federalist 10; middle of the road, 5; leaning Antifederalist/Republican, 6; and Antifederalist/Republican, 88.[49]

The rigidity of party lines is quite remarkable, especially in view of the fact that the Federalists lost substantial support as a result of Hamil-

---

[45] Henry Lee to Madison, April 3, 1790, Edward Carrington to Madison, April 30, 1790, Edmund Randolph to Madison, May 20, 1790, Madison Papers.

[46] Nov. 3, 1790, *Journal of . . . Delegates . . . 1790*, pp. 35–36.

[47] William to James, Dec. 3, 1791, James to William, Dec. 13, 1791, Madison Papers.

[48] On the districting bill, Francis Corbin thought that "Party wish runs higher than I ever knew it before upon any Legislative arrang[ement] whatever." Corbin to Madison, Jan. 7, 1792, *ibid.*

[49] The record of each legislator was compared with that of several known Federalists and Republicans who agreed among themselves 100 percent of the time. Those classified by party agreed with the party models at least 80 percent of the time. Those listed as "leaning" voted with a party on 60 to 80 percent of their votes; those in the middle of the road agreed with either party less than 60 percent. Two hundred and seventy-six men voted fewer than three times or split their votes 2–1. Percentages were calculated only for those who voted more than five times; if a delegate cast fewer votes he had to side consistently with either one party or the other in order to be classified with a party.

ton's fiscal policies. The five middle-of-the-roaders, for example, were all professed Federalists—such as Henry Lee and Francis Corbin—who opposed assumption of state debts. But the relatively small number of "trimmers" suggests that there was no major shift among the delegates from one party to another during these years. When voters became unhappy with Federalist policies, they merely elected new men. The extent of continuity can be discerned (see Table VI).[50]

There are 316 men whose stand on the Constitution is known, either through participation in the ratifying convention or through their voting in the assembly on the issues of a second convention and radical amendments. Their subsequent party affiliation can be identified (see Table VII). Lines of historical continuity are never perfect, but there does seem to be, in Virginia at least, a rather continuous pattern of party evolution. There were shifts, of course, especially among supporters of the Constitution who became Republicans. But it is also clear that a substantial majority of the Republican party were former Antifederalists. In

TABLE VI.

	Creditor faction of 1785–1787	Debtor faction of 1785–1787
Pro-Constitution in 1788–1789	26	4[a]
Anti-Constitution in 1788-1789	6[b]	28
Unknown	16	9
	—	—
	48	41

[a]Two remained Federalists; two became Republicans.
[b]Two of the six voted Federalist in 1793–1794.

TABLE VII.

Federalists in 1788		Antifederalists in 1788	
Remained Federalists	68	Became Federalists	5
Became Republicans	31	Became Republicans	49
Unknown	62	Unknown	101

---

[50] The totals in each case are higher than in Tables III and IV because they also include a few delegates who were identified only by their votes on domestic debts and taxes.

general, it can be said that the party system that appeared in the 1790s as a result of differences over national policies, domestic and foreign, was superimposed upon the existing factional alignment in Virginia.

The outbreak of war in Europe, Washington's neutrality proclamation, and the mission of Edmond Genet in the spring of 1793 created new sources of controversy among Virginians, but did not seriously disrupt existing political alignments. Their main effect was to stimulate party organization at the local level.[51] Mass meetings and petition campaigns were not new, but never before had they been so well managed or so successful in mobilizing opinion. On August 17, 1793, Federalists organized a "numerous meeting" of Richmond citizens, chaired by aging George Wythe. It passed resolutions submitted by Marshall which endorsed the neutrality proclamation and denounced foreign influence that might "lead to the introduction of foreign gold and foreign armies."[52] Popular meetings in neighboring counties soon passed similar resolutions. The language and tone differed somewhat in each case, but the extent of Federalist collusion was evident. By early September their apparatus had spread to the Shenandoah Valley. A meeting in Staunton passed resolutions drafted by Archibald Stuart— Madison's ally in the 1780s—that were virtually identical to the Richmond set.[53]

Republicans were surprised and dismayed at this Federalist initiative. Madison suspected "the cabal at Philadelphia" was behind it, but he suggested that Republicans sponsor similar meetings to determine "the real sense of the people."[54] The first was held in Caroline, where Pendleton presided over a meeting that passed resolutions vaguely endorsing the President and neutrality while denouncing all efforts to drive a wedge between the United States and France. Similar resolutions were adopted in other counties, and though the tone was vague and defensive the Republicans could count on general public support.[55] When the Federalists tried to organize another meeting in Staunton, Monroe rode across the Blue Ridge with one of Madison's addresses in hand and managed to "effectually change the current and give it a direction against the anti-Republican faction."[56]

During the next two years national issues continued to dominate Virginia politics. When Governor Henry Lee led a detachment of Vir-

---

[51] Harry Ammon, "The Genet Mission and the Development of American Political Parties," *Journal of American History*, LII (March 1966), 725–41.

[52] Richmond *Virginia Gazette and General Advertiser*, Aug. 21, 1793.

[53] *Ibid.*, Sept. 4, 11, 25, Oct. 2, 1793.

[54] Madison to Jefferson, Aug. 27, 1793, Madison Papers.

[55] Richmond *Virginia Gazette*, Sept. 25, Oct. 17, 23, 1793.

[56] Monroe to Madison, Sept. 25, 1793, Madison Papers.

ginia troops to suppress the Pennsylvania whiskey rebels in the fall of 1794, Republicans in the House of Delegates introduced a resolution claiming the governor had violated the statute which prohibited officials from holding positions under both state and federal governments. The house thereupon declared the office of governor vacant and elected Republican Robert Brooke over Federalist James Wood by a vote of 90 to 60.[57] This was the first time national issues dictated the selection of a governor.

The Whiskey Rebellion coincided with a crisis in Anglo-American relations brought on by British depredations on American commerce and lingering disputes over planter debts, retention of the Northwest posts, and intrigues among the Indians. Henry's son-in-law, Spencer Roane, told Monroe that if war became necessary, "a pretty strong Expedition into Canada, paid with the money due to british creditors, could scarcely fail. . . ."[58] In Congress, Madison introduced resolutions to curtail trade with Britain as a measure of retaliation; and, when Washington dispatched Chief Justice John Jay to negotiate a settlement, Republicans expected the worst. They disliked the use of a judge for executive embassies, and they distrusted Jay for his suggestion a decade earlier that navigation of the Mississippi be abandoned to Spain in return for commercial concessions that would have benefited the North.[59] Rumors that came out of England during Jay's negotiations were not reassuring, and Virginia Republicans were fully prepared to be dismayed at the result.[60]

After Jay returned, Washington delayed several months before submitting the treaty to the Senate; and then the Senate voted to keep its provisions secret until it was fully ratified. On June 24, 1795, Senator Henry Tazewell summarized Virginia's objections to the treaty. It set up mechanisms for the restoration of confiscated Loyalist property and the recovery of British debts without providing compensation for Negroes allegedly carried off by the British during the Revolution. It regulated the nation's trade by executive agreement, thereby depriving Congress of some of its power over commerce (notably the power to retaliate against Britian through nonintercourse). And it was likely to damage American relations with France, while restoring a colonial dependence

---

[57] Nov. 21, 1794, *Journal of . . . Delegates . . . 1794*, p. 28.

[58] Spencer Roane to Monroe, Jan. 25, 1794, Monroe Papers.

[59] Madison to Jefferson, April 28, 1794, Madison Papers; Resolutions of the Democratic Society of Wythe County, Richmond *Virginia Gazette*, July 23, 1794.

[60] Jones to Madison, Nov. 16, 1794, Madison to Jefferson, Feb. 15, 1795, Madison Papers.

upon Britain.[61] In objecting to the treaty Jefferson and Madison were preoccupied with neutral rights and national pride, but other Virginia Republicans focused on the provisions involving British creditors and Loyalist estates.[62] Virginia Federalists, however, generally approved the treaty because it kept the peace, honored old debts, and removed the British from the Northwest.[63]

Each of the issues of national policy was debated in the Virginia assembly. In the period of 1793–1796 there were eleven roll calls involving party divisions, including resolutions on Washington's French policy in 1793, commentary on Congressman William Branch Giles' efforts to investigate the treasury department, attempts to add new amendments to the Constitution, the removal of Governor Henry Lee for accepting a federal command against the whiskey rebels, and a succession of votes expressing the opinion of the house on the Jay Treaty. A total of 360 men served during these four sessions, of whom 197 (54 percent) can be identified by party, a substantial increase over previous sessions.[64] The growth of party cohesion is also evident in the decline of the middle. Only twenty delegates failed to agree with one party or the other as much as 75 percent of the time, while 114 voted with a party 100 percent of the time. There were 102 Republicans and seventy-five Federalists, which is roughly the same proportion that the two parties possessed in the 1788–1792 sessions. This suggests that the Genet mission, the Whiskey Rebellion, and the Jay Treaty were not quite as disastrous to Federalist strength in Virginia as historians commonly assume.[65] The regional breakdown was also similar to that which had existed since the Constitution (see Table VIII). The solidification of party strength in the Piedmont, Southside, and West evidenced the polarizing effect of domestic and foreign issues that arose in 1793 and after. The Middle Tidewater

---

[61] Thomas J. Farnham, "The Virginia Amendments of 1795: An Episode in the Opposition to Jay's Treaty," *Virginia Magazine of History and Biography*, 75 (Jan. 1967), 75–88.

[62] Paul Varg, *Foreign Policy of the Founding Fathers* (East Lansing, 1963), 111–12. For examples, see Daniel Hylton to Jones, Jan. 17, 1795, Robert Atkinson to Jones, Sept. 7, 1795. Joseph Jones Papers (Duke University); Stevens T. Mason to Henry Tazewell, Oct. 6, 1795, Henry Tazewell Papers (Virginia State Library); Joseph Neville to Madison, Dec. 8, 1795, Madison Papers.

[63] Risjord, "The Virginia Federalists," 499–501.

[64] One Republican and two Federalists voted on all eleven roll calls; their records were used as models. The minimum standard was three out of four agreements (75 percent), but there were only thirteen of these.

[65] It is possible, of course, that the Federalists were more conscientious in attendance and voting and, therefore, more likely to be identified. This could not be tested without undertaking to count members who cast only two ballots on the key issues. This was not statistically defensible.

TABLE VIII.

	1788–1792 Sessions			1793–1796 Sessions		
Region	Fed	Anti fed/Rep	Middle	Fed	Anti fed/Rep	Middle
Northern Neck	10	12	1	13	4	2
Middle Tidewater	7	16	2	15	12	3
Piedmont	4	11	0	6	19	3
Southside	7	37	0	2	52	3
West	22	18	1	37	15	9
Urban	1	0	1	2	0	0
Totals	51	94	5	75	102	20

SOURCE: Derived from multidimensional scaling of recorded roll-call votes in the United States Congress (collected by the Inter-University Consortium for Political and Social Research).

remained as mixed as ever, and the only important shift is in the stance of the Northern Neck. Federalist gains there were the result mostly of the party organization built in the mid-1790s by Alexandria merchant Levin Powell. He was particularly successful in the Loudoun/ Fairfax/ Fauquier part of the northern Piedmont, counties that were solidly Federalist through these years. The Federalist complexion of the Northern Neck is also reminiscent of its creditor stance in the 1780s. Indeed, the aberration is the mixed record of the area in the 1788–1792 period; and this was probably the result of personal influence more than anything else—the strong antipathy to the Constitution voiced by Mason, Grayson, and Richard Henry Lee.

In addition to the various votes which determined party loyalty in the 1793–1796 sessions, there were eight roll calls involving economic issues: four on taxation and four on various forms of debtor relief. Republican cohesion was remarkable. Using as a model William Boyce, the one Republican who voted on all eight issues, a total of fifty-one Republicans, five Federalists, nine middle-of-the-roaders, and two of unknown party agreed with him at least 75 percent of the time. It is not always clear from the *Journal* what issues were involved in the debtor-relief votes, but on the other four votes the Republicans consistently favored tax reduction or postponement.

Federalists were more divided on economic issues. One group that voted the reverse of the above Republican position on all issues contained twenty-one Federalists, five Republicans, and five in the middle. The Federalists were mostly from the Shenandoah Valley and the Tidewater, especially the Northern Neck and lower James River regions. Another group of eleven Federalists, mostly from western Virginia, voted with Republicans on tax issues but with eastern Federalists on debtor-relief issues. Despite the return of prosperity in the 1790s partisan voting still extended to economic issues. Thus the state divided regionally along roughly the same lines that it did in the 1780s, and since the political parties followed similar lines there is substantial correlation between partisan and economic voting behavior.

By the end of Washington's administration the first party system had taken shape in Virginia, and there remained only the perfection of techniques—disciplining party ranks in the legislature and improving the local machinery for mobilizing the electorate. The political tensions of the Adams administration—including the XYZ Affair, the undeclared war with France, and the alien and sedition laws—afforded both parties plenty of opportunity to perfect their organizations. At the same time they eroded Federalist strength, for the administration's belligerence toward France, its moves to enlarge the army, and its efforts to silence the Jeffersonian press were generally unpopular in Virginia. In the 1797–1799 sessions there were twenty-one roll calls involving party issues (twice as many as in any previous period), itself an indication of the increase in partisanship. The issues included statements on John Adams' conduct of foreign policy, changes in the state's presidential electoral system, and numerous resolutions protesting the alien and sedition laws and increases in the military establishment. The increased number of roll calls enables the identification of a higher percentage of the house than before (270 out of 330, or 81 percent), and it permits some assessment of the degree of party fervor (see Table IX).[66]

The amount of internal cohesion among both parties evidences the final development of the system. The legislature was virtually polarized; there was no longer much room for moderates or inconsistent behavior. The fate of John Pierce of James City County is a case in point. In the 1788–1792 period Pierce voted Antifederalist five of six times, but then in the 1793–1796 sessions he voted with the Federalists on ten of twelve roll calls. Republican Littleton Waller Tazewell, who defeated him in the spring election of 1798, observed triumphantly that Pierce had "met the reward for his inconsistency."[67] Tazewell, at least, kept track of Pierce's voting record and evidently thought the electorate did too.

Considering the dramatic changes in national public attitudes during these years—from the patriotic burst that greeted the XYZ Affair to the shrill criticism of federal taxation and the military establishment—one might expect more shifts in party allegiance.

---

[66] A minimum of 80 percent agreement was required for party categorization; "moderates" were those who voted with a party 60 to 80 percent of the time. Those who cast only three or four votes were not included unless they were perfectly consistent.

[67] Littleton W. Tazewell to Henry Tazewell, Feb. 16, 1798, Tazewell Papers.

TABLE IX.

Republicans	149
Moderate Republicans	8
Middle-of-road	7
Moderate Federalists	12
Federalists	94

Yet, of the Federalists, only four had voted Republican in previous sessions, and among the Republicans only seven had previously voted Federalist. To the extent that public opinion changed in Virginia it was reflected in the turnover among the delegates, which was higher in these years than at any time since the Constitution went into effect. Evidently, when a delegate was out of tune with his county he was quickly replaced.

The development of the party system thus enhanced the importance of the electorate. In earlier years candid appeals to the voters for support were considered bad form, but by the late 1790s democratic sentiments were creeping into the political rhetoric.[68] When John Page lost his congressional seat in 1797 to a Federalist from the Eastern Shore, he ascribed his defeat to the influence of "the Aristocrats" in the district. (Page was master of "Rosewell," a plantation of 1,750 acres and thirty slaves on the York River, while his opponent, Thomas Evans, posssessed 516 acres and six slaves in Accomac.)[69] Nevertheless, Page reassured a Williamsburg friend, "I have so perfectly trained my mind to republican Principles that it instantly submits to the will of the Majority. I am therefore perfectly reconciled to the Decision of the Electors. I thank you and your Friends who went to York to vote for me."[70]

When the spring elections of 1799 were over, Marshall observed, "There are from fifty to sixty new members. Unfortunately the strength of parties is not materially varied. The opposition maintains its majority in the house of Delegates. The consequence must be an antifederal Senator & Governor."[71] The assembly had been sending former Antifeder-

---

[68] For examples of how electioneering was equated with demagoguery, see Pendleton to Richard Henry Lee, March 14, 1785, Lee Family Papers (University of Virginia); Archibald Stuart to John Breckinridge, Oct. 21, 1785, Breckinridge Papers (Manuscript Division, Library of Congress); Madison to Randolph, Nov. 23, 1788, Madison Papers; "Articles to the Freemen of the State of Virginia," Richmond *Virginia Independent Chronicle*, March 21, 1787; "Observer to the Freeholders of the Commonwealth of Virginia," *ibid.*, March 28, 1787.

[69] Tax lists, Gloucester (1797), Accomac (1793, 1800) (Virginia State Library).

[70] John Page to St. George Tucker, March 30, 1797, Tucker-Coleman Papers.

[71] Marshall to Washington, May 16, 1799, Washington Papers.

alists to the Senate since the first federal election, but the gubernatorial election, except for Henry Lee's dismissal in 1794, was not a partisan affair. Indeed, the incumbent James Wood, a veteran of the Indian wars, was a Federalist. The governor had few powers under the constitution of 1776, but installing a Republican in the post, thought John Taylor of Caroline, would be "of immense importance by the influence it will have on public opinion." Another Republican thought the state needed a change because a "truely Republican Executive" would provide "a sure foundation for the Election of the next President."[72]

When the assembly met in the autumn, Monroe was elected governor over Federalist James Breckinridge by a vote of 111 to 44, and Federalists were purged from all offices—speaker, clerk, and public printer.[73] The Republican majority then proceeded to change the rules of the electoral system. It abolished the district system of choosing presidential electors in favor of a winner-take-all approach, thereby preventing a repetition of the two electoral votes which Virginia Federalists had cast for Adams in 1796. It also eliminated oral voting in the choice of presidential electors, so that each voter had to write in the name of each of the twenty-one electors allotted to the state. The effect was to give an advantage to the party with the best local organization. A week after these changes were adopted the Republicans held a party caucus. This meeting selected prominent figures in each county to serve as a local committee, and then it created a standing committee to supervise the activities of the county committees. The purpose behind the changes in the electoral laws became evident when the central committee distributed printed ballots containing the names of the Republican electors. It even suggested that local committees could hand them out to freeholders to be used as genuine ballots on election day.[74]

The Federalists were slightly less organized and considerably more defensive, aware that the Adams administration was quite unpopular in the state. In May 1800, they printed a list of candidates for the electoral college. An accompanying "Address to the Voters" avoided any reference to the national party, even to the point of styling itself "The American Republican Ticket." It appealed to the name of the recently deceased Washington and called for support of his "virtuous successor" without mentioning Adams by name. Avoiding any mention of such unpopular policies as the alien and sedition laws, increases in the military, and heavy taxation, it concentrated instead on Republican

---

[72] John Taylor to Jefferson, Feb. 15, 1799, *John P. Branch Historical Papers of Randolph-Macon College*, II (1908), 278–81; John Guerrant to Monroe, Oct. 14, 1799, Monroe Papers.

[73] Beeman, *Old Dominion and the New Nation*, 212–13.

[74] Cunningham, *Jeffersonian Republicans*, 194–96; Beeman, *Old Dominion and the New Nation*, 221–22.

changes in the electoral rules which placed the choice of President in the hands of a few "imposing names."[75]

The election of 1800 thus represents the ultimate maturity of the first party system. Party loyalty was a major criterion for appointment to both executive and legislative offices. Nearly all members of the legislature and all candidates for the electoral college were identified by party. Each side was actively appealing to the people for support or at least giving lip service to the principle of democracy, and each was developing sophisticated organizations to mobilize that support on election day.

Thus, from essentially personal factions in the early 1780s there evolved by 1800 political organizations with a disciplined membership, able to formulate a comprehensive program and appeal to the electorate for support. The process was gradual, with each new coalition and each new political technique built upon earlier alliances and methods. The economic issues and congressional politics of the Confederation, the Constitution, Hamilton's fiscal system, and the diplomatic problems of the 1790s—each contributed to the evolutionary process by focusing attention on issues, stimulating public debate, and engendering popular organizations.

Even in its maturity, however, the first party system was comparatively primitive by modern standards. Much would still be done by later organizers to develop more effective means of party discipline and a rhetoric that would enable the "common man" to identify with the political system. Nor should the first party system be judged by the example of a practitioner as profound and analytical as Madison. Probably a more typical product and observer of the system was the assembly "back bencher" from the Shenandoah Valley who wrote to a neighbor: "I hop that I shall be at home against Crismus not that I am tired of the buesness it is the Best Scool that I ever was at I am verry happy if I could engoy my little famuley, I have a grate oppertunity of knowing the ways of the Town, I hope that Mr. Jefferson will be Elected praesedent. . . . "[76]

---

[75] "An Address to the Voters for Electors of President and Vice President of the United States, in the State of Virginia," May 26, 1800, John Cropper Papers.

[76] William Lemon to Henry Bedinger, Nov. 23, 1796 [copy], Danske-Dandridge Papers (Duke University).

The Democratic Republicans
of New York

Alfred F. Young

Among the most admired of all the state and local studies of the 1960s was The Democratic Republicans of New York: The Origins, 1763–1797 *(Chapel Hill: University of North Carolina Press, 1967). Though cautious in his generalizations and insistent on significant changes over time, Young also found considerable continuity from the politics of the 1780s—and even from the early Revolution—to the party battles of the 1790s. His concluding chapter, which originally appeared under a different title, summarizes the findings of a fine, big book. ©1967 The University of North Carolina Press. Published for the Institute of Early American History and Culture, Williamsburg. Reprinted by permission.*

By 1797 the Democratic Republicans of New York were in full bloom, the contours of the movement clearly shaped. In the political history of New York in the early national period, four broad questions emerge to which this study was directed. Who were the Democratic Republicans? What were the issues that brought the movement into being? What was it like as an organized entity? What was its philosophy?

I

Who were the Repubicans in New York? One of the best ways to answer this question is to ask another: who were the Federalists? In the leadership of the Federalists, the continuities in New York politics from the Revolution through the 1790s were striking. The Federalist party of the mid–1790s was led by the same men who had led the conservative Whigs in the '70s and the nationalists in the '80s: Philip Schuyler, Alexander Hamilton, and John Jay above all others, James Duane, Egbert Benson, Nicholas Low, John Laurance, Stephen Van Rensselaer among the second-rank figures. These leaders were themselves of the landlord-mercantile aristocracy or were their spokesmen. There were also discontinuities. By the mid–1790s the Federalists had lost the lower manor Livingstons completely, and could not count on the upper manor branch; Gouverneur Morris was in Europe; William Duer was in jail; Duane died in 1794. They also were joined by several new clusters of leaders whose strength lay in rural areas outside the traditional domain of the landlords and merchants; former anti-Federalists like Peter Van Gaasbeck of Ulster County and John Williams of the northern frontier, and William Cooper, Charles Williamson, and Thomas Morris of the west. In New York City and the Hudson Valley they took into their councils such former Tories as Richard Harison, Josiah Hoffman, and Samuel Jones and Yankee newcomers like Rufus King, James Watson, and Ambrose Spencer. These new leaders also tended to be men at the apex of wealth and economic power in their communities, especially on the frontier.

The leadership of the Republicans showed similar continuities and discontinuities. The party was built around the nucleus of George Clinton's anti-Federalists who in the Revolution had been the leaders of the popular Whigs. The anti-Federalist leaders of 1788 in Albany, Ulster, and Dutchess counties, on Long Island and at New York City remained leaders of the Republicans through the 1790s. Yet Clinton had broken "the confederacy" of "all the great and opulent families" which he had mentioned to Rufus King in 1789. Chancellor Livingston's family which had been with him in the Revolution had rejoined him; so had the Van Cortlandts who had deserted in 1787–88. These two landed families contributed Republican congressmen in two districts, New York City and Westchester. The few anti-Federalist leaders of 1788 whom Clinton had lost—Williams, Van Gaasbeck, and Jones—were more than matched by well-known former Federalists who became active Republicans: Brockholst and Edward Livingston, James Nicholson, Samuel Osgood, and Elkanah Watson. Equally important, there were a number of active young newcomers among the Republicans like Tunis Wortman and William Keteltas who counted themselves as neither Federalist nor anti-Federalist in '88. And on the western frontier, Republicans were on the verge of acquiring a new breed of former Federalists among whom Jedediah Peck was a prototype.

The support of both Federalist and Republican leaders changed markedly between the 1780s and the 1790s. The old anti-Federalists were sustained primarily by the yeomanry, both of the substantial and poorer sort. They had created a small following among aspiring entrepreneurs—land speculators, manufacturers, would-be bankers, upstart merchants—but they had lost most of the prewar mechanic following of the popular Whigs to the Federalists. As for the tenants, even though large numbers of them voted anti-Federalist in the convention contest of '88, the leaders feared them as "mechanical creatures" of the aristocracy.

By 1797, Republicans were like the anti-Federalists in one essential: they were still primarily an agrarian party whose strongest vote came from the centers of the yeomanry. Unlike the anti-Federalists, however, Republicans had acquired an urban wing in New York City based primarily upon the mechanics.[1] Their following in this class consisted of entire trades whose interests they espoused, such as the tallow chandlers, trades in need of protection from British manufactures, and the poorer mechanics in general, especially cartmen and laborers, who, if they could not vote, turned out to damn Jay's Treaty at the "town meetings," and packed the assembly chambers to cheer William Keteltas, the ferryman's champion. Republicans also won over a good sprinkling of articulate professionals: lawyers, ministers, doctors, teachers, and young men and women in all classes who gave the movement its tone. Among merchants their degree of success is summed up by an offhand comment by the poet-editor, Philip Freneau. The daily papers, he explained to DeWitt Clinton, "were supported by a mercantile interest which as you know is not republican." He completed the sentence, returned, placed a caret mark between "not" and "republican" to make it read "not generally republican."[2] By 1797 Republicans had won over a small segment of the "mercantile interest," although a growing one.

Republicans also made inroads, though small ones, among the tenantry. In Columbia County, some of their new support was dragooned by the upper manor Livingstons, but the family was so unpredictable that they were more of a handicap than a help; some came from the small, politically inconsequential lower manor. Republicans had only limited success in exploiting the growing anti-landlord sentiment among dependents of Schuyler and Van Rensselaer at the polls. They were willing to climb to office by charging political domination by "the manor lords" but were unwilling to join tenants in challenging the landlords' property rights or the court system that upheld them. Republicans thus broke out of the mold of the popular Whigs who had scorned the tenant rebellions of '66 and '77 and Shays' Rebellion of '86, but in only a limited way.

The basis of Federalist support was also broader at the end of the Washington administration than a decade before, as their success in electing Jay in 1795 and six congressmen in 1796 indicated. To a considerable extent Federalist electoral strength continued to be a vote of economic dependents. The safest counties in the state for both gubernatorial and congressional voting were those where the landlords Philip Schuyler and Stephen Van Rensselaer predominated. In their tradi-

---

[1] See Young, "The Merchants and the Jeffersonians," *Labor History*, 5 (1964) 247–76.

[2] Philip Freneau to DeWitt Clinton, Nov. 8, 1795, DeWitt Clinton Papers, No. 35, Columbia Univ.

tional stronghold, New York City, Federalists owed a good deal of their vote to the influence of merchant over clerk and cartman, of master craftsman over journeyman and of both over laborers. And on the frontier, their newest recruits were often debtors to land projectors and land agents. But the fact remains that most Federalist support was uncoerced, a product of the appeal of their policies. In the 1780s the yeomanry of the southern district was attracted to the Federalists for their leniency to loyalism; in the 1790s a segment of the yeomanry of the Hudson Valley in Whig Clintonian counties like Ulster, Orange and Dutchess also came over, disillusioned with Clintonian policies. On the frontier their support among farmers was based on a variety of policies already analyzed. In New York City Federalists also kept a following among the "leading" and "substantial mechanics," who very likely were the more well-to-do master craftsmen and native-born or English-born mechanics. In both parties there was a subtle shift of appeal between 1788 and 1797; Republicans had to attract mercantile and mechanic support and Federalists were tugged by their new and potential yeoman constituents in the Hudson Valley and especially on the frontier.

Ethnic factors seem more important by 1797 than before. The native born and the established immigrant groups, the English, Dutch, Scotch-Irish, and Germans, divided along lines of social economic interests or political tradition. The newcomers from 1793 on, the French, Irish, and Scotch-Irish who were mostly poor, had settled in New York City and had a liberal or radical political heritage, tended to become Republican. Immigrants of English background and those who rose quickly tended to be Federalist. The largest group of newcomers to the state, the New England migrants, went en masse into the Federalist party, especially on the frontier. There, however, they leavened the party in their own Yankee image, contributing to the split of western against eastern Federalist and pioneer farmer against proprietor which paved the way for the emergence of Republicanism on the frontier.

Republicans and Federalists both drew support from almost all religious groups. This much, however, can be said of the Republicans: they obviously had far more adherents among orthodox Protestant denominations than the numerically small deists. Most deists were Republicans, but staunch Baptists like Melancton Smith and Jedediah Peck and the liberal ministers of New York City were more important in shaping the movement than Elihu Palmer, the famous blind deist, or the short-lived Deistical Society of Newburgh. The evidence also suggests that there was significant support for Republicans among Presbyterians, whose church had been synonymous with Whiggery in the Revolution; George Clinton and Aaron Burr were well known as Presbyterians and the Livingstons were heirs to the tradition of the "Presbyterian Party" of provincial days.

II

What were the issues which gave rise to the Democratic-Republican movement, bringing about the alignment just described? Noble Cunningham's generalizations that the Republican party was "a product of national rather than state politics" and that it "was a new growth that sprang from the divisions in Congress and the national government" must be modified for New York, perhaps even more than he concedes.[3] In New York, as we have said, the Republican party was built around the core of the anti-Federalist Clintonian party, the product of Governor Clinton's long tenure in the state government. Men who were attracted to Clinton by his policies and patronage, his principles and reputation, did not need national issues to stimulate them to oppose the Federalists, their traditional political enemies. Indeed the first Washington administration witnessed a duel between two masterful politicians who used the magnet of governmental power to attract substantial interests. Hamilton by his policies on funding, assumption, the tariff, and the bank, hoped to cement an array of interests to the new national government. Clinton used land grants, state investments in canals and roads, and support for manufacturing and banking to attract others and sustain his power. Clintonianism, like Hamiltonianism thus was a positive, dynamic force.

The national policies which did affect New York during Washington's first administration operated differently than most historians have assumed. The "high tone" of the new government, the "aristocracy" that loomed so large in Senator Maclay's diary simply did not strike fire as a public issue. Neither did Hamiltonian finance, at least not at its inception. The anti-Federalists did not vote against funding and the tacit understanding about the settlement of New York's debts of the Revolution to the central government assuaged hostility to assumption. Opposition rose as the orgy of speculation revealed the beneficiaries of Hamilton's program, but even after "the panic of 1792" the political kickback did not last beyond the spring elections. At the end of Washington's first term Federalists won a sweeping vote of approval in the congressional elections.

The Bank of the United States probably had the most serious repercussions within New York of any internal Hamiltonian measure, for it triggered rival business groups into a "battle of the banks." Although the "State Bank" project to counter the political combination of the Bank of the United States and the Bank of New York failed, the demand for a non-Federalist bank remained, emerging in 1799 to support Aaron Burr's more famous scheme for the Bank of Manhattan. The bank war of New York in 1791–92 also anticipated in more ways than one the

---

[3] Cunningham, *The Jeffersonian Republicans*, 256.

business rivalries and "anti-monopoly" spirit of the bank war of the Jacksonian era.

The issue of banking, combined with assumption, was also important for providing the occasion on which the Livingstons first demonstrated their opposition to Hamilton's policies. There is a more complex explanation for Chancellor Livingston's departure from the house of Federalism than his disappointment over not being appointed to high office. An ally of Governor Clinton in the Revolution, he had been slow to join Hamilton and Jay in the battle for a new federal Constitution. He had fought Hamilton on banking policy in 1784; he never favored assumption of the state debts; he also had a latent disagreement with John Jay over the French alliance. Principle thus combined with pique and pride. After 1793 when foreign affairs became crucial, Washington found that he could not bridge the gap between the Chancellor and the Federalists by patronage.

The "republican interest" that came into existence in Washington's first term would not have found a mass following had it not been for Federalist foreign policies in the second. Here the stimulus was unmistakably national and international. The French Revolution helped but it was not as divisive an issue in New York as dramatizers of the period have made it out to be. It operated, moreover, to widen a long-standing schism over the French alliance in which Robert R. Livingston, the "Gallican," and John Jay, the "anti-Gallican," had long been protagonists. British policy on the high seas and on the frontier, coupled with the Federalist response to them, created the Republican movement in New York, enabling Republicans to catch full sail the strongest winds of nationalism to blow across American political waters since the Revolution.

After men were alienated from the Federalists, Republicans found a receptive audience to renewed attacks against Hamiltonian finance. The evil effects of "the funding system" seemed more visible in the light of the burning effigies of John Jay. Even so, when the inscription for Abraham Yates's tombstone was made public in 1796:

SPECTATOR
Beneath Lies
Abraham Yates, Junior
who uniformly opposed the tyr-
rany of Britain,
and the corrupt, perfidious
funding system;
not for his own good but for the
Public Good.
He has directed this last testi-
monial of the sincerity

of his apprehensions
That it will prove most injurious
to the
Equal Rights of Man
And the essential interests of his country[4]

there probably were not many Republicans who shared the depth of feeling that burned to the last in "Rough Hewer."

After a political following was handed to them by the Federalists, the New York Republicans, it must be said, bungled their chance. They clung to Citizen Genêt after Jefferson advised them to abandon him as a liability; Cornelia Clinton's marriage to the Frenchman was symbolic. They became strident "war hawks" in the spring of 1794, alienating both the commercial interest and the frontier, and by making a last-ditch fight against Jay's Treaty in 1796 they pitted themselves against George Washington whose prestige outmatched theirs. In each crisis Federalists were able to outmaneuver the Republicans, making the issue Washington or his traducers, and war or peace with Britain. The result in New York, as elsewhere, was that Republicans were unable to consolidate their gains of 1794, the year of patriotism, thus losing the crucial presidential and congressional elections of 1796.

This extraordinary support for the Federalist party, one of the striking themes of New York politics in the 1790's, was based in large part on the widespread conviction that Federalist policies benefited the state. Hamiltonian financial measures, while they feathered the nests of a good number of wealthy New Yorkers, were also to the advantage of the state treasury as a holder of federal securities and then as an investor in bank stock. The invigoration of commerce lined the pockets of exporting farmers as well as merchants. National military power broke the back of Indian resistance and national diplomacy, however humiliating Jay's Treaty may otherwise have been, restored the forts on New York soil and established a procedure to indemnify shippers for their losses. The results were a boon to pioneer as well as proprietor on the frontier and to all in the east whose prosperity rested on foreign commerce. Federalists, in short, had an outstanding record to point to.

Secondly, Federalists, as the "outs" in the state government, exploited to the hilt Clinton's aberrations from democratic ideals. They campaigned against him for his excessive stay in office and his personal fortune. They hung the albatross of the land office sales of 1791 around his neck for a decade. They championed the "rights of suffrage" after the election "steal" of 1792. Schuyler, western state senator and father of the first canal, espoused the interests of the western district which

---

[4] *Albany Register*, July 8, 1796.

elected him. In New York City, Federalist humanitarians pioneered as abolitionists, while Ulster Clintonians still defended slavery.

Third, and most important, one face of Federalism was consistently moderate. Under the guidance of Hamilton, Schuyler, Jay, King, and Benson, the New York Federalists established a middle-of-the-road record on issue after issue. They promised amendments to the Constitution in 1788, toned down the "high" Federalists, and ran Robert Yates, a moderate anti-Federalist, against Clinton in 1789; they cooled off the western hotheads who wanted to oust Clinton by extra-legal methods after the election decision of 1792, and did an about-face in 1794, fortifying the state and adopting an embargo in order to avert war. This flexibility continued the tactic cultivated by conservative Whigs from the 1770s, based on the dictum of Robert R. Livingston to "yield to the torrent if they hoped to direct its course."[5] John Jay's career is the perfect example of this policy. A straight line of moderation runs from his role in getting the state constitution through Abraham Yates's committee in 1777, to the tactics of appeasement to get the federal Constitution through the Poughkeepsie convention in 1788, through his caution as the aggrieved victim of the "stolen" election of 1792, to his conciliatory first message as governor in 1796. This pattern suggests that the process of conservative adaptation to democratic currents began much earlier than Dixon Ryan Fox and many others allowed.

On the other hand these same Federalists had a strain of contempt for the people—a class prejudice—which was a major cause of their undoing. "Aristocracy" was a persistent issue in a state which from 1777 on elected George Clinton because it did not want a Livingston or a Schuyler as governor. It took on new meaning in the 1790s in reaction to the highhandedness of Hudson Valley landlords, western land proprietors, and New York City magistrates. In 1795, Stephen Van Rensselaer, who coerced his tenants at the polls, barely sneaked in as lieutenant-governor. In 1796 just when Federalists were recovering the ground they had lost because of Jay's Treaty, Mayor Varick by his handling of the case of the Irish ferrymen and the assembly by jailing William Keteltas almost gave the city to the Republicans. The same year pioneers on the western frontier exploded against the "Albany junto" which seemingly dictated the nominations of the district and against William Cooper, the "Bashaw of Ostego."

The violent reaction of Federalist leaders to the democratic upsurge of the mid–1790s revealed a growing rigidity. In stigmatizing the Democratic societies as "self created," the "town meetings" as the work of "the rabble," and petitions to Congress as unwarranted, Federalists

---

[5] Robert R. Livingston to William Duer, June 12, 1777, R. R. Livingston Papers, N.Y. Hist. Soc.

asserted their elitist notion of representation. Lacking confidence in their ability to win back Republicans as they had once won over followers of the popular Whigs and anti-Federalists, New York's Federalists were on the path to repression which culminated in the Alien and Sedition Laws of 1798. Years later Noah Webster in counseling Rufus King on a way out of the political debacle to which such policies had led them, resorted to the very language Robert R. Livingston had used in 1777: "They have attempted to resist the force of current opinion instead of falling into the current with a view to direct it."[6] By then, however, it was too late to repeat the techniques of the conservative holding action of the era of the Revolution.

III

What were the Republicans as an organized movement? Their achievement can be measured against the limitations of the predecessor group which they absorbed. The anti-Federalist party, in itself, was a landmark in New York's history, the first stable political group that did not center on one of the great landed families. It revolved instead around George Clinton's power as governor, not as landholder. More than a personal following, it was a loosely organized collection of the "new men" risen to power in the Revolution who were tied to Clinton by patronage, policy, and family "connections." It functioned cohesively in the state legislature but it was not put to the test as a state-wide electoral party until the gubernatorial campaign in 1789. The anti-Federalists had developed no political societies except for the shortlived Federal Republican Society of New York City and had established only one newspaper for the entire state, Thomas Greenleaf's *New York Journal and Patriotic Register*. Their rural following was unorganized, ill-informed, and provincial. To be a rank and file anti-Federalist in 1788 meant only that one voted for Governor Clinton and his followers and supported their policies.

By 1797 there clearly was a Democratic-Republican movement in New York State which embraced not only the Republican party but the Republican societies and the Republican press as well. The societies were distinct from the party, although they took part in elections on a *sub rosa* basis. But there were societies with staying power in only three counties who could not have had more than 500 members, all told. They were more "advanced" than the party and bore the stigma of "Jacobinism" which could not be pinned on local leaders elsewhere. They functioned as the "sentinels" who watched the rulers, as catalysts

---

[6] Noah Webster to Rufus King, July 6, 1807, King, ed., *Correspondence of Rufus King*, V, 37–38.

who produced the "addresses" to rally the citizenry, and as behind-the-scenes organizers. In New York City the Democratic society may be credited with perfecting the techniques of direct democratic expression: the "town meetings," the patriotic parades and celebrations, the circulation of public petitions. None of these techniques were new to Whigs who had lived through the 1770s but their scope was far broader.

By 1797 the upstate Republican societies had faded; all would disappear during the Adams administration. In the long run the myriad of other "self-created societies" which blossomed in the mid–1790s may have exerted a more profound political influence. The mechanic, fraternal, humanitarian, ethnic, religious, and militia organizations developed "the spirit of association" fundamental to a democracy. None was new to the 1790s but each in its own way expressed an awakened consciousness on the part of "the middling classes" and to a lesser extent the poor which was the essence of the Republican movement.

The Republican press was indispensable as a vehicle for the movement. With each spurt of Republican sentiment new papers were founded and old ones expanded their circulation. In the mid–1790s Greenleaf's *Journal* was joined by outright Republican papers at Newburgh, Goshen, Poughkeepsie, Kingston, and Albany; elsewhere new "impartial" and Federalist papers stimulated political discussion. The papers ran notices of meetings, nominations, and activities and reported resolutions, toasts, and orations. Most important, they teemed with articles on the issues of the day, long and short, "planted" and unsolicited. The small-town papers were jammed with "intelligence" of national, state, and European affairs, which probably kept their readers better informed on the world beyond their own village than do their counterparts today.

By the end of the era of Washington, Republicans had more of the attributes of a political party than the anti-Federalists. They had a name—usually "Republican"; their candidates often ran on a clearly labeled ticket; committees whose personnel was fairly stable from year to year made their nominations and conducted their campaigns. If Republicans ran as individuals as most still did, it was because it was expedient to avoid the party label. But political leaders knew who "their" men were. There was a process in operation; it went further in some areas, New York City, for example, than others. It also went further in national than state elections. Gubernatorial elections were the least partisan, as is indicated by the efforts of Burr and Chancellor Livingston in 1795 to secure nominations from both "interests" and by the management of the campaign by "the friends of Mr. Yates" and the "friends of Mr. Jay." Yet while the lines were looser in state elections they were essentially the same as in national affairs. In 1796 assemblymen and state senators elected without a label lined up in the state legislature on a predictable partisan basis to choose presidential electors.

Republican campaign methods did not change markedly in this period. Campaign workers made more use of newspapers, pamphlets, and broadsides but they still knew the value of "a beaver hat, an oyster supper, or a glass of grog" to sway a voter.[7] And while the voters heard more and more appeals to lofty principles, one suspects that in more than one township "a large majority gloried" at the election of their favorite because the legislature had located the new county courthouse favorably.[8] On the other hand if campaign methods did not change, it was unquestionably true that more and more people participated in the political process: in making nominations, in campaigning, and in voting.

As a party the Republicans were less unified than the anti-Federalists. Through the election of 1789 George Clinton was the undisputed anti-Federalist leader; he was indispensable for victory in gubernatorial elections and held a tight rein on the patronage. After Chancellor Livingston formed a "coalition" with Clinton to elevate Burr to the Senate in 1791, there were men with their own power base to challenge the Governor. Clinton's prestige also dropped after the land scandal and near defeat of 1792, and once Federalists gained control of the Council of Appointment in 1794 he lost the sinews of his power. As a result factionalism which was under wraps in 1792 when Burr maneuvered to replace Clinton as the Republican vice-presidential candidate was out in the open in 1795 when Clinton retired.

While there was never any love between Clinton, Livingston, and Burr, neither was there the virulent factionalism for which the New York Republicans of the early nineteenth century are so well known. If in Columbia County the Livingstons never got together with the old anti-Federalists on a congressional candidate, they worked unstintingly in harness with the Clintons against Federalist foreign policy. As a congressman Edward Livingston was untarnished in his Republicanism. If Burr sat out the gubernatorial election of 1795, the next year he ran for state senator to bolster the Republican ticket in the contest that would decide the choice of presidential electors. The incentive to oust the Federalists from national power made for cooperation if not cohesion.

If Chancellor Livingston had hopes of "directing" the Republican "torrent" by "yielding" to it, he must have been disillusioned. Control of the party was somewhat diffuse. Clinton, as long as he was governor, ran the party in the legislature together with the leading legislators. Gubernatorial nominations were made by a caucus of legislators attended by other leaders, and then were in effect endorsed at

---

[7] "Inspector," *N.Y. Evening Post*, Apr. 17, 1795.
[8] Vanderkemp, Journal, 16, N.Y. Hist. Soc., referring to the 1792 election for governor in Herkimer County.

local town and county meetings. Congressional candidates, by contrast, were chosen by the local leaders of the district; when two of the state's six Republican congressmen failed to stand firm on the crucial test of Jay's Treaty in 1796, the statewide leaders were not able to discipline them. Republican factionalism, so scorned by historians, actually was a symptom of a competition for power healthy to a new party.

By virtue of their strength in the state the New York Republicans clearly were a component of a national party; indeed, the national party appears to have been no more than a loose amalgam of the state groups. Neither Jefferson nor Madison had anything to do with organizing the New York Republicans; there would have been a Republican party in New York without them. Nor did the New Yorkers follow Madison's lead either in the fight against Hamiltonian finance in 1789–90 or in the foreign policy crisis of 1794–96 when they took a position to the "left" of the Virginians. They willingly backed Jefferson for the presidency in 1796 because of his opposition to Federalism, not because of his influence among the state party leaders. The New York Democratic Republicans thus cannot accurately be called New York Jeffersonians.

IV

What was the philosophy of the Democratic Republicans of New York? By 1797 they did, indeed, have a political credo distinct from the Federalists and in a number of ways distinct from the anti-Federalists of '88. For many young men who later achieved reputations only as hard-bitten politicians—DeWitt Clinton, Daniel Tompkins, Smith Thompson, Martin Van Buren—the 1790s were a seedbed of their Republican faith, and indeed of a youthful idealism.

First and foremost, Republicans were patriots. "After thy creator, love thy country above all things," read a catechism of the Albany Republicans entitled "The Precepts of Reason." "She alone, ought to fix thy thought and direct thy actions; thy life is hers."[9] To Republicans the battle against Jay's Treaty, a betrayal of national interest, was a holy crusade; England, a den of iniquity; "Tory," the most odious epithet in their vocabulary; Independence Day, a sacred festival; and Thomas Paine, old "Common Sense" of '76, a near saint. Republican patriots followed the progress of liberty in Europe with bated breath, took Citizen Genêt to their bosoms as a symbol of the French Revolution, and welcomed Joseph Priestley and the victims of European tyranny to America, "an asylum for the oppressed." But they did not cease to think of themselves as the true patriots, loyal to the spirit of '76. "Your drum," ex-Governor Clinton wrote to his new grandson, "Citizen

---

[9] "Precepts of Reason," *Barber and Southwick's Almanack for 1798*, unpaged.

George Clinton Genêt," is "at Granny's braced for you to beat to arms against Tories and aristocrats if necessary."[10]

Second, Republicans believed in democracy, as they testified by adopting the name Democratic for their societies, Democratic Republican for their party, and such pseudonyms as "Democratis." They discussed the concept infrequently, yet most probably would have agreed with the simple definition offered at Poughkeepsie: "a government emanating from and being under the influence of the people."[11] Unlike Federalists, Republicans believed that elected representatives should express the will of the people and, invigorated by the spirit of direct democracy, instructed officials through the resolutions of societies, public meetings, and petitions. Some Republican congressmen also believed that they had a responsibility to report on their actions to their constituents.[12] As Federalists censured the "self-created societies," denigrated the "town meetings," and jailed protesters like William Keteltas, a libertarian strain never strong in anti-Federalist thinking became more pronounced among Republicans, preparing the ground for the enunciation of a full-blown philosophy of freedom of expression by New Yorkers in the Sedition Law crisis.

Third, Republicans supported the federal Constitution. The Federalist persistence in labeling them "anti-Federalists" missed the mark completely. It was not rhetoric when a New York City orator referred to Republicans as "sincere friends to Our National Constitution."[13] By 1796, when Abraham Yates died, the old anti-Federalism lingered on primarily in such counties as Dutchess and Ulster; the other anti-Federalists had already created a mythology about 1788, maintaining that the sole issue had been whether amendments should be adopted before or after ratification. Republicans had moved toward a "strict interpretation" of the Constitution in the fight over Jay's Treaty, when they defended the legislative powers of the House of Representatives. They already thought of themselves as the "true" upholders of the Constitution against the Hamiltonians. This same strain of Constitutional literalism was also evident in the 1792 controversy over the election canvassers' decision when Clinton's defenders descended to an arid legalism, placing the letter over the spirit of the law.

---

[10] George Clinton to Citizen George Clinton Genêt, July 2, 1796, June 1, 1797, Genêt Papers, N.Y. Hist. Soc.

[11] "Gracchus," *Poughkeepsie Journal*, Mar. 17, 1801.

[12] A circular letter by Theodorus Bailey of Dutchess County, *Goshen Repository*, Feb. 11, 1794; Egbert Benson to Rufus King, Dec. 16, 1794, King Papers, N.Y. Hist. Soc., reported that Bailey also sent newspapers to the voters; Philip Van Cortlandt, Circular Letter, May 20, 1796, Van Cortlandt-Van Wyck Papers, N.Y. Pub. Lib.

[13] George Warner, *Means for the Preservation of Public Liberty . . . An Oration July 4, 1797 . . . before the General Society of Mechanics, Tammany, the Democratic and the New York Cooper Societies* (N.Y., 1797), 15, 9.

Fourth, in spite of Federalist efforts to stigmatize them as "revolutionaries," Republicans advocated change by peaceful means. In 1792 when frontier Federalists talked of redressing the canvassers' decision by the sword or a popular convention, Republicans put themselves on the side of "law and order." In 1794 they were quick to disavow the "Whiskey Rebellion." In 1796 they cheered William Keteltas' appeal for confidence in the courts for a legal redress of his unjust imprisonment. And at no time did they sanction extralegal action by tenants against their landlords.

Fifth, Republicans inherited the anti-Federalist attitude toward class. "Wherever the influence of riches are enabled to direct the choice of public offices," said George Warner, a sailmaker, "there the downfall of liberty cannot be very far remote." "Our choice," he continued, "ought only to be direct to men of TALENTS AND VIRTUE whatever their situation in life may be" and "the experience of ages confirms this opinion that a state of mediocrity is more favorable to them both." Melancton Smith had said as much at the Poughkeepsie convention; unlike the anti-Federalists who had faith only in the yeomanry, however, Warner thought of the "tradesmen, mechanics and the industrious classes of society" as the *Means for the Preservation of Public Liberty*, the title of his oration.[14] Other Republicans found a place for merchants in a coalition of "farmers, merchants, mechanics and common laboring men" necessary to defeat "great landholders and monied men."[15] None, it seems, found a place for estate holders like the Livingstons. Most Republicans, like most anti-Federalists, still believed that suffrage should be confined to the "middling classes," although Republican success among the propertyless in New York City led to some demands that the suffrage be broadened.

Sixth, Republicans were even less "agrarian" than were the anti-Federalists. Robert R. Livingston and Philip Freneau expressed a distaste for city life and a desire to retreat to a rural haven, but the patrician landlord and the sensitive poet were hardly typical of the Republican movement.[16] In the state legislature Clintonians were dedicated to the pursuit of wealth for the aspiring entrepreneur, be he land speculator or farmer, would-be banker or manufacturer. Republicans thought of themselves as advocates of "the mechanic and useful arts," a phrase that embraced the productive classes of both city and countryside.

Under the imperative of winning support from the commercial community Republicans in New York City constantly wooed "the mer-

---

[14] *Ibid.*, 13–15.

[15] "Scrutator," N.Y. *Journal*, Apr. 19, 1797.

[16] See Robert R. Livingston, "Address to the Agricultural Society of the State of New York," *New York Magazine*, 6 (1795), 95–102; Leary, *That Rascal Freneau*, 108, 260–65, 275.

cantile interest," from 1789 when they ran John Broome, president of the Chamber of Commerce for Congress, through the campaign for a third bank and the appeals by Genêt and his commercial agents, to the stand of the anti-Jay Treaty minority in the Chamber of Commerce in 1795. "The Colossus of American freedom," Congressman Edward Livingston toasted, "may it bestride the commerce of the world."[17] New York spawned no John Taylor in the 1790s.

Finally, Republicans were mild humanitarian reformers, as the activities of William Keteltas, Tunis Wortman, DeWitt Clinton, Jedediah Peck, and Elkanah Watson attest. "Every mortal is thy brother," read the Albany "Precepts of Reason," "always extend to him the helping hand. . .and always say to thyself, I am a man, nothing which interests humanity is foreign to me."[18] Republican humanitarianism for the most part, expressed middle-class sympathy for the less fortunate: the oppressed slave, the slum-ridden victims of yellow fever, the penniless immigrant, or the cruelly whipped prisoner. Republican reform sentiment was more urban than rural, more moderate rather than radical, and stopped short of a fundamental challenge to the state's political institutions or landlord system. Nevertheless ideology as well as political necessity pushed Republicans toward ridding society of its "glaring deformities."

In these democratic, libertarian, constitutionalist, humanitarian articles of faith and in their sympathy for "the middling classes," "the mechanic and useful arts," and men of "talents and virtue," Republicans were wedded to a set of convictions that would carry them beyond the immediate battles they were engaged in. In the period that followed, from 1797 to 1801 their ideals and their movement would be put to a test.

---

[17] Report of a dinner in New York City in honor of John Adams, *Whitestown Gazette*, Oct. 31, 1797.

[18] "Precepts of Reason," *Barber and Southwick's Almanack for 1798*, unpaged.

PART FOUR
Party Ideologies

By 1970 intense investigation of the early party conflict had resulted in a brilliant spectrum of competing understandings of the character, development, and social sources of political division. Each of the interpretations had become increasingly sophisticated as the scholars built on one another's work. Collectively, the modern studies added vastly to our stock of information and to our interpretive tools. But interests changed; and as this happened, it became increasingly apparent that— for all the baffling range of different views—the body of the recent literature had concentrated on a narrow set of questions. These, it now appeared, must certainly continue to be asked. And yet the very focus of the finest scholarship of the 1950s and early 1960s—concentrating so intensively on party operations, party growth, and social sources of political division—may also have produced a fundamentally misleading image of the new republic, suggesting that its early years were dominated by a sort of "politics as usual."

Comparisons are undeniably instructive, and the issues that preoccupied the writers of the early 1960s hardly seem less interesting today. By 1970, however, scholars were increasingly disturbed by the suggestion that the "first party system," as it was then familiarly called, was not so very different from the second or the third. Richard Hofstadter, as we have seen, had argued that the very concept of a party system was missing from the intellectual equipment of the nation's early years. Marshall Smelser had insisted that a better understanding of the new republic would require some means of comprehending the peculiar virulence of its political exchanges, some method of explaining why contemporaries argued with such passion and hated with such depth. The politicians of the new republic did not merely wish to see their enemies defeated and displaced. They wanted to annihilate them as a public force. Among the voters, too, the bitterness of the political division of these years has been exceeded only once in American history, and that resulted in a civil war.

A partial explanation might be found in the very newness of the new republic. Americans embarked in 1789 on an experiment that had no precedent in history. Their sense of common nationality had only recently emerged, and they had no assurance that the infant federal union—or democracy itself—would long endure.

Perhaps, however, it would be an error to assume that explanations of the differentness of early national politics can safely start with Washington's inauguration or the meeting of the first new Congress. This, indeed, had been a common habit of "Consensus" writings of the 1950s and early 1960s, which often opened with the ratification of the Constitution and attempted to explain how parties arose within the infant, national system. But another theme of rising criticism of this work insisted that we ought to breach the mental barrier traditionally erected by the launching of a new regime and see the federal government's first years as an extension of the Revolutionary era. Historians of the "Progressive" school had always stressed the continuity of the political divisions of the new republic with the factional alignments of the Revolutionary years. Maybe there was also a persistence of Revolutionary passions.

Among the first to bring these thoughts together was John R. Howe, whose newly published book, *The Changing Political Thought of John Adams*, would greatly influence subsequent inquiries. Howe's 1967 article, "Republican Thought and the Political Violence of the 1790s," *American Quarterly*, XIX, 147–165, suggested that the strident language and the often riotous behavior of this decade might be understood as consequences of a common body of assumptions, fears, and expectations that contemporaries carried with them from the Revolution. Howe was one of many scholars currently involved in an exciting reinterpretation of Revolutionary thought, which had been sparked by new discoveries about the history of eighteenth-century British thinking. As this reinterpretation flowered in the hugely influential works of Bernard Bailyn, Gordon S. Wood, and J. G. A. Pocock, its consequences for our understanding of the new republic became a central subject for the scholarly inquiries of the 1970s and 1980s.

A reconsideration of the Federalists emerged most quickly, and a different understanding of the Federalists was probably a precondition for a new interpretation of the victors in the party war, since the Republicans undoubtedly developed in response to the initiatives of their opponents. Three important books appeared in 1970 alone: James M. Banner, Jr., *To the Hartford Convention: The Federalists and the Origins of Party Politics in Massachusetts, 1789–1815* (New York: Alfred A. Knopf, 1970); Linda K. Kerber, *Federalists in Dissent: Imagery and Ideology in Jeffersonian America* (Ithaca, N.Y.: Cornell University Press, 1970); and Gerald Stourzh, *Alexander Hamilton and the Idea of Republican Government* (Stanford: Stanford University Press, 1970). Together with Howe's book on Adams, these important studies thoroughly rewrote prevailing understandings of Federalist ideas and laid a new foundation for the reinterpretation of the Jeffersonians that is the subject of this section.

Republican Ideology and the Triumph of the Constitution 1789–1793

Lance Banning

Building on the work of Pocock, Bailyn, Wood, and Howe, this article attempted to relate the quick acceptance of the Constitution and the rapid rise of party conflict to the expectations generated by republican ideas. Though I am tempted to revise it after nearly fifteen years, the essay introduced the reexamination of the Jeffersonian Republicans that was developed in The Jeffersonian Persuasion: Evolution of a Party Ideology *(Ithaca, N.Y.: Cornell University Press, 1978). It is reprinted without change from the* William and Mary Quarterly, *third series, XXXI (April, 1974), 167–188.*

In 1787 the men who signed the Constitution went home from Philadelphia determined to seek an unconditional victory for their new plan of government for the United States. To Federalists the alternative was clear: the people must accept the new plan of government or face the certain prospect of political debility and social collapse. Antifederalist convictions were equally strong. For opponents of the Constitution no threat was so outrageous, no evil so chimerical, that they could not see it lurking in the Federalist plan. If we are to listen to the participants, the struggle over the Constitution was a dispute between contending social interests over a question no less vital than the future of republican government in America and the world.[1]

---

[1] The strongest case for a conflict of social interests in the ratification contest is Jackson Turner Main, *The Antifederalists: Critics of the Constitution, 1781–1788* (Chapel Hill, N.C., 1961). Both here and in his more recent *Political Parties before the Constitution* (Chapel Hill, N.C., 1973), Main builds on the work of Charles Beard, Merrill Jensen, and Manning J. Dauer, who together construct a story of a conflict of economic interests which extended from the 1780s into the 1790s. For a contrary opinion of the ratification contest see Cecelia M. Kenyon, "Men of Little Faith: The Anti-Federalists on the Nature of Representative Government," *William and Mary Quarterly*, 3d Ser., XII (1955), 3–46. See also Robert Allen Rutland, *The Ordeal of the Constitution: The Antifederalists and the Ratification Struggle of 1787–1788* (Norman, Okla., 1966).

Yet no anticonstitutional party emerged in the new United States. As early as the spring of 1791 the Constitution was accepted on all sides as the starting point for further debates.[2] Within four years of ratification, the Republican opponents of the new administration—a party which probably included a majority of the old Antifederalists— insisted that they stood together to defend the Constitution against a threat that originated within the government itself.[3] While interest in fundamental amendments persisted for years, determined opposition to the new plan of government disappeared almost as quickly as it arose.

Too little thought has been given to this remarkable turn of events, and its most peculiar feature remains to be explained. Revolutionary France tried six constitutions in fifteen years. Most of a century of civil strife lay behind the constitutional consensus of eighteenth cen- tury England. The quick apotheosis of the American Constitution was a phenomenon without parallel in the western world. Nowhere has fundamental constitutional change been accepted with so much ease. Nowhere have so many fierce opponents of a constitutional revision been so quickly transformed into an opposition that claimed to be more loyal than the government itself. Why was America unique?

As long ago as 1835 Alexis de Tocqueville observed that America had no democratic revolution in the European sense, and therefore had no dispossessed estates to linger in inveterate enmity to the new order of affairs. Counterrevolution lacked a social base. Accordingly, a thorough explanation of the weakness of anticonstitutional tendencies in the new United States might recognize that a society without social orders may well have been a precondition for constitutional consensus. Of course, that did not make it certain that consensus would quickly

---

[2] By this time constitutional arguments had been the main support for both sides in the quarrel over Alexander Hamilton's proposal for a national bank. This was true for contestants within the administration, in Congress, and in the press.

[3] The relationship between the parties of the 1790s and the parties of the ratification contest is very much a matter of debate. Two of the best arguments for continuity are Alfred F. Young, *The Democratic Republicans of New York: The Origins, 1763–1797* (Chapel Hill, N.C., 1967), and Norman K. Risjord, "The Virginia Federalists," *Journal of Southern History,* XXXIII (1967), 486–517. On the other side see Joseph Charles, *The Origins of the American Party System: Three Essays* (Chapel Hill, N.C., 1956); Nobel E. Cunningham, Jr., *The Jeffersonian Republicans: The Formation of Party Organization, 1789–1801* (Chapel Hill, N.C., 1957); Paul Goodman, *The Democratic-Republicans of Massachusetts: Politics in a Young Republic* (Cambridge, Mass., 1964). I agree with those who conclude that ratification introduced a new situation, a new set of issues, and a significant realignment of political groups, although I also believe that Young and Risjord have shown that Antifederalists overwhelmingly became Republicans. The Federalists of 1787 divided more sharply after ratification and produced leaders for both parties, although a majority of those who voted for the Constitution probably became Federalists in the 1790s.

appear. It does not explain the peculiar inclination of so many opponents of constitutional revision to turn so abruptly to a fundamentalist defense of the plan.

Other traditional explanations ultimately come to ground on similar shoals. To account for the rapid collapse of opposition to the Constitution historians have emphasized the swift adoption of the Bill of Rights, the weakness of Antifederalist organization, the prosperity of the 1790s, and the people's trust in a venerated head of state. All these, surely, were conditions for success. Without them the Constitution might have failed. By themselves, however, they do not explain the startling kind of triumph that occurred.

The Bill of Rights may have satisfied Antifederalist demands for additional protection for valued civil liberties, but, as we shall see, it did not attempt to answer strong objections to the governmental structure of the federal plan. The venerated George Washington was at the head of the new government, but it was not entirely obvious in these early years that the president, rather than his cabinet members, would control the executive's course.[4] Prosperity did provide a beneficent climate for the new Constitution, yet we may legitimately wonder whether the effects of good times were felt strongly or swiftly enough to account for what had happened by 1791. Finally, the organizational weakness of Antifederalism cannot explain why, intellectually, the Antifederalists had no heirs. No list of conditions which favored the new government can help us more than marginally if we want to see why the opposition of the 1790s rejected Antifederalist criticisms, becoming constitutional literalists instead. To understand this we need new insight into what was happening within men's minds. What kind of mental process could produce a transformation so rapid and complete?

Part of the answer—part of it only—can be found in the nature of the ratification dispute. Americans of the Revolutionary generation shared a powerful determination to make republicanism work. The intense convictions which caused men to quarrel mightily over the proper nature of the new Constitution were coupled with a willingness on the part of nearly everyone, once the people had delivered their decision, to support a settlement that no one thought ideal. Most

---

[4] A certain ambiguity in the conceptions of the executive is evident throughout the 1790s. Particularly in the early years the veneration of Washington combined with Hamilton's role as first minister to make Republicans uncertain whether to attribute administration policy to the president or to his cabinet. Although he should have known better, Thomas Jefferson long attributed policy to Hamilton's demonic influence on the president. John Taylor of Caroline even went so far as to appeal to Washington as a kind of patriot king, urging him to veto the measures of his wicked ministers, in *An Enquiry into the Principles and Tendency of Certain Public Measures* (Philadelphia, 1794).

men entered upon the experiment with considerable suspicion but in remarkably good faith.[5]

Acquiescence in the people's decision may also have been eased for the Antifederalists because their objections to the Constitution had never reached as far as the basic principles of governmental structure around which the Convention had ordered its plan. There is a sense in which the ratification contest was a fight within the camp.[6] The dispute developed within a strong consensus which restrained disagreement within relatively narrow bounds. Few Antifederalists denied that a proper constitution should provide for a bicameral legislature within a system of balanced powers. Both sides were liberal, both republican; they agreed that the genius of the people was democratic, and they were equally committed by a shared majoritarian philosophy to abide by the verdict of the nation. For the first time in history an entire people had ratified an organic law.

Still, we must not minimize the conflict. Consensus is always more apparent in hindsight than in the midst of dispute, and even a large degree of underlying consensus leaves abundant room for serious differences of view. The quarrel over the Constitution was altogether real, a bitter disagreement of great ideological depth. Indeed, the more closely we examine the substance of Antifederalist objections to the Constitution, the more we are likely to compound our puzzlement over the ready acceptance of the fundamental law. Most Antifederalists denied that America could support a republican government of national extent. Many of them wondered whether the new Constitution was genuinely republican at all. All of them doubted that the proposed plan of government promised sufficient safeguards for the republican liberty that everyone professed to desire.[7] Elbridge Gerry called the constitution a "many headed monster; of such motley mixture, that its enemies cannot trace a feature of Democratick or Republican extract; nor have its friends the courage to denominate [it] a Monarchy, an Aristocracy, or an

---

[5] For new insights into ideological consensus (and conflict) in the new republic see John R. Howe, Jr., "Republican Thought and the Political Violence of the 1790s," *American Quarterly*, XIX (1967), 147–165; James M. Banner, Jr., *To the Hartford Convention: The Federalists and the Origins of Party Politics in Massachusetts, 1789–1815* (New York, 1970); Linda K. Kerber, *Federalists in Dissent: Imagery and Ideology in Jeffersonian America* (Ithaca, N.Y., 1970).

[6] A degree of consensus is emphasized in Cecelia M. Kenyon, ed., *The Antifederalists* (Indianapolis, Ind., 1966), xxi–cxvi.

[7] This is evident from even a cursory reading of Antifederalist materials. Kenyon, ed., *Antifederalists*, and Paul Leicester Ford, ed., *Pamphlets on the Constitution of the United States, published during its Discussion by the People, 1787–1788* (Brooklyn, N.Y., 1888).

Oligarchy."[8] Speaking for many of his fellows, George Mason predicted that "this government will commence in a moderate aristocracy; it is at present impossible to foresee whether it will, in its operation, produce a monarchy or a corrupt oppressive aristocracy; it will most probably vibrate some years between the two, and then terminate in one or the other."[9]

Inevitably the Antifederalists questioned the motives of those who had devised such a plan. The era of the American Revolution was a period of political paranoia. Social and political events were seldom conceived to have causes apart from conscious purpose, and the purposes of any group organized to have an impact on government were automatically thought of as malignant. Visions of conspiracy were endemic in these years, and Federalist conduct encouraged their play. The delegates to the Constitutional Convention debated in strict secrecy, exceeded the authority granted them by the Congress and their states, and produced a document shocking in the degree of change it proposed. Then, in support of a plan of government suspiciously similar to the old British form, they went to the people with an unshakable opposition to prior amendments or a second convention, an unseemly haste in pushing the ratification process, and tactics of questionable legality in some of the states. When these actions were added to the undisguised antipopular feelings of some of the Federalist leaders, their opponents had all the reason they required to suspect that the self-styled "better sort" had launched an aristocratic conspiracy against American liberty. Antifederalists generally viewed the Constitution as the first step in a plot to revive the tyranny of mixed monarchy or to introduce into the United States the horrors of aristocracy and despotism.[10]

These anxieties persisted after ratification was complete, and there is no reason to doubt that they were honestly felt. During the first year of the new government, Antifederalist fears of hereditary rule provoked sharp conflicts over protocol between the branches of the

---

[8] "Observations on the New Constitution and on the Federal and State Conventions," in Ford, ed., *Pamphlets on the Constitution*, 8. [editorial note: this pamphlet should have been attributed to Mercy Otis Warren]

[9] "Objections of the Hon. George Mason, to the Proposed Federal Constitution," in Kenyon, ed., *Antifederalists*, 195.

[10] The Pennsylvania Antifederalists were especially prone to charges of conspiracy. One of the best short examples of this line of attack is "The Address and Reasons of Dissent of the Minority of the Convention of the State of Pennsylvania to their Constituents,"*ibid.*, 27–60. See also Richard Henry Lee's "Letters from a Federal Farmer," in Forrest McDonald, ed., *Empire and Nation* (Englewood Cliffs, N.J., 1962), 135; Gerry, "Observations on the New Constitution," in Ford, ed., *Pamphlets on the Constitution*, 5–6; Luther Martin, "To the Citizens of Maryland," in Kenyon, ed., *Antifederalists*, 169–171.

new government, the character of presidential receptions, and a title for the head of state.[11] Moreover, it was nothing other than "monarchy," "aristocracy," and imitation of Great Britain that the developing "Republican interest" soon claimed to detect in the Federalist administration of affairs.

We return to our original problem. If Antifederalists genuinely believed that the Constitution would endanger republican government in the United States, how could they so easily accede to it? Given the nature of the Antifederalist critique, why was it that so few Republicans attributed the advance of "monarchy" and "aristocracy" to the constitutional settlement itself? How did it come to pass that, almost from the beginning of the new government, opponents of the administration chose to rest their objections on the strict words of this frail Constitution, insisting on a literal interpretation of a document that many of them had vilified on fundamental grounds?

Historians have recently given us a likely place to look for the missing element in our explanations. In the past few years, preeminently through the efforts of Bernard Bailyn and Gordon S. Wood, we have learned much about the impact on Revolutionary America of certain aspects of eighteenth-century English political thought. Colonial Americans had participated fully in the admiration for Britain's balanced constitution, and they had been particularly attracted to the opposition strands in British thought, whose critique of governmental techniques and social trends identified the development of ministerial government, parliamentary influence, and English public finance with a degeneration of the ancient constitution into a tyranny in disguise. Colonial advocates used the ideas of British oppositionists to legitimize the Revolution. The theories of classical republicans and eighteenth-century critics of ministerial rule helped define an American character and contributed fundamentally to American constitutional thought.[12]

Recently, a growing number of historians have shown that recognition of the persistent influence of inherited English thought can also contribute significantly to our understanding of politics in the new republic.[13] But there is still much more to learn through careful exploration of this universe of thought, for only its general contours have been traced. What is needed is close examination

---

[11] A good brief history of these disputes is John C. Miller, *The Federalist Era, 1789–1801* (New York, 1960), chap. I. See also James H. Hutson, "John Adams' Title Campaign," *New England Quarterly*, XLI (1968), 30–39.

[12] Bernard Bailyn, *The Ideological Origins of the American Revolution* (Cambridge, Mass., 1967), and Gordon S. Wood, *The Creation of the American Republic, 1776–1787* (Chapel Hill, N.C., 1969).

[13] See n. 5.

of the specific structure of inherited ideas, as well as fuller study of their influence. Among other things, such an examination can show that, intellectually, the Republicans of the 1790s were the "country" party of the United States. Their quarrel with Federalism was much more systematically ideological than has been seen. It rested on a complete and consistent Americanization of English opposition thought.[14] Recognizing this, we may be able to obtain new insight into the triumph of the Constitution.

In *The Creation of the American Republic* Wood argues that acceptance of the Constitution marked the end of classical politics in the United States. This is only true in a limited sense. The Federalists' great achievement, as Wood explains, was to separate the idea of a balance of governmental functions from the idea of a balance of social estates, with which it had long been joined. America's revolutionary concept of popular sovereignty made it possible to imagine a constitutional structure in which the people would be represented in all of the branches of the government, yet present in none. This concept of a balanced government which would rest in all its parts on the undifferentiated body of the people was an innovation of fundamental significance, the foundation for a new kind of state. Still, the idea of a balance of social estates, which Federalists rejected, was only part of a larger universe of classical republican thought. Its passing did not invalidate the larger structure of inherited ideas in terms of which Anglo-Americans had long perceived and formulated their social and political concerns.

Ratification of the Constitution assured the gradual rejection of the ancient habit of thinking in terms of a governmental balance of social estates, although it was years before most men would rid themselves entirely of a residual tendency to associate the branches of the new government with democracy, aristocracy, and monarchy. But this rejection did not entail repudiation of other classical concerns. Most of the inherited structure of eighteenth-century political thought persisted in America for years after 1789. And this persistence was not a matter of a shadowy half-life of fragmentary ideas. A structured universe of classical thought continued to serve as the intellectual medium through which Americans perceived the political world, and an inherited political language was the primary vehicle for the expression of their hopes and discontents. For every literate American the traditional constructs entailed particular concerns. A detailed knowledge of this inherited structure of thought is necessary if we are to understand the limits within which Americans went about the creation of a new kind of state and the ways in which they debated its virtues and defects.

---

[14] Lance Banning, "The Quarrel with Federalism: A Study in the Origins and Character of Republican Thought" (Ph.D. diss., Washington University, 1971).

From its inception in ancient times, through Niccolo Machiavelli, to its proponents in times of civil unrest in England, the theory of balanced government had been a response to the problem of constitutional instability. Among the many strengths of balanced government none was more important than the protection it was thought to offer against the tendency of any simpler constitution to degenerate into a form of government that would prove oppressive to a segment of the people, driving them to revolt. Proponents of balanced governments began with the assumption that, whenever they are able, men will pursue their individual interests at the expense of other members of the state. A simple democracy might originate, for example, in a universal determination to seek the public good. Eventually, however, human nature would have its way and the selfish interest of a majority would lead them to oppress the rest, who would then rise against the government and found an aristocratic state. Degeneration would follow every revolution in an endless cycle of political instability as long as private interest went unchecked. Only a balanced constitution offered a release. With its devices for pitting power against power and interest against interest in such a way that each group in a society would be guarded against the rapacity of the rest, a balanced government might offer a period of constitutional peace.

Of course, none of the proponents of a balanced constitution believed that the mere inauguration of a balance could change the basic characteristics of man. The concern with selfish interest and the clash of contending groups—the concern which gave rise to the theory of balanced government in the first place—demanded from its proponents unremitting attention to the stability of the state. While theorists hoped that each part of a balanced government would exert its power to protect the balance, they also expected each to attempt to expand its power at the expense of the others. Success by any part of the government in its attempts to encroach on the proper province of another meant constitutional degeneration, since the government would increasingly approximate one or another of the simpler forms. Constitutional degeneration was the technical definition of "corruption," a word which conveyed an image of progressive, organic decay. Corruption was a growing cancer which meant the inevitable destruction of the liberty and property of some social group and the ultimate dissolution of the state. Corruption was the normal direction of constitutional change.[15]

Virtually all of this traditional reasoning applied to the Constitution of the United States. Men were still selfish, power still ambitious, tyranny still a consequence of the accumulation of governmental pow-

---

[15] For fuller explanation and support see *ibid.*, chaps. 2–3.

ers in a single set of hands. The assumption of human selfishness, the very principle which required a government of divided powers, induced in America, as it had in eighteenth-century England, an expectation that the delicate balance of the Constitution would be subject to decay. Each part of the government could be expected to encroach on the spheres of the others in an attempt to seize all power for itself. In the first years of the new government a shared anticipation of constitutional decay helps account for the intensity of partisan feeling on both sides of disputes, enabling us to understand the exaggerated sense of danger that was prevalent on both sides. Fear of constitutional degeneration is an indispensable explanation for the rise of party conflict.

After years of constitutional experimentation and more than half a century of repeated analysis of the course and nature of governmental decay, Americans of 1787 had a rather clear idea of the kind of constitution they desired. It would be a balanced constitution freed from all connection with nobles, kings, and priests, and guarded with all of modern ingenuity against the openings for corruption that had ruined the British state. This was the kind of constitution the Federalists hoped they had achieved—a genuinely republican constitution which checked each part of government with the countervailing power of other parts and left no room for the rotten boroughs, parliamentary placemen, and irresponsible ministers that had destroyed constitutional liberty in England.

Antifederalists obviously disagreed. Confronted with the Constitution, many of them concluded that the small lower house—a part of government still closely associated with democracy in many minds—could never adequately represent the people.[16] Worse, it seemed entirely likely that the more aristocratic and monarchical branches of the proposed government would combine to overbear the assembly and reduce it to a sham. Federalists might take a democratic pride in a House of Representatives elected on as popular a basis as any branch of government in the states and resting on electorates so large as to

---

[16] Some excellent and geographically scattered examples are R. H. Lee, "Letters from a Federal Farmer," in McDonald, ed., *Empire and Nation*, 98, 146; Samuel Adams to R. H. Lee, Dec. 13, 1787, in Harry Alonzo Cushing, ed., *The Writings of Samuel Adams*, IV (New York, 1908), 324–325; Samuel Bryan, "Letters of 'Centinel'" [Benjamin Workman]; "The Letters of 'Philadelphiensis'"; "The Letters of 'John De Witt'"; Melancthon Smith's remarks in the "Debates of the New York Convention," all in Kenyon, ed., *Antifederalists*, 1–25, 69–87, 108, 382–389. Only by recognizing the extent to which many Americans were still thinking in terms of mixed government is it possible to understand how such a man as Gerry could have been one of the most outspoken critics of excessive democracy in the Constitutional Convention *and* one of the most bitter opponents of an undemocratic constitution. It was perfectly consistent to abhor simple democracy and yet to insist on one genuinely democratic branch in a balanced government.

defeat any scheme for bribery in elections.[17] Antifederalists saw in the small number of representatives a fertile field for bribery and executive influence and only the "shadow" of democratic representation.[18] To them the balance of the Constitution was tilted from the start, and the cooperation of president and Senate required by numerous violations of a proper separation of powers assured the eventual destruction of its democratic elements. Fear of constitutional degeneration helps explain the most incredible Antifederalist prophecies of doom.[19]

Fear of degeneration, however, was not a monopoly of a single side. When the new government was established in 1789, articulate Americans commonly anticipated constitutional decay. Many Federalists, for example, were preoccupied with an ancient set of constitutional fears. From Aristotle forward, proponents of a balanced constitution had predicted that balanced governments would degenerate in the direction of whichever element of government was strongest in the mixture. Thus, democratic commonwealths would tend to become simple democracies, while aristocratic commonwealths would tend toward simple aristocracy. Throughout the Confederation period American nationalists had been preoccupied with an excess of democracy in the states. Many of them doubted that the Constitution would suffice to end this threat. After 1789, the nationalists who remained Federalists continued to believe that the people's traditional localism and faith in a lower house were still the predominant dangers to a balanced state. The people's proclivities might lead them to confer increasing power on the most democratic branch of the federal government or to reverse the flow of power from the nation to the states. In either case the original equilibrium of the Constitution could not survive.

Other Americans—Federalists and Antifederalists alike—were impelled by a different, although equally traditional, set of concerns. Suspecting that the framers had checked democracy as much as or even more than was to be desired, distrusting the dangerous ambition which traditionally followed power, they expected threats to the stability of

---

[17] For example, Hamilton's speech of June 21, 1788, at the New York Convention, in Harold C. Syrett and Jacob E. Cooke, eds., *The Papers of Alexander Hamilton*, V (New York, 1962), 54–55, and Madison's speech of June 11, 1788, at the Virginia Convention, in Gaillard Hunt, ed., *The Writings of James Madison, Comprising his Public Papers and his Private Correspondence . . .* (New York, 1900–1910), V, 158–159.

[18] The phrase was Mason's but the belief was widely shared. Fears of a small representation and of executive influence went hand in hand. Thus, R. H. Lee said that the Constitution would make it "extremely difficult to secure the people against the fatal effects of corruption. . . . Where there is a small representation a sufficient number to carry any measure may with ease be influenced by bribes, offices, and civilities." See his "Letters from a Federal Farmer," in McDonald, ed., *Empire and Nation*, 109, 146, 149–150.

[19] For a fuller treatment of Antifederalism and the fear of corruption see Banning, "Quarrel with Federalism," 181–192.

the Constitution to proceed from its executive part. Political centralization and executive aggrandizement, the old foes of Revolutionary experience, were thought likely to pose the greatest danger to the infant state.

For both these groups in the context of American constitutionalism in 1789 the natural response was a posture of defense. Traditional ways of thinking prepared them poorly for any other poise. These men had grown up English. For them the major historical precedent for continuing opposition to a constitutional settlement was still the Tory resistance to the decisions of 1689. Americans were a nation of Whigs. They thought of Tories as proponents of unrestrained executive power, and they had been reared in a historical tradition which saw the Glorious Revolution as a saving restoration of ancient constitutional law, a standard of governmental perfection against which one could measure contemporary decline.[20] According to their favorite histories of England and of Rome, constitutional change, like water, always flowed downhill. Against the great Whig theme of constitutions in decay, only one small school of "Tory" writers supported a belief in the possibility of progressive constitutional improvement. Beset by Bolingbroke and other critics, who used Whig history to condemn the ministry of Walpole as the culmination of a steady process of decay, defenders of Sir Robert argued that the growth of ministerial influence was necessary to adjust the ancient constitution to the increasing dominance of the Commons. Valuable as history, this was also special pleading on behalf of the arch-villain of America's favorite Old Whigs. It was a "court" tradition, foreign to a people long since committed to "country" ideas.[21] A settled determination to overthrow a constitution or a persistent effort at progressive constitutional change was neither of them native to the American grain.

This is not to say that persistent discontent was unimaginable or that Americans could not conceive of constitutional change. The new plan of government was itself a constitutional revision.[22] Most of its framers originally expected that time would reveal some defects, and they made deliberate provision for amendments. Almost immediately, the nation added ten amendments of a libertarian sort. Few men were

---

[20] H. Trevor Colbourn, *The Lamp of Experience: Whig History and the Intellectual Origins of the American Revolution* (Chapel Hill, N.C., 1965).

[21] For "court" ideology and its limited influence in America see Banning, "Quarrel with Federalism," 215–232.

[22] Although the Articles of Confederation can only with difficulty be seen as an organic law, Wood has shown that the effort which led to the Constitution was aimed in large part against what many nationalists had come to see as constitutional weaknesses in the various states. By 1787 most nationalists saw the constitutions of the 1770s as aberrations from conventional good sense.

entirely happy with the Constitution, and there were always some who wanted major change. Significantly, however, generations passed without structural alterations. Once ratification was completed, most of the political nation found itself on different mental terrain. Demands for alteration now ran precisely counter to the natural paths. A great intellectual inheritance now warned against attempts at change.

To most of the Revolutionary generation, almost by definition a constitution was something to protect, a fragile structure raised from chaos in liberty's defense. The people had been consulted. Whiggish theory taught that the majority must rule. The classical republican foundations of American constitutional thought taught that a constitution, once established, changed only for the worse. To this axiom all the best authorities in political science, from Aristotle to Jean Louis De Lolme, united in assent, and all the Whig historians agreed. The recognized task of friends of liberty was neither counterrevolution nor reform. It was to guard against social and political degeneration and to force a frequent recurrence to the original principles of a free and balanced constitution.

A powerful inclination to insist on the original terms of the Constitution thus greeted the new government from its start, an inclination that seems inevitable when we have grasped the context of Anglo-American thought. In this sense, if not in others, ratification immediately altered the framework for debate. In Congress in 1789, as James Madison and his supporters sought to complete the strong central government outlined in the Convention's plan, it was members of an Antifederalist persuasion—Gerry, Richard Jackson, and John Page—who insisted on the strict words of the Constitution and cried alarm at every indication of the slightest departure therefrom. Those most suspicious of the new plan of government instinctively fought to make sure that "corruption" would never find a start. This reflexive literalism does not in itself explain the apotheosis of the Constitution, but it is essential to the explanation.

No man's thought is altogether free. Men are born into an intellectual universe where some ideas are native and others are difficult to conceive. Sometimes this intellectual universe is so well structured and has so strong a hold that it can virtually determine not only the ways in which a society will express its hopes and discontents but also the central problems with which it will be concerned.[23] In 1789 Amer-

---

[23] This conception of the development and function of ideology has been most strongly influenced by the various writings of J. G. A. Pocock, particularly *Politics, Language and Time: Essays on Political Thought and History* (New York, 1971), and by Thomas S. Kuhn, *The Structure of Scientific Revolutions* (Chicago, 1962). Also useful is Clifford Geertz, "Ideology as a Cultural System," in David E. Apter, ed., *Ideology and Discontent* (New York, 1964), 47–76.

icans lived in such a world. The heritage of classical republicanism and English opposition thought, shaped and hardened in the furnace of a great Revolution, left few men free. This universe contained no familiar ways of thinking about gradual constitutional improvement or persistent opposition to a fundamental law. It demanded a concern with preservation and assured the presence of an inclination to insist on strict adherence to original terms. A leaning toward constitutional literalism, a tendency engendered by some of the strongest currents in Anglo-American thought and powerfully reinforced by Antifederalist prophecies of constitutional decay, prepared the way for constitutional apotheosis. It also does much to explain the appearance of an opposition party which would quickly elevate the Constitution as the palladium of American liberty.

Americans of the Revolutionary generations were a nation of political physicians, expert diagnosticians of the subtlest symptoms of constitutional decay. They knew that constitutional degeneration could assume many forms, and they watched in fearful expectation for any of its signs. They knew, for example, that it might appear in the guise of a change in the moral habits of the people. Wood has shown that during the middle years of the 1780s it was the detection of a growth of popular licentiousness that led many nationalists to decide on the necessity of constitutional change. In the 1790s men of both political parties continued to watch for symptoms of this sort of decline. Similarly, as we have seen, both parties understood that constitutional degeneration could begin with a tendency by any part of government to encroach on the sphere of another. The battles in Congress in 1789 can be interpreted as products of this fear, and it seems to have been a similar concern with encroachment which started Republican leaders on the way to opposition.

In 1789, when he agreed to serve in Washington's cabinet, Thomas Jefferson declared himself more nearly a Federalist than not.[24] No one, of course, had had a more important part in the creation of a vigorous central government than Jefferson's friend, Madison. During the first year of the new government, while Jefferson made his way back from France, Madison acted as congressional leader of the forces who meant to assure a strong and independent executive power. He parted with the administration only on the questions of discrimination and national assumption of the debt, policies that Virginians considered sectionally unjust. On these issues, however, both Madison and Jefferson were

---

[24] Jefferson originally opposed some of the features of the Constitution, particularly the absence of a bill of rights and the lack of limitations on the president's right to succeed himself, but he declared himself on balance in favor of the plan.

willing to compromise for the sake of federal union.[25] The two Virginians did not move firmly into a more general opposition until they were confronted with Alexander Hamilton's proposal for a national bank. Then, already troubled by what seemed to them a growing sectional bias in the laws, they saw in the broad construction of federal powers which Hamilton advanced in support of the Bank a powerful blow at the barriers against an indefinite expansion of federal authority and, with it, the enhancement of the dangerous power of a northern majority. In response they demanded a narrow interpretation of constitutional limitations on federal authority.

Significantly, it was not the Bank itself so much as the constitutional interpretation advanced in its defense that was the original focus of the Virginians' concern. Their fears were unashamedly sectional, but they were also something more than that. From the beginning, more was implicit in Jeffersonian strict constructionism than the particularistic defense of local interests usually associated with a doctrine of states' rights. The balance of constitutional powers between the nation and the states, like the balance within the federal government between executive and legislative branches, was part of the equilibrium on which liberty and stability were thought to depend. Deviation from this equilibrium—change in any form—was constitutional corruption, a danger to the foundations of the state.[26] For Madison, accordingly, defense of the residual powers of the people and the states was no less a duty than his earlier defense of executive independence against the threat of encroachment by the legislative branch. Hamilton's broad construction of federal powers endangered not just southern interests but the fragile balance that assured a republican state. It was one of several signals that touched an alarm.[27]

Already the character of the Virginians' opposition had begun to change. At first, Jefferson and Madison feared a sectional injustice, and they concentrated their objections on specific policies and on the dan-

---

[25] James Madison to James Madison, Sr., July 31, 1790, in Hunt, ed., *Writings of Madison*, VI, 19, and these letters of Thomas Jefferson: to George Mason, June 13, 1790; to James Monroe, June 20, 1790; to Thomas Mann Randolph, June 20, 1790; to Edward Rutledge, July 4, 1790, in Julian P. Boyd *et al.*, eds., *The Papers of Thomas Jefferson*, XVI (Princeton, N.J., 1961), 493, 536–538, 540–541, 601.

[26] Accordingly the same fear of deviation from the original equilibrium worked just as strongly from the other side, where men were concerned with the people's localism. Nothing frightened Hamilton so much as early attempts by state legislatures to instruct their federal senators and representatives or to pass legislative resolutions on federal laws.

[27] By this time Jefferson especially was beginning to be upset by the writings of John Adams, Hamilton's private conversations, and the general tone of the Federalists' social style.

ger of deviation from the original balance between the nation and the states. Meanwhile, a growing number of newspaper writers and congressional critics were beginning to sense in Federalist policy a subtler and more general kind of threat. A common train of worries seems to have occurred independently to men in various stations in different parts of the country, old Federalists and Antifederalists alike.[28] It made little difference where they had stood in 1789. All were gradually attracted to an interpretation of events and definition of concerns that reflected the inherited ideology. In this process of definition, self-justification, and appeals for popular support, a true political party began to form.[29]

Over the course of the eighteenth century generations of English oppositionists had analyzed a special kind of constitutional corruption until all but the most illiterate could mark its every stage. The basic mechanism of this corruption was the subversion of legislative independence—and therefore balanced government—by an ambitious executive through the calculating use of offices, pensions, and titles to suborn the members of the legislature. The usual accompaniments of executive influence were standing armies, rising taxes, chartered corporations, and an enormous public debt.

No technique of constitutional subversion was more insidious than "governing by debt. " Since the early eighteenth century a great public debt, with a chartered bank and other privileged corporations, had been identified by English opposition writers as a mechanism designed to extend the influence of a scheming ministry from Parliament into the country at large. Like parliamentary placemen, members of privileged corporations and holders of the debt depended for their livelihoods on the continuing favor of the government. These "paper men"

---

[28] Early examples include the speeches of Jackson and Page in the second session of Congress in *The Debates and Proceedings in the Congress of the United States* . . . (Washington, D. C., 1834), 1180–1182, 1214; Benjamin Rush to James Madison, Feb. 27, 1790, in L. H. Butterfield, ed., *Letters of Benjamin Rush,,* I (Princeton, N.J., 1951), 539; the Remonstrance of the Virginia legislature against funding and assumption, Dec. 1790, in *American State Papers. Documents, Legislative and Executive, of the Congress of the United States* . . . (Washington, D.C., 1832–1861), *Finance*, I, 90–91; "Funding Bill," in *Independent Chronicle: and the Universal Advertiser* (Boston), Aug. 12, 1790.

[29] Jefferson and Madison certainly created the Republican party, but they did so by joining with and organizing a growing number of critics, some of whom arrived earlier at a consistent critical ideology than the Virginians. In *Securing the Revolution: Ideology in American Politics, 1789–1815* (Ithaca, N.Y., 1972), Richard Buel, Jr., argues that the first party system originated in a split within the Federalist leadership of 1789. If so, the triumph of the Constitution might be more easily explained. It may be, however, that Madison was the only one of a large number of significant Republican thinkers whose conduct can be described in these terms.

were not independent citizens, who could be trusted with the liberty of others, but creatures of the executive will. Preying on the public treasury in exchange for their support of the ministry, they drained a nation of its wealth. Parading their dishonesty, their subservience, and their unearned riches, these servants of corruption made a mockery of decency and honest work. The power of their riches and the influence of their licentious example undermined the virtuous habits of an entire commonwealth, whose people were thus impoverished and made fit subjects for despotism. With its servants in the legislature and its "paper men" outside, an ambitious ministry could both establish and mask its tyranny.[30]

Reared on a diet of opposition writings, many Americans of 1789 anticipated certain specific measures in any conspiratorial plot to subvert republican government, certain typical stages in any process of constitutional decay. When the new Constitution was established, in the midst of many warnings of a plot, Americans of both Federalist and Antifederalist persuasion watched every step with conscientious suspicion, fearing executive influence, distrusting a regular army, uncertain how to handle the public debt.[31] These fears were explosives to which Hamilton gradually laid a fuse. Recreating the essentials of English governmental finance, he struck men's sensitivities in their sorest point. Step by step he presented them with a threat they had to recognize, a danger which ultimately justified their anxieties. Uneasiness with the tone and tendency of the Federalists' social style and concern for sectional interests came together with a fear of executive influence on the legislature and a sense of danger to the moral foundations of republican life to suggest a consistent interpretation of administration policy and a frightening analysis of the course of the infant state.

By the end of 1792 the administration confronted a determined opposition which challenged its policies on fundamental grounds. As the full range of Hamilton's economic policy gradually became clear, Jefferson and Madison and a growing number of other critics in Congress

---

[30] The most important sources for an understanding of opposition thought are J. G. A. Pocock, "Machiavelli, Harrington, and English Political Ideologies in the Eighteenth Century," *WMQ*, 3d Ser., XXII (1965), 549–583; Isaac Kramnick, *Bolingbroke and His Circle: The Politics of Nostalgia in the Age of Walpole* (Cambridge, Mass., 1968); Caroline Robbins, *The Eighteenth-Century Commonwealthman: Studies in the Transmission, Development and Circumstance of English Liberal Thought from the Restoration of Charles II until the War with the Thirteen Colonies* (Cambridge, Mass., 1959). Neglect to this point of the American influence of the opposition criticism of "government by money" is one of several warnings against a premature assumption that we have learned as much as is necessary about these currents in English thought.

[31] Banning, "Quarrel with Federalism," 194–209, examines the workings of these fears in the first session of Congress. Two Federalists who immediately adopted a "country" frame of mind were Rush and William Maclay.

and the press could scarcely avoid a conspiratorial conclusion. United with suspicions of a conspiracy to restore mixed monarchy to the United States, the old English criticism of government by money and executive attempts to undermine the constitution again became the core of a consistent ideology of opposition to the men in power. In a process too complicated to summarize in detail, the English opposition theory which had provoked so many worries provided a model for an American version of "country" ideology.[32]

Reviving the old ideas, opponents charged that Hamilton was another Walpole, a "prime minister" whose economic program created in Congress and in the country a "phalanx" of stockholders and bank directors who were committed by their economic interests to follow his every command.[33] Stockholders and bank directors in Congress were servants of the executive branch, whose presence in the legislature destroyed its independence, endangered balanced government, and subverted the popular will.[34] In the country at large, hordes of avaricious speculators and "paper creatures" of the executive fattened on public spoils, mocking virtuous habits and forming the dissolute and privileged core for a new aristocracy. With the aid of these creatures Hamilton was directing an elaborate and effectual conspiracy to create a government of the British sort. The goal of this Federalist conspiracy could be summarized in a word. That word was "liberticide."[35]

Careful study of the public writings of the 1790s—pamphlets, broadsides, and newspaper articles—will demonstrate that condemnation of a carefully contrived conspiracy to destroy republican government was the central accusation in the Republican indictment of Federalism. The evidence suggests that party leaders believed in the actuality of this conspiracy and that they used this conviction to define their character to themselves as well as to appeal successfully for popular support.[36] As earlier in England, the criticism of executive influence

---

[32] *Ibid.*, chap. 5, traces the reconstruction of opposition ideology in detail.

[33] The first crescendo of this kind of criticism appeared in the contributions of "Franklin," "Decius," "Timon," "An American Farmer," and others to the *National Gazette* (Philadelphia) in the early months of 1793. The barrage was set off by the congressional controversy over William Branch Giles's resolutions, which were designed to force Hamilton to resign, and they seem to have been part of a careful campaign. "Franklin" was very probably Taylor; "An American Farmer" was George Logan.

[34] Taylor's *Enquiry* is probably the best single source for a recognition of the Republicans' consistent Americanization of opposition thought. This pamphlet was approved in advance by Madison, Jefferson, James Monroe, and other party leaders.

[35] Full demonstration of the nature and importance of the Republican critique is impossible in limited space. See Banning, "Quarrel with Federalism," chaps. 5–6.

[36] In addition to the examples cited below see the essays which Madison contributed to the *Natl. Gaz.* in 1792. These are reprinted in Hunt, ed., *Writings of Madison*, VI, 80–95.

on the legislature became the center of a systematic argument which, in widening circles, could ultimately encompass all manner of social and political discontents. In time, some Republicans would accuse the administration of deliberately losing an Indian war or even of provoking the Whiskey Rebellion in order to provide itself with an excuse for maintaining a dangerous standing army.[37] Charges such as these were credible to men who were convinced of the reality of a liberticide plot, although most Republicans never went this far.

Throughout the 1790s opposition to a supposed Federalist conspiracy provided the most important justification for Republican conduct and the general framework for fundamental criticism of specific Federalist plans. It gave rise to the Republican party in the first place. It prepared the party to interpret the administration's foreign policy as an attempt to ally the country with Britain and the forces of international despotism against liberty and the French. Finally, it required the party to see in the crisis legislation of 1798 the predictable culmination of a liberticide design.[38] For a party which opposed the Federalist administrations on such grounds as these, constitutional literalism was more than a pose, more than a temporary tactic in the warfare of sectional and economic interests. Defense of a republican constitution was the reason for its being.

Strict construction of the Constitution was an integral part of this libertarian response. Indeed, its eighteenth-century proponents had always had an ancient constitution on which they could insist, a settled standard against which they could measure the progress of decay. Men who feared the subversion of republican government through the subtle operation of executive influence or changes in the social and moral foundations of the state knew also that constitutional degeneration could come in plainer forms. Thus, when Hamilton employed a broad construction of constitutional authority to defend the president's power to issue a proclamation of neutrality, Madison responded with an attack on "principles which strike at the vitals of the Constitution." Hamilton's generous interpretation of executive authority was derived, in Madison's opinion, from the theory and practices of monarchical Britain. It was "pregnant with . . . consequences against which no ramparts in the constitution could defend the public liberty or scarcely the forms of republican government."[39] Its nature and consequences were

---

[37] Albert Gallatin, *An Examination of the Conduct of the Executive . . . towards the French Republic . . .* (Philadelphia, 1797), 39–41.

[38] Banning, "Quarrel with Federalism," chaps. 6–8.

[39] "Letters of Helvidius," in Hunt, ed., *Writings of Madison*, VI, 139, 151–152. "Helvidius" originally appeared in the *Gazette of the United States* (Philadelphia), between Aug. 24 and Sept. 18, 1793.

of a piece with other forms of corruption which were undermining American liberty. From Hamilton's principles "every power that can be deduced . . . will be deduced, and exercised sooner or later by those who may have an interest in so doing. The character of human nature gives this salutary warning to every sober and reflecting mind. And the history of government in all its forms and in every period of time, ratifies the danger. A people, therefore, who are so happy as to possess the inestimable blessing of a free and defined constitution cannot be too watchful against the introduction, nor too critical in tracing the consequences, of new principles and new constructions, that may remove the landmarks of power."[40]

To Republican minds, a broad interpretation of constitutional powers was one of several means by which the Federalist planned to subvert republican government in the United States. Insistence on a strict interpretation of executive authority and attacks on executive attempts to undermine the independence of the legislative branch were two of several methods of defense. Another way to maintain the original equilibrium of the Constitution was to insist on the preservation of the residual rights of the people and the states.

Particularly in the years when they could not break the Federalists' grip on the national government, the Republicans were determined to prevent federal encroachment on the remaining bastions of liberty in the states. During the crisis of 1798 Jefferson and other Republicans even considered state nullification of federal laws. This does not mean that they were primarily proponents of local rights—a traditional interpretation which creates more problems than it solves.[41] The Virginia and Kentucky Resolutions of 1798 were episodes in a broader defense of civil liberties and of republican government itself.[42] For most Republicans of the 1790s, the federal system was one of many protections for liberty in a time of dreadful peril. States' rights would naturally seem less crucial when the peril had been brought to an end.

---

[40] "Helvidius," in Hunt, ed., *Writings of Madison*, VI, 171–172

[41] An interpretation which sees Jefferson and his party *primarily* as proponents of strict construction and states' rights is at least as old as Henry Adams's famous *History of the United States during the Administrations of Jefferson and Madison* (New York, 1880–1890). Only the mistaken assumption that "the principles of 1798" were strict construction and states' rights permits Adams to see Jefferson as an apostate from his own ideals. This mistake is largely responsible for the whole great debate over the Republicans' "reversal" of belief once their party was in power. The question of the relationship between Republican principles and the conduct of the Republicans after 1800 is a legitimate problem for historical analysis, but such an analysis must begin with a better understanding of the original structure of Republican thought.

[42] Adrienne Koch and Harry Ammon, "The Virginia and Kentucky Resolutions: An Episode in Jefferson's and Madison's Defense of Civil Liberties," *WMQ*, 3d Ser., V (1948), 145–176.

Meanwhile, states' rights and strict construction were necessary parts of a systematic defense of republican liberty against a conspiratorial threat. Near the end of his long life Jefferson remembered the struggle of the 1790s in a way that made this plain. "The contests of that day," as he recalled them, "were contests of principle, between the advocates of republican and those of kingly government."[43] A faction of American monarchists, active since Revolutionary days, had seized the powers of government during the administrations of Washington and John Adams. They had systematically sought to replace the republican government with a constitution modeled on the British form. The object of their Republican opponents had been "to preserve the legislative pure and independent of the Executive, to restrain the administration to republican forms and principles, and not permit the constitution to be construed into a monarchy, and to be warped in practice into all the principles and pollutions of their favorite English model."[44]

Since the middle of the eighteenth century, in England and in America, persistent legislative minorities had reconciled their position with their belief in majority rule by means of an established ideology which explained their anomalous situation as a consequence of constitutional corruption and the subversion of the popular will. Unable to control the legislature, they claimed nevertheless to represent a genuine majority of the people, the expression of whose will had been perverted through the corrupt influence of the executive on legislative affairs. Like them, Jefferson and his party called upon this ideology to place their opposition on fundamental constitutional grounds.

In an age when political factions were normally condemned and persistent opposition to the government in power aroused suspicions of disloyalty to the state, opposition to constitutional degeneration— and that almost alone—could transmute a political faction into patriotic defenders of the common good. Men who joined together to guard against constitutional degeneration and who stood in formed opposition to an executive plot were something other than a band of factious politicians dedicated to the selfish pursuit of political power.[45] Thus, while persistent "country" worries led men to resist Federalist plans,

---

[43] "The Anas, 1791–1806," in Paul Leicester Ford, ed., *The Works of Thomas Jefferson*, I (New York, 1904), 167.

[44] *Ibid.*, 178.

[45] In *Idea of a Party System: The Rise of Legitimate Opposition in the United States, 1780–1840* (Berkeley and Los Angeles, 1969) Richard Hofstadter shows that a modern justification of party competition did not appear in America until well into the new Republic. He does not fully explore this older justification for formed opposition, but its essential connection with an opposition stance seems even clearer when we remember that Banner and Kerber have shown that the Federalists also produced their own distinctive development of the old style of criticism when they found themselves out of power in the years after 1800.

the political necessities of determined opposition pushed them inexorably toward a revival of traditional opposition ideas.

But opposition to the progress of social and political corruption
traditionally required an ancient constitution against which it could
measure the degeneration of the present day. A critique of constitutional corruption needed an accepted constitution that could be seen
to undergo a process of decay. Lacking an ancient constitution, the
Republicans instinctively settled for the next best thing. Symbolically
speaking, they made the Constitution old. Paradoxically, then, it was
the appearance of a deeply felt opposition to the policies of our first
administration which assured the quick acceptance of the Constitution
that had been committed to its care. More than the government itself,
the opposition had to have an unchallengeable constitution on which it
could rely.

The world of classical constitutionalism—a world which Americans
found inescapable in 1789—was a world with little precedent for continuing resistance to a constitutional settlement. It was a world which
hobbled anticonstitutional feelings and predisposed men to defend a
fundamental law. It drove men to oppose an energetic government at a
time when the American union was still insecure, but it compelled them
to challenge the administration, not the government itself. It forced the
Republican party to defend a sacred constitution against an executive
threat. This world of classical politics assured the quick apotheosis of
the Constitution of the United States.

Republicanism and American Foreign Policy: James Madison and the Political Economy of Commercial Discrimination, 1789 to 1794

Drew R. McCoy

The previous selection focused on political and constitutional dimensions of the influence in the new republic of traditional debates between the British opposition and the "court." This selection, which anticipated portions of The Elusive Republic: Political Economy in Jeffersonian America *(Chapel Hill: University of North Carolina Press, 1980), suggests that a familiarity with eighteenth-century British thinking can illuminate additional dimensions of the early party conflict. It is reprinted by permission from the* William and Mary Quarterly, *third series, XXXI (October, 1974), 633-646.*

In probing the political economics of leading Jeffersonian Republicans, historians have generally focused on Thomas Jefferson, to the comparative neglect of James Madison. Yet a close analysis of Madison's thought can draw cogent connections between what historians have recently discovered as "republican ideology," attitudes toward economic development, and the evolution of American commercial policy in the early national period.[1] Scholars have invariably noted the coherence

---

[1] For an excellent discussion of the growth of "republicanism" (or "republican ideology") as a concept in American historiography see Robert E. Shalhope, "Toward a Republican Synthesis: The Emergence of an Understanding of Republicanism in American Historiography," *William and Mary Quarterly*, 3d Ser., XXIX (1972), 49–80. Edmund S. Morgan has taken the first step toward linking this system of thought to economic policy in "The Puritan Ethic and the American Revolution," *ibid.*, XXIV (1967), 3–43, while Roger H. Brown's *The Republic in Peril: 1812* (New York, 1964) suggests the utility of examining American foreign policy from the general perspective of republicanism.

of Alexander Hamilton's "system," in which fiscal policy and economic growth were intimately tied to the need for amicable Anglo-American commercial relations; they have failed to develop, however, the parallel relationship between Madison's commitment to commercial discrimination against Great Britain and his approach to internal economic development.[2] An examination of Madison's commercial policy from the perspective of his republicanism can suggest that he had a "system" of his own, directed toward the fulfillment of a specific pattern of politico-economic development in the new nation.

Central to this discussion is the question of Madison's attitude toward the development of manufactures. Historians have labeled Madison as anything from a rather naive, Virginia-oriented "agrarian" to a sophisticated "mercantilist" more committed to encouraging American manufactures than even his adversary Hamilton.[3] I would suggest that although Madison was neither naive nor narrowly provincial, his aversion to the development of *large-scale* manufacturing enterprises in the United States was central to his nationalist outlook. This aversion was grounded in the web of associated ideas and prejudices known as "republicanism" and stemmed from Madison's desire to secure American economic independence. His definition of economic independence, however, differed sharply from that of many of his contemporaries, especially from Hamilton's. A careful consideration of Madison's policy of commercial discrimination during the period 1789 to 1794 can uncover the origins of that definition, show how it was expressed in concrete

---

[2] For a concise description and explanation of the Hamiltonian "system" and its incompatibility with Madison's commercial policy see Paul A. Varg, *Foreign Policies of the Founding Fathers* (East Lansing, Mich., 1963), 77–78, and Joseph Charles, *The Origins of the American Party System: Three Essays* (Chapel Hill, N.C., 1956), 13, 30–31. For related and more extensive discussions of economic thought and policy in this period see esp. Charles A. Beard's classic *Economic Origins of Jeffersonian Democracy* (New York, 1915), and E. A. J. Johnson, *The Foundations of American Economic Freedom: Government and Enterprise in the Age of Washington* (Minneapolis, Minn., 1973).

[3] For a typical "agrarian" approach see Varg, *Foreign Policies*, William Appleman Williams develops the "mercantilist" argument in *The Contours of American History* (Cleveland, 1961), esp. 111–223. Williams undoubtedly built on the analysis of Madison's biographer, Irving Brant, who stresses that Madison was strongly in favor of encouraging domestic manufactures. Brant argues, for example, that Madison had no quarrel with the general purpose of Hamilton's Report on Manufactures—"for years he had been urging the national advantage of industrial development—but objected only to the secretary's preference for bounties as a means of encouragement." *James Madison: Father of the Constitution, 1787–1800* (Indianapolis, 1950), 348, 392–393. Those scholars who take the "mercantilist" approach to Madisonian political economy stress that commercial discrimination was designed to promote the development of American manufactures. As I will argue below, this point of view misinterprets Madison's fundamental motives and the thrust of his program, while often failing to make necessary distinctions between different types of manufacturing.

policy suggestions, and further expose the interdependence of domestic
and foreign policy objectives in this critical period of ideological conflict.

As one of the more prominent members of the First Congress,
Madison moved immediately in the spring of 1789 to implement his
program for economic independence.[4] The cornerstone of that program
was commercial discrimination—a distinction in tonnage and tariff laws
between nations in and out of commercial treaty with the United States.
The target was Great Britain, which had refused since the peace of 1783
to enter into mutually acceptable commercial arrangements with its former colonies. As befitted a staunch republican and Virginia planter,
Madison bemoaned the existing structural ties between the American
and British economies. Credit, for example, was a curse used by experienced British merchants to divert American commerce from its "natural
channels." Influenced strongly by the commercial liberalism of Adam
Smith, Madison predicated his analysis on a rather vague but consistent
reference to an ideal, "natural" international economic order. Despite
political independence, Americans were still tied to the old system of
British mercantilism; not only did British merchants and capital dominate American trade, thereby restricting foreign markets for American
exports, but they directed it into "artificial" and politically dangerous
channels of dependence. Madison's aim was to remove these onerous
shackles from American commerce; his vehicle was retaliatory commercial legislation in the form of discrimination.[5]

Discrimination was designed to accomplish several purposes. First,
it would encourage the development of American shipping, an objective
dearer to Madison than to most southerners at that time. Proclaiming
to Congress that he was "a friend to the navigation of America" who
would always "be as ready to go as great lengths in favor of that
interest as any man on the floor," Madison insisted that an independent
navigation industry was necessary both for naval defense and for easy,
dependable access to foreign markets.[6] Second, discrimination would
force the British to grant America a just reciprocity in commerce; it
would occasion a relaxation of the British navigation acts and thus
loosen the deadly grip of British credit and redirect American commerce

---

[4] The proceedings and debates may be found in U.S. Congress, 1st Congress, 1st
Session, in Joseph Gales, comp., *The Debates and Proceedings in the Congress of the United
States . . . (Washington, D.C., 1834–1856),* I, 107; hereafter cited as *Annals of Congress.*

[5] *Ibid.,* 193, 209–210. In discussing British restrictions on American commerce, Madison
often stressed the more fundamental danger of political "corruption" which transcended
mere economic inconvenience; it was necessary, he argued in 1794, to consider "the
influence that may be conveyed into the public councils by a nation directing the course
of our trade by her capital, and holding so great a share in our pecuniary institutions, and
the effect that may finally ensue on our taste, our manners, and our form of government
itself." *Ibid.,* 3d Cong., 1st sess., IV, 215.

[6] *Ibid.,* 1st Cong., 1 sess., I, 247. See also 197, 290–292.

into more "natural" channels. Madison was particularly interested in promoting direct trade with France, a nation in commercial treaty with the United States, by reducing the lucrative (and unnatural) British reexport trade of American produce. Another primary target was American trade with the British West Indies, as Madison intended to force open this "most natural and valuable" channel of commerce that the British had closed to American vessels in 1783.[7] Confidence in the efficacy of commercial coercion had characterized American Revolutionary thought but never was the policy more articulately promoted and defended than by Madison in this initial period of nation building. To understand why he was convinced that an "infant country" had sufficient power to coerce the mightiest nation on the globe, it is necessary to examine the assumptions on which the rationale for discrimination was based.

From a twentieth-century perspective, Madison had a peculiar analysis of the comparative nature and strength of the American and British economies. Great Britain was in a precarious position. "Her dependence, as a commercial and manufacturing nation," Madison argued, "is so absolutely upon us that it gives a moral certainty that her restrictions will not, for her own sake, be prejudicial to our trade."[8] The United States produced "necessaries" for export—food and raw materials—and imported "superfluities" in the form of British manufactures. Great Britain was "under a double dependence on the commerce of the United States"; her West Indies could not subsist without American supplies, and her manufacturers could not subsist without American customers. Madison usually emphasized the latter dependence, asserting the general rule that "in proportion as a nation manufactures luxuries must be its disadvantage in contests of every sort with its customers."[9] The United States, on the other hand, was blessed with an economy that provided a unique and relatively untapped source of natural power. Arguing that "the produce of this country is more necessary to the rest of the world than that of other countries is to America," Madison contended that "we possess natural advantages which no other nation does." Therefore, "if we have the disposition, we have abundantly the power to vindicate our cause."[10]

Several of Madison's fellow congressmen were at a loss to penetrate this logic and hardly shared his perception either of the latent strength of an undeveloped American economy or of Britain's dependence on it. They found it difficult to regard British clothing and hardware as "su-

---

[7] *Ibid.*, 193; Madison to Jefferson, June 30, 1789, in Julian P. Boyd *et al.*, eds., *The Papers of Thomas Jefferson* (Princeton, N.J., 1950–   ), XV, 226.

[8] *Annals of Congress*, 1st Cong., 1st sess., I, 256. See also 214, 248.

[9] *Ibid.*, 3d Cong., 1st sess., IV, 157, 215–216.

[10] *Ibid.*, 1st Cong., 1st sess., I, 214.

perfluities," and, unlike Madison, they feared the dire consequences of British economic power should commercial discrimination provoke a full-scale commercial war with that nation.[11] Madison's blanket view of American imports from Britain as "superfluities" stemmed in part from his conviction that the United States had the potential to manufacture any "necessaries" that it currently imported, and that the young Republic could, if necessary in the unlikely event of a commercial war, be converted very quickly into a society of self-sufficient yeomen who spun their own clothing at home. But this in itself seems insufficient to explain Madison's extreme view of British weakness and dependence on America, a view disputed by several of his contemporaries and, most importantly, actively opposed by the secretary of the Treasury.[12]

It is apparent that Madison's weltanschauung was strongly grounded in the structured intellectual paradigm now referred to as American "republican ideology." As several scholars have recently demonstrated, the vocabulary and concepts generated by minority opposition to government in eighteenth-century England permeated the American mind throughout the Revolutionary era.[13] "Corruption" signified more than bribery or dishonesty in government; it was an ideological catchword that connoted fundamental social and moral decay. American republicanism had its immediate origins in English "country" thought, which had flourished in the wake of England's post-1688 financial revolution and the crown's increased use of an enlarged patronage power. Radical Whig "Commonwealthmen," led by John Trenchard and Thomas Gordon, had shared with the nostalgic Tory Lord Bolingbroke a moral and aesthetic aversion to certain features of the new politico-economic order consolidated under Robert Walpole.[14] To these

---

[11] Rep. John Lawrence of New York led the opposition to discrimination in Congress, *Ibid.*, 184, 212, 243. In private correspondence Congressman Fisher Ames of Massachusetts proved to be a determined foe of Madison's policy. See letters from Ames to George Richards Minot, May 27, 29, and July 2, 1789, in Seth Ames, ed., *Works of Fisher Ames*, I (Boston, 1854), 45–46, 48–50, 59.

[12] *Annals of Congress*, 1st Cong., 1st sess., I, 248. See also *ibid.*, 3d Cong., 1st sess., IV, 215, 382. For a detailed discussion of Hamilton's initial opposition to "Jeffersonian" commercial policy see the editorial note in Boyd *et al.*, eds., *Jefferson Papers*, XVIII, 516–558.

[13] Shalhope, "Toward a Republican Synthesis," WMQ, 3rd Ser., XXIX (1972), 49–80. See esp. Bernard Bailyn, *The Ideological Origins of the American Revolution* (Cambridge, Mass., 1967); Gordon S. Wood, *The Creation of the American Republic, 1776–1787* (Chapel Hill, N.C., 1969); and two essays by J. G. A. Pocock, "Civic Humanism and Its Role in Anglo-American Thought," and "Machiavelli, Harrington and English Political Ideologies in the Eighteenth Century," both reprinted with slight revisions in Pocock, *Politics, Language, and Time: Essays on Political Thought and History* (New York, 1971), 80–103, 104–147.

[14] See Caroline Robbins, *The Eighteenth-Century Commonwealthman: Studies in the Transmission, Development and Circumstance of English Liberal Thought from the Restoration of Charles II until the War with the Thirteen Colonies* (Cambridge, Mass., 1959), and Isaac Kramnick,

critics, the growth of a new system of public finance, accompanied by the emergence and development of large moneyed companies (most notably the Bank of England) and the institutionalization of a stock and money market in London, brought into existence social types (rentiers, speculators in public funds, placemen and the like) whose influence on government and society was pernicious; their predominance signaled the decline of English liberty and the corruption of the moral and social fabric. After 1760 most Americans came to share this view, and the Revolution became, in part, the necessary struggle to save America from that same corruption.[15] This "country" image of eighteenth-century England furnished the rationale for commercial discrimination, for it depicted an unhealthy, debauched society whose strength and prosperity were illusory—a society mired in fiscalism, with a national debt, privileged corporations, paper money, "stockjobbers," and all the attendant moral evils, in which large numbers of citizens, suffering under the burden of institutions incompatible with republican liberty, lacked "independence" and "virtue."[16]

Economically, then, Great Britain was "dependent" on the United States precisely because so many of its citizens were not free in either an economic or a political sense. In particular, British manufacturers of "superfluities" could never be independent, since they depended for subsistence on a capricious, often transient demand for their products. In both his essay "Fashion," published March 20, 1792, in Philip Freneau's *National Gazette*, and later in congressional debates on commercial discrimination, Madison pointed to the pathetic plight of twenty thousand English buckle manufacturers and employees who were devastated by a sudden preference for shoestrings and slippers. To him these victims of the "mutability of fashion" offered a disgusting example of "the lowest point of servility."[17] An economy characterized by such industries was particularly vulnerable to customers who exported "necessaries" that would always command a "sure market." Blessed with plentiful natural resources (primarily an abundance of open land) and a healthy political culture, the United States, by comparison, was a young and

---

Bolingbroke and His Circle: The Politics of Nostalgia in the Age of Walpole (Cambridge, Mass., 1968). Pocock develops the concept of "country" thought in the essays cited above and in the review article, "Virtue and Commerce in the Eighteenth Century," *Journal of Interdisciplinary History*, III (1972–1973), 119–134.

[15] Pocock, *Politics, Language, and Time*, 93–97. My brief description of "country" ideology and its origin is, of course, selective and oversimplified. As Pocock notes, it was part of a tradition anchored in the Florentine Renaissance and looking back to classical antiquity.

[16] For an explicit and extended development of this general argument in relation to commercial discrimination by William Branch Giles, a fellow Virginian and one of Madison's congressional allies, see *Annals of Congress*, 3d Cong., 1st sess., IV, 281–285.

[17] Gaillard Hunt, ed., *The Writings of James Madison*, VI (New York, 1906). 99–101; *Annals of Congress*, 3d Cong., 1st sess., IV, 216.

virile society of independent and industrious republicans.[18] Madison never doubted that American power was latent, sown in nature, and fully capable of shattering the British restriction on American commerce that threateded the virtue and autonomy of the new Republic.[19]

Commercial discrimination was thus to be Madison's vehicle for building an independent American economy. But his conception of economic independence did not necessarily imply extensive domestic manufactures, the development of a great home market, or a diminishing reliance on foreign markets for American agricultural exports. His intention was not to use commercial regulations as a means of raising semipermanent tariff walls to encourage "industrial growth," a balanced internal economy, and American self-sufficiency. There did exist a radical strain of republican thought in America with strong anticommercial, even anticapitalist overtones, which called for the United States to isolate itself completely from the corrupting influence of the rest of the world.[20] But other republicans, including Madison, did not share this suspicious antipathy to commerce, provided it could flow in its proper "natural" channels. They regarded commerce as a civilizing force that would expand the human mind, remove local prejudices, and extend an empire of humanity and benevolence throughout the world.[21] The retaliatory duties provided for by Madison's discrimination program were a means to this end, temporary regulations that would promote the development of an international economic order

---

[18] *Annals of Congress*, 3d Cong., 1st sess., IV, 212; "Fashion," in Hunt, ed., *Writings of Madison*, VI, 99–101.

[19] Madison could have found confirmation both of his comparative view of the American and British economies and of the potential viability of commercial coercion in Adam Smith's *Wealth of Nations* (1776). See esp. Book IV, chap. VII, pt. III, in which Smith portrays the British economy as unbalanced and dangerously precarious, particularly vulnerable to the very type of scheme Madison ws advancing 15 years later. Adam Smith, *An Inquiry into the Nature and Causes of the Wealth of Nations*, ed. Edwin Cannon (reprint ed. New York, 1937 [orig. publ. London, 1776]), 590–593.

[20] For examples of this strain of thought see Amicus, "An Essay on the Fatal Tendency of the Prevailing Luxuries, . . ." *American Museum*, II (1787), 216–220; "An Oration Delivered at Petersburgh, Virginia, on the 4th of July, 1787, . . ." *ibid.*, 419–424; and extracts from "An Enquiry into the Causes of the Present Grievances of America," *ibid.*, V (1789), 254–257. The author of the Petersburg oration bluntly asserted that "foreign trade is in its very nature subversive of the spirit of pure liberty and independence, as it destroys that simplicity of manners, native manliness of soul, and equality of station, which is the spring and peculiar excellence of a free government." *Ibid.*, II, 421.

[21] Clear statements of the economic implications of this more moderate strain of republican thought may be found in Enos Hitchcock, *An Oration: Delivered July 4, 1788, . . .* (Providence, R. I. [1788]), and William Hillhouse, Jr., *A Dissertation, in Answer to a late Lecture on the Political State of America . . .* (New Haven, Conn. [1789]). These republicans usually argued that only commerce and the demand of foreign markets could stimulate the virtues of industry and frugality among Americans.

in which restrictions would be unnecessary.[22] Madison's prescription for American economic independence did not require isolation from foreign markets as long as Americans continued to export the right kind of products—"necessaries." To be in a "dependent" relationship to a foreign customer or nation the United States would have to become a producer of whimsical "superfluities." Madison particularly regretted to see the day when Americans should resort to the production of articles like brass buckles for export; pointing to the British example, he warned that "in proportion as a nation consists of that description of citizens, and depends on external commerce, it is dependent on the consumption and caprice of other nations."[23]

In addition to dependence on foreign customers, Madison was determined to avoid another type of dependence—that of one class of citizens upon another within the United States. Here he referred in part to the problem of wage laborers who depended for subsistence upon the will of their employers. At the core of republican ideology was an intense concern with the autonomy or "independence" of the individual, and with the material or economic basis for that autonomy.[24] The individual who was "dependent" on others for subsistence was in a particularly deplorable situation, for he could be made to serve the will of his patrons, thus sacrificing the moral integrity necessary for the exercise of proper civic virtue. Once there were large numbers of "dependents" in a society, republican government was doomed. It seems clear that Madison, steeped in "republicanism," subscribed to James Harrington's maxim that the form of government followed the distribution of wealth, particularly landed wealth, and that republican government required a wide distribution of property among small independent landowners.[25] It was for this reason that Madison was so concerned with the potential economic and political ramifications of rapid population growth in America; in Europe, a human "surplus" had con-

---

[22] Madison repeatedly professed his adherence to "a very free system of commerce," in which "industry and labor are left to take their own course," free from "unjust, oppressive, and impolitic" commercial shackles. *Annals of Congress*, 1st Cong., 1st sess., I, 116. For the system to function properly between nations, however, all nations had to comply. Madison was determined to induce compliance from Great Britain.

[23] See "Fashion," in Hunt, ed., *Writings of Madison*, VI, 100–101.

[24] For a detailed discussion of the development of this concept of "independence" in 17th-century English political thought see C. B. Macpherson, *The Political Theory of Possessive Individualism: Hobbes to Locke* (Oxford, 1962). More recently, Edmund S. Morgan has discussed this matter in relation to Jefferson and the slavery problem in "Slavery and Freedom: The American Paradox," *Journal of American History*, LIX (1972–1973), 5–29.

[25] For an extended discussion of Harrington and the "balance of property" element in republican thought see Pocock, *Politics, Language, and Time*, 80–103, 104–147.

tributed to, if not induced, the general pattern of corruption, decay, and misery.[26] Madison had no aversion to household manufactures, which constituted "the natural ally of agriculture," but he did not look forward to the development of large-scale manufacturing enterprises that would employ large numbers of "dependent" wage laborers who neither owned their own land nor possessed much personal property. In his essay, "Republican Distribution of Citizens," which appeared in the *National Gazette* on March 3, 1792 (shortly after the delivery of Hamilton's Report on Manufactures to Congress), Madison wrote in reference to "the regular [i.e., nonhousehold] branches of manufacturing and mechanical industry" that "whatever is least favorable to vigor of body, to the faculties of the mind, or to the virtues or the utilities of life, instead of being forced or fostered by public authority, ought to be seen with regret as long as occupations more friendly to human happiness, lie vacant."[27] He hoped that the United States would not be forced to turn to such manufacturing or to the production of "superfluities" by the pressures of an expanding population, a contracting supply of land, or inadequate foreign markets for American agricultural surpluses. Expansion across the continent and the expansion of foreign markets were the two surest ways to forestall this calamity; both strategies were central to Madison's political economics and foreign policy.[28]

While he drew upon much of the same republican heritage as Madison, Alexander Hamilton's intellectual world had a far different texture. Influenced heavily by David Hume's defense of luxury in modern commercial society, Hamilton's republicanism was less intense, less classical, and less rigid. By the 1790s his style of thought was closer to the English "court" mainstream than to the "country" opposition that

---

[26] See Madison's several statements on this matter in the Constitutional Convention in *Notes of Debates in the Federal Convention of 1787, Reported by James Madison* (Athens, Ohio, 1966), 194, 375. In an often-cited letter to Jefferson of June 19, 1786, Madison fretted about the apparent truism that "a certain degree of misery seems inseparable from a high degree of populousness." Boyd *et al.*, eds., *Jefferson Papers*, IX, 660.

[27] Hunt, ed., *Writings of Madison*, VI, 99. See also *Notes of Debates*, 194, 375. For an example of the dependence of wage laborers on their employers in Europe as, ironically, it was extolled (in the name of efficiency) by one promoter of large-scale manufacturing in America see John F. Amelung, *Remarks on Manufactures . . .* ([Frederick, Md.], 1787). There had been a definite trend in the direction of factory production in America between 1786 and 1792; if Madison was aware of this trend, it could only have exacerbated his fears. Curtis P. Nettels, *The Emergence of a National Economy, 1775–1815* (New York, 1962), 125.

[28] See Gerald Stourzh's recent study, *Alexander Hamilton and the Idea of Republican Government* (Stanford, Calif., 1970), and Pocock, "Virtue and Commerce," *Jour. Interdisc. Hist.*, III (1972–1973), 130–131.

had predominated in Revolutionary America.[29] His economic system—tied to a funded debt, a national bank, and fluid capital—was a bold but politically explosive initiative in a society of "country" republicans who were ideologically prone to view it as an insidious replica of the system that had corrupted Augustan England. The developing opposition to Hamilton should thus be viewed on two different levels; first, on the level of strictly tactical and strategic differences among intellectuals, competing interest groups, and geographic regions, and second, on the level of ideological resistance to an alleged conspiracy to corrupt American society and smash the republican experiment by imitating British forms, manners, and institutions. This ideological resistance was triggered for Madison and many others by the scramble for the stock of the Bank of the United States on the part of speculators, (some of whom were congressmen) in the summer of 1791 and the ensuing panic of March 1792.[30] Madison was outraged by what he saw to be a corrupted legislature, manipulated by Hamilton from his vantage point in the Treasury and tied to a fiscal system that encouraged bad morals and habits in the society at large. Particularly frightening to Madison in this respect was Hamilton's Report on Manufactures, issued to Congress in December 1791.[31]

In his private correspondence Madison's objections focused on Hamilton's treatment of the "general welfare" clause of the Constitution. In urging pecuniary bounties as the best means of encouraging American manufactures, Hamilton had argued that Congress had virtually unlimited power to interpret that clause, and Madison

---

[29] See Gerald Stourzh's recent study, *Alexander Hamilton and the Idea of Republican Government* (Stanford, Calif., 1970), and Pocock, "Virtue and Commerce," *Jour. Interdisc. Hist.*, III (1972–1973), 130–131.

[30] See Madison's general correspondence during this period—for example, Madison to Jefferson, Aug. 8, 1791, in Hunt, ed., *Writings of Madison*, VI, 58n–59n, and Madison to Henry Lee, Apr. 15, 1792, in *Letters and Other Writings of James Madison*, I (Philadelphia, 1865), 553–554. Madison also published during this general period an extended series of 13 essays (of which "Fashion" and "Republican Distribution of Citizens" were a part), focusing on threats to republicanism in America. See also, in particular, "Spirit of Governments," in Hunt, ed., *Writings of Madison*, VI, 93–95. Perhaps the best discussions of the intellectual origins of the Jeffersonian side of the ideological struggle of the 1790s are two unpublished doctoral dissertations: Douglass Adair, "The Intellectual Origins of Jeffersonian Democracy" (Yale University, 1944), and Lance G. Banning, "The Quarrel with Federalism: A Study in the Origins and Character of Republican Thought" (Washington University, 1972). See esp. Chap. 5 of Banning's dissertation and his recent article, "Republican Ideology and the Triumph of the Constitution, 1789 to 1793," *WMQ*, 3d Ser., XXXI (1974), 167–188. Richard Buel, *Securing the Revolution: Ideology in American Politics, 1789–1815* (Ithaca, N.Y., 1972), fails to exploit fully the ideological depth of the "republican" opposition to Hamilton's system.

[31] The final version of the Report on Manufactures may be found in Harold C. Syrett and Jacob E. Cooke, eds., *The Papers of Alexander Hamilton*, X (New York, 1966), 230–340.

clearly feared the ominous potential of an unrestrained and "corrupted"legislature.[32] Staunch "republicans" suspected that the secretary
of the Treasury would use this spurious constitutional interpretation to
create corporate monopolies that would ruin small producers and create
unrepublican inequalities of wealth. Hamilton's Report left little doubt
that he was most interested in large-scale factory production; this was
corroborated by his aid in the establishment of a grandiose corporate
enterprise, the "Society for Useful Manufactures," at Paterson, New Jersey, which prompted an outpouring of antimonopoly rhetoric.[33] There
seems little doubt, moreover, that Hamilton's Report helped provoke
Madison's essays "Fashion" and "Republican Distribution of Citizens,"
which raised republican objections to certain types of manufacturing
enterprises.

Beyond this, the Report on Manufactures directly challenged
Madison's fundamental system of political economy and the rationale for commercial discrimination. Hamilton insisted that foreign markets, limited by the restrictions of European mercantilism, would be
increasingly insufficient for the absorption of burgeoning American
agricultural surpluses. He admitted that if the doctrine of perfectly free
commerce were universally practiced, arguments against the development of American manufactures would have great force; he contended, however, that "an opposite spirit" regulated "the general policy of
Nations," with the unfortunate consequence that "the United States are
to a certain extent in the situation of a country precluded from foreign
Commerce."[34] Hamilton's unstated assumption was that the United
States did not have the power necessary to destroy or significantly
alter the prevailing European system of commercial intercourse. He
thus denied Madison's assertion that the nature of the American economy provided power sufficient to overturn British commercial restrictions; instead, he explicitly developed the general theory that nations
with extensive manufactures had overwhelming advantages in their
intercourse with predominantly agricultural nations.[35] Since Hamilton's
view of England was not shaped by the assumptions of classical repub-

---

[32] See Report on Manufactures, *ibid.*, 302–304; Madison to Edmund Pendleton, Jan.
21, 1792, James Madison Papers, Library of Congress; and Madison to Henry Lee, Jan.
1, 1792, in Hunt, ed., *Writings of Madison*, VI, 81n.

[33] Hamilton made an indirect reference to the Society for Useful Manufactures in the
Report when he announced that "measures are already in train for prosecuting on a
large scale, the making and printing of cotton goods." Syrett and Cooke, eds., *Hamilton
Papers*, X, 328. The most thorough study of the Society and the ideological attacks on it
is in Joseph S. Davis, *Essays in the Earlier History of American Corporations*, II (Cambridge,
Mass, 1916), 349–522.

[34] Report on Manufactures in Syrett and Cooke, eds., *Hamilton Papers*, X, 262–263. See
also 256–260, 287–288.

[35] *Ibid.*, 287–290.

licanism and Country ideology, Madison's idea of American "necessaries" and British "superfluities" was totally alien to his structure of thought. For Hamilton, the insufficiency of foreign markets for American surpluses pointed directly to the need for governmental assistance in the development of domestic manufactures and a more dependable home market for American produce. The result, he argued, would be a more balanced, sectionally interdependent economy that would gradually enhance American power to the point where the United States might effectively contend for commercial reciprocity.[36]

By denying the viability of commercial coercion and asserting that the development of government-subsidized manufacturing enterprises on a large scale was necessary to insure an adequate vent for American agricultural surpluses, Hamilton put Madison in an increasingly precarious position. He threatened to sustain the momentum already generated by the establishment of public credit (largely on his terms) and the Bank of the United States, and further consolidate the "system" that Madison thought antithetical to republicanism in America. Madison's counterattack came in January 1794, on the heels of Secretary of State Thomas Jefferson's Report on Commerce, when he attempted to exploit a growing diplomatic crisis with Great Britain by reviving his program of commercial discrimination.[37] The secretary of the Treasury had frustrated Madison's repeated attempts to enact the policy into law during each session of the First Congress, in part because his "system," tied to British credit and the revenue from Anglo-American trade, could not stand the risk of a serious rupture with England.[38] Madison's 1794 resolutions touched off a momentous congressional debate in which Representative William Loughton Smith of South Carolina led the opposition by delivering a brilliant, day-long speech that had been prepared by Hamilton. Echoing the implicit assumption of the Report on Manufactures, Smith ridiculed "the impracticability and Quixotism of an attempt by violence, on the part of this young country, to break through the fetters which the universal policy of nations imposes on their intercourse with each other."[39] During the course of the debate the crisis with Britain worsened, and Madison's resolutions were put

---

[36] John C. Miller, *Alexander Hamilton: Portrait in Paradox* (New York, 1959), 292–295, 301. See also the conclusion of a speech written by Hamilton and delivered to Congress by William Loughton Smith in early 1794. *Annals of Congress*, 3d Cong., 1st sess., IV, 208.

[37] See Merrill D. Peterson, "Thomas Jefferson and Commercial Policy, 1783–1793," *WMQ*, 3d Ser., XXII (1965), 584–610.

[38] For a good account of Madison's repeated failures see Jerald A. Combs, *The Jay Treaty: Political Battleground of the Founding Fathers* (Berkeley and Los Angeles, 1970), 31–33, 50–51, 58.

[39] *Annals of Congress*, 3d Cong., 1st sess., IV, 196. For the whole debate see *ibid.* 155ff. For a secondary account see, among many others, Varg, *Foreign Policies*, 99–101.

aside in favor of more appropriate measures. While he concurred in the need for additional action, Madison stubbornly maintained that his resolutions were "in every view and in every event proper to make part of our standing laws till the principle of reciprocity be established by mutual arrangements."[40] Implementation of discrimination was to be indefinitely postponed, however, for the ultimate upshot of the 1794 crisis was the Jay Treaty, which prohibited for ten years the type of anti-British commercial program Madison had championed.

I would suggest that the full economic implications of Madison's aggressive commitment to commercial discrimination have been obscured by a failure to examine his motives within the broader context of his republicanism. Twentieth-century historians, anxious to prove that Madison was not a parochial or short-sighted agrarian, have stressed that his program would have promoted American manufactures and, therefore, that this objective must have been central to his purpose. To the limited extent that he expected his policy to encourage manufactures, however, Madison clearly spoke of those "carried on, not in public factories, but in the household or family way, which he regarded as the most important way."[41] Above all, Madison intended to demonstrate the ability of America's "natural" economic power to shatter Old World mercantilist restrictions. His primary politico-economic goal was not to stimulate manufactures but to undercut one of the key assumptions behind Hamilton's program for industrial development and insure the opening of adequate foreign markets for American agricultural surpluses. This is turn would encourage further westward expansion and, most importantly, secure the institutional and moral base for an American political economy conducive to republicanism. Viewed in this context, commercial discrimination was part of a determined attempt to perserve and expand across space the predominantly agricultural character of American society.[42] To this degree, Madison,

---

[40] Madison to Jefferson, Mar. 19, 1794, Madison Papers.

[41] *Annals of Congress*, 3d Cong., 1st sess., IV, 221. As John C. Miller notes, Madison's commitment was thus to manufacturing that could be carried on as well in the southern states as in the North or East. *The Federalist Era, 1789–1801* (New York, 1960), 144n; *Annals of Congress*, 3d Cong., 1st sess., IV, 221–222. For a parallel discussion of Jefferson's political economics and its relation to commercial policy in this period see William D. Grampp, "A Re-examination of Jeffersonian Economics," *Southern Economic Journal*, XII (1945–1946), 263–282.

[42] See Adair, "Intellectual Origins," As J. R. Pole has recently noted, Madison always feared the political ramifications of industrial growth and widespread urbanization. *Political Representation in England and the Origins of the American Republic* (London, 1966), 360–361, 530–531. For an interesting and relevant discussion of later Whig and Democratic conceptions of economic development see Major L. Wilson, "The Concept of Time and the Political Dialogue in the United States, 1828–48," *American Quarterly*, XIX (1967), 619–644.

as much as Hamilton, had a "system" in which foreign policy objectives were integral to his approach to economic development and to his vision of a future America. Hopefully, on a broader scale, this exploratory essay has suggested the need to extend our growing understanding of "republicanism" and American "republican ideology" into the areas of economic thought and foreign policy.

Commercial Farming and the "Agrarian Myth" in the Early Republic

Joyce Appleby

With the appearance of "Liberalism and the American Revolution," New England Quarterly, IL (March, 1976), 3-26, and "The Social Origins of American Revolutionary Ideology," Journal of American History, LXIV (March, 1978), 935-958, Joyce Appleby emerged as probably the leading critic of the recent reinterpretation of Revolutionary thought. "Commercial Farming and the 'Agrarian Myth,'" which was awarded the journal's best-article prize for 1982, challenged the "republican" interpretation of Jeffersonian ideas and offered an alternative that is elaborated in Capitalism and a New Social Order: The Republican Vision of the 1790s *("Anson G. Phelps Lectureship on Early American History"; New York: New York University Press, 1984). The article is reprinted by permission from the* Journal of American History, *LXVIII (March, 1982), 833-849. Copyright: Organization of American Historians, 1982.*

Nineteen forty-three marked the two-hundredth anniversary of the birth of Thomas Jefferson and the occasion for bestowing yet another honor on the Sage of Monticello. Amid salutes to Jefferson's politics and philosophy, historians and agronomists seized the opportunity to herald his contributions to scientific agriculture. Quoting from Vice-president Henry A. Wallace, M. L. Wilson claimed that farmers identified Jefferson with "the application of science to agriculture," and he then admiringly listed Jefferson's scientific achievements: the invention of a threshing machine, the improvement of the plow, the introduction of Merino sheep, and the advocacy of soil conservation.[1] August C. Miller, Jr., called Jefferson the father of American democracy and "a scientific farmer and agriculturist in the most comprehensive sense" of the term.[2] On this bicentennial anniversary, according to A. Whitney Gris-

---

[1] M. L. Wilson, "Thomas Jefferson—Farmer," *Proceedings of the American Philosophical Society*, 87 (1944), 217–19.

[2] August C. Miller, Jr., "Jefferson as an Agriculturist," *Agricultural History*, XVI (April 1942), 65.

wold, people paid tribute to Jefferson as "preeminently and above all a farmer." Noting that Jefferson's enthusiasm for farming had always included commerce, Griswold agreed with William D. Grampp that Jefferson's concern about marketing farm commodities had made him an ardent proponent of international free trade.[3] Thus, like the Department of Agriculture experts who gathered in the auditorium that bore his name, Jefferson in 1943 was depicted as an early-day New Dealer, a modernizer dedicated to helping ordinary farmers become efficient producers.

In 1955—just twelve years later—Richard Hofstadter published *The Age of Reform*, and Jefferson was captured for an altogether different historiographical tradition. Looking for the roots of the nostalgia that flowered with the Populists, Hofstadter described how Jefferson and other eighteenth-century writers had been drawn irresistibly to the "noncommercial, nonpecuniary, self-sufficient aspects of American farm life." The Jeffersonians, Hofstadter said, had created an "agrarian myth" and fashioned for the new nation a folk hero, the yeoman farmer, who was admired "not for his capacity to exploit opportunities and make money," but rather for his ability to produce a simple abundance. Underlining the mythic aspect of this literary creation, Hofstadter noted the actual profit orientation of the farmers who, he said, accepted the views of their social superiors as harmless flattery.[4]

The instantaneous popularity of Hofstadter's "agrarian myth" owes a good deal more to trends in the writing of history than to the evidentiary base upon which it rested. That, in fact, was very shaky. Hofstadter directed his readers to two writers, neither of whom drew the distinction he had made between the romantic myth of rural self-sufficiency created by writers and the reality of farming for profit acted upon by ordinary men. Griswold, whom Hofstadter claimed had produced "a full statement of the agrarian myth as it was formulated by Jefferson," in fact explored Jefferson's views on agricultural improvements and commercial expansion in order to point out that what had made sense in jefferson's day no longer held true in the twentieth century.[5] The second writer to whom Hofstadter referred, Chester E. Eisinger, addressed Hofstadter's theme of national symbols, but his freehold concept can be readily differentiated from Hofstadter's agrarian myth. Tracing the appearance of independent freehold farmers to the destruction of feudal tenures, Eisinger explained how in England the same commercial forces that destroyed the manorial system had also worked

---

[3] A. Whitney Griswold, *Farming and Democracy* (New York, 1948), 18–19, 26–32; William D. Grampp, "A Re-examination of Jeffersonian Economics," *Southern Economic Journal*, XII (Jan. 1946), 263–82.

[4] Richard Hofstadter, *The Age of Reform: From Bryan to F.D.R.* (New York, 1955), 23–24, 30.

[5] *Ibid.*, 25; Griswold, *Farming and Democracy*, 12–15.

to eliminate the small, freeholding producer. In America the reality of vacant land gave substance to a vision of a society of independent farmers; so the freehold concept, like so many other ideas, got a new lease on life by crossing the Atlantic. Where Hofstadter stressed the appeal of yeoman self-sufficiency, however, Eisinger linked the freehold concept to the emerging capitalist economy. In the era of commercial agriculture, Eisinger wrote, "not only could a man possess his own farm, but he was his own master, rising and falling by his own efforts, bargaining in a free market."[6] Thus where Hofstadter's introductory chapter juxtaposed the agrarian myth and commercial realities, Eisinger distinguished between the poetic yearning for a bygone age of peasants and the modern reality of market-oriented farmers. All of Hofstadter's sources had traced the eighteenth-century literary preoccupation with farming to the rising population and the consequent importance of food production, but Hofstadter snapped this connection between material reality and intellectual response by stressing the purely mythic power of what two of his students have recently characterized as the ideal of "'the self-sufficient yeoman' dwelling in a rural arcadia of unspoiled virtue, honest toil and rude plenty."[7]

Without looking firsthand at the literature of the 1790s, Hofstadter wrote his thesis about the nostalgic politics of the Populist era back into the earlier period. His indifference to a time that provided only a backdrop to the central drama in the age of reform is understandable. Indeed, what sustained the attractiveness of the yeoman ideal was not Hofstadter's book but a much stronger tide coursing through scholarship on eighteenth-century America. As a quick survey of titles and expository prose produced in the last twenty years will reveal, *yeoman* has become a favorite designation for the ordinary farmer of postrevolutionary America. Losing its definition as a rank in a hierarchical society of tenants, yeomen, gentlemen, and lords, it has become instead a code word for a man of simple tastes, sturdy independence, and admirable disdain for all things newfangled. In this form the yeoman archetype has become particularly congruent with the recent work of social historians, who have sought to reconstruct the basic character and structure of colonial society.

Using continuous records on family formation and landholding

---

[6] Chester E. Eisinger, "The Freehold Concept in Eighteenth-Century American Letters," *William and Mary Quarterly*, IV (Jan. 1947), 46–47. See also Chester E. Eisinger, "Land and Loyalty: Literary Expressions of Agrarian Nationalism in the Seventeenth and Eighteenth Centuries," *American Literature*, 21 (May 1949), 160–78, and Chester E. Eisinger, "The Farmer in the Eighteenth Century Almanac," *Agricultural History*, XXVIII (July 1954), 107–12.

[7] Stanley Elkins and Eric McKitrick, "Richard Hofstadter: A Progress," in *The Hofstadter Aegis: A Memorial*, ed. Stanley Elkins and Eric McKitrick (New York, 1975), 316.

patterns, these scholars have given special attention to the collective experience of whole communities. The models of the social scientists that they have employed, moreover, have encouraged them to look for the similarities between early American society and its counterpart in Europe. Where earlier historians had emphasized the idea of an America born free and modern, the new practitioners of social history have been more open to the possibility that America, too, had once been a traditional society. Indeed, they have found that, like traditional men and women of sociological theory, colonial Americans created the community solidarity and familial networks that encouraged resistance to change.[8] Instead of the contrast between old-fashioned and up-to-date that had been employed to describe the essentially external transformation from rural to industrial America, recent writings have concentrated on the connection between visible social action and invisible cultural influences. Traditional society as an abstract concept has been invested with the normative values of stability, cohesion, and neighborly concern, while the changes that came with economic development have been characterized as intrusive, exploitive, and class-biased. Where Hofstadter played off myth against reality, the new interpreters of early America are more likely to insist that a genuine conflict existed between farm communities and the modern world of money, markets, and merchants.

It is this more refined and subtle model of rural life that has turned the Jeffersonians into nostalgic men fighting a rearguard action against the forces of modernity. Thus J. G. A. Pocock has named Jefferson as the conduit through which a civic concept of virture entered "the whole tradition of American agrarian and populist messianism."[9] Less concerned with political issues, James A. Henretta has stressed the farmers' concern with protecting the lineal family from the centrifugal forces of individual enterprise and economic competition.[10] According to Lance Banning, the Republican party appealed to "the hesitations of agrarian conservatives as they experienced the stirrings of a more commercial age," while John M. Murrin has concluded that the Jeffersonians were like the English Country opposition on political and economic questions

---

[8] For a review of this literature, see John J. Waters, "From Democracy to Demography: Recent Historiography on the New England Town," in *Perspectives on Early American History: Essays in Honor of Richard B. Morris*, ed. Alden T. Vaughan and George Athan Billias (New York, 1973), 222–49.

[9] J. G. A. Pocock, "Virtue and Commerce in the Eighteenth Century," *Journal of Interdisciplinary History*,III (Summer 1972), 134. See also J. G. A. Pocock, *The Machiavellian Moment: Florentine Political Thought and the Atlantic Republican Tradition* (Princeton, 1975), ix, 529–33.

[10] James A. Henretta, "Families and Farms: *Mentalité* in Pre-Industrial America," *William and Mary Quarterly*, XXXV (Jan. 1978), 3–32.

because "they idealized the past more than the future and feared significant change, especially major economic change, as corruption and
degeneration."[11] For Drew R. McCoy the tension between tradition and
innovation is more explicit. The Jeffersonians, he has said, were forced
to reconcile classical ideals with social realities; their ambiguities and
contradictions reflected "an attempt to cling to the traditional republican
spirit of classical antiquity without disregarding the new imperatives of
a more modern commercial society."[12] In *The Elusive Republic* McCoy
has recovered the centrality of commercial policy in the Jeffersonians'
program, but he has assumed that the values of civic humanism gave
shape and direction to their recommendations.

In contrast to these characterizations of early national attitudes,
I shall argue that the new European demand for American grains—
the crops produced by most farm families from Virginia through Maryland, Pennsylvania, Delaware, New Jersey, New York, and up the Connecticut River Valley—created an unusually favorable opportunity for
ordinary men to produce for the Atlantic trade world. Far from being
viewed apprehensively, this prospect during the thirty years following the adoption of the Constitution undergirded Jefferson's optimism
about America's future as a progressive, prosperous, democratic nation.
Indeed, this anticipated participation in an expanding international
commerce in foodstuffs created the material base for a new social vision
owing little conceptually or practically to antiquity, the Renaissance,
or the mercantilists of eighteenth-century England. From this perspective, the battle between the Jeffersonians and Federalists appears not
as a conflict between the patrons of agrarian self-sufficiency and the
proponents of modern commerce, but rather as a struggle between
two different elaborations of capitalistic development in America. Jefferson becomes, not the herioc loser in a battle against modernity,
but the conspicuous winner in a contest over how the government
should serve its citizens in the first generation of the nation's territorial
expansion.

Anyone searching for the word *yeoman* in the writings of the 1790s
will be disappointed. A canvass of titles in Charles Evans's *American
Bibliography* failed to turn up the designation *yeoman* in the more than
thirty thousand works published in the United States between 1760 and
1800. The word *yeomanry* appeared only three times, all in works by a

---

[11] Lance Banning, *The Jeffersonian Persuasion: Evolution of a Party Ideology* (Ithaca, 1978),
269; John M. Murrin, "The Great Inversion, or Court versus Country: A Comparison of
the Revolution Settlements in England (1688–1721) and America (1776–1815)," in *Three
British Revolutions: 1641, 1688, 1776*, ed. J. G. A. Pocock (Princeton, 1980), 406.
[12] Drew R. McCoy, *The Elusive Republic: Political Economy in Jeffersonian America* (Chapel
Hill, 1980), 10.

single author, George Logan.[13] Noah Webster, American's first lexicographer, defined *yeoman* as "a common man, or one of the plebeians, of the first or most respectable class; a freeholder, a man free born," but went on to explain that "the word is little used in the United States, unless as a title in law proceedings...and this only in particular states." *Yeomanry*, on the other hand, was much used, according to Webster, and referred to the collective body of freeholders. "Thus the common people in America are called the yeomanry."[14] For Webster, an ardent Federalist, the word retained the social distinction of its British provenance but conveyed nothing as such about farming. I have never found the word *yeoman* in Jefferson's writings; it certainly does not appear in his one book, *Notes on the State of Virginia*, where undifferentiated people in political contexts are called "citizens," "tax-payers," or "electors"; in economic references, "husbandmen," "farmers," or "laborers"; and in social commentary, "the poor," "the most discreet and honest inhabitants," or "respectable merchants and farmers." When Jefferson spoke in theoretical terms, ordinary persons were often discussed as "individuals," as in a passage where he says the dissolution of power would leave people "as individuals to shift for themselves."[15] Like Jefferson, the writers who filled Evans's bibliography with titles chose such socially neutral nouns as *farmers, planters, husbandmen, growers, inhabitants, landowners,* or more frequently, simply *countrymen,* a term whose double meaning reflected accurately the rural location of the preponderance of American citizens.

The absence of the word *yeoman* is negative evidence only, although its occasional use by contemporary Englishmen and New Englanders suggests a lingering reference to a status designation.[16] The error in current scholarly usage, however, is not lexical, but conceptual; it points Jefferson and his party in the wrong direction. Despite Jefferson's repeated assertions that his party was animated by bold new expecta-

---

[13] Charles Evans, C. K. Shipton, R. P. Bristol, comps., *American Bibliography* (14 vols., New York, 1959); George Logan, *Letters Addressed to the Yeomanry of the United States* (Philadelphia, 1791); George Logan, *Five Letters, Addressed to the Yeomanry of the United States Containing Some Observations on the Dangerous Scheme of Governor Duer and Mr. Secretary Hamilton* (Philadelphia, 1792); George Logan, *Letters Addressed to the Yeomanry of the United States Containing Some Observations on Funding and Bank Systems* (Philadelphia, 1793).

[14] Noah Webster, *An American Dictionary of the English Language* (2 vols., New York, 1828), s.v. "Yeoman" and "Yeomanry." See also Noah Webster, *A Compendious Dictionary of the English Language* (Hartford, 1806), where *yeoman* is defined as "a gentleman-farmer, freeholder, officer."

[15] Thomas Jefferson, *Notes on the State of Virginia*, ed. William Peden (Chapel Hill, 1955), 125, 127, 130, 164–65, 213.

[16] For the use of *yeoman* in this period, see *Boston Gazette*, April 15, 1790, March 3, 1794, May 25, 1796; *Independent Chronicle* (Boston), Dec. 15, 1786, April 9, 1789.

tions for the human condition, the agrarian myth makes him a traditional, republican visionary, socially radical perhaps, but economically conservative. The assumed contradiction between democratic aspirations and economic romanticism explains why his plans were doomed to failure in competition with the hard-headed realism of an Alexander Hamilton. To this form of the argument, interpretive schemes much older than Hofstadter's have contributed a great deal. Viewed retrospectively by historians living in an industrial age, Jefferson's enthusiasm for agriculture has long been misinterpreted as an attachment to the past. So dazzling were the technological triumphs of railroad building and steam power that the age of the marvelous machines came to appear as the great divide in human history. Henry Adams offers a splendid example of this distorting perspective. Describing America in 1800, Adams said that "down to the close of the eighteenth century no change had occurred in the world which warranted practical men in assuming that great changes were to come." The connection between industrial technology and a modern mentality for him was complete, for he then went on to say, "as time passed, and as science developed man's capacity to control Nature's forces, old-fashioned conservatism vanished from society."[17] In fact, an American who was forty years old in 1800 would have seen every fixed point in his or her world dramatically transformed through violent political agitation, protracted warfare, galloping inflation, and republican revolutions. Yet for Adams the speed of travel held the human imagination in a thrall that the toppling of kings could not affect.

Two interpretative tendencies have followed from this point of view. One has been to treat proponents of agricultural development as conservative and to construe as progressive those who favored manufacturing and banking. The contrast between Jefferson cast as an agrarian romantic and Hamilton as the far-seeing capitalist comes readily to mind. The other retrospective bias has been the characterization of industrialization as an end toward which prior economic changes were inexorably moving. Both classical economic and Marxist theory have contributed to this determinism which recasts historical events as parts of a process, as stages in a sequential morphology. Under this influence, the actual human encounter with time is reversed; instead

---

[17] Henry Adams, *The United States in 1800* (Ithaca, 1955), 42. Contrast this with Duc Francois de La Rochefoucauld-Liancourt's firsthand observation that America was "a country in flux; that which is true today as regards its population, its establishments, its prices, its commerce will not be true six months from now." David J. Brandenburg, "A French Aristocrat Looks at American Farming: La Rochefoucauld-Liancourt's *Voyages dans les Etats-Unis*," *Agricultural History*, 32 (1958), 163.

of interpreting social change as the result of particular responses to a knowable past, the decisions men and women made are examined in relation to future developments unknown to them.[18] The situation in America at the end of the eighteenth century is exemplary.

Ignorant of the industrial future, Americans were nonetheless aware that their economy was being reshaped by the most important material change of the era: the rise of European population and the consequent inability of European agriculture to meet the new demand for foodstuffs. After 1755 the terms of trade between grain and all other commodities turned decisively in favor of the grains and stayed that way until the third decade of the nineteenth century.[19] In *Common Sense*, Thomas Paine dismissed colonial fears about leaving the security of the English navigation system by saying that American commerce would flourish so long as "eating is the custom of Europe."[20] Eating, of course, had long been the custom of Europeans. What made their eating habits newly relevant to Americans was their declining capacity to feed themselves. More fortunate than most of her neighbors, England benefited from a century and a half of previous agricultural improvements so that pressure from her growing population meant that harvest surpluses, which had once been exported, after mid-century were consumed at home. The withdrawal of English grains, however, created major food deficits on the Iberian peninsula. No longer able to rely upon Britain's bounteous harvests, the Spanish and Portuguese began looking anxiously across the Atlantic to North America. The impact of food shortages had a differential impact upon European nations, but for Americans the consequences, particularly after 1788, were salubrious. The long upward climb of prices enhanced the value of those crops that ordinary farmers could easily grow.[21] Combined with the strong

---

[18] For a critique of this tendency in economic history, see Robert E. Mutch, "Yeoman and Merchant in Pre-Industrial America; Eighteenth-Century Massachusetts as a Case Study," *Societas*, VII (Autumn, 1977), 279–302.

[19] B. H. Slicher Van Bath, "Eighteenth-Century Agriculture on the Continent of Europe: Evolution or Revolution?" *Agricultural History*, XLIII (Jan. 1969), 173–75.

[20] [Thomas Paine], *Common Sense, Addressed to the Inhabitants of America*, in *The Writings of Thomas Paine*, ed. Moncure Daniel Conway (4 vols., New York, 1894–1896), I, 86.

[21] For some important interpretative points in regard to agricultural productivity and to exports as its measure, see Claudia D. Goldin and Frank D. Lewis, "The Role of Exports in American Economic Growth during the Napoleonic Wars, 1793 to 1807," *Explorations in Economic History*, 17 (Jan. 1980), 6–25; William N. Parker, "Sources of Agricultural Productivity in the Nineteenth Century," *Journal of Farm Economics*, 49 (Dec. 1967), 1455–68; and Andrew Hill Clark, "Suggestions for the Geographical Study of Agricultural Change in the United States, 1790–1840," in *Farming in the New Nation: Interpreting American Agriculture, 1790–1840*, ed. Darwin P. Kelsey (Washington, 1972), 155–72.

markets in the West Indies for corn and meat products, the growth of European markets for American foodstuffs had the greatest impact on the ordinary farmer who pursued a mixed husbandry.

The first and most conspicuous response to these economic changes came in the prerevolutionary South where large planters and small farmers alike began planting wheat instead of tobacco. While soil exhaustion offered an incentive to make the switch, rising prices for grains financed the conversion. In the frontier areas of the Piedmont and Shenandoah Valley, selling grain and livestock surpluses offered a speedy avenue of integration into the Atlantic trade world.[22] As historians have recently made clear, this changeover to grains in the Upper South involved more than agricultural techniques, for the marketing of wheat and corn had a decisive influence upon the area's urban growth. The switch to grains and livestock along the Eastern Shore, the lower James, the upper Potomac, and in the Piedmont promoted in two decades the cities, towns, and hamlets that had eluded the Chesapeake region during the previous century of tobacco production. Equally important to the character of these new urban networks was capturing what Jacob M. Price has termed "the entrepreneurial headquarters" of the grain trade. Unlike tobacco, the capital and marketing profits for the commerce in food remained in American hands.[23] For planters and farmers the switch to wheat could mean liberation from British factors and merchants who controlled both the sales and purchases of Tidewater tobacco planters. Such a possibility can be read in more personal terms in the writings of the young planter George Washington, who pledged himself to economic freedom by raising wheat.[24] Fanning out from Baltimore, Norfolk, and later Richmond, an array of market towns sprang up to handle the inspection, storage, processing, and shipping of the grains and livestock being pulled into the Atlantic trade from the rural areas of North Carolina, Virginia, Maryland, and Pennsylvania. During these same years Philadelphia and New York, both drawing on a grain-raising hinterland, surpassed Boston in population, wealth, and shipping.[25]

---

[22] Robert D. Mitchell, *Commercialism and Frontier: Perspectives on the Early Shenandoah Valley* (Charlottesville, 1977), 40, 173–78; Malcolm J. Rohrbough, *The Trans-Appalachian Frontier: People, Societies, and Institutions, 1775–1850* (New York, 1978), 99–106.

[23] Carville Earle and Ronald Hoffman, "Staple Crops and Urban Development in the Eighteenth-Century South," *Perspectives in American History*, X (1976), 5–78; Jacob J. Price, "Economic Function and the Growth of American Port Towns in the Eighteenth Century," *Ibid.*, VIII (1974), 121–86.

[24] James Thomas Flexner, *George Washington: The Forge of Experience, 1732–1775* (Boston, 1965), 279–84.

[25] Price, "Economic Function and the Growth of American Port Towns," 151–60.

The dislocations of the American Revolution were followed by a five-year depression, but in 1788 a new upward surge in grain and livestock prices ushered in a thirty-year period of prosperity. Even in England the shortfall between grain production and domestic demand led to net grain imports for twenty-seven out of these thirty years. Southern European demand remained strong. A printed solicitation for American business sent from a Barcelona firm in 1796 described American wheat and flour as much esteemed and constantly in demand "in this Place & Province, which," as the handbill explained, "in years of abundance never produces more than for four Months provisions."[26] In the longer run, sustained profits in grain-raising encouraged investments in agricultural improvements and prompted heroic efforts to increase output. By 1820, especially in England, Belgium, and the Netherlands, food roduction again had caught up with population growth, and prices returned to the levels of the mid-1790s.[27] Higher yields abroad, not the end of the Napoleonic wars, curbed demand for American farm products.

Coinciding as it did with the adoption of the United States Constitution, the new climb of food prices meant not only that the market could penetrate further into the countryside but also that the national government could extend its reach with improvements in communication and transportation systems. In the single decade of the 1790s, America's 75 post offices increased to 903 while the mileage of post routes went from 1,875 to 20,817. The number of newspapers more than doubled; circulation itself increased threefold. In the middle of the decade turnpike construction began.[28] With each decadal increase in grain prices the distance wheat and flour could be carted profitably to market increased dramatically. At 1772 price levels, farmers and grain merchants could afford to ship flour 121 miles and wheat 64 to reach the grain exporting seaports of Norfolk, Baltimore, Richmond, Philadelphia, and New York. Between 1800 and 1819 the range had extended to 201 miles for flour and 143 for wheat. For the farmer who wished to earn his own teamster's wage, the distance could be

---

[26] Arabet, Gautier & Manning handbill, Barcelona, May 18, 1796, file 1215, Miscellaneous Material Regarding Philadelphia Business Concerns, 1784–1824 (Eleutherian Mills Historical Library, Wilmington, Del.). British imports of American grain can be followed in Great Britain, *Parliamentary Papers* (Commons), "An Account of the Grain of All Sorts, Meal, and Flour, Stated in Quarters, Imported into Great Britain in Each Year from January 5, 1800 to January 5, 1825" (no. 227), 1825, XX, 233–67. For the earlier period, see Great Britain, *Parliamentary Papers* (Commons), "Accounts Relating to Corn, Etc." (no. 50), 1826–1827, XVI, 487–501.

[27] Slicher Van Bath, "Eighteenth-Century Agriculture," 175.

[28] Allan R. Pred, *Urban Growth and the Circulation of Information: The United States System of Cities, 1790–1840* (Cambridge, 1973), 58–59, 80, 153.

extended further.[29] The population doubled during the first twenty-three years of the new national government, but even more important to the burgeoning trade in American foodstuffs, the preponderance of American farmers lived within marketing range of the inland waterways that flowed into the sea-lanes of the great Atlantic commerce. As the volume of grain exports grew, country stores replaced rural fairs, and millers, bakers, butchers, brewers, and tanners turned from the custom trade of their neighbors to the commercial processing of the farmer's surpluses.

For the gentlemen planters of the Upper South, the switch to wheat represented a calculated response to new market opportunities, but for the mass of ordinary farmers the growing demand for foodstuffs abroad offered an inducement to increase surpluses without giving up the basic structure of the family farm. The man with seventy-five to one hundred acres who relied principally upon his own and his family's labor to grow Indian corn and wheat and to tend his livestock and draft animals could participate in the market with increasing profits without taking the risks associated with cash crops.[30] European population growth had enhanced the value of the little man's harvests, not that of the rich man's staples. It also blurred the old textbook distinction between the commercial agriculture of the South and the subsistence farming of the North. The wheat farmer's replication of European crops was no longer a commercial liability, for it was exactly the foods and fibers indigenous to Europe that were in demand. Published prices current of American produce in Liverpool, Amsterdam, Le Havre, Bordeaux, Barcelona, Saint-Dominque, and Havana convey the situation: wheat, flour, Indian corn, clover seed, flax seed, hemp, deerskins, beeswax, staves, and timber all commanded good prices, while West Indian markets took beef, pork, fish, cider, apples, potatoes, peas, bread, lard, onions, cheese, and butter as well. The mixed husbandry through which the farmer supplied his family also fed into the stream of

---

[29] Ibid., 114. Max G. Schumacher has calculated the "approximate maximum commercial range from Baltimore and Philadelphia of wheat and flour dependent on land-carriage" for price levels in 1755 and 1772. I extended Schumacher's ratios to the price range from 1800 to 1819. Max G. Schumacher, The Northern Farmer and his Markets during the Late Colonial Period (New York, 1975), 63.

[30] As this relates to Maryland, see Paul G. E. Clemens, The Atlantic Economy and Colonial Maryland's Eastern Shore: From Tobacco to Grain (Ithaca, 1980). See also Mitchell, Commercialism and Frontier, 234; David Maldwyn Ellis, Landlords and Farmers in the Hudson-Mohawk Region, 1790–1850 (New York, 1967), 76–82; Sarah Shaver Hughes, "Elizabeth City County, Virginia, 1782–1810: The Economic and Social Structure of a Tidewater County in the Early National Years," (Ph.D. diss., College of William and Mary, 1975), 406–07; and David C. Klingaman, Colonial Virginia's Coastwise and Grain Trade (New York, 1975). For some of the theoretical implications of the market involvement of self-sufficient family farms, see Mutch, "Yeoman and Merchant," 279–302.

commerce that linked rural stores and backcountry millers to the Atlantic commerce. To be sure, as Diane Lindstrom has pointed out, the farmer's family remained his best customer, but this held true well into the nineteenth century.[31]

The diversity of demand for American farm commodities in the generation after 1788 encouraged the adoption of the up-and-down husbandry that had revolutionized English and Dutch agriculture a century earlier. Here diversification, not specialization, held the key to raising crop yields and maintaining soil fertility in an age without chemical fertilizers.[32] Livestock and wheat raising required dividing land among meadows, pastures, and fields. When these were rotated, yields could be increased and fertility maintained. Livestock fed with soil-enriching grasses could also produce manure for fields of wheat and corn. While foreign visitors judged American farmers improvident and wasteful, American writers insisted that European practices had been adapted to American needs. Fertility in the grain- and livestock-producing areas evidently held up.[33]

---

[31] Diane Lindstrom, "Southern Dependence upon Western Grain Supplies," (M.A. thesis, University of Delaware, 1969), 10. Printed prices current and merchant handbills can be sampled in manuscript files 1303, 667, 1097, 1144, 1215, and 1457 (Eleutherian Mills Historical Library). Comparisons were made between advertised export items and farm account books in the collections at the Delaware State Archives (Dover, Del.) the University of Delaware Library Special Collections (Newark, Del.); and the Historical Society of Delaware (Wilmington, Del.).

[32] Eric Kerridge, *The Agricultural Revolution* (London, 1967), 39–40, 107, 214–15, 299, 347–48.

[33] For a foreign view of American agriculture based on a tour in 1794–1795, see William Strickland, *Observations on the Agriculture of the United States of America* (London, 1801). A rebuttal is provided by William Tatham, *Communications Concerning the Agriculture and Commerce of America* (London, 1800). The controversy over William Strickland's report to the English Board of Agriculture is covered by G. Melvin Herndon, "Agriculture in America in the 1790s: An Englishman's View," *Agricultural History*, XLIX (July 1975), 505–16. Other contemporary writers who stressed both the differences and the profitability of American agriculture were Timothy Matlack, *An Oration Delivered March 16, 1780* (Philadelphia, 1780), 14–16; Francois Alexandre Frederick, duc de La Rochefoucauld-Liancourt, *Voyages dans les Etats Unis d'Amerique Fait en 1795, 1796, et 1797* (8 vols., Paris, [1799]), I, 101–17, II, 325, III, 50; John Spurrier, *The Practical Farmer* (Wilmington, Del., 1793); John A. Binns, *A Treatise on Practical Farming* (Frederick-town, Md., 1803); George Logan, *Fourteen Experiments on Agriculture* (Philadelphia, 1797); and J. B. Bordley, *Essays and Notes on Husbandry and Rural Affairs* (Philadelphia, 1801). Estimates on yields vary widely. William Guthrie estimated that yields in Delaware after fifty years of planting continued at levels of fifteen to twenty-five bushels per acre for wheat and barley and two hundred for Indian corn. William Guthrie, *A New System of Modern Geography* (2 vols., Philadelphia, 1795), II, 458. Sarah Shaver Hughes has confirmed Guthrie's conclusion that fertility held up. Hughes, "Elizabeth City County, Virginia," 90–91. An elaborate tabular computation of wages, prices, and yields done by La Rochefoucauld-Liancourt indicates yields ranging from eight to twenty-five bushels per acre for various areas in the Delaware, Maryland, and Pennsylvania wheat-raising belt. "Tabulation of Commerce in the United States, 1795–97," file 501, P. S. DuPont Office Collection (Eleutherian Mills Historical Library).

Economies of scale had practically no bearing on the enhancement of the harvests that produced the food surpluses of the eighteenth and early nineteenth centuries. Attention to detail was the key. As the agricultural writer John Dabney explained, the farmer who does not "cart out his summer dung, nor plough those lands in the fall, which he means to feed in the following spring" could not grow rich.[34] In no other husbandry was it more true that the best manure was the tread of the master's foot. Moreover, the capital investments that could improve output—folding animals, bringing uncultivated land under the plow, laying down new pastures—could be made by the ordinary farmer willing to exchange leisure for off-season labors.[35] Increasing surpluses required, above all, a better management of time and a close watch on the market. Here too the range of farm commodities in demand redounded to the benefit of the small farmer, for each nook and cranny had a potential use. Hemp, according to John Alexander Binns, could be raised on every conceivable hollow just as bee hives, whose wax commanded good prices in England, could be lodged near the ubiquitous stands of white clover.[36] The relative success of the farmers who harvested wheat in the Middle Atlantic states can be gauged by Stanley L. Engerman's findings that the wealth of the North surpassed that of the South for the first time in the period from 1774 to 1798.[37] Without any of the qualities that characterized commercial agriculture in the colonial period—slave labor, specialization, large holdings—northern farmers had been brought into the thriving trade in foodstuffs.

Although high food prices greatly increased the ambit of the market, soil and climate more rigidly delimited the domain of up-and-down husbandry. The optimal mix of livestock and grain raising depended on crops of timothy, alfalfa, and clover, which were not easily grown in the lower South where heavy rains leached the land, leaving severe lime deficiencies. Hot, humid summers exposed cattle to ticks and mosquitos which kept herds small. Agricultural improvements in these areas had

---

[34] [John Dabney], *An Address to Farmers* (Newburyport, 1796), 5. John Dabney continued: "A complete Farmer is also a man of great carefulness and solicitude; without care, the severest labor on the best of Farms, will never produce riches nor plenty."

[35] For theoretical discussion of this point, see Stephen Hymer and Stephen Resnick, "A Model of an Agrarian Economy with Nonagricultural Activities," *American Economic Review*, LIX (Sept. 1969), 493–506.

[36] John A. Binns, *A Treatise of Practical Farming* (Richmond, 1804), 63. Dabney maintained that a farmer could clear £6 profit from an acre of flax. Dabney, *Address to Farmers*, 51. Substantial British imports of American beeswax are reported in Edmund C. Burnett, "Observations of London Merchants on American Trade, 1783," *American Historical Review*, XVIII (July 1913), 776.

[37] Stanley L. Engerman, "A Reconsideration of Southern Economic growth, 1770–1860," *Agricultural History*, XLIX (April 1975), 348–49.

to await later developments in fertilizers and soil amendments.[38] In New England the thin soils and rocky terrain also barred farmers from effectively competing with the rich farmlands of the South and West. Even before the revolution, Massachusetts had become an importer of wheat.[39] The New England situation did not encourage the embrace of an expansive, market-oriented, food-raising economy. In time the reexport trade breathed new life into the mercantile sector, but manufacturing, with its very different cultural imperatives, held out the long-range prospect for development.[40] Thus, despite the easy entry into the mixed husbandry of grain and livestock raising, climate and topography drew the boarders around the wheat belt that passed through Virginia, Maryland, Delaware, Pennsylvania, New Jersey, and New York. As long as food prices remained high, the conventional divisions of North and South, subsistence and commercial, yielded to a core of common interests among American farmers, food processors, and merchants in this favored region.[41]

The acknowledged novelty of the new American nation's political experiments has too often obscured the equally strong sense contemporaries had that they were entering a new economic era as well. Gouverneur Morris, for instance, called his fellow countrymen of 1782 "the first born children of extended Commerce in modern Times."[42] Americans were repeatedly characterized as eager market participants—certainly when it came to spending and borrowing—and commerce itself was associated with a remarkable augmentation of wealth-producing possibilities. "The spirit for Trade which pervades these States is not to be restrained," George Washington wrote to James Warren in 1784. Jefferson, eager to build canals linking the Chesapeake to the interior valleys of Virginia, wrote Washington that since all the world was becoming commercial, America too must get as much as possible of this modern source of wealth and power.[43] Timothy Mat-

---

[38] Julius Rubin, "The Limits of Agricultural Progress in the Nineteenth-Century South," *Agricultural History*, XLIX (April 1975), 362–73.

[39] Klingaman, *Colonial Virginia's Coastwise and Grain Trade*, 38.

[40] Charles L. Sanford, "The Intellectual Origins and New-Worldliness of American Industry," *Journal of Economic History*, XVIII (March 1958), 1–16.

[41] For discussion of the problem of discriminating between a subsistence and a commercial agriculture, see Clark, "Suggestions." 166.

[42] Governor Morris to Matthew Ridley, Aug 6, 1782, quoted in Clarence Ver Steeg, *Robert Morris: Revolutionary Financier* (Philadelphia, 1954), 166–67.

[43] George Washington to James Warren, Oct. 7, 1785, *The Writings of George Washington, from the Original Manuscript Sources, 1745–1799*, ed. John C. Fitzpatrick (39 vols., Washington, 1931–1944), XXVIII, 290–91; Thomas Jefferson to Washington, March 15, 1784, *The Papers of Thomas Jefferson*, ed. Julian P. Boyd et al. (19 vols., Princeton, 1950–1974), VII, 26.

lack predicted for an audience in Philadelphia the rise of America to a "Height of Riches, Strength and Glory, which the fondest Imagination cannot readily conceive" going on to specify that "the Star-bespangled Genius of America . . . points to Agriculture as the stable Foundation of this rising mighty Empire."[44] Without any major technological break-through, the late-eighteenth-century economy nonetheless suggested to men that they stood on the threshold of major advances.

By isolating in time and space the golden era of grain growing in the early national period, one can see more clearly the material base upon which Jefferson built his vision of America, a vision that was both democratic and capitalistic, agrarian and commercial. It is especially the commercial component of Jefferson's program that sinks periodically from scholarly view, a submersion that can be traced to the failure to connect Jefferson's interpretation of economic developments to his political goals. Agriculture did not figure in his plans as a venerable form of production giving shelter to a traditional way of life; rather, he was responsive to every possible change in cultivation, processing, and marketing that would enhance its profitability. It was exactly the promise of progressive agricultural development that fueled his hopes that ordinary men might escape the tyranny of their social superiors both as employers and magistrates. More than most democratic reform-ers, he recognized that hierarchy rested on economic relations and a deference to the past as well as formal privilege and social custom.

The Upper South's conversion from tobacco to wheat provided the central focus for Jefferson's discussion of commerce and manu-facturing in his *Notes on the State of Virginia*. Throughout the Tide-water, planters were shifting from the old staple, tobacco, to the production of cereals. Made profitable by the sharp price increases occasioned by European and American population growth, food-stuffs were much less labor-intensive than tobacco and were therefore suitable for family farms. Large and small Virginia planters became integrated into the new grain-marketing network that connected Amer-ican producers from the James or Hudson with buyers throughout the Atlantic world. As Jefferson wrote, wheat raising "diffuses plenty and happiness among the whole," and it did so, he noted, with only moderate toil, an observation that evokes the unstated, invidious comparison with slave labor.[45] Whether talking about consumption or production, he took for granted the importance of the market in influencing developments. For instance, he predicted that wheat would continue to replace tobacco because growers in Georgia and the Mississippi Territory would be able to undersell their Chesa-peake competitors. Similarly the weevil might threaten the profits

---

[44] Matlack, *Oration*, 25.
[45] Jefferson, *Notes on the State of Virginia*, 168.

of the Virginia wheat grower, for the expense of combating the infestation would "enable other countries to undersell him." Looking to the future Jefferson hailed the "immensity of land courting the industry of the husbandman," but he assumed that the husbandman would participate in international trade. Popular taste, that final arbiter for Jefferson, guaranteed that Americans would "return as soon as they can, to the raising [of] raw materials, and exchanging them for finer manufactures than they are able to execute themselves." The country's interest, therefore, would be to "throw open the doors of commerce, and to knock off all its shackles." At the same time it was entirely natural to Jefferson to mix shrewd assessment of market realities with homiletic commentary. Thus, he said, relying on European manufacturing would forestall the corruption of "the mass of cultivators," and he condemned tobacco raising as "a culture productive in infinite wretchedness."[46]

Working with a completely commercial mode of agriculture, Jefferson projected for America a dynamic food-producing and food-selling economy which promised the best of two worlds: economic independence for the bulk of the population and a rising standard of living. Even the word *farmer* captured some of the novelty of the new prospect. As William Tatham explained to his English readers, the cultivator "who follows the ancient track of his ancestors, is called a *planter*" while he "who sows wheat, and waters meadows, is a *farmer*."[47] The concrete policy measures that emanated from this prescription for American growth were both political and economic: making new land in the national domain accessible to the individual farmer-owner, using diplomatic initiatives to open markets around the world, committing public funds to internal improvements, and, negatively, opposing fiscal measures that bore heavily upon the ordinary, rural taxpayers.[48] William N. Parker has described just what these policies meant to mid-nineteenth-century agriculture: "an ambitious farmer might buy more farms, but he gained no economies by consolidating them" because "enterprise was too vigorous and too widely diffused, competition for finance, land, and labor too intense to permit large concentrations of wealth in land." The larger

---

[46] *Ibid.*, 164–68, 174. For a description of the Founding Fathers as having "commerce-phobia," citing Jefferson's expressions of enthusiasm for free trade as the result of his years in France, see James H. Hutson, "Intellectual Foundations of Early American Diplomacy," *Diplomatic History*, 1 (Winter 1977), 6, 8.

[47] Tatham, *Communications Concerning the Agriculture and Commerce of the United States*, 46.

[48] For excellent discussions of Thomas Jefferson's commercial policies, see Merrill Peterson, "Thomas Jefferson and Commercial Policy, 1783–1793," *William and Mary Quarterly*, XXII (Oct. 1965); Richard E. Ellis, "The Political Economy of Thomas Jefferson," in *Thomas Jefferson: The Man, His World, His Influence*, ed. Lally Waymouth (New York, 1973), 81–95.

farmer, moreover, "suffered the disadvantages of the liberal land policy and the prevailing sentiment in favor of the settler."[49]

Jefferson was not alone in joining political democracy to economic freedom; these themes coalesced in a number of local movements that in time found a national base in the opposition to Hamilton's program. Typical of this new view was Logan's declaration that the sacred rights of mankind included farmers deriving "all the advantages they can from every part of the produce of their farms," a goal that required "a perfectly free commerce" and "a free unrestricted sale for the produce of their own industry."[50] In a similar spirit John Spurrier dedicated *The Practical Farmer* to Jefferson because of his interest in agricultural science and his efforts "to promote the real strength and wealth of this commonwealth" on rational principles.[51] Writing at the same time Tench Coxe described the overwhelming importance of farming to America. Capital and labor investments in agriculture were eight times those in any other pursuit, Coxe estimated. More pertinently, he gave almost exclusive attention to the range of foodstuffs produced by family labor from Virginia to Connecticut.[52]

The nationalism implicit in these descriptions of America's economic future helps explain the breadth of the Republican movement, and the emphasis upon the commercial value of the grains, livestock, and beverages produced on family farms indicates how market changes affected early national politics. Jefferson's own nationalism was closely tied to the issues of international free trade and the disposition of the national domain. In this he was representative of the Virginia nationalists who dominated American politics after 1783 and led the campaign to establish "a more perfect union" four years later. With peace and the failure of William Morris's impost scheme, attention in the Continental Congress passed to matters of vital concern to Virginians—the taking-up of western land and the marketing of America's bounteous harvests. Both goals encouraged a national perspective. To expel the British from the northwest, to ease the Indians out of Ohio territory, to negotiate new commercial treaties abroad—these things required more than confederal cooperation. Just how long-range their view was can be gauged by the passions aroused by the idea of closing the port of New Orleans at a time when settlers had reached Kentucky. The implicit social values of this southern program, as H. James Henderson has pointed out, were secular rather than religious, anticipatory rather than regressive,

---

[49] William N. Parker, "Productivity Growth in American Grain Farming: An Analysis of its 19th Century Sources," in *Reinterpretations of American Economic History*, ed. Robert Fogel and Stanley L. Engerman (New York, 1971), 178.

[50] Logan, *Five Letters*, 25, 28.

[51] Spurrier, *Practical Farmer*, iii.

[52] Tench Coxe, *A View of the United States of America* (Philadelphia, 1794), 8–9, 87–99.

individualistic rather than corporate. The leaders of the Old Dominion "looked forward to continental grandeur rather than back to ancestral virtue."[53] East of the Hudson there was little support for an expansive American republic. The stagnating Massachusetts economy made the past a more reliable guide to the future than dreams of a new age of prosperity and progress. In the middle and southern states, however, the depressed 1780s reflected less the limits of growth than the failure to unlock America's rich resources.

From Georgia to New York a hinterland ran westward that gave the new American nation what no other people had ever possessed: the material base for a citizenry of independent, industrious property holders. And Virginia, the largest and wealthiest state, produced the leaders who turned this prospect into a political program. Most national leaders recognized the economic potential in America; the question that emerged was how and in deference to which values would this potential be realized. The issues that clustered around the opening of the national domain reveal very well how choices would affect the character of American society. Manufacturing, proponents argued, would provide jobs for sons and daughters at home; uncontrolled movement into the west would scatter families.[54] Recognizing the class difference in migration rates, an article addressed to the working people of Maryland urged support for the Constitution on the grounds that the common people were more properly citizens of America than of any particular state, for many of them died far away from where they were born.[55] The congressional debates on the Land Act of 1796 swirled around the question whether these sons and daughters who moved west would become independent farmers or the tenants of land speculators. The geographic base of the Jeffersonian Republicans can be traced in the votes for 160-acre sales.[56] Because grains were raised throughout the United States and required ancillary industries for their processing and sale, the Republican program was neither regional nor, strictly speaking, agrarian. It should be emphasized that it involved neither American isolation nor a slowed pace of growth. It was in fact a form of capitalism that Jefferson seized as the ax to fell Old World institutions because free trade offered the integrative network that social authority

---

[53] H. James Henderson, "The Structure of Politics in the Continental Congress," in *Essays on the American Revolution*, ed. Stephen G. Kurtz and James H. Hutson (Chapel Hill, 1973), 188.

[54] "On American Manufactures," *American Museum or Repository of Ancient and Modern Pieces, Prose and Poetical* I (Jan. 1787), 18.

[55] *Pennsylvania Gazette*, April 2, 1788, p. 3.

[56] Rudolph M. Bell, *Party and Faction in American Politics: The House of Representatives, 1789–1801* (Westport, Conn., 1973), 85–89; Murray R. Benedict, *Farm Policies of the United States, 1790–1950: A Study of Their Origins and Development* (New York, 1953), 12–15.

supplied elsewhere. Hamilton's response to the Louisiana Purchase makes this point negatively: the extension of America's agricultural frontier, he maintained, threatened to remove citizens from the coercive power of the state.[57]

The Revolution had made possible Jefferson's vision of a great, progressive republic, but developments during the first years of independence brought to light two different threats to its fulfillment. The one was old and predictable: the tendency of the rich and mighty to control the avenues to profit and preferment. The other came from the very strength of common voters in revolutionary America. The war effort itself had democratized politics, and without royal government, the broad prerevolutionary suffrage was translated into comprehensive popular power.[58] Emboldened by the natural rights rhetoric of the resistance movement, political newcomers began to challenge the old merchant oligarchies in the cities, while their counterparts in state legislatures pushed through radical measure affecting taxation, inheritance, insolvency, debt retirement, and land sales.[59] The ensuing conflicts, which Progressive historians made familiar as part of the struggle between rich and poor, aroused fears that cannot be categorized so easily. The new aggregate power of the people channeled through popularly elected legislatures alarmed men as philosophically different as Jefferson and Hamilton, as unalike temperamentally as Benjamin Rush and Robert Livingston. When ordinary Americans used their new voting power to push for legislation favorable to themselves, they made committed democrats as well as conservatives apprehensive. The anxieties expressed during the late 1780s cannot be ascribed solely to an elitist distrust of the poor, the ill-born, and the untalented many. Men destined to become the champions of political equality found the augmentation of power in the first state governments a genuine threat. A historiographical tradition that reads all fears of popular, unrestricted governmental power as evidence of upper class sympathies is in danger of missing the most compelling political goal to emerge in late eighteenth-century America—the limitation of formal

---

[57] Gerald Stourzh, *Alexander Hamilton and the Idea of Republican Government* (Stanford, 1970), 192–93.

[58] Jackson Turner Main, "Government by the People: The American Revolution and the Democratization of the Legislatures," *William and Mary Quarterly*, XXIII (July 1966), 391–407; John Shy, "The American Revolution: The Military Conflict Considered as a Revolutionary War," in *Essays on the American Revolution* ed. Kurtz and Hutson, 21–56; Edward Countryman, "Consolidating Power in Revolutionary America: The Case of New York, 1775–1783," *Journal of Interdisciplinary History*, VI (Spring 1976), 645–77.

[59] Jon C. Teaford, *The Municipal Revolution in America: Origins of Modern Urban Government, 1650–1825* (Chicago, 1975); Jackson Turner Main, *Political Parties before the Constitution* (Chapel Hill, 1973).

authority in deference to individual freedom. Disaggregating society, the Jeffersonians redirected the sovereign people away from exercising power as a body and toward enjoying free choice as private persons. Leaders of both the Federalist and Republican parties had cooperated in 1787 because a national political framework and a unified economy were essential to their differing conceptions of America's future. The new government created by the Constitution, however, proved to be a double-edged sword for the democratic nationalists. Strong enough to provide the conditions for freedom and growth, it could also be used to concentrate power and thereby raise a new national elite.

In resisting Hamilton's policies the Republicans eschewed the very divisions that historians have dwelt upon in explaining party formation. Far from pitting merchants against farmers, rich against poor, or the commercially inclined against the self-sufficient, the Jeffersonians assumed that a freely developing economy would benefit all. The eradication of privilege and the limitation of formal power would stimulate the natural harmony of interests. Thomas Paine with his usual directness gave expression to this liberal view in the fight over Robert Morris's bank. In a republican form of government, he wrote, "public good is not a term opposed to the good of individuals; on the contrary, it is the good of every individual collected. . . . the farmer understands farming, and the merchant understands commerce; and as riches are equally the object of both, there is no occasion that either should fear that the other will seek to be poor."[60] Making a slightly different point, the Jeffersonian congressional leader, Albert Gallatin, opposed the Federalists' 1800 bankruptcy bill because its provisions could not be restricted to merchants. In America, he argued, "the different professions and trades are blended together in the same persons; the same man being frequently a farmer and a merchant, and perhaps a manufacturer."[61] What was distinctive about the Jeffersonian economic policy was not an anticommercial bias, but a commitment to growth through the unimpeded exertions of individuals whose access to economic opportunity was both protected and facilitated by government. Treated for so long as a set of self-evident truths, the flowering of liberal thought in America owed much to specific developments. The advantageous terms of trade for American farm commodities, the expulsion of Europeans and Native Americans from the trans-Appalachian west, the people's commercial tendencies that Jefferson described—all these made men and women receptive to a new conception of human nature that affirmed

---

[60] [Thomas Paine], *Dissertations on Government: The Affairs of the Bank; and Paper Money,* in *The Complete Writings of Thomas Paine,* ed. Philip S. Foner (2 vols., New York, 1945), II, 372, 399–400.

[61] *Annals of the Congress,* 5 Cong., 3 sess., Jan. 14, 1799, 2650–51.

the reciprocal influences of freedom and prosperity. What had given a sacred underpinning to Locke's contract theory was his assumption that men living under God's law were enjoined to protect the life, liberty, and property of others as well as their own. Jefferson perceived that Locke's identity of interests among the propertied could be universalized in America and thereby acquire a moral base in natural design. It was indeed a *novus ordo seclorum*.

Jeffersonian Ideology Revisited: Liberal and Classical Ideas in the New American Republic

Lance Banning

Prompted by the growing criticism of the reinterpretation of Republican ideas, this essay offered a direct rebuttal of the critics while attempting to incorporate their insights into a review of current arguments and thinking. It is not, of course, a final word, but may provide a starting point for reading later contributions. Reprinted from the William and Mary Quarterly, *third series, XLIII (January, 1986), 3–19.*

Recent studies of the Jeffersonian Republicans may leave some readers at a loss. The last fifteen years have brought a new interpretation of the character and sources of Jeffersonian ideas.[1] This "republican hypothesis" (to modify a term of Robert E. Shalhope's) is a consequence

---

[1] The new interpretation emerged as a collective product, although there are significant differences in individual views. Lance Gilbert Banning's "The Quarrel with Federalism: A Study in the Origins and Character of Republican Thought" (Ph.D. diss., Washington University, 1971) was directed by John M. Murrin, who suggested that a major portion of the argument might be summarized in the form of "Republican Ideology and the Triumph of the Constitution, 1789 to 1793," *William and Mary Quarterly*, 3d Ser., XXXI (1974), 167–188. J.G.A. Pocock, who served as second reader of the dissertation, drew upon its findings for portions of *The Machiavellian Moment: Florentine Political Thought and the Atlantic Republican Tradition* (Princeton, N.J., 1975) and for other works cited below. The dissertation also influenced Drew R. McCoy, "Republicanism and American Foreign Policy: James Madison and the Political Economy of Commercial Discrimination, 1789 to 1794," *WMQ*, 3d Ser., XXXI (1974), 633–646, and "The Republican Revolution: Political Economy in Jeffersonian America, 1776 to 1817" (Ph.D. diss., University of Virginia, 1976). All these works, in turn, profoundly influenced Banning, *The Jeffersonian Persuasion: Evolution of a Party Ideology* (Ithaca, N.Y., 1978). A similar interpretation of Jeffersonian thought was independently advanced in Forrest McDonald, *The Presidency of Thomas Jefferson* (Lawrence, Kan., 1976). Murrin, "The Great Inversion, or Court versus Country: A Comparison of the Revolution Settlements in England (1688–1721) and America (1776–1816)," in J.G.A. Pocock, ed., *Three British Revolutions: 1641, 1688, 1776* (Princeton, N.J., 1980), 368–453, is an important recent addition.

of previous reinterpretations of American Revolutionary thought.[2] Like them, it places major emphasis on the persistent influence in the new American republic of concepts, hopes, and fears that may be traced to England's seventeenth-century classical republicans and their eighteenth-century opposition heirs. As Shalhope tells us, though, the same fifteen years have also seen the rapid growth of a variegated criticism of revisionary views of Revolutionary thinking.[3] The reinterpretation of the Jeffersonians has been erected on unstable ground, and in several recent works Joyce Appleby has charged that it is simply wrong, urging a renewed attention to what might be called a "liberal hypothesis."[4] The specialists seem so at odds that general readers must be sorely puzzled and historians are faced with an imposing barrier to further study.

This article seeks to get beyond that barrier, which may not be as insurmountable as first appears. Appleby and those she criticizes are all concerned to come to closer grips with Jeffersonian opinion, an enterprise that has large stakes not only for our comprehension of the new republic but for efforts to reshape our understanding of America in the fifty years and more after the first party quarrel came to an end. There are major differences among these scholars, which can be clarified where they cannot be reconciled. When that is done, it should be evident that Appleby and her opponents have all grasped portions of important truths, that all have been incautious, and that insights from both camps must be combined for further progress. As things now stand, the literature appears to force a choice between mutually exclusive interpretations of Jeffersonian ideology—a choice we do not really have to make, and one that would impede a better understanding.

Current scholarship, writes Appleby—from Richard Hofstadter to J.G.A. Pocock, Lance Banning, John M. Murrin, and Drew R. McCoy— "points Jefferson and his party in the wrong direction," toward nos-

---

[2] Especially Bernard Bailyn, *The Ideological Origins of the American Revolution* (Cambridge, Mass., 1967), and Gordon S. Wood, *The Creation of the American Republic, 1776–1787* (Chapel Hill, N.C., 1969).

[3] Robert E. Shalhope, "Republicanism and Early American Historiography," *WMQ*, 3d Ser., XXXIX (1982), 334–356. Also useful is Daniel Walker Howe, "European Sources of Political Ideas in Jeffersonian America," *Reviews in American History*, X (December 1982), 28–44.

[4] Joyce Appleby, "Commercial Farming and the 'Agrarian Myth' in the Early Republic," *Journal of American History*, LXVIII (1982), 833–849; "What Is Still American in the Political Philosophy of Thomas Jefferson?" *WMQ*, 3d Ser., XXXIX (1982), 287–309; and *Capitalism and a New Social Order: The Republican Vision of the 1790s* (New York, 1984). See also Isaac Kramnick, "Republican Revisionism Revisited," *American Historical Review*, LXXXVII (1982), 629–664, and John Patrick Diggins, *The Lost Soul of American Politics: Virtue, Self-Interest, and the Foundations of Liberalism* (New York, 1985). Kramnick and Diggins both specifically endorse Appleby's interpretation, but neither discusses America between 1789 and 1815.

talgia for the past instead of enthusiasm for the future, toward admiration for "agrarian self-sufficiency" rather than acceptance of commercial development. This scholarship makes Jefferson "the heroic loser in a battle against modernity," whereas he was actually the "conspicuous winner in a contest over how the government should serve its citizens."[5]

Between 1755 and 1820, Appleby points out, European demand for the grain and other commodities produced by American farmers expanded dramatically, while West Indian demand continued strong. The resulting opportunity for ordinary people to prosper by producing for the Atlantic market was not viewed apprehensively by Jefferson and other Virginia nationalists. On the contrary, these changing circumstances became the material base for a new social vision that owed little to the past, that was "both democratic and capitalistic, agrarian and commercial."[6] The prospect of an expanding, improving, commercial mode of agriculture persuaded Jefferson and others that the bulk of the American people could enjoy a rising standard of living, unprecedented social and economic independence, and—with these—political freedom. From 1783, therefore, Virginia nationalists and Jeffersonian Republicans advocated policies of making new lands available to farmers, opening world markets, and developing internal improvements, while they opposed fiscal measures that would burden farmer-owners. Such policies were "neither regional nor, strictly speaking, agrarian."[7] They entailed "neither American isolation nor a slowed pace of growth." They represented, in fact, "a form of capitalism" that looked to free trade to create "the integrative network that social authority supplied elsewhere."[8] The Jeffersonians, in sum, did not pit "rich against poor, or the commercially inclined against the self-sufficient," but sought a freely developing economy that would benefit all, eradicate privilege, and "stimulate the natural harmony of interest" among the propertied that John Locke had assumed.[9] In Jeffersonian hands, expanding involvement in the Atlantic economy become the context for "the flowering of liberal thought in America."[10] It was hardly an occasion for revival of agrarian nostalgia and British opposition fears.

Proponents of the views attacked in "Commercial Farming and the 'Agrarian Myth' in the Early Republic" must first protest that they have not been carefully represented in the essay. Close examination of the

---

[5] Appleby, "Commercial Farming and 'Agrarian Myth,'" *JAH*, LXVIII (1982), 836–837.
[6] *Ibid.*, 844.
[7] *Ibid.*, 847.
[8] *Ibid.*, 848.
[9] *Ibid.*, 849.
[10] *Ibid.*

article reveals that Appleby's target is fuzzier than first appears and that she seems to make a sharper challenge to recent work than is in fact the case. The essay opens with a summary of Hofstadter's portrayal of the Jeffersonians as celebrators of the self-sufficient yeoman, although none of the recent writers has been significantly influenced by Hofstadter's point of view. Appleby repeatedly objects to an interpretation that regards the Jeffersonians as spokesmen for the self-sufficient against the commercially inclined. Yet Pocock says that Jeffersonians derived from England's seventeenth-century republicans *both* a belief that men engaged in commerce are capable of republican citizenship *and* an archetype of the landed man as the ideal, autonomous citizen; they did not oppose commerce or technological improvements but "the alliance of government, finance and standing army."[11] Banning's *Jeffersonian Persuasion* specifically denies that either English oppositionists or Jeffersonian Republicans identified their enemies as those involved in manufacturing or commerce; both groups commonly contrasted the virtuous freeholder, not with merchants or manufacturers, but with government officers, public creditors, and stockjobbers.[12] And the central theme of McCoy's *Elusive Republic* is the Jeffersonian attempt to reconcile received republican values with *rejection* of an isolated, Spartan mode of life.[13] Maintaining that the Jeffersonians conceived commercial growth as vital to the perpetuation of a virtuous citizenry, the latter book, indeed, has been our most important source for fuller understanding of the Republican commitment to free trade and to the acquisition of new lands on which American farmers would produce for the Atlantic market. Recent scholarship, in short, does not advance quite the interpretation that Appleby condemns. It may, in fact, claim some of the responsibility for arguments that she develops.

Similar objections can be raised, this time with louder voice, to the second article in which Professor Appleby elaborates her criticism of interpretations emphasizing British opposition sources of Republican ideas.[14] Jefferson's dislike of Montesquieu, she argues, hints further

---

[11] J.G.A. Pocock, ed., *The Political Works of James Harrington* (Cambridge, 1977), 151.

[12] Banning, *Jeffersonian Persuasion*, 68, 204–205, 269. See also Murrin, "Great Inversion," in Pocock, ed., *Three British Revolutions*, 417–418.

[13] American Revolutionaries did not distrust "independent artisans and mechanics" but "poverty-stricken, landless laborers, and especially those [large-scale manufactories] dependent on government subsidy and promotion." "The Revolutionaries did not seek to reject a proper degree of civilization in the name of republicanism; they wished only to stop at the point where refinement became corruption" (Drew R. McCoy, *The Elusive Republic: Political Economy in Jeffersonian America* [Chapel Hill, N.C., 1980], 65, 73). Some recent works come closer than Banning or McCoy to advancing the view Appleby condemns, as will be discussed below. I single out these books because they are the fullest presentations of recent views and are similarly selected in Appleby's second article.

[14] Appleby, "What Is Still American?" *WMQ*, 3d Ser., XXXIX (1982), 287–309.

difficulties with recent views. Jefferson strongly favored commercial developments and economic innovations about which the civic-humanist tradition was suspicious; he also held a concept of human nature radically at odds with Montesquieu's. Montesquieu was essentially an advocate of aristocratic power who believed that republics must rest on commitment to the public good and must thus be small and founded on a frugal, homogeneous citizenry. Jefferson, by contrast, accepted James Madison's alternative to the small republic. His object was not to raise power to check power in a civic arena where men would attain fulfillment by rising above self-interest, but to secure a polity that would protect the private and personal realm where men would freely exercise their faculties. He praised Destutt de Tracy's critique of Montesquieu because Tracy's analysis began with individuals, not social orders, and because it sought to eradicate social injustice by eliminating privilege and protecting a natural equality of rights.

Appleby's Jefferson, in brief, espoused a "liberal economic order" incompatible with Country ideology. He was "temperamentally at odds with the reverence for the past nurtured by civic humanism" and "repeatedly insisted that his was the party of change."[15] Claims that Jefferson was under the influence of eighteenth-century opposition thought must thus result from a misreading. Banning and McCoy, Appleby charges, have *assumed* an influence of Country ideas on the Republicans without presenting "confirming evidence" for such an influence, presuming that a search for such was "unnecessary" in light of the work of Bernard Bailyn, Gordon S. Wood, and others.[16] After 1789, Appleby concludes, the Country-minded and the Court-minded, sharing a traditional vocabulary, both become Federalists. The Jeffersonians broke more completely with the past. Placing their faith in a limited rather than a balanced government, they sought to nurture capitalist development by freeing the private energies of equal men.

A reading of *The Jeffersonian Persuasion* or *The Elusive Republic* would suffice, I trust, to refute the surprising charge that neither offers solid evidence for opposition influences on Republican ideas. It is more important to remark that Appleby's criticism of these books would be more telling if either of them really argued what she says they do. Appleby objects to works that "have depicted the thought of Americans in the 1790s as *encapsulated in* the conceptual world of Montesquieu's civic humanism"; she condemns "the recent scholarly effort to *assimilate* Jefferson into the Country party tradition of eighteenth-century England."[17] No such effort was intended by most of the authors men-

---

[15] *Ibid.*, 308, 306.
[16] *Ibid.*, 302–303.
[17] *ibid.*, 302, 288. My emphases.

tioned in her critiques, nor does it seem to me that recent scholarship
is fairly taxed with leaving the impression that there were no significant differences between the Jeffersonians and their seventeenth- and
eighteenth-century sources.

The implications of this point are too important to pass over.
Both Appleby and Isaac Kramnick, who has endorsed her point of
view, write as though the recent claims that Jeffersonians were strongly
influenced by English opposition thought are equivalent to claims for
the *identity* of Jeffersonian and opposition thinking, perhaps particularly
for an identification of the thought of the Republicans with that of Bolingbroke or Montesquieu, who both defended a traditional hierarchical
social order. Nearly everyone who has advanced these claims would
certainly deny that this has been the point. Indeed, some might com-
plain that critics have occasionally come close to standing arguments
upon their heads.[18]

For example, Appleby maintains that "historians of the early
national period have recently claimed that the classical" republicanism
that can be found in the works of John Adams "dominated American politics well into the nineteenth century."[19] None of these historians has actually advanced this notion. As early as 1977 Pocock wrote,
"It is notorious that classical republicanism was . . . transformed in the
making of the Federal Constitution and the Federalist and Republican
minds."[20] *The Jeffersonian Persuasion* explicitly accepts Wood's argument
for an "end of classical politics" and the repudiation of Adams, while
qualifying this by suggesting that rejection of the concept of a balance
of social orders did not entail an end of other traditional concerns.[21]
The Elusive Republic, accepting major arguments of Wood and Banning
while transcending their concern with political and constitutional ideas,

---

[18] An exception might be made for McDonald, *Presidency of Jefferson*, esp. 19–22: Jeffersonian ideology "was borrowed *in toto* from such Oppositionists as Charles Davenant,
John Trenchard, Thomas Gordon, James Burgh, and most especially . . . Bolingbroke. As
a well-rounded system, it is all to be found in the pages of the *Craftsman* . . . The essence
of [the Jeffersonian program was to] restore America to the pristine simplicity of an
Arcadian past." McDonald obviously wrote this book with tongue sometimes in cheek,
aiming for general readers and often seeking language designed to shock and rouse his
fellow professionals. But McDonald's other recent work presents Alexander Hamilton as
a modernizing, liberal hero and suggests that he would characterize the first American
parties in terms almost opposite to those of Appleby. This view is shared by none of the
other recent writers.

[19] Appleby, "What Is Still American?" *WMQ*, 3d Ser., XXXIX (1982), 293.

[20] Pocock, ed., *Works of Harrington*, 147.

[21] Banning, *Jeffersonian Persuasion*, 84–103. "Adams was an eighteenth-century classical
republican . . . His friends were living in a different mental world . . . Adams' failing was
his inability to comprehend the changes in the theory of a balanced constitution that the
concept of a democratic social order introduced" (*ibid.*, 97–98).

emphasizes the *ambivalence* of Republican attitudes toward manufacturing and commerce, rising from their struggle to combine a commitment to prosperity, active industry, and economic growth with a traditional distrust of the potential civic consequences of these things. Recent scholarship, in short, often actually *insists* on American departures from received ideas, most especially on American hostility to privilege and American rejection of "the distinctions of class and rank whose balancing played so central a role in classical republicanism."[22] This scholarship should not be condemned as though the authors claimed that an entire, unchanging, civic-humanist tradition persisted into the new republic. Such criticism charges it with errors never made and caricatures a thesis that requires a subtler reading.

The *Jeffersonian Persuasion*, *The Elusive Republic*, Murrin's "Great Inversion," and other titles mentioned in Appleby's critiques are all revisionary studies. All maintain that previous interpretations of America's first party quarrel were imperfect in the absence of the fuller understanding of eighteenth-century British thinking pioneered by Caroline Robbins, Pocock, Kramnick, Bailyn, and others. All argue that comprehension of the new republic's politics was incomplete without a recognition of the parallels between American disputes and the familiar exchanges between the English Court and Country, together with a fuller appreciation of the continuing American concern with concepts, hopes, and worries that may be traced to classical antiquity by way of James Harrington and Niccolo Machiavelli.

All these works display some of the characteristic weaknesses of a revisionary effort. Their authors sought to add a new dimension to existing knowledge. They attempted to revise and alter, without entirely overturning, the body of previous scholarship. In the manner of revisionists, however—emphasizing new materials and stressing differences from older views—most of them were less explicit than they might have been about received opinions they did not dispute. Most were also guilty of incautious use of language, which is the more regrettable when passages are separated from their qualifying context. Flaws such as these are certainly responsible for some of our current confusion. But this confusion will be radically compounded if we fail to see that the Country ideology or opposition thinking identified in the majority of recent studies is simply not the Country ideology described by Appleby, or if we read these works as though they have denied the major changes in received ideas effected by the Revolution.

Appleby has fastened her attention on one of several groups that together composed the eighteenth-century opposition as most recent writers have described it—the backward-looking, fearful country gen-

---

[22] Appleby, "What Is Still American?" *WMQ*, 3d Ser, XXXIX (1982), 300.

tlemen and their great Tory spokesman, Viscount Bolingbroke. She identifies the opposition heritage exclusively with Bolingbroke's reactionary posture and condemns her scholarly opponents for associating the American Republicans with Bolingbroke's or Montesquieu's world view. Two misleading consequences follow. First, arguments that Jeffersonians were influenced by some of Bolingbroke's ideas by no means necessarily imply that the Republicans adopted other aspects of the viscount's Tory thought or that revisionists believe that ideology was unaffected by the Revolution.[23] Second, an exclusive emphasis on a single aspect of a complex heritage seriously distorts the major emphases of several recent works and loses sight of their most important contributions. Revisionists have drawn attention to the influence on the Jeffersonians of civic-humanist preoccupation with virtue and corruption, to eighteenth-century concern with standing armies, public debts, executive influence, and government by money. They have stressed the Country's condemnation, not of commerce, but of financialism, mercantilism, and all-absorbing luxury.[24] Somewhere, nearly all of this has disappeared from Appleby's summary of Country thought and of the republican hypothesis.

Appleby's critiques suggest that recent scholarship has traveled ever farther down a fundamentally false trail, placing ever-growing emphasis on the nostalgic, antimodern, Country bent of Jeffersonian thinking and failing to detect a crucial change. Quite the contrary is in fact the case. *The Jeffersonian Persuasion* advanced the thesis that the

---

[23] Chapter 2 of *The Jeffersonian Persuasion* discusses Bolingbroke as one of several outstanding figures in an opposition tradition to which radical Whigs contributed fully as much as reactionary Tories. It contains only passing references to Montesquieu. Similarly, when J.G.A. Pocock writes that the stance of the 18th-century opposition was that of a "radical right," it is clear he is referring to the demand for a return to an uncorrupted constitution ("Machiavelli, Harrington, and English Political Ideologies in the Eighteenth Century," *WMQ*, 3d Ser., XXII [1965], 572). Whig or Tory, all oppositionists regarded patronage, "government by money," and much else as undesirable innovations. But British acceptance of the opposition's demand for the excision of these innovations would scarcely have been conservative in practical effects, nor were all opposition writers on the right of the political spectrum when the spectrum is defined in broader terms.

[24] It needs to be emphatically reemphasized that even in the writings of Pocock, which stress the antithesis of virtue and commerce, it is not commerce defined as exchange that is identified as a focus of 18th-century worries. Revisionists have repeatedly insisted that commerce becomes a problem in 18th-century minds when it produces luxury, enervation, and single-minded attention to acquisition and enjoyment. Similarly, it might be noted that in *Capitalism and a New Social Order* Appleby identifies the Republicans with a capitalist vision partly by defining *capitalism* in terms of buying and selling (especially among farmers). Although I do not like the rather anachronistic use of this word, I would readily agree that Jeffersonians endorsed free exchange. Different conclusions emerge, however, if we associate capitalism primarily with entrepreneurial activities and investment.

emergence and character of an opposition to Federalism "was dependent to an important and unrecognized degree on an *Americanization* of eighteenth-century opposition thought."[25] It sought not just to demonstrate a lingering regard for old ideas but to explain how specific classical and opposition concepts were *altered* in such ways that they continued to exert a vital influence in a setting very different from the one in which they had originally appeared. Since 1978, historians have focused with increasing intensity on the question how the Jeffersonians accommodated and adjusted their heritage of British opposition and classical republican ideas to their perception that the world was characterized increasingly by complexity, commercialization, specialization, and professionalism.[26] Far from being false, this trail has been productive of increasing insight—the right one to pursue.

Yet this is not to say that Appleby is altogether wrong. Revisionists *have* stressed the central influence on the Jeffersonians of British opposition thought, which had been overlooked before. In doing so, they may have given so much space and stress to what was old, inherited, and hesitant about the future at the core of Jeffersonian belief that there was need for a revitalized insistence on what was progressive and new. To the degree that recent works have mistakenly or unintentionally overemphasized the conservative characteristics of Jeffersonian thought, Appleby's work should serve as a useful corrective. She helps us see more clearly the differences between the Jeffersonians and eighteenth-century British thinkers, among them differences that the revisionists themselves insisted on and differences that they neglected but would not deliberately deny. Her influence is already working to restore a better balance and to reinforce a growing emphasis on the varieties of Jeffersonian opinion.

Saying this, however, does not settle the dispute or even probe its depths. Thus far, I have suggested that the distance between Appleby and the revisionists will seem narrower if we recognize that most of the latter have neither argued nor deliberately implied that the Jeffersonians were wholly derivative or exclusively conservative in their thinking. Even so, the gap remains a large one. For Appleby does not intend a mere corrective. Rather, seconded by Kramnick, she rejects the major thesis of the recent work and calls for a renewed attention to the advent and influence of modern liberalism. Here—and not in classical repub-

---

[25] Banning, *Jeffersonian Persuasion*, 129, Emphasis added.

[26] In addition to McCoy see, for example, Robert E. Shalhope, *John Taylor of Caroline: Pastoral Republican* (Columbia, S.C., 1980), Lawrence Delbert Cress, *Citizens in Arms: The Army and the Militia in American Society to the War of 1812* (Chapel Hill, N.C., 1982), and Ralph Ketcham, *Presidents above Party: The First American Presidency, 1789–1829* (Chapel Hill, N.C., 1984).

licanism or eighteenth-century opposition thought—we are to find a
more appropriate beginning for studies of the origins and nature of
the Jeffersonian impulse. No revisionist would wish to follow her to
this extreme. Neither is it necessary that we choose between two such
sharply irreconcilable points of view.

Analytically, of course, modern liberalism and classical republicanism are distinguishable philosophies. *Liberalism* is a label most would
use for a political philosophy that regards man as possessed of inherent
individual rights and the state as existing to protect these rights, deriving its authority from consent.[27] *Classical republicanism* is a term that
scholars have employed to identify a mode of thinking about citizenship and the polity that may be traced from Aristotle through Machiavelli and Harrington to eighteenth-century Britain and her colonies.
The two philosophies begin with different assumptions about human
nature and develop a variety of different ideas. Their incompatibility
will seem much more pronounced if we expand our use of *liberalism* to
encompass capitalism or imply a bourgeois attitude and set of values.[28]

A full-blown, modern liberalism, as Appleby and Kramnick appear
to use the term, posits a society of equal individuals who are motivated
principally if not exclusively by their passions or self-interest; it identifies a proper government as one existing to protect these individuals'
inherent rights and private pursuits. A fully classical republicanism, as
Pocock may best explain, reasons from the diverse capacities and characteristics of different social groups, whose members are political by
nature. No republicanism will still be "classical" if it is not concerned
with the individual's participation with others in civic decisions where
the needs and powers of those others must be taken into account.[29]
Liberalism, thus defined, is comfortable with economic man, with the
individual who is intent on maximizing private satisfactions and who
needs to do no more in order to serve the general good. Classical republicanism regards this merely economic man as less than fully human.
Assuming a certain tension between public good and private desires,
it will identify the unrestrained pursuit of purely private interests as
incompatible with preservation of a commonwealth.

Liberal and classical ideas were both available to eighteenth-century
Englishmen and to America's Revolutionary generation. Distinguishing

---

[27] I have no objection to identifying liberalism, if defined *this* way, particularly with
John Locke. American historians have not ordinarily gone as far as Pocock toward dis-
counting Locke's influence.

[28] As in C. B. Macpherson, *The Political Theory of Possessive Individualism: Hobbes to Locke*
(Oxford, 1962).

[29] Most helpful are Pocock, ed., *Works of Harrington*, 145–151; *Machiavellian Moment*,
115–116, 394–395, 523–527; and "Virtue and Commerce in the Eighteenth Century,"
Journal of Interdisciplinary History, III (1972), 119–134.

between them is a useful scholarly pursuit. Identifying contradictions, tensions, or confusions in the thought of any individual or group who may have held ideas derived from two ultimately irreconcilable philosophies can certainly improve our understanding. But major difficulties will arise if we suppose that the analytical distinctions we detect were evident to those we study, or if we suggest that, in America, one of two separate and competing modes of thinking displaced the other in the years before 1815.

Logically, it may be inconsistent to be simultaneously liberal and classical. Historically, it was not. Eighteenth-century opposition thought was always a complex blend of liberal and classical ideas. So was the thought of America's Revolutionary generation. Jeffersonian Republicans inherited a way of thinking that accustomed men to move immediately from the concepts of a contractual origin of government and inherent individual rights to the assertion that a balanced form of government *and* sufficient virtue to preserve that form are necessary guarantees of liberty.[30] The major novelty and most important contribution of revisionary work has not been to deny that Revolutionary Americans and Jeffersonian Republicans were Lockean and liberal, but to demonstrate that liberal ideas were only part of their inheritance, to show that other parts of the inheritance assured that Jeffersonians could never be wholly comfortable with the increasing complexity and privatization of American life. Among the most important implications of this work is the suggestion that nineteenth-century America did not begin with and may never have achieved a liberal consensus.[31]

In developing this thesis, revisionists may well have overemphasized the similarities between the Jeffersonians and British oppositionists. They may have exaggerated the classical at the expense of the liberal dimensions of Jeffersonian thought, if only by assuming that the latter had received sufficient emphasis. They may thus have left an impression that the Jeffersonians were less progressive than they really were. This is the valid element in Appleby's protest. In recognizing this, however, let us take care not to tip the balance to an opposite extreme. While it is possible to throw a brilliant light on Jeffersonian ideology by emphasizing liberal and democratic ideas—consider Daniel J. Boorstin's classic book[32]—the benefits that have accrued from recent

---

[30] For 18th-century blending of the two philosophies see *Jeffersonian Persuasion*, 55–69. The similarities between the two are as clear as their ultimate incompatibility, and the same thinkers often contributed to both. Liberalism and classical republicanism both insisted on a definition of the individual in terms of his autonomy. Both linked liberty with property. There were many points of contact and even of confusion.

[31] Cf. Louis Hartz, *The Liberal Tradition in America: An Interpretation of American Political Thought since the Revolution* (New York, 1955).

[32] Boorstin, *The Lost World of Thomas Jefferson* (Boston, 1948).

efforts to explain American disputes by reference to the exchanges
between the English Court and Country are readily apparent when we
measure how far we have come form Boorstin's point of view. While
it is true that Jeffersonians were never strictly classical in their republicanism—no one has really argued that they were—neither were they
merely liberal. Thus, although I would agree with Appleby that Federalism had both Court and Country wings, I would resist the rather con-
tradictory suggestion that the party battles of the new republic can be
described as contests pitting Federalist attachment to tradition against
a liberal, Republican commitment to change. What do we do, on this
hypothesis, with the substantial evidence that the cosmopolitan, most
thoroughly commercial, and most aggressively capitalistic segments of
new-republican society were Federalist in their politics?[33] What would
we do with evidence, which remains persuasive to my mind, for the
Country character of many Jeffersonian ideas? What, finally, would
be the consequences of this thesis for our understanding of American
developments in the years after 1815?

A premature discovery of a wholly liberal perspective holds
risks beyond those most directly related to our understanding of the
Jeffersonians. One of the most important consequences of the modern
reinterpretation of Revolutionary republicanism has been the understanding that the Revolutionaries left to their successors a lasting and
profound commitment to values and ideas that were not part of a liberal
consensus, transmitting to their heirs a more complex political tradition whose rediscovery permits important reinterpretations of American
developments and conflicts from the war of 1812 to Watergate.[34] This
does not mean that the advent of a liberal perspective is without further
value as an explanation of developments. It may mean, though, that we
are well advised not to claim too much for its explanatory benefits. Like
the concept of modernization, to which it seems to bear a resemblance,
the rise of liberalism may explain too little if it is called upon to explain
too much, too soon.

In the end, I would suggest, it is no longer possible to accept any
analysis of the first American party struggle that describes the Republicans and Federalists in terms of left versus right, liberal or progressive
versus conservative or reactionary. If revisionary work has taught us
anything, it has surely taught us that both parties were a bit of each.

---

[32] Boorstin, *The Lost World of Thomas Jefferson* (Boston, 1948).

[33] Murrin cites the most important studies, principally by authors not especially concerned with the history of ideas.

[34] For a useful discussion of some benefits of the displacement of Hartz's thesis with
a republican hypothesis see Dorothy Ross, "The Liberal Tradition Revisited and the
Republican Tradition Addressed," in John Higham and Paul K. Conkin, eds., *New
Directions in American Intellectual History* (Baltimore, 1979), 116–131.

Prepared to understand the Jeffersonians as neither unambiguously left nor unequivocally right, I find instructive Appleby's insistence that the desire to free the individual from formal restraints and to use the government to promote access to opportunity were major and essentially progressive elements of the Jeffersonian position, elements inadequately discussed in recent work. At the same time, I resist depiction of Jeffersonian Republicanism as a "flowering of liberal thought" or "a form of capitalism." We cannot simply shut our eyes to the abundant evidence that the Republicans had many reservations about the eager, unrestrained pursuit of economic opportunity and even stronger reservations about the use of government to speed the processes of economic change. Republicans *were* conservative compared to their Hamiltonian opponents *in several important respects.* Appleby is right to stress that they conceived themselves as a progressive force, as the party seeking to defend and perfect a revolutionary new order. In America, however, this new order was commonly defined as one that had escaped or rejected major political, commercial, industrial, and financial changes that had overtaken contemporary England. These novelties the Jeffersonians were determined to resist.[35]

Building on the work of Marvin Meyers and Major Wilson, Daniel Walker Howe has recently described the early nineteenth-century Whigs as neither of the left nor of the right.[36] Whigs were partial modernizers. They were comfortable with, and advocates for, economic changes about which the Jacksonians were anxious, yet they envisioned a process of modernization that would be directed, disciplined, and controlled. They were hesitant about dimensions of modernity and progress that Jacksonians were more inclined to accept: laissez-faire, equality, party competition, executive initiatives, secularization, and the like. A comparable analysis of the Federalists and Jeffersonians has yet to be achieved. Its benefits, however, may be hinted by the disagreement between Appleby and other scholars. Its development must draw from both.[37]

---

[35] Even the suggestion that both parties were conservative in some respects and progressive in others risks implying value judgments or assuming a teleological perspective. Like Appleby, I think we should avoid this, but it does seem helpful to point out that the future was hardly on the side of the independent craftsmen and small farmers whose advocates the Jeffersonians were. It was on the side of the entrepreneurial capitalists associated with Alexander Hamilton's Bank of the United States and Society for Useful Manufactures, corporations that were novel in American conditions.

[36] Howe, *The Political Culture of the American Whigs* (Chicago, 1979).

[37] A more sophisticated interpretation of the first party struggle must also link our growing understanding of party thought with our regrettably scanty information about the social sources of party division. The two most ambitious recent starts toward this are James H. Hutson, "Country, Court, and Constitution: Antifederalism and the Historians," *WMG* XXXVIII (1981), 337–368, and Murrin, "Great Inversion," in Pocock, ed., *Three British*

This seems to me entirely possible, for—to put a former point another way—recent reconstructions of Revolutionary republicanism and of Jeffersonian opinion have always recognized and sometimes even emphasized the powerful impact in America of liberal ideas (provided that we do not use too broad a definition of this word). John Locke and Algernon Sidney contributed importantly *both* to the development of a contractual philosophy *and* to the English modification of the classical republican tradition.[38] English oppositionists included theoretical republicans and Protestant dissenters as well as country gentlemen and Tory politicians, whose role may have been unduly stressed of late by both the students of republicanism and their critics. Noting this, *The Jeffersonian Persuasion* argued that the eighteenth-century opposition was moving in a democratic direction (or returning to a Harringtonian condemnation of hereditary privilege) well before the American Revolution.[39] Bailyn and Wood both attributed a large part of the transformed and transforming character of Revolutionary thought to the influence of a democratic, individualistic, natural-rights philosophy. Subsequent interpreters have been consistently concerned with the continuing transformation, not simply the persistence, of eighteenth-century concepts, a transformation they have always understood as very much a consequence of individualistic and contractual dimensions of Revolutionary thinking. These interpreters need quarrel, not with further study of this transformation or with new attempts to analyze the liberal contribution, but only with arguments that seem to urge retreat to an older, more constricted interpretive perspective, one that might deny much of the newly rediscovered complexity of Revolutionary discourse and imply an easier American adjustment to modernity than the republican hypothesis suggests.

Revolutions, 368–453. Both are valuable and impressive. Neither seems free from difficulties. The Federalists of 1787 included groups and individuals, most notably James Madison, who cannot be associated with a Court tradition. To compare the Federalists to the English Court and Antifederalists to the Country, while revealing, still seems to force materials into the misleading terms of left versus right. We should be careful, too, to avoid a definition of "Court" that would make the term nearly synonymous with pro-government or pro-commercial. Other useful attempts to link the findings of historians of party thought with those of students of party behavior include H. James Henderson, *Party Politics in the Continental Congress* (New York, 1974), and Robert Kelley, "Ideology and Political Culture from Jefferson to Nixon," *AHR*, LXXXII (1977), 531–562.

[38] One of the earliest sourcebooks for current understanding of the sources of Revolutionary thinking emphasized the contribution of 18th-century opposition writers to the preservation and transmittal to America of both republican and liberal ideas. Caroline Robbins, *The Eighteenth-Century Commonwealthman: Studies in the Transmission, Development and Circumstance of English Liberal Thought from the Restoration of Charles II until the War with the Thirteen Colonies* (Cambridge, Mass., 1959).

[39] Banning, *Jeffersonian Persuasion*, 63–64, 81. John Brewer's *Party Ideology and Popular Politics at the Accession of George III* (Cambridge, 1976) deals more fully with this issue.

If liberalism connotes adherence to an individualistic and contractual theory of the origins and limits of government, then the Jeffersonians were certainly liberals—which, however, will not help explain how they differed from the Federalists. If liberalism suggests a conception of politics in which the general good will emerge if the state respects the rights of all and individuals attend to little or nothing more than improving their private lives and voting their self-interest, then Republicans (and Federalists) were something less or something more than liberals; most did not consider self-interest a sufficient basis for citizenship, and most did not, as Boorstin would have it, regard the state as existing solely to protect an individual pursuit of private satisfactions.[40] Finally, if liberalism implies unqualified acceptance of acquisitive behavior, "a wholehearted ideology of the market," redefinition of man as "*homo oeconomicus*" rather than "*homo civicus*,"[41] or unequivocal support of an emerging commercial, industrial, and capitalistic order, then it is simply not helpful to describe the Jeffersonians as liberals. Many of their opponents were more nearly comfortable with attitudes such as these.

Jeffersonian Republicans did not oppose business, commerce, manufacturing, or every variety of social change, much less technological or managerial improvements in agriculture and communications. Neither did most of the eighteenth-century oppositionists from whom many of their ideas derived. Both Republicans and oppositionists, however, were sharply aware of the ease with which a spirit of commerce becomes an avaricious desire for private gain and self-immersed enjoyment. Both were convinced that such a spirit, together with the inequality of fortunes that it can promote, is incompatible with preservation of a commonwealth. Both believed agriculturalists to be less subject to the transition from a spirit of virtuous industry to a spirit of avaricious enjoyment than other social groups. Both believed that dangers to virtue and to the moderate level of property-holding that supports it can be accelerated by mercantilism and financialism. While they were not opposed to commerce, they did fear commercialization, which they hoped could be contained and reconciled with traditional values. They distrusted urban crowding and were horrified by the political and social consequences of English industrialization. In these ways, and in so far as governmental intervention may actually have been required in order to encourage commercialization and industrialization, they stood against modernity.

In opposing mercantilism and financialism—"unnatural" economic policies and governmental rewards to "parasites"—Jeffersonians were

---

[40] Boorstin, *Lost World of Jefferson*, esp. 190–196.
[41] Kramnick, "Republican Revisionism Revisited," *AHR*, LXXXVII (1982), 661–662.

in accord with later liberals. But they did not share the "liberal" desire to unleash the acquisitive spirit, the liberal denial of any tension between private enterprise and public good. Republicans, like nineteenth-century liberals, disapproved of governmental guidance of the economy; but, unlike liberals, they did not aim essentially at using government to nurture the conditions for a general race to get ahead. The Jeffersonians were not Jacksonians. They were still uncomfortable with the thought that uninhibited pursuit of market opportunities would automatically result in public happiness and harmony. They were even more uncomfortable with the notion that the role of the state is to facilitate the growth of capital and credit, hurrying the community into the marketplace. They held that individual improvement ought to be restrained by a residual regard for others, that private satisfactions must sometimes give way to public duties. And they suspected that this commitment to community would be endangered if commerce and manufacturing, which they accepted as the proper, narrow top of the pyramid of economic enterprise, should become too heavy for the pyramid's broad and equal agricultural base.

The irreducible difference between a strictly liberal interpretation of Jeffersonian ideology and a republican hypothesis may lie in our understanding of the way in which the Jeffersonians related the public and private spheres of life. On this point, proponents of the republican thesis can summon valuable assistance from Hannah Arendt. Arendt understood that American Revolutionaries "knew that public freedom consisted in having a share in public business, and that the activities connected with this business by no means constituted a burden but gave those who discharged them in public a feeling of happiness they could acquire nowhere else."[42] She shared the Revolutionaries' own sense of the tension between this active—and ultimately still classical—kind of liberty, and privatization. She saw, of course, that Revolutionary republicans desired the liberty to pursue their private welfare and that they sometimes even spoke as though happiness lay exclusively in the private realm. But Arendt saw, as well, that these republicans continued to define "liberty" as much in terms of freedom *to* participate actively and virtuously in politics as in terms of freedom *from* restraint. To them, she wrote,

> Tyranny . . . was a form of government in which the ruler, even though he ruled according to the laws of the realm, had monopolized for himself the right of action, banished the citizens from the public realm into the privacy of their households, and demanded of them that they mind their

---

[42] Hannah Arendt, *On Revolution* (New York, 1963), 115.

own, private business. Tyranny, in other words, deprived of public happiness, though not necessarily of private well-being, while a republic granted to every citizen the right to become "a participator in the government of affairs," the right to be seen in action.[43]

Let us follow Arendt one more step, drawing also both from advocates of the republican hypothesis and from their critics, in order to apply these thoughts to the Jeffersonian Republicans. "The Declaration of Independence," Arendt said, "still intends us to hear the term 'pursuit of happiness' in its twofold meaning: private welfare as well as the right to public happiness, the pursuit of well-being as well as being a 'participator in public affairs.' " Even during the Revolutionary period itself, she suggested—and even within Thomas Jefferson himself, we might add—the classical-republican insistence on liberty in its participatory meaning "came into conflict with ruthless and fundamentally antipolitical desires to be rid of all public cares and duties; to establish a mechanism of government administration through which men could control their rulers and still enjoy" a mode of government that would release them to attend exclusively to their private concerns.[44] The Jeffersonian Republicans undoubtedly attracted many individuals whose concerns were essentially private. It seems certain, as well, that a fundamentally antipolitical spirit encroached increasingly on the participatory ideal in the years after 1789.[45] But the republican hypothesis has shown, I think, that the men who developed a Jeffersonian persuasion and who led the Republican Party into the War of 1812 were still sufficiently classical in their thought that they could not accept the antipolitical spirit as compatible with liberty. Indeed, these Jeffersonians quarreled with the Federalists, in no small part, because so many of the latter wished to banish ordinary people from the public realm.

American Revolutionaries and Jeffersonian Republicans attempted to combine (and probably confused) concepts of liberty deriving from a classical tradition—freedom *to*—with more modern or liberal concepts that associated liberty more exclusively with the private, pregovernmental realm—freedom *from*. Historians can usefully explore

---

[43] *Ibid.*, 127. Also helpful on these matters is Trevor Colbourn, ed., *Fame and the Founding Fathers: Essays by Douglass Adair* (Chapel Hill, N.C., 1974).

[44] Arendt, *On Revolution*, 129, 133.

[45] Jan Lewis, *The Pursuit of Happiness: Family and Values in Jefferson's Virginia* (Cambridge, 1983), is an interesting, although not entirely successful, consideration of this question. Lewis stresses privatization, especially in the period after 1812, yet it seems clear that the Virginia gentry did not massively withdraw from politics even in these years when nearly all historians would agree that the 18th-century heritage was fading. Lewis also emphasizes a continuing distrust of commerce, insisting that individual opportunity and self-reliance were not embraced but dreaded. See pp. 115–116, 161–165.

resulting tensions and confusions. They should consider whether different social groups and political factions mixed liberal and classical dimensions of their heritage in different ways.[46] They will certainly wish to study changes over time. But the question need not be which set of concepts most Jeffersonians ultimately preferred. The Jeffersonians, together with their rivals, may have drawn from a coherent—which is not to say consistent—universe of thought that could contain important elements of both philosophies in a persistent, fruitful tension.[47]

The Jeffersonians were very much concerned with freedom *from* and with replacement of a social and political order grounded on hereditary privilege by an order resting on individual equality and talent. They were not the eighteenth-century British opposition. And yet they never broke entirely free from an eighteenth-century concern with freedom *to*, from a continuing insistence on public duties as well as private rights, or from a humanistic fear of merely economic man. It is, in part, because they never did that "the revolutionary notions of *public* happiness and *political* freedom have never altogether vanished from the American scene." Because of this, their heirs continue to the present to distrust the "antics

---

[46] Eric Foner, whose *Tom Paine and Revolutionary America* (New York, 1976) was published as I neared completion of *The Jeffersonian Persuasion*, suggests the presence of a distinctive and perhaps more completely liberal variety of Republicanism. Tench Coxe may have represented yet another variety of urban, cosmopolitan Republicanism. See Jacob E. Cooke, *Tench Coxe and the Early Republic* (Chapel Hill, N.C., 1978). John R. Nelson, Jr. "Alexander Hamilton and American Manufacturing: A Reexamination," *JAH*, LXV (1979), 971–995, is helpful for understanding the popular, urban appeal of Jeffersonian ideology, as, of course, is Appleby. Since 1978, it has become increasingly apparent that Jeffersonian opinion ranged across a broad spectrum. Spokesmen included reactionaries or conservatives such as John Randolph and John Taylor, together with radicals such as Joseph Priestly or Thomas Cooper, English emigres who were far more accepting of modernity. (For the range of this spectrum on the issue of a proper military force for a republic, see Cress, *Citizens in Arms*, 155–166.) The presence of such variety, however, does not exclude the possibility of identifying a core of belief that held Jeffersonians together, and I remain willing to argue both that the Republicans were bound together by the concepts explored in *The Jeffersonian Persuasion* and *The Elusive Republic* and that the thought of the great party leaders should be placed somewhere toward the middle of the party's spectrum.

[47] Some of the fruits of this tension are analyzed in Ketcham's *Presidents above Party*, which appeared after this passage was written. Ketcham, who begins by asking why Jefferson should have mentioned Bolingbroke and Thomas Paine in the same sentence as "advocates of human liberty," also offers a very useful discussion of the complementary but distinguishable contributions of Tories and radical Whigs to the opposition response to the "modern Whig" (or Court) tradition of Walpole, Mandeville, and Daniel Defoe. See pp. 3 and 55–57 *passim*.

of a society intent upon affluence and consumption."[48] The Jeffersonian perspective—and even, perhaps, our own—was a product of a Revolutionary republican discourse whose parameters proved stubbornly resistant to complete transcendence.

---

[48] Arendt, *On Revolution*, 135. Published while the present article was in press, Richard K. Matthews, *The Radical Politics of Thomas Jefferson: A Revisionist View* (Lawrence, Kan., 1984), 84–91, also draws on Arendt for a criticism of the liberal interpretation. But Matthews is almost equally opposed to the republican hypothesis.

Thomas Paine's Apostles: Radical Emigrés and the Triumph of Jeffersonian Republicanism

Michael Durey

A very recent effort to untangle the dispute about the sources and develop-ment of party thought is offered in this essay. Michael Durey is a member of the History Programme at Murdoch University, Western Australia. The article appeared in The William and Mary Quarterly, *3rd series, XLIV (October, 1987), 661–668. It is reprinted by permission of the author.*

The key to understanding eighteenth-century American political dis-course since the publication of Caroline Robbins's *The Eighteenth-Century Commonwealthman* in 1959 and Bernard Bailyn's *The Ideological Orgins of the American Revolution* in 1967 has been the recognition that political ideas from England and Scotland underpinned republican ideology. In developing Robbins's and Bailyn's insights, both for the period of the American Revolution and for the Federalist years, his-torians have tended to gravitate toward one or the other of two gen-eral interpretations. "Classical" historians, represented most forcefully by J.G.A. Pocock and Lance Banning, seek the roots of American republicanism in the political writings of James Harrington, Alger-non Sidney, John Trenchard, Thomas Gordon, Viscount Bolingbroke, and Joseph Addison.[1] In contrast, "liberal" historians such as Joyce

---

[1] Robbins, *Eighteenth-Century Commonwealthman* (Cambridge, Mass, 1959); Bailyn, *Ideo-logical Origins of the American Revolution* (Cambridge, Mass., 1967); J.G.A. Pocock, *The Machiavellian Moment: Florentine Political Thought and the Atlantic Republican Tradition* (Princeton, N.J., 1975), and "Virtue and Commerce in the Eighteenth Century," *Journal of Interdisciplinary History,* III (1972), 119–134: Lance Banning, *The Jeffersonian Persuasion: Evolution of a Party Ideology* (Ithaca, N.Y., 1978); John Murrin, "The Great Inversion, or Court versus Country: A Comparison of the Revolution Settlements in England (1688–1721) and America (1776–1816)," in Pocock, ed., *Three British Revolutions: 1641, 1688, 1776* (Princeton, N.J., 1980), 368–453.

Appleby and Isaac Kramnick include John Locke, Thomas Mun, Adam Smith, Richard Price, and Joseph Priestly.[2] The controversy over American republican ideology concerns which of these two lines of thought was the more influential in late eighteenth-century American political discourse.

Whatever the relative merits of these two approaches for an understanding of American republicanism, one notable absentee from historians' deliberations on the 1790s is Thomas Paine. This omission is surpising, for recent historiography on the Revolutionary period has emphasized both Paine's role in securing popular acceptance of Independence and his wartime political propaganda.[3] But his long-term influence in the United States has been strangely neglected. Eric Foner's perceptive study of Paine in America, for instance, deals wiith his career after 1787 in an epilogue, as if his impact on the New World rapidly diminished after the crisis years of war became a memory.[4] Kramnick notes that Paine returned in 1802 to a very different America from the one in which *Common Sense* and the *Crisis* papers created mass support for the patriot cause: "*Common Sense* was a thing of the distant past. Paine was no longer the celebrated author of the pamphlet so influential in its day. He was now the notorious author of the godless *Age of Reason*"—and, it might be added, of the bitter *Letter to George Washington*.[5] Neither Banning nor Appleby, from their different vantage points, feels it necessary to dwell on Paine's contribution to American political thought after the acceptance of the Constitution.[6]

Paine's absence becomes even stronger when it is appreciated that much of the debate on republicanism in the 1790s revolved around political and economic issues such as egalitarianism, natural rights, and national economic development, on all of which Paine wrote copiously.

---

[2] Joyce Oldham Appleby, *Economic Thought and Ideology in Seventeenth-Century England* (Princeton, N.J., 1978); "Liberalism and the American Revolution," *New England Quarterly*, XLIX (1976), 3–26; "The Social Origins of American Revolutionary Ideology," *Journal of American History*, LXIV (1978), 935–958; and "What Is Still American in the Political Philosophy of Thomas Jefferson?" *William and Mary Quarterly*, 3d Ser., XXXIX (1982), 287–309; Isaac Kramnick, "Republican Revisionism Revisited," *American Historical Review*, LXXXVII (1982), 629–664, and "Religion and Radicalism: English Political Theory in the Age of Revolution," *Political Theory*, V (1977), 505–534; John Patrick Diggins, *The Lost Soul of American Politics: Virtue, Self-Interest, and the Foundations of Liberalism* (New York, 1985).

[3] David Freeman Hawke, *Paine* (New York, 1975); David Powell, *Tom Paine: The Greatest Exile* (London, 1985).

[4] Eric Foner, *Tom Paine and Revolutionary America* (New York, 1976), chap. 7.

[5] Thomas Paine, *Common Sense*, ed. Isaac Kramnick (London, 1976), 36.

[6] Joyce Appleby, *Capitalism and a New Social Order: The Republican Vision of the 1790s* (New York, 1984), and "Republicanism in Old and New Contexts," *WMQ*, 3d Ser., XLIII (1986), 20–34; Lance Banning, "Jeffersonian Ideology Revisited: Liberal and Classical Ideas in the New American Republic," *ibid.*, 3–19.

The essence of Paine's radicalism—its singular politico-economic combination of democratic egalitarianism and support for national economic development in a market-oriented society—appears anomalous when one considers the classical-liberal debate. Paine, writes Pocock, "remains difficult to fit into any kind of category"; even *Common Sense*, the most unproblematic of his works for American politics, fails "consistently [to] echo any established radical vocabulary."[7] In other words, Paine's radicalism does not fit neatly into the categories posited by historians, for when the patriots who guided the Constitution through Congress and the state ratifying conventions split in the 1790s, they did so in a way that sundered Paine's political from his economic ideology. They divided along lines leading to a federalism that rejected democratic politics but accepted economic progress or to a republicanism that accepted egalitarian politics yet held grave reservations concerning the nation's transformation into a commercial-manufacturing society. But the general debate over republicanism in the 1790s has as one major interest the question of how, and to what extent, Jeffersonian republicanism came to incorporate a more positive attitude toward commercial development.[8] Thus, although not recognizing Paine as a formative influence, this part of the debate is concerned with the process by which Jeffersonianism moved toward a political economy that, by combining egalitarianism with an acceptance of market economics, had many of the hallmarks of Paine's own ideology.

Moreover, some historians appear to suffer from telescopic longsightedness that enables them to see the impact of political ideas dating from as far back as Machiavelli but blinds them to much closer influences. One such influence on Jeffersonian republicanism was brought to bear by the political emigrants who arrived in numbers from Britain and Ireland in the 1790s. Although many studies focusing on individual émigrés have been published, only a few have essayed an assessment of their collective role in the formation and dissemination of the republican ideology in this period.[9] As a consequence, an important dimension of republicanism has been neglected.

---

[7] J.G.A. Pocock, "The Variety of Whiggism from Exclusion to Reform: A History of Ideology and Discourse," in *Virtue, Commerce and History* (Cambridge, 1985), 276.

[8] Appleby, "What Is Still American?" *WMQ*, 3d Ser., XXXIX (1982), 287–309; Drew R. McCoy, *The Elusive Republic: Political Economy in Jeffersonian America* (Chapel Hill, N.C., 1980).

[9] Arthur Sheps, "Ideological Immigrants in Revolutionary America" in Paul Fritz and David Williams, eds., *City and Society in the Eighteenth Century* (Toronto, 1973), 231–246; Dumas Malone, *The Public Life of Thomas Cooper, 1783–1839* (New Haven, Conn., 1926); Caroline Robbins, "Honest Heretic: Joseph Priestley in America, 1794–1804," American Philosophical Society, *Proceedings*, CVI (1962), 60–76; Kim Tousley Phillips, "William Duane, Revolutionary Editor" (Ph.D. diss., University of California, Berkely, 1968);

The most impressive general analysis of the emigrants can be found in Richard Twomey's thesis of 1974, from which, unfortunately, only a small fragment has yet been published.[10] Ironically, it is Appleby who has most clearly tied the radical emigrants into American politics in the 1790s, but in such a way that their possible influence went unremarked. She has shown, by relying on James Cheetham, Thomas Paine, and especially Thomas Cooper to explicate Jeffersonian ideology, how important were their ideological and propagandist roles. Yet Appleby remained unaware that she was considering a new and significant element in the Republican equation. Recognizing that "no fewer than twenty [British radicals] played an active role in Republican politics," she nevertheless included with the "Jacobins" who arrived in the 1790s men of British extraction such as Eleazer Oswald, Blair McClenachan, William Findley, and even the West Indian-born Alexander Dallas, all of whom had left the British Isles many years previously.[11] Indiscriminately blending all those prominent in Republican politics who had connections with the British Isles, she has failed to distinguish those whose political sensibilities had been shaped less by Commonwealth ideology and the politics of the 1760s and 1770s than by the growth of popular Painite radicalism in the early 1790s and by the French Revolution.

John Ashworth has recently stated that "a definitive explication of Republican ideology will have to take full account of the factional composition of the party."[12] A major purpose of this article is to demonstrate that one important component of the Republican party in the 1790s

---

Colin Bonwick, "Joseph Priestley: Emigrant and Jeffersonian," *Enlightenment and Dissent*, II (1983), 3–26; Edward C. Carter II, "The Political Activities of Mathew Carey, Nationalist, 1760–1814" (Ph.D. diss., Bryn Mawr College, 1962); G. S. Rowell, "Benjamin Vaughan—Patriot, Scholar, Diplomat," *Magazine of History*, XXII (1916), 43–57; Willis G. Briggs, "Joseph Gales, Editor of Raleigh's First Newspaper," *North Carolina Booklet*, VII (1907), 105–130; W. T. Latimer, "David Bailie Warden, Patriot 1798," *Ulster Journal of Archeology*, XXIII (1907), 29–38; D. H. Gilpatrick, "The English Background of John Miller," *Furman Bulletin*, XX (1938), 14–20; Sir James Fergusson, *Balloon Tytler* (London, 1972); Joseph I. Shulim, "John Daly Burk: Irish Revolutionist and American Patriot," Am. Phil. Soc., *Transactions*, LIV (1964), pt. 6, 5–60.

[10] Richard Jerome Twomey, "Jacobins and Jeffersonians: Anglo-American Radicalism in the United States, 1790–1820" (Ph.D. diss., Northern Illinois University, 1974), and "Jacobins and Jeffersonians: Anglo-American Radical Ideology, 1790–1810," in Margaret Jacob and James Jacob, eds., *The Origins of Anglo-American Radicalism* (London, 1984), 284–299. The thrust of Twomey's work is to emphasize the *diversity* of the radicals in their political ideology and social composition. See *ibid.*, 285. Subsequent citations to Twomey, "Jacobins and Jeffersonians," are to the dissertation.

[11] Appleby, *Capitalism and a New Social Order*, 60–61.

[12] John Ashworth, "The Jeffersonians: Classical Republicans or Liberal Capitalists?" *Journal of American Studies*, XVIII (1984), 427.

consisted of political émigrés from Britain and Ireland, who brought with them to the "asylum for oppressed humanity"[13] a stock of political ideas acquired in the popular radical societies of the British Isles—ideas that were Painite in inspiration.

On their arrival in the United States many became deeply involved in national and local politics. Some, such as William Duane, James Thomson Callender, John Binns, and James Carey, through their writings played a significant role in national Republican politics. Others participated more in local political affairs, either through membership in Republican clubs or by working to recruit immigrant votes for the Republican cause. A surprising number gained sufficient respect from their neighbors to be asked to give Fourth of March Jeffersonian or Fourth of July Independence Day orations.[14]

Although they did not supply original ideas to American political discourse, I will argue that the émigrés helped to rearrange the priority order of some of the more contentious elements of Republicanism in the 1790s, assisting both in the defeat of Federalism and in the development of a Jeffersonian image of America's future as an egalitarian society in which agriculture, commerce, and industry interacted in harmony. What exactly their political ideology was and how effectively they broadcast their Painite message are additional concerns of this study. By examining the role of the exiles I hope to demonstrate that British radical ideology, emerging from the popular societies, was influential in the United States in the 1790s.

I

Down yonder rough beach, where the vessels attend,
I see the sad emigrants slowly descend;
Compelld by the weight of oppression and woe,
Their kindred, and native, and friends to forego.
In these drooping crouds that depart every day,
I see the true strength of the state glide away;
While countries that hail the glad strangers to shore,
Shall flourish, when Britain's proud pomp is no more.[15]

---

[13] Callender in *Recorder* (Richmond), Aug. 18, 1802.

[14] Alexander Wilson, *Oration, on the Power and Value of National Liberty* (Philadelphia, 1801); John Binns, *An Oration Commemorative of the Birth-Day of American Independence, Delivered before the Democratic Societies of the City and County of Philadelphia* (Philadelphia, 1810); John D. Burk, *An Oration, Delivered on the 4th, of March, 1803, at the Courthouse, in Petersburg: To Celebrate the Election of Thomas Jefferson, and Triumph of Republicanism* (Petersburg, Va., 1803); [Richard Dinmore], *A Long Talk, Delivered before the Tammany Society . . .* (Alexandria, Va., 1804).

[15] Alexander Wilson, "Tears of Britain," in [Thomas Crichton], *Biographical Sketches of the Late Alexander Wilson, Communicated in a Series of Letters to a Young Friend* (Paisley, Scot., 1819), 40.

Historians have failed to appreciate the significant *number* of British and Irish radicals who fled to the United States in the 1790s. Many thousands of ordinary people emigrated in that decade; most of them, claimed Callender, went "not in search of a republic, but of *bread*."[16] But the emigrants also included politically conscious exiles whose vision of the new American polity was conditioned by strongly held republican perceptions forged from Paine's political works and from their experiences in opposition to William Pitt's government. At least seventy-four can be confirmed as having been active in the popular radical movements in Britain and Ireland in the 1790s. Of these, one-half were Irish; three-fifths of the remainder were English, and two-fifths Scottish.[17]

Until the end of the eighteenth century, politics in Britain was the province of the aristocracy and the landed classes. The radical societies that were springing up by the end of 1791 reflected a new phenomenon: for the first time political awareness was becoming widespread in the British Isles. These societies represented a groundswell of opinion in favor of significant parliamentary reform as the first and essential step toward reforming social and political institutions. Avowedly constitutionalist—at least in the early years—the radicals sought by petitioning Parliament to persuade the government to reform itself.

The extent of political reformation regarded as necessary was never universally agreed upon, but the majority of men who joined the Society for Constitutional Information, the London Corresponding Society, the Society of United Irishmen, and the English provincial corresponding societies favored eventual introduction of manhood suffrage and annual parliaments. In London, reformers who desired a slighter degree of change, and who could afford the high subscriptions, joined the Friends of the People, the society of the Foxite parliamentary Whigs; two of the emigrants, Robert Merry and Benjamin Vaughan, were associated with this group. The Scottish Friends of the People, founded in July 1792, began as an amalgam of conflicting groups, with the most moderate reformers—who wanted the franchise extended only to the middle classes—trying to persuade the moderate radicals to disown the small body of revolutionary extremists. The United Irishmen, whose membership included Roman Catholics, communicants of the Church of Ireland, and Protestant Dissenters, agitated for Catholic emancipation in addition to parliamentary reform. In the early years, national

---

[16] [James Thomson Callender], *A Short History of the Nature and Consequences of the Excise Laws . . .* (Phildelphia, 1795), 45n.

[17] These are revised figures from Michael Durey, "Transatlantic Patriotism: Political Exiles and America in the Age of Revolutions," in James Walvin and Clive Emsley, eds., *Artisans, Peasants and Proletarians, 1760–1860: Essays Presented to Gwyn A. Williams* (London, 1985), 12–15. Twomey believes that there were more English radical émigrés than Irish ("Jacobins and Jeffersonians," 20–21).

independence was not a major part of the radical program in either Scotland or Ireland, although it was to become so, especially in Ireland, by 1796.[18]

The government responded to these new societies with policies of repression. In addition, in a semiofficial way, through local Church and King clubs and John Reeves's Association for the Preservation of Liberty and Property against Republicans and Levellers (founded in November 1792), the government harnessed popular loyalism in defense of the state. Thus the radicals, always a small minority, were harassed from all sides.[19]

The stage at which individual radicals decided to accept defeat and emigrate varied according to local circumstances and to the tactics used by government. Joseph Priestley and his Unitarian followers in Birmingham and London, for instance, experienced the force of Church and King mobs as early as July 1791, and Thomas Cooper's Unitarian group in Manchester was attacked by Edmund Burke in parliament in 1792. In December 1792 a mob sacked the house and shop of Matthew Falkner and William Young Birch, publishers of the radical *Manchester Herald*. In March 1793 Falkner and Birch "discontinued the *Herald* and fled before the storm" to America. In July the government indited a number of Cooper's friends on charges of sedition. They were acquitted in April 1794, but by that time most of them had decided to join Priestley and other Unitarians in the United States.[20]

One of those acquitted, James Cheetham, persevered in Manchester. His career thereafter exemplifies the way in which radicals who did not at first fold under loyalist pressure were gradually forced into seret societies aimed at overthrowing the state. By 1798 he was, with his two brothers, a member of the revolutionary United

---

[18] The literature on the popular societies in the 1790s is considerable. The last two paragraphs are based on E. P. Thompson, *The Making of the English Working Class* (London, 1969); Gwyn A. Williams, *Artisans and Sans-Culottes: Popular Movements in France and Britain during the French Revolution* (London, 1968); Albert Goodwin, *The Friends of Liberty: The English Democratic Movement in the Age of the French Revolution* (Cambridge, Mass. 1979); Edward Royle and James Walvin, *English Radicals and Reformers, 1760–1848* (Lexington, Ky., 1982); Marianne Elliott, *Partners in Revolution: The United Irishmen and France* (New Haven, Conn., 1982); Roger Wells, *Insurrection: The British Experience, 1795–1803* (Gloucester, 1983); and John D. Brims, "The Scottish Democratic Movement in the Age of the French Revolution" (Ph.D. diss., University of Edinburgh, 1983).

[19] Clive Emsley, "Repression, 'Terror' and the Rule of Law in England during the Decade of the French Revolution," *English Historical Review*, C (1985), 801–825; Goodwin, *Friends of Liberty*, 264–265.

[20] R. B. Rose, "The Priestley Riots of 1791," *Past and Present*, No. 18 (1960), 68–88; Malone, *Thomas Cooper*, 65–70, quotation on p. 69.

Englishmen. Loyalist rioters forced him to flee to America; he was carried on board ship at Liverpool in a chest marked "dry goods."[21]

In Scotland a similar combination of government repression and loyalist activism had similar results: the open radical movement collapsed and its most intransigent members laid insurrectionist plots, culminating in the Watt conspiracy of 1794. Robert Dundas, lord advocate of Scotland and a nephew of Henry Dundas, Pitt's close colleague, acted as soon as the Scottish Friends of the People held their first convention in Edinburgh in December 1792. Using the authority of a royal proclamation against seditious writing, Dundas prosecuted extremist writers such as Callender and James Tytler for seditious libel. Both failed to appear in court and were outlawed. Tytler fled to Belfast, whence he sailed to Boston in 1794. Callender escaped with his family only hours before the authorities searched his lodgings. After two months in Dublin, the Callender family set sail for Philadelphia.[22] Tytler and Callender were sensible; the Scottish courts gave extremely harsh sentences for crimes like theirs.

Radicals who persevered found themselves ostracized and their employment opportunities diminished. In her autobiography Mrs. Eliza Fletcher, wife of an Edinburgh lawyer, pointed out that "every man was considered a rebel in his heart who did not take a decided part in supporting Tory measures of government . . . Such was the terror of Liberal principles in Scotland that no man at the Bar professing these would expect a fair share of practice." In the spring of 1795 the lawyer John Craig Millar, son of a professor at Glasgow University and a moderate reformer in the Friends of the People, was unable to find professional employment. "Disgusted with the state of public affairs," he took his family to America.[23]

Schoolmasters and university professors faced the same pressures. In Scotland their every word was carefully scrutinized for "Jacobin" connotations; even the famous were not exempt.[24] And, of course, men who received patronage of any kind could not afford to arouse even slight suspicions. In London, in January 1792, the poet and playwright Robert Merry made the mistake of presenting his play "The Magician No Conjuror" at Covent Garden. (Playhouses, like newspapers, were battlegrounds for partisan propaganda.) Though Merry's play had no

---

[21] *Recorder* (Rich.), Dec. 1, 1801.

[22] Brims, "Scottish Democratic Movement," chap. 4; Fergusson, *Balloon Tytler*, 132–134; John Pringle to Henry Dundas, Jan. 7, 1793, H.O. 102/5, Public Record Office; *Recorder* (Rich.), Feb. 9, 1803.

[23] [Eliza Fletcher], *Autobiography of Mrs. Fletcher, with Letters and Other Family Memorials*, 3d ed., (Edinburgh, 1876), 65–71, quotations on pp. 66, 71; A. Hook, *Scotland and America: A Study in Cultural Relations, 1750–1835* (Glasgow, 1975), 241.

[24] Henry Cockburn, *Memorials of His Time* (Edinburgh, 1856), 85.

Jacobin signification, it satirized William Pitt as "The Magician." In June the popular actress Miss Brunton, Merry's wife, was suddenly dismissed by the theater. With the government subsidizing the theaters and Merry associated with the Friends of the People, her career was finished. After a period in France the Merrys emigrated to the United States.[25]

Under such pressures, men of progressive views found their options shrinking in the 1790s. They could recant, and hope that their sins would soon be forgiven and forgotten. Many middle-class reformers did so, especially after the Jacobins had seized control of the French Revolution and Britain went to war with France. Most radical artisans, laborers, and small shopkeepers followed suit by 1796, except, of course, in Ireland.[26] Alternatively, radicals could continue efforts to gain parliamentary reform, but this became increasingly difficult as the decade progressed: first the government stopped the spread of information by prosecuting newspaper editors and booksellers, then it banned public meetings, and, finally, it proscribed the popular societies by name. Only the most thick-skinned and intransigent could withstand this onslaught; they retaliated—in Scotland, Ireland, and England—by forming themselves into revolutionary cells.[27]

The only other viable option was emigration. The choice of country, for radicals, was confined to revolutionary France and to the republican United States. By and large, especially from 1793, only the most committed opponents of despotism, prepared to endorse the excesses of the Jacobans, fled across the Channel. United Irishmen, who realized the importance of intervention by foreign troops to the success of their intended revolution, made up the great majority of émigrés to France, where they squabbled amongst themselves in their efforts to obtain a French invasion force. Most prospective emigrants—disillusioned by the Terror, during which Paine was imprisoned and nearly executed—perceived the United States as a personally safer haven of liberty, even if its distance from Britain precluded their continued involvement in the politics of the popular societies.[28]

Most members of the popular societies in the British Isles in the 1790s were artisans, journeymen, and small shopkeepers, yet more than 70 percent of the radicals who emigrated to the United States had middleclass backgrounds or were attempting—before their political

---

[25] Lucyle Werkmeister, *A Newspaper History of England, 1792–1793* (Lincoln, Neb., 1967), 92–93.

[26] Thompson, *English Working Class*, 162–164; Williams, *Artisans*, 101.

[27] Emsley, "Repression," *Eng. Hist. Rev.*, C (1985), 825; Wells, *Insurrection, passim*.

[28] Elliott, *Partners in Revolution, passim*; Foner, *Tom Paine*, 244; Hawke, *Paine*, 291–306.

activities intervened—to rise into the solid middle ranks of society. In other words, emigration to the United States was less appealing to rank-and-file radicals, who possibly could not afford to go even if they wanted to, than to the the educated and ambitious, who expected opportunities for advancement in republican America. At least seven were qualified in medicine; the United Irishman Edward Hudson was a dentist; the English Unitarian John Edmonds Stock was an Edinburgh medical student when he become embroiled in the Watt conspiracy.[29] John Craig Millar and the United Irishmen William Sampson, Harman Blennerhassett, and Thomas Addis Emmet were lawyers or barristers, while Callender, the son of a tobacconist, claimed to have been "bred to the law."[30] Thomas Ledlie Birch was a Presbyterian minister; David Baillie Warden, James Hull, and John Miles were probationer Presbyterian ministers; Denis Driscol had been a clergyman before taking up the pen—in Ireland he edited the "wicked" *Cork Gazette* and in America the deist *Temple of Reason*—and Priestley was an eminent, if controversial, divine.[31]

Some of the émigrés had wealthy backgrounds. Thomas Cooper was a prosperous calico manufacturer until his business collapsed in 1793; the United Irishman Henry Jackson, who named his country seat "Fort Paine," was a well-to-do ironfounder.[32] When in 1798 the British army's attempt to forestall revolution by arresting most of the United Irish leadship failed, and the bloody and disastrous Irish rebellion erupted, John Devereaux, who owned an estate worth $10,000 per annum in Waterford, led 2,000 tenants against the British army. Banished, he became a merchant in Baltimore with business interests in South America, where he frequently visited. In 1815 he became a Bolivian general, returned to

---

[29] Those qualified in medicine included William James MacNeven, Stock, Reynolds, Edward Sweetman, Henry Toulmin, McLean, and Emmet. For Stock, see *Edinburgh Evening Courant* Sept. 6, 1794; *Scots Magazine*, LVI (1794), 652; and *Gentleman's Magazine*, N.S., IV (1835), 557. For Hudson, R. B. McDowell, *Ireland in the Age of Imperialism and Revolution, 1760–1801* (Oxford, 1979), 135, and *Dictionary of American Biography*, s.v. "Hudson, Edward."

[30] For Millar see Sir Francis J. Grant, *The Faculty of Advocates in Scotland, 1532–1943, with Genealogical Notes* (Edinburgh, 1944), 149, and *Autobiography of Mrs. Fltecher*, 64, 71. For Sampson, Twomey, "Jacobins and Jeffersonians," 36. For Blennerhassett, McDowell, *Ireland in the Age of Imperialism*, 134–135. For Emmet, Thomas P. Robinson, "The Life of Thomas Addis Emmet" (Ph.D. diss., New York University, 1955), 23–24. For Callender, *Recorder* (Rich.), Apr. 30, 1803.

[31] Latimer, "David Bailie Warden," *Ulster Jour. Arch.*, XXIII (1907), 29–38; A. Aspinall, *Politics and the Press, 1780–1850* (London, 1949), 62; Twomey, "Jacobins and Jeffersonians," 33–34.

[32] Malone, *Thomas Cooper*, 6; McDowell, *Ireland in the Age of Imperialism*, 480–481.

Ireland to enlist troops, and was eventually rewarded by Gen. Simón Bolívar with some of the profits of a goldmine. He died once again a rich man.[33]

At least four refugees secured professorships at American institutions of higher learning: Cooper at Central College (the University of Virginia) and at South Carolina College (the University of South Carolina); the chemist William James MacNeven at the New York College of Physicians and Surgeons; the Scotsman John Maclean at Princeton; and the United Irishman Daniel McCurtin at Washington College, Maryland. In addition, Warden was offered a professorship at Union College, Schenectady, but became for a while principal tutor at the Columbia Academy in New York, and John Wood, a Scotsman, tutored Aaron Burr's accomplished daughter. No fewer than eighteen exiles had attended university, although by no means all of these took a formal degree.[34]

Finally, nearly one-half of the émigrés were involved at one time or another in journalism and pamphleteering, and sixteen made the media their career. They ranged from hack writers Callender and James "Balloon" Tytler, who wrote much of the second edition of the *Encyclopaedia Britannica*, and struggling newspaper owners and editors such as James Carey and John Mason Williams, to successful media barons such as William Duane, John Binns, and Joseph Gales.

This résumé of the respectable social origins of so many of the radical emigrants is a reminder that Paine's ideas influenced not only the lowest classes in the 1790s.[35] It also highlights the fact that his appeal centered partly in his belief in a meritocracy. In 1792 he wrote,

> Experience, in all ages, and in all countries, has demonstrated, that it is impossible to control Nature in her distribution of mental powers. She gives them as she pleases. . . . It appears to general observation, that revolutions create genius and talents; but these events do more than bring them forward. There is in man, a mass of sense lying in a dormant state, and which, unless something exictes it into action, will descend with him, in that condition, to the grave. As it is to the advantage of society that the whole of its faculties should be employed, the construction of government ought to be such as to bring forward, by a quiet and regular operation, all that extent of capacity which never fails to appear in revolutions.[36]

---

[33] [John Binns], *Recollections of the life of John Binns* (Philadelphia, 1854), 317–318.

[34] Hook, *Scotland and America*, 241; Carter, "Political Activities of Mathew Carey," 244; *American Patriot* (Baltimore), Jan. 13, 1803.

[35] Foner, *Tom Paine*, 99.

[36] Philip S. Foner, ed., *The Life and Major Writings of Thomas Paine* (Secaucus, N.J., 1974), I, 367–368.

Much of Paine's popularity in Britain stemmed from his ability to mirror the sentiments of large numbers of people who resented their marginality in a society where a small privileged elite manipulated the levers of power. Professional men, and men aspiring to professional careers, in particular regarded their social position with ambivalence, for although they strove for independence and eminence, by tradition the lawyer, the cleric, the doctor, the teacher, and the man of letters were regarded as mere auxiliaries to the ruling elites. They were dependent satellites in a highly structured social world controlled by what Jonathon Clark has called "an *ancien régime* state."[37] At a time when the professions had neither the social status nor the popular esteem of today, and when professional power was confined to small oligarchies, many professionals found their social and economic aspirations stifled by a social structure that denied opportunities to advancement on merit. Thus to an important degree the émigrés represented the radicalism of ambitious but socially blocked classes in late eighteenth-century Britain. Their resentments multiplied when, as with most of the exiles, their dissenting religious opinions further reduced their status in the eyes of the powerful social elites.[38]

The émigrés writings echoed Paine's theme of wasted or underutilized talent. For the Reverend Thomas Dunn, in 1794, this was a perpetual condition; "from the murder of righteous Abel, down to Dr. Priestley, the first philosopher of the present age, superior integrity and superior talents have always been persecuted by narrow-minded, malignant, and wicked men." James Carey was more precise; in 1799 he claimed that John Adam's form of Federalism was no different from "the [Pittite] consitution," which aimed "above all to cramp the inventive genius and the enterprising spirit of Englishmen." For Cooper, "strength, and wisdom, and talents, and good dispositions, superior capacity of body or mind—superior industry or activity, do, and ought to create proportionate distinctions, and to bring with them their own reward."[39]

---

[37] J.C.D. Clark, *English Society, 1688–1832: Ideology, Social Structure and Political Practice during the Ancien Regime* (Cambridge, 1985). This is a sustained and brilliant argument against the "bourgeois" nature of 18th-century British society that throws new light on late 18th-century radicalism.

[38] Goodwin, *Friends of Liberty*, 65–98; Thompson, *English Working Class*, 28–58; Michael R. Watts, *The Dissenters: From the Reformation to the French Revolution* (Oxford, 1978), 478–490.

[39] Thomas Dunn, *A Discourse, Delivered in the New Dutch Church, Nassau Street . . .* (New York, 1794), 4; Timothy Telltruth [James Carey], *The Collected Wisdom of Ages, the Most Stupendous Fabric of Human Invention, the English Constitution* (Philadelphia, 1799), v; Thomas Cooper, *A Reply to Mr. Burke's Invective against Mr. Cooper, and Mr. Watt, in the House of Commons, on 30th of April, 1792* (Manchester, 1792), 22.

Under Pitt's government radicals had few illusions that their talents would be permitted effective expression. Recognizing this, Paine had written that republican government offered the best prospects of an open society. He defined republican government as one "established and conducted for the interests of the public, as well individually as collectively," and noted that "it most naturally associates with the representative form."[40] He had, since 1776, always carefully distinguished between society and government, the former a blessing, the latter "but a necessary evil."[41] The radicals accepted this distinction. Dunn, in a 1794 discourse at the New Dutch Church in Nassau Street, New York, went so far as to quote *Common Sense* almost verbatim: "At best, Government is but an imperfect remedy for the various evils of this imperfect state. 'Tis more a badge of lost innocence, than any positive advantage. SOCIETY is, indeed, a blessing; as it promotes our happiness, unites our affections. . . . Government is only a negative advantage; a mere curb upon our vices: the necessity for government . . . arises from our wickedness."[42] So pervasive was Paine's view of government that Callender, near the end of his remarkable career in the United States, even when in the name of independence and political purity he was attacking the Jeffersonians and their newly imported propagandist, Thomas Paine, still adhered to it. "Government," he declared, "is chiefly known by the expence which it occasions. It is a sort of complex constable, a *something* hired to keep the peace, and nothing more. In 'Common Sense,' Mr. Paine has fully explained this doctrine. He observes that society arises from our *wants*, and government, from our *vices*. The definition is perfect. Government is to society, what a bridle is to a horse, or a dose of salts to the human body. They produce no positive good but they prevent the existence of evil."[43]

Paine's ideal form of republican government was that of the United States, in which "representation [is] ingrafted upon democracy." The American people had solved their political problems in 1787 "by the simple operation of constructing government on the principles of society and the rights of man. . . . There the poor are not oppressed, the rich are not privileged. Industry is not mortified by the splendid extravagance of a court rioting at its expense. Their taxes are few, because their government is just; and as there is nothing to render them wretched, there is nothing to engender riots and tumults."[44] As enthusiasm for

<hr>

[40] Foner, ed., *Writings of Paine*, I, 369.

[41] Paine, *Common Sense*, ed. Kramnick, 65. This distinction can, of course, be traced back to Locke.

[42] Dunn, *Discourse Delivered in the New Dutch Church*, 13–14.

[43] *Recorder* (Rich.), Dec. 1, 1802.

[44] Foner, ed., *Writings of Paine*, I, 371, 360.

reform in Britain gave way in 1792 first to the recognition that loyalism was immensely strong, and then to despair of success, Paine's vision of America as an asylum of liberty with an exemplary political system became more and more attractive. From Dublin in April 1792 John Chambers, whose bookshop was a meeting place for the United Irishmen, informed Mathew Carey in Philadelphia that the American Constitution was increasingly admired in Europe: "even that of France shrinks from a contrast."[45] Cooper, following a short sojourn in America at the end of 1793, wrote that "there is little fault to find with the government of America, either in principle or in practice; . . . we have few [disputes] respecting political men or political measures: the present irritation of men's minds in Great Britain, and the discordant state of society on political accounts, is not known there. The government is the government *of* the people, and *for* the people."[46] A Painite utopian vision filled the radicals' minds as they took flight across the Atlantic.

II

Utopian expectations are normally disappointed when confronted with reality, and, émigrés dreams were no exception. Many radicals were unpleasantly surprised by their initial reception in America. Disembarking at New Castle in 1794, Alexander Wilson walked to Wilmington and then to Philadelphia. Virtually penniless, he and his nephew "made free to go into a good many farm-houses on the road, but saw none of that kindness and hospitality so often told of them."[47] In 1795 Wolfe Tone, the United Irishman, found the country to be "beautiful, but it is like a beautiful scene in a theatre; the effect at a proper distance is admirable, but it will not bear a minute inspection." Americans were unfriendly and selfish, and "they do fleece us émigrés at a most unmerciful rate."[48] Their poverty or even notoriety does not explain the treatment the émigrés received. A respectable English lawyer, Charles William Janson, visiting a market in 1793 with other new arrivals, soon found "that we had paid at least a halfpenny per pound more than the market price," although he conceded that in other countries "the perversion of the scriptural expression 'I was a stranger

---

[45] John Chambers to Mathew Carey, Dublin, Apr. 12, 1792, Lea and Febiger Collection, Historical Society of Pennsylvania, Philadelphia.

[46] Thomas Cooper, *Some Information Respecting America* . . . (London, 1794), 52–53.

[47] Alexander Wilson to his parents, July 25, 1794, in Clark Hunter, ed., *The Life and Letters of Alexander Wilson* (Philadelphia, 1983), 150.

[48] Joseph James St. Mark, "The Red Shamrock: United Irishmen and Revolution, 1795–1803" (Ph.D. diss., Georgetown University, 1974), 154.

and you took me in,' is perhaps still more strikingly exemplified."[49] Sooner or later, however, most émigrés came to terms with contemporary "republican mores" and settled down, usually with the assistance of radicals who had arrived earlier and who thus had already experienced the adapting process. Mathew Carey gave work to Callender, for instance, and Archibald Binny, the typefounder, assisted his fellow Scottish radical David Bruce.[50]

The émigrés' personal experiences, however, were less painful in the longer term than their dismay at Alexander Hamilton's perversion of the new Constitution. The pattern of radical reactions to Federalist policies was to some extent determined by the length of time émigrés had spent in America. The early emigrants' confidence in republican institutions *gradually* diminished as Hamilton's program systematically unfolded. Those arriving after 1795 already knew what to expect. All, however, condemned the growing convergence of Federalist policies and those of successive British governments in the eighteenth century. They had fled from the effects of such policies; many reacted in America by becoming actively involved in Jeffersonian Republican politics.

The émigrés strongly opposed Hamilton's apparent intention to recreate in America a stratified society based on finance capitalism, high taxation, a national debt, and a "placeman" system, with "the British and stock-jobbing faction" holding power only by "the countenance of England."[51] Richard Dinmore's succinct retrospective analysis of John Adams's presidency neatly underlined the émigrés' fears of Federalism. "Your national expences were encreased," he stated, and "placemen became numerous and governmental influence enormous."[52] According to Cheetham, Adams's administration "copied implicitly the acts of the English government, even in the worst and most vitiated period of its history. . . . The will of the executive became the animating principle of our federal legislature, and that will was palpably in favour of monarchy."[53] As usual, it was Callender who made the most virulent attacks on the Federalist system. Languishing in Richmond jail in 1800, he bemoaned the constitutional provision giving "an unqualified power of taxation" to Congress. "Out of every dollar which they could raise," he wrote, "at least three fourths have been misapplied. The public

---

[49] Janson, *The Stranger in America, 1793–1806* (London, 1807), 20.

[50] Mathew Carey to James Thomson Callender, Oct. 5, 1793, Lea and Febiger Letter Book, IV, 1st Ser.; Follo G. Silver, *Typefounding in America, 1787–1825* (Charlottesville, Va. 1925), 73; Twomey, "Jacobins and Jeffersonians," 66–75.

[51] [James Thomson Callender], *The Prospect before Us* (Richmond, Va., 1800), I, 101.

[52] [Dinmore], *Talk before the Tammany Society*, 13.

[53] "A Citizen of New York" [James Cheetham], *A Narrative of the Suppression, by Colonel Burr, of the History of the Administration of John Adams . . .* (New York, 1802), 6–7.

officers have rushed to public plunder, like as many dogs to a dead carcase. . . . [T]he federal government feels anxious . . . *to have a finger in every pye*; to swell the public debt as much as may be; and to raise its own power by the depression of the state governments, by the useless and endless multiplication of places, and of jobs."[54]

The émigré radicals, having discovered similar features in Federalist and Pittite policies, attacked the former with the weapons they had honed in their war against the latter. Faced in America with the menace of excessive governmental power, of a financial system supported by the state, and of a corrupt officialdom, the émigrés responded with political arguments that mingled the natural rights theories of Paine with residual elements of Commonwealth ideology. They laid much heavier emphasis on promoting the Painite vision of a socially harmonious, egalitarian, and commercialized society than on defending the older and by now—for both Britain and the United States—less relevant Commonwealth ideal of a closely integrated, realtively static, hierarchical agrarian polity. Much of the exiles' importance in America stems from the relative weighting of Commonwealth and Painite ideas in their political thought, for compared to contemporary American republican thought, theirs was more significantly informed by liberal than by classical ideology. Both American and British strains of republicanism were in transition,[55] but the latter had been developed further. Thanks to Paine's influence, British republicans were quicker to accept the benefits of a commercial society. In the battles of the Federalist decade, the émigrés' political arguments helped to nudge Jeffersonian Republicanism away from classical political thought.

Commonwealth ideology's limited appeal to the radical exiles is exemplified by their conception of virtue. Appleby has argued that in the United States "by the end of the century virtue more often referred to a private quality, a man's capacity to look out for himself and his dependents—almost the opposite of classical virtue."[56] The radicals easily accepted such a privatized version of virtue. The defrocked Irish priest and newspaper editor Denis Driscol, for instance, when extolling the middling class of free and independent citizens, equated virtue with the quintessentially personal values of honor and integrity.[57] Similarly, Cooper, while analyzing the inequities of a hierarchical society based on

---

[54] [Callender], *Prospect before Us*, II, 97, 116. Callender, of course, was incorrect to state that Congress's taxing power was unqualified.

[55] McCoy, *Elusive Republic*, 10.

[56] Appleby, *Capitalism and a New Social Order*, 15.

[57] *Am. Patriot*, Nov. 13, 1802; "A Quaker in Politics" [Joseph Priestley], "Maxims of Political Arithmetic, Applied to the Case of the United States of America" *Aurora, General Advertiser* (Philadelphia), Feb. 27, 1798.

privilege and birth, also associated virtue with personal qualities. The privileged, although ignorant and vice-ridden, received all the honors and rewards, and thus undermined the morals of those with "abilities and virtue."[58] Callender gave short shrift to the nostalgic view of a virtuous golden age under an ancient constitution. "At what era this *freedom* and *virtue* existed, no body could ever tell. . . . British annals . . . [are] full of calamity and disgrace. . . . Some people talk of restoring the constitution to its *primitive* purity. They would do well to inform us what that purity was, and where its traces are to be found."[59]

Far more important than the language of virtue for the émigrés was the language of natural rights and the ethic of individualism. Their political discourse was founded less on the Commonwealth tradition of Harrington, Sidney, Bolingbroke, and Montesquieu than on the political and economic ideas of Locke, Smith, and Paine. In all their published writings there is only one reference to Harrington—by Cooper, who in a discussion of monarchy claimed that the subject was covered "more profoundly" by Paine, Joel Barlow, and the Abbé Siéyés than by Milton, Harrington, or Sidney.[60] Only Daniel Isaac Eaton, whose sojourn in America was brief, openly espoused the ideas of Montesquieu, reprinting the section "On Liberty" from *The Spirit of Laws* in 1795. Eaton was also eccentric in believing that "talent was conferred on mankind, undoubtedly, for the promotion of public virtue."[61] Sidney was mentioned only rarely, and then usually in a general litany of heroic names that coupled him with Locke. Cheetham, in his dying speech to his children in 1810, after "raving mania" had set in, did mention Bolingbroke, but not for his political perspicacity. "With herculean strength he now raised himself from his pillow; with eyes of meteoric fierceness, he grasped his bed covering, and in most vehement but rapid articulation, exclaimed to his sons, 'Boys! study Bolingbroke for style, and Locke for sentiment. ' He spoke no more."[62]

On the other hand, the names and ideas of Locke, Smith, and "the immortal Paine" punctuate the writings of the radicals.[63] Dumas Malone showed how influential were Locke in the development of

[58] Cooper, *Reply to Mr. Burke's Invective*, 37.

[59] [James Thomson Callender], *The Political Progress of Britain; or, An Impartial History of Abuses in the Government of the British Empire* (Philadelphia, 1795), pt 2, 55–56.

[60] Cooper, *Reply to Mr. Burke's Invective*, 17.

[61] Daniel Isaac Eaton, *The Philanthropist; or, Philosophical Essays on Politics, Government, Morals and Manners* (Philadelphia), Mar. 16, 1795, I, Nov. 2, 1795, 1–3.

[62] Twomey, "Jacobins and Jeffersonians," 56–57.

[63] Cooper, *Reply to Mr. Burke's Invective*, 23.

Cooper's early views and Smith for his political economy.[64] William Duane quoted with approval both Locke and Smith in an 1804 pamphlet on banking.[65] Callender was uncharacteristically effusive. "No man," he wrote, "has done more honour to England, than Mr. Locke." He added that Smith's *Wealth of Nations* "deserves to be studied by every member of the community, as one of the most accurate, profound, and persuasive books that ever was written."[66]

It was Paine's writings above all others that spoke to the radicals' needs. The publishing history of *Rights of Man* is astonishing. Part one, published in March 1791, was promoted by the Society for Constitutional Information in London and by the new provincial radical societies. The Manchester Constitutional Society asked Cooper to abridge it for popular use, and in January 1792 Joseph Gales of the Sheffield Consitutional Society obtained Paine's consent to print the first cheap edition.[67] The book became a bestseller, but it was eclipsed by the phenomenal success of part two, published in February 1792. As many as 200,000 copies of part two, in various forms and editions, may have been distributed in the British Isles by the end of the year.[68]

The effect of *Rights of Man* on many of the émigrés was electric. Cooper told James Watt, Jr., that "it has made me still more politically mad than I ever was . . . It is choque full, crowded with good sense and demonstrative reasoning . . . I regard it as the very jewel of a book."[69] Cheetham, one of three Manchester brothers known as "the three Jacobin infidels," rushed "from tavern to tavern and from brothel to brothel with *Rights of Man* in one hand and *Age of Reason* in the other."[70] Eaton gained notoriety for repeatedly publishing Paine's works, even after they had been banned as seditious libel.[71] Incarcerated in Kilmainham jail in 1793, Dr. James Reynolds took comfort from a print of Paine hanging on the wall of his cell.[72]

---

[64] Malone, *Thomas Cooper*, 13, 98, 216.

[65] [Duane], *Observations on the Principles and Operation of Banking* (Philadelphia, 1804), 3; [Richard Dinmore], *An Exposition of the Principles of the English Jacobins . . .* , 2d ed. (Norwich, 1797), 10.

[66] [J. T. Callender], *Deformities of Dr. Samuel Johnson, Selected from His Works*, 2d ed. (London, 1782), 69, 89.

[67] Goodwin, *Friends of Liberty*, 177.

[68] Royle and Walvin, *English Radicals*, 54.

[69] Frida Knight, *The Strange Case of Thomas Walker: Ten Years in the Life of a Manchester Radical* (London, 1957), 63–64.

[70] Twomey, "Jacobins and Jeffersonians," 29–30.

[71] Daniel Lawrence McCue, Jr., "Daniel Isaac Eaton and *Politics for the People*" (Ph.D. diss., Columbia University, 1974), 90.

[72] R. R. Madden, *The United Irishmen, Their Lives and Times*, rev. ed., 4 vols. (London, 1857–1860), I, 83.

Paine was by no means an original thinker; it is possible to trace all his ideas to previous theorists, especially to those in the Lockean tradition. It was his tone that so stimulated the radicals, encouraging their sense of individual worth and desire for change. Paine, Edward Thompson has written, "destroyed with one book century-old taboos."[73] His contemptuous dismissal of the hereditary principle, his promotion of egalitarianism, individualism, and natural rights (Paine's two major points, wrote Callender, were an attack on hereditary right and a defense of equal representation),[74] and his faith in the future galvanized thousands into political action. Although some of the exiles were to have intellectual and emotional difficulties coming to terms with the deist principles in *Age of Reason*, in the 1790s they widely disseminated Painite radicalism so that it became a potent force in American Republican circles.

III

A recent examination of late eighteenth-century British radicalism shows that it consisted of two main ideological tendencies, one agrarian and the other commercial. According to Geoffrey Gallop, agrarian radicalism "exerted a powerful influence on a radical generation searching for solutions to . . . moral and political decay. The ideas of the self-sufficient village community and the independent freeholder . . . became intermixed with classical republican ideals of equality, simplicity and virtue to produce the agrarian radicalism of the late eighteenth century." In contrast, commercial radicalism "emphasised material progress and connected it with private property, self-interest and commercial society." Commercial radicals, including Paine and Priestley, "argued that the society and economy said by the agrarians to be the basis and fulfilment of the ethic of universal benevolence—the agrarian utopia—was antithetical to real human needs and aspirations. They . . . believed that commerce expanded and humanised the mind by way of increased contact and the encouragement of mutual interdependence."[75] This vision of a commercialized society appealed most to those radicals who looked to the establishment of a polity in which socially formed obstacles to growth and personal advancement were obliterated and opportunities for the exercise of talents were maximized. A commercial society obviously had more attractions for aspiring professionals than a hierarchical agrarian polity, for, as long as

---

[73] Thompson, *English Working Class*, 92; Williams, *Artisans*, 17–18.

[74] *Recorder* (Rich.), Dec. 1, 1802.

[75] Geoffrey I. Gallop, "Politics, Property and Progress: British Radical Thought, 1760–1815" (D. Phil. diss., Oxford University, 1983), 22–24.

the political, social, and educational contexts were organized to promote equality of opportunity, their chances of advancement and independence were considerably enhanced.

The émigrés' emphasis on individual freedom and opportunity made their acceptance of commercial society inevitable. It was Paine who linked individualism and commerce most clearly. "Commerce," he wrote, "is no other than the traffic of two individuals, multiplied on a scale of numbers; and by the same rule that nature intended the intercourse of two, she intended that of all."[76] Thus a commercial society had to be free and open to all. The émigré radicals strongly opposed what John Thelwall, the foremost theorist of the London Corresponding Society, called "speculation-commerce"—that is, commerce based on mercantilism, in which world trade was controlled "by a few engrossers and monopolists" who, by accumulating commodities "in the hope of exciting artificial wants" within a mercantilist system, manipulated trade to their own advantage.[77] Similarly, the views on commerce put forward by Cooper and Priestly in 1799, which some historians seem to have misinterpreted,[78] were aimed not at commerce per se but at commercial *speculation* and at government support for such artificial trade. Both men opposed the tendency of merchants to rush into the Atlantic carrying trade, opened up temporarily by the war between Britain and France, partly because the naval support necessary to defend a merchant marine increased the Federalist mania for government defense spending and the risk of war, and partly because it represented "forced" or "unnatural" trade. Merchants should be left alone to seek their own best interests, said Cooper: "prohibit nothing, but protect no speculation." If foreign commerce was threatened, it should, "like every other losing scheme . . . be left to its own fate,"[79] In like manner, Callender's oft-reprinted *Political Progress of Britain*, much admired by Jefferson, was a virulent attack not on commerce itself but on British mercantilist policies that had led to numerous wars and millions of deaths in the eighteenth century.[80]

---

[76] Foner, ed., *Writings of Paine*, I, 400.

[77] Gallop, "Politics, Property and Progress," 144.

[78] This is not the place to discuss in detail the misunderstandings, but compare Twomey, "Jacobins and Jeffersonians," 146, with McCoy, *Elusive Republic*, 176, and Appleby, *Capitalism and a New Social Order*, 88–89. Twomey's thesis is the most thorough examination of the émigrés' political economy.

[79] Twomey, "Jacobins and Jeffersonians," 146–147; [Priestley], "Maxims of Political Arithmetic," *Aurora*, Feb. 26, 1798.

[80] [James Thomson Callender], *The Political Progress of Britain; or, An Impartial Account of the Principal Abuses in the Government of This Country, from the Revolution in 1688 . . .* (Edinburgh, 1792), pt. I. It was reprinted in London in 1792 and in 1795 (by Daniel Isaac Eaton), and in America in 1794, 1795, and 1796.

"Speculation-commerce" conflicted with the radicals' vision of an open society where every individual had the same opportunities to use his talents to the full. The ideal system of commerce was "commission-commerce," whereby countries exchanged abundant commodities for scarce but desired ones.[81] In this process the state should have no role to play. As Dinmore wrote, radicals "oppose all laws which cramp industry. . . . [E]very man has a right to get his bread wherever he pleases, and by whatever honest means."[82] In the American context, "commission-commerce" condoned the supremacy of agricultural products within the nation's economy; trade links with the rest of the world were naturally to be based on the exportation of agricultural products and the importation of manufactured goods.

Thus the British and Irish radicals' political economy incorporated without difficulty Smith's—and the French physiocrats'—belief that, in a "natural" and unfettered economic world, investment would logically flow into agriculture first, then into home manufactures, and finally into domestic and foreign commerce.[83] They did not oppose either commerce or manufacturing in the 1790s; they merely argued, as did Cooper in 1799, that individual and rational investment decisions in the United States would normally favor agriculture.[84]

But at the same time some were aware, at an earlier date than most Americans and probably as a result of their anglophobia, that to be truly independent Americans ought to be ready to promote home manufacturing when favorable conditions arose. Although in 1794 Cooper felt that large-scale domestic manufacturing would be unprofitable in America as long as land was a better investment and there remained "a prejudice in favour of British goods" he was not opposed to its eventual development. His unfortunate experiences as a failed manufacturer in England partly determined his opinions; "the common lot of inventors and first improvers [is that] they usually enrich the country and impoverish themselves," he wrote bitterly. In the same year Morgan John Rhees argued that Americans should "strain every nerve to patronize their manufactural as well as their agricultural interest." Callender, too, believed in the 1790s that home manufacturing would be unprofitable, at least while the circulation of excessive paper money left wages too high and excise taxes encourage British imports, thus entombing American manufactures "in the grave of her independence." Neverthless, by

---

[81] Gallop, "Politics, Property and Progress," 144.

[82] [Dinmore], *Principles of the English Jacobins*, 8; [Priestley], "Maxims of Political Arithmetic," *Aurora*, Feb. 26, 1798.

[83] D. D. Raphael, *Adam Smith* (Oxford, 1985), 81–82.

[84] Thomas Cooper, *Political Essays, Originally Inserted in the Northumberland Gazette, with Additions* (Northumberland, Pa., 1799).

1798, trying to wean Americans from Federalist support for Britain, he was arguing for the self-sufficiency of America ("America should, like the armidilla, withdraw within her shell") in both agriculture and home manufactures, the latter being more important than foreign commerce. No one was more useful to American society, he suggested, than the "industrious and intelligent manufacturer."[85]

The radical exiles envisaged a society in which agricultural, manufacturing, and commercial pursuits were carried out in harmony, without the danger of economic class conflict. In this they again echoed Paine, who had written that "the landholder, the farmer, the manufacturer, the merchant, the tradesman, and every occupation, prospers by the aid which each receives from the other, and from the whole. Common Interest regulates their concerns."[86] As early as 1788 Mathew Carey looked to a United States where a manufacturing North and an agricultural South worked together to promote national unity. It would be "a patriotic undertaking," wrote Gales in 1802, for Americans to wear home manufactured cotton goods, for "it must be obvious . . . that every manufacture that consumes cotton, would be highly profitable to this country," most particularly to its agricultural interest. In 1806 Cheetham asserted that "if the commercial interest of this country is called upon to suffer, its *agricultural interest* cannot possibly escape. They are both too closely connected to stand alone; they must rise or fall together." And Binns in the *Democratic Press* continually emphasized the message that "manufacturing and commerce are the sisters, the friends, and the handmaidens of agriculture."[87]

In the 1790s, however, the mercantilist implications of this commercial and industrial political economy remained latent amongst the émigrés. While the Federalists held power, and state influence, in the opinion of Republicans, promoted the interests of a monied minority, anglophobia, and political necessity, the continued authority of Paine's teachings ensured radical adherence to a laissez-faire program. The alternative would merely have played into the hands of the Federalists. Under a Republican regime in the following decade, however, a mercantilist political economy become a patriotic desideratum, and as Paine's vision of a peaceful world predicated on commercial reciprocity

---

[85] Cooper, *Information Respecting America*, 59, 2; Twomey, "Jacobins and Jeffersonians," 155; James Thomas Callender, *Sketches of the History of America* (Philadelphia, 1798), 185–187, 207–209, and *Sedgwick & Co.; or, A Key to the Six Per Cent Cabinet* (Philadelphia, 1798), 87.

[86] Foner, ed., *Writings of Paine*, I, 357.

[87] Carter, "Political Activities of Mathew Carey," 160; *Raleigh Register, and North-Carolina State Gazette*, June 2, 1801, Mar. 9, Aug. 3, 1802; "Politicus" [James Cheetham], *An Impartial Enquiry into Certain Parts of the Conduct of Governor Lewis, and a Portion of the Legislature . . .* (New York, 1806), 18, 51; [Binns], *Recollections*, 164–166.

stubbornly failed to materialize, one is not surprised to find at the forefront of demands for an independent and self-sufficient United States
most of the surviving émigrés of the 1790s, including Cooper, Mathew
Carey, Binns, Gales, and Sampson.[88] Government promotion of manufactures and of the infrastructure required for a modern commercial
society was no longer regarded as creating a "forced" or "unnatural"
economy; patriotic necessity ensured its "naturalness." With its emphasis on national economic development, such a political economy still
conformed to Painite radical parameters.[89]

IV

Appleby has noted that in the 1790s the democrats in America
found "a national voice where in the past their strength had been
local."[90] Certain prerequisites were necessary for this to occur; one of
the most important was a nationwide system for disseminating information by print. In media communications in particular can be seen
most clearly the influence of the émigré radicals on the development
of Jeffersonianism. As one historian has written, "foreigners seemed to
get one sniff of printers' ink and become loyal Jeffersonians."[91]

The extent of the radicals' involvement in newspaper production
has never been fully appreciated. It has been estimated that 450 newspapers and 75 magazines were founded in the United States between
1783 and 1800.[92] The appendix indicates which ones were edited by
émigrés from 1783, when the ex-Wilkite and later Democratic Society
member John Miller founded the *South Carolina Gazette*.[93] All told, eighteen British and Irish radicals edited no fewer than 49 newspapers and
magazines, mostly in the politically sensitive middle states but at one
time or another covering all the eastern seaboard, from Georgia to Massachusetts.

It is obviously very difficult to determine their newspapers' general
influence in spreading ideas, news, and propaganda. Circulation

---

[88] "Autobiography of Mathew Carey," *New England Magazine*, 1834, letters 22, 23;
Mathew Carey, *The Olive Branch; or, Faults on Both Sides* (Philadelphia, 1814); [Binns],
Recollections, 165–166; Twomey, "Jacobins and Jeffersonians," 147–170.

[89] The best study of Paine's nationalist political economy is Foner, *Tom Paine*, esp.
chaps. 5, 6.

[90] Appleby, *Capitalism and a New Social Order*, 4.

[91] Walter Francis Brown, Jr., "John Adams and the American Press, 1797–1801: The
First Full Scale Confrontation between the Executive and the Media" (Ph.D. diss., University of Notre Dame, 1974), 45.

[92] *Ibid.*, 72.

[93] Gilpatrick, "English Background of John Miller," *Furman Bulletin*, XX (1938), 14–20;
Eugene P. Link, *Democratic-Republican Societies, 1790–1800* (New York, 1942), 90; Donald
H. Stewart, *The Opposition Press of the Federalist Period* (Albany, N.Y., 1969), 649.

figures are almost impossible to calculate, although the common practice of copying from other newspapers ensured that major views were
widely disseminated. Undoubtedly, most of these newspapers worked
on a shoestring. The émigrés' efforts were predictably weak in Federalist New England, where the United Irishman John Daly Burk briefly
edited the first daily newspaper in Boston, and elsewhere many of their
prints were ephemeral. James Carey, for example, failed with newspapers in Richmond, Charleston (twice), Savannah, Wilmington, N.C.,
and Philadelphia (three times). Still, financially insecure though his
newspapers were, their value was recognized in high places. As *Carey's
United State's Recorder*, devoted to "the American constitution" and "true
republican principles," and the *Aurora* tottered in 1798, Jefferson, who
had subscribed to Carey's first newspaper in 1792, told Madison that
"we should really exert ourselves to procure them, for if these papers
fall, republicanism will be entirely brow-beaten."[94] He then organized
a group of Philadelphia Republicans, including John Beckley, Israel
Israel, and Mathew Carey, to subsidize Callender, who was then the
assistant editor of the *Aurora*.[95] *Carey's United States' Recorder* collapsed,
partly owing to the yellow fever epidemic, but the *Aurora*, edited by
William Duane after Benjamin Franklin Bache's death in 1798, went
from strength to strength. In his first year Duane nearly doubled the
Aurora's circulation, to a peak of 1,700 subscribers.[96] As the political
crisis deepened in the last years of Adams's presidency, the Republican newspapers, with the émigrés to the fore, acted as a "conduit
between [the party's] leaders and philosophers, and the masses."[97]
Newsprint became the circulating medium that brought Republicans
together under Jefferson's banner. As Callender wrote, "it is certain
that the citizens of America derive their information almost exclusively
from newspapers."[98]

The émigré newspaper editors represented perhaps 15 to 20 percent
of all Republican printers in this period.[99] Their importance, however,
was greater than their numbers suggest, for at crucial times, espe-

---

[94] Jefferson to Madison, Apr. 26, 1798, in Worthington Chauncey Ford, ed., "Thomas
Jefferson and James Thomson Callender," *New England Historical and Genealogical Regis-
ter*, L (1896), 328n; *Carey's United States' Recorder* (Philadelphia), June 30, 1798; Carter,
"Political Activities of Mathew Carey," 200.

[95] *Recorder* (Rich.), Aug. 25, 1802.

[96] *Carey's U.S. Recorder*, Aug. 30, 1798; Ray Boston, "The Impact of 'Foreign Liars' on
the American Press (1790–1800)," *Journalism Quarterly*, L. (1973), 722–730.

[97] Steward, *Opposition Press of the Federalist Period.*, 13.

[98] *Recorder* (Rich.), Dec. 1, 1802

[99] This is an estimate. Fewer than one-half of the printers in America in the 1790s
were Republicans. If together they edited just under half of the 550 serial publications,
and individually two each, there would have been 18 emigre editors in a total of 110
Republicans.

cially in the years leading to Jefferson's victory in 1800, they controlled some of the country's most widely circulating, strategically placed newspapers. Duane, for example, developed the *Aurora* almost into a national daily; not only did it circulate beyond the borders of Pennsylvania, but many other Republican newspapers reprinted its most important political articles. In North Carolina, the Federalist Abraham Hodge, with four presses and three newspapers, held almost a monopoly of printing until Sen. Nathaniel Macon persuaded Gales to move from Philadelphia in order to establish an opposition newspaper in Raleigh. The first number of Gales's *Register* was printed in October 1799, and within a few months Hodge was forced to shift one of his newspapers from Rayetteville to Raleigh to meet the competition. It was to no avail; Gales soon had a statewide readership. After 1800, for his services to Republicanism, Gales was rewarded with the state government's printing contract.[100]

Meriwether Jones's Richmond *Examiner* had the widest circulation of any Republican newspaper in Virginia. In the crucial months from mid-1799 to early 1801, as a "Scots Correspondent," Callender wrote for it almost one hundred columns of political news and opinion, and the newspaper's circulation rose by nearly 400, an increase of about 40 percent.[101] So much more dangerous did the tone of the newspaper become after Callender's arrival that a group of young Federalists tried, unsuccessfully, to drive him out of town.[102]

Federalists perceived the émigré printers as major threats to their political supremacy. It was no accident that they regarded Duane, Cooper, and Callender as fit candidates for the rigors of the Alien and Sedition acts. If John Adams and Fisher Ames can be believed, Jefferson's election in 1800 was partly the consequence of the émigré newspapermen's concerted campaigns from 1799. In 1801 a distraught Adams lamented, "Is there no pride in American bosoms? Can their hearts endure that Callender, Duane, Cooper and Lyon should be the most influential men in the country, all foreigners and degraded characters?" Ames was equally devastated: "The newspapers are an overmatch for any Government. They will first overawe and then usurp it. This has been done; and the Jacobins owe their triumph to the unceasing use of this engine."[103]

---

[100] Briggs, "Joseph Gales, Editor of Raleigh's First Newspaper," *N.C. Booklet*, VII (1907), 117–118.

[101] *Recorder* (Rich.), May 12, 1802.

[102] *Ibid.*, Feb. 9, 1803.

[103] James Morton Smith, *Freedom's Fetters: The Alien and Sedition Laws and American Civil Liberties* (Ithaca, N.Y., 1956); Brown, "John Adams and the American Press," 272, 258. Brown argues that opposition to Adams from the High Federalist press was as important as Republican propaganda in Jefferson's election (*ibid.*, iv).

Newspapers at that time, as today, were reading material one day, fire lighters the next, effective only if, as was the case from 1799 to 1801, the message was repeatedly hammered home and widely diffused by the copying system, which, according to Ames, was precisely why the Republican press was so effective. Somewhat less ephemeral were the numerous political pamphlets published in the 1790s. Again, émigré radicals were to the fore in disseminating political information, both original and borrowed. In addition to the printers listed in the appendix to this article, at least five other émigrés—Matthew Falkner, John Chambers, Daniel Isaac Eaton, Patrick Byrne, and Thomas Stephens—published and sold books and pamphlets in this period.[104] in 1796 Callender noted a preponderance of émigré booksellers: "take away all the Scots and Irish booksellers from Philadelphia, and [a reader] could hardly supply his library. With three or four exceptions the whole trade centres among foreigners. The case is much the same in New York and Baltimore."[105]

The émigrés had a two-fold publishing strategy: they printed original materials, and they reprinted political pamphlets from overseas. Mathew Carey, for example, who was probably the most prolific publisher and certainly the greatest risk-taker in the publishing world, reprinted Mary Wollstonecraft's *Vindication of the Rights of Women* (1794), Helen Maria Williams's *Letters Containing a Sketch of the Politics of France* (1796), and Condorcet's *Outlines of an Historical View of the Progress of the Human Mind* (1796); "Citizen" Richard Lee reprinted Charles Pigott's *Political Curiosities* (1796); James Carey reprinted the *Trial of Margarot* (1794) and William Godwin's *Memoirs of Mary Wollstonecraft* (1799); and Thomas Stephens republished *The Proceedings of the Society of United Irishmen, of Dublin* (1975), and Volney's *The Law of Nature* (1796).[106] Although the émigrés had no monopoly on Paine's works, they reproduced his writings in a number of ways. Mathew Carey republished both parts of *Rights of Man* in 1796, and his brother James printed a two-volume edition of Paine's works in 1797, which could be bought with or without *The Age of Reason* and with or without Bishop Richard Watson's reply to Paine's deist pamphlets.[107]

---

[104] The major source for the publishers and printers is Charles Evans, *American Bibliography*, vols. 9–13, (Worcester, Mass., 1925–1955). Another emigre, either Alexander Kennedy or his brother James, both of whom fled Scotland in 1794 during the Watt trial, was "a theological bookseller" in Washington in 1830. See Hook, *Scotland and America*, 240; *Edinburgh Evening Courant*, May 29, Aug. 28, Sept. 4, 6, 1794; *Scots Magazine*, Oct. 1794, 627. Another Scottish émigré, Archibald Binny, manufactured most of the type for the printers in Phildelphia, including Mathew Carey. See Silver, *Typefounding in America*, 22.

[105] *Recorder* (Rich.), Apr. 3, 1802.

[106] Evans, *American Bibliography*, nos. 27592, 28122, 28590, 30257, 31010, 31516, 31634.

[107] Ibid., nos. 31174, 32633.

Some also published their own or their fellow émigrés original works. Callender wrote a second part to *The Political Progress of Britain* (1795) and *A Short History of the Excise* (1795)—both of which Mathew Carey reprinted in 1796—as well as an infamous but extraordinarily effective *History of 1796* (1797) and two volumes of *The Prospect before Us* (1800). The "O'Careys," as William Cobbett called them, published numerous squibs and satires in their private war against "Porcupine." Birch and Burk wrote histories of the United Irishmen. Cooper published his *Political Arithmetic* (1798) and *Political Essays* (1799).[108] In addition, the émigrés ensured the wide circulation of important speeches and political opinions. Mathew Carey published A. J. Dallas's *Features of Mr. Jay's Treaty* (1795), *An Address to the House of Representatives on Lord Grenville's Treaty* (1796), and Tench Coxe's *The Federalist* (1796), a defense of Jefferson. Gales printed Albert Gallatin's speech against naval expansion (1799), and Duane, at the height of the debates on the constitutionality of the Alien and Sedition acts, printed George Hay's *Essay on the Liberty of the Press* (1799).[109]

To recite this record is not to diminish the effectiveness or courage of native Republican editors and booksellers in the battle against Federalism. But throughout the 1790s Republican propaganda outlets were far fewer than those available to the Federalists, who where possible gave both state and federal patronage to politically reliable printers. The Republicans therefore needed all the help they could get, and although Callender may have exaggerated when he claimed that "it is [the newspapers'] weakness, or ability, which must decide the fate of every administration,"[110] there can be little doubt that in the propaganda battle against Federalism the radical émigré printers were of more value to the Republicans than their numbers suggest.

In the current debate on republicanism in the 1790s too little attention has been given to the role of the radical émigrés. Banning's failure to recognize their influx into the Republican party in the 1790s enables him to state that the party "was dependent to an important and unrecognized degree on an Americanization of eighteenth-century opposition thought."[111] Appleby, moreover, is only partly correct when she writes that "the particular ideas the Republicans and Federalists thought and fought with came from an English frame of reference, but it was only a frame of reference. They gave the ideas their operative meaning, working within their own situation in the polemics of the early national period."[112] This may have been true for English writers of earlier gen-

---

[108] *Ibid.*, nos. 28381, 28384, 31173, 31174, 31906, 37083, 37084.

[109] *Ibid.*, nos. 28527, 30156, 30293, 30294, 35531, 34605.

[110] *Recorder* (Rich.), Dec. 1, 1802.

[111] Banning, *Jeffersonian Persuasion*, 129.

[112] Appleby, *Capitalism and a New Social Order*, 23.

erations, but it ignores the influence of the emigrants of the 1790s. These radicals brought with them a peculiarly Painite political discourse that combined, without strain, egalitarianism, advocacy of commercial development, and a vision of unlimited progress. The Jeffersonian Republican party eventually stabilized around just such a political economy. This is certainly not to claim that the exiles determined by themselves the direction of Republican discourse; rather, it suggests that they were especially well equipped to promote Republican ideology as it developed in the Federalist decade. Their propagandizing was effective in vulgarizing Republican discourse, making it more suitable for a society that was becoming increasingly politicized and in which popular participation in politics was coming to be taken for granted. They therefore continued Paine's role of demystifying political principles and offering them to the masses.

In addition, their very foreignness helped to consolidate the Republican party, for at least before 1800, they were not burdened with the factionalism that stemmed from earlier political battles. Their perception of America, unfettered by sectional or local interests and fueled by an intense anglophobia, was predicated on a demand for national unity and independence. They instilled this demand, together with other true Painite republican sentiments, into both native-born Americans and fellow immigrants, in the latter through relief-cum-political societies such as the Hibernian Society in Philadelphia and the Friendly Sons of St. Patrick in New York, or through patriotic militia companies such as the Republican Greens.[113]

Thus recent disputes over a Court-Country dichotomy and the emergence of a commercialized republicanism in the 1790s can perhaps be resolved more satisfactorily if it is recognized that there was offered to the American public a prepackaged Painite political economy, stamped "Made in Britain," that sought to destroy Britain's other exports, both manufactured and ideological. If we are fully to appreciate the meaning of Jefferson's success in 1800, and to understand what Republicanism meant in the early national period, we cannot afford to ignore the achievements of the radical émigrés as a major component of the Jeffersonian movement.

---

[113] "Autobiography of Mathew Carey," *N. E. Mag.* (1834), letter 6; *Carey's U.S. Recorder*, May 19, 1798; St. Mark, "Red Shamrock," 147; Carter, "Political Activities of Mathew Carey," 120; Callender, *Prospect before Us*, I, 37.

APPENDIX

Radical Émigré Serial Publications

Editor	Title and Place	Dates
J. Binns	Republican Argus (Northumberland, Pa.)	1802–1807
	Democratic Press (Philadelphia)	1807–1829
J. D. Burk	Daily Advertiser (Boston)	1796
	Polar Star (Boston)	1796–1797
	Time-Piece (New York)	1798
J. T. Callender	Aurora (Philadelphia)	1797–1798
	Examiner (Richmond)	1800–1802
	Recorder (Richmond)	1802–1803
J. Carey	Virginia Gazette (Richmond)	1792
	Star (Charleston)	1793
	Georgia Journal (Savannah)	1793–1794
	Wilmington Chronicle (N. C.)	1795
	Daily Evening Gazette (Charleston)	1795
	Telegraph (Charleston)	1795
	Daily Advertiser (Philadelphia)	1797–1798
	Carey's United States' Recorder (Philadelphia)	1798
	Constitutional Diary (Philadelphia)	1799–1800
M. Carey	Pennsylvania Evening Herald (Philadelphia)	1785–1788
	Complete Counting House Companion (Philadelphia)	1785–1788
	American Museum (Philadelphia)	1787–1792
J. Cheetham	Republican Watchtower (New York)	1800–1801
	American Citizen (New York)	1801–1810
T. Cooper	Sunbury & Northumberland Gazette (Pa.)	1797
R. Davison	Messenger (Warrenton, N. C.)	1802–1809
R. Dinmore	National Magazine	1801–1802
	American Literary Advertiser (Washington, D. C.)	1802–1804
	Alexandria Expositor (Va.)	1802–1807
	Washington Expositor (D. C.)	1807–1809
D. Driscol	Temple of Reason (New York and Philadelphia)	1800–1801
	American Patriot (Baltimore)	1802–1803
	Augusta Chronicle (Ga.)	1804–1811
W. Duane	Merchants' Daily Advertiser (Philadelphia)	1797
	Philadelphia Gazette	1797–1798
	Aurora (Philadelphia)	1798–1829
	Apollo (Washington, D. C.)	1802
J. Gales	Independent Gazetteer (Philadelphia)	1796–1797
	Raleigh Register (N. C.)	1799–1833
R. Lee	American Universal Magazine (Philadelphia)	1796–1797
T. Lloyd	Merchants' Daily Advertiser (Philadelphia)	1797–1798

Radical Émigré Serial Publications (cont.)

J. Miller	*South-Carolina Gazette* (Charleston)	1783–1785
	Back Country Gazette (Pendleton, N. C.)	1795
	Miller's Weekly Messenger	1807
M. J. Rhees	*Western Sky* (Beula, Pa.)	1798
J. M. Williams	*Columbian Gazette* (New York)	1799
	Democrat (Boston)	1804
J. Wood	*Virginia Gazette* (Richmond)	1802–1804
	Western World of Kentucky (Frankfort)	1806
	Atlantic World (Washington, D. C.)	1807
	Petersburg Daily Courier (Va.)	1814

PART FIVE

The Jeffersonian Ascendancy

In American historiography, as in the national memory more broadly, the period from 1801 to 1828 was long imagined as a gray one. A few dramatic incidents aside—the Burr conspiracy, the War of 1812, the bitter battle over the admission of Missouri—it was easy to regard the era as a time of relatively placid economic growth and national expansion, rendered all the more exceptional and unexciting by the ultimate predominance of a single political party. Among historians, there have been many recent signs of a dramatic alteration of this image. Students of American society increasingly insist that fundamental changes were at work beneath the relatively uneventful surface. Political historians have been displaying rising interest in the consequences of this transformation. But although our understanding of these years has greatly changed, they probably remain as little studied as any comparable span in the whole of the national experience.

For the period before the War of 1812, there was a second reason why historians were long inclined to turn their interests elsewhere: the nine imposing volumes of Henry Adams's *History of the United States during the Administrations of Thomas Jefferson and James Madison* (New York: Charles Scribner's Sons, 1889–1891). Adams was a careful scholar and a brilliant writer. The *History* was one of the magnificent achievements of the art. Given the prevailing image of the era, few were tempted to encroach on Adams' terrain until the great expansion of the historical profession after the Second World War. When they did, they found that Adams cast as long a shadow as did Beard.

Several stubborn images have haunted modern studies of the Jeffersonian administrations. Two of them can certainly be traced to Henry Adams. First, Adams sketched the Federalists in their declining years as a persistent band of grumpy, ineffective diehards who eventually produced—and got their just comeuppance from—the sectional resistance and disloyalty that culminated in the Hartford Convention. Second, this descendent of the second president portrayed the Jeffersonians as a pragmatic party dominated by a group of Southern hypocrites who courted popularity by making some cosmetic changes in the Hamilto-

339

nian domestic system and pursuing foreign policies so cheap and ineffective that they led the nation to the brink of a catastrophe in 1812. Both
of these persistent images were solidly embedded in the literature from
which more recent scholarship has taken its departure. Also much at
work was our habitual preoccupation with the presidency itself, which
accounted in particular for the neglect of the administrations of Monroe
and John Quincy Adams. Not only was it easy to assume that years
of uninspiring presidents and single-party rule could be regarded as an
interlude between two more exciting eras; it also was natural to believe
that, after the conclusion of the war, the feeble central government had
left the nation dangerously adrift.

Among the most exciting publications of the middle 1960s, one
important study strongly reinforced this final image, which itself was
not unknown to Adams. In *The Washington Community, 1800–1828* (New
York: Columbia University Press, 1966), the political scientist James
Sterling Young set out to analyze the national leaders as a social group.
He found that the informal structure of the governing community at
Washington had amplified the sharp division of national rulers into
separate, rival groups, which was intended by the framers of the Constitution and the planners of the federal city. Separate social systems
formed around the physically divided branches of the federal government, and fragmentation was increased again by separate subsystems
centered on the rival salons of competing cabinet members and the
boardinghouses where the congressmen resided. Votes in Congress,
Young maintained, were closely correlated with the boardinghouse
affiliations of its members. The pervasive antipower attitudes of rulers
rationalized a structure in which dominance was usually denied to any
group or person; and parties proved too incohesive, even during times
of greatest stress, for party loyalty to offer an effective bond. Isolated
in the swamps on the Potomac, out of sight and out of mind of the
majority of voters, neither congressmen nor presidents were able to
provide effective guidance. After Thomas Jefferson, who often managed to transcend the fragmentation, presidents were gradually reduced
to figureheads, and the Republicans degenerated into warring factions
that were equally incapable of ruling. The result, Young argued, was
an unacknowledged crisis of profound importance. If the situation had
not changed as a result of the Jacksonian revolution, which ended popular indifference and put the force of popular opinion solidly behind a
vigorous executive, the government could not have won the Civil War.

I have found no practicable way to offer a selection from *The
Washington Community* and thus have not reprinted any of its critics.
Powerful rebuttals have been published. For example, Noble E.
Cunningham's *The Process of Government under Jefferson* (Princeton:
Princeton University Press, 1978), a highly detailed study of the way

the federal government was run, challenges Young's argument at every point. Insisting that the congressmen maintained close contacts with the voters and that national representatives selected boardinghouses on the basis of their sectional and partisan affiliations, Cunningham presents strong evidence that Jefferson's administration was very much a party operation. Young himself, however, had admitted that the first Republican administration offered some significant exceptions to his rules, and there are no equivalents to Cunningham's critique for the succeeding Jeffersonian administrations. Thus, the image powerfully presented in *The Washington Community*, together with the legacy of Henry Adams, constitutes essential background for the selections in this section, all of which are concerned with the extent of party conflict and the force of party loyalty between the victory of 1800 and the declaration of the War of 1812.

The Democratization
of American Politics

David Hackett Fischer

No one played a more important part in challenging the old impression of the Federalists—and, with it, of the Jeffersonian ascendancy itself—than David Hackett Fischer. Hindsight frequently misleads. Knowing that the Federalists were absolutely crushed in 1804 and that they never won another national election, it is easy to assume that party rivalry and party loyalties were of decreasing interest after 1801 as Federalists retreated grumblingly toward the extinction that awaited them soon after the conclusion of the War of 1812. Not surprisingly, political historians had tended to neglect these years and turn their interests toward the 1790s or the much more evident excitement of the Age of Jackson. In doing so, said Fischer, they had missed a major watershed in popular participation and even in the way that most American conservatives would henceforth play the democratic game. This selection, lightly edited and given a descriptive title, is the general introduction to The Revolution of American Conservatism: The Federalist Party in the Era of Jeffersonian Democracy *(New York: Harper and Row, 1965). Copyright ©1965 by David Hackett Fischer. Reprinted by permission of Harper and Row, Publishers, Inc.*

In the year 1810, two elderly American gentlemen reflected sadly upon what they took to be the ruins of a republic. "The times are really altered, [compared] to what they were thirty years ago," David Sewall wrote to Robert Treat Paine. "The Patriotism and genuine American spirit which then glowed is greatly depreciated, and seems degenerated into selfishness and democracy." Paine replied sympathetically, "The times are *really* altered, and that spirit which once was so successfully exerted to procure and protect the substantial liberty and happiness of the country . . . has unhappily taken the course you have described."[1]

I

No major problem in American history is more difficult to discuss reasonably—and is more in need of reasonable discussion—than the

---

[1] David Sewall to Robert Treat Paine, 27 July 1810; Paine to Sewall, 17 Aug. 1810, Robert Treat Paine Papers, Mass. Hist. Soc.; punctuation is modified throughout.

expansion of political democracy. A profusion of interpretations and a paucity of facts have together bred bewilderment and despair among serious students of the problem. Confusion is compounded, of course, by conceptual conflict. An outspoken colonial historian has argued that America was a "middle-class democracy" long before the Revolution. An eccentric politician insists that American has never been a democracy, and hopes that we shall never become one. Clearly, they are not discussing the same thing.[2]

Democracy as an ideal, as a philosophical conception, does not admit of easy explication. But the process of political democratization may be specified more simply as the expansion of voter participation within an increasingly open and free electoral process. To say this is to specify but two variables of many, but it will serve as a working definition for the purposes of this investigation.

The process of democratization has been continuous in American political history; scholars have observed and described it in every period. But it is surely true that more significant changes have occurred in some periods than in others, and that the process, though continuous, has not been constant. To examine a part of the problem is difficult because there are few fixed reference points. But perhaps it is possible to begin by agreeing upon two generalized assumptions which, though not supported by a consensus of expert opinion, would appear to be sustained by a majority (the majoritarian idea, it seems, has even invaded the academy).

The first rests upon a cluster of revisionist studies of the Jacksonian era, which conclude that the process of democratization was far advanced before Jackson reached the White House, before Tocqueville crossed the coast. "Political democracy," Marvin Meyers has written, "was the medium more than the achievement of the Jacksonian party," a precondition more than a consequence of the election of 1828. The expansive ideals of equality and liberty would, of course, continue to ramify in new and surprising ways after 1828, but by that date they had already wrought radical changes in the structure of American politics. Richard P. McCormick and J.R. Pole have recently buttressed this assumption with voting statistics.[3]

---

[2] Robert E. Brown, *Middle-Class Democracy and the Revolution in Massachusetts, 1691–1780.* (Ithaca, 1955), pp. v–viii, 401–408; Barry Goldwater, *The Conscience of a Conservative* (N.Y., 1960), pp.15–24.

[3] Marvin Meyers, *The Jacksonian Persuasion, Politics and Belief* (Stanford, 1957), p.4; Richard P. McCormick, "New Perspectives on Jacksonian Politics," *American Historical Review*, LXV (1960), 288–301; J.R. Pole, "Suffrage and Representation in Massachusetts; A Statistical Note," *William and Mary Quarterly*, 3d. ser., XIV (1957), 560; XV (1958), 412–426; "Suffrage and Representation in New Jersey, 1774 to 1844," *New Jersey Historical Society Proceedings*, LXXI (1953), 38; "Election Statistics in Pennsylvania, 1790–1840," *Pennsylvania Magazine of History and Biography*, LXXXII (1958), 217; "Constitutional Reform and Elec-

A second generalized assumption concerns the structure of American politics before 1800. Bernard Bailyn has given it intelligent expression: "Nowhere in the eighteenth-century America was there 'democracy'—middle-class or otherwise, as we use the term." The political role of the people was effectively limited, not by property qualifications for voting and officeholding, but by the much greater weight of habit and custom. "In stable governments," Fisher Ames observed, "usages become laws. Things wear a certain channel for themselves."[4] It would appear to have been thus in colonial America. A few prominent families, possessed of wealth and distinctions, monopolized offices and power in every colony.

The politics of New Hampshire were dominated during the eighteenth century by a single family, the Wentworths. In Boston, great power lay in the hands of Hutchinsons, Sewalls, Wheelwrights, and Olivers; other Massachusetts towns were controlled in similar fashion by a few families whose names regularly recur upon the lists of officeholders. In Connecticut there was an ascendancy of Allyns, Huntingtons, Pitkins, Stanleys, and Walcotts; a recent study of the structure of power in a single town, Kent, has shown the "top offices were filled by a small group or clique of the town's wealthiest men." Even in Rhode Island where, as John Adams wrote, "there has been no Clergy, no Church, and I had almost said no State, and some People say no religion, there has been a constant respect for certain old Families."[5]

The elitist pattern of politics and society in eighteenth-century New England was even more apparent in the middle and southern colonies. New York, before the War for Independence, was largely governed by Bayards and De Lanceys, Heathcotes, Johnsons, Livingstons, Coldens, Morrises, Nicollses, Pells, Philipses, Rapaljes, Remsens, Schuylers,

---

tion Statistics in Maryland, 1790–1812," *Maryland Historical Magazine*, LV (1955), 275–292; "Representation and Authority in Virginia from the Revolution to Reform," *Journal of Southern History*, XXIV (1958), 16–50; "Election Statistics in North Carolina to 1861," *ibid.*, 225–228.

[4] Bernard Bailyn, "Political Experience and Enlightenment Ideas in Eighteenth Century America," *Amer. Hist. Rev.*, LXVII (1962), 339–351, esp. 346; J.R. Pole, "Historians and the Problem of Early American Democracy," *ibid.*, LXVII (1962), 626–646; Fisher Ames to Josiah Quincy, Jan. 20, 1806, in Ames, *Works*, I, 349.

[5] Leonard W. Labaree, *Conservatism in Early American History*, 2d. edn. (Ithaca, 1959), pp. 1–31; see also Benjamin W. Labaree, *Patriots and Partisans, The Merchants of Newburyport, 1764–1815*, (Cambridge, 1962), p. 15; Robert J. Taylor, *Western Massachusetts in the Revolution* (Providence, 1954), pp. 11–26; and John Cary, "Statistical Method and the Brown Thesis on Colonial Democracy," *William and Mary Quarterly*, XX (1963), 250–264; Charles S. Grant, *Democracy in the Connecticut Frontier-Town of Kent* (New York, 1961), p. 152; Oscar Zeichner, *Connecticut's Years of Controversy, 1750–1776* (Chapel Hill, 1949), pp. 3–19; John Adams to Thomas Jefferson, Nov. 15, 1813, *Adams-Jefferson Letters*, ed. Cappon, II, 400; David S. Lovejoy, *Rhode Island Politics and the American Revolution, 1760–1776* (Providence, 1958), pp. 5–31.

Smiths, Stuyvesants, Van Cortlandts and Van Rensselaers. The predominant families of proprietary Pennsylvania were Penns, Allens, Assetons, Fishbournes, Hamiltons, Hills, Lloyds, Logans, Norrises and Pembertons; of Maryland, Bordleys, Calverts, Carrolls, Darnalls, Dulanys, Lloyds, Ogles and Taskers. Similar lists could be recited for Virginia, the Carolinas, and Georgia.[6]

The industrious researches of Robert Brown have conclusively established the important point that the political power of the colonial elite did not derive from economic restrictions upon the exercise of voting. Brown has shown that the suffrage was open, in Massachusetts, to most adult white males; and it may be granted, in Bailyn's words, that "what has been proved about the franchise in early Massachusetts—that it was open for practically the entire adult male population—can be proved to a lesser or greater extent for all the colonies." It is also true, of course, that many members of the ruling elites were parvenu, that their wealth was often new wealth. Both popular participation and social mobility were far more extensive in colonial America than in the mother country, or in any other eighteenth-century state.[7]

Nevertheless, Bagehot's phrase for nineteenth-century England, a "deferential society," would appear to describe eighteenth-century America. Men were trained from childhood to show deference to their betters, and to expect it from their inferiors. The "habit of subordination," as a Federalist later labeled it, served to cement a functional society more effectively than legislative restraints or constitutional restrictions. The dropping of a curtsy, the doffing of a cap, the raising of a deferential finger to the brow—these were the superficial symbols of a spirit which ran deep and strong in the minds and hearts of men. A fundamental distinction between the "multitude" and the "people of the better sort" expressed itself in manners, speech, and modes of dress. A nineteenth-century historian of Portsmouth, New Hampshire, recalled "earlier times, when scarlet colored broadcloth cloaks, worn by our *Warners*,

---

[6] Charles S. Sydnor, *Gentlemen Freeholders*, pp. 60–77; Jack P. Greene, *The Quest for Power* (Chapel Hill, 1963), pp. 11, *passim*; Roy Smith, *South Carolina as a Royal Province, 1719–1776* (New York, 1903), p. 87; Frederick B. Tolles, *Meeting House and Counting House* (Chapel Hill, 1948), pp. 109–143; Labaree, *Conservatism in Early American History*, pp. 1–32. The work of an older generation of historians is still useful and relevant here; see esp. Carl Lotus Becker, *History of Political Parties in the Province of New York, 1760–1776 (Madison, 1909; 2d. edn. 1960), ch. I.* Becker's conclusions on local conventions have been challenged by Luetscher; and his assumption of a restricted suffrage is open to question. But his work has permanent value for its description of social patterns and political structure.

[7] Bailyn, "Political Experience and Enlightenment Ideas," p. 346; Brown, *Middle-Class Democracy and the Revolution in Mass.*, *passim*. Robert and Katherine Brown, *Virginia, 1705–1786; Aristocracy or Democracy?* (East Lansing; 1964), *passim*.

Jaffreys, Cutts and other gentlemen of the old school of politeness, good order and decorum, warned the boys of *severe reprehension,* if not *rods* which awaited them for any neglect of respectful recognition of the approach of these august personages, by the *low bow,* or *doffed hat,* or both."[8]

The "habit of subordination" also expressed itself in the low level of voter participation in colonial elections. Despite competition between individual candidates or between rival "connexions," which often took place in an unsystematic fashion, the deferential spirit resulted in desultory attendance at the polls, and the "best people" with only occasional difficulty managed the affairs of their communities.[9]

If these assumptions about the Jacksonian era and the colonial period are correct, then it follows that between 1760 and 1820 two major changes occurred in the structure of American politics. Many more people exercised their electoral privileges. They did so within an increasingly open and free electoral process. With these hypotheses in mind, I examined the voting statistics compiled by McCormick and Pole. The work of both scholars shows that a sudden expansion of popular participation did in fact take place within a very narrow time span—the sixteen-year period from 1800 to 1816. Before 1795, participation appears to have ranged between 15 and 40 percent of adult males in nearly all states, with no clear upward tendencies. From 1796 to 1799, a slow but significant rise was perceptible, especially in the middle states. In 1800 there appears to have been a sudden jump, followed in the next few years by a falling off. But from 1804 to 1816, in a majority of states, an extraordinary surge carried voter participation in state elections to unprecedented heights—68 to 98 percent of adult males. This level has been maintained ever since, with many fluctuations, of which the most important was a falling off in the period 1824–1840, the Age of Jackson![10]

In a few states voting qualifications were eased within the period 1800–1816, but in most states they were not. The revision of suffrage

---

[8] Charles Brewster, *Rambles About Portsmouth,* 2 vols. (Portsmouth, 1869), II, 117.

[9] Brown concedes that voter participation was generally low in the colonial era. See *Middle-Class Democracy and the Revolution in Massachusetts,* pp. 51–52, 397 (the turnout in Boston in 1763, a peak figure, was low in percentage of adult males); and see Brown and Brown, *Virginia 1705–1786; Democracy or Aristocracy?,* pp. 146, 163.

[10] See statistics of McCormick and Pole, summarized in ch. IX below (Tables XXII, XXIV, XXV, pp. 370, 373–374). It will be noted that the expansion of popular participation is apparent in state elections. The Jacksonian era may have been a period of expanded voter participation in presidential contests, but not in the electoral process. A minor premise of this investigation is that more significant things were happening to the structure of American politics on the local than on the national level—more significant because the people were more interested in local affairs. Evidence appears not only in voting statistics but also in impressionist statements of contemporary observers. See, e.g., Israel Pickens to William Lenoir, Jan. 29, 1816, in the Lenoir Papers, Southern Hist. Coll., Univ. of N.C.

requirements followed, rather than preceded, the expansion of voter participation. An explanation must be found elsewhere.

The principal issues of the period, the embargoes and the War of 1812, were of course bitterly controversial, but intrinsically no more interesting than the imperial questions of the 1760s and early 1770s, or the constitutional issues of the late 1770s and 1780s, or the pressing problems of the 1790s. Why did the explosive expansion of participation come when it did? Two alternative hypotheses come to mind. First, the Jeffersonian movement might have been solely responsible for quickening popular interest in political questions, and for the expansion of the democratic principle. Seymour Lipset has summarized this possible interpretation in a sentence: "The almost unchallenged rule of the Virginia Dynasty and the Democratic-Republican Party served to legitimate national authority and democratic rights."[11] A second hypothesis would be that organized party rivalry gained a new intensity in the period 1800–1816—a two-party rivalry more competitive than ever before; and that the central and transcendent fact of competition served to stimulate an expansion of popular participation.

Standard works on the Jeffersonian era (there are remarkably few of them) tend to support the first hypothesis. They do not generally indicate that party competition was unusually keen in the period 1804–1816; indeed, most suggest the opposite, arguing that the Federalist Party was moribund after 1804, unresponsive to the Jeffersonian movement, unyielding in its stubborn conservatism, unwilling and unable to compete for popular support.[12]

---

[11] Seymour Martin Lipset, *The First New Nation* (New York, 1963), p.45.

[12] The origins of this interpretation are to be found partly in the earliest histories of the Federal Party by descendants of Federalist leaders, who emphasized what appeared to them to be the most admirable features of that political group—its honest and independent leaders who remained stubbornly loyal to their own ideals in defiance of popular opinion. There were such Federalists as these, but as a generalized view of the Federal Party it is not merely inaccurate but in the case of Dwight and Sullivan positively deceitful. It has contributed to present misunderstandings. See Theodore Dwight, *History of the Hartford Convention* (New York, 1833); William Sullivan, *Familiar Letters on Public Characters and Public Events* (Boston, 1834); Henry Cabot Lodge, *Life and Letters of George Cabot* (Boston, 1877); Charles R. King, *The Life and Correspondence of Rufus King*, 6 vols. (New York, 1894–1900); Edmund Quincy, *Life of Josiah Quincy* (Boston, 1867); Theophilus Parsons, Jr., *Memoir of Theophilus Parsons* (Boston, 1859); Octavius Pickering and C.W. Upham, *The Life of Timothy Pickering* 4 vols. (Boston, 1867–1873); William Plumer, Jr., *Life of William Plumer* (Boston, 1856); Simeon E. Baldwin, *Life and Letters of Simeon Baldwin* (New Haven, n.d.); Thomas Wentworth Higginson, *Life of Stephen Higginson (Boston, 1907)*; Richard Hildreth, *The History of the United States*, 6 vols. (New York, 1849–1856). The standard view has also developed from another tradition of filiopietism, the accumulated antipathies of the Adams family, which culminated in Henry Adams' magnificent *History of the United States*, 9 vols. (New York, 1889–1891). I have discussed this work at greater length in "The Myth of the Essex Junto," William and Mary Quarterly, 3d. ser., XXI (1964), 191–235.

2

Historians have not been attentive to the men who called themselves Federalists in the age of Jefferson. The prevailing interpretation calls to mind the Scottish poet's satirical strictures upon another great party in adversity:

> Awa, Whigs, awa!
>   Awa, Whigs, awa!
> Ye're but a pack o' traitor louns,
>   Ye'll do nae good at a'.
> Our thrissles flourish'd fresh and fair,
>   And Bonnie bloom'd our roses;
> But Whigs cam' like a frost in June,
>   And wither'd a' our posies.

Even John Bach McMaster, who openly admitted that one of the purposes of his history was to "show up" Thomas Jefferson, dismissed the Federalists after 1800 as "mere obstructionists, a sect of the political world which, of all other sects, is most to be despised." And Albert J. Beveridge, whose admiration for one Federalist, John Marshall, is well known, had little sympathy for Marshall's political friends. The Federal Party after 1800 was, in his judgment, "reduced to a grumbling company of out of date gentlemen...They had repudiated democracy, and assumed an attitude of insolent superiority, mournful of a glorious past, despairing of a worthy future."[13]

---

[13] John Bach McMaster, *A History of the People of the United States*, 9 vols. (New York, 1883–1927), II, 629; his view of Jefferson is quoted in Eric Goldman, *John Bach McMaster, American Historian* (Philadelphia, 1943), p. 123; A.J. Beveridge, *Life of John Marshall*, 4 vols. (Boston, 1916–1919), III, 256–257; IV, 6; see also James Schouler, *History of the United States under the Constitution*, 6 vols. (New York, 1881–1899), II, 430; Vernon Louis Parrington, *Main Currents in American Thought*, Harvest Books ed., 2 vols. (New York, 1927), II, 271; Claude G. Bowers, *Jefferson in Power: the Death Struggle of the Federalists* (Boston, 1936), p. 487; Henry Adams, *History of the United States*, 9 vols. (New York, 1889–1891), I, 88; Edward Channing, *A History of the United States*, 6 vols. (New York, 1905–1925), IV, 164. A Jeffersonian historian, Claude G. Bowers, began his study of Jefferson's administration with the astonishing statement that "anti-Jeffersonian historians have been much too tender with the Federalists in their days of degeneracy and treason." Mr. Bowers announced that he would set the record straight. He offered an account of the "death struggle of this once great party" as "a warning to all succeeding political parties and politicians that public opinion cannot be defied with impunity" (Bowers, pp. v–vii). For a Madisonian variant of the Jeffersonian theme see Irving Brant, *James Madison*, 6 vols. (Indianapolis, 1941–1961). Although Brant bitterly assails Henry Adams's cavalier treatment of Madison, he merely accepts Adams's interpretation of the Federalists after 1800. The economic interpretation of Charles Beard and the frontier thesis of Frederick Jackson Turner harmonized readily with this interpretation. John D. Barnhart, *Valley of Democracy; The Frontier versus the Plantation in the Ohio Valley, 1775–1818*, (Bloomington, 1953), pp. 159, 174; Homer C. Hockett, "Federalism and the West," *Essays in American History dedicated to Frederick Jackson Turner* (New York, 1910), p. 114; and "Western Influences on Political Parties to 1825," *Ohio State University Studies*, IV (1916).

Students of parties and political machinery have generally concluded that the Federalists disdained formal political organization and competition in the Jeffersonian era. George D. Luetscher, in an able and important monograph on early American politics, suggested that the Federalists were destroyed because they refused to develop an organization and to compete actively with the Jeffersonians. He contended that his rule was proved by one exception, Delaware, where Federalists did develop effective party machinery, competed energetically, and managed to retain power throughout the Jeffersonian era.[14]

There are a few exceptional works—a splendid study of Delaware politics by John A. Munroe, an excellent biography of William Plumer, and an important and provocative monograph on New York politics by Dixon Ryan Fox. But the great majority of studies of the Jeffersonian era are, understandably, centered upon the Jeffersonians. The standard interpretation of the Federalists remains unchanged from Henry Adams to the most recent surveys of the period.[15]

---

[14] George D. Luetscher, *Early Political Machinery in the United States* (Philadelphia, 1903), pp. 102–103, 150–151. Luetshcer's thesis reappears, slightly modified, in J.R. Pole, "Jeffersonian Democracy and the Federalist Dilemma in New Jersey, 1798–1812," *Proceedings of the New Jersey Hist. Soc.*, LXXIV (1956),292.

[15] John A. Munroe, *Federalist Delaware, 1775–1815* (New Brunswick, 1954); Lynn W. Turner, *William Plumer* (Chapel Hill, 1962); Dixon Ryan Fox, *The Decline of Aristocracy in the Politics of New York* (New York, 1919); Paul Goodman, *The Democratic-Republicans of Massachusetts* (Cambridge, 1964). In at least two instances, fine Jeffersonian-centered studies have accurately and suggestively appraised the activity of their opponents. See Noble Cunningham, *The Jeffersonian Republicans in Power* (Chapel Hill, 1963) and Sanford Higginbotham, *The Keystone in the Democratic Arch: Pennsylvania Politics, 1800–1816* (Harrisburg, 1952). Other Jefferson-centered studies include James Truslow Adams, *New England in the Republic* (Boston, 1926); Chilton Williamson, *Vermont in Quandary: 1763–1825* (Montpelier, 1949); William A. Robinson, *Jeffersonian Democracy in New England* (New Haven, 1916); Walter R. Fee, *The Transition from Aristocracy to Democracy in New Jersey* (Somerville, 1933); Charles Henry Ambler, *Sectionalism in Virginia from 1776 to 1861* (Chicago, 1910); Joseph I. Shulim, *The Old Dominion and Napoleon Bonaparte* (New York, 1952); Delbert H. Gilpatrick, *Jeffersonian Democracy in North Carolina, 1789–1816* (New York, 1931); John Harold Wolfe, *Jeffersonian Democracy in South Carolina* (Chapel Hill, 1940); Ulrich B. Phillips, "Georgia and State Rights," in *American Historical Association Report*, 1901, II; William T. Utter, *The Frontier State, 1803–1825*, vol. II in *The History of the State of Ohio*, ed. C.F. Wittke, (Columbus, 1942). There are two useful biographies of latter-day Federalists, Samuel Eliot Morison, *Life and letters of Harrison Gray Otis*, 2 vols. (Boston, 1913),which is discussed in my "Myth of the Essex Junto," and Morton Borden's *The Federalism of James Bayard* (New York, 1955). Both defend one Federalist while dismissing the rest in traditional fashion. Morison's work, however contains one chapter, "The Federalist Machine," which is very helpful for present purposes. For the most recent statements of the standard view see Shaw Livermore, *The Twilight of Federalism* (Princeton, 1962), pp. 6–9, 28–30; William Chambers, *Political Parties in a New Nation* (New York,1963), pp. 183 *passim*; and Lipset, *The First New Nation*, p.45. These are all works of high importance; the behavior of Federalists in the period 1800–1814 is central to none of them. Mr. Lipset's sociological insights have been very helpful in many ways; Mr. Chambers' reformulation of the role of parties in the republic—as artifacts essential to the operation of the government—was very useful; and

3

The following account is frankly revisionist. Its purpose is to suggest that a younger generation of Federalists—the most obscure leaders of a major party in American political history—responded to the Jeffersonian movement with energy, flexibility and effect. It will be argued that they deliberately tried to create popularly oriented vote-seeking political organizations which might defeat Jefferson with his own weapons. The younger Federalists successfully established these party organizations in at least ten states. They sponsored partisan newspapers and secret political societies on an unprecedented scale, and borrowed Jeffersonian electioneering techniques, rhetoric, and issues for their own elitist purposes.

The young Federalists were, of course, conspicuously unsuccessful in their effort to recover power from their opponents. They never overcame the heavy handicap of a late start, after their adversaries were well organized, after their adversaries' principles and prejudices had been widely disseminated, after Federalism itself had become a byword for repression and antirepublican ideas, a synonym for privilege and political depravity. Young Federalists were hindered by older colleagues who refused to cooperate, and even opposed any effort to borrow Jeffersonian techniques. Jeffersonians themselves proved to be extraordinarily resourceful as the rivalry became more intense. And finally, after fourteen years of slow political starvation, the chance coincidence of events at Hartford, Ghent, and New Orleans came as a crushing blow to the frail structure of the Federalist cause.

But if the young Federalists were unsuccessful in their own particular purposes, their partisan activity remains doubly significant. Firstly, by offering close competition to the Jeffersonians in a contest for popular favor, they helped to stimulate an increase in popular interest in

---

Mr. Livermore's discussion of the Federalists after their party fell apart was often suggestive. All three works relied primarily upon secondary sources in the period 1800–1814; their restatements of the standard view are evidence of the consensual support which it has attracted. Less helpful in this context is Mr. Louis Hartz' brilliantly intuitive single-factor synthesis of American history. The Federalists, he suggests, were not aristocrats but whiggish liberals who misunderstood their own society. The Federalists, he writes, "deserve all of the criticism they have received, but not for the reason they have received it. Their crime was not villainy but stupidity, and perhaps in politics a man ought to know that if he is guilty of the second, he is going to be charged with the first. What is remarkable is how long the American Whigs [and Federalists] managed to endure the strange abuse of a liberal community without waking up to the logic behind it. Here they were in a setting where the democracy was closer to them than anywhere else in the West, and yet instead of embracing it they feared it and fought it" (*The Liberal Tradition in America* [New York, 1955]), p. 101. As I hope to demonstrate, Mr. Hartz has misread the political ideals of the older Federalists and mistaken the political behavior of their younger colleagues.

politics. The fact of intensive party rivalry would explain, better than any other, the extraordinary surge of voter participation in the Jeffersonian era and other important changes which will be discussed in chapter IX.

Secondly, the political ethics and behavior of younger Federalists contrast in striking ways with the conduct of older colleagues who had grown to maturity in a different political environment. The juxtaposition of two generations of Federalist leaders is itself an important measure of change in the structure of society and politics during the New Republic.

*****

A Journey to Laputa

Linda K. Kerber

Fischer emphasized the imitation by the younger Federalists of Jeffersonian techniques for organizing voters and even for appealing to the democratic values of the people. The younger Federalists, he seemed to say, were hardly less elitist in their instincts than the generation they replaced, but the imperatives of democratic politics were such that the appeals of the competing parties sounded more and more alike. Later writers have been more inclined to stress the gulf between the Federalist and Jeffersonian perspectives. Like Fischer, they decidedly reject the old idea that Federalists were ineffective and reactionary plotters, but they attribute both the underlying commonalities between the parties and the sharpness of their clash to the complexities inherent in the Revolutionary vision. Many of these themes are evident in Kerber's Federalists in Dissent: Imagery and Ideology in Jeffersonian America *(Ithaca, N.Y.: Cornell University Press, 1970). This selection joins a portion of the preface (pp. vii–xi) with much of chapter 1 (pp. 1, 4–5, 8–22). Copyright ©1970, 1980 by Cornell University. Used by permission of the publisher, Cornell University Press.*

The Federalist image in American memory is a strange one. In a mere twenty years, from 1789 to 1809, the Federalists as a group are assumed to have reversed character; once representing statesmanship of the highest order and originality, they deteriorated, it seems, into a pack of quarreling, ill-tempered curmudgeons, the poorest losers in American history.

The sources of this changing image are multiple, and so familiar that it is necessary only to list them here. The most obvious source is the opposition, to whom the Federalists were a group of Anglophile monarchists unworthy of trust or even courtesy. . . . Furthermore, Federalist leaders were unlucky enough to quarrel and ultimately to sever relations with President John Adams. Adams, understandably, could never forgive them; neither could his son, John Quincy Adams, nor his greatgrandson, Henry Adams. The latter's volumes on the Jefferson and Madison administrations deservedly remain classics of American historical literature, but they should not be read as nonpartisan evaluation.

Finally, the Federalists have been maligned by historians who, intent on demonstrating a Jefferson–Jackson–Franklin D. Roosevelt continuity, are unable to see Jefferson's opponents as anything but mean-spirited enemies of the republic. This view can pervade the work of otherwise careful and judicious historians; Charles Grove Haines, for example, in his magisterial volume *The Role of the Supreme Court in American Government and Politics,* can speak of a "Federalist Regime" as opposed to the "Republican administrations."

More recent historical investigations have made these assessments less tenable. Thanks to the work of historians such as Shaw Livermore and Lee Benson, we are no longer so certain of a Democratic Party continuum stretching from Jefferson to Roosevelt. Leonard Levy has forced us to approach Jefferson with a willingness to acknowledge his errors as well as his wisdom, and David H. Fischer has shown that "disintegration" is neither accurate nor sufficient to describe what happened to the Federalist Party after Jefferson took office. It begins to seem possible, at least, that intelligent men of good will might have found Jeffersonian politics distasteful.

* * * * *

The opening decade of the nineteenth century was not a placid time; social changes in the post-revolutionary era created tremendous intellectual pressures from which few were insulated. The novelty of the American political experiment and the myriad problems arising from the wars of the French Revolution are only the most obvious sources of American uncertainty and concern. A social transformation, the extent of which we are only beginning to appreciate, and which was, to many, as unexpected as it was unwelcome, seems to have been experienced by the post-revolutionary generation. Americans had from the earliest days regarded their experiment as a "City upon a Hill," as an attempt, that is, to build in the new world an exemplary civilization. The proof that such a society had been built would be found, it was thought, in certain measurable accomplishments—in the obvious ones of financial stability and commercial prosperity, and in the more subtle ones of political order, cultural sophistication, and literary and scientific achievement. How fully the revolutionary generation had succeeded in any of these accomplishments was, it turned out, debatable—not only because subjective assessments necessarily vary, but because the very terms of the debate, the definitions of the desirable political and economic order, and of the proper features of scientific inquiry and literary creativity, kept changing.

The revolutionary generation had left an ambiguous legacy. It had warned Americans against organized political parties and created an embryonic two-party system; it had endorsed popular participation in government because it expected that the citizenry would continue to accept the leadership of an educated and generally conservative elite; it had defined cultural accomplishment in the traditional terms of the study of theology, the classics, and certain experimental sciences.

Was the new nation, with its tensely mobile "middling classes," its laboring groups growing in number and in skill, its bickering party organizations, its remodeled curricula which replaced classical studies with modern languages and vocationally practical information, precisely the new society of which its founders had dreamed? Obviously not, and since it was not, what was left to justify the psychic sacrifice of the Revolution?

The answers to this last question varied, and the patterns of response are far more numerous than might be suspected from the simple distinction, so common to our historiography of a generation ago, between Jeffersonians who endorsed progressive change and Federalists who resisted it. Within each party there were many varieties of political response, from the Old Republicans on the right of the Jeffersonian spectrum to the Young Federalists on the left of the opposition, and the politics of the early republic cannot wholly be understood without a scrupulous analysis of all these factions.

* * * * *

[Many] Federalists, contemplating the American scene at the opening of the nineteenth century, concluded that an ordered world was disintegrating, and that this disintegration was encouraged by an organized group of men who joined opposition to the politics of George Washington with a skepticism of established patterns of inquiry in the arts and sciences, and a guile which enabled them to weaken the cultural fabric of the republic while purporting to strengthen it. In the heat of partisan debate, awareness of contradiction easily led to accusations of hypocrisy. Prevarication and hypocrisy seemed in fact to permeate a number of Republican concerns. Southern Republicans claimed to defend the rights of man while retaining the power of life and death over their own slaves; Republicans expressed scorn for the established educational curricula and at the same time expounded the glories of an educated citizenry; furthermore they welcomed with joy the acquisition of Louisiana, which was essentially unconstitutional.

* * * * *

"I know of only two occasions," Alfred North Whitehead once remarked, "when the people in power did what needed to be done about as well as you can imagine its being possible."[1] One of these occasions Whitehead identified as the reign of Caesar Augustus; the other, the era of the framing of the American Constitution. The parallel was not unsuspected by the contemporaries and immediate descendants of the Founding Fathers; repeatedly they made clear a determination that their America be as significant as Augustan Rome: as successful in the development of political power, in the building of an empire, in the construction of a civilization.

* * * * *

The distinction between Federalist and Jeffersonian in the latter part of the early national period is as much cultural as it is political, if not more so. When Jeffersonians found that the revolution had not produced the golden age they had so confidently expected, they redefined the terms of the golden age. The Federalists tended to be men who maintained faith with the dream—and with their disappointment. Continued consciousness of disappointment makes men bitter, and the Federalists of Jefferson's time were bitter men. *Not* merely because they had lost office, patronage, and power in the election of 1800, but because America appeared to be developing a civilization which they did not understand and of which they certainly did not approve. The more they clung to their definition of what a proper Augustan age would be, the less likely it seemed that America was going to have one....Washington had embodied the American ideal. That no one took up his role, that his public style was not satisfactorily imitated, that partisan papers began to denounce him, was taken as a rejection of the neoclassic goals which Washington was assumed to have represented. For those who felt this way, attacks on Washington were not merely attacks on a man and his party, but on a whole set of cultural expectations.

* * * * *

The Roman model had come naturally to Washington, as it came to many of his contemporaries. To extend one's schooling beyond the three R's meant, in the early national period, to study the classics, and in the course of that study to learn not only the ancient languages, but to value, even to venerate, the stately Roman morality. For the remainder of their lives, men so educated would find the classical comparison the natural one to make. One of the more popular pseudonyms adopted by Federalists was "Phocion"; the writer who used it expected his readers

---

[1] Lucien Price, *Dialogues of Alfred North Whitehead* (Boston,1954), pp. 161, 203.

to know their Plutarch, and assumed that the name could stand, in a sort of intellectual shorthand, for both the elitist variant of republican political theory popular among Federalists and for the sense of rejection that tormented them in the years of the Jeffersonian ascendancy. Phocion had been an Athenian statesman of the fourth century, B.C.; a man honored for his prudence and rectitude; a highly popular general who had been reelected forty-five times, "although he was not even once present at the election, but was always absent when the people summoned and chose him," and despite the fact that he "never said or did anything to win their favour." Phocion was elected by a public which could choose its own medicine; "the Athenians," explained Plutarch, "made use of their more elegant and sprightly leaders by way of diversion, but when they wanted a commander they were always sober and serious, and called upon the severest and most sensible citizen, one who alone, or more than the rest, arrayed himself against their desires and impulses." When they eventually rejected him, Phocion complained, like the frustrated Federalist of 1801, "I have given this people much good and profitable counsel, but they will not listen to me!"[2] When Alexander Hamilton searched for the worst name he could call Aaron Burr without resorting to unprintable language, the name of Catiline came readily to mind, and his audience did not need to be reminded who Catiline had been nor why his name was odious. And to continue, after school, to read and to collect a gentleman's library meant to add to one's schoolboy editions of the ancients the works of the great English Augustans: Swift, Pope, and Dr. Johnson, who also had venerated the great heroes of the ancient world.

A classical education, a literary background in the Augustans, these were shared by most educated Americans of whatever political sympathies. But men who were disenchanted with their world found certain features of the work of the English Augustans particularly attractive. For one thing, the English Augustans were critical of contem-

---

[2] *Plutarch's Lives*, trans. Bernadotte Perrin (Cambridge, Mass., 1919), pp. 161–162, 177. Among Federalist users of the "Phocion" signature were Fisher Ames (in a series of essays in the *New-England Palladium*, April, 1801); Tapping Reeve (in the Litchfield, Conn., *Monitor*, December 9, 1803) and William Loughton Smith (in the Charleston *Courier*, 1806, published as a pamphlet called *The Numbers of Phocion...on the subject of Neutral Rights* [Charleston, S.C., 1806]. Alexander Hamilton used the name in a series of articles protesting the seizure of Loyalist property in 1783; his choice may have had certain autobiographical connotations, as John C. Miller suggests (*Alexander Hamilton: Portrait in Paradox* [New York, 1959], p. 102n). Oliver Wolcott and Smith used Phocion as their signature in their famous pamphlet attack on *The Pretensions of Thomas Jefferson to the Presidency...*(Philadelphia, 1796). Henry Steele Commager discusses this habit of "putting contemporaries into some historical niche" ("Leadership in Eighteenth-Century America and Today," in *Freedom and Order: A Commentary on the American Political Scene* [New York, 1966], p.162).

porary changes in dress, manners, and language; American Federalists too lived in an era when the forms of social intercourse were changing, and not, they were convinced, for the better. The Augustans regularly sneered at what they called "the mob," and the more the American public rejected Federalism, the more many Federalists assuaged their feelings by sneering back at the public. The Augustans knew they lived in an age of flagrant political corruption, and sought to expose it; Federalists convinced themselves that they could not have been rejected save for political corruption, and denounced the phenomenon nearly as vigorously. Finally, the American Federalist might count himself Augustan in his expectation of literary accomplishment, in the exaggeraged honor he accorded to Washington, in his gloomy cyclical reading of history.[3]

To men of such persuasion, the most useful literary form is the satire. It had been virtually the trademark of English Augustan writing from Butler to Swift, and, taking encouragement and rhetorical instruction from the great satirists of Augustan England, American Federalists scattered verse and prose satire among their jeremiads. It is not likely that Federalist pamphleteers flattered themselves they were the literary equals of Swift and Butler. They seem to have regarded satire primarily as a way of reaching the "middling classes" who failed to respond to high seriousness; given an eighteenth-century education which taught students to write by the imitation of classical models and given the obvious similarities of Augustan antipathies to their own, the Federalist turn to the Augustan model was a logical one. Federalist satire is seldom very clever, but it does help clarify those reasons for Federalist distrust of their opponents that are not linked directly to specific political issues. While their polemics attacked what the Jeffersonians did, their satire attacked what the Jeffersonians *were*, revealing in the process something of the Federalist image of the Democrat.

The satires were many and took a variety of forms. There was the witty potpourri that Washington Irving, his brother William, and James Kirke Paulding called *Salmagundi*. There were the letters of the Baron von Hartzensleigzenstoffendahl which William Tudor, Jr., wrote for the *Monthly Anthology and Boston Review*. John Sylvester John Gardiner, a Boston clergyman as pompous as his name, wrote an "Ode to Democracy" in which the lyric echoed Gray and the images imitated Pope; there were less pretentious pieces, like John Quincy Adams's

---

[3] See Lewis P. Simpson, "Federalism and the Crisis of Literary Order," *American Literature*, XXXII (1960), 253–266; and Lewis P. Simpson, ed., *The Federalist Literary Mind: Selections from the Monthly Anthology and Boston Review 1803–1811* (Baton Rouge, La., 1962), pp. 31–41, for extended discussion of this analogy.

drinking song "On the discoveries of Captain Lewis," or the sarcastic sketch signed "Buffon" that Oliver Wolcott, Jr., scribbled for the
Connecticut Courant. Federalist satirists kept returning to one seemingly
inexhaustible source of inspiration: Thomas Jefferson himself. Certain
episodes of his career, especially his flight to Monticello during the
British invasion of Virginia in 1780, and certain pieces of his writing,
especially the *Notes on Virginia* and the *First Inaugural Address*, became
particular favorites, used to the point of redundancy and at the risk,
fatal to the satirist, of boring the reader. This singleness of focus was
due less to a failure of imagination than to the habit of treating the
Republicans not as a political party but as a faction, the personal following of a single leader, bound together by personal loyalties rather
than by ideology or by political principle. According to this reasoning,
if popular faith in the person of Thomas Jefferson could be broken, the
whole opposition could be expected to fall apart.

The Federalist satirists were not a homogeneous group. Sharing primarily a technique of response to the Jeffersonian challenge, each had
some acquaintance among the others, but their interrelationship and
interaction seem insufficient to justify the rubric of "circle" or group.
Some of the satirists were primarily politicians: Josiah Quincy, for example, and his distant cousin, John Quincy Adams. Thomas Green Fessenden was educated as a lawyer, but spent most of his life as a writer
and journalist, as did Joseph Dennie. For others, political satire provided avocational distraction from a rather different sort of career: Timothy Dwight, for example, was president of Yale; Oliver Wolcott, Jr.,
after leaving the office of Secretary of the Treasury, was building a mercantile trading house in New York. Surely the satirists do not represent
a cross section of Federalist society; their family backgrounds were too
upper-class, too intellectual for that. Their fathers were too often ministers and lawyers; their own education culminated too frequently in
Harvard or Yale to make them either sociologically or geographically
typical, nor would it do to assume that they "spoke for" the Federalist party in a representative sense—if anyone, for that matter, did or
could. They were, however, authors of a particularly revealing genre of
Federalist dissent, and much of what they had to say coordinates with
criticism made in more pedestrian fashion by the more typical members
of their party. What is under examination here is one variant of what
might well be called "The Federalist Persuasion."

The most extended of these satires, and the ones that best repay
careful analysis, were "Climenole," a dozen essays written by the
Massachusetts congressman Josiah Quincy, and *Democracy Unveiled,
or Tyranny Stripped of the Garb of Patriotism*, a book-length epic "of the
Hudibrastic kind," by Thomas Green Fessenden, which enjoyed three
printings in New York and Boston. Other satires generally concentrate
on a single Democratic failing, but Quincy and Fessenden had room

to expound on all they found distressing in their opponents' views of life and politics. Fessenden was a Vermont lawyer with an erratic intellectual career, which mingled poetics and polemics. During a brief stay in England he attacked the medical profession in a versified satire called *The Terrible Tractorian*; he served a brief stint in New York City as editor of the shortlived *Weekly Inspector* in 1807, and eventually returned to New England, where he edited agricultural journals and dabbled in inventing. He wrote numerous political verses, but the most vigorous are those of *Democracy Unveiled*, which is Hudibrastic both in meter and in shared antipathies.[4]

The satire of *Democracy Unveiled* was sharp, Fessenden warned, because he "cuts to cure"; a sharpness the more necessary because "our democrats, though spitted with the arrows of satire, by the merciless wits of the age, and roasted before the slow fire of public indignation, appear to possess as little feeling as the " 'passive ox,' that graced the democratic fete in Boston, held in honor of the French revolution."[5] He intended his verses "as a sort of compendium of Federal principles."[6] In cantos headed "Mobocracy," "The Jeffersoniad," and "The Gibbet of Satire," Fessenden took exception to, among other things, Jefferson's *Notes on Virginia*, America's failure to take arms against France, Tom Paine and "the Catalines of faction," ending with the pious hope that as of 1806 "the cause of Federalism...has passed its most gloomy period. The *ebb tide* had arrived to its utmost point, and will shortly be succeeded by a flood, which will overwhelm its enemies in one prodigious ruin."[7] No accusation was too severe or vulgar for Fessenden to endorse; he spent a whole canto chortling over the tales of Jefferson's alleged dalliance with Mrs. Walker and a black slave named Sally Hemings, excusing himself with the comment that he could not be accused of libel because he did not intend to "disturb the public peace."[8]

* * * * *

---

[4] Written in iambic tetrameter, it was critical of the political tastes of the general public and of what Thomas Green Fessenden vaguely called "mobocracy." An antidemocratic note was characteristic of Augustan satire; perhaps the most quoted lines in *Hudibras* are these:

> "For as a Fly, that goes to Bed,
>   Rests with his Tail above his Head;
> So in this Mungril State of ours,
>   The Rabble are the Supreme Powers."

See Ian Jack, *Augustan Satire: Intention and Idiom in English Poetry, 1660–1750* (Oxford, 1952), pp. 34,41.

[5] [Fessenden], *Democracy Unveiled, or Tyranny Stripped of the Garb of Patriotism, by Christopher Caustic, L.L.D.*, 3d ed. (New York, 1806), I,viii,116.

[6] *Ibid.*, I, xvi.

[7] *Ibid.*, II, 147, 214–215.

Unfortunately for Fessenden, most readers of his satires were probably already anti-Jeffersonian. At any rate, no one seems to have sued him for libel.

Josiah Quincy wrote "Climenole" in 1804, most of it in the dull months between his first election to Congress and the opening of the session. Quincy was to amass an impressively long bibliography in the course of a varied career as lawyer, congressman, judge, mayor of Boston and president of Harvard College, but virtually all of the items in it were published versions of speeches he had made or polemical pamphlets intended to endorse or attack projected legislation. "Climenole" was his sole imaginative effort, a *tour de force* written to please an old friend and college classmate, Joseph Dennie.[9] Its arrangement is peculiarly convoluted. The "I" of the narrative is not Josiah Quincy, Federalist, but Slaveslap Kiddnap, Republican author of a fictitious book called "Memorabilia Democratica" of which Quincy purports to be merely the reviewer. The expressions of temperament and principle in the essays are thus supposed to be Republican rather than Federalist, and the absurdities in them so patent that the Republican party is condemned out of its own mouth.[10]

Quincy's rhetorical intention was to use ridicule to arouse hatred; like Fessenden, he could be nasty and at times vulgar. He found the proof-sheets of "Memorabilia Democratica," the author of "Climenole" tells the reader, among the waste papers used by Republicans, who "seldom returned from congress hall, without having their animal economy in a most deranged and turbulent state;— for being hard pressed by the federalists, and also gagged by the votes of their own party, the noxious humours, which used to vapour through the mouth, were driven to other channels." The name "Climenole" was well chosen: it was the name Jonathan Swift had given to the servants in the country of Laputa which Gulliver visited in his third voyage, who were responsible

---

[8] *Ibid.*, I, xviii.

[9] Dennie, founder and editor of the *Port Folio*, best known and most widely circulated of Federalist periodicals, was habitually in need of new contributions and constantly badgered old friends for aid. Once Quincy had obliged him with a few installments that he probably did not intend to continue, Dennie pressed him for more, and the mixture of flattery and appeal to an honorable commitment was enough to result in a total of twelve installments. The later ones were widely spaced in time, and the series eventually petered out. See also Edmund Quincy, *Life of Josiah Quincy* (Boston, 1867), p.32.

[10] This form was not uncommon. In 1803 the Charleston *Courier* printed a series of satirical letters signed "Habakkuk Hoecake," who pretended to be a Jeffersonian, the better to satirize them: "We drink, and smoke segars, and talk about state affairs, and argue sometimes so warmly, that we are upon the point of gouging...you know it would be a disgrace to democrats not to disagree, it it were for nothing else but to shew that every man has a right to do as he pleases" (February 22).

for warning their extremely absentminded masters when to speak and when to listen. "This flapper is likewise employed diligently to attend his master in his walks, and upon occasion to give him a soft flap on his eyes, because he is always so wrapped up in cogitation, that he is in manifest danger of falling down every precipice, and bouncing his head against every post, and in the streets, of justling others."[11] Quincy had chosen a striking and perceptive illustration of the relation many Federalists of his generation conceived they had with a largely Republican public. If the Federalist could not awaken the public to the dangers of democracy, then he could at least act the protective role of the flapper, the climenole, to alert the absentminded public to the dangers it ran, to keep it from "falling down every precipice." If the master refused to heed and continued to "bounce his head against every post," the fault would not rest with the weaker party. It was just such a definition of their role that congressional Federalists had developed in the years since the black day that Thomas Jefferson had been elected President and the Federalist opposition was tempted (as a minority still, in 1804, was tempted) to sit silently by while the nation inevitably proceeded to Hell in a Handbasket. If the Federalists were to be flappers, they would have to pity their opponents as well as hate them; this sort of ambivalence was a fairly standard Federalist characteristic.

Quincy was not the first Federalist to find Gulliver's Third Voyage highly useful source of instructive parallel. References to Laputa appear and reappear in Federalist satirical prose.[12] Why Federalists should have fastened on Gulliver's third voyage, the least popular, most disjointed section of the *Travels*, is easily explained by the similarity of Swift's enmities to the Federalists' own. Federalists found that Swift had, as Quakers say, "spoken to their condition." The hero of the Third Voyage is Lord Munodi, a man with whom the Federalists could readily identify. Munodi, though out of power, retains his good judgment and perceptively discerns the weaknesses of his opponents' schemes. "While Lord Munodi tries to hold on to the living past, which is the universally sound, the Balnibarbians sacrifice all to the pride which they project into a utopian future."[13] Substitute Federalist for Lord Munodi, Jeffersonian for Balnibarbian, and we have a statement of the Federalist definition of America's central problem. The language of Laputa, there-

---

[11] "Climenole. A Review, Political and Literary.—No. 2," *Port Folio*, February 4, 1804 (all installments of "Climenole" appeared in *Port Folio* in 1804; the periodical name will be omitted in subsequent references); Jonathan Swift, *Travels into Several Remote Nations of the World. By Captain Lemuel Gulliver* (London, 1726), II, 26.

[12] E.g., Charleston *Courier*, March 14, 26, 1803; *The Ordeal*, March 25, 1809.

[13] Martin Price, *Swift's Rhetorical Art: A Study in Structure and Meaning* (New Haven, 1953), p.83.

fore, appears and reappears in Federalist satire. In Quincy's work the parallels are drawn so extensively that even the scatology so typical of Swiftian rhetoric and so foreign to Quincy's pompous, starch prose, appears in "Climenole."[14]

Swift's satire had been directed against abstract and impractical scientific investigations, represented in fact by those that were carried on in his own day by the Royal Society of London, and in his fiction by the inhabitants of the Flying Island of Laputa, who were too engrossed in abstract speculations to cope with commonsensical problems.[15] The investigations conducted at the Grand Academy at Lagado were, as Marjorie Nicolson has demonstrated, direct lampoons of actual experiments reported in the *Transactions* of the Royal Society.[16] Swift's variants included schemes for building houses "by beginning at the roof and working downwards to the foundation," substituting spider webs for silkworm thread, and the investigations of a man who "had been eight years upon a project for extracting sunbeams out of cucumbers, which were to be put into vials hermetically sealed, and let out to warm the air in raw inclement summers."[17]

Swift's Laputan imagery proved useful to those who wished to satirize, not the Royal Society, but the Jeffersonian Republicans. One of the earliest uses, in a Fourth of July oration delivered in New Haven in 1799 by David Daggett, is engagingly entitled "Sunbeams May Be Extracted from Cucumbers, But the Process Is Tedious." Daggett prefaced a long list of recent developments he deplored in travel, in agriculture, in education, in morals as well as in politics, by the comment:

> These [Laputan] theorists were very patient, industrious, and laborious in their pursuits—had a high reputation for their singular proficiency, and were regarded as prodigies in science. The common laborers and mechanics were...despised for their stupid and oldfashioned manner of acquiring property and character. If the inquiry had been made whether any of these projects had succeeded, it would have been readily answered that they had not; but they were reasonable, their principles just—and of course, that [they] must ultimately produce the objects in view. . . . If a further enquiry had been made what would be the great excellence

---

[14] See Edward J. Rosenheim, Jr., *Swift and the Satirist's Art* (Chicago, 1963), pp. 230–232; Normal O. Brown, *Life Against Death* (Middletown, Conn.,1959),pp. 179–201.

[15] Laputa, the Flying Island, hovers over the domains of its monarch; Lagado, the capital city of these domains, houses a Grand Academy. Swift's description of the investigations undertaken at the Academy is a particularly pointed thrust at the Royal Society and the "new science" of Descartes, Kepler, and Newton, which had become in Swift's time fairly standard objects of Augustan attack.

[16] "The Scientific Background of Swift's Voyage to Laputa," *Science and Imagination* (Ithaca, N.Y., 1956), pp. 117–118. See also Nicolson, "Swift's 'Flying Island' in the Voyage to Laputa,"*Annals of Science*, II (1937), 405–430.

[17] Swift, II, 65, 66–67, 63.

of marble pin-cushions, or the superior advantage of a breed of naked sheep, the answer would have been, it is unphilosophical to ask such questions.[18]

Washington Irving's early satires abound in Swiftian imagery. Jefferson's "projects" are the targets of satire, both in *Salmagundi* and in the chapters on William the Testy in Dietrich Knickerbocker's *History of New York*. Irving reported that William "was exceedingly fond of trying philosophical and political experiments...much given to mechanical inventions— contructing patent smoke-jacks—carts that went before the horses, and especially erecting windmills." His enemies had the effrontery to suggest "that his head was turned by his experiments, and that he really thought to manage his government as he did his mills—by mere wind![19] *The New-England Palladium* published a series of satires on modern trends in education and religion headed "The Projector";[20] a poem critical of Joel Barlow's proposals for naval reforms stigmatized him as "Most nobel of Projectors."[21] The Hudson, New York, *Balance* ran a poem about

> a gentleman, whose head
> Was full of philosophic notions.

Among the notions was the idea that

> To root up weeds their [*sic*] is no reason,
> Against the *rights of plants* 'tis treason.
> Each has an equal right to live.

Projector-like, he embarks on the experiment, and orders his servant to let the weeds alone.

---

[18] *Sun Beams May Be Extracted from Cucumbers, But the Process Is Tedious, An Oration Pronounced on the Fourth of July, 1799, at the Request of the Citizens of New Haven* (New Haven,1799),pp. 6–7. Daggett made it clear that he believed similar strictures should apply to the recent social and political developments he deplored.

[19] Washington Irving, William Irving, and James Kirke Paulding, *Salmagundi; or, the Whim Whams and Opinions of Launcelot Langstaff, Esq. & Others* (London,1811),I,46; Washington Irving, *A History of New York, from the Beginning of the World to the End of the Dutch Dynasty...by Dietrich Knickerbocker* (New York,1809), I, 194, 197–198, 217. Irving's debt to Swift is explored in William L. Hedges, *Washington Irving: An American Study— 1802–1832* (Baltimore,1965), pp. 47–48, 58, 61, 76–78, and in Martin Roth, *Washington Irving's Contributions to "The Corrector"* (Minneapolis,1968), pp.33–34, 37–38, 66.

[20] *New-England Palladium*, January 2, 6, 13, 20, 23, 1801. The similarity of the angle of vision (a satire reputedly provided by a Republican, who is made to condemn himself), the reference to Laputa, and the easy availability of the *Palladium* to Quincy suggest that this series may have provided the model for "Climenole," or even that Quincy had written it himself. Another possible author of the *Palladium* series is David Daggett.

[21] "Native Poetry," *New-England Palladium*, April 21, 1801.

>   And why should wheat and barley thrive,
>   Despotic tyrants of the field?

The result, of course, is disaster, and the story is told as an object lesson to anyone who should contemplate becoming a "Philosophical Farmer."[22]

Now, the appearance of the word "philosophical" in any Federalist tract signals invective ahead. Federalists seem to have associated the word with the French "philosophe" (which of course is not the same thing) and used the adjective to describe all that they wished to denounce, all they wished to associate with French revolutionary theory and practice, and subsequently all they deplored in Jeffersonian ideology. When a Federalist said something was philosophical, he was saying what Burke had said about the French Revolution: that it was visionary, that it was ludicrously impractical, and likely to prove dangerously unsound in practice. Another way of saying the same thing was provided by Jonathan Swift in the language of Laputa, a society formed and ruined by men who walked with their heads literally in the clouds (the island hovered in the atmosphere) and their feet dangling over precipices; a land where agriculture had been ruined by "scientific" schemes purporting to increase productivity beyond natural limits, a land where men refused to recognize the limitations of common sense, and tempted disaster by seeking to do what only God can do, as exemplified by the attempt to build houses by working downwards from the roof, imitating "the proceeding of this Sovereign Architect in the Frame of this great Building of the Universe...he began at the Roof, and Builded downwards, and in that process, suspended the inferior parts of the World upon the superior."[23]

"Never," warned Noah Webster in a Fourth of July Address, "...let us exchange our civil and religious institutions for the wild theories of crazy projectors; or the sober, industrious moral habits of our country, for experiments in atheism and lawless democracy. *Experience* is a safe pilot; but experiment is a dangerous ocean, full of rocks and shoals."[24] To the Federalist mind, Jeffersonians were Laputans, committed to an abstract impracticality which would, if not deterred, tear apart the cultural fabric of the young republic. All the famous Jeffersonian rhetoric about man's capacity to construct a better world from new blueprints was so much high-flown nonsense. It

---

[22] Hudson, New York, *Balance*, August 28, 1804.

[23] Swift, II, 65. See R.L. Colie, "Some Paradoxes in the Language of Things," *Reason and the Imagination*, ed. J.A. Mazzeo (New York, 1962), p.128.

[24] *An Oration Pronounced Before the Citizens of New Haven on the Anniversary of the Independence of the United States* (New Haven, 1798), p.15.

was given to man only to remodel his world, not to remake it, and then only with the greatest caution. Anything else was visionary, dangerous, "philosophical"—in short, Laputan. The Revolution and Constitution-making had been renovatory enough. The Federalist had been willing to build a new Jerusalem; he was not anxious to be absorbed into an effort to build a new Laputa.

The Presidency of
Thomas Jefferson:
The Triumph and the Perils
of Republican Ideals

Forrest McDonald

"To build a new Laputa," this selection may suggest, describes the Jeffersonian endeavor all too well. But if McDonald is unusual in his decided condemnation of Republican objectives, his perspective offers several striking insights. And many recent students of the Jeffersonians have been as thoroughly impressed as he or Kerber with the depth of the continuing distrust between the first two parties and the differences between their visions of the new republic's future. Henry Adams' insistence that the new administration cared a great deal more for popularity than for "the principles of '98" has been subjected to increasing criticism as historians have moved away from the consensual interpretations of the 1950s. But nowhere is the Jeffersonian commitment to a different vision emphasized more strongly or denounced more wittily than in McDonald's The Presidency of Thomas Jefferson *("American Presidency Series"; Lawrence: University Press of Kansas, 1976). The following excerpts are from pages 17–22, 36–37, 38–40, 41–44, 53–54, 96, 115–117, 139, and 162–165. Copyright ©1976 by the University Press of Kansas; reprinted by permission.*

Anglo-Americans, like the English themselves, were by and large non-ideological people, but in 1800 the country was divided into two fiercely antagonistic ideological camps. In a loose, general sort of way, and with allowance for a number of exceptions, it can be said that the rival ideologies derived from contrasting views of the nature of man. The first view, that associated with the Hamiltonian Federalists, was premised upon the belief that man, while capable of noble and even altruistic behavior, could never entirely escape the influence of his inborn baser passions—especially ambition and avarice, the love of power and the love of money. The second, that espoused by the Jeffersonian Republicans, held that man was born with a tabula rasa, with virtually boundless

capacity for becoming good or evil, depending upon the wholesome-
ness of the environment in which he grew. From the premise of the first
it followed that government should recognize the evil drives of men as
individuals, but check them and even harness them in such a way that
they would work for the general good of society as a whole. From the
premise of the second it followed that government should work to rid
society of as many evils as possible—including, to a very large extent,
the worst of evils, government itself. The one was positive, the other
negative; the one sought to do good, the other to eradicate evil.

But the ideological division was more specifically focused than that.
The High Federalists believed in and had fashioned a governmental
system modeled upon the one that began to emerge in England after
the Glorious Revolution of 1688 and was brought to maturity under the
leadership of Sir Robert Walpole during the 1720s and 1730s. In part
the system worked on the basis of what has often, simple-mindedly,
been regarded as the essence of Hamiltonianism: tying the interests of
the wealthy to those of the national government or, more accurately,
inducing people of all ranks to act in the general interest by making
it profitable for them to do so. But the genius of Hamilton's system
ran much deeper. He erected a complex set of interrelated institutions,
based upon the monetization of the public debt, which made it virtually impossible for anyone to pursue power and wealth successfully
except through the framework of those institutions, and which simultaneously delimited and dictated the possible courses of government
activity, so that government had no choice but to function in the public interest as Hamilton saw it. For instance, servicing the public debt,
on which the whole superstructure rested, required a regular source
of revenue that was necessarily derived largely from duties on imports
from Great Britain. For that reason the United States could not go to
war with Britain except at the risk of national bankruptcy, but could
fight Revolutionary France or France's ally Spain, which were owners
of territories that the United States avidly desired. Hamilton regarded
this as the proper American foreign policy, at least for a time; and
should circumstances change, he was perfectly capable of redefining
the rules and rerigging the institutions so as to dictate another policy. In
domestic affairs, a wide range of implications of his system was equally
inescapable.

The Jeffersonian Republicans regarded this scheme of things as
utterly wicked, even as the English Opposition had regarded Walpole's
system. Indeed, though the Jeffersonians borrowed some of their ideas
from James Harrington and other seventeenth-century writers and some
from John Locke, their ideology was borrowed *in toto* from such Oppositionists as Charles Davenant, John Trenchard, Thomas Gordon, James
Burgh, and most especially Henry St. John, First Viscount Bolingbroke.

As a well-rounded system, it is all to be found in the pages of the *Crafts-man*, an Oppositionist journal that Bolingbroke published from 1726 to 1737. The Republicans adjusted the ideology to fit the circumstances, to fit the United States Constitution and the "ministry" of Alexander Hamilton rather than the British constitution and the ministry of Robert Walpole; but that was all, and astonishingly little adjustment was necessary.

The Bolingbroke-Oppositionist *cum* Jeffersonian Republican ideology ran as follows. Corruption was everywhere, it was true; but given a proper environment, that need not be the way of things. Mankind could be rejuvenated through education and self-discipline, but that was possible only in the context of a life style that exalted living on, owning, and working the land. Only the land could give people the independence and unhurried existence that were prerequisite to self-improvement.

In some Edenic past, "the people"—which both Bolingbroke and Jefferson understood to mean the gentry and the solid yeomanry, and not to include aristocrats, money jobbers, priests, or the scum in the cities—had enjoyed the proper atmosphere, and therefore had been happy. Relationshps were based upon agriculture and its "handmaiden" commerce, upon ownership of land, honest labor in the earth, craftsmanship in the cities, and free trade between individuals. All men revered God, respected their fellows, deferred to their betters, and knew their place. Because they were secure in their sense of place, they were also secure in their identities and their sense of values; and manly virtue, honor, and public spirit governed their conduct.

Then a serpent invaded the garden. To Bolingbroke, the evil started with the Glorious Revolution, which begat two bastard offspring: the Financial Revolution and the system of government by ministry, rather than the system of separation of powers that had been embodied in the ancient English constitution. To Jefferson, things were slightly more complex. America had been spared the corruption that had poisoned England until the accession of George III, and when it began to infest America, the spirit of 1776 had saved the day. Yet the American Revolution, because of the Hamiltonians, was ultimately undermined in just the way the English revolution had been: both were waged to check executive power, and both ended in the worst form of executive tyranny, ministerial government. The instrument of corruption in both instances was money—not "real" money, gold and silver, but artificial money in the form of public debt, bank notes, stocks, and other kinds of paper—the acquisition of which had nothing to do with either land or labor. Government ministers assiduously encouraged people to traffic in such paper, and with that stimulus the pursuit of easy wealth proved irresistible. A frenzy for gambling, stockjobbing, and paper shuffling permeated the highest councils of state and spread among the people themselves. Manly virtue gave way to effeminacy and vice; public spirit succumbed to extravagance, venality, and corruption.

Jefferson never tired of telling a story which, to him, epitomized what had gone wrong. Early in Washington's first administration, Jefferson recalled, he had been engaged in a friendly discussion of political principles with Hamilton and Vice-President Adams. Jefferson had maintained that an agrarian republic was most conducive to human happiness. Adams disagreed and, to Jefferson's horror, said that monarchy was better, that if the British government were purged of corruption it would be the best system ever devised. Hamilton, to the astonishment of both his listeners, declared that if the British system were purged of corruption it would not work: it was, he said, the most perfect system of government as it stood, for corruption was the most suitable engine of effective government.

In the matter of foreign relations, Republicans opposed the corrupt new order on two interrelated sets of grounds, with the same logic and often the same language that the Oppositionists had used earlier. One was that it entangled the nation with foreign powers, making independent, self-determined action impossible. Not only had Hamilton's system prevented the United States from siding with Revolutionary France against Britain in the early 1790s—which the Republicans believed to be the moral course, as well as the one most advantageous to the country—but it continually subjected America to alien influences because foreigners owned a large percentage of the public debt and the stock of the Bank of the United States. This involvement, in turn, gave rise to the second set of grounds for objection: foreign entanglements necessitated standing armies and navies, the support of which added to an already oppressive tax burden. The gentry and yeomanry, the Republicans believed, had been carrying more than their share of the tax load, even when taxes had been mainly in the form of import duties; and when excise taxes were levied specifically to support the military during the quasi war with France in 1798, the new burden fell almost exclusively on the landed. Taxes to support standing armies and navies were doubly galling because a professional military corps, as a class distinct from the people, was a threat to liberty in its own right, and it could also be unleashed to collect taxes by force, thus making the people pay for their own oppression. (English Oppositionists had been afraid of standing armies, but not of navies, for they had regarded a strong naval establishment as necessary for the protection of British commerce. The American Republicans' fear of standing armies was largely abstract, since they believed that the traditional American reliance on militias would prevent the rise of dangerous armies; but their hostility to navies was immediate and strong, for navies seemed most likely to involve the

United States in fighting, and besides, navies cost a lot of money for upkeep even when they were not actively employed.)

Given all that, a revolution in the form of a return to first principles was called for. The several branches of government must be put back into constitutional balance, the moneychangers must be ousted from the temples, the gentry and yeomanry must be restored to suprema- cy, commerce must be returned to its subordinate role as agriculture's handmaiden, and the values of the agrarian way of life must be cher- ished anew. In the undertaking, the Republicans had reason for hope— as, in reality, Bolingbroke and his circle had not—for it could all be done within the framework of the Constitution. The Constitution made it possible for the Republicans to gain control of the national government, and should they prove able to do so, only two major tasks needed to be done. The first was to purge government of extreme, irreconcilable monarchists. Jefferson believed that this could be done quickly and eas- ily, for he thought that all but a handful of the people in government were men of sound and honorable principles. The second was to pay off the public debt as rapidly as possible, since that was the wellspring of the whole system of corruption. This would not be easy; but with good management, honest administration, and rigid economy, Jeffer- son believed that it could be accomplished within sixteen years.

That was the Republicans' ideology and the essence of their pro- gram: restore the separation of powers through the voluntary restraint of virtuous officials, cast out the monarchists and the money men, repeal the most oppressive of taxes, slash expenses, pay off the public debt, and thus restore America to the pristine simplicity of an Arcadian past.

* * * * *

To a considerable extent, Jefferson's success in bringing his policies into execution was due to his departure from the methods followed by his predecessors in regard to appointments at the highest levels. Washington had sought to find the best available man for every posi- tion and had given little if any thought to policies. Adams had retained Washington's cabinet, mainly because public office had proved to be a frightful consumer of reputations and therefore replacements were not easy to find; only gradually and timorously had he fired disloyal or incompetent subordinates and replaced them with men more to his liking. Jefferson, from the start, surrounded himself only with dedicat- ed, loyal Republicans whose principles were the same as his own. To be sure, his appointments to the less important cabinet posts—Henry Dearborn of Maine (Massachusetts) as secretary of war, Robert Smith of the Baltimore Smiths as secretary of the navy, Levi Lincoln of Massachusetts as attorney general, and Gideon Granger of Connecticut as postmaster general—were made with political considerations in mind, and a certain mediocrity was the result. To head the State and Treasury departments, however, Jefferson opted for brilliance as well as for solid principles, and James Madison and Albert Gallatin joined him to form a virtual triumvirate—though always with the understanding that they stood to him as the second and third consuls stood to Napoleon.

* * * * *

A similar arrangement marked the relations between the executive and legislative branches of government. Jefferson established a rapport with Congress that neither of his predecessors and few if any of his successors could match. He used none of the techniques that are usually associated with "strong" presidents—popular pressure, naked power, bribery, flattery, cajolery, blackmail, or shrewd trading—yet he had but to suggest legislation and it was almost invariably forthcoming.

In no small measure the achievement was based upon the way Jefferson dealt with the congressmen personally. Officially he stood aloof from them, maintaining a wall of absolute separation between the branches. Beginning with his first annual message in December of 1801, he abandoned the traditional practice of appearing in person before Congress, sending written communications, usually quite brief, by a messenger instead. In point of political form, that was a radical break from a ritual that had originated with the English Crown and Parliament and had been followed in both state and national government in the United States. In point of practice, the change reflected Jefferson's realization that he was simply no good at dealing with men in the aggregate: his inaugural address, for instance, was a rhetorical and political gem, but it was delivered in a voice so unprepossessing that few could even hear it, much less be inspired by it. Rather, his touch, to be effective, had to be personal. To that end he feted all the congressmen, in carefully chosen groups, at a rotation of dinner parties, where—in an environment of seemingly casual elegance—he maintained the same kind of comfortable, informal atmosphere that prevailed in cabinet mettings.

Always unwigged, somtimes dressed in frayed homespun and rundown slippers, the president put his guests at their ease with the folksy, open hospitality of a country squire; but the dinner (prepared by a French chef and accompanied by a magnificent selection of French wines) was likely to be the finest the legislators had ever tasted, and the conversation was regularly the most fascinating they ever heard. Jefferson always led the conversation, dazzling his guests by talking with equal ease of architecture, history, science, theology, music, math-

ematics, or art—everything but current politics, which subject was
forbidden. Reading between the lines of the accounts of these occasions,
one sometimes suspects that the talk was more brilliant than deep and
that it frequently had the flavor of a lecture by Polonius. Moreover, the
congressmen were for the most part a mediocre lot, having less talent,
wealth, education, and social experience than their predecessors in the
early Federalist Congresses. In any event, Jefferson's guests were usually overwhelmed: few congressmen were immune to the president's
personality, and most returned to the congressional pit with renewed
faith in his wisdom and virtue.

There was more, of course, to Jefferson's power over the national
legislature than his magnetism at dinner, but that was a cardinal
element. Another element was his deployment of Gallatin as the administration's unofficial liaison man with Congress. Gallatin knew and was
on friendly terms with most Republican congressmen, having served for
some time as their floor leader, and he could work informally with them
on proposed legislation without violating their sensibilities in regard to
executive encroachment. That made it possible for the president to have
an effective voice in making legislative policy, and yet avoid Hamiltonian trappings of a monarchical-ministerial system.

Still another element was the Republicans' system of organization
in Congress. Republican members of both houses met in caucuses to
determine policy, and that was normally enough to establish all the
discipline necessary for carrying out the party's program. There was,
however, always a danger of factionalism within the party, and in order
to check factional disputes, something extra was needed. In part, this
was provided by investing the Speaker of the House with great power, and by choosing as Speaker Nathaniel Macon of North Carolina—
a plodding, sincere, impeccably honest man whose lack of imagination and guile would have made him trustworthy even if his purity of
Republican principles had not.

The next necessity was for a floor leader, which by recent custom devolved upon the chairman of the Ways and Means Committee.
There some friction developed. The chief pretender to both roles was
William Branch Giles of Virginia, who had earlier served as Madison's
ablest lieutenant when Madison headed the "republican interest" in
Congress; but instead, Macon appointed another Virginian as head of
Ways and Means—his brilliant, caustic, erratic twenty-eight-year-old
friend, John Randolph of Roanoke. Giles, as it happened, soon became
ill and returned home, and when he came back to Washington, it was as
a member of the Senate, in which he promptly became the president's
leading spokesman. Meanwhile, Randolph took over as the Republicans' floor leader in the House, which caused the president some
discomfort. Randolph was a man of pure political principles, but he was

also a bit crazy, and was devoid, as well, of ability to compromise. His close friends in the House—Macon, Joseph Nicholson of Maryland, and Joseph Bryan of Georgia—exercised some moderating influence upon him; but Jefferson, sensing that he might one day prove a menace, sought vainly to find a leader to replace him.

* * * * *

A great deal of the Republicans' program for reform was negative, which is to say that it was aimed at undoing as much of Federalism as possible. In short order, for example, Congress repealed those of the Alien and Sedition Acts that had not already expired, Jefferson pardoned all ten persons (mostly Republican newspaper publishers) who had been convicted under the Sedition Act, and Congress voted to restore with interest all fines that had been levied under the act. Almost as quickly, Congress abolished most of the internal taxes—the hated excise, carriage, and direct property taxes—that Federalists had enacted in 1798 to help pay for the quasi war with France. As part of the same package, Congress set about the business of reducing the military establishment and slashing army and naval appropriations.

The task of undoing the Hamiltonian system fell mainly upon Gallatin. Gallatin's primary goal, which Jefferson not only shared but repeatedly said was the most important tangible objective of his presidency, was to reduce the public debt and ultimately abolish it. The ideological underpinning of this aspiration, as indicated, was the belief that debt, public or private, was inherently bad, and that the national debt as created and managed by the Hamiltonians was doubly so because it infected American government and society with the noxious germs of the corrupt British system. Gallatin also accepted Republican ideology in regard to taxes, which meant, after the internal taxes were repealed, that approximately 90 percent of all federal revenues came from a single source, namely, duties on imports. Gallatin believed that if people were relieved of onerous taxes in normal circumstances, they would gladly pay them during a war or in other emergency situations. He also believed that the best way for a government to build its credit was to pay its debts. Hamilton's view, on the other hand, was that Gallatin was making a dangerous mistake on both counts, that the public debt and the machinery and legislation for collecting all forms of taxes must be kept at least nominally operative at all times, so that they might be readily expanded or activated during emergencies.

The revenue structure thus being a "given," Gallatin sought to achieve his goal by cutting expenditures. Like most Republicans (and like most reformers at most times), he was entirely convinced that civilian expenditures of the government were extremely wasteful, and

he instituted a vigorous program designed to eliminate the waste. With
the wholehearted cooperation of both Congress and the president,
he infused the government with a regularity and efficiency that the
more freewheeling Federalists had never practiced. Appropriations, for
instance, had previously been voted in lump sums by departments,
and department heads and other high officials were left free to use the
money at their discretion—with the result that funds intended for one
purpose were often used for another. Indeed, money had sometimes
been spent with no authorization at all, Congress being presented with
a bill after the fact. The Republicans in Congress never went so far as
to adopt Gallatin's recommendation for line-budget appropriations—
ironically, because they trusted him implicitly and did not want to tie
his hands—but they did make their appropriations much more specific
than the Federalists had, and Gallatin policed every expenditure with
meticulous care.

It turned out, however, that precious little waste was there to
remove. The Federalists, for all their cavalier manners, proved not to
have been throwing money around needlessly, and though irregulari-
ties had been common, actual peculation or other wrongdoing had been
almost nonexistent. Thus, despite his zeal and his precisely methodical
administration, Gallatin was unable to make any appreciable dent in
civilian expenditures.

That left the military. Under legislation passed March 16, 1802, the
army was cut to one regiment of artillery and two of infantry and to
a total strength of 3,350 officers and men. All soldiers that were super-
numerary to this establishment were discharged with a modest bonus.
No provision was made for a quartermaster general or commissary;
instead, economy was effected by placing the army's pay master general
in charge of clothing the troops and by vesting military agents, one at
each post, with authority to feed and supply the soldiers. Economy was
not the sole purpose of this reform: the Jeffersonians aimed at creating a
small but well-trained army and at placing the main burden of national
defense upon the militias. Toward the first end, positive steps were
taken, for the same basic law of 1802 established the Army Corps of
Engineers and the military academy at West Point; but Congress balked
at the president's proposal to reorganize the militia system and infuse
it with discipline. The result was expensive economy, for the army was
rendered so small as to be ineffectual and nothing was provided in its
place.

Efforts to trim the naval budget were likewise less than satisfactory.
The Federalists had, on the eve of Jefferson's inaugural, voted to dis-
pose of all the smaller vessels acquired since the Navy Department had
been created in 1798, to pare down to thirteen frigates—which were,
by the way, the best fighting ships of their class in the world—and

to keep only six of them in active service, the others to be laid up in ports. To maintain the reduced establishment, they appropriated only $3 million a year. The Jeffersonians promptly laid up the remaining frigates, suspended construction and all but minimal maintenance, and cut the annual appropriation to $1 million.

In regard to the navy as to the army, however, Jefferson and Gallatin had a positive program, or rather what more properly might be called a pet idea. They believed that navies were more of a menace than a boon, not only because they entailed an arrogantly aristocratic officer caste but also because they extended a nation's hostile boundaries and thus its likelihood of stumbling into war. What was needed was an inexpensive potential for defense without the potential for mischief that accompanied an attacking force, and the Jeffersonian answer was the maritime equivalent of militias, namely gunboats. According to Jeffersonian theory, gunboats measuring about fifty feet in length, of shallow draft, equipped with oars as well as sails, and armed with one or two cannon were ideally suited to protect American harbors from foreign marauders, and had the added advantage of costing very little for construction or maintenance. Following that theory, the Jefferson administration was prepared to let the nation's magnificent Humphreys frigates rot at the wharves, and in 1805 it began to build a "mosquito fleet" of gunboats in their place.

The long-range implications of these false economies were to reduce the military capacities of the United States to virtually nothing, and thus to tie the nation's hands in its foreign relations far more than Hamiltonian policy ever had. On a different scale they seemed justified, for the fiscal soundness they seemed to make possible promised to strengthen the country more than a temporary loss of military potential weakened it. But there was the rub: for reasons quite beyond the administration's control (and to be described later), average peacetime expenditures for military purposes actually increased rather than decreased while Jefferson was in office.

And yet, under Gallatin's management the United States government was able, during the presidency of Thomas Jefferson, to reduce its debt from $80 million to $57 million and to accumulate an additional treasury surplus of $14 million, despite the unanticipated expenditure of $15 million for the purchase of the Louisiana Territory. The key factor in this impressive achievement was an abnormal circumstance that blinded Jefferson and Gallatin to some harsh realities and would, in time, lead them quite astray: because of the profits of the neutral carrying trade, and ultimately because of the policies of the British government which permitted that trade, American commerce was inordinately prosperous during Jefferson's first few years in office, and with that prosperity the revenues of the American government were inordinately swollen. In sum, the success of the Jefferson administration in purging American government of corrupt British influence was directly dependent upon the will of the British government.

* * * * *

Domestic reform was only half of the Jeffersonian revolution, for the basis of America's relations with other nations also wanted a fundamental reordering. In immediate and practical terms, it is true, the Jeffersonians sought pretty much the same things in foreign relations that the Federalists did. In orientation, style, and philosophical outlook, however, their approach was quite different. The Jeffersonians changed the reference point of American foreign policy from northern commercial centers to the southern plantation. They changed the style from that of Hamilton and Adams (who were both, though in separate ways, quite in the European tradition) to that of Virginia and Thomas Jefferson. And they changed the ideological base, from Walpolean to Bolingbrokean.

In Viscount Bolingbroke's plan of opposition to the Financial Revolution, obsession with independence was the international counterpart of obsession with retiring the public debt at home, and so it was with the Jeffersonians. In his inaugural address, Jefferson spoke of a need to avoid "entangling alliances" with all nations, but his attitude was rooted far deeper than in a mere concern with formal treaties between governments. As secretary of state, he had seen the United States turn its back on Revolutionary France, despite a treaty of friendship and alliance, because America's financial and commercial commitments made it dependent upon the favor of Great Britain, and he was determined to rid his country of all such shackles. Yet even that was not all. Independence, or self-reliance, was at the very core of the eighteenth-century gentry's notion of manhood, and virtue and manhood were interchangeable concepts: a nation could not simultaneously be virtuous and dependent, any more than a man could simultaneously be a gentleman and a sycophant. The trouble was that the game of international relations, as it was played in the courts of Europe, turned not upon manly virtue but upon wile, intrigue, and hypocrisy. Moreover, as Jefferson knew from personal experience, it was a seductive game; and Jefferson was determined to keep his nation out of it, even as a once-burned, twice-wise father steers his sons away from gambling houses and harlots. On this subject he was almost fanatical. He would avoid intimacy with the powers of the Old World as he would avoid a vile and fatal contamination; he used such words as "cankers" and "sores" in talking of Europe's society, and "madmen" and "tyrants" to describe its rulers; he thanked an "overruling Providence" for being "separated by nature and a wide ocean" from a Europe that he described as the "exterminating havoc of one quarter of the globe."

Jefferson's way of implementing his foreign policy was uniquely his own, and it corresponded closely to his style in handling domestic affairs. Madison played, in the international arena, a role that was a counterpart to the one that Gallatin played in the domestic: he was all propriety, reserve, caution, and protocol, and he worked himself to the emaciation point into the bargain. The president assumed a manner that seemingly clashed with but in fact complemented the secretary of state's stiff formality, treating diplomats with calculated casualness, with a threadbare and homey simplicity that was somehow elegant, with a New-World innocence that was somehow sophisticated and cosmopolitan, with an insistence upon equality that somehow demonstrated his superiority.

For a time that style was as persuasive in foreign affairs as it was in domestic: as president, Jefferson was a superb diplomat. But there were two crucial weaknesses in his approach to it. One was implicit in the ideology of Republicanism. The Republicans' world-view included a naive, secularized form of demonology in which certain groups were rigidly typed as evil; and high on their list of devils was the government of Great Britain. Accordingly, they failed to understand that the British people were entirely loyal to Crown and country and that indeed they tended to despise Americans for having rebelled against mother England. Moreover, Republicans were incapable of recognizing or admitting that the United States was inherently dependent upon Britain in some respects and was her natural ally in others; and thus when they had to deal with her at all, they felt partly sullied and partly as if they were doing her a favor.

The second shortcoming was related to the first: consciously or unconsciously downgrading as well as distrusting Great Britain, Jefferson, like most Republicans, never fully grasped the significance—to Britain and to the United States—of British sea power, and he never fully understood that what happened on the seas was as important as, and inextricably connected with, what happened on the battlefields and at the negotiating tables. Thus he virtually took the seas for granted as he concentrated his efforts, single-mindedly, on the next major goal of American foreign policy, the acquisition of West Florida. He assumed that commerical prosperity and the attendant burgeoning of federal revenues—without which most of his achievements would have been impossible—would continue to come as a matter of course, as if they were due to America as a right. They came, in fact, only at the suffrance of the hated British government; but so far was Jefferson from facing this harsh reality that he even expected to be able to use the Royal Navy when it suited his convenience.

* * * * *

Jefferson's second term [thus became] a painful ordeal. Disappointment and frustration followed one another in endless succession, and before the term was half over, events at home as well as on and beyond the seas had ceased to respond to his bidding. It is customary, in accounting for the calamity of his second term, to attribute it to circumstances. He was a man of high ideals and lofty moral principles, as the accounting usually reads, who was caught between the hungry British shark and the even more ravenous Napoleonic tiger, and he strove nobly but in vain to extricate his administration and his country from an impossible situation.

The truth is at once simpler and more complex: the failings were of Jefferson's own making, and they flowed logically if not inevitably from the interaction between Republican ideology and the policies adopted during Jefferson's first term. The primary goals of the Republican revolution, sought with obsessive zeal, were retirement of the public debt and territorial expansion, specifically the acquisition of Spanish territory on the southern and southwestern frontiers of the United States. Given world circumstances, both ends might have been most efficaciously pursued by a policy of accommodation with Great Britain and a policy of aggressive opportunism toward Spain and its ally France. The Jefferson administration followed quite the opposite course, and yet because of special conditions that prevailed during the first term it registered spectacular successes both in managing the debt and in expanding the nation's boundaries. But those special conditions had vanished by the winter of 1805–1806, never to return; and a policy of accommodation with Britain and aggressiveness toward France and Spain now became the *only* policy that was consistent with the primary aims of Jeffersonian Republicanism.

And therein lay the dilemma the Jeffersonians had made for themselves: they simply could not follow the necessary path. As to bellicosity, they were willing to fight Spain (a pushover) and did not fear war with Britain (they could always "defend" the United States by staying off the seas); but they were possessed of an uneasy feeling, rational or otherwise, that a war with France could mean loss of territory to Napoleon's seemingly invincible armies. To the Jeffersonians, no foreign policy that entailed such a risk was thinkable. As to accommodation with Britain, there were several barriers they could not overcome. One barrier was ideological and psychological. Since opposition to the

English system lay at the very heart of the Republican revolution, to make common cause with England was to join hands with the devil. Another was more involved. The Jeffersonians, having emasculated the American armed forces in the interest of economy, were left with no way of making themselves heard abroad except through diplomacy and a professed moral commitment to abstract principles of international law. The British, given the conditions necessary to their continued existence as a sovereign nation, found it impossible to comport themselves strictly within the limits of those principles. They depended for their survival upon mastery of the seas, and though they were (after Pitt's death) willing to make concessions to the United States that they made to no other nation, they could not and would not waive their "right" to impress British seaman from foreign vessels and to issue orders determining who could trade with whom and in what commodities. Since both of these practices were in violation of the international law to which the Jeffersonians were committed, the Jeffersonians could not sanction them without compromising their moral integrity. Moreover, in that regard they were also bound by practical political considerations. For more than twelve years the Republicans had consistently and vigorously protested British naval policies, and they could not suddenly abandon that posture without a total loss of face. Finally, and perhaps most vitally, for the Jeffersonians to reach an accommodation with Britain on Britain's terms—however reasonable those terms might be— would have been to admit the obvious but unutterable fact that the success of the Revolution of 1800 was directly dependent upon the good will of Great Britain. In other words, for the Revolution of 1800 to continue to succeed, it would have to deny and contradict itself.

* * * * *

As a system of national policy, Jeffersonian Republicanism was bankrupt by the summer of 1807. By fall, the president himself began to suffer what amounted to a paralysis of will. He had always had a tendency, when faced with difficult or unpleasant decisions, to procrastinate in the hope that changing circumstances would improve his options; but now every change deepened his dilemma, and he simply could not think of anything reasonable to do.

Indecisiveness and self-doubt are scarcely the stuff of presidential leadership in times of national danger. But until December Jefferson could not move, he could only wait—without knowing what he was waiting for and without knowing what he would do when it came. In this vacuum, James Madison emerged with a far-fetched scheme that became administration policy. At first, Jefferson distrusted and failed to understand the policy, and Gallatin flatly disapproved it, but in the course of a few months the president came to embrace it and regard it as his own. He also rationalized it as a noble effort to avoid both war and submission to tyranny, and set out to enforce it with fanatical zeal.

The name of the scheme was embargo. In its name, Thomas Jefferson conducted a fifteen-month reign of oppression and repression that was unprecedented in American history and would not be matched for another hundred and ten years, when Jefferson's ideological heir Woodrow Wilson occupied the presidency.

* * * * *

[The Jeffersonians] remained remarkably true to their principles throughout Jefferson's presidency—despite charges to the contrary by a host of critics, ranging from Alexander Hamilton to Henry Adams to Leonard Levy. Moreover, they were remarkably successful in accomplishing what they set out to do. They set out to destroy the complex financial mechanism that Hamilton had built around the public debt, and they went a long way toward that goal—so close that if war could have been avoided for another eight years, their success might have been total. They also set out to secure the frontiers of the United States by expanding the country's territorial domain into the vast wilderness, and they succeeded so well that it became possible to dream that the United States could remain a nation of uncorrupted farmers for a thousand years to come.

And yet on the broader scale they failed, and failed calamitously —not because of their own shortcomings, but because their system was incompatible with the immediate current of events, with the broad sweep of history, and with the nature of man and society. As an abstract idea, Bolingbrokism *cum* Jeffersonian Republicanism may have been flawless, and it was certainly appealing. In the real world, it contradicted and destroyed itself.

At the core of the Republicans' thinking lay the assumption, almost Marxian in its naiveté, that only two things must be done to remake America as an ideal society and a beacon unto mankind. First, the public debt must be extinguished, for with it would die stockjobbing, paper-shuffling, "monopoly" banking, excisemen, placemen, and all the other instrumentalities of corruption that the Walpole/Hamilton system "artificially" created. Second, governmental power must be confined to its constitutional limits, which implied reduction of the functions of government but also, and more importantly, meant adherence to the rules of the separation of powers—that being the only legitimate method, in their view, whereby a free government could exercise its authority. If ancient ways were thus restored, the Jeffersonians believed, liberty and independence would inevitably follow. In turn, liberty and independence—by which they meant the absence of governmental restraint or favor and the absence of effective interference from foreign powers—would make it possible for every man, equal in rights but not in talents, to pursue happiness in his own way and to find his own "natural" level in the natural order.

Things did not work out that way, especially in regard to relations with foreign powers: far from freeing the country from foreign interference, Republican policy sorely impaired the nation's ability to determine its own destiny. In their eagerness to retire the public debt, the Jeffersonians tried diligently to economize. Toward that end they slashed military and naval appropriations so much as to render the United States incapable of defending itself—at a time when the entire Western world was at war. Simultaneously, in their haste to destroy all vestiges of the Hamiltonian system, the Jeffersonians abolished virtually all internal taxes. This relieved the farmers and planters of an onerous tax burden and arrested the proliferation of hated excisemen, but it also made national revenues almost totally dependent upon duties on imports—which meant dependent upon the uninterrupted flow of international commerce, which in turn depended upon the will of Napoleon Bonaparte and the ministers of King George III.

For two or three years the Jeffersonians were extremely lucky. That is to say, during that period the kaleidoscope of events in Europe turned briefly and flukishly in their favor. They obtained Louisiana as a result of a concatenation of circumstances that was wildly improbable and was never to be repeated. They were able to pay off much of the public debt and to accumulate sizable treasury surpluses because Great Britain, out of consideration for its own interests, allowed the Americans to engage in a trade of debatable legality, thus swelling the volume of American imports and, concomitantly, the revenues flowing into the United States Treasury.

From 1803 onward, however, each turn of the international wheel was less favorable to the United States. By 1805 it was apparent that West Florida—for which the Jeffersonians hungered almost obsessively, since its strategic and economic value was considerably greater than that of all Louisiana excepting New Orleans—would not become American in the way that Louisiana had. In the same year it began to be clear that the British would not long continue to allow the United States to grow wealthy by trading with Britain's mortal enemies.

But for their ideology, the Jeffersonians could have reversed their earlier policy stance, embraced Britain, and become hostile toward France and Spain, thus enabling the nation to continue to prosper and expand. Given their ideological commitment, they could not do so. Moreover, given the consequences of their actions so far, they lacked the strength to make even a token show of force against Great Britain. Thus in 1807, when both Britain and France forbade the United States to engage in international commerce except as tributaries to themselves, the embargo—a policy of pusillanimity and bungling, billed as a noble experiment in peaceful coercion—was the only course open to them.

At home, as they became ever more deeply impaled upon the horns of their self-created international dilemma, the Jeffersonians became progressively less tolerant of opposition or criticism. From the beginning they had shown considerable disdain for the federal courts; as Jefferson's second term wore on, this disdain degenerated into contempt for due process of law and for law itself. Thus the embargo became a program of domestic tyranny in inverse ratio to its ineffectiveness as an instrument of international policy: the more the policy was found wanting, the more rigorously was it enforced.

The embargo, then, both as a bankrupt foreign policy and as a reign of domestic oppression, was not a sudden aberration but the logical and virtually certain outcome of the Jeffersonian ideology put into practice: the ideology's yield was dependence rather than independence, oppression rather than liberty.

Jeffersonian Divisions

Richard E. Ellis

Historians of party ideologies insist that differences between the Federalists and the Republicans were more important for a long while after 1801 than differences within the parties. Historians of governmental operations during Jefferson's administration have increasingly agreed. But there are certainly political historians who do not see the party struggle as the most illuminating aspect of these years, including some who would suggest, as the Progressives did, that deeper, more enduring conflicts had persisted in the nation since the eve of Independence. Among the most instructive studies from this point of view is Richard Ellis' The Jeffersonian Crisis: Courts and Politics in the Young Republic *(New York: Oxford University Press, 1971).*

The Jeffersonian Crisis *is a history of the dispute over the judiciary during Jefferson's administration, both on the national level and in Kentucky, Pennsylvania, and Massachusetts. It focuses throughout on divisions within the Republican Party and concludes with the acquittal of Supreme Court Justice Samuel Chase, whose impeachment marked the peak, as Ellis represents it, of a radical Republican challenge to moderates in both political parties. Ellis argues that the struggle over the judiciary was a vivid part of an extended conflict over just how democratic the American Revolution was to be. Radical Republicans preferred an elected, responsible judiciary and a simplified code of laws. They tended to be hostile to lawyers and the common law alike. Moderates, by contrast— Jeffersonians as well as Federalists—defended a judiciary holding office during good behavior, together with a uniform system of law removed from immediate popular demands. The clash between conservatives and democrats, the book suggests, coincided after 1801, as it had done since Revolutionary days, with deep divisions between rational and evangelical religions, between "a provincial, anti-intellectual, agrarian democracy...and a highly rationalized, elite-directed commercial society" (p. 261).*

The structure of The Jeffersonian Crisis *defeated my desire to offer excerpts. But Ellis has restated several of its central themes in "The Persistence of Antifederalism after 1789," published in* Beyond Confederation: Origins of the Constitution and American National Identity, *ed. Richard Beeman, Stephen Botein, and Edward C. Carter II (Chapel Hill: University of North Carolina Press, 1987), 295–314. Pages 295–307 of this essay are reprinted by permission. Copyright ©1987 The University of North Carolina Press. Published for the Institute of Early American History and Culture, Williamsburg.*

The Antifederalists, like most of history's losers, have not been treated very kindly. Until fairly recently, the tendency has been either to ignore them or simply to dismiss them as "men of little faith," who have only a peripheral place in the American political or constitutional tradition.[1] In the past two decades, however, a growing number of professional scholars have taken a fresh look at the Antifederalist opposition to the Constitution; they have concluded that they were an articulate and formidable group who not only offered a searching, intelligent, and coherent criticism of the proposed new government but also spoke the views of a substantial portion of the population, perhaps even a majority of Americans.[2] It still remains unclear, however, what happened to the Antifederalists and their opposition to the Constitution after the new government went into effect. For at this point the Antifederalists have generally been abandoned by scholars. Most students of the 1790s tend to deny that there is any connection between the struggle over the adoption of the United States Constitution and the party battles that followed, or they argue that the Antifederalists generally accepted the Constitution as a fait accompli and abandoned the struggle.[3] Sometimes

---

[1] Edmund S. Morgan, *The Birth of the Republic, 1763–89* (Chicago, 1956), 131; Cecelia M. Kenyon, "Men of Little Faith: The Anti-Federalists on the Nature of Representative Government," *William and Mary Quarterly*, XII (1955), 3–43; Benjamin Fletcher Wright, *Consensus and Continuity, 1776–1787* (Boston, 1958); Stanley M. Elkins and Eric McKitrick, "The Founding Fathers: Young Men of the Revolution," *Political Science Quarterly*, LXXVI (1961), 181–216.

[2] Michael Lienesch, "In Defense of the Anti-federalists," *History of Political Thought*, IV (Spring, 1983), 65–87; Jennifer Nedelsky, "Continuing Democratic Politics: Anti-Federalists, Federalists, and the Constitution," *Harvard Law Review*, XCVI (1982), 340–360; John P. Kaminski, "Antifederalism and the Perils of Homogenized History: A Review Essay," *Rhode Island History*, XLII (Feb. 1983), 30–37; Herbert J. Storing, ed., *The Complete Anti-Federalist*, 7 vols. (Chicago, 1981); Jackson Turner Main, *The Antifederalists: Critics of the Constitution, 1781–1787* (Chapel Hill, N.C., 1961); Robert Allen Rutland, *The Ordeal of the Constitution: The Antifederalists and the Ratification Struggle of 1787–1788* (Norman, Okla., 1966).

[3] See, in particular, Lance Banning, "Republican Ideology and the Triumph of the Constitution, 1789–1793," *WMQ*, 3d Ser., XXXI (1974), 167–188; and *The Jeffersonian Persuasion: Evolution of a Party Ideology* (Ithaca, N.Y.,1978). Most treatments of the 1790s generally ignore the question of what happened to the Antifederalists after the adoption of the United States Constitution. Joseph Charles, *The Origins of the American Party System: Three Essays* (New York,1961); Noble E. Cunningham, Jr., *The Jeffersonian Republicans: The Formation of Party Organization, 1789–1801* (Chapel Hill, N.C., 1957); Richard Buel, Jr., *Securing the American Revolution: Ideology in American Politics, 1789–1815* (Ithaca, N.Y., 1972); Rudolf M. Bell, *Party and Faction in American Politics: The House of Representatives, 1789–1801* (Westport, Conn.,1973); Mary P. Ryan, "Party Formation in the United States Congress, 1789 to 1796: A Quantitative Analysis," *WMQ*, 3d Ser., XXVIII (1971), 523–542; Paul Goodman, *The Democratic-Republicans of Massachusetts: Politics in a Young Republic* (Cambridge, Mass., 1964); Carl E. Prince, *New Jersey's Jeffersonian Republicans: The Genesis of an Early Party Machine, 1789–1817* (Chapel Hill,N.C., 1967); William Nisbet Chambers, *Political Parties in a New Nation: The American Experience, 1776–1809* (New York, 1963).

the struggle over the ratification of the Constitution is traced through Congress's adoption of the Bill of Rights, but this is viewed exclusively as an aftermath of the ratification struggle, and not as a harbinger. A few historians have begun to examine the first congressional elections and have found some indication that Antifederalism persisted, and others have suggested that the political alignments that existed on the state level during the 1780s continued into the early 1790s. But the significance of these findings has not been fully explored, and they have not had much impact.[4]

This is unfortunate. For while it is understandable now, nearly two hundred years later, that the United State Constitution should inspire awe and even reverence, and it is comforting to some to believe that it has always inspired awe and reverence, it is undeniable that the Constitution was not very popular when it was first adopted. Moreover, the opposition to the kind of central government created by the Constitution and the desire to alter its structure fundamentally were an integral and dynamic part of American political culture well into the nineteenth century.

II

To understand why the Antifederalists remained an influential (if not quite dominant) force in American politics in the years after 1788, one must examine the amendments they proposed to the United States Constitution at the various ratifying conventions (Massachusetts, South Carolina, New Hampshire, Maryland, Virginia, New York, and North Carolina) and compare them with the Bill of Rights, for there were important differences. The amendments proposed by the states fall into two categories. The first limited the authority of the central government over individuals in a number of key areas by providing protection for freedom of religion, freedom of the press, and the rights to assemble, petition, and bear arms. Prohibitions were demanded against the quartering of troops and unreasonable search for and seizure of evidence. Still others guaranteed due process in criminal trials by demanding grand jury indictments, speedy public trials, the assistance of counsel,

---

[4] Steven R. Boyd, *The Politics of Opposition: Antifederalists and the Acceptance of the Constitution* (Millwood, N.Y., 1979); Merrill Jensen *et al.*, eds., *The Documentary History of the First Federal Elections,1788–1790* (Madison, Wis., 1976); John Zvesper, *Political Philosophy and Rhetoric: A Study of the Origins of American Party Politics* (Cambridge, 1977), esp .88–93; Joyce Appleby, *Capitalism and a New Social Order: The Republican Vision of the 1790s* (New York,1984); Norman K. Risjord, *Chesapeake Politics, 1781–1800* (New York,1978); Jerome J. Nadelhaft, *The Disorders of War: The Revolution in South Carolina* (Orono,Me.,1981); Alfred F. Young, *The Democratic Republicans of New York: The Origins, 1763–1797* (Chapel Hill, N.C.,1967).

the right of a jury trial, and protection from excessive bail and fines and cruel and unusual punishments.

The amendments of the second group were both substantive and structural. They expressed Antifederalist concern about the centralizing tendencies inherent in the new government, the federal government's control of the purse and the sword, the various limitations placed upon the power of the states, the way the president was elected, the long terms of United States senators, the authority of the federal judiciary, and the ratio of representation in the House of Representatives. Among other things they provided limitations upon the federal government's power to levy taxes, restricted the jurisdiction of the federal courts, and stipulated that the militia remain under the control of the states. Every state convention that submitted amendments also included one, often at the top of its list, stipulating that all those powers not "expressly" delegated to the federal government be retained by the states.[5]

The First Congress took up the matter of amendments to the Constitution in September 1789. Although the supporters of the new government had pledged themselves to do this and President George Washington even alluded to it in his inaugural address, many Federalists were extremely apprehensive of what the results might be. They feared, in particular, that the adoption of amendments might destroy what had been accomplished at Philadelphia. Some even suggested that the question of amendments be permanently tabled. But James Madison, who was more responsible than any other individual for the final form the Constitution had taken, insisted that the issue of amendments be directly faced. In pursuing this course, Madison was motivated by a mixture of reasons. His honor was at stake, since he had personally guaranteed the Virginia ratifying convention that he would support the move to amend the Constitution. He also recognized that failure to amend the Constitution would fuel the movement for a second constitutional convention, which was in many ways a more dangerous alternative. Finally, in 1789, Madison could have few illusions about the extent of Antifederalist strength, especially in Virginia, where Patrick Henry had blocked his election to the United States Senate. In addition, Madison had won his seat in the House of Representatives only

---

[5] The proposed amendments may be found in Jonathan Elliot, ed., *The Debates in the Several State Conventions on the Adoption of the Federal Constitution...* (Philadelphia, 1836), II, 177, 550–553, III, 657–661, IV, 243–247. U.S. Department of State, *Documentary History of the Constitution of the United States, 1786–1870* (Washington, D.C., 1894–1905), II, 139–142, 190–192. There is an incomplete but convenient list of the proposed amendments in Edward Dumbauld, *The Bill of Rights and What It Means Today* (Norman, Okla., 1957), 173–205.

after a close contest with James Monroe, who had opposed the adoption of the Constitution.[6]

To deal with the dilemma of how to go along with amendments to the Constitution without fundamentally altering either the power or structure of the newly created central government, Madison arranged to be appointed head of the committee considering the recommendations of the state ratifying conventions. Carefully culling the various proposals, Congress under Madison's leadership submitted twelve amendments to the states for approval. Of these, ten were eventually adopted. Of the two rejected amendments, one increased the number of representatives, and the other prevented members of Congress from benefiting from increases in compensation. Of the ten amendments that make up the Bill of Rights, the first nine protected the rights of individuals. Only the tenth dealt with the problem of distributing power between the states and the federal government, and the way it was written did not satisfy many Antifederalists. The Tenth Amendment stipulates, "The powers not delegated to the United States by the Constitution, nor prohibited by it to the States, are reserved to the States respectively, or to the people." Taking their cue from the second article of the Articles of Confederation, the Antifederalists tried to alter it to read, "The powers not *expressly* delegated to the United States by the Constitution...are reserved to the states...," but they were unsuccessful.[7]

Richard Henry Lee described the amendments finally proposed by Congress as "mutilated and enfeebled," and William Grayson judged them to be "good for nothing."[8] In other words, the Bill of Rights, as finally adopted, did not lay to rest the concerns of many Antifederalists about the kind of central government created by the United States Constitution. As a result, the question of how power was to be distributed between the state and federal governments was to remain the central constitutional and political issue in American history until the Civil War.

---

[6] For Virginia policies following the adoption of the United States Constitution, see Richard R. Beeman, *The Old Dominion and the New Nation, 1788–1801* (Lexington, Ky., 1972). This is one of the few attempts to look at the persistence of Antifederalist thought after 1788. It has not received the attention it deserves.

[7] On the drafting of the Bill of Rights, see Bernard Schwartz, *The Great Rights of Mankind: A History of the American Bill of Rights* (New York, 1977); and Robert Allen Rutland, *The Birth of the Bill of Rights, 1776–1791* (Chapel Hill, N.C.,1955); Dumbauld, *The Bill of Rights*, 206–222. Almost nothing has been done on the ratification procedure followed in the different states.

[8] Richard Henry Lee to [Francis Lightfoot Lee], Sept. 13, 1789, in James Curtis Ballagh, ed., *The Letters of Richard Henry Lee* (New York, 1911–1914), II, 500; William Grayson to Patrick Henry, Sept.29, 1789, in William Wirt Henry, ed., *Patrick Henry: Life, Correspondence, and Speeches* (New York, 1891), III, 406.

Careful analysis of the fight over ratification indicates that, once local and special considerations are taken into account, the main division was between the cosmopolitan and commercial-minded Americans who favored adoption and the provincial rural types who were either outside or on the periphery of the market economy that opposed the new government. The opponents of the Constitution were strongest in those areas farthest away from urban areas and navigable waterways, areas to be found in northern New England, western Massachusetts, central and western Pennsylvania, backcountry South Carolina and Georgia, New York, Virginia, and North Carolina.[9]

The social, economic, and geographical conditions that undergirded Antifederalism and made its localist appeal so attractive to so many people did not suddenly change after 1789, but continued to exist well into the nineteenth century. In many ways Antifederalism was much more than simple opposition to the United States Constitution or a demand for amendments. It was a way of viewing the world. It was the political and constitutional expression of tradition-oriented people who distrusted change and who desired to live in a society and under a government that was as simple and immediately under their control as was possible. It was a world view that was also in many ways decidedly anticommercial and precapitalist.[10]

III

The struggle over the adoption of the United States Constitution did not so much create divisions as reflect them, and this caused problems for Jefferson and Madison, who had their own vision for the economic development of the United States and who became unhappy over many of the domestic programs and the foreign policies that were adopted by Alexander Hamilton and the Federalists in the early 1790s. For their opposition to the government did not include a desire to alter the Constitution fundamentally. It is for this reason that their criticism of Federalist policies took the form of a demand for a strict, or a literal, interpretation of the powers granted by the Constitution, and not for clarifying amendments.

Throughout the early 1790s Jefferson's and, especially, Madison's opposition to Federalist policies tended to be cautious and measured. Although they sometimes recognized the Antifederalists as useful allies, they also tended to dissociate themselves carefully from many of their

---

[9] Main, conclusion to *Antifederalists*, 249–281; and *Political Parties before the Constitution* (Chapel Hill, N.C., 1973). See also Orin Grant Libby, *The Geographical Distribution of the Vote of the Thirteen States on the Federal Constitution, 1787–8* (Madison, Wis., 1894).

[10] Richard E. Ellis, *The Jeffersonian Crisis: Courts and Politics in the Young Republic* (New York, 1971), 250–284.

forms of opposition. For example, Madison was critical of Hamilton's proposal to fund the domestic portion of the national debt at face value with back interest. But instead of adopting the Antifederalist position, which would have repudiated that portion of the debt which provided enormous profits for speculators and would have reduced the amount of taxes to be levied, Madison instead *ineffectively* and confusedly proposed that the federal government discriminate between original holders and speculators. Madison wanted to pay the speculators the highest market value at the time of their purchase and to give the balance to the original holder. This proposal would not have reduced either the total amount of the national debt or the amount of taxes needed to pay it off.[11]

Slowly and haltingly, the Republican party was formed between 1792 and 1796. The consolidating tendencies evinced by the passage of the Judiciary Act of 1789, the assumption of the state debts, the creation of the national bank, and the levying of internal taxes bore out to many the fears expressed by the Antifederalists during the ratification struggle, and most Antifederalists became Republicans. But the Republican party was made up not only of Antifederalists but also of people who had supported the adoption of the Constitution. It was not so much an absorption or even an amalgamation of the two groups, but an uneasy alliance. The differences between them were real enough in 1792, when George Clinton decided to oppose John Adams for the vice-presidency. Jefferson and Madison were, at best, lukewarm to this development, because they viewed the governor of New York as the Antifederalist candidate.[12]

Tension between the two groups also emerged during the struggle over the Jay Treaty. Madison, who started out as a vigorous opponent of its adoption, became increasingly hesitant and eventually withdrew from the fight at a key point, as extremist elements on the Republican side, both on the state level and in Congress, turned the battle into a struggle over the Constitution itself. The Virginia legislature proposed a series of amendments that would have required the approval of both houses of Congress (not just the Senate) for a treaty to go into effect, limited the term of senators to three years, removed the power to try impeachments from the Senate, and prohibited federal judges from holding any other office at the same time. Although these proposals were not formally endorsed by the legislature of any other state, they did gain the approval of a number of prominent Antifederalists, including Samuel Adams, then gov-

---

[11] E. James Ferguson, *The Power of the Purse: A History of American Public Finance* (Chapel Hill, N.C., 1961), 297–342.

[12] Thomas Jefferson to James Madison, June 10, 1792, in William T. Hutchinson *et al.*, eds., *The Papers of James Madison* (Chicago, Charlottesville, 1962), XIV, 316.

ernor of Massachusetts. Within the House of Representatives there were various proposals which, had they been adopted, would have seriously weakened the power of the president.[13]

Despite the tensions that existed between the two wings of the party, the coalition in opposition to the policies of the Washington administration made sense. Disunited, each group would remain an ineffective minority. In particular, for the Antifederalists, an alliance with former supporters of the adoption of the Constitution would mean help from leaders who had the experience and the connections to launch a national campaign. This is something at which the Antifederalists, who tended to be ideologues lacking in organizational skills and particularist in outlook, were not very adept, as the struggle over the adoption of the United States Constitution had revealed.

Equally important, it allowed the opponents of the Constitution to shed the name "Antifederalist," which they themselves had not chosen. It had been successfully foisted on them by the supporters of ratification in the 1787–1788 struggle, who preempted the term "Federalist" for themselves, even though, in many ways, it more accurately described their opponents. That the term "Antifederalist" stayed with the opponents of the Constitution through the early 1790s and generally down to this day is part of the penalty for losing perhaps the most crucial political battle in American history. Therefore, when the Antifederalists, with only a few key exceptions moved into the Republican party, they eagerly embraced the opportunity to be known as Republicans.[14]

The coalition of the two most important groups opposed to the policies of John Adams's administration in the latter part of the 1790s proved to be a formidable development that culminated not simply in the defeat of the Federalists but in their permanent vanquishment. The high point of Republican opposition came in 1798–1799 with the adoption of the Kentucky and Virginia resolutions (drafted by Jefferson and Madison, respectively), with their emphasis upon fear of the central government's power and upon the rights of the states.

These resolutions not only denounced the Alien and Sedition Acts as unconstitutional but also contained an elaborate theory of the Union.

---

[13] Stephen G. Kurtz, *The Presidency of John Adams: The Collapse of Federalism, 1795–1800* (Philadelphia, 1957), 21–23, 35–36, 40–45, 48–50, 64–65; Bell, *Party and Faction in American Politics*, 54–56; Thomas J. Farnham, "The Virginia Amendments of 1795: An Episode in the Opposition to Jay's Treaty," *Virginia Magazine of History and Biography*, LXXV (1967), 75–88; "To the Legislature of Massachusetts, January 19, 1796," in Harry Alonzo Cushing, ed., *The Writings of Samuel Adams* (New York, 1904–1908) IV, 386–393.

[14] Those exceptions were Patrick Henry, Luther Martin, and Samuel Chase, whose conversions to the Federalist party have never been adequately explained, but who appear to have been motivated by personal and idiosyncratic reasons.

The federal government, they argued, was one of limited and specifically delegated powers and a product of the compact made between the different states in 1787–1788. The Kentucky and Virginia resolutions also took issue with the Federalist claim that the United States Supreme Court was the exclusive and final arbiter of constitutional questions. The Court, it was asserted, was a creature of the Constitution, and to give it the power of judicial review would be to make, as Jefferson argued in the Kentucky Resolutions, "its discretion, and not the Constitution, the measure of its powers." According to the Kentucky and Virginia resolutions, should the federal government assume a power not granted to it, each state as a party to the compact had the right to declare the law unconstitutional; and since Congress exceeded its constitutional powers when it adopted the Alien and Sedition Acts, the state of Kentucky declared these to be "not law" and "altogether void and of no force."[15]

In actuality, at least where Jefferson and Madison were concerned, the rhetoric of the Kentucky and Virginia resolutions was a good deal more extreme than their reality. They were never meant to be a prescription for action. Even though both states declared the Alien and Sedition Acts to be unconstitutional, no official attempt was actually made to prevent the enforcement of the laws by federal officials within the boundaries of Kentucky and Virginia. The resolutions were issued for political effect to rally the Republican opposition, to reaffirm the Revolutionary tradition whereby the defense of personal and civil liberty was joined to states' rights, and to offer a theory of the origins and nature of the national government that undercut the constitutional basis for the Federalist program of centralization. In this sense the resolutions were an enormous success, as they played an important role in helping Jefferson obtain the presidency in 1800.

But other Republicans wanted more than simply a victory for Jefferson in 1800. John Randolph, an influential Virginia congressman, expressed the feelings of this group when he observed, "In this quarter we think that the great work is only begun: and that without *substantial reform*, we shall have little reason to congratulate ourselves on the mere change of *men*." These Republicans wanted substantive changes in the Constitution and a definite weakening of the principles of nationalism that had been unleashed by the achievement of 1787–1788. In particular, they wanted to reduce the power of the president and the federal judiciary, make the latter more amenable to popular control, and more precisely define and restrict the prerogatives of the

---

[15] Adrienne Koch and Harry Ammon, "The Virginia and Kentucky Resolutions: An Episode in Jefferson's and Madison's Defense of Civil Liberties," *WMQ*, 3rd Ser., V (1948), 145–176.

central government.[16] In later years these demands became known as the Spirit, or Principles, of 1798, and for many Jeffersonians, especially those who became known as Old Republicans, the base from which they were to measure the apostasy, as they viewed it, of the leaders of the Republican party after 1801.

As president, Jefferson refused to launch an attack on the Constitution. He removed some Federalists from office and repealed the Judiciary Act of 1801, but did not ask for amendments to weaken the power of the federal government. Instead, he established the precedent that, when the out party comes to power in the United States, it changes the personnel and the policies of the government, but not the government itself. Disappointed but undaunted, the Old Republicans, led by John Randolph, who from 1801 to 1805 was the Spirit of 1798 incarnate, proceeded to attack the federal judiciary by broadly defining the impeachment process and thereby raising constitutional questions about the nature of judicial independence. But this, too, was thwarted in the impeachment trial of Samuel Chase when Jefferson made no attempt to impose party regularity and allowed enough Republican senators to vote not guilty and put an end to the attack on the federal judiciary. If anything, Jefferson, as president, expanded the powers of the national government, through the purchase of Louisiana, the building of a national road, and the adoption and enforcement of his controversial embargo policy.[17]

When Jefferson stepped down from the presidency in 1808, a vigorous, if uncoordinated and unsuccessful, attempt was made to prevent Madison, who clearly was the leader of the pro-Constitution wing of the Republican party, from succeeding him. George Clinton and James Monroe, both of whom opposed the adoption of the Constitution in 1787–1788, were his chief rivals, but the congressional caucus, which had the final say, stuck by Madison.[18] During his first term in office Madison revealed his constitutional nationalism in a number of impor-

---

[16] John Randolph to Joseph H. Nicholson, July 26, 1801, Nicholson Papers; William Branch Giles to Thomas Jefferson, June 1, 1801, Jefferson Papers, both at Library of Congress, Washington, D.C.; *Examiner* (Richmond), Oct. 20, 1801.

[17] Ellis, *The Jeffersonian Crisis*, 19–107; Richard Hofstadter, *The Idea of a Party System: The Rise of Legitimate Opposition in the United States, 1780–1840* (Berkeley, Calif., 1969), 122–169. On Jefferson's attitude toward the Constitution and the related problem of the economic development of the United States, see also Richard E. Ellis, "The Political Economy of Thomas Jefferson," in Lally Weymouth, ed., *Thomas Jefferson: The Man, His World, His Influence* (London, 1973), 81–95.

[18] Harry Ammon, "James Monroe and the Election of 1808 in Virginia," *WMQ*, 3rd Ser., XX (1963), 33–56.

tant ways. When the governor of the state of Pennsylvania, with the approval of the legislature, moved to prevent the enforcement of the Supreme Court's decision in *United States v. Peters*, Madison threatened to use force and compelled the state to back down. In fact, the militia officer who, under the authority of the state, had led the resistance to the federal marshal in charge of enforcing the high court's decree was arrested, tried, and convicted.[19] Although he was eventually pardoned by the president, for humanitarian reasons, this pardon did not come until the principle of federal supremacy had been established. Madison also, over the objections of many Republicans, even Jefferson's, appointed Joseph Story, who turned out to be an even more extreme nationalist than John Marshall, to the United States Supreme Court.[20] Madison also endorsed the move to recharter the first Bank of the United States.

Despite the ability of nationalist-oriented Republicans to preserve the integrity of the Constitution and increase the power of the federal government, their need to stay in power, their constant fear of a Federalist revival, and their desire to avoid, if at all possible, an open division in the party required that some recognition be given to those Republicans whose roots lay in Antifederalism. Consequently, the person selected to be vice-president came from that wing of the party. Aaron Burr, the unsuccessful Republican vice-presidential candidate in 1796 and the vice-president from 1801 to 1805, had been very circumspect during the struggle over the adoption of the Constitution in New York, but he was viewed by many as basically opposing its adoption and was initially proposed for the post by Melancton Smith, a prominent Antifederalist. George Clinton, vice-president from 1805 to 1812, was, of course, a vigorous and open opponent of the Constitution in 1787–1788. And Elbridge Gerry, vice-president from 1813 until his death in 1814, although a member of the Philadelphia Convention in 1787, had refused to endorse the new government. Neither Burr nor Gerry had much impact on Republican policy, but Clinton definitely made his presence felt when, as presiding officer, following a tie vote in the United States Senate, he killed, for constitutional reasons, the bill to recharter the first Bank of the United States.

---

[19] Kenneth W. Treacy, "The Olmstead Case, 1778–1809," *Western Political Quarterly*, X (1957), 675–691; William O. Douglas, "Interposition and the *Peters* Case, 1787–1809," *Stanford Law Review*, IX (1956–1957), 3–12; Sanford W. Higginbotham, *The Keystone in the Democratic Arch: Pennsylvania Politics, 1800–1816* (Harrisburg, Pa., 1952), 177–204.

[20] Morgan D. Dowd, "Justice Story and the Politics of Appointment," *American Journal of Legal History*, IX (1965), 265–285; R. Kent Newmyer, *Supreme Court Justice Joseph Story: Statesman of the Old Republic* (Chapel Hill, N.C., 1985), 70–71.

Beginning in 1811, a major political revolution, one that has barely been touched on by historians of the period, began to take place in the Republican party.[21] After several years of drifting on foreign policy issues, which were further complicated by various personal and policy differences among the more nationalist Republicans, Madison decided to take control of matters by going to war with Great Britain in 1812. Before doing so, however, he had to make his peace with the old Antifederalist wing of the party. He did this by reconciling with James Monroe and making him secretary of state and his heir apparent. Madison also developed good relations with Governor Daniel Tompkins of New York, known as "the farmer's boy," who had inherited George Clinton's political supporters, and gained the support of Governor Simon Snyder of Pennsylvania, the political leader of the small farmers from the more economically backward areas of the state. He also obtained the backing of Spencer Roane, the politically influential judge of the Virginia Court of Appeals who had had close political and personal ties to Patrick Henry (Roane married Henry's daughter) and who had actively opposed the adoption of the Constitution by the Old Dominion.

The Country was swept by a spirit of nationalism following the end of the War of 1812, but there was more opposition to the expansion of the federal government's power than is generally recognized. To be sure, the second Bank of the United States was chartered, but the vote was a close one (eighty to seventy-one in the House and twenty-two to twelve in the Senate). Most of those who voted against the bank were Old Republican types, and the measure passed only when it received the support of a number of states' rights Republicans who adandoned their constitutional scruples and voted in favor of the bank because they believed it was the only way to achieve economic stability following the chaos of the war years and the proliferation of state banks since 1811. The nationalists, or New Republicans (as they were beginning to be called), were much less successful in establishing a federal program of internal improvements. The bonus bill vote was eighty-six to eighty-four in the House and twenty to fifteen in the Senate; and Madison, who supported the measure on policy grounds, vetoed it because he believed it unconstitutional. In his veto message he specifically rejected the "necessary and proper" clause, the federal government's "power to regulate commerce among the several states," and its obligation "to provide for the common defense and general welfare" as justification for such a program.

---

[21] Although the events leading to the War of 1812 have been closely examined, almost no work has been done on the effect of the coming of the war on the Republican party.

Why did Madison do this? There is no question but that he was motivated by a genuine belief in a truly federal system of government in which there was "a definite partition of powers between the General and State Governments" and was fearful "that no adequate landmarks would be left by the constructive extension of the powers of Congress as proposed in the bill" should the extreme nationalist arguments of John C. Calhoun and Henry Clay, who were the bill's chief supporters, be followed.[22]

He also was aware, however, that there was considerable opposition to the measure from Old Republicans and other advocates of states' rights, a group whose support had been crucial for the recent war effort. In addition, it is clear that by 1817 there existed considerable popular discontent with the nationalist direction in which Congress was taking the country. A number of states moved to try to tax the second Bank of the United States out of existence. But the opposition to congressional policies found an even more effective way to express itself. In 1816, the Fourteenth Congress voted to increase the salaries of its members, and there was an enormous reaction in the fall elections. Incumbents ran into so much hostility at home that most members of Congress decided not to run for reelection or were defeated if they did run. Two-thirds of the members of the House of Representatives were replaced in what is probably the largest single turnover in American history.[23] What makes this development significant is that the right of congressmen to increase their own salaries had been prohibited in one of the amendments that had actually been submitted to the states by Congress as part of the Bill of Rights, but that amendment had not been ratified. It is yet further indication that the issues and the resentments that had been raised in the fight over the adoption of the Constitution continued to smolder and even explode well into the nineteenth century. The huge turnover that took place in the congressional election of 1816 put a halt to any further nationalist legislation. What few internal improvement bills did squeak through as a consequence of logrolling activities were generally vetoed by James Monroe, who had succeeded Madison in 1817. John Quincy Adams, who urged Congress not "to be Palsied by will of its Constituents," was the first president to support the view

---

[22] "Veto Message," Mar. 3, 1817, in Gaillard Hunt, ed., *The Writings of James Madison* (New York, 1900–1901), VIII, 386–388.

[23] George Dangerfield, *The Awakening of American Nationalism, 1815–1828* (New York, 1965), 16; Henry Adams, *History of the United States of America during the Administrations of Thomas Jefferson and James Madison, 1801–1816* (New York, 1891–1896), IX, 119–122, 134–138, 144–146; George T. Blakey, "Rendezvous with Republicanism: John Pope vs. Henry Clay in 1816," *Indiana Magazine of History*, LXII (1966), 233–250. See also Gerald Gunther, ed., *John Marshall's Defense of McCulloch v. Maryland* (Stanford, Calif., 1969).

that Congress had the authority to create a federal program of internal improvements, but by the time he entered the White House in 1825, the Jacksonian revolution had already begun, and relatively few measures were adopted.

The Republic in Peril, 1812: Party Loyalty and War

Roger H. Brown

*Differences among Republicans were so apparent during Madison's admin-
istration that participants in the extended scholarly debate about the causes
of the War of 1812 searched everywhere except in congressmen's allegiance
to their party. But party loyalty and the persistent influence of the clashing
ideologies that had appeared soon after the creation of the federal system
may have been a critical ingredient in the decision for a "second war for
independence." This was the central argument of Roger Brown's* The
Republic in Peril: 1812 *(New York: Columbia University Press, 1964).
This selection is from pages 44–66, 73, 76, 78, 83–84, and 186–191,
reprinted by permission. Copyright ©1964 Columbia University Press.*

Disunity and division characterized the congressional decision that in
June, 1812, brought war with Great Britain. By a vote of 79–49 the
House of Representatives authorized war on June 4. By a margin of
19–13 the Senate passed the measure on June 17. Ninety-eight members of Congress approved and 62 opposed the declaration of war.
Casting an eye over the nation's nineteenth-century wars with Mexico
and Spain, one notes that in 1846 and 1898 Congress twice again failed
unanimously to agree on war. But neither of these later conflicts began
with the national legislature so badly torn by conflicting sentiment, with
majority and minority so close to balance.[1]

Sectional interpretations of pro- and antiwar motivation have dominated twentieth-century writing on the War of 1812. Modern historians
with the notable exception of Bradford Perkins have viewed the division in sentiment as between a prowar south and west and an antiwar
northeast. An economic interpretation of the causes of war holds that
ruinously low cotton and grain prices in the south and west aroused war
feeling against Great Britain and her blockade of Continental markets.
An expansionist thesis locates the primary thrust of war sentiment in
frontier aspirations for Canada and Florida. Historians explain northeastern opposition to the war on the basis of reluctance to give up
profitable overseas commerce with Great Britain and fear of naval bom-
bardment and military attack.[2] Although sectional interests played a

part in the final war decision, this problem is more clearly understood as a party division than a sectional one. Contemporaries understood the line of division as primarily between Republicans and Federalists . . . The war vote itself is more consistent with a party than a sectional interpretation. With some exceptions the congressional split followed party lines. All members for war were Republican while 40 Federalists and 22 Republicans who bolted from party ranks stood in opposition. A breakdown of the antiwar vote by geographical regions shows 31 Federalists from the northeast and 9 Federalists from the south—not a consistent sectional line-up. Of 22 Republican votes against war, it is true that 18 came from the northeast, only 2 from the south, and 2 from the west. But a geographical breakdown of the Republican vote for war shows 46 from the south, 12 from the west, and 40 from the northeast—again not a sectional pattern.[3]

President Madison and Secretary Monroe believed that the impasse over the Orders in Council could be broken only by a resort to force and that failure to bring force to bear against Great Britain constituted submission....Republicans from all sections of the country, in letters to relatives, local party leaders, and constituents, stated similar views. Members from the south, the northeast, and the west had come to believe that all means short of war had failed and that the country had no other alternative. . . .

Recent writing on the causes of war in 1812 supports this position. Norman Risjord, Bradford Perkins, and Reginald Horsman, in publications that have appeared within the last three years, agree in locating the basis for war in a feeling that the peaceful policies of diplomacy and commercial restrictions, operative since 1806, no longer offered hope of redress. Nevertheless, on the matter of when and how Republicans reached this consensus, significant differences occur among these writers. Risjord and Horsman see the process as one of gradual conversion, a process that began with the agitation of the "war hawks" as early as 1809, then gathered strength and numbers as more "conservative" Republicans gradually joined their ranks. Perkins, on the other hand, finds no "war hawks" until late 1811, when by word and action a belligerent wing of the party began forcing peace-minded "scarecrow men" and "moderates" into hostilities. . . .[4]

Neither of the two most famous members of the 12th Congress— Henry Clay of Kentucky and John C. Calhoun of South Carolina— supported war until late 1811. Both men played important roles in the final march towards hostilities. Clay, as speaker, appointed the standing committees and almost certainly packed them with men who agreed with his views. During the session he worked closely with the administration and helped shape and guide much of its program through the House. A telling document in the Monroe papers shows

Clay working out details with the Secretary of State for a brief embargo as a preliminary to war. Calhoun had an important share in the final drafting of the war manifesto and it was he who introduced the war resolution to be voted upon on June 1. Both men, as their letters and speeches clearly demonstrate, believed the country had before it only the two alternatives of war or submission.

There is no clear evidence that Clay and Calhoun had been for war before the fall of 1811. Contrary to frequent accounts, Clay had not pressed for war in 1810 when addressing Congress. True, he had at that time told the assembly that when commercial restrictions were abandoned he was for "resistance by the sword" and that the "conquest of Canada" was "in your power." But he also made it clear in the same speech that the time for forcible resistance had not yet come. He had then proposed either a more stringent nonimportation law or congressional authorization for arming merchant ships to take effect after another negotiating attempt. In the early months of 1811 he intimated that Britain might still repeal her Orders in Council. In August, 1811, he told a party associate that repeal was possible, but that if Britain did not follow France's example in repealing her edicts, war would be "inevitable." During the war session he said again and again, in public and private statements, that war had now become necessary owing to British intransigence.[5] Nor did Calhoun advocate war before the fall of 1811. Nowhere in the recently published first volume of his papers is there any indication that before that time he believed war necessary. His biographer, Charles M. Wiltse, hypothesizes that Calhoun campaigned for Congress in 1810 on a war program.[6] Yet during the war session Calhoun showed considerable concern as to how his constituents were taking the prospect of a coming British war. His letters suggest he did not know just what kind of response the war would evoke in South Carolina. Would he have been unsure of public reaction had he campaigned and been elected on a war platform? There are other indications that he shared the position of Clay and the great majority of other Republicans. "Experience," he told a friend, had proved commercial restriction and negotiation to be "improper for us." Their effects had been "distrust at home and contempt abroad." Again, he told a correspondent in May, 1812, that war "has become unavoidable," military preparations having been no more successful in bringing England to yield than all other efforts.[7]

Furthermore, members made it very plain that Republican support for war rested on the view that now no other course had become possible. Military preparation was a matter "on which we have no choice but to act," said Jonathan Roberts of Pennsylvania. The President had called for military legislation "under circumstances that present no alternative but a vigorous preparation for resistance, or, as has been frequently observed during this debate, 'unconditional submission.'" Nathaniel Macon of North Carolina declared that "to attempt another negotiation would be useless; every effort has been made in that way that could be made. Indeed, no one has yet said that he wished another. Is there a man in the House that wishes another attempt at negotiation, or one that wishes to go to war if it could possibly be avoided? " Perhaps Felix Grundy of Tennessee gave the best testimony on the matter:

> At the opening of the present session of Congress, the President informed us that every effort to settle our differences with Great Britain by friendly negotiation had been employed without effect. Under such circumstances, as every other expedient had failed, we determined that the only justifiable course left was to put the nation in arms, and by force redress the violated rights and honor of an injured and insulted people.

As Bradford Perkins has accurately perceived: "Most congressmen came to Washington in the fall of 1811 unpledged, probably undecided."[8]

Precisely when and how did the Republican majority reach the view that no alternative remained but war? A close study of congressional correspondence for the period November, 1811, to June, 1812, showed that widespread agreement developed among Republican members during the first month of the session. In July, 1811, after the position of the British government had been fully developed through negotiations with Foster, President Madison had issued a proclamation summoning Congress some weeks earlier than originally planned. During late summer, at Montpelier in Virginia, he had reached his decision for war. His recommendations, together with the documents exchanged between Monroe and Foster in their July negotiations, greeted Congress at its November convening. But the President did not state clearly his personal reasons for recommending force. His message recommended military preparations, but did not analyze in detail the reasons for making this recommendation. Great Britain, Madison noted laconically, had refused to repeal her Orders and had taken a new and more advanced position that indicated greater intransigence than ever. This action led him to believe that Congress would feel the necessity of putting the nation "into an armour and attitude demanded by the crisis."

The facts communicated by the President threw congressional Republicans into a quandary. They agreed a "crisis" was at hand. Nonimportation had failed to shake Great Britain. Now the Napoleonic Decrees as they affected American neutral commerce no longer seemed in force, Britain's defense of her own system as retaliation was untenable. Yet in addition to denying the fact of French repeal, Foster had indicated that Britian had no intention of repealing her Orders even if she were to accept, as fact, repeal of the French Decrees. France must repeal her Decrees to the extent they prohibited importation into the Continent of productions and manufactures made in Britian when owned or carried by neutrals. So impossible did this demand appear that its very existence proved Britain would not yield. Meanwhile, on the high seas, British cruisers seized American vessels not complying with the Orders in Council—according to one report in circulation, 100 were lost within six months. Republicans agreed it was necessary to do something to protect American commerce. As George Poindexter, delegate from the Mississippi Territory, observed, shortly after the President's message had been received by Congress: "We cannot tell what will be done, until the Committees report. No one has suggested a specific measure; but all agree *that something must be done.*" In a similar state of mind Felix Grundy told the Governor of Tennessee that "something must be done, or we shall loose [sic] our respectability abroad and even cease to respect ourselves.[9]

To observers, the month following the President's message seemed a period of much confusion. Actually, it was a time of slow groping towards common ground, a time when members revolved, canvassed, and discussed various opinions and possibilities . . . Among those quickly reaching a decision that war was necessary was Henry Clay. As early as the previous August he had been over the possibilities and foreseen "inevitable" war if Britain continued to hold fast; he must have made up his mind the moment he learned the contents of Foster's hand. Perhaps Republican members he picked for the Foreign Relations Committee—Porter, Calhoun, Grundy, Desha, John A. Harper of New Hampshire, and Ebenezer Seaver of Massachusetts—had arrived at a similar conclusion; would he have chosen a majority that did not agree with him or the President?[10]

In this situation, as Congressman William Lowndes of South Carolina observed, "the want of some controuling or at least concentrating influence" was "very obvious." On such a basis members could predict the impending committee reports would afford the necessary rallying point. Calhoun noted that members were "generally very anxious as to the course that will be persued" and predicted that the report of his committee "will in a great measure determine the course that will be persued." The committees in both House and Senate invited the Executive to discuss its views in detail. Charles Tait of Georgia, a member of the Senate committee, told how Secretary of State Monroe appeared before his group and explained "with utmost frankness the views of the Admin," giving assurances that "the utmost harmony prevails in the Cabinet and that they mean bona fide to enter into the Contest" unless Britain relaxed. Likewise the Secretary appeared before the House committee, where he made known as one committee member put it, the *"motives,* the *views* and the *wishes* of the Executive."[11]

On November 29 Chairman Porter of the House committee presented the report of the Republican majority. The report reviewed past efforts to induce repeal of the Orders in council—embargo, nonintercourse, and nonimportation laws, repeated negotiations and appeals to justice—all unsuccessful. It restated what everybody knew, that Britain had not only refused to admit the fact of French repeal of edicts affecting American neutral rights but had demanded that France repeal provisions affecting British trade with the Continent as a precondition of her own repeal. It stated what everybody knew too, that Britain was seizing and condemning American vessels. Also it cited, as the second of "the great causes of complaint against Great Britain," the impressment of American seamen into the British navy, a practice it described as "carried on with unabated rigor and severity." The time has come, the report proclaimed, when we "must now tamely and quietly submit, or we must resist by those means which God has placed within our reach"—armed force...

During November members had looked towards the impending report of the Foreign Relations Committee as a crucial determinant of future events. With presentation of the report on November 29 opinion began moving swiftly towards a consensus. It is clear that the document made an impact on Republicans and brought into sharper focus incipient ideas and tentative postions.[12]

No Republican member genuinely hoped for war or joined the consensus that war was now necessary with any other feeling than deep reluctance and regret. Thus Nathaniel Macon asked the rhetorical question of his congressional colleagues whether there was "a man in the House" who "wishes to go to war if it could possibly be avoided?" John A. Harper avowed: "I pray to God, that he may open the eyes of the British Government to the interests of their renowned nation, and save us, them, and the world, from the evils of the impending conflict." Jonathan Roberts accurately perceived this mood when he wrote in January: "There seems to be no disposition to relax our war measures but I believe every body would be exceeding glad to remain at peace. The federalists seem sanguine the orders in council will be revoked. I confess I hardly allow myself to hope it."[13] These men did not minimize or close their eyes to the disadvantages and evils of war. Historians have portrayed the leaders as bellicose, fervent, and heedless as to the evils of war. A reading of their correspondence suggests that this does not do them justice. A few Republicans foresaw danger in a standing army, a swollen national debt, corruption of public virtue, and a possible alliance with Napoleon. All foresaw hardships and dangers in war—casualties, expenses, taxes, and commercial and business losses. The nation's military and naval establishments were weak. Thirty years had gone by since the nation had fought a war, and few men were experienced in supply, recruitment, strategy, and tactics under actual war conditions. There was great concern as to whether public opinion would wholeheartedly and unitedly support war against Great Britain at this time with all the hardships and sacrifices it entailed, and which Federalists were bound to exploit . . .[14]

It was quite true that a good deal was said in debate to suggest that some Republicans were spoiling for a fight with Great Britain. Men did wax belligerent, they did ignore or minimize the evils of war, and they did predict quick and easy victory. They talked heatedly and emotionally of accumulated British aggressions on national rights and honor— Orders in Council, impressment, British-incited Indian attacks, the *Chesapeake* outrage, and much else. In vivid colors they painted the horrors of American sailors enslaved on British men-of-war and of Indian scalping raids against frontier women and children, the indiginity of American vessels seized on our own coasts, the insulting repudiation of the Erskine agreement, and the growing hardship of the southern and western farmer. They seemed eager for war, for a chance to get revenge for half a decade of unredressed injuries and insults. Yet one should consider the situation they were then facing. The country needed to be aroused. The recruitment of men for the new army, the subscription to the $11,000,000 loan, and the conversion of business operations to a war footing all required that the war seem credible and worthy of sacrifice to private citizens. But how were these objects to be met, except by oratory that received a wide circulation through the newspapers? The President's statements were infrequent and couched in restrained, almost cryptic tones. No new blatant insult, like the *Chesapeake* affair or the Erskine repudiation, had occurred in 1811 to stir national feeling. Britain had once again refused to repeal her Orders, but in terms requiring a better understanding of the complex web of diplomacy than the ordinary citizen possessed. A British envoy had laid out his government's position in an exchange of notes with an American secretary of state which are not easy even for the historian to understand. When many men, Federalists, were telling their friends and constituents that the war was a fraud, the task of rousing the country became. . .even more difficult. Finally, heavy concentration of belligerent speeches during the December debates suggests the possible operation of another motive. A faint hope remained that Great Britain only needed convincing that the Republican majority genuinely meant war and she would repeal her Orders. Was it not well therefore to show her we meant business? In summary, the speeches of individual congressmen afford a false impression of eagerness for war. Fiery, belligerent, and oblivious of the consequences as they may seem at first glance, they give a less accurate picture of prevailing reluctance than do private letters . . .

On the existence of a conflict between "war hawks" and "peacemen" within the party, the evidence is also far from conclusive. There was no consistent division within the party over war measures—the army, navy, taxes, or recess—that might reveal such a struggle; the same men may be found on both sides of these issues at different times. There were Republicans who were very supicious of "bluffers" in their own party—Grundy was one. But suspicion does not prove fact. Grundy was suspicious of Madison and Monroe who were not bluffing, even though at times they might seem to have been.[15]

The great majority of Republicans—south, north, and west—rallied to the idea of war when party leaders had assured everyone that all honorable, pacific measures had been tried and that no choice remained between war and submission. This meant confidence that Jefferson, Madison, and their advisers had earnestly and honestly sought accommodation with both belligerents. It meant acceptance of Henry Clay's avowal: "Not a man in the nation could really doubt the sincerity with which those in power have sought, by all honorable pacific means, to protect the interests of the country." Or of John Sevier's claim: "Our Government have tried negociation until it is exhausted, and there is no doubt in my mind the Executive have observed the most perfect uprightness, and impartial neutrality." In 1812 only men who trusted Jefferson and Madison in their leadership of party and country held such sentiments. These were administration Republicans, men who had agreed with the Virginians on the main outlines of their domestic and foreign policies and who trusted their personal competence and devotion to the Republic. This did not include Federalists, antiadministration Republicans like John Randolph of Roanoke, or Clintonians. But that is another story.[16]

To say all this is not to disclaim the importance of leadership in the Republican march towards the final June declaration of war. Clay and Calhoun deservedly won reputations for their role in shaping and guiding the Republican war program through the Congress. Their energy and determination impressed members of both parties at the time, and their contribution to the business of legislating the means of war was vital.[17] Without their presence Congress might have become paralyzed in squabbles over the details of war legislation. Nor is it contended that Republicans were generally agreed on the manner and timing of hostilities. A sizable group in the party wanted an undeclared limited maritime war instead of the full-scale hostilities that a declaration of war would bring. Some of the same men, and others, wanted to postpone hostilities until the nation was more adequately prepared. But these were differences over strategy, not over the fundamental question of war or peace. It is contended, however, that the main body of the Republican party did not separate into two factions that differed during most of the session over the questions of war or peace; that the great majority of Republicans reached a consensus that no acceptable peaceful alternative remained between the end of July, 1811 (the Foster negotiations), and the end of November, 1811 (the report of the House Foreign Relations Committee); and that the great majority came to this decision with no little regret and reluctance, however eager some might appear in their speeches. Given these conditions, perhaps the time has come for us to relegate a misleading term—"the war hawks of 1812"—to the realm of partisan misunderstanding and historical mythology.

There remains a crucial problem. Republicans rejected submission and chose war. They regarded this choice as a choice between evils, and they took the lesser—war. They were reluctant to go to war. They would have been happy to avoid it. What might they have anticipated from submission that outweighed the risks and evils of war? Why did Republicans prefer war as a less dangerous course than submission?...

Concerns larger than assured commerce, national sovereignty, and national honor were at stake. Republicans thought of themselves as defenders of republicanism against enemies both at home and abroad. Certainly the economic consequences of submission concerned many. Certainly the threat to national independence caused worry; certainly, too, did the matter of personal and public self-respect. But Republicans in 1812 feared above all else that submission would threaten their control of the nation's political life and draw odium down upon republican government. No other possibility could have so overweighed the predicted dangers and evils of war, or evoked such dire forecasts at the thought of submission...

Ever since the Revolution American leaders had been conscious of the unproven capacity of their republic to function effectively in the jungle of international life. The question was still unanswered whether a government made up entirely of elected members possessed enough unity of purpose and firmness of will to give full protection to vital national interests—by force if necessary. Years of temporizing and postponement in the face of European maritime aggression—negotiation after negotiation, restriction after commerical restriction—had deepened doubts as to the competence of the present American form of government. Perhaps, after all, republicanism was (as Washington once put it) "ideal & fallacious." Thus, Henry Clay, deploring the fear of British power in the "councils of the nation" and its influence on the retreat from the embargo in 1809, referred to "that dishonorable repeal which has so much tarnished the character of your Government." It was of the utmost importance to dispell all doubt as to the capacity of republican government and to avoid giving any further proof of weakness...[19]

Such expressions reveal how Republicans linked the prestige of republicanism to the issue of war versus submission. Submission would demonstrate that republican government lacked energy, staying power, the ability to organize and bring to bear the will and strength of the nation. In the event of submission, would republicanism survive? It seemed possible that it would not. Proven inability to ensure such vital concerns as the economic interests of citizens, national sovereignty, and national honor might destroy the faith of all America in the republican form of government . . .

At the Constitutional Convention in 1787 Madison had labored to save republicanism. His efforts to organize opposition to the Federalists in the 1790s had been to save this precious form of government. In 1812 he was again concerned . . . It was [this] concern that dictated a passage in the Annual Message of November, 1812, where he reviewed the course of British aggression.

> To have shrunk under such circumstances from manly resistance would have been a degradation blasting our best and proudest hopes; it would have struck us from the high rank where the virtuous struggles of our fathers had placed us, and have betrayed the magnificent legacy which we hold in trust for future generations.

There was also the Second Inaugural Address in which the President stated that war had not been declared by the United States until all hope of accommodation had been exhausted, "nor until this last appeal could not longer be delayed without breaking down the spirit of the nation, destroying all confidence in itself and in its political institutions, and either perpetuating a state of disgraceful suffering or regaining by more costly sacrifices and more severe struggles our lost rank and respect among independent powers . . . "

The Jefferson administration took office in 1801 determined to check a presumed swing towards monarchy and preserve the government from Federalist control. Facing problem of commercial depredation and impressment brought on by the Napoleonic wars, Jefferson and his advisers determined they must protect commerce if reputation was to be preserved abroad and public confidence upheld at home. Commercial restriction and negotiation afforded the means by which he and his successor sought to attain these ends. By mid-1811 it became clear that these weapons were useless in the contest with Great Britain. The inducements of nonimportation, embargo, nonintercourse, the Macon law, and possible conflict with France had failed; the presumed repeal of the French Decrees as they affected American neutral rights had produced no comparable British action; Britain continued her seizures and not only refused to repeal her Orders as they affected American neutral commerce, but made demands that revealed determination to make them codeterminate with her struggle with France. The Madison administration saw that no course remained but war or submission. Madison, Monroe, and their party associates in Congress and in the country at large believed submission would gravely imperil the very objects they had long sought. Aside from economic privation, infringement of national sovereignty, and the loss of national honor and morale, submission would work grave injury to the party and to the prestige of republicanism. Republicans rejected submission and reluctantly took the other alternative. Preparing for war they endeavored to use the threat of military force in a final effort to induce repeal. When this too failed the President recommended war—a war that would put an end to impressment as well.

Sentiment in Congress on the question of war divided closely along party lines, Republican and Federalist. The great majority of Republicans supported war because they, like the President, saw no other option. They concurred with the reasoning which led the President and secretary of state to this conclusion. They were able to agree because they trusted the good faith and integrity of all past efforts to achieve settlement. They could agree to Henry Clay's avowal that: "Not a man in the nation could really doubt the sincerity with which those in power have sought, by all honorable pacific means, to protect the interests of the country."[19] Had these policies and negotiations been the work of Federalists they would doubtless have opposed them. But they were not; they were the work of fellow Republicans, men who could be trusted . . .

The year 1812 for the student of our early history bears an heretofore unperceived meaning. The waning prestige of republicanism in 1787 had given deep urgency to the movement that produced a new blueprint of republican government—the Constitution. By 1812 republicanism seemed again in peril. Contemporaries perceived the parallel between the two periods. The present moment, exclaimed Calhoun of South Carolina, "is a period of the greatest moment to our country. No period since the formation of our constitution has been equally important." Once again men felt that a momentous outcome hung in balance. We must consider our actions with great care, urged William King of North Carolina, "when the destinies of the country are about to be launched on an untried ocean, and when the doubt is about to be solved, whether our Republican Government is alike calculated to support us through the trials and difficulties of war, and guide us in safety down the gentle current of peace."[20]

Nor did the sense of urgency concerning republicanism and the party dissipate after war began. The nation had shown it could declare war. It must now show that it could wage war. A letter from Secretary Monroe to Senator William H. Crawford reveals a continuing concern. Would the Senator call to discuss candidates to head a confused and leaderless War Department, asked the Secretary, at a particularly low point in American fortunes? "This is the time when the arrangements that are to insure success to the republican party & to free government for our country, are to be made, or which will lay the foundation for their overthrow." From the Virginia son-in-law of the Secretary of State,

George Hay, a state party leader, came this warning. "According to my limited views of the state of things in the UStates, this is the crisis of the republican cause. If it sustains the present shock, it will prevail and flourish for many years. The undivided strength of its friends ought therefore to be exerted with the utmost vigilance and circumspection." A speedy recruitment of an efficient military force, wrote William W. Bibb of Georgia in 1814, involved "the safety, if not the very existence of this free government." Only with news of the Peace of Ghent did there come relief from the sense of crisis. There had been disasters in this war, but also triumphs. Johnathan Roberts spoke for many when in 1815 in a letter to his brother he appraised the war. It had not been a defeat or even a stalemate but a victory—for the party and for republicanism.

> We have not got a stipulation about impressments & orders in council nor about indemnity—But victory perches on our banner & the talisman of invincibility no longer pertains to the tyrants of the Ocean—But the triumph over the Aristocrats & Monarchists is equally glorious with that over the enemy—Is is the triumph of virtue over vice of republican men & republican principles over the advocates & doctrines of Tyranny.[21]

There would be future crises which would call into doubt the energy and staying power of the American Republic. But to many Americans like Roberts the War of 1812 was one long stride in the march towards permanency.

Notes

1. *Annals of Congress*, 12th Cong., 1st Sess., pp. 297, 1637, The *Annals* reports the Senate vote as 19 to 13. The roll call actually shows only 12 negative votes, but Pope of Kentucky, missing on the roll call, voted against war. Josiah Bartlett, Jr., to Ezra Bartlett, 18 Je 12, Bartlett MS, LC; Thomas D. Clark, "Kentucky in the Northwest Campaign," in William T. Utter and others, *After Tippecanoe: Some Aspects of the War of 1812* (East Lansing, Mich 1963), pp. 84–85.

2. Margaret K. Latimer, "South Carolina—A Protagonist of the War of 1812," *American Historical Review*, LXI (1955–56), 914–29, and George R. Taylor, "Agrarian Discontent in the Mississippi Valley Preceding the War of 1812," *Journal of Political Economy*, XXXIX (1931), 471–505, stress southern and western economic distress. Julius Pratt, *Expansionists of 1812*, makes the classic statement of the expansionist thesis. A. L. Burt, *The United States, Great Britain, and British North America* (New Haven, Conn., 1940), pp. 306–10, and Reginald Horsman, *Causes of the War of 1812*, pp. 175–76, argue the case of northeastern opposition. Leading textbooks follow, with minor variations, the sectional approach.

3. For a convenient listing of members according to party affiliation, see Nile's *Weekly Register*, 30 N 11. I have taken the Mason-Dixon line east to Delaware as dividing south from north and the Appalachian barrier as demarcating the west. Bradford Perkins in *Prologue to War*, pp. 407–17, has perceived the party basis of voting.

4. Norman K. Risjord, "1812: Conservatives, War Hawks, and the Nation's Honor," *William and Mary Quarterly*, XVIII (1961), pp. 196–210, especially 205–7; Horsman, *Causes of the War of 1812*, pp. 156–57, 177, 182–87, 222–23, 266–67; Perkins, *Prologue to War*, pp. 267, 343–50, 373–74, 392, 406–7, 415–16, 432–37.

5. Clay Speeches, 22 F 10, 28 D 10; Clay to Caesar Rodney, 11 Ja 11, 7 Mr 11, 17 Ag

11, Clay Speech, 31 D 11, Clay to ?, 28 F 12, to Thomas Bodley, 12 My 12, Clay, *Papers*, I, 448–52, 515, 522, 546, 574, 609, 633, 653.

6. Charles M. Wiltse, *John C. Calhoun, Nationalist, 1782–1828* (New York, 1944), pp. 51–53. Mr. Wiltse's evidence for his statement that Calhoun campaigned for Congress in 1810 on a war platform is, in my judgement, inconclusive. I can find no supporting evidence in the cited *Correspondence*. Other evidence cited by Mr. Wiltse consists of personal reminiscences, an anonymous campaign biography, and a personal memoir. But neither Ebenezer Smith Thomas's *Reminiscences*, the *Life of John C. Calhoun*, nor Colonel W. Pinkney Starke's *Account of Calhoun's Early Life* states explicitly that the campaign of 1810 turned on the issue of war, or that Calhoun at that time advocated war. The most these sources suggest is that South Carolina voters were disgusted with members of the 10th Congress who had voted to repeal the embargo.

7. Calhoun to Patrick Calhoun, 24 Ja 12, to Patrick Noble, 22 Mr 12, 17 Je 12, to James Macbribe, 17 F 12, to Virgil Maxcy, 2 My 12, Calhoun Speech, 12 D 11, Calhoun, *Papers*, I, 89–90, 95–96, 126, 91, 76.

8. Roberts, Macon, and Grundy in *Annals*, 12th Cong., 1st Sess., pp. 502, 505, 493, 661, 1139; Perkins, *Prologue to War*, p. 267.

9. Madison's Third Annual Message, 5 N 11, Madison, *Writings*, VIII, 158–65; Thomas Rodgers to Jonathan Roberts, 17 N 11, Roberts MS, HSP; John Sevier to George W. Sevier, 13 Ja 12, "Some letters of John Sevier," pp. 62–63; George Poindexter to Cowles Mead, 11 N 11, Poindexter MS, Mississippi Dept. Archives and History; Grundy to Willie Blount, 18 N 11, quoted in Joseph H. Parks, *Felix Grundy: Champion of Democracy* (Baton Rouge, La., 1940), p. 37.

10. Thomas B. Cooke to Governor Daniel B. Tompkins, 6 N 11, Tompkins MS, Box 7, Package 1, NYSL; Macon to Nicholson, 21 N 11, Nicholson MS, LC; Peleg Tallman to William King, 18 N 11, King MS, Maine HS; Clay to Caesar Rodney, 17 Ag 11, Clay, *Papers*, I, 574; Joseph C. Cabell to John H. Cocke, 31 N 11, Cabell MS, VaU; *Annals*, 12th Cong., 1st Sess., P. 343.

11. Lowndes to Wife, 7 N 11, Lowndes MS (copies), UNC; Calhoun to Patrick Calhoun, 14 N 11, Calhoun, *Papers*, I, 63; Tait to Governor David Mitchell, 10 Ja 12, Gratz Collection, HSP; John A. Harper to William Plumer, 2 D 11, Plumer MS, LC.

12. W. W. Bibb to William Jones, 1 D 11, Jones MS, GaHS; Stevenson Archer to Elijah Davis, 4 D 11 (photostats, vertical file), MdHS; Hugh Nelson to Joseph Cabell, 28 D 11, Cabell MS, VaU.

13. Macon and Harper in *Annals*, 12th Cong., 1st Sess., pp. 661, 655; Roberts to Matthew Roberts, 25 Ja 12, Roberts MS, HSP.

14. W. W. Bibb to William Jones, 1 D 11, Jones MS, GaHS; Charles Tait to Governor David Mitchell, 10 Ja 12, Gratz Collection, HSP, to Thomas Carr, 1 Mr 12, Carr Collection, GaU; Hugh Nelson to Charles Everette, 16 D 11, Nelson MS, LC; Gideon Granger to Jong Tod, 26 D 11, Granger MS, LC; Paul Hamilton to Morton A. Waring, 4 N 11, 25 Jl 12, Hamilton MS, USC; William Eustis to Henry Dearborn, 28 Ja 12, Dearborn MS, MHS; Richard Rush to Charles Jared Ingersoll, 10 My 12, Ingersoll MS, HSP.

15. *Annals*, 1st Cong., 1st Sess., pp. 564, 617, 1003, 1069, 1353; Grundy to Jackson, 28 N 11, 12 F 12, Jackson, *Correspondence*, I, 208, 215; Charles Cutts to William Plumer, 11 D 11, Plumer MS, LC.

16. Clay Speech, 31 D 11, Clay, *Papers*, 1, 609; Sevier to George W. Sevier, 13 Ja 12, "Some Unpublished Letters of Sevier," pp. 62–63.

17. Jonathan Roberts to Matthew Roberts, 20 My 12, Roberts MS, HSP; John A. Harper to William Plumer, 2 D 11, Plumer MS, LC; William Reed to Timothy Pickering, 18 F 12, Pickering MS, MHS.

18. Washington to John Jay, 1 Ag 86, Department of State, *Documentary History of the Constitution* (Washington, D. C., 1905), IV, 20; Clay in *Annals*, 11th Cong., 3rd Sess., pp. 63–64.

19. Clay Speech, 31 D 11, Clay, *Papers*, I, 609.

20. Calhoun to James Macbribe, 17 F 12, Calhoun, *Papers*, I, 90; King in *Annals*, 12th Cong., 1st Sess., p. 516.

21. Monroe to Crawford, 3 D 12, *The Writings of James Monroe*, ed. by Stanislaus M. Hamilton (New York, 1898–1903), V, 227; Geroge Hay to Monroe, 1 N 12, Monroe MS, NYPL; W. W. Bibb to William Jones, 31 O 14, Jones MS, GaHS; Roberts to Matthew Roberts, 17 F 15, Roberts MS, HSP.

PART SIX

The End of an Era

As Roger Brown suggests, the Peace of Ghent, which brought the War of 1812 to a conclusion, also proved a landmark in the early party struggle. By any prudent calculus of gain or loss, the War of 1812 might seem a masterpiece of folly. Nineteen months of warfare ultimately went for naught. Boundaries were unaltered by the treaty. Prewar arguments about impressment and the rights of neutrals continued unresolved. Few Americans, however, were disposed to make such simple calculations. After all, the war had not been fought for merely prudent reasons. National honor and the reputation of republican government had also seemed at stake, and both appeared to have been vindicated by the struggle. Andrew Jackson's stunning triumph at the Battle of New Orleans abundantly redeemed the earlier American reverses in the field, and news of Jackson's victory arrived in the Atlantic states just before the news of peace. Americans, accordingly, believed they had fought a second war for independence and had won. If little had been gained, nothing had been lost in conflict with the greatest empire on the earth. A war whose practical objectives went completely unfulfilled thus had enormous meaning in the end.

Independence, to be sure, had never really been at risk. For Britain, war with the United States was a surprising outcome of a quarrel that had seemed a lesser evil than a relaxation of the struggle of the French. Once Bonaparte was vanquished, little could be gained by further prosecution of the lesser war. British statesmen blanched at military estimates of the commitments necessary to defeat, much less to subjugate, the new United States. And yet, for the Americans, the peace did bring a sort of second independence. In the War of 1812, the youthful nation had endured the strongest test that any European state was likely to present. And not until this test was passed did both the European powers and Americans themselves feel confident that the American Republic would persist.

Even the experiment in federal union seemed a great deal more secure with the conclusion of the war. Through all the years since the adoption of the Constitution, every difference over policy had seemed a

difference over principle as well, and conflicts over Revolutionary principles had repeatedly led to threats of sectional secessions. Undoubtedly
the passing years had strengthened national feelings, but the failure of
the federal experiment had never seemed more imminent than in the
final months of the war.

After years of Jeffersonian experiments with economic warfare,
New England was bitterly alienated from federal policy, as the United
States had entered on the War of 1812. During the struggle, wealthy
Yankees declined to lend money to a government that tottered on the
edge of bankruptcy. Legislatures passed resolutions condemning the
war. New England governors refused to permit their militias to be used
outside the borders of their states. Too often, noncooperation shaded
into trading with the enemy, schemes for the disruption of the union,
and talk about a separate peace.

Most New Englanders were not disloyal, but enough of them were
angry that, in December 1814, a convention met in Hartford, Conneticut
to consider the section's grievances against the nation. The majority of
delegates easily overrode the few secessionist plotters, but the convention did agree on several demands designed to protect New England
from a Southern and Western majority in Washington. It called for constitutional amendments that would break Virginia's grip on the presidency by limiting the office to a single term and forbidding successive
elections of men from the same state; that would reduce the number of
Southern congressmen by ending the representation of three-fifths of
the slaves; that would limit any embargo to sixty days; and that would
require a two-thirds majority in Congress to admit new states, provide for commerical retaliation, or declare a war. Acquiescence in these
changes might have crippled the central government, but the convention sent a committee to Washington with a manifesto that promised
a second convention and hinted at more drastic action if the demands
should be refused.

Despite New England's noncooperation, the administration managed to conduct the war—and did so, we might note—without resorting to repressive measures such as those of 1798. Not only that, it also
happened that the Hartford manifesto reached the federal city just in
time for celebration of the Battle of New Orleans. In consequence, New
England's effort to extort constitutional change under pressure of war
appeared both foolish and disloyal. James Madison and the Republicans
finished the war with far more prestige than thay had at its beginning,
while the reputation of New England Federalists was damaged beyond
repair. National pride moved massively behind the victors. Within a
few more years, for all essential purposes, the Republicans were the
only party left. In 1824, John Adams' son succeeded James Monroe as
the fourth Republican president.

For all of this, survival in the War of 1812 had not been easy, and the conflict taught hard lessons to Republicans as well. Party principles had joined with lack of planning, poor administration, and the alienation of New England to brew a bitter stew. For years, the Jeffersonian Republicans in Congress had resisted peacetime military forces. They had repealed internal taxes and refused to recharter Hamilton's national bank.   Thus, in 1812, the new United States had callenged Europe's most successful empire with a naval force of sixteen ships and a regular army of less than 7,000 well-trained men. Congress authorized new military forces on the eve of war, but ships could not be built in time to join the conflict. Enlistments in the army were painfully slow, so that the regulars carried the largest part of the burden only in the northern campaign of 1814. Meanwhile, the best American militia sat home in New England, and Western soldiers enjoyed a very mixed sucess. Meanwhile, too, the government was a financial cripple. Congress authorized internal taxes as it moved toward the war, but revenues were slow in coming in. Even when they did, the funds were all too meager.   And without a national bank, the Treasury had no dependable source of ready loans and no easy way to transfer funds from one part of the country to another. Against a less distracted, more determined foe, the burning of the federal city might have been the least of consequent humiliations.

Early in 1815, President Madison recommended a peacetime army of 20,000 men. In his annual message of December 5, 1815, the great architect of the old Republicanism called on Congress to consider federal support for certain internal improvements, tariff protection for the fragile industries that had emerged during the troubles with England, and creation of a new national bank. In 1816, Congress overwhelmingly adopted all of his suggestions. The implications of these actions were profound. Coming in connection with the self-destruction of the Federalists—and followed three years later by the first financial panic and the bitter sectional collision over the admission of Missouri—they signaled the conclusion of the first party struggle and the advent of a different age.

The Great Inversion, or Court versus Country: A Comparison of the Revolution Settlements in England (1688–1721) and America (1776–1816)

John M. Murrin

This tour de force of comparative and synthetic scholarship is hard to match for its encompassing review of nearly all the ground that has been covered in this volume. Murrin seeks the highest vantage and the broadest view. No less importantly, he seeks to fuse much of the most impressive scholarship from the distinctive, frequently competing schools represented in the earlier selections. "The Great Inversion" first appeared in Three British Revolutions: 1641, 1688, 1776, *ed. J.G.A. Pocock (Princeton: Princeton University Press, 1980), 368–453. This excerpt, taken from pages 377 and 407–428, offers Murrin's observations on the party struggle and its resolution. Copyright ©1980 by Princeton University Press. Reprinted with permission of Princeton University Press.*

Much can be learned by contrasting America's "Revolution Settlement" through the War of 1812 with that of England through the Hanoverian Succession and the rise of Sir Robert Walpole. To an almost incredible degree, American events after 1789 mimicked or even repeated English developments of a century before. America's Revolution Settlement resembles the remake of an old movie classic, except that the new producer has altered the ending to suit the changing tastes of his audience.

Note first the striking similarities. Each Revolution bequeathed intense, brutal party conflict to the next generation, a struggle that mobilized unprecedented numbers of voters, only to yield to a period of one-party rule—the Whig Oligarchy in Britain, the Era of Good Feelings in America. In both cases, because nobody really believed in parties, the contenders sought to destroy or at least absorb one another, not to perpetuate some kind of "party system." The division between Whig and Tory in Britain closely parallels the split between Federalists and Republicans in the United States, with Hamilton assuming the role of Junto Whigs or Walpole, and Jefferson serving as Tory or "Country" gentry—better still, as the "patriot" opposition to Walpole that had united Tories with Real Whigs in the 1730s; for Jefferson took his nomenclature from the late seventeenth century and would have hated to be called a Tory.

Indeed virtually all of England's central issues reappeared in America once Hamilton and his admirers launched their own financial revolution in the 1790s—an overt response to unresolved problems from the Revolutionary War. Hamilton took a debt that had sunk, depending upon the type of security and the provisions individual states had made for redemption, to anywhere from ten to thirty cents on the dollar and funded it at par, creating some of the grosser windfall profits in American history. Nearly all of this gain went to speculators rather than exsoldiers or planters, as entrepreneurs from New York City, Philadelphia, and Baltimore raced through the Southern backcountry to buy every available security before the local inhabitants (including local speculators) could learn how valuable they were.[1] Thus many Southerners saw only losses for themselves in these arrangements, and New York's Clintonian faction, which had already been forced to surrender lucrative port duties to the government, was not won over, despite the state's gains. But Hamilton's assumption of state debts meant an immense flow of capital into New England and Pennsylvania, sharply reducing the need for direct taxes there and instantly lowering political temperatures. Certainly for New England, Court politics on a national scale worked wonders that had been utterly impossible when attempted at the state level in the 1780s.

In 1791 Hamilton chartered the Bank of the United States, America's direct copy of the Bank of England. In place of England's great recoinage of the 1690s, the United States government established its own coinage and persuaded "the American Newton," David Rittenhouse, to take charge of the mint, a task Sir Issac had accepted a century before.[2] Not surprisingly, the New York Stock Exchange also dates from the 1790s, doubtless contributing to a "projecting spirit" that far exceeded anything Defoe's generation had known. By 1792 the speculations of Hamilton's associate, William Duer, had produced the republic's first financial panic. "The stock buyers count him out," complained Jefferson, "and the credit and fate of the nation seem to hang on the desperate throws and plunges of gambling scoundrels."[3] "No man of reflection, who had ever attended to the South Sea Bubble, in England, or that of [John] Law in France, and who applied the lessons of the past to the present time," he added in another letter, "could fail to foresee the issue tho' he might not calculate the moment at which it would happen." The national debt, he admitted, had to be paid. Indeed, unlike Hamilton, he was determined to pay it off as rapidly as possible and end the government's dependence upon the financial community. "But all that stuff called scrip, of whatever description, was folly or roguery, and yet, under a resemblance to genuine public paper, it buoyed itself up to par with that. It has been a severe lesson: yet such is the public cullability [sic] in the hands of cunning & unprincipled men, that it is doomed by nature to receive these lessons once in an age at least."[4]

No mere panic could restrain the "projecting spirit" set loose in the 1790s. Led by Eli Whitney's cotton gin and Robert Fulton's steamboat, the number of federal patents nearly doubled in every five-year period from 1790 through 1814. By 1802 it had reached a level thrice England's peak of the 1690s, which, incidentally, rested on a population base that was nearly identical: 5.5 million people.[5] Similarly the number of American banks exploded from four in 1791 to 29 by 1800, 89 in 1811 when the Bank of the United States expired, 246 by 1816, and over 300 at the onset of the Panic of 1819.[6] Oceanic commerce, mostly stagnant since 1774, grew at an astounding rate. America's $20 million worth of exports in 1790 had multiplied more than five times by 1807, led by the nation's reexport trade as the world's only major neutral carrier after 1793. An even more solid achievement, because it did not rest on European wartime conditions, was the fourfold increase in shipping engaged in coastal and internal trade—about double the rate of population growth. Indeed shipping profited enormously from the overall boom. In 1790 American vessels controlled only 40 percent of the value of American imports and exports. Just six years later this figure had lept to 92 percent. The tonnage of American registered bottoms tripled between 1790 and 1810, approaching two-thirds of Britain's on a much smaller population base, while American shipbuilding may have roughly equaled the entire British empire's between 1800 and Jefferson's embargo of late 1807.[7] Frantic expansion of this sort created unprecented extremes of wealth and soon stimulated great concern among the upper and middle classes about the problem of the poor.[8]

Other similarities abound. In every crisis with Indians or foreign powers in the 1790s, Federalists inched the government closer to the statist model first articulated by Continental officers and investors in the crucial war years, 1779–1783.[9] For a time the leverage provided by the debt gave Hamilton a virtual placeman system for controlling Congress under a "prime minister"—creating, in effect, a national faction such as Madison thought he had rendered impossible in the persuasive argument of Federalist Number 10. Through the whiskey excise Hamilton hoped to establish beyond question the government's power to tax internally. This Court measure provoked a rebellion in western Pennsylvania within a few years. As the republic verged on war with France, the Federalists extended their imitation of England with the stamp and land taxes of 1798, the second of which touched of Fries' Rebellion in 1799. Federalist repression of this mild and rather comic outburst, combined with the virulent nativism of the government's policy toward aliens, rapidly drove church Germans over to the opposition and forever alienated Pennsylvania from the party of Washington, Hamilton, and John Adams.[10] Hamilton closely supervised the creation of a true standing army at the end of the decade, and Congress added a navy designed to win respect for the American merchant vessels on the high seas.[11] Especially after the Jay Treaty, Federalists pursued a pro-British and anti-French foreign policy, partly because the funding program depending for its solvency upon customs duties derived from British trade. (On the other hand, the Federalists, far more than their opponents, took serious steps to limit this dependence by attempting to develop internal revenues as a partial alternative.) Jeffersonians, most of them sincere admirers of the French Revolution, took the opposite approach on these questions. Yet as the new army, the Sedition Act, hysterical nativism, and the threat of electoral reform to guarantee a federalist presidential succession in 1800 all revealed, Hamiltonian statism possessed a high potential for coercing dissent, which Federalists honestly equated with disloyalty. In their hierarchy of political values, liberty and equality had become subordinate to public order and energetic government.[12]

For that matter, just as Whigs and Tories agreed after 1689 that violent protest was no longer acceptable politics, so Federalists and probably a large majority of Republicans accepted Washington's argument that once a government had been validly established by popular consent, it could be changed only be peaceful means. But in America each party still applauded the violent resistance of the Revolutionary War, unlike England where the Civil Wars seemed indecently excessive to virtually the entire governing class by 1689. In this sense, whiskey rebels and others with similar ideas still had a viable tradition to invoke. Yet on balance the similarities with England appear to outweigh the differences even on this issue.[13]

Nevertheless the two Revolutions came out so differently that the result, to steal a phrase from R. R. Palmer, might well be called America's "Great Inversion" of England's Revolutionary Settlement.[14] The Court won in England, and the Country in America. Surely one reason was the contrasting pattern of international involvement. While Britain warred with France in all but six years from 1689 to 1714, the United States remained at peace in all but six years from 1789 to 1815 (if we omit Indian conflicts from the comparison). When the republic did go to war, many of the pressures that had transformed England after 1689 appeared instantly in America: an enlarged army, a small but proficient navy, and internal revenues during the quasiwar with France. All of these devices plus improved coastal defenses and a new Bank of the United States reappeared during or immediately following the War of 1812.

But because America's political antagonisms had a strong sectional base, protracted war with any great power would almost certainly have destroyed the fragile Union long before it could have transformed itself into a modern state, which, in the world of 1800, meant above all a government able to fight other governments effectively for an indefinite period. Even more than Englishmen of 1700, Americans could not agree on who their natural enemy was, or, as Washington stressed with peculiar force in his Farewell Address, whether they had one at all. Southern planters, who resented their continuing colonial dependence on British markets for their staples, often did regard Britain as a natural enemy. So did West Indian export merchants in the 1790s when the British took to plundering American vessels in the Caribbean, while merchants specializing in British imports completed this revival of the pattern of 1769 by opposing commercial sanctions and rallying to neutrality and the Jay mission.[15] Yankees, on the other hand, responded similarily to the prospect of war with France. Resurrecting ancestral memories of the traumatic struggles along New England's borders from 1689 to 1763, they evidently still did regard the French as natural enemies, a popish people doomed either to Jacobin anarchy, or, especially after the rise of Napoleon, to slavish government.

Thus any major war mobilized hostile interests quite capable of paralyzing the government. Conflict with France soon generated threats of nullification and even disunion in the Anglophobic South after 1798. War with Britain provoked an overt danger of secession in Francophobic New England in 1814. A timely peace defused the crisis in each case. Yet in a real sense Americans could agree to live together only so long as they did not have to experience or share the pressures inevitably associated with a modern central government, and even that minimal understanding was to collapse by 1861.

Two other differences between Augustan England and federal America help to explain the political contrast. The first point is impressionistic but probably accurate, although its dimensions remain uncertain. Compared with England, the United States simply lacked a national governing class, that is, one that had intermarried across state boundaries.

The Revolution, and particularly the resulting comradeship among Continental Line officers, undoubtedly stimulated something of the kind, later perpetuated in the Society of the Cincinnati; and while the national capital remained in Philadelphia in the 1790s, High Federalists did everything they could socially to act like a true governing class. But relatively few New Englanders seem to have married outside their region, and while the phenomenon was more common elsewhere, it required—almost by definition—more than a generation for the effects to be felt.[16]

The final contrast may well outweigh the others. By 1700 England had certainly acquired an integrated economy with London at its center, but the United States would achieve nothing fully comparable until the generation after 1815 or even 1840. The Revolution reversed the prevailing trend toward improved, imperial economic efficiency without creating a national, American economy. Many parts of the republic, awkwardly enough, still traded more with the former empire than with the rest of the Union. American vessels (not American produce) were now excluded from the British West Indies, and where about a third of the empire's ships (but not a third of its tonnage) had been built in the colonies as of 1774, Britain now preferred to construct her own at significantly greater cost. American shipbuilding recovered only in the 1790s, mostly as a byproduct of European war. Similarily the Mediterranean trade, a rapidly expanding sector before Lexington, utterly collapsed for a quarter-century because American vessels had no navy to protect them from Barbary pirates. The sheer uncertainties of these years, and not the solidity of economic opportunity in the new republic, probably explain the appearance of economic scramblers like William Duer, riding a spectacular cycle from boom to bust. Because imports from Britain, mostly in British ships, did revive after the Revolution, beginning with the famous glut of 1783–1784, the overall pattern seemed ironic in the extreme until perhaps 1793. The mercantile heirs of the loyalists, primarily British importers and overwhelmingly Federalist politically, appeared to be doing much better than merchants who concentrated in areas that patriots had once dominated. From this perspective, if the Revolution really was fundamentally an economic movement, somebody had miscalculated rather badly.[17]

To be sure, coastal and internal trade expanded more rapidly than American exports (not counting reexports). The margin was about 3:2 from 1790 to 1807 and much more decisive thereafter until war disrupted everything. By 1820 intra-American trade would finally catch up with American foreign trade. And in the decades 1790 to 1810, greater New York City displayed unmistakable signs of its rapid emergence as the continent's center of communications. But as a central city it still could not compare with London, even the London of 1700. As of the War of 1812, the United States was still a less efficient and less integrated economic entity than the old empire had been. By the time this situation began to change in the generation after 1815, the political configuration of the republic had already been defined in a way that excluded the British Court option.[18]

Thus the results of the two Revolutions differed markedly. In Britain the Court Whigs won and kept central control over the new Hanoverian dynasty, Parliament, the debt, the bank, high finance, the major corporations, the army, the navy, the bureaucracy, and the vast network of patronage. In the United States the Country opposition of Thomas Jefferson, which defined its aspirations very much in classic British terms, captured the central government in 1801 and held it. Compared with the Tory revival in Britain a century before, which had regained control of Parliament and the ministry in the last years of Anne's reign, the later Federalist resurgence that fell only one state short of retaking the presidency in 1812 was a less spectacular threat. And as a national force, Federalists disintegrated much more rapidly after 1815 than British Tories had after 1714.[19]

Yet Federalists and Republicans were not mere shadows of earlier Whigs and Tories, dueling awkwardly after 1789 in the sunrise of Europe's new revolutionary age. The American parties showed much fainter tendencies to shift polarities in the course of their struggles, even after the Republicans gained power and the Federalists found themselves in the uncongenial role of a permanent opposition. Both overwhelmingly rejected hereditary monarchy, although they differed considerably over how broadly they construed this repudiation. The etiquette Hamilton devised for President Washington strongly evoked monarchical traditions, his opponents strictly objected, while John Adams' passionate campaign for titles in 1789 and his insistence that functionally the Constitution really had created a monarchy caused him no end of polemical discomfort.[20] To suspicious Republicans, the Federalists seemed to give their secret away whenever John Allen and Uriah Tracy, two avowed monarchists from the unlikely state of Connecticut where not even appointive governors had ever taken root, opened their sarcastic and vituperative mouths. Convinced that "the herd have begun to walk on their hind legs," Tracy raged that "it was a damned farce to suppose that a republican government could exist," and that even America must finally have its own aristocracy and king.[21]

As in England, however, each party had discernable Court and Country wings, the normal results of frantic coalition building in times of stress. Among the Federalists, Allen and Tracy represented the extreme, not the norm. But Hamilton's policies explicitly emulated English Court techniques, and on the whole John Adams, the unyielding Country ideologue of 1775, agreed with him. Although he never abandoned his hostility to standing armies, Adams endorsed funding, assumption, the Bank, the Jay mission and treaty, and at first greatly admired Hamilton. "The Secretary of the Treasury is so able, and has done so well," he wrote in 1791, "that I have scarcely permitted myself to think very closely whether he could or could not have done better," although he did believe that Hamilton should have pushed harder for internal revenues. Adams found speculation deplorable but inevitable. "The funding system is the hair shirt which our sinful country must wear as a propitiation for her past dishonesty," he explained. "The only way to get rid of speculation is to hasten the rise of our stocks to the standard beyond which they cannot ascend." Fear of disunion and disorder now outweighed the dangers of malignant power that had tormented him in the 1770s. "The rivalries already arisen between the State Sovereignties and the National Sovereignty, and the other rivalries which if not already in action, will soon appear between Ministers of State and between the Legislative, executive and judicial powers give me more serious apprehension, than National Debt, Indian Wars and Algerine depredations—that is, the three issues out of which a national bureaucracy, army, navy, and their accompanying patronage already seemed likely to emerge.[22] Eventually of course, Adams and Hamilton did split, mostly over the army issue after 1798. Yet even in the 1790s some Federalists opposed each Hamiltonian measure, sometimes on explicit "Country" grounds. Once out of power, a few of them could develop these themes more fully, as when Senator Isaac Tichenor of Vermont fumed against James Monroe—of all people—for overlavish support of a standing army during the War of 1812. On the whole, however, the rarity of such defections is far more striking. Although younger Federalists copied Republican styles of mass politics, they held strongly to their old policies. In 1811 they voted unanimously to recharter the Bank which, despite the administration's support, died at Republican hands.[23]

More fascinating are tensions among the Republicans. In several respects Republican attitudes, like popular upheaval during the Revolution, strayed past the accepted boundaries of Country ideology. Republicans often extended to any navy the kind of rhetoric aimed at a standing army in England, where Country thinkers saw the navy as a politically safe *alternative* to larger armies. When Republicans extended the suffrage beyond property holders, they clearly outran neo-Harringtonian prescriptions, but this trend—common among northern Republicans by 1800 or so—did not become widespread in the more orthodox South until the Jacksonian era.[24] Similarly when radical Republicans fought to repudiate English common law for simplified codes or digests, they attacked a major prop to Country ideolology in England and hence rang alarm bells through their own party. The Sedition Act of 1798 persuaded virtually all Republicans that no such thing as a common-law crime should exist under federal jurisdiction.[25] But at the state level moderate Republicans combined successfully almost everywhere with Federalists to protect common law.[26] Even Jefferson, who at times could sound quite radical on this theme, retreated hastily when confronted with an ominously viable alternative—French civil law in Louisiana.[27]

This issue aside, Jefferson fits the specifications for a Country ideologue almost perfectly. Country terminology happily avoids the muddle Jeffersonian scholars usually get into when they worry about whether, or how and why, an "agrarian" like Jefferson could advocate commercial expansion and internal improvements of so many different kinds, including "manufacturing" after 1807. Evidently he was not really an "agrarian" after all.[28] But as Pocock and McCoy have shown, Country thinkers believed that commerce was a basic civilizing force and that the exchange of agricultural surpluses for other necessities strengthened the economic viability of the virtuous landowner. They were indeed suspicious of immense cities, of luxuries which might "effeminate" virtuous and "manly" qualities, and of the money power by which people who did no work and performed no visible useful function got rich at someone else's expense. Confined to the household level, manufacturers were acceptably virtuous. Jefferson matches the model on all these points, even if his deep Anglophobia inclined him to quote Scots more often than Englishmen.[29]

Jefferson agreed that the Revolutionary War debt had to be paid, but he loathed funding systems and the very idea of a permanent debt. To redeem this obligation, his "wise and frugal government" had to spend less than it received. Always fearful of banks, he tried to prevent the chartering of the Bank of the United States in 1791, and after it expired he attempted to prove with logarithms in 1813 that the republic could not afford banks.[30] Speculative booms and busts appalled him and made him tremble for the nation's future, whether in 1792 or 1819.[31] He opposed any standing army beyond a decentralized, frontier, constabulary force, although he did support the West Point Academy as a place through which its officers could be rotated to learn the technical side of their trade.[32] Like English Country spokesmen, he favored a navy if only to regain for America's agricultural surpluses the world markets that the Revolution had closed. Thus he launched the Barbary War to keep open the newly revived Mediterranean trade.[33] Only with assured overseas markets could the United States remain agricultural, prosperous, and free of undue dependence upon British credit and buyers.

Madison and Gallatin shared most of these values. Madison was less given to rhetoric about the tree of liberty and the blood of tyrants, and as an author of *The Federalist*, perhaps more inclined to praise public order. Although he and Gallatin reconciled themselves to the Bank in a way that Jefferson never did, Madison's economics involved the same concern—to protect America's agricultural surpluses by making the rest of the world bid for them competitively. He and Gallatin seemed more skeptical than Jefferson about the navy. Could the United States afford one large enough to make a real difference? Indeed for Gallatin, retirement of the debt overruled almost all other considerations and strongly reinforced his deep antimilitarist beliefs. Only when the government had an assured surplus revenue should it start to think seriously about fleets and internal improvements. Madison did agree with Hamilton that population pressure would eventually force the United States to follow the economic pattern of Europe—sprawling cities, huge manufacturers, and the network of social dependencies that these phenomena involved. But while Hamilton's policies tried to hasten this trend in the interests of national strength, Madison—much to Hamilton's surprise—struggled to postpone the evil day in the name of republican virtue.[34]

Nevertheless the Jeffersonians did attract a number of "Court" Republicans, defined here as men whose social and economic values resembled Hamilton's much more closely than Jefferson's, Madison's, or Gallatin's. General Samuel Smith of Baltimore—wealthy merchant, Revolutionary War hero, and strong advocate of the Federal Constitution—entered Congress as a Hamiltonian. "Gentlemen might speak of equality," he scoffed in an early speech, "but in practice the thing was impossible." Yet he soon went over to the opposition when the Washington administration did nothing to protect his ships against British depredations in the Caribbean. Always a bit contemptuous of Jefferson's idealism and Madison's policies, he vainly tried to arrange an accord between Jefferson and Adams in 1800. Although he rarely got his way with the administration on commercial policy after 1801, his brother did become Jefferson's Secretary of the Navy, and Samuel did serve in a frustrating role as the administration's chief link with the merchant community.[35] Jacob Crowninshield, a Salem merchant who made his fortune after 1790 in the far Eastern and Continental European trades, had acquired a strong dislike for the British during the course of doing so. Quite logically, his experience and attitude brought him into the Republican Party.[36] Elbridge Gerry of Massachusetts followed a more tortuous path from antifederalist with a keen distrust of the people in 1787–1788 (the people of New England, he told the Philadelphia Convention, "have . . . the wildest ideas of Government in the world"), to Hamiltonian with an anti-Southern bias a few years later, to Adams Federalist, to Jeffersonian.[37] Like Smith, he hoped Jefferson would acquiesce in Adams' reelection in 1800, in exchange for the succession in 1804. John Armstrong's strange career led him from authorship of the extremely inflammatory Newburgh broadsides in 1783 to the secretaryship of war in Madison's cabinet.[38] In New York the Clintonian, Livingston, and Burr factions all had conspicuous entrepreneurial elements that would make possible a coalition of moderate Republicans and Federalists against Madison's reelection in 1812.[39]

Whatever Burr's famous conspiracy was really about, one element of it represented the ultimate danger to liberty in Country terms. Burr actively tried to subvert the officer corps of both navy and army, and he did bring the army's commanding general, James Wilkinson, into his scheme. Despite his killing of Hamilton, he apparently had considerable Federalist support. Emphasizing "the weakness and imbecility of the federal government" under Jefferson, Burr boasted to one potential recruit "that with two hundred men, he could drive Congress with the president at its head into the river Potomac" and "that with five hundred men, he could take possession of New York." Wilkinson tried to win over a reluctant major by arguing "that the very existence of an army and democracy was incompatible; that Republics were ungrateful; jealous of armies and military merit; and made no provision for the superannuated and worn out officers . . . who were left to starve." The major stayed out of the conspiracy, but he agreed with the general's opinion. Interestingly, in the cypher used between Burr and Wilkinson, 76 meant "democracy," 89 stood for "aristocracy," and 96 represented the navy.[40]

Pennsylvania produced a small but active group of Court Republicans. Merchants and manufacturers such as Tench Coxe, John Nicholson, John Swanwick, Charles Pettit, and Blair McCleanachan, plus the able lawyer Daniel Cunyngham Clymer, entered the 1790s either as overt Hamiltonians or with principles difficult to distinguish from Hamilton's, but each of these men eventually defected to the Republicans. Their motives varied from dissatisfaction with the funding program (Pettit and McCleanachan demanded even better terms for security holders), to an interest in manufacturing with Anglophobic implications that Hamilton did not share (Coxe and possibly Nicholson), to ethnic and social resentment against Federalist snobbery (McCleanachan again, and Swanwick). Quite a rarity among Jeffersonians, Coxe had been a loyalist during the Revolution, while Swanwick was the son of a British placeman and loyalist. Swanwick also entered public life while a younger member in the mercantile firm of Robert Morris, "financier of the Revolution" and arch-Federalist.[41] As Federalism rapidly collapsed in Pennsylvania after 1800, such men often found themselves working with Federalists against radical Republicans, such as Michael Leib. Yet moderate Republicans always remained in command. Their support of Madison made the difference in his reelection in 1812.

The Court-Country paradigm heavily colored nearly all participants' perceptions of the issues and personalities of the era. The political rhetoric of the age implicitly assumed a spectrum of possibilities from an extreme Court position on the right, through Hamiltonianism, then various stages of moderation in the middle, then a pure Country position on the left, and on to radical Jacobinism (most evident, perhaps, in Pennsylvania) as a new option on the extreme left. Wherever one stood on this spectrum, he was likely to suspect anyone to his right of sinister conspiracies against liberty. Hamilton so accused Burr, Adams attacked Hamilton, Jefferson and Madison indicted Adams, John Randolph and the Quids denounced Madison, and Michael Leib raged against Gallatin in these terms. Conversely, everybody to one's left had to be flirting with disorder and anarchy. High Federalists never quite trusted John Adams, for they remembered his radicalism of the 1770s. Jefferson, of course, was to them a hopeless demagogue. For example, even after four years of mild Republican rule, Fisher Ames still expected a dawning age of democratic terror. "Our days are made heavy with the pressure of anxiety, and our nights restless with visions of horror," he groaned in the placid year of 1805. "We listen to the clank of chains and overhear the whispers of assassins. We mark the barbarous dissonance of mingled rage and triumph in the yell of an infatuated mob, we see the dismal glare of their burnings and scent the loathsome steam of human victims offered in sacrifice." Even a brief glimpse of reality only drove him to deeper despair, for as he confessed in the same essay, "there are not many, perhaps not five hundred even among the federalists, who yet allow themselves to view the progress of licentiousness as so speedy, so sure, and so fatal, as the deplorable experience of our country shows that it is . . ."[42] Somewhat more genially, the moderate Republican governor of Pennsylvania, Thomas McKean, remarked of the radicals: "who is there to control the wanton passions of men, suddenly raised to power and frisking in the pasture of true liberty, yet not sufficiently secured by proper barriers?"[43] Even when they went past conventional Country positions, men still used the rhetoric. Opponents of common law attacked its malignant corruptions. Many Republicans denounced a navy with arguments borrowed from the classic controversy over standing armies.

Yet when they faced one another, Federalists and Republicans accurately recognized what were basically Court and Country coalitions, respectively. Both parties also understood that westward expansion and the continuing immigration of non-English elements strongly favored the Republicans over the Federalists. But only when their own position had become quite hopeless did Federalists seriously try to exploit the Republicans' most conspicuous weakness—African slavery.[44]

Although most American historians like to boast that Federalists and Republicans created the world's first example of a modern party system, Ronald Formisano, a close student of the "second American party system," has challenged this view. To him the contrast between Hamiltonians and Jeffersonians embodied the antiparty deferential values of the eighteenth century more than it anticipated the mass parties of the 1840s. Federalist decline was so rapid and complete that no "system" ever existed for very long, and in any case, state and national politics were far from integrated along party lines.[45] However we define the threshold that permits use of the term "party system," these strictures, by emphasizing the underlying similarities between Augustan Britain and Federalist-Jeffersonian America, nicely support a central argument of this chapter.

Finally, did Republicans really take on Federalist traits after 1801 until by 1816 they "out-Federalized the Federalists?" Did the responsibilities of power turn the Country into the Court? Did Republicans switch positions much as English Whigs had a century before? Certainly the "Old Republicans" (or "Quids") who prided themselves on faithfulness to "the principles of '98" believed that too much of Hamilton had sneaked inside Jefferson, and historians since Henry Adams have found the theme equally attractive. To be sure, Jefferson was not as radical after 1801 as some of his earlier pronouncements had hinted he might be. Much to Gallatin's relief, he did not interfere with the Bank. Although he and Madison had questioned the value and desirability of the burgeoning reexport trade in the 1790s, they decided to defend it when it came under British attack after 1806. But they resorted to the more drastic embargo, rich as it was in Revolutionary precedents, only when Britain challenged American access to European markets for agricultural products.[46] Yet in 1816 Republicans did enact a second Bank of the United States and the nation's first protective tariff, while Madison vetoed an internal improvements bill solely on constitutional grounds.

Still, the argument is fairly weak. Even after 1816 Republicans differed from their antagonists far more than they resembled them.[47] Before 1812 and again after 1816, they worked consistently and successfully to pay off the national debt, a commitment that would survive in American politics until World War II. All internal taxes were repealed as soon as possible, another legacy that endured into the present century. The army and navy were again reduced to prewar size. Even during the war of 1812 Madison's government attempted none of the repressive measures that Federalists had inflicted upon Republicans in 1798. More than any other single factor, the regional lopsidedness of the two parties tended to keep both safely within their respective traditions.

The very success of Republicans in assimilating ex-Federalists did attract alien souls to the coalition, including for the first time a powerful Northern element committed to heavy manufactures. Yet the Tarriff of

1816 was designed merely as a temporary response to British dump-
ing tactics and, in any case, had little Southern support—almost none
by 1820.[48] As early as 1813 Jefferson complained "that in proportion
as avarice and corruption advance on us from the north and east, the
principles of free government are to retire to the agricultural states of
the south and west, as their last asylum and bulwark."[49] Momentarily
he seemed correct, but the pattern did not take hold. Occasional deviations aside, Jeffersonian and Jacksonian government held amazingly
steadfast in protecting its virtue from the corrupting influences of economic modernity. By the 1830s things had been righted once again, and
the most commercial elements began to organize separately as National
Republicans before they finally emerged as the Whig Party. Jackson
dismantled the Bank, and South Carolina the tariff. In one state legislature after another, Democrats displayed their suspicions of corporations, America's over-mighty subjects. In New York City, men of truly
great wealth gathered almost unanimously under the Whig banner by
1840.[50] The United States became in the 1830s the only country in the
world that I know of to repay its entire national debt and then fret
virtuously about how to spend, or not spend, its surplus revenue.

Similarly the federal government remained minuscule, a midget
institution in a giant land. It had almost no internal functions except
the postal system and the sale of western lands. It role scarcely went
beyond what would have pleased even most Antifederalists in the
1780s, the use of port duties and the revenue from land sales to meet its
own limited expenses. Thus when the Adams administration occupied
Washington, D.C. for the first time in 1800, congressmen and senators
physically outnumbered executive officials and clerks combined! This
ratio slipped very little over the next thirty years.[51] The American army
of five to ten thousand men held fast at a level roughly comparable
to Charles II's weak force, even though by 1830 the population of the
United States would be double that of England in the 1680s, and the
difference in per capita wealth must have been much greater. To take
a guess, the American navy must have not exceeded the strength of
the Tudor fleet of three centuries earlier, despite the fantastic growth
of commercial shipping after 1790.[52]

Can we explain this contrast by defining the United States as naturally a "Country" society, so committed to the principles of English
opposition ideology that alternatives were scarcely conceivable, much
less attainable?[53] Court principles as we have seen, did take root as
far south as Maryland in the provincial era, and after a devastating setback in the Revolution, they reappeared in the 1780s and, in the next
decade, came amazingly close to defining the new government's character for an indefinite future. Without the French Revolution, which
gave Republicans the leverage to organize voters on an unprecedented

scale and take possession of Pennsylvania and New York, Federalists might have triumphed even when outnumbered. After all, England's natural majority, the Tories, managed to lose to the Whigs by 1714. At this level the consensus school has a compelling point to make, for a broader electorate than Britain's, organized into nearly equal districts and constantly stimulated by westward expansion and immigration, gave the French example something to work with and thus contributed decisively to Jefferson's "Revolution of 1800."[54]

But at another level the vital difference between Britain and America was not so much the voting population or even ethnic and religious pluralism, but the South. From this perspective, Country principles did become inseparable from American politics after the titanic battles of the 1790s, not because everybody shared them, but because they overwhelmingly characterized a region that established something close to political hegemony within the republic after 1801. Had the Union begun and ended north of the Potomac, Federalists probably could have created a variant of Britain in America, with themselves as a genuine ruling class presiding over a modernizing economy. And American politics would have acquired a more overt class basis. But slaveholding planters, by dominating the federal government without serious interruption from 1801 to 1861, made regional Country principles into national political practices until the party of Lincoln emerged to threaten everything they cherished. In response they tried to withdraw into a smaller union that could sustain their system, but were smashed into submission by invading armies from the industrial North. Even then, whenever the South remained free to function openly in national politics, it severely limited Northern options. A united South could still tip the balance in a closely divided North. To take only the most conspicuous example, no incumbent Northern president ever won reelection until William McKinley in 1900, except Lincoln while the South was out of the Union, and Grant with the aid of Reconstruction governments and votes. No incumbent Southerner ever failed to gain reelection until John Tyler was repudiated by his own party in 1844 and James K. Polk chose not to run again four years later. The decision of 1800 had enduring effects for a full century of presidential politics, another good reason for considering it an essential element in America's Revolution Settlement.[55]

Yet the political defeat of Federalism did not destroy the old Court forces in American society at large. In league with Republican moderates, they retained control of the judicial system which they used, often despite the known wishes of state and national legislatures, to encourage the redistribution of property in favor of wealthy entrepreneurs—the complex process by which "instrumentalism" evolved into "legal formalism" between the Revolution and the Civil War.[56] They discovered that they did not have to dominate politics or the central government to manipulate America's vast resources. In fact the mid-century judicial barriers against legislative interference probably seemed more valuable than any possible benefits that active political participation could bring. Thus, reluctantly at first but inevitably nonetheless, they largely abandoned national politics to the "plain republicans" and shifted their activities—and most of the potential for "corruption"—to the state and local levels of the Northeast and later the Northwest where their enterprise, booster-ism, ability, and greed ran amok across the land. Rapidly transforming Jefferson's "fee-simple empire" into the world's most commercial and industrial society, they soon outstripped the regulatory capabilities of local jurisdictions while Jeffersonian and Jacksonian opponents stood impotent guard over the inactive virtue of the central government. For that matter, the very inexpensiveness of democratic government may have contributed significantly to the frantic pace of industrial growth, for in the United States—unlike Britain—the government's military and naval needs, or even its civil expenditures, provided almost no drain upon the nation's productive resources. Even the Civil War proclaimed only a temporary interruption, and not a permanent change, in this pattern.[57]

In this way the Great Inversion became complete. America's Revolution Settlement centralized the Country and decentralized and largely depoliticized the Court. Big money, quite capable of buying a state legislature here or there and hence of acquiring real weight in the Senate by the 1880s, otherwise would not again play a sustained role in national politics between Jefferson's victory and the Hanna-McKinley triumph of 1896.[58] Because a decentralized and depoliticized Court is a contradiction in terms, this result merely stresses the decisiveness and permanence of the Settlement. Court politics, a real option before 1801, had become impossible by 1815. One is tempted to add the old cliche, that the Republicans won all the battles but evidently lost the war, except that the same verdict also applies to the Federalists—if we assume that their deepest aspiration was general recognition and acceptance of their status as a ruling class. Both parties would be equally appalled by what the United States has in fact become.

Notes

1. Whitney K. Bates, "Northern Speculators and Southern State Debts: 1790" *WMQ*, 19 (1962), 30–48.

2. Bray Hammond, *Banks and Politics in America from the Revolution to the Civil War* (Princeton, 1957), ch. 5; Brooke Hindle, *David Rittenhouse* (Princeton, 1964), pp. 331–32.

3. Jefferson, quoted in Robert Sobel, *The Big Board: A History of the New York Stock Market* (New York, 1965), p. 19. Cf. Robert F. Jones, "William Duer and the Business of Government in the Era of the American Revolution," *WMQ*, 32 (1975), 393–416.

4. Jefferson to Henry Remsen, 14 April 1792, quoted in Nathan Schachner, *Thomas Jefferson, a Biography* (New York, 1951–57), I, 466.

5. Calculated from *U. S. Hist. Stats.*, II, 959.

6. Hammond, *Banks and Politics*, pp. 144–45, 190.

7. Computed from *U. S. Hist. Stats.*, II, 750–51, 886, and B. R. Mitchell and Phyllis Deane, *Abstract of British Historical Statistics* (Cambridge, 1962). pp. 217, 220.

8. David Hackett Fischer, *America, A Social History Volume. I: The Main Lines of the Subject* (forthcoming) discusses the new polarization of wealth in this period, as does Edward Pessen for a slightly later era in his "The Egalitarian Myth and the American Social Reality: Wealth, Mobility, and Equality in the 'Era of the Common Man'," *AHR*, 76 (1971), 989–1034. Although the numbers of poor began to increase rapidly in colonial cities around 1750, poverty inspired major reform movements only in the 1790s. Gary B. Nash, "Urban Wealth and Poverty in PreRevolutionary America," *J Intdis. H*, 6 (1975–76), 545–84; Nash, "Social Change and the Growth of Prerevolutionary Radicalism," in *The American Revolution*, ed. Young, pp. 3–36; Young, *Democratic Republicans*, pp. 252–56, 518–45. Cf. David J. Rothman, *The Discovery of the Asylum: Social Order and Disorder in the New Republic* (Boston, 1971) especially chs. 1, 7.

9. Richard H. Kohn, *Eagle and Sword: The Beginnings of the Military Establishment in America, 1783–1802* (New York, 1975).

10. Poorly discussed in the secondary literature, the internal taxes of the Adams administration can be followed in *American State Papers: Finance* (Washington, 1832–59), I, 579–80, 616–22, 681–88, 718–27; Kohn, *Eagle and Sword*, pp. 157–73; Keller, "Diversity and Democracy," ch. 7.

11. Kohn, *Eagle and Sword*, chs, 10–13; Marshall Smelser, *The Congress Founds the Navy* (Notre Dame, Ind., 1959).

12. Jerald A. Combs, *The Jay Treaty: Political Battleground of the Founding Fathers* (Berkeley, 1970); Buel, *Securing the Revolution*, chs. 7–12—a major revision of Leonard W. Levy's *Freedom of Speech and Press in Early American History: Legacy of Supression* (Cambridge, Mass., 1960) which, at least on the question of seditious libel, finds little difference between Federalists and Republicans. On the Disputed Elections Bill, designed to guarantee a Federalist succession in 1800, see Buel, pp. 208–10, and Albert J. Beveridge, *The Life of John Marshall*, (Boston, 1916–19), II, 452–58.

13. I am not aware of any study of American ideas of public order and revolution in the 1790s.

14. Palmer, "The Great Inversion: America and Europe in the Eighteenth-Century Revolution," in *Ideas in History: Essays presented to Louis Gottschalk by his Former Students* (Durham, N.C., 1965), pp. 3–19.

15. Fischer, *Revolution of American Conservatism*, pp. 207–8; Young, *Democratic Republicans*, pp. 42, 47, 455; Paul Goodman, *The Democratic Republicans of Massachusetts: Politics in a Young Republic* (Cambridge, Mass., 1964), ch. 5.

16. Wallace Evan Davies, "The Society of the Cincinnati in New England, 1783–1800," *WMQ*, 5 (1948), 3–25, and Ethel E. Rasmussen, "Democratic Environment–Aristocratic Aspiration," *PMHB*, 90 (1966), 155–82, are both highly suggestive, especially when contrasted with James Sterling Young, *The Washington Community, 1800–1828* (New York, 1966.) The point about intermarriage derives mostly from reading hundreds of biographical sketches of graduates of Harvard, Yale, and Princeton, but I have never attempted to measure the differences. James McLachlan, author of *Princetonians, 1748–1768: A Biographical Dictionary* (Princeton, 1977) shares this opinion.

17. Charles R. Ritcheson, *Aftermath of Revolution: British Policy toward the United States, 1783–1795* (New York, 1969); Hutchins, *American Maritime Industries*, chs.6–8; James A. Field, Jr., *America and the Mediterranean World, 1776–1882* (Princeton, 1969), pp. 27–49; Jones, "William Duer"; McCoy, "The Republican Revolution," p. 182.

18. *U.S. Hist. Stats.*, II, 750, 886; Allen R. Pred, *Urban Growth and the Circulation of Information: The United States System of Cities, 1790–1840* (Cambridge, Mass., 1973), pp. 28–29 and *passim*.

19. G.W. Trevelyan, *England Under Queen Anne: The Peace and the Protestant Succession* (London, 1934) remains the fullest narrative of the Tory resurgence. For the Federalist revival and its limitations, see Fischer, *Revolution of American Conservatism;* Harry W. Fritz, "The Collapse of Party: President, Congress, and the Decline of Party Action, 1807–1817" (Ph.D. dissertation, Washington University, 1970): James M. Banner, Jr., *To the Hartford Convention: The Federalists and the Origins of Party Politics in Massachusetts, 1789–1815* (New York, 1970); Victor Sapio, "Maryland's Federalist Revival, 1808–1812," *MHM*, 64 (1969), 1–17; James H. Broussard, "Regional Pride and Republican Politics: The Fatal Weakness of Southern Federalism, 1800–1815," *South Atlantic Quarterly*, 73 (1974), 23–33; J.C.A. Stagg, "James Madison and the 'Malcontents': The Political Origins of the War of 1812," *WMQ*, 33 (1976), 557–85; Norman K. Risjord, "Election of 1812," in *History of American Presidential Elections, 1789–1968*, ed. Arthur M. Schlesinger, Jr. (New York, 1971), I, 249–72; Irving Brant, *James Madison: Commander-In-Chief, 1812–1836* (Indianapolis, 1961), ch. 8; Frank A. Cassell, "The Great Baltimore Riot of 1812," *MHM*, 70 (1975), 241–59.

20. On presidential etiquette, compare Broadus Mitchell, *Alexander Hamilton: The National Adventure, 1788–1804* (New York, 1962), p. 13, with Jefferson's view, in *The Life and Selected Writings of Thomas Jefferson*, ed. Adrienne Koch and William Peden (New York, 1944) pp. 175–76. On Adams, see James H. Hutson, "John Adams' Title Campaign," *New England Quarterly*, 41 (1968), 30–39; Wood, *Creation of the American Republic*, ch. 14; Manning J. Dauer, *The Adams Federalists* (Baltimore, 1953), ch.3. Cf. James D. Tagg, "Benjamin Franklin Bache's Attack on George Washington," *PMHB*, 100 (1976), 191–230.

21. Fischer, *Revolution of American Conservatism*, pp. 22–23.

22. Adams to Councillor Trumbull, 31 March 1791; Adams to Henry Marchant, 3 March 1792, *John Adams Letter Book, 1789–1793*, pp. 158, 168–69, Massachusetts Historical Society, Microfilms of the Adams Papers owned by the Adams Manuscript Trust, Part II, Reel 115 (Boston, 1955), quoted with permission. See also John R. Howe, Jr., *The Changing Political Thought of John Adams* (Princeton, 1966), especially chs. 4, 7; Joyce Appleby, "The New Republican Synthesis and the Changing Political Ideas of John Adams," *American Quarterly*, 25 (1973), 578–95.

23. Dauer, *Adams Federalists* contains much useful information about alignments on specific issues; Richard A. Harrison, sketch of Issac Tichenor, *Princetonians: A Biographical Dictionary*, II (forthcoming). For the bank issue in 1811, see Hammond, *Banks and Politics*, p. 224.

24. For English Country support of naval power, see John Trenchard and Thomas Gordon, *Cato's Letters: or, Essays on Liberty, Civil and Religious, and Other Important Subjects*, 6th ed. (London, 1755), II, No. 64. For the argument against standing armies, see *ibid.*, III, Nos. 94–95, and Trenchard, *An Argument Shewing, that a Standing Army is Inconsistent with a Free Government, and Absolutely Destructive to the Constitution of the English Monarchy* (London, 1697); see also Lois G. Schwoerer, *"No Standing Armies!" The Anti-Army Ideology in Seventeenth Century England* (Baltimore, 1974). Republican use of these arguments against a navy can be followed throughout Smelser's *Congress Founds the Navy*. On suffrage, see Chilton Williamson, *American Suffrage from Property to Democracy, 1760–1860* (Princeton, 1960), especially chs. 8–9.

25. Levy, *Legacy of Suppression*, especially pp. 238–48, and ch. 6, *passim*.

26. Richard E. Ellis, *The Jeffersonian Crisis: Courts and Politics in the Young Republic* (New York, 1971).

27. George Dargo, *Jefferson's Louisiana: Politics and the Clash of Legal Traditions* (Cambridge, Mass., 1975).

28. Examples include Richard E. Ellis "The Political Economy of Thomas Jefferson," in *Thomas Jefferson: The Man, his World, his Influence*, ed. Lally Weymouth (London, 1973), pp. 81–95; and Marshall Smelser, *The Democratic Republic, 1801–1815* (New York, 1968), especially ch.1. These references are not in any sense meant to be invidious. The present

writer was equally or more perplexed by Jefferson's economic views until the appearance of Pocock's "Virtue and Commerce" and McCoy's "Republican Revolution."

29. *Ibid.* Garry Wills nicely developed Jefferson's preference for Scottish over English writers in the first of three lectures on Jefferson delivered at Princeton University, fall term, 1975.

30. Jefferson's *Anas* (available in numerous editions) contains his strictures on Hamiltonian finance. For his views on banks in 1813, see Hammond, *Banks and Politics*, p. 195.

31. For Jefferson's reaction to the Panic of 1819, which left him insolvent because he had underwritten a friend's obligation, see his letter to John Adams, 7 November 1819, *The Adams-Jefferson Letters: The Complete Correspondence between Thomas Jefferson and Abigail and John Adams*, ed. Lester J. Cappon (Chapel Hill, 1959), II, 546–47.

32. Kohn, *Eagle and Sword*, pp. 253, 262, 302–3. For the very narrow role of the West Point Military Academy before the War of 1812, see Edward C. Boynton, *History of West Point and Its Military Importance during the American Revolution: And the Origin and Progress of the United States Military Academy* (New York, 1964), chs. 10–11.

33. Julia A. Macleod, "Jefferson and the Navy: A Defense," *Huntington Library Quarterly*, 8 (1944–45), 153–84.

34. On Madison, see McCoy, "Republican Revolution," pp. 114, 120, 128–29, 166, 179, 212, 254, 256–57, 271–73, 296–97, 305–9, 311; on Gallatin, see Henry Adams, *The Life of Albert Gallatin* (Philadelphia, 1879), especially pp. 218–19, 270–74, 304, 321–22, 362; and Alexander S. Balinky, "Albert Gallatin, Naval Foe," *PMHB*, 82 (1958), 293–304; Balinky, "Gallatin's Theory of War Finance," *WMQ*, 16 (1959), 73-82.

35. Frank A. Cassell, *Merchant Congressman in the Young Republic: Samuel Smith of Maryland, 1752–1839* (Madison, 1971). The quotation is from p. 49.

36. William T. Whitney, Jr., "The Crowninshields of Salem, 1800–1808: A Study in the Politics of Commercial Growth," Essex Institute, *Historical Collections*, 94 (1958), 1–36, 79–118; John H. Reinoehl, "Some Remarks on the American trade: Jacob Crowninshield to James Madison, 1806," *HMQ*, 16 (1959), 83–118.

37. George A. Billias, *Elbridge Gerry, Founding Father and Republican Statesman* (New York, 1976), especially chs. 11, 16, 19. For the quotation, see *The Records of the Federal Convention of 1787*, ed. Max Farrand, rev. ed. (New Haven, 1937), I, 123.

38. C. Edward Skeen, "Mr. Madison's Secretary of War," *PMHB*, 100 (1976), 336–55.

39. Young, *Democratic Republicans*, pp. 243–50.

40. *The Case of Aaron Burr*, ed. V.B. Reed and J.D. Williams (Boston, 1960), pp. 119–22, 154, 174, 178.

41. Richard A. Harrison's sketch of Clymer, in *Princetonians*, II, (forthcoming); Jacob E. Cooke, "Tench Coxe, Alexander Hamilton, and the Encouragement of American Manufactures," *WMQ*, 32 (1975), 369–92; Cooke, "Tench Coxe, American Economist: The Limitations of Economic Thought in the Early Nationalist Era," *Pennsylvania History*, 42 (1975), 267–89; Robert D. Arbuckle, "John Nicholson and the Attempt to Promote Pennsylvania Industry in the 1790s," *ibid.*, 42 (1975), 99–114, Roland M. Baumann, "Heads I Win, Tails You Lose': The Public Creditors and the Assumption Issue in Pennsylvania, 1790–1802," *ibid.*, 44 (1977), 195–232; Baumann, "John Swanwick: Spokesman for 'Merchant-Republicanism' in Philadelphia, 1790–1798," *PMHB*, 97 (1973), 131–82.

42. *Works of Fisher Ames*, ed. Seth Ames (Boston, 1854), II, 354.

43. Adams, *Gallatin*, p. 313.

44. Donald L. Robinson, *Slavery in the Structure of American Politics, 1765–1820* (New York, 1971).

45. Formisano, "Deferential-Participant Politics: The Early Republic's Political Culture, 1789–1840," *American Political Science Review*, 68 (1974), 473–87. Cf., Paul Goodman, "The First American Party System," in *The American Party Systems: Stages of Political Development*,

ed. William M. Chambers and Walter Dean Burnham (New York, 1967), pp. 56–89; Sneddon, "State Politics in the 1790's," *passim*.

46. McCoy, "The Republican Revolution," pp. 251–57. The range of disagreement and factionalism among republicans can be gleaned from Norman K. Risjord, *The Old Republicans: Southern Conservatism in the Age of Jefferson* (New York, 1965); Kim T. Phillips, "William Duane, Philadelphia's Democratic Republicans and the Origins of Modern Politics," *PMHB*, 101 (1977), 365–87; and John S. Pancake, 'The Invisibles': A Chapter in the Opposition to President Madison," *Journal of Southern History*, 21 (1955), 17–37.

47. Smelser, *The Democratic Republic*, ch. 15. Even New York's General Incorporation Law of 1811 was aimed primarily at stimulating household manufacturing. See Ronald E. Seavoy, "Laws to Encourage Manufacturing: New York Policy and the 1811 General Incorporation Statute," *Business History Review*, 46 (1972), 85–95.

48. Norris W. Preyer, "Southern Support of the Tariff of 1816—A Reappraisal," *Journal of Southern History*, 25 (1959), 306–22.

49. Jefferson to Henry Middleton, 8 January 1813, *Writings*, ed. Lipscomb, XIII, 203.

50. For major revisions of Bray Hammond's entrepreneurial interpretation of the bank war, see Jean Alexander Wilburn, *Biddle's Bank: The Crucial Years* (New York, 1967); James R. Sharp, *The Jacksonians versus the Banks: Politics in the States after the Panic of 1837* (New York, 1970). See also Frank Otto Gattell, "Money and Party in Jacksonian America: A Quantitative Look at New York City's Men of Quality," *Political Science Quarterly*, 82 (1967), 235–52; Herbert Ershkowitz and William G. Shade, "Consensus or Conflict? Political Behavior in the State Legislatures during the Jacksonian Era," *JAH*, 58 (1971–72), 591–621.

51. Young, *The Washington Community*, 31, Table 2.

52. *U.S. Hist. Stats.*, II, 1142.

53. A major theme of Bailyn's *Origins of American Politics*.

54. Brown, *Middle-Class Democracy*. But by denying the impact of either deference or conflicting interests on colonial and revolutionary politics, Brown deprives the subject of the contingencies it obviously possessed as late as 1800 or even 1812. Young's *Democratic Republicans* carefully documents Clintonian mobilization of poorer voters as the 1790s progressed. Pole, *Political Representation*, Appendix II, provides statistics on voter turnout in several states. See also J.G.A. Pocock, "The Classical Theory of Deference" *AHR*, 81 (1976), 516–23; Lance Banning, "Jeffersonian Ideology and the French Revolution: A Question of Liberticide at Home," *Studies in Burke and His Times*, 17 (1976), 5–26.

55. Among many possible items, see especially Richard H. Brown, "The Missouri Crisis, Slavery, and the Politics of Jacksonianism," *South Atlantic Quarterly*, 65 (1966), 55–72; and Robert Kelley's brilliant synthesis, "Ideology and Political Culture from Jefferson to Nixon," *AHR*, 82 (1977), 531–62.

56. Morton J. Horwitz, "The Emergence of an Instrumental Conception of American Law, 1780–1820," *Perspectives in American History*, 5 (1971), 287–326; Horwitz, "The Rise of Legal Formalism," *American Journal of Legal History*, 19 (1975), 251–64; Gerard W. Gawalt, "Sources of Anti-Lawyer Sentiment in Massachusetts, 1740–1840," *ibid.*, 14 (1970), 283–307; William E. Nelson, *Americanization of the Common Law: The Impact of Legal Change on Massachusetts Society, 1760–1830* (Cambridge, Mass., 1975), chs. 8–9, especially pp. 173–74.

57. Richard D. Brown, *Modernization: The Transformation of American Life, 1600–1865* (New York, 1976), and his "The Emergence of Urban Society in Rural Massachusetts, 1760–1820," *JAH*, 61 (1974–75), 29–51, nicely develop a number of these themes. Peter Temin, *The Jacksonian Economy* (New York, 1969), demonstrates the government's trivial role in the economy, while Pred's *Urban Growth* charts what is really the emergence of a national economy. C. Vann Woodward, "The Age of Reinterpretation," *AHR*, 66 (1960–61), 1–19, stresses America's "free security" after 1815.

58. Richard J. Jensen, *The Winning of the Midwest: Social and Political Conflict, 1888–1896* (Chicago, 1971); Wallace D. Farnham, 'The Weakened Spring of Government': A Study in Nineteenth-Century American History," *AHR*, 68 (1962–63), 662–80; Pocock, "Classical Theory of Deference," p. 523.

The Missouri Crisis, Slavery, and the Politics of Jacksonianism

Richard H. Brown

As Murrin says, the Jeffersonian ascendency can also be interpreted as the beginning of a Southern dominance of national affairs that would persist into the 1850s. Ironically, however, Southern dominance may always have depended on the section's leadership of a political party that did not appeal exclusively to any single region. Both Republicans and Federalists had always had their strongest bastions in distinctive sections of the country, but both had always had an interregional appeal; party loyalties had often overridden, and had always helped contain, the sectional hostilities that they had never wholly hidden. Thus, the quick collapse of party competition during James Monroe's administration threatened a political division of a very different sort. Seen in this perspective, the Missouri crisis was, at once, another signal of the termination of the early party struggle and a lesson that would not be lost on younger politicians who were starting to believe that party conflict might be something other than an evil. This article appeared in the South Atlantic Quarterly, *LXV (Winter, 1966), 55-72. Copyright 1966 by Duke University Press; reprinted by permission.*

From the inauguration of Washington until the Civil War the South was in the saddle of national politics. This is the central fact in American political history to 1860. To it there are no exceptions, not even in that period when the "common man" stormed the ramparts of government under the banner of Andrew Jackson. In Jackson's day the chief agent of Southern power was a Northern man with Southern principles, Martin Van Buren of New York. It was he who put together the party coalition which Andrew Jackson led to power. That coalition had its wellsprings in the dramatic crisis over slavery in Missouri, the first great public airing of the slavery question in ante bellum America.

I

More than anything else, what made Southern dominance in national politics possible was a basic homogeneity in the Southern electorate. In the early nineteenth century, to be sure, the South was far from monolithic. In terms of economic interest and social classes it was scarcely more homogeneous than the North. But under the diversity of interests which characterized Southern life in most respects there ran one single compelling idea which virtually united all Southerners, and which governed their participation in national affairs. This was that the institution of slavery should not be dealt with from outside the South. Whatever the merits of the institution—and Southerners violently disagreed about this, never more than in the 1820s—the presence of the slave was a fact too critical, too sensitive, too perilous for all of Southern society to be dealt with by those not directly affected. Slavery must remain a Southern question. In the ante bellum period a Southern politician of whatever party forgot this at his peril. A Northern politician might perceive it to his profit. There had been, Martin Van Buren noted with satisfaction late in life, a "remarkable consistency in the political positions" of Southern public men. With characteristic insouciance the Little Magician attributed this consistency to the natural superiority of republican principles which led them to win out in a region relatively untainted by the monied interest. But his partisan friend Rufus King, Van Buren admitted, ascribed it to the "black strap" of Southern slavery.

The insistence that slavery was uniquely a Southern concern, not to be touched by outsiders, had been from the outset a *sine qua non* for Southern participation in national politics. It underlay the Constitution and its creation of a government of limited powers, without which Southern participation would have been unthinkable. And when in the 1790s Jefferson and Madison perceived that a constitution was only the first step in guaranteeing Southern security, because a constitution meant what those who governed under it said it meant, it led to the creation of the first national political party to protect that constitution against change by interpretation. The party which they constructed converted a Southern minority into a national majority through alliance with congenial interests outside the South. Organically, it represented an alliance between New York and Virginia, pulling between them Pennsylvania, and after them North Carolina, Georgia, and (at first) Kentucky and Tennessee, all states strongly subject to Virginia's influence. At bottom it rested on the support of people who lived on that rich belt of fertile farmland which stretched from the Great Lakes across upstate New York and Pennsylvania, southward through the Southern piedmont into Georgia, entirely oblivious of the Mason-Dixon line. North as well as South it was an area of prosperous, well-settled small farms. More farmers than capitalists, its residents wanted little from government but to be let alone. Resting his party on them, Jefferson had found a formula for national politics which at the same time was a formula for Southern preeminence. It would hold good to the Civil War.

So long as the Federalists remained an effective opposition, Jefferson's party worked as a party should. It maintained its identity in relation to the opposition by a moderate and pragmatic advocacy of strict construction of the Constitution. Because it had competition, it could maintain discipline. It responded to its constituent elements because it depended on them for support. But eventually its very success was its undoing. After 1815, stirred by the nationalism of the postwar era, and with the Federalists in decline, the Republicans took up Federalist positions on a number of the great public issues of the day, sweeping all before them as they did. The Federalists gave up the ghost. In the Era of Good Feelings which followed, everybody began to call himself a Republican, and a new theory of party amalgamation preached the doctrine that party division was bad and that a one-party system best served the national interest. Only gradually did it become apparent that in victory the Republican party had lost its identity—and its usefulness. As the party of the whole nation it ceased to be responsible to any particular elements in its constituency. It ceased to be responsive to the South.

When it did, and because it did, it invited the Missouri crisis of 1819–1820, and that crisis in turn revealed the basis for a possible configuration of national parties which eventually would divide the nation free against slave. As John Quincy Adams put it, the crisis had revealed "the basis for a new organization of parties . . . here was a new party ready formed, . . . terrible to the whole Union, but portentously terrible to the South—threatening in its progress the emancipation of all their slaves, threatening in its immediate effect that Southern domination which has swayed the Union for the last twenty years." Because it did so, Jefferson, in equally famous phrase, "considered it at once as the knell of the Union."

Adams and Jefferson were not alone in perceiving the significance of what had happened. Scarcely a contemporary missed the point. Historians quote them by the dozens as prophets—but usually *only* as prophets. In fact the Missouri crisis gave rise not to prophecy alone, but to action. It led to an urgent and finally successful attempt to revive the old Jeffersonian party and with it the Jeffersonian formula for Southern preeminence. The resuscitation of that party would be the most important story in American politics in the decades which followed.

II

In Jefferson's day the tie between slavery, strict construction of the Constitution, and the Republican party was implicit, not explicit. After Missouri it was explicit, and commented upon time and again in both public and private discussion. Perceptive Southerners saw (1)

that unless effective means were taken to quiet discussion of the question, slavery might be used at any time in the future to force the South
into a permanent minority in the Union, endangering all its interests;
and (2) that if the loose constitutional construction of the day were
allowed to prevail, the time might come when the government would
be held to have the power to deal with slavery. Vital to preventing
both of these—to keeping the slavery question quiet and to gaining a
reassertion of strict construction principles—was the reestablishment of
conditions which would make the party in power responsive once again
to the South.

Not only did the Missouri crisis make these matters clear, but
it shaped the conditions which would govern what followed. In the
South it gave marked impetus to a reaction against the nationalism and
amalgamationism of postwar Republicanism and handed the offensive
to a hardy band of Old Republican politicians who had been crying
in the wilderness since 1816. In the early 1820s the struggle between
Old Republicans and New would be the stuff of Southern politics, and
on the strength of the new imperatives to which the Missouri conflict
gave rise the Old Republicans would carry off the victory in state after
Southern state, providing thereby a base of power on which a new strict
construction party could be reared.

For precisely the same reason that it gave the offensive to the Old
Republicans of the South—because it portrayed the tie between slavery and party in starkest form—the Missouri crisis put Northern Old
Republicans on the defense. Doing so, it handed the keys to national
party success thereafter to whatever Northern leader could surmount
charges of being pro-Southern and command the necessary Northern
votes to bring the party to power. For that reason Thomas Jefferson's
formula for national politics would become, when resurrected, Martin
Van Buren's formula for national politics. What has long been recognized as happening to the Democratic party in the forties and fifties
happened in fact in 1820. After Missouri and down to the Civil War the
revised formula for Southern preeminence would involve the elevation
to the presidency of Southerners who were predominantly Westerners
in the public eye, or of Northern men with Southern principles.

Because they shaped the context of what was to come, the reactions
to the Missouri crisis in the two citadels of Old Republican power,
Richmond and Albany, were significant. Each cast its light ahead. As
the donnybrook mounted in Congress in the winter of 1820, the Virginia
capital was reported to be as "agitated as if affected by all the Vol-
canic Eruptions of Vesuvius." At the heart of the clamor were the Old
Republicans of the Richmond Junto, particularly Thomas Ritchie's famous *Enquirer*, which spoke for the Junto and had been for years the
most influential newspaper in the South. Associates of Jefferson,

architects of Southern power, the Old Republicans were not long in perceiving the political implications of the crisis. Conviction grew in their minds that the point of Northern agitation was not Missouri at all but to use slavery as an anvil on which to forge a new party which would carry either Rufus King or DeWitt Clinton of New York to the presidency and force the South from power forever. But what excited them even more was the enormity of the price of peace which alone seemed likely to avert the disaster. This was the so-called Thomas Proviso, amending the Missouri bill to draw the ill-fated 36°30′ line across the Louisiana Purchase, prohibiting slavery in the territory to the north, giving up the lion's share to freedom.

No sooner had the proviso been introduced in Congress than the temper of the Old Republicans boiled over, and with prescient glances to the future they leapt to the attack. Ritchie challenged the constitutionality of the proviso at once in the *Enquirer*, a quarter century before Calhoun would work out the subtle dialectic of a Southern legal position. Nathaniel Macon agreed. "To compromise is to acknowledge the right of Congress to interfere and to legislate on the subject," he wrote; "this would be acknowledging too much." Equally important was the fact that, by prohibiting slavery in most of the West, the proviso forecast a course of national development ultimately intolerable to the South because, as Spencer Roane put it to Monroe, Southerners could not consent to be "dammed up in a land of Slaves." As the debates thundered to their climax, Ritchie in two separate editorials predicted that if the proviso passed, the South must in due time have Texas. "If we are cooped up on the north," he wrote with grim prophecy, "we must have elbow room to the west."

When finally the Southern Old Republicans tacitly consented to the Missouri Compromise, it was therefore not so much a measure of illusion about what the South had given up, as of how desperately necessary they felt peace to be. They had yielded not so much in the spirit of a bargain as in the spirit of a man caught in a holdup, who yields his fortune rather than risk his life in the hope that he may live to see a better day and perhaps even to get his fortune back. As Ritchie summed it up when news of the settlement reached Richmond, "Instead of joy, we scarcely ever recollect to have tasted of a bitterer cup." That they tasted it at all was because of the manipulative genius of Henry Clay, who managed to bring up the separate parts of the compromise separately in the House, enabling the Old Republicans to provide him his margin of victory on the closely contested Missouri bill while they saved their pride by voting to the end against the Thomas Proviso. They had not bound themselves by their votes to the proviso, as Ritchie warned they should not. If it was cold comfort for the moment, it was potent with significance for the future.

In fact, the vote on the proviso illuminated an important division in Southern sentiment. Thirty-seven slave state congressmen opposed it, while thirty-nine voted for it. On the surface the line of division ran along the Appalachian crest and the Potomac, pointing out seemingly a distinction in interest between the South Atlantic states on the one hand and those in the Southwest and mid-Atlantic regions on the other—between those states most characteristically Southern and those which in 1820 were essentially more Western or Northern in outlook. More fundamental, within each section it divided Southerners between those who were more sensitive to the relationship of slavery to politics and those who were less so; between those who thought the party formula for Southern preeminence and defense important and those who thought parties outmoded; between particularists and postwar Republican nationalists; between the proponents of an old Republican polity and the proponents of a new one as defined in the years of postwar exuberance; between those closest to Jefferson, such as the Richmond Junto and Macon, and those closest to Monroe, such as Calhoun. It was a division which prefigured Southern political struggles of the twenties. When two years later 70 percent of those congressmen from the South Atlantic states who had opposed the Thomas Proviso returned to the next Congress, compared to 39 percent of those who had supported it, it was a measure of the resurgence of Old Republicanism. Two years after that, in the chaotic presidential election of 1824, the Southerners who had opposed the proviso were the Southerners who sought to sustain the party caucus as a method of nominating in a vain attempt to restore old party discipline. Four years after that they marched back to power at last under the banner of Andrew Jackson, restoring to effectiveness in so doing a political system intended to make future Missouri crises impossible, and committed in due time to rectify the Thomas Proviso.

Equally important to the reaction in Richmond was what went on in Albany. There command of the state's Old Republicans was in the hands of the Bucktails, a group of which State Senator Martin Van Buren, at thirty-eight, was already master spirit. Opposed to the Bucktails was Governor DeWitt Clinton, an erstwhile Republican who drew a good deal of his support from former Federalists. With the Bucktails committed to the old Virginia–New York alliance, the Missouri question offered Clinton a heaven-sent opportunity; indeed there were those who suspected the ambitious governor of playing God himself and helping to precipitate the crisis. Whether or not this was true, Clinton tried desperately while the storm was raging in Washington to get a commitment from the Bucktails which would stamp them as proslavery, but the Bucktails acted cautiously. When a large meeting was called in Albany to indorse the prohibition of slavery in Missouri, Van Buren found it convenient to be off on circuit. When the Clintonians whipped a resolution indorsing the restriction through the legislature, not a Bucktail raised a voice in dissent. But for all their caution against public commitment it was generally understood both in Washington and New York that the Bucktails were anxious for peace, and that they supported the corporal's guard of Northern Republicans in congress who, retreating finally from the Missouri prohibition, made peace possible. Several of the Bucktail newspapers said as much, and despite the lack of public commitment on the part of party leaders, more than one Clintonian newspaper would brand them the "Slave Ticket" in the legislative elections which followed.

In private, Van Buren left no doubt where he stood, or where he meant to go once the storm had passed. No sooner had the compromise been adopted in Washington than the Little Magician got off a letter to his friendly rival Rufus King, promising at "some future day" to give that veteran Federalist his own views on the expediency of making slavery a party question, and remarking meanwhile that notwithstanding the strong public interest in the Missouri question, "the excitement which exists in regard to it, or which is likely to arise from it, is not so great as you suppose." It was a singularly important assessment of Northern public opinion for a politican who had fallen heir to a tattered Southern alliance, and in it King apprehensively saw the panorama of forty years of national politics stretching before him:

> The inveteracy of party feelings in the Eastern States [he wrote a friend], the hopes of influence and distinction by taking part in favor of the slave States, which call themselves, and are spoken of by others as the truly republican States and the peculiar friends of liberty, will keep alive & sustain a body considerably numerous, and who will have sufficient influence, to preserve to the slave States their disproportionate, I might say exclusive, dominance over the Union.

Twenty months after that, in the late fall of 1821, Van Buren set off for Washington as a newly elected United States senator. With his party having taken the measure of Clinton in the meantime, he carried with him into the lion's den of presidential politics effective command of the thirty-six uncommitted electoral votes of New York. If he would be the most disinterested statesman in all the land, he could not avoid for long the responsibility that went with that power. It was an opportunity to be used for large purposes or small, as a man might choose, and the Little Magician lost no time in indicating his intended course. Within weeks of his arrival he was pulling the strings of the New York delegation in the House to bring about return of the speakership to the slave states, from whom it had been wrested by a straight sectional vote upon Clay's retirement the year before. The new speaker was P. P. Barbour of Virginia, a leader of the Old Republican reaction in the South. Three months after that Van Buren was on his way to Richmond to plan the resurrection of the Old Republican Party.

That he should do so was partly for reasons of personal ambition, partly because the Bucktails after years of frustrating struggle with Clinton had their own clear reasons for wanting to redraw party lines. Beyond this there would appear to be the simple fact that Van Buren believed implicitly in the whole system of republican polity as Thomas Jefferson had staked it out. Committed to the principle of the least possible government, the Republican party was the defender of that republican liberty which was the sole political concern of the disinterested agrarian constituency for which, through life, Van Buren saw himself as a spokesman, and which constituted the majority of Americans. That majority was strongest where it was purest, least subject to the corrupting power of money. That was in the South. Slavery was a lesser issue than republicanism. Nor was it by any means clear in 1820 that agitation was the best way to deal with it. For while some who were nominally Old Republicans, such as Senator William Smith of South Carolina, were beginning to argue that slavery was a positive good, it was generally true that no men in America were more honestly committed to the notion that the institution was wrong than those men of Jeffersonian conscience who were the Old Republicans of the South. Eleven years later, in 1831, some of them would mount in the Virginia legislature the last great effort south of the Mason-Dixon line to abolish slavery. It required no very extended rationalization to argue in 1820 that the whole perplexing question would be best left in their hands, even if in fact the North had the right to take it up. Particularly was this true when, as Van Buren put it, the motives of those in the North who sought to take it up were "rather [more] political than philanthropical." Because he believed as he did, Van Buren's efforts to revive party distinctions and restore the Old Republican Party were to be more than a mere matter of machinations with politicians, looking toward the making of the Democratic party. He looked to Southern power, and he would quiet the slavery question if he could. He was dealing with the root principle of the whole structure of ante bellum politics.

III

In the long history of the American presidency no election appears quite so formless as that of 1824. With no competing party to force unity on the Republicans, candidates who could not command the party nomination were free to defy it. They did so, charging that "King Caucus" was undemocratic. Eventually no fewer than four candidates competed down to the wire, each a Republican, every man for himself. Because they divided the electoral votes between them, none came close to a majority, and the election went to the House of Representatives. There, with the help of Henry Clay, John Quincy Adams outpolled the popular Andrew Jackson and the caucus nominee, William H. Crawford of Georgia, and carried off the prize.

Historians, viewing that election, look at King Caucus too much through the eyes of its opponents, who stated that the caucus represented an in-group of political officeholders attached to Crawford and anxious to preserve their own political power. In fact it was the Old Republicans who organized the caucus, not so much to sustain Crawford and preserve power as to revive the Virginia–New York party and regain power. They took up Crawford unenthusiastically because he came closest to the Old Republican pattern, and because he alone of all the candidates could hope to carry Virginia. They took up the caucus at the behest of Van Buren after two years of searching for a method of nominating which would command the support of all, because four years after Missouri the only hope of winning New York for a Southern candidate was to present him, however unpopularly, as the official party nominee.

Hidden in the currents and crosscurrents of that campaign was the reiterated issue of party versus amalgamation. Behind it, in turn, were repeated pleas by Old Republican presses, North and South alike, that unless genuine Republicans agreed on a method of choosing a candidate the division must be along sectional lines, in which case a Federalist or proto-Federalist might sneak into the White House. Behind it too was the repeated warning that party organization alone would make democracy work. Without it, the Old Republicans correctly prophesied, the election would end up in the House of Representatives, subject to the worst kind of political intrigue, and with the votes of the smallest states the equals of those of populous Virginia and New York.

When the caucus failed it was because amalgamation had destroyed the levers which made party discipline possible. Exhortation could not restore them. Meantime the issue of democracy had been turned against the advocates of party, because in key states like New York and North Carolina they tried to use the power of the party organizations for Crawford, bucking more popular candidates such as Jackson and Adams. It was a bogus issue. The real issue was whether a party was necessary to make democracy work, and because they were more nearly right than their opponents about this, and the election in the House shortly proved it, the Old Republicans would recover quickly after 1824, after Crawford and the caucus issue were politically dead. Let circumstances limit the number of candidates, and tie up party and democracy on the same side, and the results would be different another time.

In the campaign of 1824 and the years immediately following, the slavery issue was never far below the surface. The Denmark Vesey conspiracy for an insurrection in Charleston (now a subject of controversy among historians) was to contemporaries a grim reminder of the Missouri debates, and it was attributed publicly to Rufus King's speeches on the Missouri question. In 1823–1824 some Southerners suspected that an attempt by Secretary of State Adams to conclude a slave trade convention with Great Britain was an attempt to reap the benefit of Northern anti-slavery sentiment; and some, notably Representative John Floyd of Virginia, sought to turn the tables on Adams by attacking him for allegedly ceding Texas to Spain in the Florida treaty, thus ceding what Floyd called "two slaveholding states" and costing "the Southern interest" four Senators.

Old Republicans made no bones about their concern over the issue, or their fear that it might be turned against them. In the summer of 1823 an illuminating editorial debate broke out between the New York *American*, which spoke the thoughts of the old Federalists in New York, and the Richmond *Enquirer*. So vehemently had the *American* picked up a report of a plan to revise the Illinois constitution to admit slavery that Ritchie charged its editors with reviving the slave question to put New York into the lap of the "Universal Yankee Nation" and to put the South under the "ban of the Empire." "Call it the Missouri question, the Illinois question, what you please; it was the *Slave question*," Ritchie shrilled, which the *American* was seeking to get up for political purposes. Shortly, the Albany *Argus* got into the argument. The *Argus*, which got its signals from Van Buren and spoke the thought of New York's Old Republicans, charged the *American* with trying to revive the slave question to "abrogate the old party distinctions" and "organize new ones, founded in the territorial prejudices of the people." "The more general question of the North and South," the *Argus* warned, "will be urged to the uttermost, by those who can never triumph when they meet the democracy of the country, openly, and with the hostility they bear towards it." Over and over the debate rang out the argument that the attempt to revive party distinctions was an attempt to allay sectional prejudices, and by the time the debate was over only the most obtuse citizen could have missed the point.

Nor was the election of Adams destined to calm Southern fears on issues having to do with slavery. A series of incidents early in 1825 suggested that the New Englander's election had made antislavery advocates more bold, and Southern tempers grew shorter in the summer of 1825 than they had been at any time since Missouri. One of the incidents was a reported argument before the Supreme Court in the case of the South Carolina Negro Seaman's Act by Attorney General William Wirt, stating that slavery was "inconsistent with the laws of God and nature." A second was a resolution offered in the Senate a scant nine days after Adams' election by Rufus King, proposing to turn the proceeds from the sale of western lands to the emancipation and export of slaves, through the agency of the American Colonization Society. In the same week the New Jersey legislature proposed a system of foreign colonization which "would, in due time, effect the entire emancipation of the slaves in our country." John Floyd enclosed a copy of the New Jersey resolution to Claiborne Gooch, Ritchie's silent partner on the *Enquirer*, with salient warning:

> Long before this manifestation I have believed, connected with the Missouri question, would come up the general question of slavery, upon the principles avowed by Rufus King in the Senate. . . .
> If this indication is well received, who can tell, after the elevation of Mr. A. to the presidency—that he, of Missouri effort, or DeWitt C. or some such aspirant, may not, for the sake of that office, fan this flame— to array the non-slaveholding States against the Slaveholding states, and finally quiet our clamor or opposition, by the application of the slaves knife to our throats. Think of this much, and often.

Meantime, the New York *Commercial Advertiser* expressed publicly the hope that Adams' administration would introduce "a new era, when the northern, eastern, and non-slaveholding states, will assume an attitude in the Union, proportionate to their moral and physical power." Ritchie responded hotly in an editorial asking what the designs of such a combination would be against the "southern and *slave-holding states*." Soon in Georgia the Old Republican Governor George M. Troup, at the instigation of Senator John M. Berrien, put before the legislature a request for resolutions stating slavery to be exclusively within the control of the states and asking that the federal government "abstain from intermeddling." In May there was another violent editorial exchange between the New York *American* and the *Enquirer*, growing out of an *American* editorial which attacked the "slave press" and taunted the South with the comment that "the sceptre has departed from Judah, and those who have long ruled must be content to obey." Ritchie picked up the taunt as a challenge to the South, admitting that slavery was evil but insisting pointedly that the South had "too much at stake" to allow decisions on the matter by men ignorant of Southern "habits, manners, and forms of society." Ultimately, the Virginian concluded belligerently, Southern defense would be found in the traditional mechanisms of national politics: "Mr. John Adams the 2d is now upon his trial, [and] his friends consult as little his own interest as the public good, by conjuring up these prejudices against the *Slave people*. Should they persevere in their misguided policy, it will require no prophet to foretell that the son will share the fate of his father."

With the slavery issue thus drawn taut, the Old Republicans recovered quickly from the setback of 1824. Calhoun's inveterate foe William Smith was returned to the Senate from South Carolina, completing for the moment an Old Republican sweep of the South Atlantic states begun in 1821, a sweep which put Calhoun's political career in jeopardy and forced the Carolinian, now vice president, to break with Adams. For the Old Republicans, moreover, Adams made an infinitely better target than Monroe. The high-toned nationalism of the New Englander, combined with popular revulsion to the alleged bargain which secured his election, put the kiss of death on amalgamation as a political theory. The stage was set, under more favorable circumstances, for the Old Republicans to try again.

IV

For all the illuminating insights into Jacksonianism to which Americans have been treated in recent years, Jacksonian politics are still interpreted in Victorian terms, along classic lines descended from an early biographer of Jackson, James Parton, who recorded them one hundred years ago. To the Victorians, it is perhaps not too much to say, most of history could be ultimately attributed either to whores or to the unbridled pursuit of ambition. It was a simple view of history, and the Jacksonians got both barrels, one through the beguiling story of Peggy Eaton, the other through the notion of a sterile and essentially meaningless struggle for the succession between Van Buren and Calhoun. As Parton quaintly put it, "the political history of the United States, for the last thirty years, dates from the moment when the soft hand of Mr. Van Buren touched Mrs. Eaton's knocker."

When finally it rode to power, the Jacksonian party was made up of two clearly discernible and distinct wings. One comprised the original Jacksonians, those who had supported him in 1824 when he ran on his own, bereft, like all the rest, of party, and nearly of allies. As measured in that election this strength was predominantly in the West. It spilled over into a few states east of the mountains, most notably Pennsylvania, where the chaos of the existing political structure enabled Jackson as military hero to ride roughshod over all the rest. But this was all. The Western vote, especially when shared with Clay, amounted in electoral terms to little. Even with the votes of the Carolinas, thrown to him gratuitously by Calhoun and counting one-quarter of his total, he was far short of an electoral majority. To get even this much he had been formally before the public for two years, and all his considerable natural appeal as a Westerner and a hero had gone into the bargain.

After 1824 Jackson found himself the candidate of a combined opposition. The concrete measure of difference between defeat in 1824 and victory in 1828 was the Old Republican strength of the South Atlantic states and New York, brought to the Jackson camp carefully tended and carefully drilled by Van Buren. Nearly equal in size to the original Jackson following, they constituted a political faction far older, far more permanent, far more purposeful, far better led, and in the long run far more important. Their purposes were set forth by Van Buren in a notable letter to Ritchie in January, 1827, proposing support of the old hero. Such support, as the New Yorker put it, would be "the best and probably the only practicable mode of concentrating the entire vote of the opposition & of effecting what is of still greater importance, the substantial reorganization of the Old Republican Party." It would "restore a better state of things, by combining Genl Jackson's personal popularity with the portion of old party feeling yet remaining." It would aid Republicans of the North and middle states "by substituting *party principle* for *personal preference* as one of the leading points in the contest. . . . Instead of the question being between a northern and Southern man, it would be whether or not the ties, which have hitherto bound together a great political party should be severed." Most important, its effects would be highly salutary for the South:

> We must always have party distinctions and the old ones are the best of which the nature of the case admits. Political combinations between the inhabitants of the different states are unavoidable & the most natural & beneficial to the country is that between the planters of the South and the plain Republicans of the north. The country has once flourished under a party thus constituted & may again. It would take longer than our lives (even if it were practicable) to create new party feelings to keep those masses together. If the old ones are suppressed, geographical divisions founded on local interests or, what is worse prejudices between free and slave holding states will inevitably take their place. Party attachment in former times furnished a complete antidote for sectional prejudices by producing counteracting feelings. It was not until that defence had been broken down that the clamour agt. Southern Influence and African Slavery could be made effectual in the North . . . Formerly, attacks upon Southern Republicans were regarded by those of the north as assaults upon their political brethren & resented accordingly. This all powerful sympathy has been much weakened, if not, destroyed by the amalgamating policy. . . it can & ought to be revived.

Lastly, Van Buren noted, a Jackson administration brought to power by the "concerted effort of a political party, holding in the main, to certain tenets & opposed to certain prevailing principles" would be a far different thing from one brought to power by the popularity of a military hero alone. An administration brought to power by Old Republican votes would be governed by Old Republican principles. Van Buren would make himself the guarantor of that.

Because the Jacksonian party was what it was, Jacksonian policy was what it was, and Jacksonian politics as well. Because the administration rested on an Old Republican alliance which bridged the Mason-Dixon line and linked New York with the Old South, the two most important steps in the development of Jacksonian policy were the veto of the Maysville Road bill and the veto of the bill to recharter the Bank of the United States. Whatever the social and economic consequences of each, they were in their origins political measures, designed to solidify and hold together the Old Republican party; and they were predicated, each of them, on a strict construction of the Constitution. And, too, because its political base was what it was, the one great question of public policy which nearly brought the administration to disaster, one with which it could not deal and never did, was the tariff.

No less important, it was the structure of the Jackson party which gave meaning to—and dictated the course of—that struggle between Van Buren and Calhoun which bulks so large in the politics of the Jackson years. It was far more than an empty struggle for the succession. Its essence was competition between two conflicting ideas as to how best to protect Southern security in the Union, and thus, inferentially, how to preserve the Union itself. One of those ideas was the old Jeffersonian idea, resuscitated by Van Buren, sustained by the Jackson party and by the Democratic party until the Civil War. It was that Southern security rested ultimately on the maintenance in national office of a political party which would be responsive to the South because dependent on it for election. A political answer, not a doctrinaire one, it was product of the practical, pragmatic, and thoroughly political minds of Thomas Jefferson and Martin Van Buren. It depended for its success on the winning of national elections by a party which would maintain its identity in relation to the opposition as a states' rights-strict construction party, but which would at the same time be moderate, flexible, pragmatic in tone, able to win support in the North as well as the South if it would serve its purpose.

Counter to this was the proposition developed by John C. Calhoun. Last of the Southern nationalists, Calhoun had held to his position through 1824, long after the Old Republicans had routed Southern nationalism in every state but his own. In the mid-twenties, with his own political strength at rock bottom, his hold slipping even in South Carolina, Calhoun made his portentous switch from Nationalist to Sectionalist, squaring the two in his own mind with the development of a counter theory to that of the Jeffersonians. This was that Southern security was dependent in the last analysis on the maintenance of an effective Southern power to veto anything it didn't like—thus nullification—and that failing, on the right to secede. In contrast to the political and moderate remedy of the Old Republicans, this was a constitutional remedy, product of the brilliant legal, doctrinaire, and essentially nonpolitical mind of the great Carolinian.

That Van Buren won out over Calhoun in the Jackson years had nothing to do fundamentally with Mrs. Eaton or with a long chronicle of personal intrigue. It had everything to do with the fact that the

Old Republican moderates controlled the South, all but South Carolina, almost that, in the twenties. While Calhoun brought only South Carolina and some personal support in Congress to the Jackson fold, Van Buren brought all the rest of the South, and New York as well. The fact was not lost on Jackson or his Tennessee friends, either before his election or after. Van Buren's triumph over Calhoun was won not on Washington backstairs after 1829 but on the Southern hustings in the early twenties. Two years before it came to power the Jackson party was already, in fact, a Jackson–Van Buren party.

V

There were postscripts, too, which harked back to the structure of the Jackson party, to the Missouri question, and to the political prophecies of Thomas Ritchie, woven into the very fabric of the party by the skilled political weaver from New York. First of these was that the Jackson party, the issue once raised, was committed to Texas. When in 1844 a new drumfire of antislavery sentiment in the North made it impossible for Van Buren to honor that commitment, Ritchie and Van Buren, after nearly a quarter century of fruitful political teamwork, would part company, and Van Buren would give up leadership of the party he had created. After 1844 the party of the Jeffersonian formula sustained itself in the face of the rising slavery issue by giving vent to its expansionist tendencies; and the Northern man with Southern principles who replaced Van Buren was in fact a Northwestern man with Southern principles, Stephen A. Douglas of Illinois. It was to be Douglas, governed by the irresistible logic of the party structure, who carried through Congress finally, in 1854, the repeal of the Missouri Compromise. And when three years after that the Supreme Court in the Dred Scott decision held the Thomas Proviso of the Missouri Compromise unconstitutional, as Ritchie and Nathaniel Macon had said it was thirty-seven years before, who were the judges who comprised the majority? Of six, one had been appointed in 1846 by "Young Hickory" James K. Polk, a second in 1853 by the next successful Democrat, Franklin Pierce. The four others were James M. Wayne of Georgia, coadjutor of Van Buren's Georgia lieutenant John Forsyth, appointed to the court by Jackson in 1835; Roger B. Taney of Maryland, appointed by Jackson in 1836; John Catron, Van Buren campaign manager in Tennessee, appointed by Jackson in 1837; and Peter V. Daniel of Virginia, long-time member of the Richmond Junto, confidante of Thomas Ritchie, appointed in 1841 by Van Buren.

Changing Concepts of Party
in the United States
New York, 1815–1828

Michael Wallace

It is not among the objects of this collection to represent the scholarship concerned with the transition from the first party struggle to the second. Still, it seems advisable to close by coming back, full circle, to the point at which we started. Michael Wallace wrote this article while working on his doctorate as a student at Columbia. His findings were incorporated by his mentor, Richard Hofstadter, in The Idea of a Party System. *The following selection is from the* The American Historical Review, LXXIV *(December, 1968), 453–460, 470–482, and 489–491. It is reprinted by permission.*

During the first thirty years of its existence the United States developed, quite unintentionally, a party system. Organized popular parties regularly contested for power; Federalists and Republicans fought passionately and acrimoniously in Congress and cabinet, in town squares and county courthouses throughout the nation. The evidence of party spirit alarmed many Americans, for the existence of parties and their constant contention violated powerful and ancient traditions of proper political behavior. According to canons inherited from British and colonial thought and practice, parties were evil: they were associations of factious men bent on self-aggrandizement. Political competition was evil: the ideal society was one where unity and consensus prevailed, where the national interest was peacefully determined by national leaders. Because partisan behavior violated normal ethical standards, many men, politicians among them, saw in the rise of parties a sign of moral decline. Not until a new generation of politicians emerged—men who had been raised in parties and had grown to maturity in a world that included party competition as a fixture of political life—were Americans able to reevaluate the ancient traditions and establish new ones that justified their political activities.

Much of this reevaluation and development of new ideals took place in New York State in the 1820s.[1] There a group of professional politicians, leaders of the Republican party known as the Albany Regency, developed the modern concept of a political party and declared party associations to be eminently desirable. They adhered to a set of values that insisted on preserving, not destroying, political parties. They denounced and derided the consensus ideal and praised permanent political competition as being beneficial to society.

This essay will examine the ideas of these politicians. It will begin with their new definition of a political party, move to the new code of political morality that declared loyalty to party to be of the highest value, and conclude with their gradual rejection of the consensus tradition.

The regency politicians justified their political party by distinguishing it from the parties characteristic of English and colonial American politics. They asserted that while the old type of party had been a personal clique satisfying nothing but the greed and whims of its aristocratic leaders—thus meriting the odium it had received—the new type of party was a popular, democratically run organization that enabled the people to participate in government; it was, therefore, praiseworthy. By distinguishing between old and new parties, and by applying the epithets of the antiparty tradition only to the former, they freed their own association from condemnation. They were able to make this distinction because in fact the parties they were familiar with were quite different from their eighteenth-century forebears: the regency ratified a change that had already occurred.

In eighteenth-century England, "parties," "factions," or "connections" were cliques of parliamentary notables, organized about one or more prominent leaders. They were held together primarily by hopes of obtaining office. As Sir Lewis Namier tells us, "whoever in the eighteenth century had the 'attractive power' of office, received an accession of followers, and whoever retained it for some time was able to form a party." In addition to patronage, kinship and friendship were the basic ligaments of these primary political units. Lacking an organizational basis, however, these connections were quite unstable: "Such parties . . . were bound to melt, . . . for the basis of the various groups

---

[1] I do not claim that only New Yorkers advanced the ideas I am about to discuss, but only that they present us with certain archetypal positions. Investigations of the reflections of politicians in other states during this period, particularly Pennsylvania, Massachusetts, and North Carolina, might uncover similar configurations of ideas. For some New Jersey attitudes, primarily concerning the caucus, see Carl Prince, *New Jersey's Jeffersonian Republicans: The Genesis of a Party Machine, 1789–1817* (Chapel Hill, N.C., 1967).

was eminently personal."[2] Several such groups would merge to form the coalitions that made up ministries, but these coalitions were themselves highly unstable and in a crisis tended to dissolve into their constituent elements. Denominations such as Whig and Tory were often meaningful designations, but they denoted broad stylistic and ideological characteristics, not cohesive structures. "There were no proper party organizations . . . though party names and cant were current."[3]

Colonial politics in New York adhered to the English pattern: an intricate interplay of family cliques that occurred largely within the confines of the Assembly. This is not to say that contests were simply affairs of personal pique; significant economic and social interests were often at stake. Yet the processes of adjustment and reconciliation of interests were not carried on through the medium of such stable groupings of political parties. The units of political organization were shifting alliances of patrician families or elite individuals: New York's political history was a dense tangle of Livingstonians and DeLanceyites, of Lewisites, Burrites, and Clintonians.[4]

From the Revolution to the 1820s, the English model of party was altered, and a distinctively American form emerged. The Revolution forced the elite factions, whose power had been rooted in connections with England, social prestige, or economic power, to turn to the public, to attempt to bolster their positions by soliciting mass support; this increased dependency on the legitimizing power of numbers produced what one historian has called a shift from a politics of status to a politics of opinion. The mobilization of popular support behind specific political positions or leaders became increasingly crucial in American politics, and the political party emerged as the mechanism for organizing that support. In the 1780s and 1790s, debate over such national issues as the adoption of the Constitution, the Hamiltonian program, the Jay Treaty, and the Genêt mission drew great numbers of previously uninvolved

---

[2] Lewis B. Namier, *England in the Age of the American Revolution* (London, 1930), 242–43.

[3] *Id.*, *The Structure of Politics at the Accession of George III* (New York, 1961), x. On the personal, nonorganizational quality of politics in this period, see also Richard Pares, *King George III and the Politicians* (Oxford, Eng., 1953), 74–82; Ivor Bulmer-Thomas, *Growth of the British Party System* (2 vols., London, 1967), I, 8; Archibald S. Foord, *His Majesty's Opposition, 1714–1830* (Oxford, Eng., 1964), 23. For the earlier part of the eighteenth century, see Robert Walcott, Jr., *English Politics in the Early Eighteenth Century* (Cambridge, Mass., 1956); and J. H. Plumb, *The Origins of Political Stability in England, 1675–1725* (Boston, 1967).

[4] See Stanley Katz, *Newcastle's New York: Anglo-American Politics, 1732–1753* (Cambridge, Mass., 1968); Dixon Ryan Fox, *The Decline of Aristocracy in the Politics of New York* (Torchbook ed., New York, 1965); Jabez D. Hammond, *The History of Political Parties in the State of New York* (2 vols., New York, 1846), I; Alfred Young, *The Democratic Republicans of New York: The Origins, 1763–1797* (Chapel Hill, N.C., 1967).

people into the expanding political parties. The parties changed from cliques in Congress to popular associations, as men sought to influence the composition and character of political leadership by concerted action at the polls.[5]

Parties began to develop identities, personas, that were separable from the personalities and positions of their leaders; structures, too, were becoming less communal, more impersonal, as parties stretched to absorb ever-larger numbers of adherents. Changing terminology marked the process: in New York, where DeLanceyites had fought Livingstonians, Federalists now fought Republicans. Yet by the War of 1812 the process was far from complete: the New York Republican party, for instance, remained primarily a coalition of family factions, which tended to fracture repeatedly along the lines of its component parts. The first generation of party members, generally unaware of the larger processes at work, maintained a greater allegiance to their personal factions than to the larger entity, the party. The structure, function, size, and scope of the party had changed, but not men's attitudes toward it. Because the transformation was unplanned, a series of *ad hoc* reactions to events, the conception of party remained unchanged. What looked like a modern party had evolved, but because change had preceded intellectual awareness, old attitudes toward parties prevailed.

In New York, after the War of 1812, a new conception of party emerged, modeled more closely on reality; in turn, the new definition of what a party ought to be legitimated existing structures. This reevaluation developed out of what at first seemed just one more intraparty feud among New York Republicans, but that rapidly took a new and significant turn. The focus of the struggle was De Witt Clinton, in 1817 the leader of the party. Clinton held to the old view of party: he was a patrician politican who considered the party his personal property.

---

[5] The literature on the development of parties is extensive; see, e.g., Carl Becker, *History of Political Parties in the Province of New York* (Madison, Wis., 1909); Lloyd Irving Rudolph, "The Meaning of Party: From the Politics of Status to the Politics of Opinion in Eighteenth-Century England and America," doctoral dissertation, Harvard University, 1956; Harry Ammon, "The Genêt Mission and the Development of American Political Parties," *Journal of American History*, LII (Mar. 1966), 725–41; Joseph Charles, *The Origins of the American Party System* (New York, 1961); William Nisbet Chambers, *Political Parties in a New Nation: The American Experience, 1776–1809* (New York, 1963); Roy Nichols, *The Invention of the American Political Parties* (New York, 1967); Paul Goodman, "The First American Party System," in *The American Party Systems*, ed. William Nisbet Chambers and Walter Dean Burnham (New York, 1967); Noble Cunningham, *The Jeffersonian Republicans: The Formation of Party Organization, 1789–1801* (Chapel Hill, N.C., 1957), and *The Jeffersonian Republicans in Power: Party Operations, 1801–1809* (Chapel Hill, N.C., 1963); William Nisbet Chambers, "Parties and Nation-Building in America" in *Political Parties and Political Development*, ed. Joseph LaPalombara and Myron Weiner (Princeton, N.J., 1966).

This attitude is not surprising, given the nature of his career. Clinton assumed his position of leadership effortlessly, inheriting control of the faction that had been led by his uncle, George Clinton, New York's Revolutionary War governor. Despite the fact that the organization he headed in 1817 was quite different from what it had been when he entered politics in the 1790s, his style of leadership remained characteristic of the earlier period. Snobbish, spiteful, and supercilious, he was forbiddingly aristocratic. He craved flattery, he rejected advice from subordinates that conflicted with his own political judgments, and he directed the party largely as he saw fit. Above all, he dispensed the rewards of the party—political patronage and party nominations—as he pleased, often to personal friends, often to Federalists at the expense of deserving Republicans.[6]

This type of leadership became increasingly unacceptable to a group of younger politicians in the party. As the party had become richer, more powerful, more obviously a vital route to a successful career in public life, many men whose allegiance lay not to any person or family but to the party itself had joined the organization. Inevitably such men would resent the idiosyncratic and unpredictable quality of party life, particularly the capricious dispensation of party rewards. Beginning about 1817, a group of these younger politicians known as the Bucktails began a quiet campaign to oust Clinton from the leadership. They were not interested merely in substituting one set of leaders for another. Rather their position may be likened to that of a group of young executives in a family firm who think that the business is being misrun because familial, not managerial, standards govern its operation.

By 1819 the Bucktails, who included such able men as Martin Van Buren, Benjamin Franklin Butler, Silas Wright, William Learned Marcy, and Azariah Cutting Flagg, felt ready to challenge Clinton openly. At first they attacked him personally, charging that he put his own interests above those of the organization. "De Witt Clinton, has acted incompatibly with his situation as the head of the republican party of this state, and in direct hostility to its best interest and prosperity. . . ."[7] "Personal aggrandizement," they declared, "has been his personal max-

---

[6] For Clinton's approach to parties, see John Bigelow, "De Witt Clinton as a Politician," *Harper's*, L (Dec. 1874), 409–17, 563–71; Hammond, *History of Political Parties*, I, 360, 461–62, 489–90; II, 269–74; Michael P. Lagana, "De Witt Clinton and Martin Van Buren: Political Managers in New York State, 1812–1822," master's thesis, Columbia University, 1963, 92–100, 103–105, Chap. VI; Samuel P. Orth, *Five American Politicians* (Cleveland, 1906), 90–91, 93, 107; Fox, *Decline of Aristocracy*, 194–228; Alvin Kass, *Politics in New York State, 1800–1830* (Syracuse, N.Y., 1965), 17.

[7] Republican meeting of the city of Hudson, in New York *National Advocate*, Feb. 10, 1820.

im, even at the sacrifice of the republican party."[8] As one Bucktail wrote in the Albany *Argus*, the organ of the insurgents, "notwithstanding his capacity, his manners are too repulsive, his temper too capricious and imperious, his deportment too dictatorial and tyrannical to acquire the affections or retain the confidence of any party."[9]

The Bucktails wanted to go beyond indicating Clinton's personal style and to get at the anachronistic system of personal politics that he represented. Yet it was difficult to criticize Clinton's kind of leadership within the traditional framework of ideas about parties, for he was acting in accord with centuries-old standards of behavior. They were thus forced to proclaim a new definition of party and new standards of proper behavior for party politicians that would discredit both Clinton and his style of politics. They accomplished this task by adopting the rhetoric of democracy and egalitarianism and applying it to intra-party organization. Parties, they declared, should be democratic associations, run by the majority of the membership. It was a simple assertion, but it immediately put them in a position of strength. The ideal was virtually unassailable; to undermine the Bucktail position, critics would have to denounce republicanism itself—in the 1820s a political impossibility. Republican ideals became the Bucktails' weapons, and they were weapons that Clinton could not counter.

The Bucktails asserted that a party organized about an individual or patrician family was unacceptable as it was not republican. Personal parties were not parties at all, but factions, aristocratic remnants from the deferential days of colonial politics. Clinton was denounced as "raising up not only an aristocracy, but what has more hideous features, a species of monarchy."[10] He was "the chieftain and head of an aristocracy"; his followers, "governed by no principle or party discipline," were "servile dependents . . . solely devoted to his views"; they were a "dangerous faction, bearing the badge of his family name," and solely concerned with "ministering to personal ambition."[11] His patronage policy was denounced, not simply as unfair, but as producing undemocratic concentrations of power: "Devotion to the person of a chief becomes a passport to public distinction, and servility to men in power is rewarded . . . by honors and emoluments."   In sum, Clinton's whole vision of politics, "characterized by personal attachments on the one hand and by personal antipathies on the other," was "highly prejudicial to the

---

[8] Republican meeting of Redhook, in Albany *Argus*, Jan. 21, 1820.

[9] *Ibid.*, Oct. 22, 1824.

[10] Broadside, Oct. 15, 1824, in Broadside Collection [hereafer cited as BC], New York Public Library.

[11]*National Advocate*, Feb. 25, 1820; Albany *Argus*, Oct. 22, 1824; Dec. 10, 1819.

interests of the people, and if successful [would] have a tendency to subvert our republican form of government."[12]

The proper form of political organization in a democratic state, the Bucktails argued, was not a personal faction but a political party. A true party was not the property of a man or a family, but transcended any of its members. Like a corporation it outlived its officers and did not, as had been the rule, expire when its leaders died or were removed from office. The proper party was "bound to the fortunes of no aspiring chief."[13] A political party, moreover, was responsible to the mass of its members: it was a democratic organization. The "cardinal maxim with the great republican party [should be] . . . always to seek for, and when ascertained, always to follow the will of the majority."[14] Politicians like Clinton, who felt themselves to be above the majority, could no longer be tolerated. "Those who refuse to 'abide by the fairly expressed will of the majority' . . . forfeit all claims to the character of republicans, and become recreant to the principles of that party."[15] This did not mean an end to leadership: "Republicans know full well that . . . some must bear the brunt of the battle, and that to some hands must be consigned the interest and honor of the party; the system, the management, the labor and the anxiety." But leaders were expected to consider themselves the instruments or agents of an organization, not its owners. He "whose talents and zeal have benefitted the republican party will be supported as long as he consults the interests and ascendancy of that party, and no longer."[16] The proper criteria for advancement were faithful dedication to the party and long service in its support, not pedigree or property.

By these standards, Van Buren was a model party leader. He proclaimed his obligation to the organization: "There are few men in the state," he told a gathering of the faithful, "more indebted to the favor of the Republican Party than myself and none more willing to acknowledge it."[17] He rose to power in the prescribed fashion: "We speak of

---

[12] *Ibid.*, Feb. 11, 1820. Another writer insisted that "the fatal rock upon which the democracy of this state has heretofore run their bark, is an undue attachment to individuals." (*Ibid.*, Oct. 21, 1826.) As early as 1817 Marcy declared that "if republicans are to be put down because they have more devotion to the cause than to an Individual I shall consider it a duty and an honor to be arrayed in opposition to such an administration." (Marcy to John Bailey, Aug. 30, 1817, quoted in Robert Remini, "The Early Political Career of Martin Van Buren," doctoral dissertation, Columbia University, 1951, 203.)

[13] Albany *Argus*, Jan. 21, 1820.

[14] *Journal of the Senate of the State of New-York; at Their Forty-seventh Session, Begun and Held at the Capitol in the City of Albany, the Fourth of January 1824* [hereafter cited as New York Senate *Journal*, 1824] (Albany, 1824), 18.

[15] Albany *Argus*, Jan. 19, 1824.

[16] *National Advocate*, Nov. 17, 1821.

[17] Draft of speech to be read at Herkimer Convention, Oct. 3, 1826, Martin Van Buren Papers, Library of Congress.

him with pride," declared a mass meeting of Albany Republicans in 1820, "because without the influence of fortune, or the factitious aid of a family name, he has, by his entire devotion to the republican cause, raised himself to the first grade as a statesman and a patriot."[18]

By 1820 the Bucktail revolt had succeeded. Largely because they were able to convince many of the party that they were more faithful to the organization and the will of its majority than was Clinton, they managed to oust Clinton and his adherents; they then appropriated the apparatus and symbols of the Republican party entirely for themselves. Despite vigorous protests at being read out of the party because they failed to measure up to the new criteria, the Clintonians were relegated to the status of a distinct personal party.[19] Van Buren and his fellow Republicans entrenched themselves in the legislature and all of the executive branch but the governorship and came to be characterized, by Clintonian and Federalist opponents, as the Albany Regency.[20]

The Bucktails thus succeeded in distinguishing between party and faction in both the theory and actuality of New York politics. A party (such as their own) was a democratically structured, permanent organization; a faction (such as the Clintonians) was a transient, aristocratic, personal clique. "On one side is arrayed the old republican party, and on the other the followers of a man."[21] Personal factions were bad:

---

[18] Albany *Argus*, Feb. 29, 1820.

[19] The Clintonians were outraged at being displaced by younger men for not adhering to the new party discipline. Their complaints are evident in a revealing pamphlet, *The Martling Man*, written either by Clinton himself or by his lieutenant, Pierre C. Van Wyck. The narrator remarks that "times appear to be much changed since the days of George Clinton. Here I am, just as good a man as ever, just as true a Republican, . . . [and all my] part and lot in the election is, to be appointed on a ward committee, and to do a duty at the polls and to scour round through the cellars and groceries to buy up votes, and for what? to elect a set of young men, of whom I know but little and care less." After many reflections on the old, independent days, the hero decides to reject the new-style politics: "hereafter I will have none of your committees, or caucuses, or tricks; . . . as to your regular modes, and all that make us drill soldiers, . . . if I can find the old Republicans again, I'll join them; if I cannot, why I'll be independent and vote as I please." (*The Martling Man, or Says I to Myself, How is This?* [New York, 1819], 5–6, 8.) Another disaffected member was James Tallmadge, who declared that "these old men who are now marked as irregulars, understand and observe the principle of the republican party; while these new converts who have thrust themselves into places and set up as leaders of party discipline, know nothing . . . To approve of caucus nominations, and obey their leader, is the extent of their education and of their political principles." (*Speech of James Tallmadge, Esq. on the subject of Caucus to Nominate a President given in the House of Assembly, 26th January, 1824* [Albany, 1824], II.)

[20] For a short account of the Albany Regency, see Robert V. Remini, "The Albany Regency," *New York History*, XXXIX (Oct. 1958), 341–55. Also useful are *id.*, "Early Political Career of Martin Van Buren"; Ivor D. Spencer, "William L. Marcy and the Albany Regency," doctoral dissertation, Brown University, 1940; John Garraty, *Silas Wright* (New York, 1949); Kass, *Politics in New York State*.

[21] Albany *Argus*, Oct. 22, 1824.

they were aristocratic and concerned only with enriching their leader. But parties were good: they allowed all members an equal voice; gave all members an equal chance to rise to positions of leadership and to receive party nominations for important elective positions; and provided all members an equal chance at receiving patronage, now no longer dispensed at the whim of an arbitrary leader. The degree to which the newer politicians rejected the antiparty tradition and the personal basis of politics can be seen in their extraordinary degree of attachment to their organization. They went far beyond merely justifying the existence of their party in ideological and practical terms and developed a system of political discipline that enjoined every politician, at whatever cost to himself, to preserve and perpetuate the party.

Because their goal was the preservation of the party, the politicians lost interest in other, more ideological objectives. This is evident from their election appeals and campaign rhetoric. There were virtually no substantive planks in regency platforms—no programs of internal improvements, no plans for expanded education or agricultural improvements, no demands for expansion of the franchise, virtually no demands at all. There were many declarations that Republicans were the party of democracy, and their opponents the standard-bearers of aristocracy, but these were either vague statements asserting differences in temperament and style or, when made specific, differences in the structure of their organizations. Their basic campaign appeal was aimed at those who already identified with them, and it was simple enough: now is the time for all good men to come to the aid of their party. Most of their political advertisements were in fact apolitical; they were calls to the colors, exhortations to keep the organizational faith. Classic in its simplicity was this broadside: "Republicans, will you abandon that party which has done so much for your country? Remember the dying words of the brave Lawrence and 'DON'T GIVE UP THE SHIP!!'"[22] Republicans were reminded of their party's glorious history. "Let scenes gone by, and blessings enjoyed, arouse every republican to a sense of his duty. Remember that republicans saved the nation from anarchy; that republicans stood firm in the 'trying times' of '98; ... O Ye patriots of '76! Ye preservers of Democracy in '98; ye defenders of our rights in '12, '13, '14; come forth . . ."[23] The most popular issues in regency campaigns were those that had been safely dead for twenty years. Republicans were enjoined to ignore objections to particular regency policies, as they were simply threats to the safety of the organization; complaints about the defeat of the electoral bill, while seemingly legitimate, masked an insidious design. "It is not a

---

[22] Broadside, Oct. 15, 1824, *ibid.*
[23] Courtland *Courier*, quoted in Albany *Argus*, Oct. 15, 1824.

question about the electoral law . . . that is now pending. It is whether the republican party shall stand or fall."[24]

Such ideological urges as Republicans had were satisfied by their association in a democratic political party. Unlike the party's founders, they felt no need to use the party to achieve certain goals, for the perpetuation of a democratic organization was goal enough. The second-generation politicians were operational democrats.[25]

The "defense" of party association outlined in the preceding pages was relatively simple. Except for harnessing the legitimizing force of majoritarianism, the Republicans had merely recognized and ratified actual changes in the structure and function of parties. The more serious traditional rejection of party had always been closely associated with the rejection of political competition; to justify party fully, it was necessary to justify competition.

In eighteenth-century England parties had been frowned upon less because of their form than because their very existence was believed to be the sign of a flawed society. The ideal state was thought to be one without parties, without political competition—a society of consensus, unity, and harmony. The model for the state was the family. The familial metaphor was persistent in British political philosophy, finding its most extensive elaboration in Robert Filmer, and it remained powerful in the eighteenth century. In 1738, for example, Lord Bolingbroke wrote that "the true image of a free people . . . is that of a patriarchal family, where the head and all the members are united by one common interest, and animated by one common spirit: and where, if any are perverse enough to have another, they will be soon borne down by the superiority of those who have the same." For Bolingbroke, parties, almost by definition, were collections of perverse souls, for they perpetuated contention and division. He called for their elimination, a principal task for his "patriot king." "Instead of abetting the divisions of his people,

---

[24] *Ibid.*, Oct. 22, 1824.

[25] Not only were what were called "abstract" principles increasingly ignored because of the overriding concern with organizational support, but, in the rush of politics, they were increasingly betrayed. Edwin Croswell, editor of the Albany *Argus*, reflected on the problems the incontrovertibly democratic electoral bill raised for the party: "Admit the general correctness of it & yet is this the proper time for its introduction? Ought the question of expediency to be entirely disregarded; or ought it with Republicans, to be one of the first consideration?" (Croswell to Flagg, Dec. 9, 1823, Flagg Papers.) Expediency triumphed increasingly. The notion that legislators should vote as their constituents wished also became a hindrance to men like Marcy, who wanted legislators to vote as their party directed. "Some timid men who wish well to the democratic party are apprehensive that the current of public opinion runs so strong that it cannot be resisted . Too many are . . . popularity hunters." (Marcy to Van Buren, Dec. 14, 1823, Van Buren Papers.)

he will endeavor to unite them, and to be himself the centre of their union: instead of putting himself at the head of one party in order to govern his people, he will put himself at the head of his people in order to govern, or more properly to subdue, all parties."[26] This dream of a unified state, beyond and above political competition, was the theoretical ideal of most men in eighteenth-century England, and there were many who went beyond mere dreaming: a large part of the lives of men like the Earl of Chatham and George III was spent in trying to reshape the stubborn, factious reality of British political life to conform to the ideal of a unified, broad-bottomed state.[27]

The strength of the tradition, despite constant rebuffs in practice, lay in the continuing centrality of the monarchy. It was difficult to praise competition between the several political units of the state as invigorating and beneficial when one of those units was the king, the repository of much of the legitimacy of the state. Competition with the monarch was not competition, but opposition, and in the eighteenth century opposition still inferred disloyalty.[28] Still, opposition persisted, and it was justified increasingly by appeals to another powerful ideal: freedom. One could not limit the power of the king or his ministers if one adopted the attitude that uniformity and tranquillity transcended all other virtues: freedom and conformity, it was perceived, were often mutually exclusive. By the 1820s, Archibald Foord finds, the legitimacy of opposition to the government was widely granted; the permanent existence of His Majesty's Opposition, as it was called in 1826, was accepted as part of the constitution. Yet although the necessity for opposition was, with varying degrees of reluctance, accepted, the ideal of consensus remained powerful, certainly throughout the eighteenth century, and even in the nineteenth it echoed in the conception of the Ministry of All the Talents of 1806–1807. While occasional appreciations of political competition for its own sake can be found sprinkled throughout the century preceding the Reform Bill of 1832, they were, as Caroline Robbins notes, exceptions to the rule. "It should be emphasized that [those who accepted party] were many fewer than those who condemned party and faction, advocated uniformity of opinion, and praised nonpartisan public service."[29]

---

[26] "The Idea of a Patriot King," in *Works of Lord Bolingbroke* (4 vols., Philadelphia, 1841), II, 402.

[27] See Bulmer-Thomas, *Growth of the British Party System*, I, 30; Pares, *King George III and the Politicians*, 116–17.

[28] See Lewis B. Namier, "Monarchy and the Party System," in *Personalities and Powers* (Torchbook ed., New York, 1965).

[29] Caroline Robbins, " 'Discordant Parties': A Study of the Acceptance of Party by Englishmen," *Political Science Quarterly*, LXXIII (Dec. 1958), 505. The reevaluations of a man like Burke were not accepted in his own day. "Only the consecration of party by

In England's former colonies, the consensus ideal was also dominant, and parties were also denounced. This might at first appear surprising, for the inhibiting factor of the monarchy had been removed. Legitimacy was no longer immutably fixed, but resided in whoever captured the apparatus of government. Yet despite changed conditions, Americans adhered to English attitudes. They had of course been educated in the antiparty tradition, which they had received from all points of the political spectrum; it was the view of men like John Trenchard and Thomas Gordon, as well as Bolingbroke.[30] But there were other, peculiarly American factors, that perpetuated hostility to organized competition. For one thing, the major opponents of the Revolution, those who might have formed the nucleus of a determined opposition, had left the country in great numbers; this relieved much of the pressure for reevaluating the tradition. Secondly, the new government was an experiment in republicanism, isolated in a world of hostile monarchies. The leaders of the new nation were convinced that republics were delicate and fragile constructions, peculiarly susceptible to destruction by party virulence. To borrow Bernard Bailyn's phrase, the surface of public life was brittle, and Americans feared party contention might shatter it.[31] Finally, the desire to ensure freedom by limiting power, which had been a major force behind the growth of the English countertradition, was thought sufficiently assured here by the constitutional mechanisms of checks and balances within the government itself: by incorporating opposition into the system, the need for parties in the United States had been eliminated.

For all these reasons there were few indeed who disagreed with Washington's classic restatement of the consensus ideal in his Farewell Address. Warning his countrymen against "the baneful effects of the spirit of party," he insisted that partisan conflict "serves always to distract the public councils and enfeeble the public administration"; that it "agitates the community with ill-founded jealousies and false alarms"; that it "kindles the animosity of one part against another"; and that it was therefore definitely "a spirit not to be encouraged."[32] Despite Washington's words, reality remained refractory. At bottom the

---

the success of the two-party system in Victoria's day has deceived posterity into thinking that Burke had the better of the argument in his own generation." (Pares, *King George III and the Politicians*, 117; see also Foord, *His Majesty's Opposition*, I, 470.)

[30]See *The English Libertarian Heritage: From the Writings of John Trenchard and Thomas Gordon in the Independent Whig and Cato's Letters*, ed. David L. Jacobson (New York, 1965), xliii-xliv, 45–50, 53–54.

[31] See the excellent essay by John R. Howe, Jr., "Republican Thought and the Political Violence of the 1790's," *American Quarterly*, XIX (Summer 1967), esp. 154–60.

[32] "Farewell Address," in *A Compilation of Messages and Papers of the Presidents, 1789–1897*, ed. James D. Richardson (10 vols., Washington, D.C., 1896), I, 231 ff.

consensus ideal rested on the view that a "national interest" existed, a common good that rational men could agree upon. But in the young republic men agreed upon very little. To Washington's dismay, parties formed, advancing conceptions of the proper organization of society and the structure of government, representing conflicting economic and social interests, pressing differing views on foreign policy, contesting particular actions of the administration. And these parties were even more obnoxious to upholders of the old tradition than were English parties, to their detractors, for they represented not merely parliamentary cliques but popular movements, reaching deep down into society. Unheralded, unplanned for, and, for most Americans, unwanted, the first party system had come into being.[33]

The growth of political competition had little impact on the consensus ideal. Departure from ideals seldom changes them, for the deviations are attributed rather to a lack of virtue in the transgressors than to lack of validity in the ideals themselves. Usually denunciations of violators grow shriller, and the virtue of the tradition is insisted on the more ferociously. That is what happened in the United States in the early nineteenth century. Although there were glimmerings of a reevaluation of the consensus mentality during the Federalist and Jeffersonian eras—stray remarks about the value of party competition in the writings of Thomas Jefferson, Robert Goodloe Harper, Fisher Ames, and John Adams coexist with more conventional denunciations of party, and James Madison achieved a major break-through on the subject of interest groups, though not political parties—the voices seem lost and isolated, exceptions that prove the rule.[34] The intellectual lag behind institutional practice increased.

---

[33] See note 5, above.

[34] The idea of the beneficence of political conflict had a life of its own, which, of course, antedated the regency years. Yet, although much research is required before anything approaching a fair assessment of the strength of proparty ideas in eighteenth-century America may be made, I feel tentatively justified in my assertion that the tradition had neither deep nor sturdy roots. Milton Klein asserts, however, that party competition flourished in New York in the eighteenth century and that the endless deprecations of party politics were simply rhetorical flourishes. "The political temper of the colony of New York can better be judged by the way men *acted* rather than by the way they *spoke* of parties and factions. . . . The newspaper references to the desirability of political peace and harmony are no more than pious bows to a theoretical ideal." (Milton Klein, "Politics and Personalities in Colonial New York," *New York History*, XLVII [Jan. 1966], 5.) But it is precisely my point that there was a tension between practice and preachment, that everyday behavior was felt to violate accepted standards of political propriety. Paul Goodman has noted that this tension existed as late as the 1790s and 1800s. And it had marked consequences for the way men thought about the legitimacy of political opposition. Goodman notes that slowly "political parties came to be recognized as institutions essential to the survival of free government, providing an orderly means of articulating the majority's wishes and settling differences among contending

After 1815 an attempt was made to align theory and practice, but in a reactionary fashion: men tried to reshape reality to conform to the older ideals. The bitter animosities of the War of 1812 had convinced many that parties had to be eliminated. The most popular political book of the day was Mathew Carey's *The Olive Branch: or Faults on Both Sides, Federal and Democratic—A Serious Appeal on the Necessity of Mutual Forgiveness and Harmony, Dedicated to a Beloved but Bleeding Country, Torn in Pieces by Factious and Ruinous Contests for Power.*[35] Peace in 1815, marking the passing of older issues, oriented to foreign policy, seemed a perfect opportunity to eliminate conflict. The nation's political leaders, noting the decline of the Federalist party, declared that political divisions were a thing of the past, that a time of harmony, unity, and consensus had arrived. It was to be an Era of Good Feelings in which the remnants of parties would come together in a celebration of national unity.

The idea of Good Feelings was professed nationally by men of the stature of James Monroe, John Quincy Adams, and Andrew Jackson. In his inaugural address, Monroe declared that parties were not needed. Echoing Bolingbroke, he announced that "the American people constitute one great family with a common interest." The national interest was so obvious that there could be no deviation from it. "Discord," he declared, "does not belong to our system."[36] Privately Monroe noted that a "great undertaking" would be to "exterminate all party divisions in our country."[37] Adams declared too that he would "break up the remnant of old party distinctions, and bring the whole people together

---

groups." (Goodman, "First American Party System," 57.) I suggest that the beginnings of this change are to be found in the 1810s and 1820s. On the background of thought on parties, see esp. Richard Hofstadter's forthcoming study, tentatively entitled "Jeffersonian Democracy and Political Parties" (Berkeley, Calif., [1969]); see also Bernard Bailyn's superlative work *The Origins of American Politics* (New York, 1968), esp. 124–31; Nichols, *Invention of the American Political Parties*, 231–32, 257; *The Making of the American Party System*, ed. Noble Cunningham (Englewood Cliffs, N.J., 1965), 17–20, 23–25; id., *Jeffersonian Republicans in Power*, 303.

[35] Edward C. Carter II, "Mathew Carey and 'The Olive Branch,' 1814–1818," *Pennsylvania Magazine of History and Biography*, LXXIX (Oct. 1965), 399, 409.

[36] *Messages and Papers*, ed. Richardson, III, 10.

[37] Monroe to Jackson, Dec. 14, 1816, in *Writings of James Monroe*, ed. Stanislaus Murray Hamilton (7 vols., New York, 1901), V, 346. "Many men," continued Monroe, "very distinguished for their talents are of the opinion that . . . free government cannot exist without parties. This is not my opinion. . . . That the ancient republics were always divided into parties; that the English government is maintained by an opposition . . . I well know. But I think that the cause of these divisions is to be found in certain defects of those governments, rather than in human nature; and that we have happily avoided those defects in our system." (*Ibid.*) To Madison he wrote: "surely our government may get on and prosper without the existence of parties. I have always considered their existence as the curse of the country. . . ." (Monroe to Madison, May 10, 1822, *ibid.*, VI, 151, 289–91.)

in sentiment as much as possible."[38] In his inaugural address, he asserted that party competition had ended; "the baneful weed of party strife" had been uprooted. It remained for those who had "heretofore followed the standards of political party" to make "one effort of magnanimity, one sacrifice of prejudice and passion," that of "discarding every remnant of rancor against each other" and "embracing as countrymen and friends."[39] And in 1817 Jackson wrote President Monroe that "party and party feelings ought to be laid out of view." "Now," he argued, "is the time to exterminate that monster called party spirit."[40]

This was the standard approach to parties and political competition in the 1820s. Against this background, the innovations of the regency politicians in New York once again take on special interest. The attitudes they had evolved toward their opponents in the normal course of political life determined to a large extent how they would react when the Good Feelings persuasion was advanced and used against them on their home grounds in 1824.

The primary goal of regency politicians was to preserve their party. This is of utmost importance for understanding their attitudes toward their opponents in New York politics. Their goal was not to destroy, overwhelm, or eliminate their opponents; they were not ideologues bent on the destruction of evildoers. They were able, therefore, to realize that the continued existence of an opposition was necessary, from the perspective of perpetuating their own party; opposition was highly useful, a constant spur to their own party's discipline. While the party might, it was argued, "suffer temporary defeats" in the interparty struggle, "it is certain to acquire additional strength . . . by the attacks of adverse parties." Indeed, the party was "most in jeopardy when an opposition is not sufficiently defined."[41] As another writer noted, "there is such a thing as a party being too strong; a small and firm majority is more to be relied upon than an overwhelming and loose one."[42] The politicians were aware that during "the contest between the great rival parties . . . each found in the strength of the other a powerful motive of union and vigor."[43]

This need for opposition led to a fertile paradox. The Federalists and their latter-day avatars, the Clintonians, were, of course, guilty

---

[38] John Quincy Adams, *Memoirs of John Quincy Adams*, ed. Charles Francis Adams (12 vols., Philadelphia, 1874–77), VI, 474.

[39] *Messages and Papers*, ed. Richardson, III, 294.

[40] Printed in Albany *Argus*, May 18, 1824.

[41] *Ibid.*, Apr. 9, 1824.

[42] *National Advocate*, Nov. 14, 1821.

[43] Albany *Argus*, Mar. 5, 1824; see also Van Buren's remark: "In the Senate we will stand as strong as we could possibly wish, more might endanger our harmony." (Van Buren to Daniel Evans, May 10, 1819, Van Buren Papers.)

of heinous political sins: they were aristocrats, personalists, factional-
ists, no-party heretics. Yet they were also the opposition. As a consequence, the Federalist party (a label Republicans attached to their
major opponents of the moment), while condemned, was simultaneously praised; it was the strong, flourishing, and virtuous organization
to which Republicans would accede should it obtain the support of the
state's majority. From the need for a sustained opposition came verbal
bouquets like the following:

> From the first organization of the government . . . this country has been
> divided into two great parties. . . . Neither party has yielded to the other in
> the zeal with which it has sought to procure concert among its members,
> or to give ascendancy to its principles, and although we may lament the
> occasional inconsistencies and the dangerous excesses into which both
> have unavoidably been betrayed, . . . we cannot for a minute admit that
> the majority of either have been actuated by any other than the purest,
> the most patriotic, and the most disinterested motives.[44]

The *Argus* declared that "we wish not to be understood as having the
slightest objection to the maintenance of the old federal party, broadly
and with the spirit of other times." The two competing parties, the
paper observed, "have existed among us almost from the formation of
our constitution, and we are content with their present organization."[45]
    The regency, then, had no desire to eliminate its opponents. Rather
it hoped for a "tranquil though determined opposition."[46] It is significant that during the 1820s the word "opposition" itself gained popularity in Republican circles. They noted things in "the conduct of the
Opposition which afford both amusement and instruction"; rejoiced in
frustrating "the hopes and expectations of the Opposition"; and discussed in their papers "the views and opinions of what may now be
termed the Opposition to the Democratic Party."[47]
    This acceptance of the continued existence of their opponents
engendered a sportsmanlike attitude toward the competition. The
Oneida *Observer* asserted that Republicans should "exercise a liberal
and tolerant spirit toward political opponents, and . . . treat them
with a moderation and courtesy which shall leave them no reason for
complaint. . . . We feel disposed to allow purity of motives in general to
political opponents and as individuals to reciprocate sentiments of good
will and esteem."[48] The Albany *Argus* also stressed a spirit of moderation: "It is right that the Clintonians should have their meetings; we

---

[44] Albany *Argus*, Apr. 4, 1824.
[45] *Ibid.*, Oct. 8, 1824.
[46] Cooperstown *Watch Tower*, quoted *ibid.*, Oct. 15, 1824.
[47] *Ibid.*, Sept. 17, Apr. 20, 9, 1824.
[48] Quoted *ibid.*, Apr. 27, 1824.

care not how they organize . . . [and] we shall avoid disturbing their conventions. . . . To interfere with the meetings of the opposing party, is blackguardism; it betrays a little, mean spirit, that an intelligent, high minded man would disown."[49] Governor Enos Throop, a regency man, observed that "political parties, at the present day, sobered by past experience, leave scope for the exercise of all the charities and courtesies of life, between opposing members. Their spirit does not enter into families to engender hate, nor into social and religious societies to create dissensions, and to produce bitter and destructive enmities."[50] To be sure, to outsiders it appeared that New York politicians lived in a state of perpetual civil war, but, the natives argued, this impression resulted from misunderstanding. One paper attempted to reassure a visitor who had protested against the bitterness of a local election that Republicans got on splendidly with their opponents:

> At the late election in the first ward, when the federalists in that ward mustered powerful, beat us by two or three hundred, did not we democrats visit their committee room, and most pacifically eat their crackers, drink their beer, and smoke their segars? To be sure we did; and if Mr. Gales had favored us with a month's residence, he would have discovered that this bitter feeling was all smoke, only visible on days of election.[51]

Republican politicians even envisioned occasionally ceding power to their enemies. They had, after all, done it often enough. Alternating in power with political opponents was a recurring experience. Yet they had a theoretical justification for this alternation that allowed them to deal with ejection from power quite calmly: they applied the doctrine of majoritarianism to interparty relations, a process less elegantly known as the spoils system. Just as they thought that the minority of the party must submit to the greater number, so they thought that the party that obtained a majority of the votes of the state should rule completely, until such time as the minority party managed to convert itself into the majority party. As the National Advocate put it, "when a great political change takes place—when one party completely triumphs over another, it is then to be expected that a change is also to take place in the offices. The very circumstance of victory supposes a reformation or alteration in the order of things."[52] Regency men insisted that the victorious party had the right to all the offices. This was not vindictive but democratic. As Van Buren noted, this had been Jefferson's policy:

---

[49] Ibid., Oct. 5, 1824.

[50] Messages from the Governors, ed. Charles Z. Lincoln (II vols., Albany, N.Y., 1909), III, 276.

[51] National Advocate, Nov. 15, 1821.

[52] Ibid., Apr. 30, 1818.

True to his trust, he not only administered the government upon the principles for which a majority of the People had shown their preference, but he carried the spirit of that preference into his appointments to office to an extent sufficient to establish the predominance of those principles in every branch of the public service. This he did, not by way of punishing obnoxious opinions, or to gratify personal antipathies, but to give full effect to the will of the majority.[53]

But while the spoils system enshrined Marcy's dictum, "to the victors belong the spoils," it also carried with it the vitally important idea that when the party found itself outvoted, it would submit gracefully to blanket proscription. As Van Buren informed the 1821 constitutional convention, "that the majority should govern was a fundamental maxim in all free governments; and when his political opponents acquired the ascendancy, he was content that they should have it in their power to bestow the offices of the government."[54] As the *National Advocate* put it, "we will surrender nothing voluntarily to our opponents; let them fight and conquer, as the democratic party has done, and we will submit quietly. . . ."[55]

These were the attitudes regency politicians developed toward their opponents amid daily political struggles. Their lack of ideological fervor and their emphasis on preserving their institution contributed to a lowering of the political temperature. In the cooler atmosphere of the 1820s the politicians perceived that an opposition was necessary, and they came to think in terms of the continued existence of two parties, each sincere, legitimate, and capable of administering the government. Within this framework of attitudes a reevaluation of the consensus ideal could easily emerge. But ideas seldom spring forth without some encouragement, no matter how conducive the times. A stimulus was needed, some reason to force the regency men to think about their political universe and to make them articulate their attitudes toward political parties. The stimulus came in the mid-twenties with a barrage of antiparty criticism from their New York opponents. Only when confronted with a severe challenge to their habits and practices would they formulate a rebuttal. A brief look

---

[53] Van Buren, "Autobiography," ed. Fitzpatrick, 123.

[54] *Proceedings and Debates of the Convention of 1821*, ed. Nathaniel Carter and William L. Stone (Albany, N.Y., 1821), 354.

[55] *National Advocate*, May 31, 1822. They often did submit quietly; Van Buren in particular set an example in 1819 when he was removed as attorney general by Clinton. He informed the governor through intermediaries that "he might rest assured that he would hear of no personal complaints from me or my friends on account of my removal," cheerily admitting that he would have done the same were he Clinton. (Van Buren, "Autobiography," ed. Fitzpatrick, 93.) On the other hand, they often violated their own precepts and resorted to various evasions to retain office after losing an election.

at the position of the New York antiparty spokesmen may help us understand what provoked the regency response.

The New York opponents of the Albany Regency, drawing on the antiparty spirit of the national leaders, reasserted the old consensus ideal. Clinton, for example, declared that the clash of parties has "rent us asunder, degraded our character, and impaired our ability for doing good."[56] He too felt there was no need for division:

> I hardly understand the nomenclature of parties. They are all republicans, and yet a portion of the people assume the title of republican, as an exclusive right. . . . It is easy to see that the difference is nominal—that the whole controversy is about office, and that the country is constantly assailed by ambitious demagogues for the purpose of gratifying their cupidity.[57]

Many New Yorkers shared Clinton's attitude. They correctly observed that no deep differences of principle divided the parties: "We ask [the regency] to lay down what it considers to be the republican creed, and then to designate any considerable body of men in this country whom it would not embrace.[58] But they went on to conclude that no matters of controversy remained that required opposing political organizations. "What does the great mass of the people . . . care for party? Why should the people be divided into a thousand different interests without knowing for what, and made hostile to each other, when their true and only interest is to be united?"[59] Many assumed that the politicians, with their vested interest in discord, were perpetuating artificial divisions among a happy and passive people. Regency leaders like Erastus Root were charged with engaging in a "mean and contemptible effort to revive party names, and to excite prejudices by cant phrases."[60]

The solution was obvious: eliminate parties. If one could "knock aside all artificial arrangements and the whole machinery of party," it would prevent the "citizens of the state having their sentiments perverted by intrigue and corruption."[61] If parties could not be exorcised, they could at least be merged and amalgamated, particularly as there existed no difference between them. The critics proclaimed an end of parties. The Federalists, "having no longer any ground of principle to stand on, [have] necessarily ceased to exist as a party."[62] Again "[both parties] have manifested a willingness to drop old animosities and obso-

---

[56] *Messages from the Governors*, ed. Lincoln, II, 54–55.

[57] Cited in Denis Tilden Lynch, *An Epoch and a Man: Martin Van Buren and His Times* (New York, 1929), 240.

[58] Albany *Argus*, Sept. 12, 1823.

[59] New York *Statesman*, June 17, 1823.

[60] *Ibid.*, Oct. 31, 1824.

[61] *Ibid.*, June 27, 1823.

[62] Albany *Argus*, Sept. 12, 1823.

lete names, and to unite with their former political opponents."[63] And again, "the barriers of party are completely broken down and the lines of political demarcation cannot be again drawn."[64]

When it became apparent that the Republicans had no intention of merging with their opponents, much less of dissolving, the antiparty men moved beyond rhetoric. They organized. They formed, of all things, a party, an antiparty party, a party to end parties. The People's party, formed in 1823 by Clintonians, Federalists, and dissident Republicans, appealed to the electorate "not in the spirit of *party* warfare, for this is emphatically the cause of the People."[65] "We contend," the People's men declared, "not for the aggrandizement of a party of men, leagued together for selfish purposes, but for a great COMMON CAUSE, interesting to the people of this state."[66] Their candidates were picked "without reference to PARTY POLITICS," as it had been deemed "best to sacrifice party considerations on the altar of public good."[67] They offered their party as a means whereby members of all groups could unite, but it was highly unlikely that many regency Republicans would be lured into support of the fledgling party in light of the candidate it chose to support in 1824—De Witt Clinton. Yet here a theoretical assault on party was linked to a potentially powerful organization and a popular candidate. If the antiparty message appealed to many in the electorate, the regency was in trouble. The emergence of the People's party threatened regency hegemony and forced its members to defend the party system that had evolved in New York. This they consciously set about to do. As the Albany *Argus* stated, "The doctrines of dissolution and amalgamation . . . must be met and resisted."[68]

The regency defense against the amalgamation attack took five forms. Their first, most parochial, and probably most effective position was that the philosophy of amalgamation, for all its seeming disinterestedness, was actually an opposition trick, the purpose of which was not to unite the country but to destroy the Republican party. Secondly,

---

[63] Albany *Register*, Jan. 11, 1820.

[64] New York *Statesman*, Sept. 20, 1824.

[65] *Address of the Democratic Republicans of the City of Albany to the Electors of the State of New York* (Albany, N.Y., 1824), 3.

[66] New York *Statesman*, Sept. 20, 1824.

[67] Rochester *Telegraph*, Nov. 5, 1823.

[68] Albany *Argus*, May 14, 1824. There was another, equally conscious conflict on the national level, waged primarily against Monroe. Van Buren reminisced about the "degree of odium" brought upon him by his staunch resistance to amalgamation doctrines "within the precincts of the White House and in most of the circles, political and social, of Washington." "The noisy revels," he recalled, "of bacchanalians in the Inner Sanctuary could not be more unwelcome sounds to devout worshippers than was this peal of the party tocsin in the ears of those who glorified the 'Era of Good Feeling.'" (Van Buren, "Autobiography," ed. Fitzpatrick, 126.)

on a more theoretical level, regency Republicans denied that parties had dissolved, but rather that they continued in undiminished strength, a result traceable to powerful ideological and historical forces perpetuating them, which the Good Feelings men had ignored. Thirdly, they rejected the entire vision of a society based on consensus; the proper political universe was characterized by constant contention; the truly moral man was not one who put himself above party, but was a committed partisan. Fourthly, echoing the English justification of opposition, they declared that parties had to exist in a free state, that the elimination of parties occurred only under despotism. Fifthly, and most broadly, they declared that, for several reasons, competition between parties benefited the state.

Paradoxically, party competition bound the country together. Here was one of the shrewdest observations that the politicians made. While only in its formative stages in the 1820s, this idea would quickly enter the main current of antebellum thought. Van Buren and his colleagues realized that contrary to antiparty mythology, the really divisive threat to the nation was not party, but section. Party associations that cut across sectional lines were, in fact, an antidote to interregional stress. The Good Feelings men, by calling for the elimination of parties, were exacerbating sectionalism. Republicans accused them of wanting "to ABROGATE THE OLD PARTY DISTINCTIONS" in order to "organize new ones founded in the territorial prejudices of the people."[69] The consequence of abolishing the old political distinctions would be "to array republicans against each other under such new and artificial distinctions . . . as geographical locations, such as North and South, East and West."[70] Van Buren rested much of his case for the maintenance of the old parties on this ground: "We must always have party distinctions, and the old ones are the best. . . . If the old ones are suppressed, geographical differences founded on local instincts or what is worse, prejudices between free & slave holding states will inevitably take their place."[71]

Finally, contests between political parties benefited society by eliminating the fierce contentions of personal parties. Decrying the "cant and self-interests" that "utter lamentations over the prevalence of party division and the exhibition of party feelings," Butler wrote that

---

[69] Albany *Argus,* Aug. 1, 1823.

[70] *Ibid.,* Apr. 9, 1824.

[71] Van Buren to Thomas Ritchie, Jan. 13, 1827, Van Buren Papers. See also Albany *Argus* (Jan. 13, 1824): "When men are governed by a common principle, which is fully indulged and equally operative in all parts of the country, the agency of party conduces to the public good. But the political opinions of the same men, when actuated by feelings of a sectional character are directly the reverse. What is *party* in the one case, is *faction* in the other."

we are not of that fastidious sect which can desire the extinction of the old parties—which would sweep away the associations . . . and give us in their stead the bitter contentions of personal feuds, and the degrading personalities of an individual vassalage. . . . The old divisions are virtues which we . . . cherish. The contests which grow out of them are salutary and needful efforts for the preservation of the community.[72]

It was now obvious, as Throop noted, that it was "one of the peculiar benefits of a well-regulated party spirit in a commonwealth, that it employs the passions actively in a milder mood, and thus shuts the door against faction. . . ."[73]

By the end of the 1820s, the amalgamation attack had been met, the consensus tradition rejected. "Let us be greeted no more," demanded the Albany *Argus*, "by the cant and whining about the extinction of party feelings and the impropriety of endeavoring to keep them alive."[74] "Parties of some sort must exist. 'Tis in the nature and genius of our government."[75]

---

[72] *Ibid.*, Oct. 22, 1824.

[73] *Messages from the Governors*, ed. Lincoln, III, 276. See also Albany *Argus* (Oct. 8, 1824): "[Parties] are in themselves checks upon the passions, the ambition, and the usurpations of individuals. . . . In their absence, personal factions, private feuds, and all the acrimonious feelings of local contentions would not fail to spring up."

[74] *Ibid.*

[75] *Ibid.*, Nov. 26, 1824. Even in the quiet aftermath of the election of 1824, with Clinton triumphantly installed in the statehouse proclaiming an end of parties, the Albany *Argus* insisted that the calm would soon pass. "The present calm is delusive and unnatural. Political divisions are inseparable from our habits and our institutions. . . ." (*Ibid.*, Apr. 1, 1825.) The ideas of the regency men were still in the minority, in state and nation, in the 1820s, but they would spread until, by the end of the century, they had become axioms of American political thought, clichés of the popular mind. (See David Rothman, *Politics and Power* [New York, 1966], Chap. VIII.) For some of Van Buren's later formulations of his party philosophy, see Max M. Mintz, "The Political Ideas of Martin Van Buren," *New York History*, XXX (Oct. 1949), 422–48. I deal with the development of the ideas set forth in this essay in my dissertation in progress, "Changing Concepts of Party in the United States, 1815–1865."